TUDOR AND STUART BRITAIN

1471–1714

TUDOR
AND STUART BRITAIN
1471-1714

Roger Lockyer

LECTURER IN HISTORY AT ROYAL HOLLOWAY COLLEGE,
UNIVERSITY OF LONDON

LONGMAN

LONGMAN GROUP LIMITED
London

Associated companies, branches and representatives
throughout the world

© Roger Lockyer 1964

First published 1964
Twelfth impression 1979

Printed in Hong Kong by
Sing Cheong Printing Co Ltd

ISBN 0 582 31465 8

Cover: from *The Noble Art of Venerie or Hunting*
by George Turberville (1575)
reproduced by courtesy of The British Library

FOR BRIAN

Preface

So much work has been done on the Tudor and Stuart period during the last twenty-five years that many long-accepted assumptions and interpretations have now been modified—sometimes out of all recognition. The debate continues, often furiously, and since no end to it ... :d, in this book, to show the direc- ... d to give an interim report. I have ... ly, on secondary material, of which ... e attempted in the bibliography to ... wishes to pursue certain topics in ... book of this size.

... ancy, now Master of Marlborough ... ing and writing are not incompat- ... g Edward's School, Birmingham, ... Mr R. C. Latham, of Royal Hollo- ... London, for his interest and en- ... rton, of Bedford College in the ... rough the typescript and saved me ... course, responsible for those that ... opinions expressed in the following ... e Pearson-Gee for her invaluable

... me much more than I ever taught ... to clarify my ideas. My thanks and ... my colleagues at Lancing College, ... olloway College, for the stimulus ... ided.

... rian Rawson, for the many hours ... reading and commenting on the manuscript. This may not be a good book, but without his knowledge, good humour, perseverance and infinite patience, it would have been very much worse.

R. W. L.

London 1964

Foreword

TRADITIONALLY speaking, modern English history starts with the accession of Henry VII in 1485. Yet no revolutionary change took place in that year. The forces at work in English life were much the same after Bosworth as before. Disorder and the keeping of private armies continued to disturb the kingdom, particularly the remoter areas, for at least another century; and as for the gradual restoration of royal authority, this had started long before the first Tudor came to the throne. There was, indeed, no sudden break between medieval and modern England. The institutions of Tudor government, including the monarchy itself, the Council, Parliament and the law courts, were all products of the Middle Ages, and the medieval Catholic Church survived for nearly half a century after Henry Tudor's victory. The main reason for choosing 1485 was that it seemed to mark the re-emergence of strong monarchy after a hundred years of weakness and disorder culminating in civil war. In fact, however, the restoration began under Edward IV, and the methods used by the first Tudor were little more than a development of those adumbrated by his great Yorkist predecessor. Taken in isolation, the work of Henry VII seems very much more revolutionary than it was, but in fact strong royal government, and all that flowed from it, began to revive in the years that followed Edward IV's victory at Tewkesbury in 1471. For this reason the following history of Tudor and Stuart Britain starts with the reign of a Yorkist king.

Contents

MAPS

FAMILY TREES

nstruction in an academic
ng a broad plan to serve the
library based-instruction wil
details about BI in later

E INFORMATION GATHERING EASIE

imes INDEX. 1851-1974

The PARTIES
the First Reps.

I

Preview: Tudor and Stuart England

THE new monarchies which emerged in Europe in the late fifteenth century marked the end of a long period of stagnation. Not everywhere had been depressed. In north Germany, for instance, the towns of the Hanseatic League had built up a commercial empire that covered much of northern Europe, including Britain, while, further south, the Italian city-states were enjoying prosperity and a dazzling display of artistic genius. Even in those countries which were most affected, the picture was not one of unrelieved gloom. In England, for example, the merchants of London were flourishing, and Southampton was growing rich on the profits of trade with Italy. But these were the exceptions. Generally speaking, western Europe had been declining since the Black Death. Repeated attacks of bubonic plague decimated populations and lowered the vitality of those who survived. Land was left uncultivated because there were not enough men to work it, villages were abandoned, and towns decayed as the number of inhabitants shrank. In Winchester there were nearly a thousand empty houses in 1430, and twenty years later Lincoln was said to have only two hundred citizens.

As if natural disasters were not enough, human ones were added to them, and as the fifteenth century drew to a close the devastations of plague were increased by the horrors of war. In Spain, the Christian princes were struggling to drive the Moors out of the peninsula; Germany was rent by sporadic civil war; while in central Europe successive emperors had to stamp out heresy among their Bohemian subjects and to try to hold back the advance of Turkish power.

In the west, France and England were fighting each other in the Hundred Years War. Widespread devastation was the result, as armies battled and undisciplined bands of soldiers roamed the countryside in search of food and plunder, holding the inhabitants to ransom. A general spiritual and physical malaise had undermined the political and economic structure of Europe, and violence had become an accepted condition of life. A century later, Shakespeare evoked the desolate scene, in the speech which he put into the mouth of the Duke of Burgundy:

> And as our vineyards, fallows, meads and hedges,
> Defective in their natures, grow to wildness,
> Even so our horses and ourselves and children
> Have lost, or do not learn for want of time,
> The sciences that should become our country;
> But grow like savages, as soldiers will,
> That nothing do but meditate on blood.[1]

All this was changing by the time Edward IV regained the English throne in 1471. The attacks of plague bred a natural resistance among those who survived, and the decline in population seems to have been checked by 1500 at the latest. With more mouths to feed, demand for food and for land increased, and this activity injected new optimism and vitality into people who had earlier been deprived of hope. Just as depression had fed upon depression, so recovery stimulated recovery, and the period which had opened with the Black Death ended with the Renaissance and the expansion of Europe into a new world.

'Renaissance' is a convenient shorthand way of summarising the revival of Europe in the late Middle Ages. As a term, however, it has its dangers, for it implies a complete break with the past and ignores the continuity that is typical of all human societies, however rapid their rate of change. There was no sudden, cataclysmic break between the medieval and modern worlds. Roman law, which seemed to be the ideal instrument for despotism and came to be associated with the monarchs and states of the sixteenth century, had long been a subject of study in medieval universities; Greek texts were known to the medieval world, usually through Latin translations; capitalism, which is one of the hallmarks of modern society, had its origins in medieval Italy; and the blend of ruthlessness and realism which Machiavelli advocated for the 'new monarchs' of Europe had already found expression in the rulers of medieval France.

Yet the rate of change did undoubtedly quicken in the last decades of the fifteenth century, and the revival of the arts and letters of the

[1] Shakespeare. *King Henry V*, V:2.

ancient world provided the justification for new attitudes, even if it did not create them. In classical Greece and Rome, man had been the centre of the world, and even gods were conceived in human form. This was not true of the Middle Ages, which contrasted the puny efforts of man with the effortless majesty of God and saw no merit in human achievement unless it was directed towards a spiritual end. The Renaissance marked the re-emergence of the individual. Painters and sculptors studied the human form, scholars set their own private judgement against that of institutions and traditions, while explorers defied the accepted boundaries of the world, and with a courage equal to that of the ancient heroes sailed across unknown seas and brought forgotten worlds into the light of day.

The voyages of Columbus and Vasco da Gama were made possible by the desire of the rulers of Spain and Portugal to extend the kingdom of God upon earth. But the purpose of these voyages was lost in the novelty and excitement of the achievement itself, and the ultimate effect was to weaken the authority of the Catholic Church. The discovery of America and of a sea-route to India forced back the frontiers not only of the known world but also of human intelligence. They demonstrated, more dramatically than any medieval disputation, the hollowness of traditional authority. Long-accepted explanations, even when they were embodied in an institution, could no longer stand against the evidence of individual experience.

This was shown most dramatically in the changing attitude towards the universe. The accepted picture was that of Ptolemy and Aristotle, in which the sun, stars and planets revolved in fixed circles around a stationary earth. This was challenged by Copernicus, who in 1543 put forward the theory that the sun was the centre of the universe, and that the earth and other planets moved in circles round it, spinning on their own axes as they did so. His explanation was received at first with indifference or hostility, but the work of other investigators, including Kepler, Tycho Brahe and Galileo, confirmed the truth of his hypothesis. All those who resented the idea of change, or who had a vested interest in preserving the established system, fought against this new philosophy, and the early scientists were frequently persecuted. But they were, like Columbus and da Gama, men of great perseverance and courage, and they could not abandon the truth which they had seen with their own eyes. The individualism of the Renaissance, and the study of Greek science to which it had given rise, brought about a revolutionary change in habits of thought, shifting the emphasis from 'received' truth to 'experienced' truth. Before the end of the seventeenth century the new philosophy had won, and the ceaseless speculation and experimentation to which it gave rise created a world very different from that of either the Middle Ages or the Renaissance, and much closer in spirit to the one in which we live today.

Throughout Europe the breakdown in medieval patterns of thought and organisation released energy which found its outlet in disorder, and the problem was how to create political institutions which could contain this new vitality. The answer was found in strong dynastic government. The wars which closed the Middle Ages concentrated power in the hands of military leaders, and if the King could assert his position as the greatest of these leaders, and buttress his claim with victories, he became the focus of incipient national consciousness. This development was encouraged in France and Spain by the struggle for control of the rich cities of northern Italy, which did not end until the middle of the sixteenth century. War is an expression of society as a whole, and the King was the symbol of this unity. By virtue of his position he could command large quantities of men and of money. Representative institutions, which might have limited monarchical power, tended to be identified with local interests, and were swept aside in the process of unification.

English society, like the rest of Europe, was being transformed in the late fifteenth and sixteenth centuries. In the years after the Black Death, when labour was in short supply, many villeins were able to improve their status and become either leaseholders, secure in possession of their land as long as the lease lasted, or copyholders, whose conditions and length of tenure had been fixed by the manorial court. The emancipation of the villeins was a gradual process, not completed until the seventeenth century, but it had a profound effect upon rural life. The manorial system, while never as rigid as the lawyers made it appear, had given the peasant security of tenure as long as he accepted his lowly status. Now he was subjected to forces of economic change as population mounted and pressure on land increased. The revolution which took place in the lower levels of English society had none of the dramatic quality of the Renaissance or Reformation, but for the illiterate poor—who were, after all, the great majority of the English population—it was the only change that mattered.

In the upper levels of society the relationship of the smaller landowners to the greater, and of the greater landowners to the Crown, was also changing. The smaller landowners were gentlemen—men, that is, who bore no title, except perhaps that of knight, but who were often quite wealthy and conscious of the dignity that successive generations of landholding had given to their families. They had originally been dependent on the greater landowners, owing military service in return for protection, but this idealised relationship rapidly changed as war became a matter for professionals and the gentlemen-soldiers turned into gentlemen-farmers. By the middle of the fourteenth century the feudal relationship had been replaced by a bastard form, based not so much upon land as on money and force. A great lord could build up the range of his influence and extend it beyond the boundaries of his actual estates by bribing officials and using gangs of retainers to terrorise anyone who stood in his way.

The number of these great lords was limited. They came from perhaps a dozen families which, like the Nevilles, Percies and de la Poles, had consolidated their estates by intermarriage, and become princely in all but name. As a result of Edward III's policy of marrying his children to his more powerful subjects, the greater magnates were related to the Crown, and it was their ambition which led to the sordid dynastic struggles dignified by the name of the Wars of the Roses. When the House of Lancaster claimed the throne in 1399, it was setting an example soon followed by the House of York.

The enfeebled Crown was weakened still further by the strain of the long war against France. The effect of war on the continental states was, ultimately, to strengthen the monarchy, but in England the opposite was true. One reason for this was that the war was fought abroad, and the English King could not call on his subjects to close their ranks behind him in face of the invader. Another reason was that the King had to rely on the magnates for men, thereby subsidising private armies with royal money, while for supplies he was largely dependent upon loans from his richer subjects and on parliamentary grants. The result was a weak Crown, and defeat in France made matters worse: instead of being, like the Kings of France and Spain, the symbol of national defence and national victory, the last Lancastrian King of England came to symbolise defeat and incompetence.

When the greater barons fought each other for the royal title they destroyed the effectiveness of central government, but at the same time they preserved the Crown. Had they been content to carve up England into separate principalities, the monarchy might have declined into insignificance, or disappeared altogether; but the tradition of kingly rule was too potent to be ignored, and the big magnates were near enough in blood and fortune to the Crown to make it worth struggling for that greatest of all dignities. As a result, the shadow, if not the substance, of royal authority survived. It remained a shadow until the magnates committed political suicide in the Wars of the Roses. Then, and only then, could the smaller property-owners assert their independence and look to the Crown for a lead. This was the situation when Edward IV was restored to the throne in 1471, and the alliance between the Crown and the gentry became one of the bases of the 'new monarchy'.

The alliance had a profound effect upon the character of English government. In France and Spain the revival of royal power led to despotism, and on the face of it this might well have happened in England. Edward IV and Henry VII were certainly as popular as their fellow-monarchs, and they made themselves as wealthy; but for men, either to administer or to fight for them, they remained dependent upon the property-owners. These supported the King because they valued the restoration of order, upon which the preservation of their property-rights depended. But the implied condition of their support was that these property-rights should not be challenged.

For defence of their position they looked to the common law. Many country gentlemen had received some training in the law at one of the Inns of Court, but even those who had not were usually familiar with its language and assumptions. Such knowledge was very useful to them, for the disorders of the fifteenth century led to many disputed claims about ownership of land, and when an anarchic society is brought to heel, its bellicose instincts find expression in litigation. The common law had grown out of land law and existed to preserve the rights of property-owners, who regarded it with veneration as the accumulated wisdom of countless generations. Such respect was exaggerated, since the common law was untidy and archaic, while its processes were inadequate, and in many European states, including Scotland, the sixteenth century saw the reception of Roman law, to replace a jumble of local customs. But no reception took place in England. The common law, with all its deficiencies, was too well established, and had the strength of the property-owners behind it.

Even so it was threatened by the expanding judicial work of the royal Council and other prerogative courts. These often included lawyers among their officials—the Chief Justices of King's Bench and

Common Pleas were, for instance, members of the court of Star Chamber—but they used common sense rather than common law and were mainly concerned with ensuring obedience to the royal will. By the middle of the seventeenth century the common lawyers had come to hate these administrative tribunals, and joined with Parliament to destroy them. But the threat which these courts offered was, though real enough, exaggerated. Their main concern, in the Tudor period at any rate, was the preservation of order, and there was one severe limitation on their power: they could not deprive a subject of his land.

Had the early Tudors wished to destroy the political strength of the gentry they would have been faced with a very difficult proposition. For one thing there were no other allies available. The magnates were weakened and were, in any case, dangerous partners for the monarchy which they had nearly destroyed; as for the Church, this was no longer the powerful institution it had once been, and could not stand firm against secular interests. Without allies, the only possibility was brute force, but the cost of maintaining a standing army and a salaried civil service with which to administer the country was more than any Tudor monarch could consider. Royal government remained dependent, therefore, upon the gentry who, as Justices of the Peace, controlled local administration. They were the medium through which the King's will was transmitted to the localities, but in the process of transmission, high-sounding and authoritarian statements of principles were often distorted and emasculated.

The problem resolved itself eventually into one of money. The King was expected to live off his own resources, like any other landowner, and could call on his subjects for assistance only in exceptional circumstances. He had no right to levy money from them without their consent. Money was property, and property was guarded by the common law. The only institution which could overrule the common law, and legitimately open the purse-strings of the King's subjects, was Parliament. This body was, however, effectively controlled by the property-owners. In order to raise sufficient money to make a despotism possible, the King would have had to gain the assent of the very people who were most opposed to such a project. Although the Tudors were popular they could hardly expect their subjects to abandon rights which they valued almost as much as life itself. The love of the Commons, as Shakespeare knew, 'Lies in their purses; and whoso empties them, By so much fills their hearts with deadly hate'.

The only solution was for the King to build up his private resources until they could, if he wished, finance absolutism. Henry VII did this by re-endowing the Crown with land on a big scale, and making the royal estates his greatest single source of revenue. There was no apparent reason why his successors should not have continued his good work, adding to their estates by escheat and confiscation. But two checks effectively prevented this. The first was war. A successful war might well increase the power and prestige of a monarch and help the process of unification by stressing national, as distinct from local and individual, needs. But war had become, by the sixteenth century, a very expensive pastime: mercenaries and trains of artillery could, in a few months, consume the profits of years of economy, particularly from about 1520 onwards, when the second check began to operate. This was a rapid and remorseless price rise which sent costs soaring. War, which had always been expensive, now became prohibitively so, and Henry VIII could not hope to expand his income from land at anything like the rate at which prices were increasing.

A second re-endowment of the Crown was needed if Henry VII's work in restoring royal finances was not to be undone. Aristocratic estates had earlier gone to swell the King's revenue; now it was the turn of the Church. By the sixteenth century this was no longer the powerful institution that in Becket's day had defied and defeated an earlier Henry. The papacy had never really recovered from the 'Babylonish Captivity' of the late fourteenth and fifteenth centuries, when the Kings of France had dominated it and forced successive Popes to abandon Rome in favour of Avignon. This humiliating dependence came to an end only with the Great Schism, when there were two Popes, and, at one time, three, each claiming to be the only legitimate heir of St Peter and each excommunicating the others.

It had looked as though control of the Church might pass from the Popes to general councils, but Martin V checked this Conciliar Movement and restored effective supremacy before he died in 1431, and from then onwards the Popes were, in effect, absolute monarchs. But the 'new papacy', like the 'new monarchy', based its power upon wealth, and the Church became a highly organised tax-gathering machine. As wealth accumulated, holiness declined, and the ideal of 'spiritual poverty' became increasingly remote from the reality of clerical riches. The result was widespread anti-clericalism, particularly among the educated laymen—who demonstrated, by their very existence, the hollowness of the Church's claim to a monopoly of culture and learning. Such men were not irreligious, but were acutely dissatisfied with the authoritarianism and obscurantism of the Catholic Church. They made their protest in the name of conscience, and their individualism was given enormous encouragement by the Renaissance. They could now call upon the learning of the ancient world to give weight to their private judgements, and they found in the texts edited by Erasmus a source of authority as old as the Church itself.

Corruption was obviously caused by wealth, and there were many who thought that the Church would be purer if it divested itself of property. Since it refused to take this action, the duty could be held to devolve upon the lay magistrate, and the princes of Europe were quick to seize their opportunity. In England, Henry VIII dissolved the monasteries and started the process of plundering the Church that was to continue throughout the entire Tudor period. The Crown again became so rich that despotism seemed inevitable, but this second re-endowment was, in fact, no more successful than the first in turning a limited monarchy into an absolute one. There were many reasons for this failure. Perhaps most important was the fact that a property transaction of such magnitude would not have been recognised by the common-law courts without the approval of Parliament, and the property-owners who dominated that institution claimed their reward for cooperation in a large share of the profits. The re-endowment of the Crown was made possible only by the re-endowment of the gentry.

The property-owners' share of church plunder increased in size as the Crown unloaded more and more of its own portion. It did this in order to meet the costs of war, for Henry VIII, in the closing years of his reign, made a belated bid for glory by once again leading an army into France. There was no compelling reason for this, but war is a political necessity for actual or aspiring despots, since it unites the country behind the man who embodies the national will to victory and diverts attention from domestic discontents. Henry was victorious, but the prestige which this brought him, and which strengthened the Crown, was achieved only at the cost of seriously weakening the structure of royal finances. By confiscating monastic lands Henry had merely obscured the fact that the system of taxation needed radical overhaul. Changes did take place in financial organisation under the Tudors, but the government, at a time when it was constantly expanding its range, remained largely dependent upon the antiquated machinery and narrow scope of the feudal monarchy. Tudor and Stuart statesmen acted and spoke as though they could control every aspect of English life, but they could not afford the machinery that a centralised state demands. All too often their brave efforts to make a penny do the work of a pound led only to irritation and a general sense of frustration.

The attack on the Church's property had a further disadvantage in that it opened the gates to an attack on the Crown itself. There was a natural alliance between Roman Catholicism and despotism, for the Popes were as absolute, in their own sphere, as any temporal prince, and the ecclesiastical hierarchy was an invaluable instrument for the control of the state. It was not by coincidence that the most powerful European princes were Roman Catholic. The basis of protestantism is, as its name asserts, protest—the protest of individual conscience against accepted dogmas, of 'experienced' truth against 'revealed' truth. Henry VIII instinctively appreciated the disruptive nature of protestantism. He wished to preserve the structure of the Catholic Church while changing its head. The King was to be Pope in his own country. But the individualism of which the Crown had made use, to justify its attack on papal pretensions, was an ally as dangerous as the medieval magnates had once been. For if conscience told a man not to obey the Pope, it could also tell him not to obey the King, and caesaro-papism was no more acceptable to the protestant conscience than papism pure and simple had been.

The real victors in the battle with the Church were the laity. And the leaders of the laity were the property-owners, increasingly impatient of restrictions upon their accumulation of wealth. The protest against authoritarianism in the Church was matched by the challenge to absolutism in the state, and, as the sixteenth century drew to its close, vociferous protestants found a sympathetic hearing among landholders who objected to the royal Council's attempt to restrict enclosure, among common lawyers who resented the expansion of administrative justice through prerogative courts, and among the majority of merchants who objected to the way in which the Crown confined lucrative areas of trade to privileged minority groups.

Merchants were of increasing importance in English life. The discovery of a sea-route to India and the Far East opened up dazzling prospects of wealth, and the Tudor and Stuart period saw an expansion of trade to cover most of the known world. As merchants contributed more and more to their own and the nation's wealth, they insisted that their voice should be heard in matters which affected them. A minority of very rich merchants was in favour of restricted trade and rigid royal control. These were the men who were doing well out of the existing system, and could see nothing but disadvantage in the prospect of change. But most of the merchants—those who had not yet arrived at the summit of wealth—were closer to the gentry in their critical attitude towards the restrictive practices of Elizabeth and the early Stuarts.

By the 1620s the term 'Country' was being used to describe all those who, for economic, religious or political reasons, were increasingly opposed to the policies of the Crown. The desire for freedom from too close a control by central government was common to landowners, lawyers and merchants, and they found a natural means of expression in protestantism, particularly of the extreme and uncompromising type which asserted the individual's direct accountability to God for his thoughts and actions. They linked up, too, with the men of science, whose freedom of expression was inhibited by the dead hand of orthodoxy, and with the writers—particularly pamphleteers—who wanted an end to literary censorship.

A hundred years after Henry VII's death the monarchy was almost as weak as it had been at his accession. The realisation of this by the early Stuarts revived the impulse towards despotism. There was little new about their aims or methods, and the language of Stuart despotism was simply the theoretical statement of Tudor practice, but the revolt of the laity had gone so far that a return to the caesaro-papism of Henry VIII could have been carried out only at the risk of civil war. Two great themes of sixteenth- and seventeenth-century history—the strengthening of authority, and the assertion of individual freedom—had come into conflict: order, which had at first been the ally of liberty, had become its enemy.

The opposition to Charles I united under the banner of puritanism, but it included moderate anglicans and undogmatic Independents to whom the orthodoxies of presbyterianism were just as unacceptable as those of the Laudian or Roman Catholic variety. Puritanism had become, in fact, the religion of the laity, the rallying point for all those who opposed the clerical control of lay life. But the 'Country' was more than simply a negative protest against the 'Court'. It had positive policies of its own. In foreign affairs, for instance, it wanted an aggress-ive, expansionist policy, directed against the despotic monarchies of Europe, particularly Spain; while at home it encouraged the wealthier members of society to set up charitable trusts and thereby help the poor to help themselves instead of depending upon the initiative of the central government. To call the revolt of the 'Country' the 'Puritan Revolution' is to confine it within too narrow limits. 'Puritanism' is, like 'Renaissance', a word of many meanings; in its widest sense it went beyond religion and embraced nearly every aspect of social, economic, intellectual and political life.

The Civil War and Interregnum resulted in the defeat of clericalism, not only the Laudian but also the puritan variety (for 'New Presbyter', as Milton came to recognise, 'is but old Priest writ large'). The 'Country' was united in opposing despotism, but when it came to power it broke up into quarrelling factions. The presbyterians, for instance, who had preached freedom of conscience against the authoritarianism of Laud, now showed that they had claimed freedom only so that they could establish their own particular brand of intolerance and replace the tyranny of bishops with the tyranny of presbyters. The property-owners, also, who had claimed the right to pursue their own interests, unhindered by central government, now found their words echoed by the real commons of England—the common people, assembled in the army, who were a much graver threat to property-rights than any royal despotism. In short, the period which ran from the summoning of the Long Parliament in 1640 until its dissolution twenty years later, taught the gentry that they had seriously underrated the problem of order. Charles I's government had inclined to tyranny, but their own attitudes had encouraged anarchy. A feeble royal despotism had been replaced by a powerful military dictatorship, and intolerant anglicans had been replaced by intolerant puritans.

The experience of civil war and dictatorship made a return to traditional patterns of government inevitable. But both sides, 'Court' and 'Country', had modified their attitudes, and although the names remained and were revived for later use, they had changed their connotations. The monarchy was restored in 1660, but it had to abandon its alliance with clericalism. Charles II was himself a symbol of the change that had taken place. His worldliness and indifference to religion would have horrified his martyred father, but they were the conditions on which the monarchy was acceptable, as was shown when James II, accused of attempting a Catholic revival, was promptly driven out by his subjects.

Authoritarianism in the state was also abandoned, and the prerogative courts were not restored. The common law, the guardian of property, had triumphed, and the lay property-owners were left secure in possession of their wealth. They were also left, as Justices of the Peace, to control local life, since the royal Council abandoned the benevolent paternalism that had been its characteristic since 1471. In return for these concessions the property-owners made their own. They accepted the restored monarchy rather than risk anarchy, and they rejected puritanism, which had lost its general significance now that the struggle against despotism was over, and had been left, in its narrowly religious sense, as a protestant version of clericalism.

The triumph of the lay property-owners, already given philosophical justification by John Locke, was confirmed by the revolution of 1688. The victory found expression in the sovereignty of Parliament (elected by men of property for men of property), which at last accepted the financial obligations that it had had been unwilling to meet while royal power was still a threat, and provided a fiscal system more in tune with the needs of the age. In local life it led to the rule of the squires, free from restraint either by central government or by the Church. Sir Roger de Coverley, it will be recalled, liked to doze throughout the sermon, whereas his seventeenth-century predecessors would have taken notes and later examined the state of their own conscience.

The defeat of authoritarianism resulted in greater freedom of expression. The Press was left unmuzzled, as was shown by the development of newspapers and the savage pamphlet war that parties engaged in. Men of science were free to meet, at the Royal Society and elsewhere, to carry out their experiments and publish the results without fear of persecution. Trade also expanded as restrictions were removed, although the merchant oligarchs, who controlled the chartered companies and had earlier supported Charles I, switched their allegiance to Parliament and clung on to power. London, which had led the opposition to the Crown, rapidly became the commercial capital of the world, and created instruments, like the Bank of England, the Stock Exchange and Lloyds, to facilitate the flow of wealth. 'Praise-God Barebones', the puritan fanatic who gave his name to Cromwell's 'Parliament of Saints', had symbolised the passion of that earlier period. His son, Nicholas Barbon, is remembered, significantly enough, not for his religious views, but as the most daring speculative builder of his day, and the founder of fire insurance in England.

There was another side of the picture, though one that was largely ignored by the Whig historians of the nineteenth century, who continued fighting the battle against Stuart absolutism long after it had been won. The autocratic monarchy of the Tudors and early Stuarts had unified England not only by bringing outlying areas under the control of a single jurisdiction, but also by caring for the community as a whole. The Tudor Poor Laws, the Enclosure Acts, the Statute of Artificers and Apprentices, were, like the constant supervision of the royal Council, the expression of an organic view of the state. The price paid for this was a closed society, in which freedom of expression was repressed for the sake of stability. The defeat of paternalism led to a much more open society, but the sense of community was lessened, and although men were now free to get rich they were also free to starve. For over a hundred years after the Glorious Revolution social problems were left largely to private and local initiative, and the unified society of the Tudors and early Stuarts split, under the impact of industrialisation, into the Two Nations described by Disraeli.

There were other losses also. Christopher Hill has contrasted the 'iconoclasm, austerity, introspection and insular patriotism' of the 'Country' with the 'sensuousness, courtly magnificence, rhetorical drama, and an internationalism of counter-reformation monarchies' of the 'Court'.[1] These courtly qualities were conspicuously absent from Hanoverian England, and the lay view of life, deprived of its puritan fervour, was spiritually arid. At the distance of several centuries it is possible to applaud the victory of lay individualism while regretting the heavy losses it entailed. Only the Whig historian would claim that the winning side had a monopoly of virtue.

Even in the field of political institutions the victory of the property-owners was not all gain. Edward IV and Henry VII had created a strong monarchy in order to check the ambitions of over-mighty subjects and force them to consider more than their own self-interest. The defeat of strong monarchy in the seventeenth century left a political vacuum which was eventually filled by a new magnate class, wealthier and perhaps more civilised than its medieval counterpart, but just as greedy of riches and power. There was not much to choose, where political virtue was concerned, between the Percies, Nevilles and de la Poles in the earlier period, and the Walpoles, Pelhams and Grenvilles in the later.

Political power in England lay with the landed classes until well into the reign of Queen Victoria, and the greater the landowner the more power he held. The period from about 1530 to 1640 was eccentric to the normal pattern, for the gentry were the smaller property-owners and yet they rose to political predominance. They took over from a declining aristocracy and gave birth to a new one, but it is not simply by chance that their period of predominance coincides with the

[1] *The Intellectual Origins of the English Revolution*, p. 290.

rule of strong monarchy in England. The alliance between the Crown and gentry has been frequently, and accurately, described as a great source of strength for royal government, but the converse is also true. The predominance of the gentry was a reflection of the strength of the Crown, and when the Commons abolished the monarchy in 1649 they took the first step towards making themselves once again the pawns of the Lords.

2

The New Monarchy

The End of the Wars of the Roses

IN 1471 Edward IV was twenty-nine. He had come to the throne ten years earlier, but had been driven into exile by a Lancastrian counter-attack. In 1470 he set out from his refuge in Burgundy, landed in Yorkshire with a small army and, by defeating the Lancastrian forces at Tewkesbury in May 1471, made himself master of England. From then until his death twelve years later he was undisputed King, although his enemies were busy plotting against him across the seas.

Edward was a strikingly handsome man, with an ease of manner that made him very popular. Women in particular found him irresist-ible—a state of affairs of which he took repeated advantage. He seemed at first glance to be little more than a pleasure-loving rake, but although this was a part of the picture, there was more to it. Exile and hard fighting had given him a knowledge of men's weaknesses and a resilience that helped him not only to regain the throne but also to hold it against determined opposition. He had many of the virtues—as well as the vices—that Charles II was later to display, and both Kings had a cynical realism that enabled them to survive and to triumph where men of greater principle might well have failed.

When Edward died, in 1483, he left his throne to his son and name-sake, the twelve-year-old Edward V. But the real ruler of England was Richard, Duke of Gloucester, the brother of Edward IV. Richard is traditionally one of the great villains of English history, and Tudor historians painted an unforgettable picture of the royal Satan: 'little of stature, ill featured of limbs, crook-backed, his left shoulder much higher than his right, hard-favoured of visage . . . malicious, wrathful, envious.' How true a picture this is, it is now impossible to say, but there is certainly no reason to believe that Richard was kind-hearted or unambitious. Whether or not he really did murder Edward V and his brother, the Princes in the Tower, he would certainly have been capable of it. Bad men were not, however, necessarily bad kings, and by taking the crown himself and showing a firmness worthy of Edward IV, Richard avoided possible anarchy.

When Henry Tudor, Earl of Richmond and leader of the Lancastrians, defeated and killed Richard III at Bosworth in 1485, he checked the restoration of royal authority that had been steadily proceeding. It seemed as though the Wars of the Roses were about to break out again, and disorder was widespread. For several years Henry was concerned mainly with establishing himself on the throne, for the Yorkists did not regard their defeat as final. In 1487 they put forward Lambert Simnel, the son of an obscure tradesman, as the Earl of Warwick, Richard III's nephew and therefore the chief Yorkist claimant to the throne. Henry, who had the real Earl of Warwick in the Tower of London, paraded him publicly through the streets, but this gesture alone could not avert the Yorkist threat. Simnel and the Yorkist lords had landed in Lancashire and were marching south. Henry only saved his throne by fighting for it. In June 1487 he met the Yorkist army at Stoke near Newark, and destroyed it. Simnel was captured and allowed to relapse into obscurity as a turnspit in the royal kitchens.

Although this revolt had been easily crushed, the Yorkists were not defeated. Neither were they reconciled to Tudor rule by Henry's conciliatory gesture of marrying Edward IV's daughter, Elizabeth of York, shortly after his accession to the throne. In 1491 they put forward Perkin Warbeck, the son of a Tournai merchant, as Richard, Duke of York, the brother of Edward V and one of the Princes in the Tower. Warbeck learnt his part well, and was accepted by the King of France and by Edward IV's sister, Margaret of Burgundy—who both had good reasons for intriguing against the new King of England. In July 1495 Warbeck appeared off Deal and landed a number of men, while prudently remaining on board himself. The invaders were quickly rounded up by the sheriff of Kent, so Warbeck sailed off first to Ireland and then to Scotland to try his luck. James IV of Scotland, who was suspicious of English power, welcomed the *soi-disant* Duke of York, and in September 1496 a Scottish army poured across the border and invaded the northern counties. Warbeck, who was with the troops, called upon 'his' subjects to rise against the Tudor usurper, but they showed remarkably little inclination to do so. The Scots, who could not plunge deep into England without support from the English, turned their attack into a raiding expedition and returned home. Warbeck had no choice but to go with them. A year later he tried his fortunes in Cornwall, where the inhabitants had just risen against Henry VII because of his demands for taxation. But although a large number of men came in to join Warbeck, he could not capture Exeter, the key to the west country, and as success eluded him his followers slipped away. In the end he abandoned the struggle and his ambitions, and threw himself on Henry's mercy. Henry kept him in prison for two years, until another impostor appeared, claiming to be the Earl of Warwick. The King realised that he would have no peace while the Yorkist claimants remained alive, since their mere existence encouraged rebellion. In November 1499, Warwick and Warbeck, the real earl and the false duke, were both tried for treason, condemned and executed.

Henry was now well established on the throne. He had been recognised by the princes of Europe, he had sons to succeed him, and the longer he kept the crown the more secure he became. Yet he could never afford to relax his watch, for the Yorkists were still plotting and waiting for their opportunity. As late as 1503, when the King lay sick, it was reported from Calais that a number of important officials assembled there discussed what would happen after Henry's death. 'Some of them', said the informant, 'spake of my lord of Buckingham, saying that he was a noble man and would be a royal ruler. Other there were that spake . . . of Edmund de la Pole. But none of them spake of my lord prince.' Yet when Henry died in 1509 his son succeeded him without difficulty. This showed that, despite the relapse into disorder which followed the death of Richard III, royal authority had been effectively restored.

The Revival of Royal Power. I: The Council

The revival of royal power was carried out through the household and Council. There had for long been an inner and an outer ring in the administration. In the early Middle Ages the expansion of royal government had led to specialisation, and within the King's household departments emerged to deal with finance and secretarial business. These departments, the Exchequer and Chancery, gradually moved out of Court and acquired their own routines, but they were still under royal control. As the barons became more powerful, however, and more politically ambitious, they forced their own nominees into these great offices, so as to take over the administration. But the King's household was perpetually fecund. While the barons were taking over the outer ring, an inner ring of household offices was being created, and the Wardrobe or Chamber by-passed the old-established offices and left them only the trappings of power. In times of emergency a determined King could govern his country through the household offices. They were flexible and informal, not yet hamstrung by the formalisation that made the Exchequer, for instance, so ponderous and long-winded in its functioning. Edward IV and Henry VII found within their own household an efficient machine that only needed to be set to work.

The mainspring of royal government was the King's Council, but from the early fourteenth century onwards the magnates claimed a larger and larger share in this body, and, eventually came to dominate it. Asserting that they were the King's natural advisers, they had made him accept them whether he wanted to or not. By the time Edward IV came to the throne the Council was a large, aristocratic body, functioning more or less independently of the Crown. Edward had no use for such an institution. He wanted something much more immediately under his control. The old-type baronial Council disappeared along with the baronage itself, and it was for long supposed that Edward ruled without out a Council. But although the evidence is slender, it is clear that Edward had a Council very similar to the early Tudor one.

The names survive of over two hundred persons in Henry VII's reign called 'Councillors'—meaning, presumably, that they had taken a special oath to advise the sovereign—and they can be divided up, as can Edward's Councillors, into a group of nobles, a group of clerics, and a large 'official' element made up of lawyers and country gentlemen. The similarity between the Yorkist and the Tudor body extends not only to structure but even to individuals, since out of forty of Edward IV's Councillors alive after 1485, at least half were Councillors to Henry VII. Trained and efficient men were not, after all, so easily come by that any monarch could afford to deprive himself of their services simply because they had fought for the other side. Neither were Yorkists and Lancastrians separate and unmixable elements, like oil and water. Many people, particularly of the country gentry and lawyer sections of society, were prepared to serve the Crown no matter who was wearing it.

There was not much sign under Henry VII, any more than there had been under Edward IV, of a deliberate attempt to oust nobles from the Council. The baronage as a group had only a shadow of its former power, but individual nobles were still men of great estates, and therefore of great influence. Under Henry, several of the most important positions in the administration were held by men who came from long-ennobled families. The Lord Admiral and Constable of the Tower, for instance, was John de Vere, thirteenth Earl of Oxford; while Thomas Howard, Earl of Surrey, who had actually fought against Henry at Bosworth, emerged from three years' imprisonment in the Tower to take a leading place in the royal Council, and to become one of Henry's best soldiers.

Clerics outnumbered nobles in the Council, and played as big a part as they had done throughout the Middle Ages. Henry VII's most trusted adviser was John Morton, who became Chancellor in 1487 and was to be a Cardinal and Archbishop of Canterbury before his death. Among the others were Richard Fox, the King's Secretary and later Keeper of the Privy Seal, who rose to be Bishop of Winchester; and William Warham, who succeeded Morton as Chancellor and also became Archbishop of Canterbury. The big advantage of these men, from Henry's point of view, was that they were well educated, could be rewarded for service to the state by promotion in the Church—which cost the King nothing—and left no legitimate heirs to claim either their wealth or their office.

As well as nobles and clerics, the late-Yorkist and early-Tudor Council included the judges and law officers of the Crown. There was nothing new in this. The element of novelty was to be found in the 'official' element in the Council, made up of men who were 'new' only in the sense that they did not belong to the handful of great families which had controlled English life in the preceding century. These were the men whom Warbeck denounced as 'caitiffs', but they were far removed from the ordinary people. The majority were country gentlemen, who had been trained in either civil or common law. Empson was the only prominent member of Henry's Council to come from a bourgeois background—his father was a person of some importance in the town of Towcester—and the idea that Henry VII surrounded himself with 'middle-class men' is very misleading. England was a predominantly rural country, with only a small middle class of merchants. The gentry, whose numbers and importance in the royal administration were steadily increasing, were close in blood and social assumptions to the aristocracy, and counted themselves among the upper ranks of English society.

The Council existed to advise the King and to translate the royal will into action. There was no fixed membership, and the numbers varied from meeting to meeting. Yet in spite of its fluctuating membership, the Council was more than the sum of its separate meetings. A number of permanent officials, peers and lawyers, were frequent attenders and formed, in effect though not in name, an inner circle. They were full-time administrators and attended the King not only during the law-terms, when most of the business was transacted, but during vacations as well. This 'Council attendant' was a skeleton staff which simply merged into the larger body when a full meeting took place. Its members included the great officers of state—the Chancellor, Treasurer and Privy Seal—and such officials as Bray, Daubeny and Guildford, who were among the most trusted of Henry VII's servants. The King himself was the heart of the Council, giving it a cohesion and continuity that it would not otherwise have possessed. Both Edward and Henry were frequently, if not usually, present at meetings, and the Council was an extension of the royal personality. It was, in practice as well as in theory, the King-in-Council, and its twin characteristics were, as Bindoff says, 'complete dependence upon the King, and omnicompetence under him'.[1]

The Council's range of work was enormous, and it made no distinction between judicial and administrative business. It sat regularly in term time and used for its meetings the two rooms that made up the Star Chamber. Its advisory and administrative functions were probably the most important part of its work, although much of this can only be inferred, since the Council had no seal of its own and had to use the Signet or Privy Seal to authenticate its decisions. Councillors offered advice to the King on matters of policy, and framed letters, warrants, proclamations and all the other documents necessary to execute the royal will.

Most of the surviving records show the Council functioning as a court of justice. It was the ideal body for dealing with complaints involving a great landowner, whose influence might easily pervert a local jury or sheriff, for in the Council sat the King and the great men of his realm and they were not to be browbeaten. They summoned offenders before them, however great, and, if they thought injustice had been done, would not hesitate to summon the jury as well, order it to change its verdict, and fine individual members.

Cases usually began with a petition addressed to the King, and

[1] *Tudor England*, p. 61.

conciliar procedure was very different from that of the common law courts. There was, for instance no jury, and the defendant was put on oath to answer questions truthfully. The accepted picture of Henry VII's Council, sitting as a court in Star Chamber, is that of a stern tribunal, summoning before it over-mighty offenders, and more or less superseding the common law courts in cases of livery (the keeping of uniformed retainers) and maintenance (the supporting of unjust claims in a court by violence or threats). Yet the surviving records, which, though only a fragment, are presumably an average cross section, do not support this picture. The Council rarely dealt with cases of maintenance, bribing of juries, dereliction of duty by sheriffs, or the keeping of retainers. Many of the offences that came before it were concerned with rioting, for the country was still very disordered and local magnates had acquired the habit of taking the law into their own hands. Even so, the Council rarely initiated action. It waited for complaints to be made to it, and then often passed cases on to the King's Bench to deal with. Under Henry VII in fact, the Council was far more concerned with settling disputes between private individuals or between corporations, particularly in cases, such as libel or slander, for which common law provided no adequate remedy.

Punishments were surprisingly light. Heavy fines were rarely inflicted and whipping or mutilation was unknown. As the historian of Henry VII's Council comments: 'It was surely the mildest-mannered tribunal that ever sentenced a criminal, considerate in its procedure, gentle in its punishments, and failing altogether to live up to the reputation of ruthlessness that the Star Chamber has enjoyed since the seventeenth century.'[1]

The moderation of the Council in Star Chamber does not mean that Edward IV, Richard III and Henry VII were not alive to the need to repress disorder. They had good reason to be. In 1486 for instance, the Prior of Leominster complained that a local Justice of the Peace had attacked his monastery with one hundred and sixty armed men, who tore down a large tree which they used as a battering-ram to breach the walls of the monastic gaol and free the prisoners inside. Much of the disorder throughout England sprang from the practice of keeping retainers. Edward IV's Parliaments passed Acts against this, and Henry's did the same: but the Act of 1504 admitted that little had been done to check this evil, and three years later it was revealed that Lord Bergavenny had extended his influence over a large part of

[1] C. G. Bayne, *Select Cases in the Council of Henry VII*, p. clxxii.

Kent and retained to his service a small army of nearly five hundred men. Henry VII's reign saw a great deal of new machinery—most of it short-lived—set up to deal with the most urgent problems. In 1487, for instance, the so-called 'Star-Chamber Act' set up a special court to try offences against public order, particularly those in which juries were concerned. This new court does not seem to have been very effective: its importance is historical, in that Stuart lawyers assumed that the Act creating it was the origin of the Court of Star Chamber. In fact, Star Chamber as a court was no more than a formalisation of the Council's judicial activity—which was, of course, medieval in origin.

Although Henry VII did not create the Court of Star Chamber, he was apparently responsible for the small 'Council Learned in the Law'. The dozen or so members of this were all Councillors, and included Empson and Dudley. They sat as a committee of the Council, and took the initiative in collecting debts owed to the Crown and in bringing defaulters to justice. On the face of it there was nothing particularly significant about such business, but the Council Learned was in fact one of the ways by which Henry VII brought his greater subjects to heel. Dudley's account book survives and shows how the system worked. A landowner accused of keeping retainers or of evading the payment of feudal dues to the Crown would be faced with the alternative of being sued in the common law courts or of paying a fine to settle the matter. The costs of legal action were high; and most of the accused preferred to admit their guilt and pay up. This procedure was swifter, more effective and less public than a lawsuit, but it smacked of blackmail and made Empson and Dudley hated by the politically important section of the population, who were not used to being called to account for their actions. Many noblemen figure in Dudley's list. The Earl of Northumberland, for instance, was fined £10,000 for ravishing one of the King's wards. He had to pay £5,000 down: the balance was held over him as a threat, to be collected in case of future misbehaviour. The King had more to gain by such actions than merely sums of money. Fines for keeping too many retainers struck at one of the most potent sources of disorder, while those for premature occupation of lands brought home to property-holders the need for a legal title, duly recorded.

The areas on the borders of Wales and Scotland were remote from London and particularly liable to disorder. When Edward IV's son was born, in 1470, he was created Prince of Wales, and a council was appointed to look after his estates. By 1476 this council had acquired judicial functions, and was supervising the enforcement of law and order throughout the principality and the marcher lordships which separated it from England. This council lapsed at Edward's death, but Henry VII appointed a similar council for his son, Prince Arthur. The young prince was given a large number of the Crown's marcher lordships, including the great Earldom of March, as well as the Principality, and thus became direct ruler over a large part of Wales. Even after his death the council continued its work, and the marcher lords, who had previously been semi-independent magnates, were forced to acknowledge the authority of the Crown.

To control the north of England, where the great border families of Percy, Neville and Dacre ruled like independent princes, Edward IV appointed his brother Richard, Duke of Gloucester. Richard ruled the north well, and when he became King he kept a council there under the presidency of his nephew, the Earl of Lincoln. In Henry VII's reign there may have been an intermittent council in the north, but generally speaking control slipped back into the hands of the Percies. Even so, Henry asserted his supremacy, and the changing position of the northern magnates was shown when the Earl of Northumberland was killed trying to suppress a riot that had broken out at Thirsk against the King's tax-collectors. Percies were more used to fighting against the Crown than dying in the King's service: now the situation was changing.

No outline of late Yorkist and early Tudor administration would be complete that left out the personality of the monarch. The institutions of government were old; it was the strong will behind them that was new. Much of the achievement of Edward IV and Henry VII was due simply to their energy and determination. When disorder broke out in East Anglia, Edward appointed one of his household officers as sheriff and publicly declared that, though he could ill spare so valuable a man, he had sent him down 'to set a rule in the country', and in 1464 Edward himself went on a tour of the most disturbed districts to make sure that order was enforced and justice administered. Richard and Henry were also constantly on the move, asserting the royal authority simply by making their presence known.

Henry had none of Edward IV's easy charm, but he shared the same iron determination to hold his throne. He had a shadowy claim by blood, being descended, through his mother, from Edward III, but his real title came from brute strength. He had killed Richard III and taken his crown: he would remain King as long as he could defeat all challengers. He was only twenty-eight when he triumphed at Bosworth, and had spent much of his life in exile. The portraits show a clean-cut face with a Roman nose, but they also suggest what his contemporaries remarked about him—a watchful reserve that allowed little or no intimacy. Bacon, in his *Life of King Henry VII*, commented that if he had been a 'private man he would have been termed proud; but in a wise Prince it was but keeping of distance'. Because he was a good judge of men, Henry was not jealous of ability, and was served as well as, if not better than, any other Tudor sovereign. He did not have the streak of vindictiveness that was to emerge in his son, and although he would not shirk from killing his enemies, he preferred to take their money and let them live. After the failure of Warbeck's rising in the west country, for instance, Henry appointed commissioners to fine all those who had taken part and eventually added nearly £15,000 to his treasury.

The legend of the miser King obscures the true image of the ruler who deliberately cultivated pomp and ceremony in order to raise the throne above the reach of even the greatest noble. Like most men Henry loved money, and between 1491 and 1503 he spent more than £100,000 on jewellery, but this was more than a miser's inexplicable greed. The medieval monarchy had collapsed because it had become so poor. Henry knew that if the Crown was to be made strong again, it must first be made rich.

The Revival of Royal Power. II: Finance

There was nothing new about Henry's financial system, except its thoroughness. Edward IV had revived the Chamber and made it the centre of his financial organisation. The Exchequer was by-passed because its methods were too cumbersome and its traditional routine made it insufficiently flexible to meet the demands of the Crown. Edward had removed at least part of his lands from Exchequer control. Henry eventually went further and ordered that all receipts from Crown lands were to be paid to the Treasurer of the Chamber. Other items of revenue were gradually transferred until the Exchequer was left with only the 'ancient revenue', made up of the '*firma comitatus*' and the '*firma burgi*' (long-established annual payments made by counties and boroughs), and the Customs. The Duchy of Lancaster, a model of estate administration, continued to handle its own revenues. Everything else went to the Chamber. Under Henry VI the Treasurer of

B*

the Chamber had handled, at the most, £2,000 a year; under Edward IV the amount fluctuated violently, though it occasionally reached £50,000. By the time Henry VII died the Chamber was receiving about £100,000 a year—nearly ten times as much as the amount paid into the Exchequer.

Since the Exchequer did not handle the bulk of the revenue, it could hardly audit it. Henry VII continued Edward IV's practice of appointing officials to audit specific accounts. He had no need of a permanent audit office, since he was his own finance minister, controlling expenditure and regularly inspecting and initialling the Treasurer's accounts. Henry paid particular attention to land revenues, and made the royal estates the foundation of the Crown's wealth. By Act of Parliament, in 1486, he took back into the Crown's possession many of the lands which had been allowed to slip from its grasp in the preceding thirty years of civil war, and throughout his reign he added to this endowment by confiscating the estates of his enemies. In the first year of his reign the net income from land, after the costs of the household and other charges had been met, was a mere £4,000, but by the end of the reign this figure had increased to £30,000. Customs did not show so striking an increase, though the Book of Rates was revised in 1507 and greater stability in England and abroad encouraged the flow of trade. By the end of the reign the gross yield was still only £40,000 a year, and although this was a large sum it did not reflect the increasing wealth of the merchant class. The failure to tap this source effectively was to be a fundamental weakness of Tudor finance.[1]

While the merchants contributed only moderately to royal income, the landowners were forced to pay heavily. The King was, in feudal theory, lord of the manor of England, and the big landowners were his tenants. Feudalism as a military and social system was in decay, but strong monarchy saw its revival as a financial system. The King could demand extraordinary 'aids', such as those which Parliament granted for the knighting of Prince Arthur and the marriage of Princess Margaret. More important were the 'incidents' which had to be paid every time death occurred in a landholding family. If the tenant left no heir, then the Crown exercised the right of escheat and took charge of his estates. Where an heiress succeeded, the Crown either made her pay for freedom to choose a husband or else married her off

---

[1] These figures, and the conclusions drawn from them, may have to be modified in the light of B. P. Wolffe's article on 'Henry VII's Land Revenues and Chamber Finance' (see Bibliography).

to the highest bidder. If the heir was a boy, he became a royal ward, and the Crown would take over his estates until he became of age, or would sell the guardianship for a large sum of money. In either case the unfortunate ward's lands would probably be exploited by those who, in theory, were responsible for safeguarding them.

Landholders resented this land tax—since that, in effect, is what it was—as a threat to the prosperity of their estates, and frequently concealed information about changes that had taken place. Edward IV appointed commissions to enquire into feudal tenures and make sure that he was not being cheated of his rights. Henry VII did the same, and some idea of the resistance offered by landed families is given by the fact that out of the last fifty post-mortem inquisitions calendared for Henry's reign—these were enquiries held after the death of a land-holder, to record the change of tenure—well over half report that the existence of under-age heirs had been deliberately concealed.

Edward and Henry both dabbled in trade on their own account. Edward's agents bought up wool and tin, and shipped these to con-tinental markets, while Henry made £15,000 from the sale of alum in 1505-6. They showed the same readiness to exploit every source of income open to them, by levying loans and gifts. Edward borrowed money from an Italian financier and from the City of London, but most of these loans had been repaid by his death. Henry took a forced loan in 1486, but this likewise was repaid, and his credit stood high. 'Bene-volences' were another matter. Edward IV's demands for 'voluntary' gifts as a sign of the *benevolentia*, or goodwill, which his richer subjects bore him, had been so bitterly resented that a statute of Richard III's reign declared them to be illegal. Nevertheless, Henry raised bene-volences on the grounds of urgent military need. On the face of it, this was an arbitrary exercise of the royal will, but in fact the tax system was rigged in favour of the richer subjects, and benevolences were one way—admittedly crude and unsatisfactory—of making the most prosperous section of the population contribute a fairer share towards the King's expenses. Yet it remains true that the "new mon-archy', so efficient in administration and expenditure, clung to anti-quated methods of collecting money. Henry VII was perhaps strong enough to have reformed the entire financial system, even at the risk of offending the landowners and merchants whose support he needed. But he never did so, nor did his son, and later monarchs were in no position to solve the problem.

For extraordinary supplies of money Henry turned to Parliament, but he did this as rarely as possible, preferring to follow the example of Edward IV, who told the Commons in 1467: 'I purpose to live upon my own, and not to charge my subjects but in great and urgent causes concerning the weal of themselves and also the defence of them, and of this my realm.' Any parliamentary taxation was liable to arouse resentment, or even open rebellion, as in the case of the Cornish rising This alone would account for the fact that Edward, who reigned for twenty-one years, only met six Parliaments, while Henry, who reigned for twenty-nine years, was content with seven. Parliament was, in any case, still too closely identified with the feudal magnates who had made it the focus of their opposition to the Crown. Yet this identification was largely accidental. Parliament reflected the balance of power within the country at any given moment. When the barons controlled the country, they controlled Parliament, and the same was to be true of the landed gentry. By the time Henry VII's first Parliament met, however, the power of the feudal baronage had been broken; fifty-three lay lords had been summoned to the last Parliament to meet before the Wars of the Roses broke out, but only twenty-nine received a summons to the first Parliament of Henry VII. Many ancienth uoses had died out in the male line or had passed into the hands of minors, while the baronage as a whole had poured out its wealth in fighting and had lost the political influence which money had given it. Henry was himself the greatest of all the barons, the residuary legatee of many noble families. In his own right he was Earl of Richmond, and as King he was heir not only to the great duchy of Lancaster but also to the Yorkist lands, including the earldoms of March and Warwick. The duchy of Cornwall and earldom of Chester were also annexed to the Crown, and more lands and titles were added throughout the reign by escheat and confiscation. Henry was the first English King for over a century not to be surrounded by magnates whose combined wealth and influence were greater than his own. He was in no hurry to alter so agreeable a situation. He created a mere five new peerages during his reign, and at his death there was only one duke left in England. A Stuart judge, looking back on this transformation a century later, saw its significance. 'Time hath his revolutions', he said. 'There must be a period and an end to all temporal things, *Finis Rerum*, an end of names and dignities and whatsoever is terrene. For where is Bohun? Where is Mowbray? Where is Mortimer? Nay, which is more and most of all, where is Plantagenet? They are interred in the urns and sepulchres of mortality.'

The Commons were not yet as important as the Lords, but they were increasing in independence. Since Edward III's reign their assent had been essential to money Bills, and in 1489 the judges declared that an Act of Parliament was not valid unless the Commons had agreed to it. In the later Middle Ages many constituencies had resented sending a member to Parliament at their expense, but this attitude was slowly changing. The increasing importance of the Commons was shown by the presence there of many of the King's Councillors, who, although technically members of the Lords, preferred to exert their influence in the Lower House.

The main function of Parliament, in Henry VII's reign, was to vote money. The standard parliamentary grant, the Tenth and Fifteenth, had originally been a charge on movable property, but had ossified into a fixed levy of about £30,000. Each county knew how much it would be expected to pay, and the incidence of the tax took little note of changes in the distribution of wealth. For this reason a change was made in 1487, when commissioners were appointed to assess individual incomes and tax them at the rate of ten per cent. The innovation was resented, and riots were widespread, but the experiment was repeated in the next reign and eventually produced the subsidy, the main parliamentary tax in Tudor and early Stuart England.

Hostility in Parliament to Henry's demands for money was not to be expected, especially as the King was always careful to explain the circumstances—usually war or the threat of war—which made such demands necessary. The last grant came in 1496, when Parliament voted £120,000 to meet the cost of Perkin Warbeck's invasion and the Scottish war. But according to Roper, who wrote the life of his father-in-law, Sir Thomas More, the King asked the Parliament of 1504 for a grant when there was no obvious need. More, who was a member of the Commons, persuaded the House to reject this demand, 'so that one of the King's privy chamber . . . being present thereat, brought word to the King out of the Parliament House that a beardless boy had disappointed all his purposes'. Henry, according to Roper's account, was furious, and showed his anger by sending More's father to the Tower for an imaginary offence and keeping him there until he paid £100 fine.

Edward IV and Henry VII summoned Parliaments not only to get money but also to unify the kingdom by crushing those who challenged their authority. Individual offenders were dealt with by Acts of Attainder—one hundred and thirty-eight of them passed in Henry's reign—while other Acts struck at privileged bodies. The Act of 1504 ordering corporations not to make any regulations unless they were first approved by the Crown, and the Acts limiting benefit of clergy, were examples of the way in which Parliament was used to establish the principle that all rights derived from the Crown and that there was one ruler, and one only, in England.

The Revival of Royal Power. III: Foreign Policy

One of the main reasons for the collapse of the medieval monarchy had been the enormous cost of the long war against France. Neither Edward nor Henry could afford to uphold the English Kings' claim to the French throne. Yet kings were expected to fight, and it seemed as if the only alternatives were a bankrupting war or an inglorious peace. Edward IV found a way out of this dilemma. In 1474 he allied with the Duke of Burgundy against France, called on Parliament to vote supplies, and led a fine army across the Channel. The French King, however, had no more desire for war than Edward, and offered terms which Edward accepted. By the treaty of Picquigny Edward agreed to withdraw his troops from France—while maintaining his theoretical claim to the French throne—in return for a large cash payment and a pension for life. This profitable example was closely followed by Henry VII. He sent an army to Brittany to try to prevent the French King from annexing the strategically important seaboard duchy, but when this failed he invaded France in person. Charles VIII, now that he had secured Brittany, saw no point in more fighting. A treaty was signed at Etaples in 1492, by which the French King bound himself not to assist pretenders to the English throne and to pay Henry an annual pension. Henry returned to England triumphant, and richer than when he had set out.

As the Tudor dynasty became more firmly settled on the throne, it was accepted by the European ruling families, and marriage negotiations were started. As early as 1489 it was agreed, in the Treaty of Medina del Campo, that Henry's eldest son, Prince Arthur, should eventually marry Catherine of Aragon, daughter of the King of Spain. The marriage did not actually take place until 1501, when the young princess landed in England, and it lasted only a few months, for in the following year Arthur died. Ferdinand wanted to keep the English alliance which the marriage had symbolised, and Henry was reluctant to lose the dowry, so negotiations were opened for a second marriage, this time between Catherine and Henry's second son Prince

Henry. There were difficulties to be overcome, including the fact that a papal dispensation was needed to set aside the law of the Church that a man may not marry his brother's widow. Agreement was eventually reached, but by the time the marriage actually took place Henry VII was dead. Before his death he had arranged another alliance of great significance for the future. In an attempt to put an end to the perpetual tension between England and Scotland he married his daughter Margaret to James IV in 1503. As a step towards peace the marriage was a failure, but it led to the eventual fusion of the two kingdoms under one dynasty.

A 'New' Monarchy?

By the time Henry died he was one of the richest kings in Europe. He left little actual money, but his plate and jewels and the debts outstanding to him were worth several million pounds in modern currency. He made the English Crown so rich that it might have survived even the extravagance of Henry VIII, but for the effect of inflation and war. As Bacon wrote: 'having every day occasion to take notice of the necessities and shifts for money of other great princes, abroad, it did the better by comparison set off to him the felicity of full coffers'.

The wealth of the Crown was one of the most novel aspects of the so-called 'new monarchy' of Edward IV and Henry VII. Institutionally speaking, there was little that was new about the reign of either monarch. The Council was medieval, Chamber finance was not essentially different from the Wardrobe administration of the fourteenth century, and as for the use of 'new men', this was as old as the monarchy itself. The real change had taken place not in the King's household but in English society, and the transformation was not confined to England. Throughout much of western Europe the erosion of medieval political and economic ideals had brought about unified states under powerful, centralised, princely governments. The important difference, however, between France and Spain on the one hand, and England on the other, was that the rulers of the two continental states were able to build up large standing armies and could control the provinces through salaried royal officials. Edward and Henry never created a salaried civil service with a strong police-army behind it. There were elements of despotism in their government, particularly the prerogative courts and the all-powerful royal Council, but there were also other elements, such as the common law and the reliance on country gentlemen for local government, that pulled in the opposite direction. Edward and Henry might have tried to create, in England, despotic monarchy on the Spanish pattern, and the novelty of their position lies in the fact that they might have succeeded. But instead of remodelling English administration and using the royal Council, as their French and Spanish contemporaries did, to invade and take over all other departments of government, they chose the easier course of pumping new blood and new vigour into the existing system. The significance of the 'New Monarchs' in the history of Tudor and Stuart Britain comes mainly from the fact that they preserved so much of the past.

3

King and Cardinal

Henry VIII

THE accession of Henry VIII, a handsome, energetic young man, not yet eighteen, effectively closed the struggle between rival houses for the throne. While through his father he was the heir to Lancaster, through his mother he was the descendant of York, and as John Skelton, his tutor and later laureate, declared:

> The Rose both white and red
> In one Rose now doth grow.

Henry's looks were commented on by many foreign observers. The Venetian ambassador reported that the new King 'is the handsomest potentate I ever set eyes on . . . with auburn hair combed straight and short in the French fashion, and a round face so very beautiful that it would become a pretty woman', and others pointed the contrast between the reserved, calculating Henry VII and his apparently open-hearted, impulsive son.

Henry's character, however, remains a puzzle. Throughout the first half of his reign he devoted his days to hunting and his nights to feasting and love, content to leave routine administration and the formulation of policy to Wolsey. He was never a mere cipher and occasionally interfered with Wolsey's arrangements, but in the late 1520s he suddenly emerged as a controlling figure in English politics, and remained for the rest of his reign much nearer the heart of government than he had ever been before. The extent to which he actually initiated policy has almost certainly been exaggerated. The playboy did not turn into an elder statesman overnight, and because he kept his distaste for the day-to-day business of government—reading documents, weighing opinions, working out consistent policies—the initiative

rested with his servants, particularly when they were men of outstanding ability, like Wolsey and Thomas Cromwell. Yet however secure
Henry's ministers seemed to be in their position, the King was never
dependent on them. Their policies were effective only because he
approved of them, and when, in a dark mood of anger or suspicion, he
chose to seize the initiative himself, he swept his advisers out of his
way with a ruthlessness unrestrained by gratitude or fear. While these
sporadic outbursts of energy lasted he remained, in fact as well as in
title, master of England.

For the first twenty years of his reign this arrogant, imperious
young man was content to play the prince and let others govern for
him. Having been kept very much in the background by Henry VII
he found the business of government unfamiliar and uncongenial and
preferred, like many a child of the second generation, to enjoy the
magnificent inheritance that his father had handed on to him. Only in
one incident did a hint of later attitudes appear. Empson and Dudley
had served his father faithfully and had done more than any other of
Henry VII's Councillors to build up the wealth of the Crown which the
young King was now consuming. But their zeal in the royal service
had made them very unpopular with the richer and politically influential section of English society. Henry VIII, looking around for
some gesture that would win him easy popularity and signal the advent
of a new and more relaxed reign, saw his opportunity. Empson and
Dudley were tried on a trumped-up charge of treason, and executed.
Lack of gratitude was to be one of the most typical of Henry's characteristics.

Wolsey. I: The Rise to Power

For the first few years of the new reign Henry relied on his father's
Councillors, but it was not long before Thomas Wolsey worked his
way into the King's confidence and established a monopoly of royal
favour that was to last for nearly twenty years. Wolsey was born in
late 1472 or early 1473, the son of an Ipswich butcher and cattle
dealer. For an ambitious and talented boy, not born into the upper
ranks of late medieval society, the Church was the only possible
opening, and Wolsey soon entered it. By the age of fifteen he was at
Magdalen College, Oxford, where his contemporaries called him the
'Boy-Bachelor', and he was befriended by the Marquis of Dorset,
whose children he had taught at Magdalen College School. Dorset, a

nobleman of high birth, was prominent among Henry VII's Councillors and presumably recommended Wolsey to others of his circle.
The ambitious clergyman soon came to the notice of Henry VII,
who employed him on several diplomatic missions and was apparently
impressed by his intelligence, his ability and his enormous capacity for
hard work.

Wolsey suffered a temporary eclipse in the early days of the new
reign, but quickly established his hold on the young King by persuading him, in the words of Cavendish, the Cardinal's biographer, 'to
follow his desire and appetite, nothing minding to travail in the busy
affairs of this realm'.

Henry, being young and rich, lacked nothing but glory. His father
had held aloof from the struggle between France and Spain for control
of Italy, but Henry only wanted a convenient excuse to intervene.
He did not have long to wait. By 1510 France held the upper hand and
the Italian states were chafing at their impotence. One of the most
important of these states was the central bloc ruled over by the Pope,
and Julius II, the embodiment of the temporal glory of the papacy,
was building up a Holy League against France. It consisted of the
Papal States, Venice, Switzerland and Spain, and the English King was
invited by his father-in-law, Ferdinand of Spain, to join the alliance.
Henry was delighted to demonstrate his devotion to the papacy at the
same time as he struck a blow at England's traditional enemy, and plans
for an invasion were set on foot. The vision of peace and enlightenment which Henry's accession had seemed to bring with it turned out
to be a mirage. Erasmus, the great Dutch scholar, wrote sadly from
London: 'I was dreaming of an age that was really golden and isles
that were happy, when that Julian trumpet summoned all the world
to arms.'

An English attempt at invading south-west France was an inglorious
failure, but Wolsey prepared another and larger expedition and spared
no effort to make sure that it succeeded. The King went in person to
Calais to take command of the army that Wolsey had concentrated
there, and struck south-east towards Tournai. On 15 August 1513
a French relieving force fled so rapidly that the engagement was
christened 'The Battle of the Spurs', and Tournai fell into the hands
of the English. Henry had won the glory he coveted and rewarded the
man who had made it possible. Wolsey was appointed Bishop of
Tournai, and shortly afterwards he was elevated to the see of Lincoln.

By 1514 Wolsey was Archbishop of York, but while William

Warham remained alive he could not hope to be Archbishop of Canterbury and head of the Church in England. Only a legate *a latere*, sent 'from the side of' the Pope, could supersede the Archbishop within his own province, and such appointments were made only in exceptional circumstances and for a limited period. Wolsey, however, was determined to rule the English Church, and with Henry's encouragement he pressed the Pope to make him *Legatus a latere* for life. Such a demand was preposterous, since Wolsey had never even been to Rome, but the Pope, caught between the millstones of France and Spain, could not afford to offend so valuable and loyal an ally as the King of England. In 1515 Wolsey was made a cardinal; by 1524 he was *legatus a latere* for life, and could extend into the administration of the Church the process of unification that Henry VII had applied to the state. Since, in 1515, he had also been appointed Chancellor, he was now the effective head of both Church and state, implying by his position a type and degree of unification far more inclusive than anything Henry VII had dreamed of.

Wolsey. II: The Problem of Church Reform

Wolsey had the power, as *legatus a latere*, to intervene in every diocese, overriding the authority of bishops and archbishops alike. He had demanded this power on the nominal grounds that he wished to reform the Church, and reform was certainly needed. There was a growing volume of complaint from the laity against pluralism and non-residence and against the high fees charged for probate and mortuary. Within the Church itself there was also a reform movement, and this was given new vitality by the Christian Renaissance, spread throughout Europe by Erasmus of Rotterdam.

Erasmus, born in 1466, was among the first to realise that the literary treasures of the ancient world included not only the pagan classics but also the fundamental Christian texts—the Bible and the writings of the early fathers. He began collating manuscripts, and produced editions of these texts which were soon circulating all over Europe.

Even before Erasmus started his work the new learning had spread to England. In 1478 the first printing press at Oxford was set up, and at about the same time an Italian scholar was brought over to the university to inaugurate the study of Greek. Among his pupils was William Grocyn, who in his turn inspired a number of young men, including

Thomas Linacre, Thomas More and John Colet. With them the
humanist movement in England—the study of man and his relationship to God—came of age. Colet visited Italy, where he studied the
early fathers, and returned to Oxford to lecture on St Paul. It was there
that Erasmus met him when, in 1497-98, he came to England to learn
Greek. The two men felt an immediate sympathy with each other and
Colet introduced Erasmus to his circle of friends. Erasmus was delighted. 'I have lost little', he wrote, 'in not going to Italy. When Colet
speaks I might be listening to Plato. Linacre is as deep and acute a
thinker as I have ever met with. Grocyn is a mine of knowledge; and
nature never formed a sweeter and happier disposition than that of
Thomas More.'

Erasmus, Colet, More and their friends were all inspired by love for
the Church, which they longed to cleanse of its corruption so that it
could meet the challenge of an age in which Renaissance paganism
and the bursting of the geographical bounds of the medieval world
were dissolving so many established institutions and beliefs. All the
reformers needed was a programme and a head, and they would
eagerly have supported Wolsey if he had given a lead.

This was at least a possibility. Wolsey chose Colet to preach the
sermon at the magnificent ceremony in which he received the red hat
of a cardinal, and he had a real interest in education. But whatever
Wolsey had in mind, he did nothing. He came instead to epitomise all
the abuses of the Church. He always held one other bishopric as well
as his Archbishopric of York, thereby introducing episcopal pluralism
to England, and he had non-resident Italians appointed to the sees of
Salisbury, Worcester and Llandaff, to whom he paid a fixed salary so
that he could pocket the surplus. He had himself elected Abbot of St
Albans, one of the richest monasteries in England, although he was not
and never had been a monk. He interfered in every diocese, appointing
his own protégés, regardless of the rights of patrons, and set up
legatine courts to which he summoned men from all over England. He
charged large sums for probate and was notoriously greedy for riches.
He was non-resident on a princely scale, never even visiting three of
his sees and first entering the diocese of York sixteen years after he had
been made Archbishop.

In an age when the laxness of clerical morals was under savage
criticism, Wolsey set an example by having an illegitimate son, on
whom he showered lucrative Church offices, and an illegitimate
daughter whom he placed in a nunnery. Colet had complained of

'pride of life', but even he could hardly have envisaged Wolsey's magnificence. The Cardinal-Legate lived on a princely scale, appearing in public in silk and velvet and expecting great noblemen to perform menial household duties for him. Cavendish spends several pages merely listing the members of his household, and estimates that he had at least five hundred persons employed in his service. He lived in state at Hampton Court, which he created, or at York Place, which Henry later turned into Whitehall. Cavendish describes him going to Westminster Hall 'with two great crosses of silver borne before him, with also two great pillars of silver, and his Sergeant-at-Arms with a great mace of silver gilt. Then his gentlemen-ushers cried and said, "On, my lords and masters. Make way for my lord's grace." '

Far from aiding the reformers, Wolsey did their cause harm by being himself so glaring an abuse. More than that, he also brought into contempt and hatred the papacy from which his ecclesiastical authority was derived and which was the only institution powerful enough to purify the Church from within. Wolsey made an occasional gesture of reform. He dissolved twenty-nine monasteries on the grounds that they were hopelessly decayed, and used their confiscated property to endow the colleges which he was building at Ipswich and Oxford. But even in this case his motives were mixed. The colleges were, like some of the philanthropic trusts which millionaires leave behind them today, an ostentatious charity designed mainly to perpetuate the glory of the founder. One observer reported that at Cardinal College (now Christ Church), Oxford, Wolsey's arms were emblazoned on every stone.

The anti-clericalism aroused by the pomp and greed of the Church was nowhere stronger than in London, as was demonstrated in 1514 when the case of Richard Hunne created a public scandal. Hunne, a London merchant of some wealth, had the misfortune to lose his infant son. When he went to arrange the burial, the parson demanded as a mortuary fee the robe in which the child had been christened. Hunne regarded this as extortionate, refused to pay, and was sued by the parson in a Church court. He countered by accusing the parson of a breach of praemunire,[1] and indicted him in King's Bench. The praemunire case collapsed, but Hunne was by that time in an ecclesiastical prison, charged with heresy. There was no evidence that he was a heretic, but if he were simply released it would seem like an admission of defeat by the Church and Hunne would become a popular

[1] See below, p. 55.

hero. While the Bishop of London was considering this tricky problem it solved itself. Hunne was found hanging in his cell and it was given out that he had committed suicide. The law required, however, that an inquest should be held, and a coroner's jury of London citizens was duly empanelled. The jurors examined Hunne's body and found marks on it strongly suggesting that he had been strangled. They thereupon returned a verdict of murder and named the Bishop's chancellor and his accomplices as the murderers.

The Bishop of London wrote to Wolsey pleading that the case should be dealt with by the royal Council on the grounds that 'if my chancellor be tried by any twelve men in London, they be so maliciously set *in favorem haereticae pravitatis* that they will cast and condemn my clerk though he were as innocent as Abel'. Before the matter could go further, Parliament met early in 1515. The Commons had before them the Criminous Clerks Act of 1512 which ordered that clerics in minor orders who committed criminal offences were to be judged by lay courts. This Act was temporary and had expired, but the Commons sent up a Bill to the Lords to revive it. The Lords, dominated by the spiritual peers, rejected the Commons' Bill and when, later in 1515, the Lower House once again sent up the Bill, the Lords again rejected it.

At the same time as Parliament met, Convocation also assembled and the Abbot of Winchcombe, Richard Kidderminster, used the occasion of his opening sermon to assert that all clergy, low as well as high, should be exempt from lay jurisdiction. The enraged Commons called upon the temporal lords—a significant conjunction—to join with them in an appeal to the King, and a conference was held, in Henry's presence, at Blackfriars, where a doctor of divinity called Henry Standish argued the case against Kidderminster. Convocation, angered that any cleric should dare attack the privileges of his own order, summoned Standish to answer charges before it, but Standish appealed to the King. He was joined in this by the Commons and temporal lords, still smarting under the rejection of the Criminous Clerks Act and with the Hunne scandal alive in their minds. They called upon the King to maintain his temporal jurisdiction, which the clergy were seeking to invade.

A second conference then took place at Blackfriars, at which the judges gave their verdict that the clergy who had taken part in the citation of Standish had derogated the King's rights and infringed the Statute of Praemunire. At a subsequent assembly of the Lords and

Commons in the King's presence Wolsey, as representative of the clergy of England, knelt before Henry to plead for royal favour on the grounds that Convocation had never intended to invade his prerogative, and to ask that the case might be sent for final judgement to Rome. Henry refused this, and in a speech full of significance because it represents his own opinion, unprompted by any of those advisers on whom he was sometimes to seem so dependent, he declared that: 'We are, by the sufferance of God, King of England, and the Kings of England in time past never had any superior but God. Know therefore that we will maintain the rights of the Crown in this matter like our progenitors. . . . You interpret your decrees at your pleasure, but as for me, I will never consent to your desire, any more than my progenitors have done.'

There the matter ended. Convocation dropped its attack on Standish, who eventually rose through royal favour to be a bishop, while the murderers of Hunne were allowed to go unpunished. The controversy, however, remained alive, and More was arguing the case against Hunne years later, on the eve of the Reformation Parliament.

Wolsey. III: Judicial and Financial Policies

While this dispute between lay and clerical power was simmering, Wolsey became Chancellor, having pestered Archbishop Warham into resigning the Great Seal in 1515. The Chancellor was, by tradition, the greatest man in the kingdom under the King, and this was certainly true of Wolsey. He had all the powers, and more, of a modern prime minister, without any Parliament or public opinion to call him to account. As long as he pleased the King, nothing short of a successful revolution could dislodge him.

As Chancellor he presided in his own court of Chancery, in which the formalism and rigidity of the common law were softened by principles derived mainly from common sense. Chancery suited Wolsey well and contemporaries bear witness to the volume of work transacted by it during his term of office. As the King's chief minister, Wolsey was also closely associated with the royal Council sitting as a court in Star Chamber and frequently presided there. During his long ascendancy the judicial business of the Council became its principal work, since Wolsey absorbed most of the administrative and advisory functions himself. The Council-court in Star Chamber had lapsed on Henry VII's death, but Wolsey revived it and by his unremitting use of it turned it from an aspect of the King's Council into a formal court. During term-time Wolsey was usually present in Chancery and Star Chamber, and Cavendish describes how he would 'repair into Chancery and [would sit] there until eleven of the clock, hearing suitors and determining of divers matters. And from thence he would divers times go into the Star Chamber, as occasion did serve, where he spared neither high nor low, but judged every estate according to their merits and deserts.'

Wolsey made many enemies by the firmness with which he enforced the law. The landowners were angered by the commissions he set up to inquire into depopulating enclosures; the great nobles were offended when he fined them heavily for keeping too many retainers. Great men, Wolsey included, were surrounded by a cloud of menial servants, and it was difficult to draw the dividing line between just enough and too many. The Duke of Buckingham, for instance, asserted in 1521 that he could not, without loss of dignity and danger to himself, travel from one country house to another without three or four hundred armed men in attendance on him. Wolsey had to decide himself whether or not a subject was becoming 'over-mighty', whether he needed teaching the 'new law of the Star Chamber'— which was not, in fact, a new law, but a new vigour in the enforcement of existing laws. His victims were quick to complain. Skelton, the poet, was one of their mouthpieces.

> In the Star Chamber he nods and becks
> And beareth him there so stout
> That no man dare rout,   [riot]
> Duke, earl, baron nor lord,
> But to his sentence must accord;
> Whether he be knight or squire
> All men must follow his desire.

Star Chamber was only one, although the greatest, of the prerogative courts. There was also the Court of Requests, set up to hear the complaints of poor men. This was a Yorkist institution, revived by Henry VII some years after his accession, and the pressure of business under Wolsey turned it into a formal court, with its own staff and its own procedures. To govern the unruly north of England, Wolsey reverted to Richard III's idea of a council, and set up one under the nominal presidency of the Duke of Richmond, Henry VIII's illegitimate son. This was intended as a sort of Court of Requests for the north, to protect the poor against enclosures and rack-renting, and it exercised a criminal and civil jurisdiction similar to that of the Council in London. It could not, however, control the big men, such as Northumberland and Dacre, who were left in charge of the marches, and its work was confined mainly to Yorkshire.

Wolsey's strength was in administration and, not surprisingly, he had little time for a body like Parliament which did not fit in with his autocratic conceptions of government. Parliament had to be summoned in 1514 and 1515, to vote supplies for the French war, but nothing was left of the money when war broke out again in 1522. Forced loans were raised, which brought in £350,000, but this was still £50,000 less than the cost of the campaigns against France and the Scots. To make up the deficit Parliament was summoned again in 1523.

The Commons were in an ugly temper. They had subsidised the wars of Henry VII without complaining, because the demands made on them were infrequent and relatively light, and because they approved of his policies. Henry VIII's campaigns, however, were inspired by no obvious need. They were widely regarded as Wolsey's wars, and there was resentment at the great sums demanded. Wolsey asked for a tax of four shillings in the pound, to bring in £800,000, but the Commons were prepared to grant only half this sum and even then insisted that collection should be spread over two years.

Wolsey went down to the Commons himself and told them he was 'from the King's own person sent hither unto you for the preservation of yourselves and all the realm. I think it meet you give me a reasonable answer.' But no one would open his mouth, and Wolsey had to retreat before what he called 'a marvellous obstinate silence'. A subsidy was eventually voted, though it still did not equal the sum Wolsey demanded, and Convocation made a grant of half the annual income of all benefices, to be paid over five years.

More money was needed in 1525 if advantage was to be taken of the French defeat at Pavia,[1] and Wolsey sent out commissioners to raise an 'Amicable Loan'. All over the country there was resistance, even in London where Wolsey was his own chief commissioner. Henry was forced to intervene, stop the collection of the grant, and give free pardon to all those who had opposed it. This was Wolsey's first real check, and it showed just how stubborn resistance could be, inside and outside Parliament, to demands for money to meet the costs of a policy which did not have popular appeal.

[1] See below, p. 45.

Wolsey. IV: Foreign Policy

Wolsey used to be credited with inventing the 'balance of power' as the controlling principle of England's foreign policy, but such a concept would have been alien to his way of thinking. England was not strong enough to make much difference when thrown into the balance against heavyweights like France, Spain and the Holy Roman Empire. Wolsey's policy was to back the winner in the hope that he would share in the profits of victory. As he grew more powerful, however, a new influence made itself felt in his attitude. He hoped to reach the summit of earthly authority by becoming Pope, and, to ingratiate himself with the papal court, he made England follow the lead of Rome. Since the Pope was in fact tacking alternately from France to Spain in an effort to steer an independent course, Wolsey also seemed to be balancing one great power against another. But Rome called the tune, and the balancing was done not in the interests of England but in those of the Holy See.

The opening phase of Henry VIII's foreign policy, in which Wolsey made his name, ended with peace signed between England and France in 1514 and a marriage between the senile Louis XII and Henry's sister, Mary. The wedding festivities and the attraction of a beautiful young bride were too much for the ageing King, who collapsed and died shortly after the marriage. He was succeeded by the youthful, charming and impetuous Francis I, and Henry, who had hitherto been the golden boy among European monarchs, felt his brilliance outshone by this ambitious new arrival. Two years later an even brighter star flared into the European sky, for in 1516 Ferdinand of Spain died and was succeeded by his grandson, the sixteen-year-old Charles.

Three years later, in January 1519, Charles's paternal grandfather, the Emperor Maximilian, died and the German prince-electors met to decide on a new ruler. The young King of Spain was the obvious candidate, but Francis I, who dreaded the thought of his rival adding an empire to his already great dominions, put himself forward as a rival and distributed money on a lavish scale. Even Henry VIII made it clear that he was prepared to accept the imperial dignity, and added his trickle to the flood of Spanish and French gold that was pouring into the hands of the electoral princes.

In fact there was never much doubt about the outcome. The Electors took everybody's money gratefully, but in June they elected

Charles as Emperor. To Francis I it seemed as though France was now encircled by imperial power—on her northern frontier, the Netherlands; on her eastern frontier, Luxemburg and Franche Comté; and, in the south, Spain herself. Only by keeping Italy under French control could he hope to break out of this stranglehold.

Francis and Charles both made overtures for an English alliance, and in 1520 Henry and Francis met amid scenes of unprecedented splendour at the Field of the Cloth of Gold. Wolsey, however, was already waiting on the Pope, and the Pope could not rest in peace while the armies which Francis I had despatched in the first year of his reign still straddled northern and central Italy. He was building up a coalition against France, and Wolsey followed suit. Immediately before and immediately after the Field of the Cloth of Gold, unpublicised meetings took place between Henry VIII and Charles V at which an alliance was agreed upon.

Charles, in return for English assistance, gave Wolsey a pension and promised to support his candidature for the papacy when the occasion arose. Wolsey did not have to wait long. In December 1521 Pope Leo died and the cardinals met to elect his successor. Charles, however, had no wish to see the ambitious Wolsey at the head of the church universal, and recommended to the conclave his former tutor, Adrian, who was duly elected. In the only scrutiny at which Wolsey's name was considered, he received a mere seven out of thirty-nine votes. Wolsey was disappointed and suspicious, but Charles assured him of his support on the next occasion and the Cardinal had little choice but to swallow his resentment.

In the spring of 1522 the Emperor was received with great state in England and war was declared against France. But England gained nothing from the war, except the cost of fighting it. Even Wolsey's personal ambitions were disappointed, for when Pope Adrian died in September 1523 the Emperor did not even make a pretence of putting forward Wolsey's claim, and an Italian was elected as Clement VII. Wolsey was furious and stood ostentatiously aloof from the imperial alliance. His personal motives coincided with his public ones, since the Emperor had made himself master of Italy in the campaign of 1522-23 and the new Pope was already making overtures to France.

England remained the nominal ally of the Emperor, but took no part in the war during 1524. A French envoy was secretly received by Henry, and England moved appreciably nearer the Holy League which Clement was building up against the Emperor. Unfortunately for Wolsey he had switched sides too soon. In February 1525 the French Army was shattered at Pavia and Francis I became a prisoner of the Emperor. The Pope set to work to build up another coalition against Charles, and England gradually moved towards open war against the Emperor. The formal declaration of war took place in 1528, but Henry's treasury was empty and his subjects were unenthusiastic. Wolsey had to look for encouragement to Italy, where the armies of England's new ally were winning brilliant successes. But their triumph was short-lived. On 21 June 1529 the French army was routed at Landriano, and Charles became the unchallenged master of Italy.

Wolsey. V: The Divorce Problem and the Reformation

Even before Landriano was fought the Pope had decided to come to terms with the Emperor, and in June 1529 he concluded the Treaty of Barcelona. Early the following month Francis and Charles made peace at Cambrai, and the long struggle was, for the moment, over. Wolsey was conspicuously absent from all this peacemaking, for he had abandoned Charles V too soon to profit from the imperial victory. He had also made an enemy of the Emperor at the very moment when he most needed his support, for on the same day that Landriano was fought, a remarkable scene was taking place at Blackfriars, where Henry and Catherine his wife appeared before Wolsey and a fellow legate to answer charges that their marriage was invalid.

There had been difficulties about the marriage from the beginning, for according to Leviticus, if a man marries his brother's widow, 'it is an unclean thing; he hath uncovered his brother's nakedness; they shall be childless'.[1] A papal dispensation had been necessary before the marriage could take place, but there was some doubt about whether the Pope had any authority to dispense with the law when it had the sanction of holy scripture behind it. Although the dispensation was eventually issued in late 1504, the marriage was still delayed—mainly because the dowry had not all been paid—and in June 1505 Henry, who was not quite fourteen at the time, made a formal protest against the validity of the proposed union. He was no doubt prompted in this by his father, who was having second thoughts on the advisability of a Spanish alliance, but the only effect was to delay the marriage, which did not take place until June 1509, several months after Henry VII's death.

[1] *Leviticus* 20:21.

The marriage seems to have been reasonably happy, but unfortunately for the Queen her children died at birth, or soon after, except for a daughter, Mary, born in 1516. By 1525 Catherine was forty, all hope of a male heir had gone, and Henry was in a quandary. As a conventionally devout man he was afraid that his failure to obtain the longed-for son might be a sign of the punishment threatened in Leviticus. A male heir seemed vital if the Tudor dynasty was to survive. It was not even certain that a woman had the right to ascend the throne. The last female ruler of England had been Matilda, whose, reign had been marred by civil war, and the memory of the Wars of the Roses was still very much alive. Henry was conscious that he was only the second of his dynasty, and that several of his subjects had a claim to the throne superior to his own as far as descent was concerned. For this reason he had Edmund Stafford, Duke of Buckingham, executed in 1521, and he also considered making his bastard son, the Duke of Richmond, his legitimate heir. It is not clear what would eventually have happened had not the matter been brought to a head by Henry's falling in love with Anne Boleyn, whose sister was already his mistress. Henry's love-letters to Anne show how deeply the King's passions had been aroused, but Anne refused to become Henry's mistress and stood firm in the hopes of a crown. But in any case the King needed her as his wife if the children she bore him were to be legitimate. By early 1527 Henry was determined to put an end to his marriage with Catherine and had made this clear to his chief minister. Wolsey may well have been in favour of annulment, since he did not yet know whom Henry intended as his second wife. The divorce of Catherine, who was Charles V's aunt, would hurt the Emperor's pride, and might lead to a French marriage, which would fit in nicely with Wolsey's plans.

What one Pope had done only another could undo. Julius II had issued the original dispensation; Clement VII was now asked to declare that his predecessor had acted *ultra vires* and that no Pope could set aside the law of the Church in this particular case. Henry had no reason to expect difficulties. Popes usually gave a sympathetic hearing to princely petitioners and Henry was an ardent supporter of the papacy and had been rewarded by the title *Fidei Defensor* for defending it against the attacks of Luther. He was therefore eager for Rome to judge his case, since he was convinced that the verdict would be in his favour. In a way this attitude was hypocritical, particularly as he played down his passion for Anne Boleyn. But the King was a proud, self-willed man, whose conscience walked hand-in-hand with his inclinations. What mattered was not what he believed, but what he professed to believe, and the actions that sprang therefrom.

Henry was unfortunate in that his appeal to Rome took place at a time when the supremacy of the papacy was being challenged on all sides. The Popes had become patrons of the arts on a grand scale and they made Rome the cultural capital of the Christian world, but to pay for their magnificence and for the intricate diplomatic manœuvrings that were forced upon them as temporal rulers of a large Italian state, they turned the Church into a machine for raising money.

The worldliness of the papacy and Church was apparent and caused a reaction throughout Europe. Lollardy in England had been a violently anti-clerical movement, and the failure of the Church to satisfy spiritual needs had been shown by the spread of semi-mystical movements— such as that of the Brethren of the Common Life in the Lower Rhineland—which, while they were not heretical, sought their inspiration outside the established hierarchy. This failure on the Church's part must not be exaggerated. Many people still found in it a satis-factory expression of their spiritual life, but like any great institution it was weighed down by the burden of its own administration, so concerned with running its own affairs that it could not stand outside itself and review its aims and methods. Everything depended on the Pope, and Martin V's successors were, unfortunately, too interested in finance, administration and diplomacy to meet the spiritual needs of the Christian world.

Erasmus and his friends, the advocates of the new learning, might have goaded the Church into reforming itself, but the opposition they met from the established authorities frequently drove them into bitter denunciations that prepared the way for more violent reformers. Colet, for instance, denounced place-hunting clergymen, who ran 'yea, almost out of breath, from one benefice to another' with an arrogance more suited to 'the high lordship and power of the world' than to 'the humble bishopric of Christ'. By exposing the weaknesses of the Church which they loved, they provided ammunition for those who hated it. Erasmus went further. His edition of the New Testament which appeared in 1516, with the Greek text printed face to face with the Latin translation, put into the hands of the influential minority who could read it a source of authority on the Christian faith to which they could appeal against the traditions of the Church and the decrees of the Pope: as Stephen Gardiner commented later, it was Erasmus who laid the egg which Luther hatched.

Erasmus and his friends may be accused of putting too much faith in the effectiveness of the unfettered intellect, but they could hardly have foreseen the way in which reform would eventually reach the Church. In 1517—the very year in which Luther nailed his theses to the door of the church at Wittenberg—Erasmus was writing: 'At the present moment I could almost wish to be young again, for no other reason but this, that I anticipate the near approach of a golden age. I am led to a confident hope that not only morality and Christian piety but also a genuine and purer literature may come to renewed life and greater splendour.'

The Catholic Church did, indeed, stand on the threshold of a new age in 1517, but the opening years of this were to be dominated not by Erasmus but by Luther. This astonishing man, a Saxon miner's son, who became a friar, was drawing huge audiences to the lectures on biblical theology which he was delivering at the University of Wittenberg. He was obsessed with a sense of his own sinfulness and of man's inability to do good. It came to him as a revelation that every individual's way to salvation was by allowing God to infuse his entire being, and that this could be done only by faith.

Luther's challenge of 1517 was directly inspired by the worldliness of the papacy. Julius II had pulled down old St Peter's, the shrine of saints, and had ordered Bramante to build a magnificent cathedral more in keeping with the pre-eminence of the first of the apostles and the dignity of his successors. To pay for this masterpiece indulgence-sellers were despatched throughout Europe. Indulgences were, in effect, charters which released the individual purchaser, or the person in whose name he bought, from a stated amount of penance—the outward act of contrition which the sinner had to make as a sign of his inward repentance and as an aid to it. Accumulated penance had to be worked out by the departed soul in purgatory, but in the mid-fifteenth century the Pope had extended the competence of indulgences to this sphere as well. The living could now pay money to liberate the dead.

The question of man's sinfulness was at the core of Luther's theology and it seemed to him blasphemous that the ignorant multitudes should be encouraged to persevere in their sinful state by purchasing worthless pieces of parchment. He determined to challenge the validity of indulgences, and to do so in the accepted manner. As a prelude to public disputation he wrote out ninety-five theses and fixed them to the church door—the public noticeboard of Wittenberg. This was a gesture of limited significance, but in the context of contemporary Germany, seething with discontent of all kinds, it grew into a major challenge. In a number of powerfully written pamphlets Luther elaborated his doctrine that human nature was utterly corrupted and enslaved by sin and that the only hope of salvation was faith in God. Good works, in the accepted sense of pious observances, acts of charity, pilgrimages, etc., could not affect the basic corruption of the soul. Without faith they were of no value: with faith they were unnecessary. The Catholic Church, with its elaborate hierarchy, its shrines, pilgrimages, relics and indulgences, was irrelevant to the human condition.

Luther's ideas found a quick response in England, particularly at Cambridge, where the new learning had already brought the Catholic Church under attack. By the 1520s an evangelical group of Cambridge dons was meeting at the White Horse Tavern, which acquired the nickname of 'Little Germany'. The leaders were Thomas Bilney and Robert Barnes, a former friar who had belonged to the same order as Luther. Among the pupils of Barnes was another ex-friar, Miles Coverdale, who was, by the mid-1520s, preaching against image-worship and confession.

The leading figure of the early years of the Reformation in England was William Tyndale, who lectured in divinity at Cambridge. He was horrified at the way in which the externals of worship were accepted without any real understanding of their meaning, and he described how 'thousands, while the priest pattereth St John's Gospel in Latin over their heads, . . . cross so much as their heels and the very soles of their feet, and believe that if it be done in the time that he readeth the Gospel (and else not) that there shall no mischance happen to them that day'. Tyndale felt that the only hope of bringing back the masses to a true understanding of the fundamentals of religion lay in giving them a vernacular Bible, and he asked permission from the Bishop of London to undertake the task of translation. When this was refused he took refuge in Germany, and by 1524 had completed his translation of the New Testament. Copies were soon circulating in England and were among the 'Lutheran books' which were burned in public bonfires, such as that at St Paul's which took place in Wolsey's presence in 1526.

Lutheran ideas circulating among the intelligentsia linked up with

CTSB

residual Lollardy in the lower levels of English society. The Lollards were the spiritual descendants of Wycliffe and the forerunners of English puritanism. They maintained that the Bible was the sole source of authority. They rejected Popes, bishops and all ecclesiastical hierarchy, denied the existence of purgatory, and did not believe in transubstantiation. Their attitude was far more extreme than that of Luther, and the established Church had persecuted Lollards ever since their first appearance. In the thirteen years before Luther there were nearly four hundred prosecutions for heresy in England, leading to death by burning in at least twenty-seven cases, and the majority of those convicted could be described as Lollards. The link-up of old Lollard and new Lutheran was symbolised by a meeting that took place in 1527 between two Essex Lollards and Robert Barnes. They had come up to London especially to see this man of whom they had heard, and told him how they had begun to convert their vicar to Wycliffe's doctrines. They also showed him some manuscript copies of parts of the Lollard Bible. But Barnes showed a tolerant contempt for this old-fashioned version of the Scriptures and, before parting with them, sold them a copy of Tyndale's translation of the New Testament.

The majority of the English people were orthodox, but anti-clericalism and criticism of abuses could shift imperceptibly into an attack upon doctrines. Many devout catholics condemned the worldliness of the monks and asked what good purpose such people served. More's reply, that the prayers of the monks shortened the torments of souls in purgatory, showed how close was the connexion between institutions and doctrines. The same was true of Henry's actions. In putting pressure on the Pope to grant him an annulment of his marriage, he attacked the corruption of the papacy as an institution. But this struck a quick response in the anti-clerical, xenophobe Commons and among the Lollard–Lutheran groups. By attacking the Pope, Henry unleashed forces over which he had little control and which were to transform the narrowly political issues into something far greater and more radical.

The first stage of the divorce case centred on the attempt to obtain a favourable papal decision. There was no intention at this stage of breaking with Rome since, as far as Henry could tell, the Pope would fall in with his wishes. He even went so far as to ask the Pope for a dispensation permitting him to marry Anne, whose sister had been his mistress. The theological impediment to such a marriage was precisely the same as that which, Henry claimed, invalidated his union with Catherine of Aragon—if a man may not marry his brother's widow, neither may he marry his mistress's sister—yet while the King denied papal competence in the one case, he was eager to accept it in the other. This suggests that Henry's real aim was to marry Ann Boleyn, and that other considerations, however sincerely held, were secondary. Wolsey can hardly have relished the prospect of having Anne as Queen, since she was the niece of the Duke of Norfolk, his rival and enemy, and was also suspected of Lutheran leanings. But Wolsey, as he later told his fellow legate, Cardinal Campeggio, considered that Henry must be allowed to have his way, since otherwise the Church would be endangered.

Campeggio was sent by Pope Clement VII to join Wolsey in judging 'the King's great matter'. Clement was trying to pursue two irreconcilable policies at the same time. To avoid offending Catherine's nephew, Charles V, who was defending the Catholic Church against Lutherans at home and Turks abroad, the Pope wanted to postpone any clear-cut action and keep the final decision in his own hands. Yet he also wished to conciliate Henry, the Defender of the Faith, and Henry insisted that the two legates should be given authority to pass final judgement in his case.

Clement played a double game. He gave Campeggio a papal bull in which he promised to accept the legates' decision and not recall the case to Rome, but he also told Campeggio that after showing this to Henry and Wolsey, as proof of papal goodwill, he was then to destroy it. Privately he ordered Campeggio not to pronounce judgement without first obtaining papal approval, for 'if so great an injury be done to the Emperor [by a decision in Henry's favour] all hope is lost of universal peace and the Church cannot escape utter ruin, as it is entirely in the power of the Emperor's servants . . . Delay as much as possible.'

Campeggio did not relish this double-dealing. 'I do not see,' he wrote to the papal secretary, 'supposing the King cannot be got from his opinion, how without scandal we can delay what, by our own commission, we have to proceed with and try. It will easily seem to them that I have been sent to gull them, and they may be furious about it.' He took as long as he could on his journey, and did not arrive in London until October 1528. Since Catherine, in spite of the promptings of the two legates, refused to abandon her conjugal rights, a trial was inevitable, and in January 1529 Henry sent Stephen Gardiner to Rome to threaten that unless a speedy decision was given the King would renounce his allegiance to the papal see. The legatine court at last opened at Blackfriars in May 1529. Catherine was not expected to be present, but on 21 June, the day on which the Emperor's hold on Italy was confirmed by the rout of the French at Landriano, she appeared and made an impassioned and moving speech asserting the validity of her marriage. She finished her oration by sweeping across the courtroom and kneeling at Henry's feet. The King was moved to tears, and publicly declared that 'she hath been to me as true, obedient and as conformable a wife as I could in my fancy wish or desire'. But he had no intention of abandoning his policy. His desire for Anne and the need to safeguard the succession were more powerful than mere sentiment.

The King confidently expected a favourable judgement when the court reassembled in July 1529. But Campeggio, who had received no further order from Rome, played for time by announcing that no decision could be given until after a three-month summer vacation. The court never, in fact, met again, and Henry's anger was expressed by his brother-in-law, the Duke of Suffolk, who stepped forward and 'spake these words with a stout and hault countenance. "It was never merry in England whilst we had cardinals among us." Which words were set forth with such a vehement countenance that all men marvelled what he intended.'

Wolsey. VI: The Fall from Power

Anger swiftly turned to action. The King had no further use for Wolsey, and Parliament was summoned so that an Act of Attainder could be passed against the fallen favourite. But the act was not needed. Wolsey, when commanded to appear before the judges to answer charges that by publishing his Bulls of appointment as papal legate he had broken the Statute of Praemunire, pleaded guilty. As in Standish's case he prostrated himself and the Church before royal authority. The independence for which Becket had died was abandoned without a protest, and the Pope never lifted a finger to save his viceroy.

Wolsey's palaces and colleges passed to the Crown as punishment for his offence, and the fallen legate journeyed slowly towards his province of York, which he entered for the first time since his appointment sixteen years earlier. He could not, however, shake off the habit of power, and was secretly negotiating with Francis I and the Emperor for their support in persuading Henry to restore him to favour. His servant, Thomas Cromwell, wrote to warn him that his enemies were still suspicious of him. 'Some allege you keep too great a house and are continually building. . . . I think you happy you are now at liberty to serve God and banish all vain desires of the world.' But the vain desires of the world still dazzled Wolsey, and he planned a magnificent enthronement for himself in York Minster. Before the ceremony could take place he was arrested on a charge of high treason, and sent towards London. He got no further than Leicester Abbey, where on 29 November 1530 he died, lamenting that 'if I had served God as diligently as I have done the King, He would not have given me over in my grey hairs'.

Wolsey was a great prince of the Church in a tradition so alien to modern assumptions that it is difficult to comprehend him. Yet he was not without his virtues. He promoted learning, and made his household a focus for men of intelligence and ability—like Richard Sampson, Richard Pace, Cuthbert Tunstall and Thomas Cromwell—where they learned how to serve the state. He was also tolerant, preferring to burn heretical books rather than the heretics themselves; and although he rose to power by royal favour he was not unworthy of it, for he had an enormous capacity for work, and knew how to win men:

> Lofty and sour to them that loved him not;
> But to those men that sought him, sweet as summer.[1]

Wolsey showed that the Church could be united and brought under the same governor as the state. He also made a lay reaction probable, by failing to reform abuses and by epitomising the arrogance and worldliness of the Catholic Church and papacy—no legate was appointed to take his place, and his successor as Chancellor was a layman, Sir Thomas More. He also showed, by his fall, that even the greatest dignities were as flimsy paper beneath the weight of royal authority. There was, however, nothing inevitable about the events that followed. Cardinal Ximenes in Spain and Cardinal Amboise in France were at least as powerful as Wolsey, yet they did not open the gates to religious reformation. Wolsey showed the King the possibilities of power: it was left to Henry and Thomas Cromwell to turn these into realities.

[1] Shakespeare, *King Henry VIII*, IV:ii.

4

The Break with Rome

The Reformation Parliament

THE Parliament which met in November 1529 had been summoned
to deal with Wolsey, but Wolsey had capitulated without a struggle
and there was no other obvious work for it to do. Henry was now his
own chief minister, and although he had no intention, at this stage,
of breaking with Rome, the possibility was not ruled out. By this date,
Denmark, Sweden and much of north Germany had already repudiated
papal supremacy, and the profits of this had gone to the temporal
princes. Henry had an eye to profit, and he regarded himself as certainly the equal, if not the superior, of the northern monarchs. Long
before he met Cromwell he believed that he was wearer of an imperial
crown—indeed he not only told Thomas More this, but he added the
unexpected information that he had received this crown from the
Pope.

While Henry had an exalted conception of the power and dignity
of his position, he did not see how this could serve his immediate
purpose. What he proposed to do was not to break with Rome but to
drive the Pope into a satisfactory settlement. For this reason he gave
Parliament its head in November 1529 and encouraged it to voice the
prevailing anti-clerical sentiment. This was genuine enough and the
Commons passed a number of Bills limiting the fees to be charged for
probate and mortuary, restricting abuses of sanctuary, and forbidding
pluralities and non-residence. The spiritual lords did not accept these
measures with equanimity. Although they had failed to initiate reform
themselves, they resented action by the lay power, and the Bill to
limit probate fees provoked Bishop Fisher to an angry outburst: 'now
with the Commons is nothing but "Down with the Church!" and all
this me seemeth is for lack of faith only.' It was probably in this session
that the Commons started drawing up the list of grievances against the

Church which was to take shape in 1532 as the Supplication against the Ordinaries.

Henry's next step was prompted by a chance meeting between two of his Councillors and Thomas Cranmer, an obscure Cambridge don. Cranmer pointed out that the real issue was whether the command that a man must not marry his brother's widow was based on canon law, which could be set aside by the Pope, or on God's law, which was irrevocable. This was a matter for theologians to settle, not lawyers, and it was decided to appeal to the universities of Europe. Should they declare in Henry's favour, as he anticipated, the Pope could then be called on to act. The King was pleased with the idea, which offered at least some positive action, and throughout 1530 his envoys were at work in England and abroad collecting opinions. But the verdicts, even though the majority were favourable, did little to advance Henry's cause. It was well known that lavish bribes had been distributed to obtain the right answers, and the verdicts were never formally presented to the Pope.

So far Henry's manœuvres had led to nothing. He therefore decided to exploit anti-clerical sentiment by bringing the clergy of England to heel. Writs were issued early in 1531 against all the clergy of England, on the grounds that merely by exercising their ecclesiastical jurisdiction they had committed an offence. The accusation was based on the Great Statute of Praemunire of 1353 (repeated, in stronger terms, in 1393), which declared that 'anyone drawing the King's subjects out of the realm on pleas, the cognisance whereof belongs to the King's courts, or impeaching the judgement given in those courts, shall . . . be put out of the King's protection, his lands and goods forfeited and his body imprisoned at the King's pleasure'.

The terms of the statute were so imprecise that they could be held to make any recognition of papal jurisdiction in England an offence, and in January 1531 Convocation decided to make a peace-offering of £100,000 to the King. Henry, however, ordered the clergy to make explicit admission that they had broken the law and that their gift was offered for a royal pardon of their offence. They were also told to style the King 'Protector and Supreme Head of the English Church and Clergy'. Opinion in Convocation was divided, but eventually a compromise formula was accepted, in which the clergy acknowledged the King as 'their singular protector, only and supreme lord, and, as far as the law of Christ allows, even Supreme Head'. Henry was satisfied with his victory, and an Act of 1531 formally granted the clergy pardon for their offence in view of their generous gift. The Commons were quick to realise that they had also been accessories, by accepting Wolsey's jurisdiction, and another Act was passed in which Henry confirmed the royal pardon of his lay subjects. In their case the pardon was free.

Negotiations with Rome continued, but Henry was no nearer a solution. The Pope was still hoping that the King, tired of delay, would abandon hope of annulling his marriage. Clement was not, as is often implied, the servile tool of the Emperor. At least Charles V did not think so when he burst out to the papal nuncio in November 1531 that 'it was a strange and abominable proceeding that to suit the lust of two fools a law suit should be held up and such an outrageous stain inflicted on a Queen who had been blameless'. The Pope was anxious to avoid a rupture with England, but he formally warned Henry to put Anne away and restore Catherine to conjugal rights pending the decision of the papal court. Henry was in a dilemma, for the threats and assertions which had served his predecessors in the late Middle Ages had not resolved his conflict with Rome. Up to this point the threat of a complete rupture had been held in the background, as an ultimate sanction. Now the King's bluff had been called, and he had either to go on to more extreme measures or to pull back. Henry's pride and personal concern in the divorce drove him forward, and at this juncture the policy he needed was proposed to him by Thomas Cromwell.

Thomas Cromwell

Cromwell had been born in or about the year of Bosworth, the son of a Putney blacksmith and brewer. He became a roving soldier in Italy, entered the service of the Frescobaldi, a famous banking family, and from there went to the Netherlands, where he made a living as a business consultant. This early experience was invaluable to him since it gave him first-hand knowledge of Renaissance Italy—the Italy of Machiavelli and Cesare Borgia. The tone of Italian politics was amoral and empirical, and the emphasis was upon the strength of the state rather than the rights of the individual. In the light of his experience the dispute about whether Cromwell ever actually read *The Prince* seems irrelevant. He knew at first hand the world it described. He also knew the trading world that had its centre in the north Italian city states, Antwerp and London, and that valued efficiency and good administration as money-making virtues.

After his return to England in 1512 or thereabouts, Cromwell took up the study of common law, and in 1523 he entered Parliament. Already he was looking to politics to fulfil his ambition and his choice of Parliament showed where his interests lay. The following year he became a member of Wolsey's household, where he was employed chiefly upon the dissolution of the twenty-nine monasteries whose endowments the Cardinal was using for the benefit of his new colleges. In Wolsey's household Cromwell had a close view of the way of life of higher ecclesiastics and their immediate entourage. He knew how corrupt the Church was, yet he was not violently anti-clerical nor without faith. In the will which he drew up in 1529 he left £20 to poor householders to pray for his soul and £5 to the orders of friars to pray for him. He also instructed his executors to arrange for masses to be sung for his soul for seven years by 'an *honest* and *continent* priest'. The adjectives are significant.

When Wolsey fell, it looked as though Cromwell would fall with him, so closely had he been identified with his master's policy, but he told Cavendish that he would go to Court, where he would, in his favourite phrase, 'either make or mar ere I come again'. In London he was informed that the King had no objection to his becoming burgess, and an old friend found him a seat at Taunton. Cromwell did not desert his former master and was apparently responsible for defeating the proposal to pass a Bill of Attainder against Wolsey. But he had to make his own way in the political world, and he quickly became a prominent figure in the Reformation Parliament, sitting on a number of Commons' committees and taking a leading part in drawing up the list of complaints against the Church which aroused Fisher's anger. The King was now his patron, and it was probably in the early months of 1530 that Cromwell took the oath required of those who entered royal service. By the end of that year he had been sworn a member of the Council, and since Wolsey was by this time dead he was now free to look to his own advantage. By the end of 1531 he was recognised in the Commons as one of the King's chief spokesmen and he was gradually entering the inner ring of Henry's advisers.

From the beginning of 1532 Cromwell's vigour and sense of direction began to make themselves apparent in the King's affairs. Parliament reassembled in January and the question of grievances against the Church was raised again. Cromwell had ready a draft document based on the list which he and his fellow-members had drawn up in 1529. This draft was now accepted by the Commons and became the

c*

'Supplication against the Ordinaries'—the judges in spiritual courts, usually the bishop or his deputy.

In March 1532 Henry received the Supplication and passed it to Convocation to consider. The bishops took a firm stand against it and declared that the Church's authority to make laws of its own was 'grounded upon the Scripture of God and determination of Holy Church, which must also be a rule and square to try the justice of all laws, as well spiritual as temporal'. This answer was worthy of Becket, but it also shows how blind the leaders of the Church were to the real faults in their organisation, and particularly in its courts. In April Henry received the clergy's answer and passed it on to the Speaker with a broad hint of his own attitude. 'We think their answer will smally please you, for it seemeth to us very slender. You be a great sort of wise men. I doubt not but you will look circumspectly on the matter, and we will be indifferent between you.' This sign of royal dissatisfaction set debate going again in Convocation, and Henry made it known that he would not accept any reply unless it agreed that no Church laws should be valid until they had been approved by a committee of his choice. The bishops, threatened by a hostile alliance between King and Commons, gave way and signed the 'Submission', accepting Henry's demands. It was left to a layman to make the only challenging gesture. On the day after the 'Submission' was presented to Henry, Sir Thomas More resigned the Chancellorship.

While the English clergy were being brought to heel, the Pope was being threatened with a cut in his revenues. For many centuries annates—the payment by newly appointed bishops of their first year's income to the Pope—had been a grievance. Now, in 1532, the Act in Conditional Restraint of Annates forbade the payment of these dues to Rome, but left it to the King to decide when this prohibition should be put into effect.

Care was taken in the Act to present this action in as conservative a manner as possible—the removal, by an orthodox and devout monarch, of a long-standing abuse—and this conservative presentation of the Henrician reformation partly explains the lack of opposition from the bishops. They could not see at what point or on what grounds to take their stand, and having accepted the early measures they found themselves committed to all that followed. They may have had reservations about certain actions, but they felt bound by the biblical commandment to fear God and honour the King, particularly a King who was such an ardent defender of the established church against heresy. In the early 1530s, for instance, at least half a dozen heretics were burned, including Thomas Bilney—one of the leaders of the 'Little Germany' group at Cambridge ten years earlier—and in March 1532, at the very moment when Convocation was debating what reply to make to the Supplication against the Ordinaries, the King told Latimer, who had been accused of heresy, that 'I will not take upon me now to be a suitor to the bishops for you unless you promise to do penance as ye have deserved, and never to preach any such things again. Ye shall else only get from me a faggot to burn you.' Warham was one of the few who saw that the key issue was the sovereignty of the Pope and that once this had been abandoned the Church would be left at the mercy of the King. But Warham died in August 1532 and the King chose as his successor Thomas Cranmer.

Thomas Cranmer

Cranmer, born four years after Bosworth, became a fellow of Jesus College, Cambridge, and although he had to give up his fellowship when he married, he was restored to it again after his first wife's death. It was while he was lecturing in divinity at the university that the chance meeting took place with Gardiner and Fox, the King's Secretary and Almoner, from which there eventually emerged the scheme to consult the universities of Europe. This brought Cranmer into royal service, and it was during an embassy to Charles V in 1532 that he met some of the Lutheran leaders and took the niece of one of them as his second wife, in spite of his priest's orders. The Lutherans, who did not regard marriage as a sacrament, saw no reason why a man should not marry his brother's widow, and were therefore unsympathetic to Henry VIII. It may have been because Cranmer shared their views that he found the news of his appointment as Archbishop so unwelcome, and delayed his return to England as long as possible.

But if Cranmer hoped that the King would change his mind, he was mistaken. Cranmer was the ideal man for Henry, since he believed in royal supremacy over the Church and dreaded the disorder that uncontrolled reform might lead to. Henry had gone through a form of marriage with Anne Boleyn, now pregnant, in January 1533, but it was essential that this should be formally confirmed so that the child—which no one doubted would be the longed-for male heir—would be legitimate. To give the new Archbishop's decision the fullest possible authority it was important that nothing should be lacking in the formalities of his appointment. The Pope issued the necessary Bulls without difficulty. He did not know much about Cranmer and he was pleased to be able to gratify Henry without giving offence to the Emperor. He was also aware that Henry had not yet made permanent the restraint of annates, and that a conciliatory move on his part might persuade the King to delay such action indefinitely.

In March 1533 Cranmer was formally consecrated, but immediately before the ceremony he read aloud a protestation, declaring that when he took the customary oaths of allegiance to the Pope it would be with the reservation that his duty to the King came first. When, many years later, he was on trial and was called on to explain this perjury, he replied, 'That which I did, I did by the best learned men's advice I could get at that time.' Two months later he opened a court as Archbishop and *legatus natus* and in due course pronounced judgement that Henry's so-called marriage with Catherine had never been valid and that the King must stop living in sin with this woman who was not his wife—a provision that Henry found easy to fulfil since he had been living apart from Catherine ever since the divorce proceedings first opened. On Whitsunday 1533 the Archbishop crowned Anne as Queen in Westminster Abbey. A few months later, on 7 September, the longed-for child was born. Unfortunately for Anne it was a daughter, and Henry did not bother to hide his anger and disappointment. The baby girl was given the name Elizabeth.

Royal Supremacy. I: The Achievement[1]

To prevent an appeal by Catherine against Cranmer's verdict the Act of Appeals was passed. This Act marks the point at which Cromwell turned Henry's vague assertions of imperial sovereignty into an actual jurisdictional supremacy based on statute, against which there could be no appeal. The fate of successful revolutionaries is that their daring innovations become the commonplaces of succeeding generations, and this is true of Cromwell. The supremacy of statute and of the nation state has been taken for granted for so long that it seems inevitable. This was not the case in Henrician England, in spite of the growing influence of the civil lawyers, with their insistence that law is

[1] The argument in this section is based upon the interpretation of Dr Elton (see Bibliography). His views, however, have not been accepted without criticism. The article by Penry Williams and G. L. Harriss, 'A Revolution in Tudor History?' (*Past & Present*, No. 25, July 1963) is a useful corrective.

the will of the sovereign. The idea still prevailed that law was something far superior to mortal man and his institutions; that it was the immutable and indestructible morality of the whole natural world.

Cromwell had every reason to anticipate opposition to his policy, particularly as his rejection of papal sovereignty threatened to produce chaos at the very moment when the catholic faith was being challenged by heresy. If the clergy had refused to co-operate, Cromwell's programme could hardly have been carried out. As for the laity, their xenophobic anti-clericalism had persuaded them to challenge the Pope, but they might well draw back from an open break. Only a small amount of opposition was needed to make the King intervene against his minister, as Wolsey had found out at the time of the 'amicable grant'. All these and other problems faced Cromwell when he brought forward the Act of Appeals in March 1533.

The Act is carefully conservative in form, not claiming a new authority but restoring an old one and asserting 'that this realm of England is an empire, and so hath been accepted in the world, governed by one supreme head and King having the dignity and royal estate of the imperial Crown of the same, unto whom a body politic, compact of all sorts and degrees of people divided in terms and by names of spirituality and temporalty, be bounden and owe to bear next to God a natural and humble obedience'. Since the King had no superior on earth it followed that there could be no appeal from his jurisdiction, and the Act therefore made arrangements for final judgement in all cases to be given by courts within the King's jurisdiction. The unity of all laws, under the co-ordinating authority of the King, was thereby established: so also was the confusion between ecclesiastical and secular authority which was to haunt Tudor and Stuart England by making religious nonconformity a political offence and by equating heresy with treason.

Now that an open act of defiance had been committed, the Pope was goaded into action. In July 1533 he quashed Cranmer's verdict and excommunicated him and the other bishops who had taken part in the proceedings. Henry was given until September to take back Catherine, failing which he would be excommunicated. Cromwell immediately set on foot a propaganda campaign against the papacy, and the *Articles*, published in late 1533, referred to 'the bishop of Rome, by some men called the Pope'. This was not simply an insult; it was a reminder that the Pope was a bishop, like any other bishop, and had no authority outside his own diocese.

The denial of papal supremacy left the English Church, from an administrative point of view, without an effective head, and further legislation was needed to replace the Pope by the King. In 1534 the Act in Absolute Restraint of Annates confirmed Henry's letters patent cutting off this source of papal revenue. It also laid down that in future bishops and abbots were to be elected only after the issue of a *congé d'élire* containing the name of the person the King had chosen. If the chapter failed to elect the person so named its members would be liable to the penalties prescribed in the Statute of Praemunire. Another Act of 1534, asserting that the realm had been impoverished by 'intolerable exactions of great sums of money', forbade the payment to Rome of Peter's Pence—an annual tribute regularly paid since the reign of the Conqueror—and prohibited the sale of papal dispensations in England.

Hope of any reconciliation with Rome had by now been abandoned and in March 1534 Clement at last gave judgement in favour of Catherine. In November of that year Parliament put the coping-stone upon the new structure of the Church in England by passing the Act of Supremacy. This did not grant a parliamentary title to Henry, since the declared assumption of the Henrician Reformation was that Kings of England had always held this supremacy, even though papal usurpations had for some time prevented them from exercising it. 'The King's Majesty justly and rightfully is', in the words of the Act, supreme head of the Church of England'. A Treason Act of the same year made it an offence to attempt by any means, including writing and speaking, to deprive the King and his heirs of their titles or to accuse them of heresy or tyranny. The heirs in question were named by the Succession Act of March 1534 as the children of the Boleyn marriage, and all subjects were ordered to take an oath accepting this.

Sir Thomas More, former Lord Chancellor, and John Fisher, Bishop of Rochester, refused to take the oath and were imprisoned. More claimed that he was 'not bound to change my conscience and conform it to the counsel of one realm, against the general counsel of Christendom'. His appeal from the law of the state to 'the law of God and His Holy Church' worried Lord Chancellor Audley, who was presiding at his trial, and he asked the Lord Chief Justice for his opinion. The Lord Chief Justice replied that 'if the act of Parliament be not unlawful, then is not the indictment in my conscience insufficient'. This reply went to the heart of the matter. More was executed because he denied the sovereignty of statute, upon which Henry and Cromwell built the Tudor state. His idealism and his appeal to conscience, as well as his courage and humanity, make More's execution seem a flagrant example of tyrannical injustice. Yet his opponents were also idealists who saw the way of salvation, in this world and the next, leading from the secular state which acknowledged no earthly superior. Before twentieth-century Englishmen commit their sympathies whole-heartedly to More's side it is as well to remember that historically and in fact they belong to the party of his opponents.

The assumption of Henry and Cromwell that anyone who refused whole-heartedly to accept the royal supremacy was a potential traitor was confirmed in Fisher's case, for Chapuys's reports over the past two years had quoted 'that excellent and holy man, the Bishop of Rochester' as calling for prompt action and strong measures on the part of the Emperor against the King. In May 1535 the Pope created Fisher a cardinal. Henry took this as a personal affront and swore that by the time the red hat arrived Fisher would not have a head to put it on. The following month Fisher, found guilty of treason, was executed. More had to wait until July, when he was executed, appropriately enough, on the eve of the feast of St Thomas Becket.

More and Fisher were the most important victims of the 'Terror', the stage common to every revolution when the leaders or potential leaders of a conservative reaction are struck down. The Henrician terror was a small-scale affair. There was no attempt to wipe out a whole class, as in France and Russia at a later date, but Henry made it clear that he would not tolerate open opposition to his will. Elizabeth Barton, 'the Nun of Kent', a visionary whose revelations had given her a great reputation, was executed in 1534, along with her accomplices, for prophesying the King's death. The following year, while More and Fisher were awaiting judgement, a number of monks from the London Charterhouse were hanged, drawn and quartered for denying the royal supremacy. This show of force was apparently sufficient. No leader emerged to challenge the policy of the Crown.

Royal Supremacy. II: The Theoretical Foundations

By the middle of 1535 Henry and Cromwell had accomplished the first stage of their revolution by destroying papal authority in England and making the King supreme head of the English Church. There were theoretical as well as legal foundations to the royal supremacy.

Most obvious, perhaps, was the justification of expediency: intervention by the King was necessary because the Church would not reform itself. The failure of the Conciliar Movement had left the papacy so powerful that a non-papal, autonomous reform movement within the Catholic Church was inconceivable. The only power which could effectively challenge papal claims and set reform on foot without causing chaos was the lay ruler. For this reason the early reformers, including Luther, appealed to the prince.

But there were good grounds for princely intervention, quite apart from expediency. The Bible showed the Jewish Kings of the Old Testament exercising authority over the Church, while in the New Testament St Paul had written, 'There is no power but of God: the powers that be are ordained of God. Whosoever therefore resisteth the power resisteth the ordinance of God: and they that resist shall receive to themselves damnation.'[1]

The evidence of Scripture was reinforced by the appeal to history. In the ancient world Constantine's authority had been accepted by the early Christian Church, and his position, the reformers claimed, had been inherited by the lay princes of Europe. Until Becket, English rulers, while acknowledging the spiritual leadership of the Pope, had not tolerated any interference in the day-to-day administration of the Church. It was Becket who embodied the full Hildebrandine theory that the Church was a monarchy ruled over by the Pope and that the princes of Europe were the Pope's feudal vassals. The rulers of late medieval England had moved a long way from this subordinate position, but Henry VIII consciously took up the struggle where his great namesake and predecessor had abandoned it, and the memory of Becket was very much alive among both the King's supporters and his opponents. Warham, for instance, in the protestation which he drew up in 1532 against the threatened indictment of the clergy for a breach of praemunire, declared that he would rather suffer martyrdom 'than in my conscience to confess this article to be a praemunire, for which St Thomas died'. The same memory prompted Henry in 1538 to order the destruction of St Thomas's shrine at Canterbury and to forbid the celebration of his feast on the grounds that 'there appeareth nothing in his life and exterior or conversation whereby he should be called a saint, but rather a rebel and traitor to his prince'.

The reformers drew a distinction between *Potestas Jurisdictionis*, or the right to exercise jurisdiction over the Church, and the *Potestas*

[1] *Romans* 13: 1, 2.

Ordinis, the right to exercise spiritual powers. The Henrician Reformation was the transfer to the Crown of the *Potestas Jurisdictionis*: the *Potestas Ordinis* remained in the hands of bishops. The appeal to history, and the distinction between the two types of ecclesiastical authority, account for the tone of the statutes which brought about the destruction of papal rule. History and the Bible, it was held, showed that the *Potestas Jurisdictionis* belonged of right to the lay ruler; all that remained was to remove papal usurpations and to restore to the King his rightful authority. The argument was a strong one and it carried many waverers with it.

Conservatives and radicals both appealed to royal authority. The conservatives were afraid that without royal protection the Church would fall victim to radical attack; better a state Church with catholic doctrine than the heresies of Zürich. The radicals, on the other hand, hoped that by destroying papal supremacy the King would open the way to a Church reformed in doctrine as well as government. Gardiner, who belonged to the conservatives, wrote that 'the King, yea, though he be an infidel, representeth the image of God upon earth'. Tyndale, who stood at the opposite extreme from Gardiner and was eventually to be burnt as a heretic, agreed with him on this point. 'He that judgeth the King', he wrote, 'judgeth God, and he that resisteth the King resisteth God.' For those whose consciences were less scrupulous than More's—that is to say the vast majority—obedience to the prince was sufficient in itself, and largely replaced dependence on relics, indulgences and outward observances which had previously given hope of salvation to men well aware of their wicked ways but unable to abandon them. Now they could take refuge with Shakespeare's soldier: 'we know enough if we know we are the King's subjects. If his cause be wrong, our obedience to the King wipes the crime of it out of us.' It was left in the play to the disguised Henry V to make the rejoinder of the later reformers: 'Every subject's duty is the King's. But every subject's soul is his own.'[1]

Obedience to the sovereign became a religious duty not only because the sovereign was the head of the Church but also because society as a whole, organised under the King, was assumed to have a spiritual function. It was this belief that explains the otherwise paradoxical combination of worldliness and deep religious feeling in the men and women of early Tudor England. Their worldliness—desire for money, lands, honours, titles and glory—led to the adulation of

[1] Shakespeare, *King Henry V*, IV:i.

the monarch from whom such things flowed. Yet at the same time their awareness of God and sin and the need for salvation suffused the secular society and its secular head with a spiritual purpose. This was true not only of England but of other countries, whether they were communities like Calvin's Geneva, where the state was conceived to be an aspect of the Church, or those like catholic France and Lutheran Germany, where the Church was subordinate to the lay magistrate. In all these the state, whether it was a city, principality or kingdom, became the unit in 'which and around which matters spiritual were organised.

In England the new society was mapped out by writers like Thomas Starkey, who were the direct heirs of the early sixteenth-century humanists. These men were products of the Renaissance. They had studied the learning of the ancient world, particularly Greece, and wished to apply their knowledge to the benefit of Church and state. Cardinal College[1] was a centre of humanist studies, and Thomas Starkey was among those students already at Oxford whom Wolsey persuaded to transfer to his new foundation. In the years following Wolsey's fall many of the scholars who had been at Cardinal College, and would normally have gone on from there to be trained in Wolsey's household, found refuge in the circle of Reginald Pole.

Pole was a member of a great family, connected by blood to the throne itself, and he was to become famous as a scholar and humanist. His household at Padua (where his studies were paid for by Henry VIII) became a centre for such English scholars as Starkey and Thomas Lupset—one of the leading figures in the academic world, a friend of Erasmus and lecturer in Greek at Oxford. But the even development of English humanist studies was broken up by the divorce question. Pole was too big a name for Henry to ignore and the King put pressure on him to give a favourable opinion. Pole was at first far from clear about his own attitude, but Starkey saw in the rise of Thomas Cromwell an opportunity to reform society on humanist lines, and in 1534 he left Pole at Padua to return permanently to England. Starkey assumed that Pole would eventually take the King's part and that English humanists would continue the tradition of service to the state which Wolsey had encouraged. But in 1536 Pole published his *Pro Ecclesiasticae Unitatis Defensione* which came out clearly against the King. From then onwards Henry regarded Pole as his enemy.

Starkey, meanwhile, was working for Cromwell. His most famous work, *A Dialogue between Pole and Lupset*, was not published until the

[1] See above, p. 38.

nineteenth century, but his *Exhortation to Unity and Obedience* was produced in 1536 by the King's printer. For Starkey, following Aristotle, the state marked the triumph of civilised man over his brute instincts: 'good policy is nothing else but the order and rule of a multitude of men, as it were conspiring together to live in all virtue and honesty.' The contrast between the humanism of Starkey and that of More is nowhere more striking than in their attitude to the state. Starkey revered it; More despised it, and described it as 'nothing but a conspiracy of rich men procuring their own commodities under the name and title of common wealth'.

did More despise the state?

For Starkey the Bible was the sole source of authority. What it commanded was, by definition, good; what it condemned was bad. But on those topics about which it was silent—for instance, papal power—society should decide for itself. These topics were the *adiaphora*, 'matters indifferent', which were not essential to salvation and belonged by right, as well as by expediency, to the sphere of authority of the lay ruler. Starkey recommended a middle course between the extremes of total preservation and total rejection, maintaining for instance that ceremonies and traditions, being *adiaphora*, should be permitted in so far as they were 'things convenient to maintain unity' and as long as they were not repugnant to 'God's word nor to good civility'. In this he was sketching out the position that the Anglican Church was eventually to make its own.

The humanists were not the only scholars of whom Cromwell made use. His own inclination and the needs of the hour led him into the circle of radical reformers, of whom Tyndale was the most important. Tyndale was a refugee in the Netherlands, where in 1528 he published *The Obedience of a Christian Man*, in which he declared that even a bad king was better than chaos, for 'it is better to suffer one tyrant than many'. This book came into the hands of Henry, who found much in it of which he approved. But when Cromwell sent an agent to Antwerp to persuade Tyndale to come out openly in support of the King, Tyndale demanded that Henry should first agree to promote radical reform by officially licensing a version of the Bible in English. Henry was not, at that time, prepared to accept such a condition, and angrily broke off the negotiations. A few years later Tyndale's hiding-place was betrayed, and he was burnt at Antwerp as a heretic. He had appealed to the lay prince and the lay prince struck him down. He died praying God to open the King of England's eyes.

Unlike Tyndale, most of the extremists were prepared to work with Henry on the destruction of papal authority, which they regarded as the first stage of the purification of the Church. Their support made the Henrician Reformation more extreme than it appeared to be on the surface and occasionally drove it beyond a mere transfer of *Potestas Jurisdictionis*. Among those who came over to Henry's side were Latimer, who recanted his radical opinions for the time being, and Robert Barnes, the Cambridge reformer. Throughout the 1530s the government was gradually moving away from rigid orthodoxy. In 1535, for instance, royal injunctions were issued to the universities, abolishing courses and degrees in canon law, and ordering that all divinity lectures should be 'according to the true sense of the Scriptures' and that all students should study the Bible privately. The following year saw the publication of the Ten Articles defining the doctrinal position of the Church of England. On the sacraments of the altar, baptism and penance these were relatively orthodox, but prayers to saints and special rites and ceremonies were permitted only on the understanding that they were simply reminders of spiritual truths, and not, as catholics maintained, themselves means to obtain new graces from God. In the same year in which the Ten Articles appeared another of the great ambitions of the radical reformers was fulfilled, when Cromwell was appointed Vicar-General with orders to exercise the King's supremacy over the monasteries.

The Dissolution of the Monasteries. I: Visitation

The obvious intention behind Cromwell's appointment was an attack upon Church wealth, for the King was short of money. The wars of the early part of his reign had consumed Henry VII's treasure, there were troubles in Ireland, and from all over England came reports of opposition to payment of taxes. The need for money was all the more pressing since the Pope had declared Henry deposed and there was a possibility that Charles V and Francis I would combine to invade England.

The monasteries were a temptation to men hungry for money. The heyday of the monks had been in the thirteenth and fourteenth centuries when their studies in divinity and canon law had made them the intellectual leaders of Christendom. But the fifteenth century saw on the Continent the spread of the new learning with its emphasis on classics and philosophy, and although this did not affect England until the reign of Henry VII, English education had also shifted its emphasis towards the study of common and civil law. While the pattern of education was changing, so also were assumptions about the Christian life. The place of the Church was held to be in the world, though not of it, and there was no longer any instinctive sympathy with the monastic ideal. This was shown by the decline in the number of novices, and by the drying up of legacies. Colet, for instance, who was both an ascetic and a contemplative, left his money to found a school, and it is a reflection on the monastic life that he and More, who were both in a sense 'natural monks', did not enter the cloister.

In England the intellectual attack on the monks ranged from the rapier thrusts of Erasmus to the bludgeoning tactics of Simon Fish. Erasmus wrote in his *Enchiridion* of 1504: 'Do we not see members of the most austere monastic orders maintaining that the essence of perfection lies in ceremonies or in a fixed quantity of psalmody or in manual labour? And if you come to close quarters with these men and question them on spiritual matters you will scarcely find one who does not walk according to the flesh.' Most of Erasmus's friends would have agreed with his criticism of monastic life, but he was prepared to go much further and welcome the abolition of monasteries altogether. Simon Fish's complaint, published in 1528, took the form of a *Supplication for the Beggars* who declared that they were being deprived of their legitimate livelihood by 'another sort, not of impotent but of strong, puissant and counterfeit holy and idle beggars'.

The violence of Fish's attack might be thought to have blunted its impact, but in fact it was so widely circulated that More replied to it with a *Supplication of Souls,* in which he reminded his readers that the prayers of the monks helped to shorten the period which souls had to spend in purgatory. Fish's attack and More's reply show how a criticism of abuses (the laziness of monks) could shift imperceptibly into an attack upon doctrine (the existence of purgatory). But only after they had unleashed their assault on the Church did the reformers turn their attention to what they believed in and wished to preserve. In these early days they were much clearer on what they hated, and they focused the full fury of their invective on the monks and the monastic ideal.

The monasteries of early Tudor England had still not recovered from the Black Death which had halved their population and wiped out some communities altogether. Monastic revenues were now so large, relative to the number of monks, that they encouraged worldliness, and the reports of episcopal visitors in the century preceding the Dissolution show how standards were declining. Feasting had replaced fasting, dress was extravagant, services were poorly attended. Sometimes there were more serious faults. In 1514, for instance, the Prior of Walsingham was a notoriously dissolute and evil liver, who wore luxurious and ostentatious clothes, kept his own private jester, and paid for all this by stealing monastic plate and jewels. Visitation could be very effective, but visitors varied in quality, and too often the punishments they prescribed were absurdly inadequate for the offence, or else were not enforced. In 1491, for instance, a deacon of Langley Priory cut off another monk's hand in a violent brawl. He was sentenced by the visitor to perpetual exile and imprisonment in another house, but six years later he was back again at Langley, this time as sub-prior.

Richard Redman, abbot of the Premonstratensian house at Shap from 1458 to 1505, is an example of a conscientious visitor. He toured the twenty-nine abbeys under his care at regular intervals of three or four years, taking about three months for each circuit. He did his job well and was obviously concerned to keep up the high quality of the houses for which he was responsible. Another of the outstanding figures in English monasticism of this period was Marmaduke Huby, abbot of the Cistercian house of Fountains from 1494 until 1526. Huby is remembered, among other things, as the builder of the great tower at Fountains, and in this particular aspect of their life the monasteries were far from decadent. Building went on throughout the Wars of the Roses and continued without a break right up to the Dissolution. Peterborough's fan vaulting dates from the period immediately preceding Wolsey's fall, and the last priors of Bath had not finished the magnificent work they had set going when the royal commissioners arrived to take over.

Some monasteries ran a school for the poor children of the neighbourhood, while they trained the sons of the rich in the abbot's household. The education of the monks themselves was, however, frequently neglected, particularly the obligation to send them to university. The failure of the orders to educate their members was a serious weakness in an age that saw an increasing number of learned laymen, for it meant that the monks could not meet the intellectual challenge of the Renaissance. Even the fine libraries which many monasteries possessed were out of date, and the connexion of monasteries with literature and learning waned with the decline of the handwritten book. A high musical tradition was maintained in some big houses where the numbers permitted it. Robert Fayrfax directed the music at St Albans

Cîteau

during the first twenty years of the sixteenth century, and at Waltham Abbey Thomas Tallis was organist and choirmaster for some years before the Dissolution. Elsewhere, numbers were usually too small for music to play more than a minor part in the life and worship of the monastery.

In charity and hospitality the same decline is recorded. Almsgiving may have averaged the stipulated one-tenth of monastic revenues, but it was indiscriminate and did little to relieve the genuine problem of poverty. Hospitality was a traditional duty of monasteries and was important, particularly in the north of England where inns were rare. The disadvantage of this was that it brought lay people into the cloister, unless, as at Glastonbury and St Albans, a separate inn was built for guests.

There were, on the eve of the Dissolution, about eight hundred and fifty monastic houses, including friaries, varying enormously in population and wealth. Westminster and Glastonbury, for instance, had incomes of nearly £4,000 a year, but some of the smaller houses were heavily in debt. The total annual income of all the houses was about £165,500, derived mainly from their estates, which amounted to a quarter of all the cultivated land in England. Much of this income went on running the estates and maintaining the worship of God, but it still seems an excessive amount for the eleven thousand monks and nuns who benefited from it, and the wealth of the monasteries made them an easy target for criticism and envy. It is true that moral standards were low and that the frequent instances of rushed or neglected services were a denial of the very purpose for which monasteries had been created. But however much they may have deserved their fate, the fact remains that they were dissolved because they were rich while the King was relatively poor.

There were many precedents for dissolution. Edward III and Henry V had suppressed alien priories, and one or two English houses had been put down, but the first systematic dissolution had been carried out by Wolsey. Between Wolsey's fall and the Dissolution no major suppressions took place, but in 1532 the Augustinian canons at Aldgate went bankrupt and handed their house over to the King. This was the first instance of monastic property not being used for a religious or charitable purpose.

Thomas Cromwell had been Wolsey's agent in suppressing twenty-nine monasteries, and was therefore well fitted for the larger task. The commissioners whom he sent round to collect oaths to the succession and supremacy met little opposition, and by the end of 1535 all except a handful of monks had rejected the Pope and accepted the King as head of the Church. The Observant Friars held out until Henry suppressed their seven houses in 1534, while the Bridgettines of Syon gave in only after their head, Richard Reynolds, had been executed. The only other opposition came from members of the London Charterhouse, following the example set by their prior, John Houghton, of whom Knowles writes: 'the strict monastic life brought to blossom for the last time on English soil a character of the rarest strength and beauty—a last flowering, a winter rose, of English medieval monachism.'[1] Houghton and two other Carthusian priors refused to take the oath of supremacy and were executed, and eighteen Carthusians suffered death before the London Charterhouse was effectively subdued.

In 1535 Cromwell, as Vicar-General, ordered an assessment to be made of the wealth of the Church. This was a remarkable administrative feat. Commissioners were appointed for each diocese to find out all the sources of Church revenue and their returns were incorporated in the *Valor Ecclesiasticus*, a sixteenth-century Domesday Book of the Church. The same year also saw a general visitation of the monasteries. Cromwell's agents in this were an odd assortment. Four of them, Richard Layton, Thomas Legh, John Tregonwell and John London, were trained in civil law, while the fifth, John ap Rice, was a common lawyer. These men have had a bad press among historians, but they were typical of the government servants of their day, who knew that their position and profits depended on ingratiating themselves with their master. Probity and independence of mind were not qualities demanded of them. They were required simply to produce damning evidence for a verdict already decided on, and this they did.

The main aim of the commissioners' enquiries was to discover the financial state of every house and to elicit as many examples as they could of superstitious practices and immoral conduct. Where mild measures were of no avail they resorted to threats, and ap Rice described Legh at work: 'at Burton he behaved very insolently . . . at Bradstock and elsewhere he made no less ruffling with the heads than he did at Burton . . . wherever he comes he handles the fathers very roughly.' They travelled at great speed. When Legh and Layton were working in the north they visited at least a hundred and twenty monasteries in two months and covered more than a thousand miles. Even had they

[1] David Knowles, *The Religious Orders in England*, vol. III, p. 224.

wished to make a thorough inquiry into the state of any house they did not have time to do so, in spite of the fact that some districts, including the whole of Lincolnshire, appear to have been left out of the visitation altogether.

The Dissolution of the Monasteries. II: Suppression of the Smaller Houses

Before the commissioners' work was half finished Cromwell decided to destroy the smaller monasteries by statute. The reports from his visitors, although incomplete, had given him sufficient lurid evidence to shock the Commons, and there may have been a feeling, even among those who wanted the monastic life to continue, that the smaller monasteries had the weakest claim to preservation, and that if the King was allowed to take these he might be willing to leave the remainder alone. In 1536 the Dissolution Act ordered the suppression of all houses whose incomes fell below £200 a year 'forasmuch as manifest sin, vicious, carnal and abominable living is daily used and committed' among them. They were contrasted with the 'great solemn monasteries of this realm wherein, thanks be to God, religion is right well kept and observed'.

The Act affected some three hundred monastic houses. To enforce it new commissions were appointed in each county, consisting of a mixture of local gentry and officials. Reports from these men make revealing comparison with those of Layton, Legh and their colleagues, since they show that there was no ill-feeling towards the religious and their houses on the part of the local population and that many of the charges of Cromwell's men were either unfounded or else based on a misinterpretation of the facts.

Some indication of the hold of the enclosed life on the religious themselves is given by comparing the number of those who, when they were offered the opportunity, left the cloister altogether, with those who transferred to a large house. The figures are not entirely satisfactory since many of the weaker members of a community would doubtless have abandoned it after the visit of Cromwell's agents, without waiting for the dissolution commissioners to arrive: in eight Norfolk monasteries, for instance, numbers had dropped during this period from sixty-nine to thirty-two. But Cromwell can hardly have believed that the monks were all itching to leave a life that meant nothing to them, since he made provision for about a quarter of the smaller houses to remain in existence to contain the large number of religious who wished to stay. The number varied from region to region, but for the country as a whole the proportion of men who abandoned the religious life was about forty per cent; for women it was much lower, only about ten per cent. This striking difference between the sexes does not necessarily mean that nuns were more fitted for the monastic life. It is rather the case that they had little to gain from leaving the cloister, since the vow of chastity was regarded as binding on both men and women, and whereas an ex-monk could hope to find employment as a secular priest, an ex-nun, vowed to chastity in a world where the only vocation of women was child-bearing, had little prospect of happiness. On the other hand, staying in the monastic life meant being transferred to another monastery, and this could be a bleak prospect for men and women who had grown to love their house and those who lived in it. The destruction of English monasticism was carried out in a remarkably dispassionate manner, but for hundreds of men and women it meant bewilderment, misery and regret.

Neither the King nor his chief minister was yet committed to total dissolution of all the monasteries. Henry actually revived the suppressed house at Bisham as 'King Henry's new monastery of the Holy Trinity', and he also placed some Premonstratensian canonesses in the buildings of Stixwold to pray for the good estate of himself and his late wife, Queen Jane. The total destruction of the monasteries only seems to have been decided on after revolt had come in the shape of the Pilgrimage of Grace, and had been defeated.

The Dissolution of the Monasteries. III: The Pilgrimage of Grace and Suppression of the Larger Houses

The Pilgrimage of Grace was the first big challenge to the policy of Cromwell and his master. In 1536 three commissions were at work in Lincolnshire, of which one was concerned with dissolving the smaller monasteries and another with assessing and collecting the subsidy, while the third was busy enquiring into the state of life of the parish clergy. The rumour spread that this third commission was only the prelude to a large-scale suppression of parish churches, and an inflammatory sermon preached by the Vicar of Louth led to a rising in October 1536. This spread rapidly to other districts, and soon York-shire and the north were in open rebellion.

Economic grievances played a big part in this. Bad harvests had sent the price of grain soaring, while enclosures had caused much hardship. The gentry were, as always, bitter about the Statute of Uses,[1] and in a part of England which was traditionally feudal in its reverence for great and ancient families there was angry contempt for men like Thomas Cromwell. The way in which he interfered in legal matters and summoned whole juries to appear in the Star Chamber was particularly resented. As one Yorkshire knight wrote: 'his servants, and eke his servants' servants, think to have the law in every place here ordered at their commandment, and will take upon them to command sheriff [and] Justices of the Peace . . . in their master's name at their pleasure.'

The Lincolnshire rising collapsed without fighting because the gentlemen and common people could not agree, but in Yorkshire Robert Aske, gentleman and lawyer, had emerged as leader of the rebels and he was joined by some of the great men of the county. Aske was an idealist, who gave to the rebellion most of its spiritual quality. He proclaimed in October 1536 at York that 'we have taken [this pilgrimage] for the preservation of Christ's Church, of this realm of England, the King our sovereign lord, the nobility and commons of the same' from the King's evil advisers. His loyalty to the King was genuine, and he and Henry probably shared many of the same assumptions about religion. Aske wanted the monasteries preserved because 'in the north parts [they] gave great alms to poor men and laudably served God . . . and by occasion of the said suppression the divine service of Almighty God is much minished'.

The Duke of Norfolk confirmed, in a letter to the King, that the abbeys were much loved in the north, but the Pilgrimage was not papalist, and although the common people were probably sympathetic to the old order it was economic rather than religious grievances that stung them into revolt. The list drawn up by the great assembly of Pilgrims which met at Pontefract in December 1536 included demands that land should be held by customary tenure instead of labour services, that 'gressoms' (ingress or entrance fines, payable before a tenant could take over his property) should be limited, that the statutes against enclosure should be enforced, and that villein blood should be removed from the King's Council.

These demands show that the Pilgrimage was, economically as well as religiously, a conservative revolt, a protest from those north parts of England whose way of life was changing much more slowly than that

[1] See below, p. 91.

of the south. As with the Lincolnshire rebels there was no suggestion of an alternative government to Henry's. The Pilgrims relied on persuading the King to accept their proposals, and probably believed that he was secretly in sympathy with them and only needed evidence of their support to shake off the evil men who surrounded him. This touching and quite unjustified belief of the common people that the King was on their side seems a little absurd, but then they had no one else in whom they could put their trust. The strength of the Tudor monarchy sprang from the fact that the only alternative to royal rule was anarchy.

The revolt was serious enough for Henry to call the Duke of Norfolk out of the sulky semi-retirement into which Cromwell's rise to power had driven him. Norfolk was the King's best soldier, and the Pilgrims could hardly complain about his 'villein blood', nor about that of his colleague, the Earl of Shrewsbury. Norfolk had assembled a large army, but his men were not all reliable and he was short of money. He therefore made offers to the Pilgrims that amounted to free pardon, although he had no intention of keeping his word and asked the King 'to take in good part whatsoever promise I shall make to the rebels . . . for surely I shall observe no part thereof . . . thinking and reputing that none oath or promise made by policy to serve you, mine only master and sovereign, can distain me, who shall rather be torn in a million of pieces rather than to show one point of cowardice or untruth to your majesty'. The tone of the letter shows Norfolk's reverence for the King and his fear of Henry's anger. To modern ears there is something nauseating about the blend of sycophancy and humble abasement, but such terms imply a false relationship, whereas Norfolk's letter reflects the reality of the situation. Henry was so powerful that his subjects loved and feared him and made it their pride to obey him. Norfolk had little reason to feel grateful to his master, and with an army under his command could easily have betrayed the King. But he remained faithful.

Distrust between gentry and commons was already beginning to cripple the Yorkshire rising as it had the Lincolnshire one. In December 1536 Norfolk promised to lay the rebels' demands before Parliament and in return for this and a guarantee of free pardon Aske and the other leaders agreed to persuade the unwilling commons to lay down their arms. Aske had betrayed the revolution, and yet it had never had any real chance of succeeding. Henry could not be coerced into changing his policy, and since Aske never considered dethroning the King he had no alternative but to trust him.

As the rebels dispersed, Norfolk and his men moved in and started their work of retribution. As usual in a state which had no effective police force or standing army, savage punishments were used as a deterrent. The Duke was in Cumberland in February, putting into effect Henry's commands to 'cause such dreadful execution upon a good number of the inhabitants, hanging them on trees, quartering them, and setting the quarters in every town, as shall be a fearful warning'. Altogether more than two hundred prisoners were put to death: they included Aske and the other leaders who were sent to London, tried in May 1537 on charges of treason, and executed in June. Henry's repression was all the more savage because the Pilgrimage had shown up the Crown's military weakness. He did not put down the rebellion; it collapsed under its own weight. Had there been more ruthless leadership and some agreement about objectives, Henry's throne might have toppled.

Now that the threat to their policy had come and gone, Henry and Cromwell were able to develop their plans with much greater freedom. In Yorkshire the big abbeys had stood aloof from the revolt, but in Cumberland and Lancashire the Cistercians had supported it. The dispossessed monks of Sawley, for instance, had returned to their house, which they turned into a propaganda centre for the Pilgrims. Henry showed his anger by ordering 'the said Abbot and certain of the chief of the monks to be hanged upon long pieces of timber, or otherwise, out of the steeple', and he used a few isolated examples, of which this was one, to justify the suppression of all the remaining monasteries. In the winter of 1537 Thomas Cromwell's commissioners were again sent out to take surrenders, and they seized on any suspicion of opposition to strike hard and reinforce the lesson of the Pilgrimage. Robert Hobbes, Abbot of Woburn, was charged with treason for denying the royal supremacy, condemned, and hanged outside his own monastery. The heads of three other big houses, Colchester, Reading and Glastonbury, were also executed.

With the great abbeys fell the friaries, though these houses were so poor that they yielded little in the way of movable property. The increasing radicalism of the government was shown by a concurrent attack on the shrines of England. Early in 1538 the tomb of St Edmund at Bury was dismantled. It was followed by the Precious Blood of Hailes, and then the great shrine of St Thomas at Canterbury was stripped of its jewels and precious metals, which were sent off in wagon-loads to the King's treasury. The end of this orgy of destruction and dissolution came in April 1540 when the Abbey of Waltham, the last survivor of centuries of English monasticism, surrendered to the commissioners. With the respect for legal forms that characterised the Henrician Reformation, a second Act of Dissolution was passed in 1539, confirming all surrenders that had been and were to take place, and formally vesting the surrendered property in the Crown.[1]

The Dissolution of the Monasteries. IV: The Dispossessed

Movables, such as plate and jewels, were sent up to the royal treasury. The rest was sold on the spot, including the lead from the roofs, which was stripped off and melted down. In some places, such as Lewes and Chertsey, the buildings were razed to the ground, while elsewhere they were left to casual plunder. This work was done so well at Sempringham that the shrine of St Gilbert, with its great tower and two adjoining cloisters, completely disappeared and even the site was forgotten, though it stood in open country; while at Walsingham an Elizabethan poet described how:

> Level, level with the ground
> The towers do lie
> Which with their golden, glittering tops
> Pierced once to the sky.

Where a monastic site was sold the new owner was in theory bound to dismantle the church and conventual buildings, but this was an expensive business and the non-habitable parts were often pillaged for building material, as at Fountains, then left to picturesque decay. A few were adapted for other purposes, like Malmesbury, where a rich clothier set up a factory; and in some cases, as at Bolton, Pershore and Tewkesbury, the local parish bought the monastic church to use as its own.

Luckiest of all houses were those which survived as cathedral churches, either for established sees, such as Canterbury, Durham and Winchester, or for the six new ones—Westminster, Gloucester, Peterborough, Chester, Oxford and Bristol—which Henry created. In these there was a considerable continuity of personnel. At Winchester, for instance, all except four of the monks became secular canons of the cathedral, while at Durham about half the community stayed on in its new capacity. The new sees were tokens of a much greater

---

[1] The economic consequences of the Dissolution are considered in Chapter 7.

reorganisation of the Church, which was never put into effect. Many of the English dioceses were too big, and Henry had himself sketched out a plan for thirteen new ones, making use of monastic buildings and land. But in the event the fear of invasion and the heavy expenditure on defence works made the need for ready cash overriding. The only other reform, minor but long overdue, was the endowment of new chairs at the two universities in Greek, Hebrew, Theology, Law and Medicine.

The dispossessed monks and nuns, were provided for by the government. Heads of houses were well treated, particularly if they co-operated with the dissolution commissioners and did not attempt private deals with the property entrusted to them. About thirty ex-abbots became bishops within a few years after the dissolution and the rest, received pensions which were at worst adequate and at best luxurious. Some abbots and priors retired to country houses, perhaps near their former home or even on part of its property, and not a few married— at the risk of being called to account later for breaking their vow of chastity—and added their names to the roll of county families.

The monks also were given pensions, except for those who had abandoned the monastic life before the surrender of the larger houses began. These pensions, averaging £5 10s per annum, were enough to exist on in 1539, but they took no account of inflation. By 1550, £5 was the wage of an unskilled labourer, and monks who had no resources other than their pension must have been near starvation level. They did not, in any case, receive the full amount. In most years the King and his successors took an ecclesiastical tenth, which was duly deducted from the pensions, and 4d in the pound was payable to the Court of Augmentations to cover the expenses of administering the grants. The pensioner lost between ten and twelve per cent of his meagre income, and in the case of nuns, whose pensions were minute, this made a big difference: a list of 1573, for instance, shows a number of aged nuns losing 4s out of their meagre grant of £2 6s 8d. Pensions were apparently paid regularly right up to the death of the last pensioner early in the seventeenth century, except for brief periods, as in 1552-53, when the government was desperately short of money.

It is not possible to draw up a balance sheet for the monasteries, putting their prayers and their example of the spiritual life on one side, and their corruption and laxity on the other. Any estimate of profit and loss must be a personal one. Henry and Cromwell, at least, were satisfied, for the minister had fulfilled his promise to make his master the richest King England had ever known, and the threat of bankruptcy had been pushed beyond the immediate horizon. Those who bought monastic property from the Crown were also presumably satisfied, since they had added to their land and prestige and were determined that the transfer from religious to lay ownership which had taken place should never be reversed. Only the eleven thousand monks and nuns and their dependants had good reason to be dissatisfied with the sudden blow that had transformed their lives and tumbled them out of the security of the cloister into an indifferent world.

5

King and Minister

THE year 1539 marks the apogee of Thomas Cromwell. Not only had he forged the weapons with which Henry swept away papal authority in England, humbled the Church and destroyed the monasteries: he had also remodelled English government in a way that Dr Elton calls revolutionary because it resulted in a really new monarchy, based on Parliament and working through bureaucratic institutions which had a life of their own.

The Privy Council

The royal Council was, as always, the heart of the administration, but successive attempts from the fifteenth century onwards to give it a definite and permanent pattern had failed. Wolsey's Council was still, in effect, that of the Yorkists and early Tudors—a fluctuating body, with the number of Councillors present varying from meeting to meeting and never representing more than a small fraction of those who were eligible. Henry VIII, like his father, had a number of Councillors in permanent attendance on him, but he occasionally complained that he was starved of advisers because the majority were waiting on the Cardinal. In 1522, for instance, he called for more Councillors, so that strangers and visitors should not 'find him so bare, without some noble and wise sage personages about him', but although the Eltham Ordinance of 1526 nominated twenty members of the Council who were to be permanently attendant upon the King it does not seem that this reform ever came into effect. Following Wolsey's fall the Council increased in importance, since Henry, having burnt his fingers with Wolsey, preferred a small ring of advisers to a single minister. Yet although the inner ring followed the King wherever he went, while the outer ring remained in London where it met daily, the Council was still one body and was too large and amorphous for convenience. Thomas Cromwell could have been, like Wolsey, a threat to the Council, but instead he was probably responsible for putting into effect the principle laid down in the Eltham Ordinances by turning the inner ring of Councillors attendant upon the King into an institution and making it the real centre of the administration. By 1540 this inner ring, or Privy Council, was sufficiently distinct from the rest of the Council to have its own clerk and minute book. The Privy Council, which numbered about nineteen members, consisted of nobles, clerics and household officials. The noble group included representatives of old families, such as Thomas Howard, Duke of Norfolk, and John de Vere, Earl of Oxford, as well as newly created peers, like Cromwell himself (who became a baron in 1536) and Sir John Russell, later Earl of Bedford. The clerical group, headed by Archbishop Cranmer, included Cuthbert Tunstall of Durham and Richard Sampson of Chichester. The household was represented by the treasurer, Sir William Fitzwilliam, the controller, Sir William Paulet, and the vice-chamberlain, Sir William Kingston.

The Council had an existence of its own and the King was rarely, if ever, present, at meetings. When Cromwell was at the height of his power he and the King decided matters of policy between them, but the Council continued dealing with a wide range of government business—receiving ambassadors, drafting despatches, discussing foreign affairs and issuing administrative orders. The Council was nicely balanced between autonomy and dependence. It could act on its own initiative, but at the same time it was immediately responsive to the King's will. This dual personality was demonstrated towards the end of the reign, when the more conservative Councillors were plotting Cranmer's downfall. Henry allowed them to go ahead, but at the same time he warned his Archbishop what was afoot, and told him to 'appeal . . . to our person and give to them this ring . . . which ring they well know that I use it to none other purpose but to call matters from the Council unto mine own hands'. The King and his Councillors were obviously used to working at a distance from each other. This was due partly to Henry's laziness, his reluctance to involve himself in the day-to-day work of government, but it would not have been possible unless Cromwell had created an administrative machine capable of working on its own.

The Secretaryship

In the late Yorkist and early Tudor period the King's Secretary was his private servant, looking after his correspondence, keeping the Signet and being frequently employed on diplomatic missions. It was Cromwell who made the Secretary into a public figure. He saw the advantage of an office that had an indeterminate range of authority and indefinite possibilities of expansion. The Chancellorship had too many judicial and routine duties attached to it for Cromwell's purposes, and it did not give control over the all-important financial administration, which was centred in the household. Cromwell replaced Stephen Gardiner as Secretary in April 1534, and from then on he dealt with every aspect of royal government, establishing the pattern that was to be followed by his successors, particularly the Cecils. This expansion of the Secretaryship was not unique to England. The sixteenth century in Europe was the age of kings, and as monarchs established themselves and reduced feudal and ecclesiastical franchises their choice determined who was to be the chief officer of state. The governmental and judicial institutions of the Middle Ages had been as much a product of the community as of the ruler. They needed streamlining to make them fit the needs of absolutism.

The increasing prestige of the Secretaryship was shown by its change of status. The Eltham Ordinances placed the Secretary, for purposes of precedence, in the fourth group of officials, but by 1539 he came immediately after the great officers of state. The Secretary's importance declined after 1540 when Cromwell gave up the office, but the Secretaryship, although only a shadow of its former self, remained the most convenient channel for transmitting the royal will. When the power of the Crown revived once again after the intermission of Edward VI, the Secretaryship revived with·it.

Financial Administration

Cromwell's reorganising genius is nowhere shown more clearly than in the financial administration. Under Henry VII the King's Chamber had become the clearing-house for the Crown's moneys, by-passing the Exchequer, and this remained the case while Sir John Heron, the Treasurer of the Chamber, was alive. After his death the office remained vacant for a time because Wolsey, with his omnivorous appetite for power, exercised a close control over financial administration and needed little more than clerks to carry out his will. By the time Cromwell rose to power a new Treasurer of the Chamber had been appointed, otherwise he would doubtless have reserved this position for himself. Instead, he occupied three comparatively minor offices and used these as a base from which he gradually extended his control over the entire financial administration. The fact that he was able to do so shows that household administration was still as fluid as it had been in Henry VII's day, but reorganisation became essential when, after 1536, money from the dissolved monasteries started pouring in at such a rate that the household offices could not cope with it. An Act of 1536 set up a special department, 'The Court of the Augmentations of the Revenues of the King's Crown', to deal with all the problems arising from the disposal of monastic lands and property. This was a court of record controlled by its own chancellor, treasurer, attorney and solicitor, and issuing documents under its own seal. As a piece of administrative engineering Augmentations was remarkably successful, particularly when contrasted with the makeshift organisation of the older household departments like the Chamber, and its statutory basis, for which Cromwell was responsible, gave it a considerable degree of autonomy.

By the time Cromwell fell from power he had reorganised the royal finances by channelling them into six main departments. Oldest of these was the Exchequer, which continued to collect and control the ancient revenues of the Crown, consisting of the county and borough farms and the Customs, as well as the profits of justice. Next came the Duchy of Lancaster, which survived as an independent unit because its organisation was highly efficient and had provided a model for Augmentations. The Chamber kept its control over all Crown lands other than recent acquisitions, but Cromwell pulled it out of the household by merging it with the office of general surveyors, which had been set up to do the auditing that Henry VII had done for himself. Not until 1542, however, after Cromwell's fall, was the final stage reached when an Act was passed setting up a formal Court of General Surveyors, controlled by the Treasurer of the Chamber and the two surveyors of Crown lands, and provided with its own clerk and its own seal.

Although the Court of Augmentations handled all the new land revenues of the Crown, the ecclesiastical revenues went to a separate department. An Act of 1534 had transferred First Fruits (or Annates) and Tenths to the Crown, but no new machinery was created to handle this money until after Cromwell's fall. An Act of that year (1540) created a Court of First Fruits and Tenths on the now familiar lines, and the same development took place with the sixth branch of the King's revenue, that which came from his feudal rights over wards. This old and important source of profit had been particularly exploited under Henry VII, but after his death there was considerable confusion. It was left to Cromwell to restore order and efficiency by creating a formal Court of Wards, and he introduced an Act for this purpose into the House of Lords a week before his fall.

Cromwell's success in remodelling the financial administration to meet the needs of a new age was considerable, though a great deal of wasteful duplication remained—particularly at a local level, since the representatives of all six courts, instead of combining their work, scavenged the counties for their respective masters. The new machinery would not have functioned smoothly had it not been for Cromwell's vigilance and energy, and as Dr Elton says, 'what distinguished him was his personal and direct control of every aspect of the day-to-day government of the country'.[1] It is at least questionable how far this particular aspect of Cromwell's work can be described as 'revolutionary'. Direct control by the King had given way to direct control by the King's favourite, but the source of authority was the same, and as long as the Court remained at or near the centre of political life (which it did until the late seventeenth century) administration depended very much upon the will of the sovereign. This was particularly so under strong rulers like Henry VIII and Elizabeth, and it is no coincidence that the most effective ministers were servants of the most effective sovereigns. Not until the power of the Crown began to wane, after 1660, could departments like the Treasury really move out of Court and acquire a considerable degree of independence even in the formulation of policy.

Not a great deal of the superstructure of Cromwell's administration survived. The Privy Council, for instance, which seemed to have a life of its own, independent of royal initiative, reverted to its pre-Cromwellian shape after Henry VIII's death. By 1553 it had forty members, including second-rank officials, and not until Elizabeth restored strong monarchy was it again reduced to a manageable size. As for the financial courts, these were swallowed up by the revived Exchequer, and only Wards and the Duchy of Lancaster preserved

[1] G. R. Elton, *The Tudor Revolution in Government*, p. 158.

their independent existence. The reformed Exchequer showed in its internal organisation the ground plan of Cromwell's system, but its very size and complexity made it more of an autonomous department than anything Cromwell had created. Independence of close royal control, either by the King or his favourite, was best achieved by a large organisation with traditions of its own—hence the strength of the Exchequer, which had centuries of existence behind it and had survived many vicissitudes.

Better administration, as well as the confiscation of monastic property, sent the King's revenue soaring. Before Cromwell's rise to power it averaged £100,000 a year, of which the Exchequer and Chamber accounted for £40,000 each, the Duchy of Lancaster for £13,000 and the Master of the Wards for the remaining £7,000. Cromwell trebled this annual revenue by adding to it £140,000 from monastic lands—over half from rents, the rest from outright sales—and £70,000 from First Fruits and clerical subsidies. Even when deductions are made for the sales of lands and goods which, in theory at least, were not recurrent, Henry still received in the 1540s considerably more than twice his pre-Comwellian revenue. Much of the increase was immediately swallowed up by heavy spending—the cost of the royal household, for instance, rose from £25,000 to £45,000 a year, while the Pilgrimage of Grace cost £50,000 to put down—and in the late 1530s the King was often short of ready cash. But he was living well within his income, in spite of mounting inflation: the royal revenue was now adequate for everything except war.

Local Administration

Cromwell's hand is to be seen in local as well as central administration. The north was still a major problem, and Cuthbert Tunstall, Bishop of Durham, who had been appointed head of the Council in the North Parts, was unable to keep order because of the power of local magnates like the Dacres and Percies. Unrest was also caused by the economic grievances of the common people, of whom Norfolk wrote to Cromwell in October 1536: 'God knows they may well be called poor caitiffs, for at their fleeing they lost horse, harness, and all they had upon them, and what with the spoiling of them now and the gressing of them so marvellously sore in time past and with increasing of lords' rents by enclosing . . . the border is sore weakened and especially Westmoreland!'

As soon as the Pilgrimage of Grace had been suppressed, the council in the north was reorganised, probably by Cromwell, on a permanent basis. A new council was appointed which was to deal solely with administration and justice and, unlike its predecessors, was not to be responsible for managing the royal estates in the north. The head of this council was the Lord President—the first being Cuthbert Tunstall —and his colleagues included three or four peers, half a dozen knights and half a dozen common and civil lawyers. The council was given full jurisdiction in civil and criminal matters within the area north of the Humber which it controlled, and in this respect it was more powerful even than the Council in London. This reorganisation of 1537 marks the real beginning of the permanent Council of the North, and from then until its dissolution a century later, the line of presidents was unbroken. Throughout the Tudor and early Stuart period it was the instrument whereby the Crown tried to enforce order in the remoter parts of the realm. It did its work well, but the north remained dangerously isolated. Revolt broke out there again in Elizabeth's reign, and the appointment of a strong man like Wentworth in the seventeenth century shows how much of a menace local independence and disorder still were.

The Council in the Marches of Wales was a direct descendant of the body which had administered Edward IV's marcher lands. Wolsey revived and reconstituted this council in 1525, but it was not very effective in putting down disorder. Cromwell therefore set up a formal council, similar to that later developed in the north. In 1536 an Act incorporated the Principality of Wales with England, thereby bringing the territories of the marcher lords within the county organisation as far as justice was concerned. This gave the Council of Wales effective jurisdiction throughout the whole country and border area. From its headquarters at Ludlow it dealt with the complaints of the poor and the offences committed by rich and powerful men, but after 1543 its common law jurisdiction came into conflict with that of the four newly created courts of Great Session, and quarrels between the two blunted the effectiveness of the Council.

A third short-lived council was set up in the west, probably in 1539. It may well have been prompted by fear of invasion, since the west country was otherwise quiet. Sir John Russell was created Baron Russell and given a large share of the monastic estates in Devon and Cornwall so that he could act as the King's lieutenant, but the Council as such had no obvious function and did not long survive Cromwell's fall.

Parliament

The most enduring achievement of Henry and Cromwell was the transformation of Parliament's place in the English constitution. Wolsey had used Parliament as rarely as he could, but Cromwell was a Parliament man and had deliberately chosen this route to a political career. He was among the first to translate into actual fact the enormous potentialities of statute, and the number of Acts of Parliament passed during his period of office shows the use he made of this particular device. The twenty-two years from Henry VII's death until Cromwell's accession to power had seen the passing of almost one hundred and fifty public Acts, but in the brief eight years of Cromwell's ascendancy the number rose to two hundred: the corresponding figure for Elizabeth's reign of forty-five years was just under eighty.

These figures partly reflect the quantity of legislation needed to carry through the break with Rome, but they also demonstrate Cromwell's attitude. Even those actions of Cromwell which appear to detract from Parliament's power are susceptible of a different interpretation. The 1534 Act, for instance, which made spoken words treason and seemed to be a despotic measure, was in fact putting on a statutory footing an interpretation already accepted by the courts of common law. As for the Proclamations Act of 1539, which used to be regarded as the high-water mark of Tudor despotism, it was more of a limitation on it, since it shifted the legal basis of proclamations from the royal prerogative to statute. Proclamations, which had long been part of the accepted law of the land, were apparently being disregarded. It was now ordered that they should be 'obeyed, observed and kept as though they were made by Act of Parliament', but it was explicitly stated that this parliamentary action had been taken so that the King might not be driven 'to extend the liberty and supremacy of his regal power and dignity by wilfulness of froward subjects'.

From 1529 onwards the part played by Parliament in legislation increased so enormously in size and importance that the King's government exerted all its considerable influence to make sure that at least no obvious malcontents were elected. Some boroughs were effectively in the Crown's control, and approved men could simply be nominated for these. Others were under the influence of some landed family, which would often be amenable to polite pressure. Shire elections were more difficult to influence, but these were usually determined by

the local interests of county families rather than by any national
political issues. In Henry VIII's reign, as in that of his father, more and
more of the King's Councillors who were eligible for a seat in the
Lords preferred to stand for election to the Commons. The 1529
Parliament contained a large number of men specially sworn to
the King as Councillors, and the Pilgrims of 1536 complained that 'the
old custom was that none of the King's servants should be of the
commons house, yet most of the [present] house were the King's
servants'.

Cromwell paid particular attention to elections. In 1534 he was busy
revising the list of members of the Commons so that he could get a
clear picture of what changes had taken place and decide who to
recommend as candidates at by-elections. Two years later he intervened directly at Canterbury, putting forward the names of two men
for election as burgesses. The sheriff replied that the election had
already taken place by the time the minister's letter arrived, but
Cromwell refused to accept this rebuff and wrote at once to the sheriff,
ordering him to 'proceed to a new [election] and elect those other,
according to the tenor of the former letters to you directed for that
purpose, without failing so to do, as the King's trust and expectation is
in you, and as ye intend to avoid his Highness's displeasure, at your
peril'. The two government-sponsored candidates were duly elected.

Much more evidence of Cromwell's activity survives for the
election of 1539, and in March of that year he informed the King that
'I and other of your Grace's council here do study and employ ourselves daily upon those affairs that concern your Grace's Parliament . . .
to bring all things so to pass that your Majesty had never more tractable
Parliament'. Cromwell was not concerned to build up a group of his
own within the Commons—indeed it was this very Parliament that
passed an Act of Attainder against him—but to use all legitimate means
to make sure that the new Commons would cooperate loyally with
the King at a time when the complications of foreign and religious
policy made the situation extremely difficult. In this aim he was entirely successful.

Cromwell's active interest was not confined to elections. Even before
Parliament met he would be busy with memoranda and drafts of Bills,
and he had a staff of expert advisers, among them the judges, working
for him. His frequent corrections and insertions in the drafts show his
infinite capacity for taking pains, and it was by this laborious attention to detail that he, like the Cecils after him, charted a reasonably

D*

smooth passage for government measures. His own inside experience of the Commons at work was no doubt invaluable in this.

Parliament, however, was not a subservient body. At the beginning of every session the Speaker made a formal claim for freedom of speech, though the limits of this were not clearly defined. Roper's account of More's petition as Speaker in 1523 implies a claim for absolute freedom for the Commons to have 'licence and pardon freely, without doubt of your dreadful displeasure, every man to discharge his conscience and boldly in everything incident among, declare his advice. And whatsoever happeneth any man to say, it may like your noble Majesty of your inestimable goodness to take all in good part, interpreting every man's words (how uncunningly soever they be couched) to proceed yet of a good zeal towards the profit of your realm and honour of your royal person.' More was not asking that members should have the right to initiate discussion, but that they should feel free to speak their minds on the issues presented to them. Henry's reply is not recorded, but as a rule he encouraged the Commons to speak freely because he had nothing to fear from them. His enemies were their enemies, and their voice was likely to be raised not in opposition to royal policy but in support of it. The formal claim for freedom of speech must be put into the context of early Tudor assumptions about the relationship between King and subjects.

Henry was remarkably tolerant of those members who dared oppose him. It did not, after all, very much matter what was said in the Commons. Debates were not publicly reported and there are no private journals surviving for this period. As long as the outcome of a debate was satisfactory the discussion which preceded it had little practical significance. Henry could afford to laugh at isolated examples of individuality. In 1529, for instance, John Petite, a member for London, objected to a Bill cancelling the King's debts, on the grounds that while he was content to accept this himself, he could not speak for his neighbours, who might suffer from it. Henry took no offence, but it was reported that he used occasionally to 'ask in Parliament time, in his weighty affairs, if Petite were of his side'. Similarly, when Sir George Throckmorton opposed the Act of Appeals, the King merely sent for him, made him a speech justifying royal policy, and allowed him to return to the Commons. Of course members knew that if they really angered the King his wrath could be terrible, and the Privy

Councillors in the House were the eyes and ears of the sovereign, always ready to report to their master anything that was said against him.

On the face of it Parliament was subservient and meekly passed Acts registering the King's various changes of wife and heirs, making it treason to assert in one year what it had been treason to deny the year before. It voted large sums of money, it attainted the King's enemies, it passed the Proclamations Act, and in 1544 it released the King from the obligation to pay his debts. Yet subservience, with its implication of being crushed beneath the tyrant's heel, is not an accurate term to describe the attitude of members of Parliament in Henry's reign. There was opposition, and not all statutes had an easy passage.

The Act in Restraint of Appeals of 1533 was only accepted by the Commons after they had amended it, and in the following year they refused to accept the original draft of the Act making spoken words treason. One of the most striking examples of parliamentary independence was the treatment given to the Statute of Proclamations. It may well be that, as Elton suggests, the first draft of this Bill provided for the enforcement of proclamations in courts of common law, and that amendments in the Lords removed this provision and substituted a special tribunal instead. Whatever Cromwell's intention, Parliament was suspicious of any measure that had a flavour of despotism about it. A collection of landholders and common lawyers knew very well what protection the law offered to property-rights, and was determined to maintain it. From this, no doubt, came the clause inserted in the Act, forbidding proclamations to interfere with the life or property of the subject.

The same acute sensitiveness caused a prolonged struggle over the Statute of Uses. In theory land held by feudal tenure could not be bequeathed. On the death of the tenant it reverted to the King, who regranted it to the heir only after the feudal incidents—relief, wardship, marriage, livery—had been met. To avoid these exactions, many landholders made over all or part of their land to a third person to hold in trust for the heir. The nominal owner was not, in fact, the user of the land, and since this device, the 'use', could be repeated indefinitely, a large amount of land was passing out of the King's control. The history of a Northamptonshire family, the Brudenells of Deene Park, describes how old Drew Brudenell, on his death-bed in 1490, sent for his younger brother Robert to whom he transferred all his estates, commanding him to hold them in trust for the two young heirs,

Drew's sons. Robert later on bought out his nephews and became possessed in his own right of the Brudenell estates. In the spring of 1530 when he was nearly seventy and felt that he had not long to live, he sent for his sons and in their presence called one of his tenants to his bedside, 'and, giving him a handful of good Deene earth, bid him take seisin in the name of all his manors and tenements, thereby making him trustee for carrying out his directions for their disposal'.[1]

It was this practice which Henry determined to check. At first, in 1529, he was willing to bargain with the Commons. He offered to accept 'uses' on parts of landholders' estates, and to make them enforceable at common law, on condition that there was no attempt to evade feudal obligations on the remainder. The Commons, however, rejected this proposal, and when a similar measure was introduced in 1532 it met with a similar fate. Henry sent for a delegation from the Commons and hectored them. 'Me thinketh that you should not contend with me that . . . am your sovereign lord and King, considering that I seek peace and quietness of you . . . I assure you, if you will not take some reasonable end now, when it is offered, I will search out the extremity of the law and then will I not offer you so much again.'

Henry was as good as his word. At this stage he might have agreed to accept feudal dues on only a half, or even less, of the land involved, but when stubborn opposition prevented this compromise, he consulted the judges and won the common lawyers over to him. In 1536 the Statute of Uses was at last accepted by both Houses and became law. The 'use' was now legalised and could be enforced in common law courts, but in cases where it had been created for no other purpose than to avoid feudal obligations, the user of the land was to be treated as though he was the heir in law as well as in practice.

The Statute of Uses is important in many ways. It showed how vigorously the royal will could be opposed in Parliament, and yet it also demonstrated the great power of the King, who could force landholders to accept a measure from which they stood to lose. Only after his victory was assured did Henry make concessions. In 1540 the Statute of Wills restored to those who held by free tenure the right to bequeath their lands. Those who held by feudal tenure (an increasing number because of the creation of new feudal tenures on monastic property) were allowed to bequeath two-thirds of their land, but only on condition that the new owner should pay all the feudal incidents

[1] Joan Wake, *The Brudenells of Deene*, p. 32.

that would have been due if it had reverted to the Crown and been regranted. Henry valued his feudal rights and the income they brought him so much that he would not willingly part with them, even if refusal to do so meant alienating his most influential subjects.

Because he had no reason to fear the increase of the Commons' power, Henry in fact nourished it by encouraging the Lower House to assert its own privileges. As a result of Strode's case in 1512 it was enacted that members of Parliament, being judges of the highest court in the land, should not be subject to suits in inferior courts during the time when Parliament was sitting. Until Henry's reign, if a member of the Commons were arrested during the session the Speaker applied to the Lord Chancellor for a writ ordering his release, but as the Commons felt their strength they began to flex their muscles. In 1543 they made the proud assertion that their House was not simply a part of the High Court of Parliament but was a court in its own right. The occasion for this declaration was the arrest for debt of George Ferrers, one of the King's servants and member for Plymouth. The Commons sent their Serjeant-at-Arms to fetch him from the London gaol where he was lodged, but the jailer and the sheriffs of London refused to recognise this unprecedented authority, and when the Serjeant-at-Arms tried to claim the prisoner there was a brawl in which his mace was broken. When the Commons heard of this affray they complained immediately to the Lords, who declared that contempt had been shown and offered to issue a writ then and there. The Commons, however, insisted on enforcing their own privileges, 'being in a clear opinion that all commandments and other acts of proceeding from the Nether House were to be done and executed by their Serjeant without writ, only by show of his mace, which was his warrant'. The sheriffs of London had by this time realised the error they had made, in fact if not in law, and when the Serjeant appeared before them again they handed over their prisoner. The Commons made this precedent doubly binding by ordering the imprisonment of the sheriffs and other officers who had resisted the Serjeant.

Henry heard of these proceedings and consulted the judges before summoning a delegation of the Commons to present themselves before him. When they appeared he praised them for the way in which they had asserted their privileges. Ferrers, he said, should have been privileged in any case because he was the servant of his King, who, being a member of Parliament, had privilege for his servants like any other member. Henry went further than this, however, and developed his favourite theme that he and his people were an organic unity. Since the King and the two Houses formed one body, any injury offered to a member was an injury to himself. 'We be informed by our judges that we at no time stand so highly in our estate royal as in the time of Parliament, wherein we as head and you as members are conjoined and knit together into one body politic, so as whatsoever offence or injury (during that time) is offered to the meanest member of the House is to be judged as done against our person and the whole court of Parliament.'

Not only in theory but in practice as well Parliament became in Henry's reign an integral part of the constitution. This is shown by the increased length of sessions. In the twenty-four years of Henry VII's reign there were seven Parliaments, which met for a total length of some twenty-five weeks, but the last eighteen years of Henry VIII's reign saw five Parliaments whose sessions occupied one hundred and thirty-six weeks. Longer sessions were accompanied by a change in the nature of Parliamentary work. The Acts of the Reformation Parliament showed that there was nothing, not even matters spiritual, with which it was not competent to deal. Henry was stating little more than the truth when he told the Pope that 'the discussions in the English Parliament are free and unrestricted. The Crown has no power to limit their debates or to control the votes of the members. They determine everything for themselves as the interests of the commonwealth require.' The Crown could in fact put pressure on members, but coercion was rarely needed, for King, Lords and Commons were engaged in the same task of building a secular society, spiritually as well as materially self-sufficient—an organic society, the harmony and interrelation of whose parts was a microcosm of the divine order throughout the universe.

Cromwell's View of the State

Since Thomas Cromwell did more than any other single person, with the exception of Henry VIII, to complete the building of an autarchic secular state in England, under the sovereignty of King-in-Parliament, it is not surprising that around him gathered a group of 'Commonwealth men', who believed that since the state existed for the good of all, the government should take positive steps to reform society and bring it more into line with the ideal. Prominent among these men was Thomas Starkey, whose attitude to religion has already been considered. He wrote in his *Exhortation* of 1536: 'the civil life is, to man, natural and by nature convenient'; and in his unpublished *Dialogue* he proposed an assortment of reforms designed to improve English society. Starkey had a vision of what England might be, and the aim of these measures was to bring nearer the time when he would see in his own country 'a people united in love and amity as members of one body, ever having the commonweal before their eyes, without regard of their own vain pleasures'.[1] This idealistic view of the state was unique to England at that particular period and the preambles to the statutes of the 1530s show that Cromwell was in considerable sympathy with it.

The ideal of the sovereign state was not Machiavelli's, though Cromwell is often held to be Machiavelli's disciple. He may have read *The Prince*: he must at least have heard of it. But he was closer in his attitude to Marsilio of Padua, who published his *Defensor Pacis* in the early fourteenth century. In Marsilio's day, as in Cromwell's, the main threat to peace and good order seemed to come from papal claims to paramountcy. Marsilio devoted much of his work to showing that papal claims were not grounded in Scripture and that the right to govern was inherent not in the Vicar of Rome but in the people themselves. Christ, he said, specifically disclaimed any temporal ambition, and submitted himself to the lay magistrate: the clergy should therefore be under the authority of the people. The Church, according to Marsilio, was not merely the ecclesiastical hierarchy, but the general body of believers. The people were simultaneously a lay and a spiritual society.

Cromwell's interest in Marsilio is shown by the fact that he commissioned William Marshall to translate the *Defensor Pacis* and advanced him money for its publication in 1535. He encouraged Starkey to send a copy to Pole and suggested to Marshall that he should use its arguments against the recalcitrant Carthusians. For Marsilio the supreme legislator was the body of the people, translated by Marshall as 'Parliament', and Cromwell's use of statute to carry through the revolutionary changes of the break with Rome suggests that in this, as in his views on papal authority, he was also close to Marsilio. Elton has shown that Maitland was wrong in his view of Cromwell as a champion of royal absolutism based on Roman law against the traditional common law liberties of England. There were, indeed, civilians in the circle of Henry's advisers, but they were not prominent among Cromwell's friends. His closest associates were men like Audley, the

[1] J. W. Allen, *Political Thought in the Sixteenth Century*, p. 151.

Lord Chancellor, and Rich, Chancellor of Augmentations, who were both common lawyers.

It is possible that in administration as distinct from justice (though the two were not always easily distinguishable) Cromwell was in favour of a more direct expression of the royal will than was possible under the existing system, based as it was upon the voluntary unpaid service of local gentlemen. This had many advantages, not least its cheapness, but country gentlemen were not easily controlled by the central government, and they were amateurs. Cromwell on the other hand was a professional administrator and preferred paid professionals to unpaid amateurs. Had he stayed in power longer he might have built up a network of councils to control the whole country. These would not have undermined the common law—the councils in Wales and the north were specifically given common law jurisdiction—nor would they have been a challenge to Parliament's authority, since they were either based upon or regulated by statute. They would have reduced the administrative significance not of judges and members of Parliament but of local gentlemen, and the whole country would have been controlled by a system of interlocking councils, similar in principle to Cromwell's new pattern of financial administration.

Such a system would have helped complete the unification of the country that the Yorkists had begun, but its cost was considerable. The Council of the North demanded more than £1,000 a year and the Council of Wales only a little less, while the estimate for the annual expenditure on the Council of the West was £1,230. These sums compared unfavourably with the unpaid work of the Justices of the Peace, and the councils were not popular with members of Parliament, jealous of their privileged position as country gentlemen, and common lawyers, alarmed at the possible diminution in the sources of profit open to them. It was not by chance that the Council of the West died with Cromwell, and three years after his fall an Act of Parliament cut at another council by setting up four new common law courts to administer justice throughout Wales.

Cromwell and the Church of England

Cromwell left his mark upon the Church of England as well as upon the state. He was not an irreligious man, though he had little time for ceremonies, and he supported those who wished to see the Bible translated into English. John Foxe, the martyrologist, reports that

Cromwell learned the whole of Erasmus's New Testament by heart while travelling to Rome and back, and although this story ought to be taken with a pinch of salt there is evidence that Cromwell was in touch with Miles Coverdale when Coverdale was still a friar at Cambridge.

Miles Coverdale had begun a translation of the complete Bible, and when this was finished and printed, in October 1535, Cromwell showed a copy to the King who passed it on to Gardiner and other bishops to examine. When they reluctantly agreed that there were no heresies in it, Henry commanded, 'then in God's name let it go abroad among our people'. This was provided for by the Injunctions drawn up by Cromwell and issued in October 1538, which required all the clergy to provide 'on this side the Feast of Easter next coming, one book of the whole Bible of the largest volume in English' to be set up in a convenient place in every parish church, where the people might go and read it.

In spite of the order to provide a copy of the Bible in English, there was still no single authorised version available. Since the Church author-ities showed no signs of producing one, it is not surprising that the radicals took the lead. Cromwell commissioned Coverdale to produce an authoritative edition. This, the Great Bible, appeared after many vicissitudes in 1539 and a royal proclamation of May 1541 ordered that it should be made available in accordance with the Injunctions of 1538, except in cases where another version had already been provided. Cranmer wrote the Preface, and this particular Bible is often called after him, but it was in fact Coverdale's work. The bishops, however, were far from satisfied with the Great Bible, which was too radical in its language for their taste, and after 1541 no more copies were printed until Edward VI's reign brought the extremists to power. Its appear-ance and authorisation had been largely due to Thomas Cromwell, and was one of his most enduring contributions to English life.

The Fall of Cromwell

By the time the Great Bible began to appear, Cromwell's ascendancy was nearing its end. The conservative and reactionary forces, suspicious of the radical tendencies of his religious policy, combined to destroy him at the very moment when Cromwell was deeply entangled in the intricacies of Henry's diplomacy. The remarkable oscillations in the King's policy in the late 1530s were largely a reflection of the European situation, although they also show the restless dissatisfaction of a religious conservative who found himself being pushed by the course of events into positions that were really unacceptable to him. In January 1536 Catherine of Aragon died, and in the following May, Anne Boleyn was executed: she had failed to produce the male heir Henry needed, and accounts of her love affairs with other men had infuriated the possessive and disappointed King. He was now free from all impediments, and could make an unchallengeable marriage. His third wife, Jane Seymour, the daughter of a Wiltshire knight, fulfilled Henry's hopes at last by giving him a boy prince, Edward, in October 1537, but she died shortly afterwards. Now that Henry had his heir and was no longer saddled with a doubtful marriage the original reasons for breaking with Rome had disappeared. But the King could not draw back, even if he had wished to. The links with Rome, so swiftly cut, could not swiftly be remade, particularly as the landed classes would never abandon their monastic property.

Henry claimed, probably honestly, that he feared nothing so long as France and the Empire were at loggerheads. When these two powers seemed likely to make a *rapprochement*, he had to look to his own defences. Throughout most of 1536 he was in the enviable position of being courted by both of the continental powers, but in 1538 Charles and Francis agreed on a truce, and England was threatened. Henry was optimistic and willing to wait and see what happened, but Cromwell preferred to open negotiations with the protestant German princes. By mid-1538 three German divines were in England, trying to work out a formula upon which the anti-catholic Churches might combine. But Henry, by insisting on clerical celibacy and communion in one kind,[1] made their task impossible. In 1539 news reached England that the agreement between Charles and Francis had broken down, and the German envoys were promptly sent home again.

Whenever danger receded, Henry was anxious to display his orthodoxy and prevent the drift of England towards radicalism. There was also a need for some definition of faith, since the political break with Rome had opened the way to doctrinal innovations of bewildering variety, while the authorisation of an English version of the Bible had encouraged discord and deepened the hostility of the various groups towards each other. Parliament was summoned early in 1539, to give sanction to a statement of faith, but the government was not clear about its policy. This in itself was a sign that Cromwell's

---

[1] Catholics make their communion by taking bread alone, since they believe that the body and blood of Christ are jointly present in each of the consecrated elements.

hold over the King was weakening, and the meeting of Parliament made his position even less secure, since it brought to Court men like Norfolk and Gardiner who were his rivals in politics and his enemies in religion. Cromwell could look for support only to the radical group in which Cranmer was prominent, and he would probably have liked a Lutheran alliance to reinforce his own position. But he adhered to the principle of royal supremacy, which had been his guide, and told the German envoys that 'the world being at this time what it was, he would believe even as his master the King believed'.

The King came down on the conservative side and chose the Duke of Norfolk to submit a number of propositions on religion to Parliament. These were the basis for the Act of Six Articles, which defined the catholic doctrine of the non-papal Church of England. The first article was concerned with transubstantiation, and declared 'that in the most blessed Sacrament of the altar, by the strength and efficacy of Christ's mighty word, it being spoken by the priest, is present really, under the, form of bread and wine, the natural body and blood of our Saviour, Jesu Christ'. The second denied the necessity of communion in two kinds, since both the elements were present in each sacrament. The third and fourth insisted on clerical celibacy and the maintenance of vows of chastity, while the last two articles affirmed the validity of private Masses and auricular confession. The English Church was now definitely committed to an orthodox position, and anyone denying these articles was to be burnt as a heretic.

No sooner had the Six Articles become law than the news came of a *rapprochement* between Francis and Charles. Expenditure on defence works was stepped up, the Fleet was concentrated at Portsmouth, and a number of artillery castles (most of which, such as that at Camber, survive) were built along the south coast. Cromwell revived his plans for a German alliance, and negotiations were set on foot for a marriage between Henry and Anne, sister of the Duke of Cleves who, although himself a catholic, was brother-in-law of one of the greatest of the Lutheran princes, the Elector of Saxony. In October a treaty was signed and in January 1540 the marriage took place. These events suggest that Cromwell had managed to check the conservative reaction and was now firmly back in the saddle. But he had tied the King to a rigid foreign alliance and, worst of all, to a woman whom Henry found repulsive. The likelihood was that as soon as Charles and Francis quarrelled again, Henry would break out of the strait-jacket that Cromwell had persuaded him to put on.

In April 1540 Parliament reassembled. Cromwell was still apparently in control and the King showed his approval by making him Earl of Essex and Great Chamberlain. But in May a new threat developed, for Henry fell in love with Catherine Howard, Norfolk's niece. Cromwell was trapped. If, as Henry insisted, he arranged a divorce for the King, the only result would be to put his enemies in a powerful position at the heart of government. He was in the same dilemma that had defeated Wolsey, and the feature common to both cases was the hatred of the Howard family for upstarts.

Cromwell began to strike out wildly at his enemies. Without consulting the King he ordered the arrest of Gardiner's associate Richard Sampson, Bishop of Chichester, and rumours were circulated that he planned to arrest five more conservative bishops. Gardiner and Norfolk determined to strike while they were still able to. They managed to convince the King that Cromwell was a Lutheran heretic, working to overthrow the Catholic Church that Henry had created. On 10 June 1540, Cromwell was arrested as he entered the Council chamber, and hurled his cap to the ground in fury, while Norfolk tore the Garter insignia from him. A Bill of Attainder was rapidly passed through Parliament, condemning the fallen minister as a heretic and traitor. The charges were so general that Cromwell could draw up no effective rebuttal of them. 'I have meddled in so many matters under your Highness', he wrote to Henry, 'that I am not able to answer them all.' He was kept alive for six weeks so that he could give evidence in the divorce action between Henry and Anne of Cleves, and then, on 28 July, was led to the scaffold.

Cromwell's death deprived Henry of 'such a servant', in Cranmer's words, 'in wisdom, diligence, faithfulness and experience, as no prince in this realm ever had'. To him must go much of the credit for establishing the supremacy of secular law in an absolute and independent state, and of embodying that supremacy in King-in-Parliament. He could not, of course, have done this by himself. Without the creation of a strong dynasty by Henry VII the Church would never have been overthrown; without the passions generated by Luther the revolution might have been stillborn; and without the arrogant courage of Henry VIII it might have been checked in mid-course. Cromwell was also dependent on the foundations laid during the late Middle Ages, before the Wars of the Roses brought constitutional growth to a halt, for it was the later Plantagenets and the early Lancastrians who first asserted the claims of the national state against the international Church.

and made statute their weapon. Henry and Cromwell between them brought this development to the point where a new monarchy was, in effect, created—supreme in state and Church, triumphant over barons and clergy alike, but at its most absolute only when it acted in harmony with the two Houses of Parliament, in which the whole nation was held to be represented.

The Closing Years of the Reign

Henry did not appoint another chief minister to replace Cromwell. Gardiner and Norfolk were his principal advisers, but the King took most of the decisions himself, while routine work was dealt with by the Privy Council. Cromwell's fall marked a triumph for conservative reaction, but the suppleness of Henry's attitude was shown in July 1540 when Barnes and two other 'Lutherans' were burned as heretics while three 'Papists' were hanged as traitors. Along with Cromwell, Henry rid himself of the Cleves marriage, which was declared invalid in July 1540, and on the day of Cromwell's execution he secretly married Catherine Howard. It seemed as though they were very happy, but in late 1541 Cranmer brought to the King's attention a paper charging the Queen with misconduct both before and after her marriage. Henry appointed a commission to enquire into charges against Catherine, and this found them proved. Catherine's accomplices were executed late in 1541, and in February of the following year the Queen herself was condemned by Act of Attainder, and shortly afterwards beheaded. Not until July 1543 did Henry remarry. This time he chose a widow of protestant inclinations, Catherine Parr, and she kept her hold on the King's affections until his death.

The closing years of the reign were marked by the struggle between protestant and catholic factions for control of the Council. Henry held the balance between the two groups. His catholic sympathies inclined him to the side of the conservatives, but he was a practical politician, who would not endanger the stability of his realm by too violently reactionary a programme. As early as July 1540 he had ordered that there should be no more persecution under the Statute of Six Articles, and although there was sporadic enforcement in later years the last purge took place in July 1543, when a number of Windsor men were executed for heresy, and John Marbeck, the composer, was only saved by a royal pardon.

Nevertheless, there was a swing to the right in religion. An Act of

1543 condemned all unauthorised versions of the Bible and forbade persons below the degree of gentleman to study even the permitted version at home. The Act also promised that some definition of doctrine would be forthcoming. *The Institution of a Christian Man*, usually called the *Bishops' Book*, had appeared in 1537, and Henry had licensed it for three years, though he was careful not to give it his official approval. Compared with the Ten Articles of 1536 this was a 'catholic' document, but it was apparently not to the liking of Gardiner and the conservative element in Henry's Council. In 1543 came the publication of *The Necessary Doctrine and Erudition of any Christian Man*, which received Henry's approval and is therefore known as the *King's Book*. This was markedly anti-Lutheran, and denied predestination and justification by faith alone.

1543 marked the climax of the catholic reaction and culminated in Gardiner's open attack upon Cranmer, who had been introducing many reforms, particularly the removal of images, into his diocese. From this year dates the incident of the ring, referred to earlier, in which Cranmer was saved by the King. Henry seems to have had a genuine affection for Cranmer, whose simple goodness he appreciated. Cromwell once said to the Archbishop: 'You were born in a happy hour, I suppose, for do or say what you will, the King will always well take it at your hand. And I must needs confess that in some things I have complained of you unto His Majesty, but all in vain, for he will never give credit against you, whatsoever is laid to your charge.' Cranmer survived, and although he could not put all his projects into effect—a book of homilies, for instance, and a codification of Church law—because of opposition from his fellow bishops or from Henry, he did, in June 1544, produce a Litany in English. This has been adopted, virtually unchanged, in all succeeding forms of service, and survives today in the Prayer-Book—a wonderful example, in its balanced cadences and majestic rhythms, of the English language as it came to flower.

Cranmer wrote the Litany at the King's command, so that men might pray for the disturbed state of the Christian world. The disturbance was made worse by Henry's own ambition. With nothing particularly pressing in domestic affairs, his youthful desire for military glory revived and he allied with his old enemy, Charles V, against an even older enemy, the King of France. In July 1544 Henry crossed to France with a large, well-equipped army and laid siege to Boulogne, which surrendered in September. Charles V made peace with Francis I, but Henry refused to surrender Boulogne, and the war continued until June 1546. By a treaty signed in that month Francis promised to pay Henry a pension as long as the King lived, and agreed to let the English keep Boulogne until 1554.

The war cost over two million pounds and undid much of Cromwell's good work in restoring royal finances. The King called on Parliament for support, and in most years from 1540 to 1547 he collected two parliamentary grants, and in 1546 three. This reflects the increased power of the Crown as well as the increasing prosperity of the country. As Dietz says: 'Taxes which would have dethroned a Yorkist could be paid without grudging to further the personal ends of a popular King.'[1] These grants brought in about £650,000— an enormous sum, which could hardly have been raised unless the subsidy, with its higher yield, had come to supplant the stereotyped tenth and fifteenth. There were also forced loans and benevolences which brought in another quarter of a million. The demand for benevolences aroused protests from many quarters, including the City of London. One alderman was imprisoned until he paid up. Henry determined to make an example of another 'who for the defence of the realm and for the continuance of his quiet life . . . could not find in his heart to disburse a small quantity of his substance'. He was sent to serve in the army against the Scots, and the commander was instructed to put him in the front line, so that he could taste the dangers endured by the ordinary soldier. He was eventually captured by the enemy and had to pay ransom. This colourful incident is not simply an illustration of the unpleasant consequences of opposing the royal will. It also demonstrates Henry's conviction that his subjects ought to contribute to the expense of what he chose to call a 'just war', and his readiness to ride roughshod over the susceptibilities of the merchant class whenever individual members of it dared to stand in his way.

The clergy were heavily taxed as well as the laity, but the total from all sources still fell short of the needs of the Crown. In August 1545 Lord Chancellor Wriothesley wrote despairingly to the Council: 'this year and last year the King has spent about £1,300,000. His subsidy and benevolence ministering scant £300,000, and the lands being consumed and the plate of the realm molten and coined, I lament the danger of the time to come. . . . And yet you write to me still Pay! Pay! Prepare for this and for that!'

Crown lands were sold to meet the deficit, and before his death

[1] F. C. Dietz, *English Government Finance, 1485-1558*, p. 162.

Henry.VIII had parted with two-thirds of the monastic estates, most of them sold to raise capital for his war. The currency was debased, outstanding debts were gathered in, loans were raised in Antwerp, Germany and Italy, and there was even a plan to unload accumulated reserves of lead—mainly from melted-down monastic roofs—on to the European market. In spite of all these expedients the royal finances were crippled, and Henry left his son an empty treasury, a debased currency and diminishing estates. The annexation of monastic property had completed the work begun by Edward IV and Henry VII of making land revenues the basis of royal wealth, and had restored to the Crown the flexibility that late-medieval rulers had lost. The end of Henry VIII's reign saw the process reversed. As land was sold off and income declined it became necessary to tap other sources, and this immediately involved problems of precedent and consent. Tudor despotism—if, indeed, it had ever been more than a possibility— became increasingly unlikely after the 1540s.

Henry's main concern in his closing years was that his son Edward should succeed him without difficulty. This meant making some concessions to the reformers, since their following throughout the country was obviously great, and a compromise with them was his only hope of maintaining unity in the realm. He valued unity more than anything else, and in his speech to his last Parliament in November 1545 he pleaded for an end to discord. 'Behold then what love and charity is amongst you, when the one calleth the other "Heretic!" and "Anabaptist!", and he calleth him again "Papist!", "Hypocrite!" and "Pharisee!" Be these tokens of charity amongst you? Are these signs of fraternal love between you?' He had not, he said, given them the English Bible in order to encourage them to discord. 'I am very sorry to know and hear how unreverently that most precious jewel, the Word of God, is disputed, rhymed, sung and jangled in every ale-house and tavern, contrary to the true meaning and doctrine of the same. And yet I am even as much sorry that the readers of the same follow it, in doing, so faintly and coldly: for of this I am sure, that charity was never so faint among you. . . . Love, dread and serve God (to the which I as your supreme head and sovereign lord require you) and then I doubt not but that love and league that I spoke of in the beginning shall never be dissolved or broken between us.'

It was a masterly speech, for Henry, like his daughter, knew how to move men's hearts by the power of words. His genuine concern for harmony in the body politic drove him closer to the reformers. The ablest man in his Council, and one who would probably have most influence over the young prince, was Edward Seymour, Earl of Hertford, the prince's uncle and a known 'reformer'. His influence, and that of John Dudley, Viscount Lisle (son of Henry VII's notorious minister), was pushing Norfolk, Gardiner and the conservative, catholic element into the background. By the end of 1546 Gardiner was absent from Court, in virtual disgrace, and rumours were afoot that bishops were to become salaried officials of the state and have their property confiscated. An Act of 1545 had already ordered the dissolution of the chantries, and commissioners were being appointed to carry it out.

Against this background counter-revolutionary plotting took place, which led, in December 1546, to the arrest of the Duke of Norfolk and his son, the Earl of Surrey—a fine poet, but an arrogant and unstable young aristocrat. Henry was a sick man, so huge with dropsy that he had to be carried upstairs, bloated, suspicious (as he always had been) and in constant pain. He was determined to strike down anybody who stood in the way of his son's inheritance, and it was typical of his attitude that he set aside his own conservative religious feelings when it came to the question of appointing a regency Council for his son, and gave the protestants a majority in it.[1] Surrey was tried for treason and condemned, and an Act of Attainder was passed against him and his father when Parliament reassembled in January 1547. Surrey was executed on 19 January and Norfolk's execution was fixed for the 28th. But on the night of the 27th Henry died, his hand in Cranmer's, and Norfolk was saved.

Henry inspired affection as well as respect among those who knew him, but his famous bluff good-fellowship concealed an iron will. He was proud and arrogant, and the habit of power from an early age led him to love no man or woman except in so far as he could use them. Yet his achievement was triumphant. He established his dynasty and his throne so securely that they were not shaken by the accession of a boy and two women, and he epitomised that blend of accessible and condescending majesty which Englishmen of the day responded to. England was an emergent state, and the passions that divided the country made impossible the liberal and peaceful pursuit of political

[1] It seems unlikely, in fact, that Henry was aware of the implications of his appointments, or that he ever considered any permanent reversal of his conservative religious policy. Cf. Lacy Baldwin Smith, 'Henry VIII and the Protestant Triumph', *American Historical Review*, Vol. 71, 1966.

aims. Henry was right when he stressed the need for unity, and this was his achievement—the extension of royal authority to incorporate all other jurisdictions. Medieval franchises, privileged corporations, the international papacy—all were to be subordinated to a single will. Men of More's persuasion could have no place in Henry's England, since they would never accept the overriding authority of the secular power and were therefore, from the very nature of their beliefs, disloyal. If men wished to survive they had to conform, for as the Earl of Northumberland told his son some time in 1523, the King's ill-will was 'intolerable for any subject to sustain. . . . His displeasure and indignation were sufficient to cast me and all my posterity into utter subversion and dissolution.'

When the greatest noblemen in the realm stood in such fear of the King it was clear that the anarchy of the Wars of the Roses was a thing of the past. Henry gave England stability and identity, concentrating the various forces at work in English life—nationalist stirrings, hatred of Rome, desire for profit, impatience with old ways and awareness of new horizons—into a single consciousness. A Roman Catholic, Hilaire Belloc, wrote the most appropriate epitaph on Henry's reign when he observed that 'in no other society is the worship of the corporate body of the nation exalted to such a height; and this worship of the native country as an idol . . . is the main cause of English homogeneity'.[1]

[1] Hilaire Belloc, *Essays of a Catholic Layman in England*, 'v. The Conversion of England', p. 94.

6

Edward VI and Mary

Edward VI

TUDOR sovereigns were far removed from ordinary men, and if the language in which they were addresssd (and in which they spoke of themselves) sounds absurdly inflated to modern ears, this is because we divorce it from the historical context. The ruler was a mortal man or woman, but the authority was godlike. This was a role beyond the capacity of any human being, but the circumstances of the age demanded that it should be filled. Little wonder that Henry, who knew his own strength and the demands made on it, could not envisage a woman playing the part. It needed a man's toughness, and when in October 1537 Jane Seymour gave birth to a boy-prince, it seemed that Henry's policy had been successful. Latimer, who was renowned for his plain speaking, was hardly exaggerating when he wrote to Cromwell: 'here is no less rejoicing at the birth of our prince, whom we hungered for so long, than there was at the birth of John the Baptist. . . . We have now the stop of vain trusts . . . and the stay of vain expectations.'

Prince Edward was a robust, quick-witted boy, and was carefully groomed for the part he was to play. From the day he was born he lived in state, surrounded by the magnificent but inhuman ceremonial of the Tudor Court, and not surprisingly, he learned to conceal his private feelings behind a mask of regality that later observers mistook for a chilly reserve. He was quickly set to work to acquire the learning expected of a Renaissance prince, and by the time John Cheke was appointed his tutor in 1544 Edward was well grounded in Latin and Greek and, of course, in the Bible—the future head of the Church would need a knowledge of theology at least equal to that of his bishops.

Henry had prevented his kingdom from falling into the feeble hands of a woman ruler, but he could not avoid the almost equally unwelcome prospect of a minority. Parliament had given him authority to bequeath the Crown as he wished, and in his will he made Edward his heir, with Mary and Elizabeth, in that order, next in line. He also appointed a regency Council in which the conservatives were at a disadvantage. Their lay leader, the Duke of Norfolk, had been disgraced and was in the Tower awaiting execution when Henry died, while Stephen Gardiner, Bishop of Winchester and the most prominent ecclesiastic in the conservative ranks, was not named as one of the Council. The leadership of the conservative group therefore rested with Wriothesley and Tunstall, neither of them very powerful, while against them were ranged the radicals led by Edward's uncle, the Earl of Hertford, and Archbishop Cranmer.

Protector Somerset

Henry made no provision for a protectorate, although he did not specifically exclude this, but he could not control events from the grave. Even before he was dead the Earl of Hertford was scheming to take effective power into his own hands, and his accomplice, Sir William Paget, one of the King's Secretaries, was later to remind him, of the plotting that had taken place 'in the gallery at Westminster, before the breath was out of the body of the King that dead is'. Hertford quickly took possession of Edward and rode with him to London. By the time the Councillors assembled Hertford and Paget had done their work, and the first official act of the Council was to ignore the spirit if not the letter of Henry's will by appointing Hertford 'Protector of all the realms and dominions of the King's majesty that now is, and . . . governor of his most royal person.' The new Protector immediately paid his debt to those who had made his bid for power successful. Paget announced that Henry had drawn up an honours list before his death and that this would now be put into effect. Hertford was created Duke of Somerset; Wriothesley, who had protested against the setting aside of Henry's will, was persuaded to drop his opposition in return for the Earldom of Southampton; while John Dudley, one of the strongest characters on the Council, was made Earl of Warwick.

For the next three years Somerset controlled the destinies of England and showed a tolerance and a love of justice that were in marked contrast to the duplicity and bigotry of most of his contemporaries.

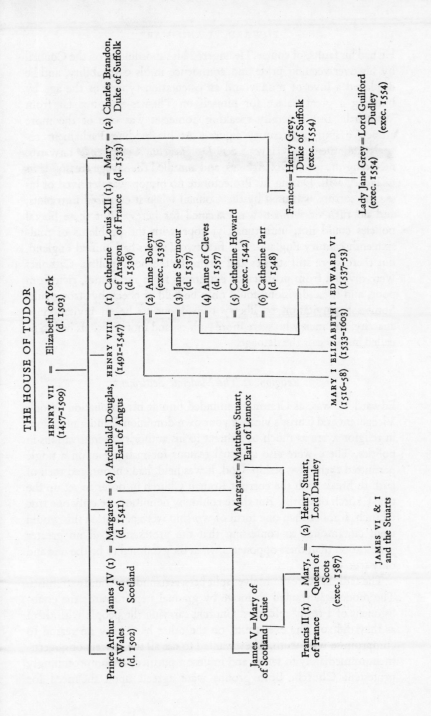

THE HOUSE OF TUDOR

HENRY VII = Elizabeth of York
(1457-1509)   (d. 1503)

Prince Arthur   James IV (1) Margaret = (2) Archibald Douglas,   HENRY VIII = (1) Catherine   Louis XII (1) = Mary = (2) Charles Brandon,
of Wales   of   (d. 1541)   Earl of Angus   (1491-1547)   of Aragon   of France   (d. 1533)   Duke of Suffolk
(d. 1502)   Scotland   (d. 1536)

                                                                              = (2) Anne Boleyn
                                                                                    (exec. 1536)

                                                                              = (3) Jane Seymour
                                                                                    (d. 1537)

                                                                              = (4) Anne of Cleves
                                                                                    (d. 1557)

                                                                              = (5) Catherine Howard
                                                                                    (exec. 1542)

                                                                              = (6) Catherine Parr
                                                                                    (d. 1548)

                                              Margaret = Matthew Stuart,   MARY I   ELIZABETH I   EDWARD VI
                                                         Earl of Lennox   (1516-58) (1533-1603)   (1537-53)

James V = Mary of Scotland   Henry Stuart,
          Guise   Lord Darnley

Francis II (1) = Mary, = (2)
of France   Queen of Scots
                (exec. 1587)

                                          JAMES VI & I
                                          and the Stuarts

Frances = Henry Grey,
          Duke of Suffolk
          (exec. 1554)

Lady Jane Grey = Lord Guilford
(exec. 1554)   Dudley
                 (exec. 1554)

He had his faults, of course. He angered his subordinates on the Council by his overweening pride and confidence in his own ability, and he displayed a love of money and an ostentation typical of the age by building a great palace for himself on Thames-side, not far from Whitehall. But generally speaking Somerset was one of the more attractive sixteenth-century figures. At his bidding Parliament repealed all the heresy laws from *De Haeretico Comburendo* onwards, including the act of Six Articles, and annulled the savage treason laws of Henry VIII. During his Protectorate no bishop was deprived of his see, no torture was used by the Council when it enquired into plots, and no man or woman was executed for heresy. But these liberal policies could not, unfortunately, cope with the problems of mid-sixteenth-century England. The first two Tudors had unified England, but there were still stresses and strains in the body politic. Catholics were divided from protestants, extremists from moderates, rich from poor, and these divisions could only be held in check by strong rule. Somerset's invitation to liberty turned out to be an invitation to anarchy, and men who were more ruthless and more efficient had to be called in to repair the damage.

Religion. I: The Moderate Settlement

Edward VI was, as Cranmer reminded him at his coronation, 'God's Vicegerent and Christ's vicar in your own dominions', and innovations in religion were as much of a threat to his authority as innovations in politics. There were also spiritual reasons for insisting upon a single permitted form of worship. God, it was held, had encouraged men of faith to break with the corrupt Roman Church in order to set up the true Church of Christ. But there could, by definition, be only one true Church. If more than one form of worship were permitted this would seem tantamount to confessing that the protestants had no greater justification than their opponents when they claimed to be the one and only true Church.

The radicals were themselves split between moderates and extremists. The moderates wanted to move by gradual steps towards the establishment of a really reformed Church, carrying the people with them as they did so. The extremists, on the other hand, saw no reason to compromise with truth. They wanted to use all the powers of government immediately to set up and impose a purified, uncompromisingly protestant Church. Both groups were agreed upon the need for reform; they differed only on the timing of it. Fortunately for the moderates two of the most important men in England, Somerset and Cranmer, were of their persuasion, and the rate of change was gradual.

The extremists objected that the reformation of the Church was proceeding at too slow a pace, even though a statute of 1547 ordered the dissolution of all chantries and gild chapels, and the confiscation of their endowments, on the grounds that prayers for the dead were no longer necessary now that the existence of purgatory had been denied. Apart from this act of plunder, Somerset moved warily in an attempt to carry public opinion with him, but he did not dare leave Gardiner, the influential catholic leader, at liberty. The Council ordered Gardiner to preach before the King in favour of the religious changes that had taken place over the previous twenty years, but even though he obeyed this command he was sent to the Tower, where he remained throughout the rest of Edward's reign. By the middle of 1548 Cranmer was at work upon a new definition of the doctrines of the English Church. His own attitude was gradually becoming more extreme and he was anxious to produce a formulary that should be acceptable to the continental reformers and perhaps provide a basis for the unification of the protestant churches that he longed to see.

Cranmer had already invited a number of distinguished European reformers to England. In late 1547 Peter Martyr Vermigli arrived from Strasburg, one of the centres of the reform movement on the Continent, and was appointed Professor of Divinity at Oxford early in 1548. After the defeat of the German protestants by the Emperor Charles V many more refugees found their way to England. John à Lasco, who was largely responsible for arguing Cranmer out of his belief in the real presence, arrived in September 1548 and in the spring of the following year came two of the leading Strasburg reformers, Martin Bucer and Paul Fagius. Cranmer had also invited to England Philip Melancthon, Luther's friend and one of the most influential reformers of his day. But Melancthon was unwilling to leave Germany when the protestant cause was threatened, and this, combined with Luther's death in 1546 and the success of the imperial armies in checking protestantism, accounts for the decline of the influence of the Lutherans in England. The early English reformers had looked to Luther, but their heirs in the mid-1540s took Calvin and Zwingli as their masters.

Lutheran doctrines were, however, the most obvious foreign

influence on the first Prayer-Book of Edward VI's reign, which was authorised by Parliament in January 1549 for use from the following Whit Sunday. This Book, which Cranmer had written entirely in English, gave the Church of England, for the first time in its long history, one form of worship and one only. The Act of Uniformity which authorised the Book provided penalties for any clergyman who refused to use it or who used any other service, but it did not require laymen to attend their parish churches to hear it. Cranmer's assumption was that the obvious merits of the Book would encourage its acceptance, and on all disputed matters he phrased his magnificent prose in such a way that more than one interpretation could be made of it. This was particularly true of the communion service, which referred to the 'Sacrament of the body of Christ' and the 'Sacrament of the blood' and ordered the priest to say, as he administered them, 'The body [blood] of our Lord Jesus Christ which was given [shed] for thee, preserve thy body and soul unto everlasting life'.

Such wording could be held to imply the real presence, and this was the interpretation Gardiner gave to it from his prison in the Tower. Cranmer himself denied that he had ever intended to permit traces of such a belief to remain in the Prayer-Book, and indeed his position was shifting so rapidly that by the time the Book was in use the Archbishop, urged on by the continental reformers, was already considering a revised and more extreme version of it. The controversy between Cranmer and Gardiner shows the development of Cranmer's views. The Archbishop had publicly maintained his belief in the real presence in 1537, but by 1550 he could write: 'What availeth it to take away beads, pardons, pilgrimages, and such other like popery, so long as two chief roots remain unpulled up? . . . The very body of the tree, or rather the roots of the weeds, is the popish doctrine of transubstantiation, of the real presence of Christ's flesh and blood in the sacrament of the altar (as they call it) and of the sacrifice and oblation of Christ made by the priest, for the salvation of the quick and the dead.'

The Western Rising and Ket's Rebellion

The fact that the first Prayer-Book, with its provision for auricular confession and its prayers for the dead, was acceptable to Gardiner made it unacceptable to the extremists. Yet there were many Catholics who found it too protestant for their taste. Among these were the villagers of Sampford Courtenay in Devonshire who on Whit Monday

1549 forced their parish priest to stop using the new Prayer-Book and made him celebrate mass according to the Latin rite. Their rebellion quickly spread to neighbouring parishes and soon the west country was up in arms. The form of worship prescribed by the new Book was, said the rebels, 'like a Christmas game', and they asked for the restoration of 'our old service of matins, mass, evensong and procession in Latin, as it was before'. It was useless for Somerset to assure them that the new Prayer-Book was 'none other but the old: the selfsame words in English which were in Latin, saving a few things taken out'. The rebels had risen, like their forefathers in Henry VII's reign, to defend the old order, and their resentment was directed against the whole process of unification which had made them merely a subordinate part of a greater political community, with which they were largely out of sympathy. But under the third Tudor, as under the first, rebellion was bound to fail because its leaders had no alternative to offer to royal government. The landowners, particularly those who held monastic estates, were ardent defenders of the new order, and one of the greatest of them, Lord Russell, was put in charge of the forces that were hastily gathered to crush the rising. In July 1549 he fought his way through to Exeter and by the end of the following month the rebellion was at an end. Its leaders were sent to London to be hanged. Lesser men were strung up all over the west country as a warning to any who felt inclined to follow their example.

While Russell was putting down the Western Rising a far more serious rebellion broke out in Norfolk. This was also a conservative revolt, but the rebels in this case were protesting not against the religious changes, which they explicitly accepted, but against the less easily definable economic forces that were transforming their lives. The Protector had listened to the complaints that poured in to him against enclosures, and had consulted with the humanists at Court on the best measures to take. These men, of whom Starkey, Latimer and John Hales were the most influential, had all More's hatred of oppression, but were closer to Starkey in their assumption that England was an organic society which existed to serve a moral and not simply a material end. To the assertion that every man's property was his own, to do as he liked with, Hales replied: 'it may not be lawful for every man to use his own as him listeth, but every man must use that he hath to the most benefit of his country.'

The same ideal prompted Somerset in June 1548 to issue a proclamation against enclosure, and he followed the example of Wolsey by setting up commissions to tour those counties that had suffered badly from it. He met opposition from the landlords, who used all their influence to make the commissions' work impossible, and in the Council itself there was a group led by Warwick—whose own park had been ploughed up on the grounds that it was an illegal enclosure—which regarded any concessions to the peasants as a dangerous weakening of the authority of government. But Somerset was a proud man, convinced of the justice of his cause, and was prepared to force his policy through against any opposition. 'Maugre the devil, private profit, self-love, money, and such like the devil's instruments', he declared, 'it shall go forward!' In May 1549 he issued a second proclamation against enclosures, and in June, four days after the outbreak of the Western Rising, he gave a general pardon to all those who had taken the law into their own hands and thrown down fences.

It seemed to the peasants as though they and Somerset were allied against the forces of private profit, and their anger was directed at the landlords who were sabotaging the work of the commissioners. Norfolk was seething with discontent, and by early July sporadic risings had coalesced into a general rebellion. The rebels gathered at Wymondham, where they chose as their leader Robert Ket, a well-to-do tradesman. With him at their head they advanced on Norwich throwing down fences as they went, and set up camp to the north of the city on Mousehold Heath. For six weeks Ket ruled the thousands of men who had flocked to join him, and, with the help of an elected council, kept good order and discipline. It was a remarkable demonstration of self-government, and it showed the quality of the rebels. They were not a motiveless rabble but a company of small farmers, peasant cultivators, gathered together in defence of their traditional rights and confident that the Protector would approve their action.

The main grievance, as revealed in the list drawn up by the rebels, was not enclosure but the overstocking of commons. Much of the county was well suited to sheep-farming, and the peasants, who had little land of their own, were dependent upon their right of common pasture. A few sheep could make a big difference to a man's income, and when a lord increased the number of animals he turned out to graze he threatened the peasants' livelihood. Significantly absent from the list was any demand for a return to the old ways in religion. The rebels used the new Prayer-Book for public services, and among those who were summoned to preach to the thousands assembled on Mousehold Heath was Matthew Parker, the future Archbishop.

Somerset's natural sympathies lay with the rebels, and he hated the thought of bloodshed. 'Content yourselves, good people', he had told the west countrymen. 'Do not with this rage and fury drive yourselves to the sword, your wives and children to famine and hunger.' But he could not ignore the threat to order, and if he would not act there were others in the Council who were ready to do so. Warwick was the obvious man. Having helped Russell put down the Western Rising he had an army ready to crush Ket and his men. In August he made his way swiftly north with ten thousand men at his back. Norwich, which the rebels had captured, was taken by storm, and the camp on Mousehold Heath was encircled. Ket gave the order to move out rather than face starvation, and this was Warwick's opportunity. He sent his cavalry in among the rebels and turned the retreat into a rout. By the end of August the Norfolk rebellion was over. A special commission was set up to deal with prisoners, of whom forty-nine were hanged at Norwich. Ket and his brother were tried in London on a charge of treason and sent back to Norfolk in December to be executed.

The Fall of Somerset

Ket's fall was followed by Somerset's. Opposition to the Protector's 'weak' policy had been growing in the Council, and now that Warwick, a very ambitious man, had control of the army, he was in a position to dictate terms. Somerset was with the King at Hampton Court in October 1549 when the news of Warwick's intrigues with the Council reached him. He seems to have contemplated resistance and he hurried the King away to Windsor, which was easier to defend. Resistance was, however, out of the question. Somerset had alienated too many of the Council by his arrogance and his passion for social justice, and although he was the idol of the common people they could not protect him against Warwick's mercenaries. In October he gave himself up to Warwick and was sent to the Tower. There he remained until the following February, when he was released. This ostentatious gesture of conciliation on Warwick's part served its turn by giving the new ruler of England time to gain the young King's entire confidence and to establish himself so firmly that he could ignore opposition. By the end of 1551 he was ready to destroy Somerset, who was always a potential threat, especially as he had lost none of his hold on the affections of the people. In October 1551 Somerset was arrested on a charge of treason, and in January the following year he was executed on Tower Hill, showing no sign of fear and publicly affirming that he had been 'ever glad of the furtherance and helping forward of the common wealth of this realm'.

Religion. II: Northumberland and the Extremist Settlement

Somerset had been associated with a policy of moderate protestantism, and it seemed at first as though his fall might be the signal for a catholic reaction. Cranmer had, after all, been Somerset's supporter, while Warwick had allied with Wriothesley, the leader of the catholic group in the Council. But whatever hopes the catholics had, they were not destined to be fulfilled. Although later, on the scaffold, Warwick proclaimed his adherence to the Roman Church, he gave no evidence of this attachment during his lifetime. His religious attitude seems to have been determined almost entirely by economic considerations, and under his leadership the attack upon the Church was set going again. The radicals hailed him as a true reformer—Hooper, for instance, who had such scruples about wearing vestments that he tried to refuse appointment to the see of Gloucester, called Warwick 'that most faithful and intrepid soldier of Christ'—and the young King was also taken in. Edward's rigidly protestant education had inclined him to the radicals and he listened willingly to Warwick's plans for removing the remaining traces of popery from the English Church. The Earl did not proclaim himself Protector: that title had too many associations with Somerset. He preferred to bring the King forward and use him as a shield behind which he could effectively control policy.

With Warwick in power the pace of the religious reformation quickened. In November 1550 the Council ordered that all remaining altars were to be destroyed and replaced by a simple wooden table, on the grounds that 'the use of an altar is to make sacrifice upon', while 'the use of a table is to serve for men to eat upon'. Just over a year later, in 1552, Cranmer produced his second Prayer-Book. This was a much more uncompromisingly protestant formulary than its predecessor. The first Book had referred to the 'Sacrament of the body' and the 'Sacrament of the blood', but these savoured too much of the doctrine of transubstantiation which Cranmer had now completely rejected. He replaced them by 'the bread' and 'the cup', and instructed the priest to say 'Take and eat this, in remembrance that Christ died for thee, and feed on him in thy heart by faith, with thanksgiving.'

Cranmer did not intend to leave any loophole in the new order of service whereby Gardiner and his fellow catholics might bring in the real presence once again. Albs, vestments and copes were no longer to be worn by the officiating priest, since they served only to emphasise the unacceptable catholic belief in the separateness of the clergy, who alone could bring about the miracle of transforming bread and wine into the body and blood. At Cranmer's insistence the communicant was still required to kneel when receiving the sacrament, but the Council inserted the notorious Black Rubric declaring that 'it is not meant thereby, that any adoration is done, or ought to be done. . . . For as concerning the sacramental bread and wine, they remain still in their very natural substances, and therefore may not be adored, for that were idolatry to be abhorred of all faithful Christians.'

The new Prayer-Book was enforced by the second Act of Uniformity, which commanded everyone to attend church on Sundays and prescribed imprisonment for those found present at a service other than that provided in the Prayer-Book. Somerset's policy of gradualness had been abandoned: protestantism was now to be imposed by force. The doctrines of the Church of England were further defined by the publication of the Forty-two Articles in 1553, which confirmed, among other things, Cranmer's abandonment of his belief in transubstantiation.

Warwick had little love for Cranmer and it may be true that, as the Archbishop told Queen Mary in the next reign, Warwick was planning to destroy him. The two men were of profoundly different temperaments. Cranmer, personally gentle but difficult to move until his conscience persuaded him, wanted to preserve the historical continuity of the English Church. Warwick, on the other hand, was a natural extremist: having thrown in his lot with the reformers he regarded moderation and compromise as weakness. The fiery Scottish reformer, John Knox, was more to his taste, and he wrote to Cecil in 1552: 'For Heaven's sake make Knox Bishop of Rochester. He will be a whetstone to Cranmer, who needs one.'

Warwick had no love for the Church because he was out to despoil it, and his period of power saw widespread destruction. In hundreds of parish churches stained glass windows were smashed, tombs were broken up and statues removed or decapitated, on the grounds that they encouraged idolatry. In 1551 the confiscation of church plate was ordered, except for the minimum required for carrying out services. At the universities, libraries were searched for heretical books, which were then destroyed, and the marked decline in the number of degrees awarded at Oxford in Edward VI's reign—an average of just over thirty a year compared with nearly one hundred and thirty in the opening three decades of the century—suggests that education was suffering.

In October 1551 Warwick was created Duke of Northumberland. He suffered much at the time—and ever since—from the comparison with Somerset, 'the good Duke', who was a far more humane man. But Somerset had also been arrogant and self-seeking, and his ambitious foreign policies put an intolerable strain on English finances. His invasion of Scotland, for instance, although it was designed to aid the protestant cause in that country, served only to drive the Scots into the arms of France. A military solution of the Scottish problem was simply not possible at that stage without expenditure on a scale that even Somerset could not contemplate, and the attempt to impose one led to open war with France. Northumberland abandoned his predecessor's forward policy and left the Scots to themselves. He also brought the French war to a close in March 1550 by surrendering Boulogne. Neither of these actions was glorious, but they relieved the strain on the Exchequer, and Northumberland showed by his attempt to reform the coinage in September 1551 that he was alive to economic realities. Boulogne was of no real value. The prosperity of England was to be sought rather in overseas trade, and Northumberland encouraged this by promoting voyages of exploration and by revoking, in 1552, the privileges of the Hanseatic League.

Northumberland had his father's virtues. He was ruthless and efficient, and much of the hatred he aroused came from his determination that the property-owners should not entirely evade their financial obligations. His success was shown by the rise in receipts from the Court of Wards, contrasted with the steep decline under Somerset. Northumberland displayed his ruthlessness by the harsh way in which he put down the two rebellions of the reign, and he had little love for the lower orders, yet even here his record is not entirely black. Somerset's concern for the welfare of the peasants had produced chaos and revolt: Northumberland allowed agrarian reform to continue, but not at such a disruptive pace.

His efficiency, unfortunately, extended into the field of money-grabbing. Somerset had done well out of office, but Northumberland set an example of plunder which was widely followed. The members of the Council, for instance, voted themselves royal estates worth

£30,000 a year, and the rule that all monastic and Church lands sold by the Crown were to be held by feudal tenure, to preserve the valuable financial obligations, was relaxed. The result was continued public insolvency, and a committee appointed to enquire into the financial situation in 1551 revealed that the total net income of the government amounted to a little under £170,000, of which ordinary expenditure consumed all but £36,550. From this tiny surplus had to be met extraordinary expenditure, yet garrisons alone cost £80,000 a year and the foreign debt amounted to a quarter of a million pounds. By September the government was virtually bankrupt and many payments were suspended, including monastic pensions. Crown lands were unloaded on to the market and brought in over £150,000, but still more money was needed. Northumberland reluctantly decided to summon Parliament and ask for a subsidy. Such a move was not likely to make him any more popular. Subsidies were usually demanded only in time of war, when the necessity for them was obvious, although even then they were not always granted without difficulty. By 1552, however, the country had been at peace for nearly two years, and Northumberland's appeal for money fell on unsympathetic ears.

Public confidence was not inspired by the continuing plunder of the Church. Ponet, who succeeded Gardiner as Bishop of Winchester in 1551, gave all the endowments of his see to Northumberland in return for a pension of two thousand marks, and Hooper—who eventually accepted both vestments and the bishopric of Gloucester—came to a similar arrangement. The new see of Westminster was suppressed as unnecessary, and in the last months of his rule Northumberland was preparing to suppress the rich see of Durham and transfer the greater part of its revenues to the Crown and himself. Much of the money plundered from the Church did, in fact, go into the Crown's coffers, but Northumberland was so identified with the government that it was impossible to say whether his efficient exploitation of all available resources was directed to public or to private ends. The only obvious truth was that the Duke and his cronies were making big profits at a time when they were pleading national bankruptcy, and Northumberland knew what the attitude of the Commons was likely to be when they met. He told Cecil to be careful not 'to seem to make a count to the Commons of his Majesty's liberality and bountifulness in augmenting or advancing of his nobles, or of his benevolence showed to any his good servants, lest you might thereby make them wanton and give them occasion to take hold of your own arguments'.

Edward VI's Death and Northumberland's Fall

The subsidy, which was eventually voted, came too late to save Northumberland. He ruled in the name of Edward VI, but by early 1553 it was clear that the fifteen-year-old King had not much longer to live. By bringing him forward and making him play a man's role in the government, Northumberland had subjected the boy to an unbearable strain. His robust health declined and a chill turned to congestion of the lungs. Northumberland knew that the King's death would shortly be followed by his own, for the heir to the throne was Edward's half-sister, Mary, who had refused to abandon her mother's faith. There seemed little reason to doubt that when she ascended the throne she would remove the protestant ministers and restore England to communion with Rome. The only way to avoid this fate was to change the succession. Henry VIII had bequeathed the Crown by will: Northumberland persuaded the dying Edward that he must do the same, and that his duty to God demanded the nomination of a protestant heir.

The person chosen by Northumberland for this onerous role was the fifteen-year-old Lady Jane Grey, descended from Henry VII through the second marriage of his daughter Mary with Charles Brandon, Duke of Suffolk. The nearest protestant claimant was, in fact, Elizabeth, but she was ruled out on the nominal grounds that she might take as husband a foreign and papist prince. To avoid the same fate befalling Lady Jane she was ordered to marry Northumberland's fourth son, Lord Guilford Dudley. The marriage took place, much against Jane's will, on 25 May 1553. At about the same time Edward drew up his 'device' in which he left the throne to Lady Jane and her male descendants: Mary and Elizabeth were both ruled out as illegitimate. The leading figures in the government—Councillors, judges and bishops—were called on to add their signature to the 'device'. Some tried to withhold their assent, but Northumberland and the King would not permit this.

Edward died after an agonising illness, on 6 July 1553. The news was kept secret for three days while messages were sent out to the Lords-Lieutenant, who controlled the counties. Then the Lady Jane was proclaimed Queen. But Mary, who had her father's spirit, raised her standard at Framlingham and called on all those who loved the Tudor dynasty to follow her. Supporters quickly came in. The common

people had little love for Northumberland, whom they regarded
as the ally of the oppressing landlords, and among the more influential
members of the community there was suspicion of the Duke's motives
in marrying his son to the new Queen. It seemed as though the new
nobility was copying the example of the old, and preparing to plunge
England into more Wars of the Roses merely to further its private
ambitions. The eastern counties came out in support of Mary, and the
Councillors at London, quick to scent the changing wind, proclaimed
her Queen. The Duke, who had taken his small force no further than
Cambridge, followed suit, for his army had melted away. By the end
of July he was a prisoner in the Tower, and on 3 August Mary entered
London in triumph. The next day the Duke of Norfolk and bishop
Gardiner were released from their long imprisonment. The catholic
reaction had begun.

Mary

Queen Mary was thirty-seven when the death of her half-brother
brought her to the throne, and the catholics rejoiced at the prospect
of a reign in which England should be restored to the see of Rome.
Success seemed certain, for the Queen herself was popular. Those who
had flocked to join her at Framlingham were, like the citizens of
London who threw their hats in the air and cheered the news of Mary's
success, inspired by more than dislike of Northumberland. Mary had
shown her courage by raising her standard in the face of what must
have seemed formidable odds, and for years before that she had resisted
all the efforts of Edward VI's protestant ministers to make her abandon
the Mass. When a deputation of Councillors waited on her in August
1551 to make her change her mind, she proudly refused and reminded
these upstarts that her father had 'made the more part of you out of
nothing'. Her stubbornness, her courage and her pride were typically
Tudor, and she was not without that other characteristic of her family
—charm. Charles V's ambassador thought she was too accessible and
too innocent of the arts and subterfuges of politics. 'I know the Queen
to be good,' he wrote, 'easily influenced, inexpert in worldly matters,
and a novice all round', and the years that followed were in many ways
to confirm this judgement. For Mary politics were an aspect of
religion and morality. Principle came first and she could see no virtue
in compromise. The simplicity of her approach, combined with her
natural stubbornness, explains why this kindly, well-intentioned
woman became a symbol of intolerance and cruelty.

E*

The opening of the reign was marked, however, by lenience. Northumberland was executed along with two of his accomplices, but otherwise there were no reprisals. Lady Jane and her husband were condemned to death, as was Archbishop Cranmer, but Mary intervened to save them from execution, and they were held prisoner in the Tower. Cranmer could have fled abroad rather than face the accession of a catholic monarch but he chose not to do so. He was typical of the early reformers in his reverence for royal authority, and to have fled out of Mary's jurisdiction would have meant abandoning one of the main articles of his faith. Another consideration which persuaded him to stay at home was the prevailing uncertainty about Mary's intentions. Cranmer may have thought she merely intended to restore the Henrician settlement, and Mary herself told her Council that she 'meaneth graciously not to compel or constrain other men's consciences otherwise than . . . through the opening of His word unto men by godly, virtuous, learned preachers'.

Religion. III: Protestant Exile and Catholic Reaction

The foreign reformers, who had come to England in the reign of Edward VI, were encouraged to leave the country, and no obstacle was put in the way of English protestants who wished to go into exile rather than live under a Catholic ruler. Peter Martyr made his way to Strasburg, from where he reported that 'English youths have come over to us in great numbers within a few days, partly from Oxford and partly from Cambridge; whom many godly merchants are bringing up to learning, that should it please God to restore religion to its former state in that kingdom, they may be of some benefit to the Church of England'. Other congregations of exiles settled at Frankfurt, and elsewhere in France, Germany and Switzerland. This was not the result of any sudden panic, for Mary's accession had been foreseen and careful plans had been made to preserve the protestant English Church in exile until such time as it could be re-established in its native country. Nearly eight hundred people, most of them from the upper levels of English society, went into voluntary exile It is not certain who were the brains behind this movement, but it seems likely that William Cecil—that astute and cunning politician who had served both Somerset and Northumberland and managed to preserve his person and his estates intact—was one of the principal organisers.

Mary appointed as Lord Chancellor and her chief minister Stephen

Gardiner, now, at the age of fifty-six, restored to freedom once again. She also looked for advice to the imperial ambassador, for she was half Spanish by birth, and ties of blood as well as religion made her desire some sort of alliance with the Habsburgs. Charles V was well aware of this and encouraged the idea of a marriage between Mary and his son Philip. In the struggle which was still going on between the Empire and France, England could be a useful ally. For this reason he did his best to keep out of England Reginald Pole, whom the Pope had appointed as legate. Pole was a man of great integrity, who, like Mary, made his policy follow his principles instead of vice versa. But he was also an English aristocrat who would swiftly sense the antagonism of his fellow-countrymen towards Spain and would try to steer Mary on more independent courses. Charles recognised this and put pressure on the Pope to keep Pole kicking his heels in Europe for more than a year after he should have been in London.

With Gardiner to advise her, Mary planned to restore the catholic faith in England. Of Edward VI's bishops, four, including Miles Coverdale, fled to the Continent; another four, including Cranmer, Ridley and Hooper were imprisoned; and four more were deprived. Five Henrician bishops, who had been expelled from their sees under Northumberland, were now restored: they included Gardiner, who returned to Winchester, Tunstall, who went back to Durham, and Bonner, who became Bishop of London. These administrative changes were carried out by virtue of the royal supremacy, even though this particular dignity was repugnant to Mary, but more fundamental changes in the structure of the English Church needed a greater authority. Accordingly, in October 1553 the first Parliament of the reign was summoned to undo the work of its predecessors under Edward VI. By the first Statute of Repeal it wiped out much of Cranmer's work. The reformed liturgy, the two Books of Common Prayer, the administration of the sacrament under both kinds and the existence of a married clergy were all declared to be illegal, and the clock was turned back to the closing years of Henry VIII.

The Spanish Match

The Statute of Repeal had a difficult passage through Parliament, since many of the members were protestants, and on the third reading in the Commons just under a third of those present voted against the Act. This opposition did not spring from disloyalty towards Mary It was caused rather by a fear that the next step would be the confiscation of monastic property and its restoration to the Church—a proceeding which would have been anathema to the many property-holders who sat in both Lords and Commons. It also sprang from a deep-seated hostility towards papal claims, and it is significant that in all the legislation of this Parliament, no mention was made of the Pope. The basic loyalty on which Mary could, in the last resort, rely was weakened by her desire for a Spanish marriage. For her the advantages of such a match outweighed all its disadvantages. It would give her the support of a catholic husband and link her kingdom with the greatest catholic power on the Continent, and when a deputation from the Lords and Commons pleaded with her to take an English husband she brushed them aside with the proud reply that 'Parliament was not accustomed to use such language to the Kings of England, nor was it suitable or respectful that it should do so. . . . She would choose according as God inspired her.' Charles V was, of course, in favour of the plan, and arrangements went ahead for a marriage between the Queen and Philip of Spain.

The news of the projected Spanish marriage caused dismay. The first two Tudors had unified their realm by stressing the common allegiance that all Englishmen had towards their sovereign and by asserting the independence of their kingdom from all foreign jurisdictions. Now it seemed as though this work would be undone. England would be subjected to a Spanish King, and, what was worse, would almost certainly be dragged into the conflict between the Habsburgs and the Valois rulers of France, from which she had nothing to gain. The effect of Henry VIII's policy had been to cut England off from the Continent and encourage the growth of the xenophobia that foreigners later remarked on. Mary failed to appreciate this and to see that her popularity and her strength depended upon the degree to which she could identify herself with this pronounced sense of Englishness. Instead, she linked her cause and the cause of her faith with a hated foreign power, and thereby made sure of ultimate failure.

The terms of marriage were agreed upon in January 1554. Philip was to be called King and was to assist Mary in the government of the country, but the Queen alone was to appoint to all offices in Church and state, and was to choose only Englishmen: there was to be no Spanish take-over. While these terms were being drawn up, a group of conspirators was plotting to make sure that they would never come into effect. Sir Thomas Wyatt, son of one of the finest poets of early

Tudor England, planned a revolt against Mary, with simultaneous risings throughout England. He had promises of support from France, and it may be that Mary's half-sister, Princess Elizabeth, was also in the secret. The ultimate aims of the conspirators were not clear, nor were they ever to become so, for Wyatt was betrayed and when he raised his standard in Kent there were no simultaneous risings elsewhere. Nevertheless, he collected several thousand men and marched on London. The situation was serious and the City might have fallen to the rebels had not Mary, with her accustomed courage, ridden to the Guildhall, where she appealed to the citizens to remain faithful to her Her bold move succeeded. The bridges were held against Wyatt and when he forced his way into the City from the Surrey side he found no one to support him. In the end he surrendered without fighting, and was immediately sent off to the Tower.

Although Wyatt's rebellion had been defeated it had come dangerously near success, and over a hundred of the rank and file were condemned to death, forty-six of them being hanged in London in a single day. Wyatt himself was executed and so were Lady Jane Grey and her husband, even though they had not taken part in the rebellion. Mary had learnt, like her father, that those who stood close to the throne were a constant menace, however innocent their intentions. Princess Elizabeth, another suspect and not, perhaps, an innocent one, was imprisoned in the Tower. For some weeks her life was in danger, but she was so popular that her execution would have raised an outcry. Nothing could be proved against her, and in the end she was allowed to leave London and live quietly in the country.

The failure of Wyatt's rebellion cleared the way for the Spanish marriage. Parliament accepted the proposed terms in April 1554 and in the following July, Gardiner, whose objections had been overcome, married Mary and Philip in the cathedral church of his diocese of Winchester. On personal grounds the marriage was a failure. Philip had little love for his wife, whom he found unattractive, and although at first Mary could blind herself to this, she could not ignore her husband's increasingly prolonged absences. She longed for a child, but even this was denied her. The failure of her marriage gradually soured Mary. She who had devoted her life to the restoration of the true Church in England had to accept the fact that her work would be in vain, for she would be succeeded by the protestant Elizabeth.

Persecution

In November 1554, Reginald Pole, the cardinal legate, at last arrived in England. Not since Wolsey's fall had a legate *a latere* controlled English affairs, and Pole was a very different man from Wolsey. He shared Mary's devotion to the Catholic Church and wished to see England restored to full communion with Rome. This would not be possible, however, until the nation had expressed publicly its desire for forgiveness. Parliament, which was held to epitomise the nation and which had shared the responsibility for schism, would have to take the initiative in asking for absolution. On the last day of November 1554 a joint session of both Houses took place at which Mary and Philip, as well as the Legate, were present. Gardiner, as Lord Chancellor, read aloud a petition asking for pardon and reconciliation, which Pole accepted. Then, while all present kneeled, the cardinal legate pronounced absolution and declared the kingdom of England restored to the unity of Christ's Church.

Pole was anxious to avoid any impression that he was prepared to bargain with Parliament, yet it is doubtful if the reconciliation would have been carried through so smoothly had he not made it known that he was empowered by his commission to confirm all holders of monastic property in possession of their estates. The Second Statute of Repeal confirmed this implicit bargain. It started by repealing all those statutes passed against Rome since the fall of Wolsey, but it also declared that the holders of monastic lands might 'without scruple of conscience enjoy them, without impeachment or trouble by pretence of any General Council, canons, or ecclesiastical laws, and clear from all dangers of the censures of the Church'. In this way the landowners who controlled Parliament took themselves back into the Roman Church without parting with any of the profits of secession.

The second Statute of Repeal was preceded by an Act reviving the heresy laws. It is not clear who advised Mary to begin the persecution of heretics, but much of the responsibility for this must rest on her alone. There was nothing new, of course, about the burning of heretics, and intolerance was not confined to catholics. Heresy was regarded as a crime against society, and like all crimes it was punishable. The modern alternative of allowing the free expression of all varieties of faith, was inconceivable in the sixteenth century. Not only was each group convinced that it was the sole possessor of truth; there was the additional complication that in a matter which made all the difference between eternal life and eternal damnation there could be no room for compromise. Just as a man's predatory instincts had to be restrained by fear of the hangman's knot, so his susceptibility to the devil's wiles had to be restrained by the stake.

Between February 1555 and November 1558 just under three hundred men and women were burnt for heresy. The punishment of death by burning was an appallingly cruel one, but it was not this that shocked contemporaries—after all, in an age that knew nothing of anaesthetics, a great deal of pain had to be endured by everybody at one time or another, and the taste for public executions, bear-baiting and cock-fighting suggests a callousness that blunted susceptibilities. It is also doubtful whether the fact that the victims were executed for heresy would have aroused much sympathy for them. What made the Marian persecution so unpopular was the way in which it struck down the small offender while letting most of the big ones go scot-free. The lead in searching out heretics was taken by the lay authorities, and all too often the accused would find himself judged by a man who had been an active propagator of protestant doctrines under Edward VI. When Thomas Watts, a linen draper of a small Essex town, was brought before a Justice of the Peace who asked him 'Who hath been thy schoolmaster to teach thee this gear, or where didst thou first learn this religion?', Watts replied: 'Forsooth, even of you sir. You taught it me, and none more than you. For in King Edward's days in open session you spoke against this religion now used; no preacher more.' The list of martyrs under Mary includes only nine people who were described as gentlemen. Just over a quarter of those burned were in holy orders; the rest came from the lower levels of English society, and included weavers, fullers, shearmen, tailors, hosiers, cappers, husbandmen, labourers, brewers and butchers. None of these men could, by reason of their very insignificance, be a real threat to Mary's Church. They were the representatives of the common people, and by striking them down Mary went a long way towards destroying the reverence and goodwill that Tudor subjects felt for their sovereigns.

The executions can hardly have advanced the catholic cause. Henry VIII had found it necessary to martyr a few heretics in order to maintain orthodoxy, and on the whole he had been successful. The far greater number of Mary's brief reign is a sign of failure: if thirty fires would not burn out heresy it was unlikely that three hundred would do so. Protestantism had not dug deep roots in English life, for Northumberland and his bishops had imposed changes of doctrine far too rapidly and had associated the extremist reformation of the Church with their own greed and graft. But Mary repeated Northumberland's mistake of trying to do too much too quickly, and the fact that her motives, unlike his, were pure, made no difference to the result. Protestant pamphleteers, at home and on the Continent, were swift to, take advantage of this error, and the accession of Elizabeth was followed by the publication of John Foxe's *Book of Martyrs*, which recorded in loving and gruesome detail the lives and deaths of all those who had been put to death by the Queen. Foxe's book came to be almost as widely read, in England, as the Bible. Mary had given the English protestant church its martyrs; Foxe made sure that their deeds would be an inspiration to generations of those who came after.

The government hoped that the threat of execution would be enough to drive protestants to recant, and one big success would have made this far more likely. This is why it put so much pressure on Cranmer to make public confession of his errors. Cranmer, Ridley, Hooper and Latimer had all been imprisoned. Hooper was burnt in the early days of the persecution, and Latimer and Ridley went to the flames at Oxford in October 1555. Cranmer was left alone to decide what to do. He was in a genuine dilemma since royal supremacy was for him an article of faith, yet by accepting the commands of his sovereign lady Mary he would be going against what his own conscience told him to be true. It was doubts about his own position, as much as fear, that led him to recant, but at the last moment he changed his mind. Led out to die at Oxford in March 1556, he denounced his recantation as 'things written with my hand, contrary to the truth which I thought in my heart, and written for fear of death and to save my life if it might be', and he plunged his hand into the flames so that it might never have the opportunity to betray him again.

Cranmer's dilemma was shared by many protestants. The early reformers in England and on the Continent had transferred to the King the reverence that Roman Catholics gave to the Pope, and had elevated royal authority because it seemed the best possible security against papal claims. Now, however, the royal supremacy, which had been created to destroy the Roman Church in England, was being used to rebuild it, and protestants had to reconsider their attitude. The first of the Marian martyrs had shown the way when he appealed from the monarch to the word of God, unto which, he said, 'must all men—

king and queen, emperor, parliament and general councils—obey. The Word obeyeth no man. It cannot be changed nor altered.' In this way Mary's reign helped to create the puritan challenge to royal supremacy.

Whatever Pole thought of the burnings—and there is no reason to suppose that he disapproved of them—he realised that they would be of little use without a more positive approach towards the problem of converting England to catholicism. Thirteen new bishops had been appointed, and none of them owed his high place to state service. A new spirit was in the air, and when Pole opened the synod which met in December 1555 he laid a far-reaching reform programme before it. But his plans were stillborn, for in May of that year a new Pope, Paul IV, had been elected. Paul IV suspected heresy everywhere and he was also violently anti-Spanish, since he wanted to free Italy from the Habsburg yoke. Charles V had abdicated all his possessions in October 1555, and papal fury was now concentrated on Charles's son, Philip, King of Spain, Italy and England. While Pole was addressing the synod that seemed to promise a new era for the Catholic Church in England, Paul IV was negotiating a treaty of alliance with France. Philip II, in reply, sent the Spanish general, the Duke of Alva, to occupy the papal states. Paul promptly excommunicated Philip and withdrew all his representatives from the King's dominions. He also deprived Pole of his legateship, and ordered him to return to Rome to answer charges of heresy.

Mary, a devout daughter of the Catholic Church, was in the invidious position of being married to an excommunicate husband and having as her chief adviser a suspected heretic. The situation would have been comic had it not been so full of tragic implications, and even had Mary lived it is at least possible that England would again have seceded from the Roman Church. Rather than lose Pole, Mary forbade him to return to Rome, and petitioned the Pope to restore him to his legateship. Her support of Philip was made clear when in June 1557 she declared war on his enemy, France. The war was a failure. Calais, the last English stronghold on the Continent, had poor defences and an insufficient garrison. When French troops appeared before it in January 1558, the city was forced to surrender. It was, in the words of A. L. Rowse, 'England's most fortunate defeat',[1] for English power and prosperity lay in expansion across the seas and not in the revival of futile dreams of European empire. But Calais had

[1] *The Expansion of Elizabethan England*, p. 9.

been a symbol, even though a hollow one, of English greatness, and its loss was one more nail in Mary's coffin. She and her Church were now allied not only with persecution and foreign domination but with inglorious failure as well.

Financial Reorganisation and the Closing Years of the Reign

In one sphere only—that of finance—could Mary's government claim success, but although the long-term effects of the reorganisation of the Crown's finances were to be most important, this was an unspectacular business that could not compensate for flaws in the government's public image. Nevertheless, the achievement was a real one. Mary carefully husbanded her resources. The sale of Crown lands was cut to a minimum, and the expenses of the household, which, in the last year of Edward's reign, had totalled more than £55,000, were reduced to under £40,000 by the time Mary died. The financial machinery was overhauled to make it less wasteful, and the Courts of Augmentations and First Fruits were amalgamated with the Exchequer. Annuities and pensions to courtiers, which under Edward had reached £20,000 a year, were cut to £6,000, and the temptation to debase the coinage again was resisted.

The continuing price rise made more positive measures necessary. The main source of royal revenue was the income from Crown lands, and this was increased by bringing the level of rents and entry fines into closer relation with that which obtained on private property. The result of this more realistic appraisal of values was that the annual net income from Crown lands rose to £70,000—more than double what it had been when Mary came to the throne. The same realism was shown in the attempt to tax trade more efficiently. In 1558 a new Book of Rates was issued, in which duties were increased by an average of seventy-five per cent, and the revenue from Customs consequently rose from £25,000 at the beginning of the reign to over £80,000 at the end. Elizabeth profited from her sister's work in this as in other respects, and although the merchants never contributed as much to the national purse as their increasing share of the nation's wealth would have justified, the revenue from Customs came to be more important to the Crown than its income from land. Generally speaking, the administration of royal finances under Mary was efficient and productive, and although the Queen voluntarily reduced her income by surrendering First Fruits and Tenths to the Church and by restor-

ing the abbey of Westminster, she checked the decline towards bankruptcy that had set in during the last years of Henry VIII and left
Elizabeth relatively solid foundations on which to build.

Financial reorganisation and religious reformation had this in
common—they both needed time for their full effect to be felt. But
time was not granted to Mary. Disappointment had aged and soured
her. She loved her husband, but he obviously cared little for her. She
loved her people, but they remained stubbornly addicted to religious
attitudes which to her were sinful. She loved the Roman Church,
but was in open conflict with the Pope who ruled it. Above all she
loved God, and yet He had denied her the child who would have
satisfied not only her maternal instincts but also her need for a catholic
successor to preserve and continue the work which she had begun. By
the autumn of 1558 she was very ill and spent long periods in a coma,
during which, so she told her attendants, she had good dreams and saw
'many little children like angels play before her, singing pleasing notes'.
Early on the morning of 17 November she died in her palace of St
James. On the other side of the river, Reginald Pole, who had been
Archbishop of Canterbury since the formal deprivation of Cranmer
in 1556, was also lying ill in his palace at Lambeth. He survived Mary
by only a few hours. The catholic reaction ended as abruptly as it had
begun.

7

Tudor England

The Price Rise

AN increase in population and a steep rise in prices determined much of the course of English history—political and religious, as well as economic—in the Tudor and Stuart period. The hundred years preceding Bosworth had seen recurrent attacks of plague which wiped out about a third of the population and produced an acute labour shortage. Land was abundant, demand was small, and prices and rents were consequently low. This situation was already changing by the time Henry VII came to the throne, for economic security and growing immunity to plague had halted the decline in population, and although there are no reliable figures it seems likely that by 1600 there were about four million people living in England—perhaps twice as many as there had been at the time of Bosworth.

As the population mounted, so did the demand for food. This could at first be met by taking back into cultivation land that had been allowed to go waste, but after this supply had been used up there was no obvious way of increasing food production without a revolutionary improvement in agricultural techniques. An increasing demand was thwarted by a more or less static supply, and the result was a rise in prices—which, by the 1520s, were nearly forty per cent higher than they had been in the late fifteenth century. Henry VIII and his ministers were powerless in face of this phenomenon which they could neither understand nor control, and the Crown suffered particularly since it was a big buyer of goods and services and now had to pay more for both. In an effort to keep the Crown's income ahead of rising prices Wolsey debased the currency in 1526, but this remedy, which had much to be said for it at a time when coin was in short supply, merely increased the rate of inflation when it was repeated by Henry VIII and Protector Somerset later in the century. The quantity of pure metal in silver coins was cut by seventy-five per cent and in gold coins by twenty-five per cent. The Crown made an immediate profit, but in the absence of that public confidence which enables currency to be taken at its face value the true worth of new coins was determined by their pure metal content. Since this was so low, more coins were demanded for goods, the value of money dropped even further and the rise in prices accelerated.

This situation was probably made worse by the influx of gold and silver into Europe from the Spanish possessions in South America, though it is far from certain that much of this bullion actually reached England. English merchants did, it is true, trade with Spain and the Spanish Netherlands, but they imported more than they exported, and there was no question of Spanish gold and silver pouring into England as a result of a favourable trade balance. Even when bullion did find its way across the Channel much of it was turned into plate—highly esteemed as a sign of wealth and as an investment that maintained its real value—and was never minted.

Enclosures and the Wool Trade

By the end of the sixteenth century the price of foodstuffs had trebled and the cost of living mounted daily. Landlords suffered at first because they could not increase their rents to keep pace with the price rise, but as soon as leases expired many landlords hastened to take their share of the profits either by farming land directly or by putting up rents and demanding a large payment for the granting of a lease. Because land was in short supply there was no shortage of bidders, and generally speaking rents kept pace with prices and occasionally outstripped them.

Big tenant-farmers, who were growing for the market and could put up their prices, could afford to pay high rents, but not the smaller men—peasant cultivators who had taken stability for granted and assumed that the value of money was as unchanging as the pattern of the seasons. Many were evicted from their holdings or else accepted a rent that was beyond their capacity to pay and lived in poverty. Not surprisingly they hated the landlords, and 'rack-renting' and increased payments ('gressoms') for entering upon tenancies drove many of them to join revolts such as the Pilgrimage of Grace and Ket's Rebellion. Hugh Latimer, who became Bishop of Worcester in 1535, made himself the spokesman of these small men and bitterly attacked 'you

landlords, you rent-raisers . . . you have for your possessions yearly
too much. For that here before went for £20 or £40 by year (which
is an honest portion to be had gratis in one lordship of another man's
sweat and labour) now is let for £50 or £100 by year. Of this *too
much* cometh this monstrous and portentous dearth made by man.'

Rack-renting and extortionate gressoms were very real evils, but
many landowners were threatened with a decline in their living
standards unless they enclosed all or part of their estates in order to
farm more efficiently. A great deal of enclosure, either of arable strips
in the open fields or of communal pasture-land, had already taken place
by 1500, much of it by agreement. The grievance came when agreement was impossible and the landlord acted alone, evicting tenants-at-
will and buying out freeholders. There was no obvious alternative
work for these men, since industry was only slowly expanding and the
demand for manufactured products was bound to be small at a period
when the majority of the people spent the greater part of their income
on rent and food. The evicted men took to the roads and became one of
the major problems of the day: 'The sixteenth century', in the words
of Tawney, 'lives in terror of the tramp.'[1]

On the land from which tenants had been evicted sheep or cattle
would be set to graze, for these fetched a high price and cost little in
labour to look after them. Meat prices went up throughout the century,
particularly for those farmers who were near enough to supply the
growing London market, and sheep were of great value, both for their
meat and for their wool. The pace of enclosure was dictated by the
flourishing state of the export trade in wool and woollen cloth, which
by 1600 accounted for over eighty per cent of all English exports.
English wool was of fine quality and the growing European demand
for it sent the price moving upwards from as early as 1450, well before
grain prices started to rise. This was an incentive to landowners to
enclose their estates and turn them over to sheep, particularly as
enclosure made possible careful breeding to produce bigger and hardier
animals. Sheep farming was carried out on a large scale—one sixteenth-
century Norfolk landowner, for instance, owned more than fifteen
thousand animals—but the ordinary peasant working in the open fields
would usually have one or two sheep which he put out to graze on the
common pasture. Even when a landlord did not enclose he would often
increase the number of sheep he kept on the common and gradually
squeeze out the poorer men. Complaints against this practice were at

[1] *The Agrarian Problem in the Sixteenth Century*, p. 268.

least as frequent as those against enclosure, and the Norfolk peasants who joined Ket's Rebellion were primarily concerned to put an end to overstocking of commons.

In the early sixteenth century large quantities of raw wool were exported, mainly by the Company of the Staple, which had a virtual monopoly. The English cloth industry, however, was rapidly expanding, and wool exports declined as those of woollen cloth mounted. At the beginning of Henry VIII's reign about eighty thousand pieces of cloth were exported every year, but by the time Henry died the figure was nearer one hundred and twenty thousand. The demand for cloth was apparently limitless, and more and more landowners went over to pasture farming. But in 1551 the foreign market collapsed and prices fell steeply. This did not halt the process of enclosure, but it slowed it down, and even though wool prices slowly climbed again they did not keep pace, this time, with the price of wheat. By 1600 it was more profitable to grow grain than to rear sheep, and the conversion of arable to pasture was effectively checked.

The wool merchant was widely blamed for the enclosures that took place in the sixteenth century, causing much unrest. Sir Thomas More spoke of sheep devouring men, and John Hales,[1] in the *Discourse of the Common Weal of this Realm of England* written in 1549, made the husbandmen say: 'these enclosures do undo us all, for they make us pay dearer for our land that we occupy ... all is taken up for pastures, either for sheep or for grazing of cattle. So that I have known of late a dozen ploughs within less compass than six miles about me laid down within these seven years; and where forty persons had their livings, now one man and his shepherd hath all.' Enclosure was largely confined to the Midland counties, where the soil was suitable for pasture, and in Leicestershire, for instance, more than a third of the villages were affected by it. Yet although enclosure took place on a big scale and pamphleteers attacked it as a social cancer, it did not bring about the total transformation that might have been expected. Northamptonshire, to take one example, was well suited for sheep farming, but in 1712 it was described as mainly unenclosed, and over half its area was open when the enclosure commissioners of the late eighteenth century set to work.

Tudor enclosures obviously shocked the national conscience far more than the actual amount that took place would seem to warrant. One reason for this was the widespread, but inaccurate, assumption that

[1] Or Sir Thomas Smith. The authorship of the *Discourse* is still disputed.

enclosure was always and inevitably accompanied by engrossing—
the throwing together of two or more farms so that they could be
treated as a single unit. When this did happen, some of the buildings
that were no longer required would be left to decay, and there were
instances of whole villages being treated in this way, so that they
vanished altogether. Yet although the outcry against depopulating
enclosures was particularly loud in the 1540s, they were by this date
extremely rare. The heyday of the evicting landlord had been the late
fifteenth century when labour was in short supply, but prejudice
against enclosures died hard and the term was used in a general way to
describe any action that led to agrarian discontent.

Tudor governments, with their lack of any police force or standing
army, were sensitive to symptoms of unrest and tried to check depopulation and enclosures in general. They valued the peasant as a tax-
payer and potential soldier, and they were afraid that enclosures for
sheep would so reduce the area available for corn growing that
England would become dependent for food supplies on the goodwill
of other powers. Between 1489 and 1597 eleven Acts were passed
against depopulation; and eight royal commissions—the last of them
appointed in 1636—were instructed to investigate the rate and consequences of agrarian change. The number of Acts and commissions
shows how determined the government was, but it also demonstrates
its ineffectiveness. Landlords were too powerful to be easily coerced,
particularly when, as Justices of the Peace, they were the people
responsible for enforcing the government's orders, and legislation has
seldom been effective in holding back economic change.

Peasant cultivators were not absolutely powerless when confronted
by an 'improving' landlord. Freeholders could claim the protection of
the common law courts if their tenure was threatened, but they were
usually in a minority. Most of the inhabitants of a manor were copyholders—men who had a copy of the manorial court roll recording
the terms of their leases, which were usually for one or more lives.
Copyholders could appeal to the Court of Chancery or to Star
Chamber for protection, but they were often ignorant men, not con-
versant with the technicalities of the law, who could be browbeaten
by an unscrupulous landlord. Even when legal action was taken it was
not always immediately effective. The inhabitants of the Northamptonshire village of Thingden, for example, had to fight their lord, John
Mulsho, in Star Chamber and other courts for forty years, from
1498 to 1538. Not surprisingly they often despaired and were goaded

into direct action, and Mulsho's depositions describe how 'not contented with the throwing down of the said ditches and hedges and
destroying of the wood [they] riotously assembled themselves and
with force and arms hewed and cut up the gate-posts and supports of
the gates that belonged to the said closes'.

Hardly a year passed without reports of riotous assemblies to throw
down enclosures, and humanists like More, Lupset, Starkey and Hales
put forward proposals to check evicting landlords. But Thomas Cromwell, their champion, was too busy with the Dissolution, and fell from
power before he could accomplish anything. Their chance came with
Somerset, who was renowned for his love of justice and revived the
Court of Requests for poor men, which met under his own eye in
Somerset House. At Hales's suggestion Somerset persuaded Parliament
to pass an Act, in March 1549, imposing a poll-tax on sheep. The idea
of this was that farmers would hardly convert their land from arable to
pasture if, in so doing, they laid themselves open to heavy taxation.
This Act, which caused widespread resentment among farmers and
wool merchants, marks the climax of the attempt to hold back
agrarian change by legislation, and it failed. Peasant unrest against the
activities of landlords in Norfolk burst out in Ket's Rebellion, which
brought down Somerset, the peasant's champion, and replaced him
with Northumberland. The change of ruler did not bring an end to
agrarian reform, for although Northumberland was more sympathetic
to sheep-owners than to peasant cultivators and quickly secured the
repeal of the poll-tax, an Act passed by his second Parliament made it
an offence for anyone to convert to pasture land that had been under
the plough since 1509, and prosecution of enclosers continued, though
at a declining rate. The significance of Somerset's fall is that it coincided
with the collapse of the overseas market for English cloth, and it was
this which succeeded where government action had failed, and
checked the spread of enclosures for sheep.

Vagabondage and Poverty

Tudor statesmen did not have to be told about the problems caused
by agrarian change. Most of them were themselves landowners, and in
London itself, the seat of government, the population was swelling
rapidly as the beggars came to town. The stability of the Tudor state
was threatened by these hunger marchers, and the government tried
to stop them moving. An Act of 1495 ordered that vagabonds were to

be sent back to their native parishes, and in 1501 the Justices of the Peace were made responsible for seeing that this was carried out.

By the 1530s the problem of vagabondage had become part of the bigger problem of relieving poverty. There had always been poverty in England, of course, but it had never seemed so urgent as it did in the sixteenth century, when the end of foreign and civil war, and the subsequent reduction in numbers of retainers, reduced opportunities of employment. Enclosures, which took most of the blame for upsetting the pattern of rural life, were only symptoms of more fundamental changes, for the manorial economy which had dominated the Middle Ages was already being transformed by the time Henry VII came to the throne. The medieval villein, who had been the property of his lord, could count on being looked after in the way most men care for their possessions, but Tudor England saw the end of villeinage and its replacement by copyhold and leasehold—tenures which were freer and for that reason left the tenant unprotected to face a changing world.

The Church continued to stimulate corporate and individual acts of charity, but in most of western Europe in the sixteenth century the state took over the responsibility for poor relief. The first result of this in England was an Act of 1531, which came, significantly enough, five years before the dissolution of the monasteries—once held to have created the whole problem by depriving the poor of monastic alms. The 1531 Act assumed that the cause of beggary was idleness—'mother and root of all vices'—but it drew an important distinction between 'aged, poor and impotent persons' who could not work and were therefore to be licensed to beg, and 'persons being whole and mighty in body and able to labour'. Any able-bodied idler was to be arrested and 'tied to the end of a cart naked and . . . beaten with whips throughout the same market town or other place till his body be bloody'. After this treatment he was to be returned to his native parish 'and there put himself to labour, like as a true man oweth to do'.

The 1531 Act failed because it assumed, wrongly, that there was enough employment available for those willing to work. The next piece of legislation came from the group of humanists who surrounded Thomas Cromwell, and it showed, as might have been expected, awareness of the fact that poverty was produced mainly by the organisation of society, and that the community must accept responsibility for the welfare of its poorer members. The Act ordered every parish to 'succour, find and keep all and every of the same poor people by way of voluntary and charitable alms . . . in such wise as none of them of very necessity shall be compelled to wander idly and go openly in begging'.

The assumption behind this Act was that every parish knew its own poor, but while this may have been true of rural parishes it was not so of towns. The weakness of Tudor paternalism was that it had very little information to go on. Cromwell realised the need for statistics and in 1538 made an attempt to establish accurate population figures by ordering all parishes to record baptisms, marriages and deaths; but he fell from power before he could enforce this, and his proposals were quietly dropped. Yet such information was essential if the problem of poverty was to be adequately dealt with, and at Coventry in 1547 and Norwich in 1570 censuses of the poor were carried out in an attempt to discover what caused poverty and how best it might be relieved.

These far-sighted measures were not made the basis of a national programme, for the landowners who dominated Parliament preferred more forceful methods. The notorious Statute of 1547 ordered that vagabonds were to be branded and enslaved for two years, and that if they attempted to escape from their master they should be enslaved for life or executed. This Statute was repealed in 1550—after Northumberland had taken over from Somerset—and the old remedy of punishing the idle poor and returning them to their parishes was revived. An Act of 1552 ordered the appointment in every parish of two collectors of alms, who were to 'gently ask and demand of every man and woman what they of their charity will be contented to give weekly towards the relief of the poor', but voluntary almsgiving failed to produce sufficient money and in 1563 compulsion was applied. Anyone refusing to contribute to funds for poor relief was to be sent before the Justices of the Peace who could, if they saw fit, levy his contribution by distraint and send him to prison to meditate upon the evil of his unsocial ways.

The Tudor system of poor relief was finally extended and defined by the Act of 1598 which was confirmed, with only minor changes, in 1601. The distinction between able-bodied and 'impotent' poor was maintained, and vagabonds were still to be whipped and sent back to their native parishes or else set to compulsory work in special Houses of Correction. As for the 'poor impotent people' they were to be provided by the parish with 'convenient Houses of Dwelling', and the money to build and maintain these was to be raised by a compulsory poor rate, collected by Overseers of the Poor, who were to be appointed by and responsible to the local Justices of the Peace. The Act also provided that if any parish was unable to raise sufficient money to meet its obligations, the Justices could order other parishes to assist it. This comprehensive poor law, the fruit of long discussion by Burghley, Whitgift and others, was gradually put into effect, and by the time the civil war broke out it was working in all except the remoter parts of the country. It was typical of Tudor paternalism in its combination of harsh punishment for those who broke out of the restraints imposed upon them and acceptance of responsibility for those who could not fend for themselves. It lasted, with constant modification, until the nineteenth century.[1]

Another example of Tudor paternalism was the great Statute of Artificers, or Apprentices, of 1563. This was closely linked with the problem of poverty, which it attempted to solve by mobilising the entire labour force of the country. All craftsmen were to serve an apprenticeship of seven years, during which time they were to be under the control of their master, while anyone who was not employed in a craft was to be set to work in agriculture. Justices of the Peace were empowered to regulate wage rates by annual assessments, and it seemed as though the problems of poverty, unemployment, vagabondage and rising prices would all be settled by this comprehensive Act. The reality, of course, was very different, for without statistical information and an army of civil servants such an ambitious programme could not possibly be made effective. Apprenticeship was enforced only in crafts which were short of men, or by gilds and companies which chose to take advantage of the letter of the law. It was not required for unskilled jobs, and judicial interpretation weakened the Act by excluding from its provisions all crafts which had sprung up after 1563. The only people who were forced to work in agriculture were pauper children, and as for wage assessments, although these were carried out well into the eighteenth century, they seem to have had little effect on wages and prices, which found their own level. The Statute of Artificers was significant as an attempt to translate humanist beliefs about the unity and interdependence of society into practical economic terms, but it also showed what limitations such a programme imposed on individual liberty. The property-owners who sat in Parliament were prepared to accept these limitations on the property-less, but when, in the seventeenth century, they were called on to subordinate their own freedom of action to the requirements of the state, they renounced the whole conception.

[1] For the important part played by individual and corporate charity in the attack on poverty, see below, p. 152.

A Changing Society. I: The Crown

The property-owners were themselves affected by the economic changes of the sixteenth century. The Crown, which was not only the biggest landowner but also the biggest buyer in the country, could not expand its income to keep pace with the rise in prices, and the independence which the endowments of Henry VII and Henry VIII had given it was being tightly circumscribed by the time Elizabeth died. New taxes on trade were needed, but such measures were impossible without the cooperation of Parliament, and the later Tudors relied instead on land sales which mortgaged the future to provide for the present. Ruthless exploitation of royal estates might have solved the financial problem, but the Crown had to set an example to other landlords, and the reorganisation which would have saved money would also have cut out many of the titles and offices which the monarch needed to reward his servants. A shrewd observer, writing in 1641, explained that the Duchy of Lancaster had never been annexed to the Exchequer because 'though it would have saved the King money, yet the chancellor's place and other places which were rewards for service would have been taken away. And it is as necessary for princes to have places of preferment to prefer servants of merit as money in their Exchequer.'

A Changing Society. II: The Nobility

For the aristocracy the price rise was simply one of a number of influences which combined to make them less important, politically, than the gentry. They remained the upper section of English society, but they were far from being a closed caste. Half the noble families existing when Henry VII came to the throne had become extinct in the male line by the time of Henry VIII's death, because of the natural failure of heirs, helped on by a number of attainders. This heavy wastage rate was obscured by the granting of new titles, and the majority of peerages created by Henry VIII were rewards for service to the Crown. The older nobility was not excluded from the administration, but if individual members were employed it was because the King wished to employ them and not because of any prescriptive right on their part. When the Duke of Norfolk, for instance, dared to suggest that the border lands in the north of England ought to be ruled by noblemen, the Council was quick to disillusion him. The King, said its reply, would choose whom he liked to serve him, and if he 'appoint the meanest man to rule there, is not his Grace's authority sufficient?' Norfolk's son, the Earl of Surrey, who resented, like his father, the decline of aristocratic power, died on the scaffold protesting that the King 'would deny the noble blood around him and employ none but mean creatures'.

The nobles were a small group, drawn, in the eighty years between Elizabeth's accession and the civil war, from just over one hundred and fifty families. They were great landowners but, like the Crown, they had an example to set, and only those who were desperate for money resorted to rack-renting and eviction. By 1570 most nobles had ceased to farm their lands directly, and preferred to let their estates to tenant farmers. The mineral rights, of course, remained theirs, and the nobility played a big part in the development of lead-mining and iron-smelting, but although they included among their ranks George Talbot, sixth Earl of Shrewsbury, whom one historian[1] describes as 'the most active entrepreneur in the country', they were not, generally speaking, prominent in the list of those capitalists who were expanding trade and establishing new industries.

The nobles looked to other sources for money—to royal favour, with all that it meant in the way of pensions and sinecures; to advantageous marriages; and to the profits of buccaneering expeditions. They needed as much money as they could lay their hands on, for they were addicted to conspicuous consumption. They built huge houses for themselves, spent vast sums of money on entertaining, extravagant clothes, jewellery, plate and numerous law suits. The days of armed retainers had gone, but households were still large and the Earl of Derby, for instance, had a hundred and fifty men on his pay-roll in 1590. Service to the Queen, leading an embassy or a military expedition, could eat up a small fortune, and even those who did not play a big part in public life had to spend heavily on educating their children, giving hospitality to their neighbours, and generally maintaining the extravagant display expected of a nobleman. Many nobles were heavily in debt—though this was not necessarily a sign of decline—and their failure to exploit their estates shifted the balance of economic and political power in favour of the gentry.

[1] Lawrence Stone in *The Nobility in Business*, p. 19 (included in a collection of papers under the general title of *The Entrepreneur*, published by the Economic History Society in April 1957).

A Changing Society. III: The Gentry and the Monastic Lands

The 'Rise of the Gentry' has become one of the clichés of Tudor and Stuart history and has caused so much dispute that it is difficult to say how much of the interpretation originally put forward by Tawney survives. Tawney, as an economic historian, was concerned to trace the links between the political preponderance of the Commons in the century after 1540 and the changes in landownership which had taken place during that period. He found that the gentry were indeed buying up land on a big scale, and that while the nobles remained the largest individual owners of land, the gentry, as a group, held more. Much of the argument that has raged over this delightfully convenient equating of economic and political power has been concerned with defining who exactly the gentry were. The difficulty arises from the fact that modern assumptions about social status are largely the reflection of an urbanised, industrial, fluid society, and the term 'middle class', for instance, with all that it implies about horizontal divisions, only came into current use in the second half of the eighteenth century when the Industrial Revolution was already destroying the old social order. Tudor and Stuart England was not, of course, a static society—wealth could bring a man into the upper ranks before, as after, the Industrial Revolution—but tradition played a big part in it. So also did vertical divisions, such as family ties, which could give to people of little wealth or apparent distinction a status that is extremely hard to describe.

Even if a 'gentleman' is defined simply as a substantial landowner who did not possess a peerage, it is still difficult to delimit the group to which he belonged. The most prominent figures are often the hardest to place. The Cecils, to take one example, started as smaller gentry, but rose into the aristocracy, and there were many other families that followed the same course. At the other end of the scale it is virtually impossible to distinguish between the lesser gentry and the upper yeomanry.

The amount of land that a family held at any time gives an indication of its status, but the sixteenth century saw enormous changes in landownership consequent upon the dissolution of the monasteries, and the historian is faced with the problem not only of finding out who was enriched by this process but also of where the money came from and whether those who profited belonged to any definable group. Not everybody who called himself a gentleman was prospering in this period. Recusancy might cripple one family, extravagance another, incompetence or sheer bad luck a third. In parts of the country—like Northamptonshire, for instance, which was ideal for sheep—agriculture alone was profitable enough for a landowner to flourish and extend his estates, while in other parts some extra source of income—the law, perhaps, or trade, or marriage to an heiress—was needed. Much depended, also, upon personal characteristics. One man might make a handsome profit out of holding public office while another would merely acquire extravagant habits that led him to live above his income: one man would run his estates with ruthless and profitable efficiency, while his neighbour would be held back by timidity, social conventions, tender-heartedness or simply lack of interest and ability.

The gentry were already important in local life and in Parliament before the dissolution of the monasteries took place, but the redistribution of land which followed the dissolution gave them a much bigger stake in the country and accelerated their rise to political predominance. Henry's lack of ready cash to pay for defence works was so crippling that part of the monastic property was sold off immediately while most of the remainder was disposed of in the ensuing hundred years. In the 1540s the standard purchase price was fixed at twenty times the estimated annual profit, and at this rate there were plenty of bidders. A third of the land went to peers and courtiers; and those who—like the Dukes of Norfolk and Suffolk, and the Earl of Hertford, future Lord Protector —happened to be in favour at the time added considerably to their estates. Some courtiers were lucky enough to get consolidated blocks of land which gave them territorial predominance in certain areas: Russell, who became the biggest landowner in the west country, was one example, and Wriothesley, who controlled Hampshire from the great house he built out of Titchfield Abbey, was another.

Officials of the Court of Augmentations also did well for themselves, eventually acquiring about one-seventh of the land disposed of, but there is no evidence of widespread speculation by groups of London business men. When Londoners did buy up land they were usually investing for themselves or acting as agents for country gentlemen who could not spare the time or energy to appear personally before the Court of Augmentations. It was these country gentlemen, medium-sized landowners whose families had often been long established in their counties, who bought up the greater part of the land that was available. Some merchants and lawyers took the opportunity to acquire estates and turn themselves into landed gentry, but it seems that, in the words of Professor Habakkuk, 'the number of new families established on the basis of monastic property was smaller than most discussions on the subject imply, and certainly small in relation to the total number of landed families'.[1]

Only a very small proportion of monastic property was given away. The rest was sold, but the new owner had to accept the financial obligations of a tenant-in-chief, and submit to wardship, relief, livery and all the other hated feudal incidents. The Crown profited from this anachronistic feudal revival, but only at the cost of a great deal of ill-will. By the time the chantry lands were disposed of, under Edward VI, the Crown was too weak to insist on its feudal rights, and many of the grants made in that reign conceded free ownership, without obligation. The new owners were not all hard-faced men determined to apply business techniques to their new estates. The majority were already landholders, but for this reason they knew the value of land, and since they had often borrowed money on a large scale in order to extend their estates they had to run them at a profit. Where monastic lands had been under-exploited they were now forced into the general pattern of bigger entry fines, higher rents, and enclosure.

Economically speaking, then, the gentry did not so much 'rise' as 'extend'. The new owners of monastic land were often already members of the Commons, or were to become so, and their attitude towards Mary's second Statute of Repeal shows how determined they were not to part with their acquisitions. Their possession of monastic property tied them to the protestant reformation and encouraged the spread of puritanism among them as the surest safeguard against a catholic restoration. It also made them aware of the substantial share they now had in their own country, and they were no longer content to play a secondary role in legislation and administration. By disposing of the monastic spoils to the gentry Henry VIII and his successors created a formidable rival to the monarchy itself.

The expansion of the gentry's authority is nowhere more apparent than in local administration. From Mary's reign onwards the nominal head of every county was the Lord-Lieutenant, usually a nobleman, but the effective rulers were the thirty or forty gentlemen who were appointed Justices of the Peace. They exercised a double function as judges and administrators. As judges they dealt with a variety of minor offences, and four times a year they came together at quarter sessions to

[1] H. J. Habakkuk, 'The Market for Monastic Property 1539-1630' (*Economic History Review*, Vol. 10, No. 3, April 1958).

FTSB

consider more serious crimes. The Justices were not lawyers, but they included men with legal training, of whom ('quorum') at least one had to be present at every meeting. These men formed an élite, but all the Justices, whether of the Quorum or not, held a respected and coveted position.

At their meetings the Justices acted as administrators, taking oaths of loyalty, binding apprentices, fixing wages and doing a hundred and one other things that were necessary for the smooth functioning of local government. In the Tudor period their duties were constantly increased and they were made responsible for enforcing the various poor laws and the complicated provisions of the Statute of Artificers. In time of rebellion they were expected to raise men in support of the Crown, and without the loyalty of the Justices no government could possibly have survived. The Council always found itself in difficulty when it called on the Justices to put into operation laws which ran counter to their own interests as landowners. Many Justices, for instance, turned a blind eye to enclosure, while in Elizabeth's reign the Justices of Lancashire were notorious for their refusal to impose fines on recusant gentry.

The Crown had limited powers of coercion, and could remove a man from the Commission of the Peace—a social humiliation which Justices were anxious to avoid. In the case of enclosures, special commissioners were occasionally appointed to supervise and supplement the work of the Justices, and the Privy Council was perpetually sending out letters of encouragement and rebuke. The surprising thing about this system is that it worked, and there are many examples of Justices loyally executing policies that were distasteful to them. This was because of the close relationship between them and the Council—a relationship that neither side was anxious to strain. One of the main reasons for the failure of the early Stuarts was that so many of their policies were unacceptable to the landowners that the co-operation of Justices of the Peace could no longer be taken for granted, and the Council lost the diplomatic touch that had smoothed over differences in the sixteenth century.

A Changing Society. IV: The Merchants and Overseas Expansion

'It is not our conquests,' said one seventeenth-century writer, 'but our commerce; it is not our swords, but our sails, that first spread the English name in Barbary, and thence came into Turkey, Armenia,

Muscovy, Arabia, Persia, India, China, and indeed over and about the world.' For the first half of the sixteenth century, however, there was little to suggest that the English would eventually take a leading part in the phenomenal expansion of western Europe over the oceans. English commercial energies were fully occupied in the lucrative cloth trade with the Netherlands. Raw wool was exported to Calais by the Company of the Staple, but heavy taxation had depressed this trade, and as the century wore on more and more English wool went to native manufacturers. The production of cloth was the big business of Tudor England, and the chief exporters were the Merchant Adventurers of London, who were granted a charter by Henry VII. Their overseas headquarters was Antwerp, from where English cloth found its way all over Europe, and as long as trade flourished between England and the Netherlands there was no capital to spare for oceanic ventures, nor was there any incentive to engage in them.

Henry VII, however, was concerned to expand English trade, since Customs duties gave him a share of the profits. By commercial treaties with the Baltic states he tried to break the stranglehold of the Hanseatic League of merchants, who had a big depot—the Steelyard—in London and enjoyed privileges greater even than those granted to English merchants. In this attempt he failed, because the Hanseatic League was well entrenched in the valuable Baltic trade, and without its goodwill the essential supply of naval stores would have been interrupted. The Hanse merchants remained important in English commerce until after 1550, when the increase in English shipping and the growth of continental rivals to the Hanse gradually eroded the profits and the privileged position of the League. Henry VII was more successful in breaking the monopoly of Venice in Mediterranean trade, and English merchants were building up a flourishing commerce with Italy when they, like the Venetians, were checked by the westward expansion of Turkish power.

Shortage of shipping was a hindrance to the growth of English commerce, and Henry attempted to remedy this at the very beginning of his reign by a Navigation Act which forbade merchants to use foreign ships when English ones were available. By encouraging the building of merchant ships, by creating the nucleus of a royal navy, and by claiming for his subjects a greater share of European trade, Henry VII set the pattern which the commercial development of England was to follow in the next two centuries. His prescience was also shown by his patronage of the Cabots, who in 1496 were granted letters patent 'to sail to all parts, regions and coasts of the eastern, western and northern sea' in the hope of finding a short sea route to those oriental lands in which spices and precious metals were to be found. John Cabot sighted Newfoundland and came back with glowing reports of the cod fisheries there, but he still believed that Asia lay on the far side of the Atlantic, and set out on a second expedition from which he never returned.

Under Henry VIII there was little exploring activity, for the cloth trade continued to flourish and Henry's money and energy were consumed in the vain dream of rebuilding an English empire in France. By 1550, however, the quality of English cloth was declining and over-production had glutted the European market. New outlets were needed, and the initiative was taken by the Duke of Northumberland, who claimed, at this late date, a share for England in the great adventure of overseas exploration that had so far been left largely to Portugal and Spain. Since the two catholic powers controlled the southern approaches to the orient English attention was concentrated on finding northern passages, particularly as the cold climate of these regions offered good prospects for the sale of woollen cloth. In 1554 Willoughby and Chancellor set sail to find a north-east passage to Cathay. They did not succeed, and Willoughby died in the attempt, but Chancellor made his way into the White Sea and from there journeyed to Moscow, where he appeared at the court of Ivan the Terrible. This epic journey inaugurated a flourishing trade between England and Russia, and led to the formation of the Muscovy Company.

The revival of English overseas expansion, which Northumberland had begun, bore fruit in the reign of Elizabeth. The cloth trade picked up again, particularly after the recoinage carried out by Cecil in 1560 at the suggestion of Sir Thomas Gresham, a prominent London merchant and the Queen's financial adviser, but the Netherlands market was far from stable even before the outbreak of rebellion in 1572. Elizabeth's accession took place at a time when the price rise and unemployment had so seriously upset the English economy that Cecil planned the authoritarian solution sketched out in the Statute of Artificers. It also coincided with a fundamental change in the European power pattern. The long struggle between Valois France and Habsburg Spain was virtually over by 1560, and Spain had emerged as the strongest power in Europe. The religious and political ambitions of Philip II were a threat to England, and they produced a reaction which drove English seamen to infringe the Spanish monopoly of the New World and to challenge Spanish supremacy at sea.

In 1562 John Hawkins set out on the first of three voyages in which he collected slaves from the West African coast and shipped them to the Spanish colonies in America. The Spanish government resented this heretic invasion of the New World, even though it was a peaceful one, and on his third voyage Hawkins only just escaped alive from a surprise attack made on his ships while he was sheltering in the harbour of San Juan de Ulloa. This news reached England at a time when Elizabeth was putting pressure on Philip in hopes of persuading him to moderate his aggressive policy in the Netherlands. The only effective way in which she could show Philip that her wishes must not be lightly disregarded was by attacks on Spanish shipping, and she encouraged— and sometimes contributed money to—the many expeditions which set out for the New World. Most famous of these was Drake's ex-expedition of 1577. He passed through the Magellan Straits, sailed up the west coast of America where he captured a heavily laden treasure-ship, and returned to England by way of the Indian Ocean and Cape of Good Hope. Not only did he have the glory of being the first English circumnavigator; he also gave back to the shareholders in the expedition a profit estimated at nearly five thousand per cent. The desire to emulate his exploits and to get rich quickly sent many more English sailors to the Spanish Main and created a legend that haunted, and in many ways distorted, the politics of Stuart England.

English seamen were short of bases in the New World, and the first attempts at colonisation were designed to provide these. Sir Walter Ralegh obtained a patent for an American colony in 1584, and in the following year a settlement was established on Roanoke Island in the area that Ralegh christened, in honour of his Queen, Virginia. The colony managed to survive, short of supplies, only until the following year, when Drake, returning from one of his voyages, took the settlers home with him. A second attempt in 1587 was no more successful, for although the colonists were once again established on Roanoke they were then deserted for several years, since all English shipping was needed in home waters to face the threat of the Armada. Infant colonies could not, unfortunately, survive without supplies and reinforcements from the mother country, and by the time Grenville returned to Roanoke in 1591 the settlers had disappeared without trace.

Colonisation was encouraged in Elizabeth's reign by writers and politicians who held that England was overpopulated and that the best way of dealing with the unemployment problem was by exporting surplus labour. Richard Hakluyt put this point of view strongly in his *Discourse of the Western Planting*, published in 1584. He was one of a number of writers whose aim was to make the English aware of the glittering prizes that waited for them across the ocean. The last vestiges of a continental empire had disappeared with the loss of Calais: England's main task now, said Hakluyt, should be to close the gap which the initiative of the catholic powers had opened in overseas exploration, and to claim at least part of the profits of the New World for England. To inspire his countrymen he wrote a magnificent history of the *Principal Navigations, Voyages and Discoveries of the English Nation*, which was published, appropriately enough, in the year following the defeat of the Armada.

By the time Elizabeth died no English colony had been successfully established in the New World, but English sailors were to be seen in all quarters of the earth. As the Hanseatic League declined, the English Eastland Company took its place in trade with the Baltic, while the Muscovy Company built up a flourishing trade with Russia. In the Mediterranean, English commerce revived in the last decades of the sixteenth century and Leghorn became a great market for cloth. Further east the merchants of the Levant Company took over much of the trade of Venice, now in decline, and transmitted to the western world the spices and riches of the East. For this, however, they were dependent upon the uncertain goodwill of the Turks, and they were already trying to establish direct communication with India and the Spice Islands by sea. Vasco da Gama had shown as early as 1499 that this could be done, and Drake's voyages had proved that English seamen were just as good as Portuguese ones. The Levant merchants therefore took a prominent part in the discussions that led, in 1599, to the fateful decision 'to set forth a voyage this present year to the East Indies and other the Islands and Countries thereabouts, and there to make trade'. On the last day of 1600 the Queen issued a royal charter to these adventurers and thereby began the official career of the East India Company.

The expansion of English trade was accompanied, though not equalled, by an expansion of industry. Paper and gunpowder mills were established, and English cannon became so famous that a profitable export trade was built up in them. Improvements in ventilating and drainage systems made possible the increased exploitation of mineral resources, and this was particularly true of coal. Elizabethan

England was short of timber, much of which was consumed by the iron industry of the Kent and Sussex Weald. As timber prices soared, coal became more popular, and 'sea-coals' from Newcastle were poisoning the London atmosphere long before the Queen's reign was over.

London was the centre of English commerce, and 'outports' such as Bristol and Southampton declined in the sixteenth century. By 1600 more than three-quarters of all English trade went through London, and the capital city had become a magnet, attracting to itself rich and poor from all over the country, as well as religious refugees from the Continent. The Privy Council was alarmed at the perpetual increase in the city's population and tried to check it by forbidding new building, but nothing could hold back the growth of London, which was pressing up against its medieval walls and extending beyond them towards Westminster, Smithfield and Shoreditch. The rulers of this wealthy community were the Lord Mayor and Aldermen who were drawn from the more important livery companies, such as the Mercers, Goldsmiths and Drapers, and one of the sights of London was the Royal Exchange, built by Sir Thomas Gresham in 1568 as a place where merchants could congregate and do business.

The dominance of London was felt—and often resented—throughout England, and one writer commented bitterly that 'no gentleman can be content to have either cap, coat, doublet, hose or shirt made in his country, but they must have their gear from London'. One reason for this was that the political unification of England, which the Tudors had carried out, had been accompanied by an economic unification. In spite of poor communications traders were travelling all over the country, knitting even the remoter counties into the general pattern, and as overseas trade increased London became a huge warehouse from which foreign products were distributed throughout the length and breadth of England.

The flow of trade slowly eroded local autonomies, and it also blurred the lines of division that cut off one section of society from another. Many of the most successful merchants came from the poorer, underprivileged groups, but they, or at least their descendants, were accepted into the upper ranks. Queen Elizabeth herself was descended from Sir Geoffrey Boleyn, who had been Lord Mayor of London in the fifteenth century, and a number of the leading figures in Stuart England, including Oliver Cromwell, John Hampden and Danby, were grandchildren of London aldermen. The tension between tradition and innovation, stability and fluidity, accounts for the vigour—exploding at times into violence—of English society in the sixteenth and seventeenth centuries.

The paternalism of a great deal of Tudor legislation sprang from the belief that the hierarchical structure of society was a reflection of that divine order which was assumed to hold the universe in place. But to many merchants, particularly those who had risen from little or nothing, paternalism was anathema. They believed that God's will, like that of the King, took no account of rank, and that society as a whole should help its more unfortunate members to help themselves; if God wished to keep a man down, He would do so, but human institutions must not be allowed to stand in the way of those whom God wished to advance. Paternalism produced the poor laws, but this generalised form of relief was no more acceptable to the merchants than indiscriminate monastic almsgiving had been. They set an example by contributing more than half of the vast sums of money provided for private charities which were, in the long run, probably more effective than state aid to the poor. One historian[1] has estimated that this voluntary giving accounted for more than ninety per cent of the total volume of poor relief in the hundred and fifty years before the Restoration, while taxes raised under the provisions of the various poor laws contributed a mere seven per cent. These figures give a striking indication of the incentive to self-help that was fostered by the merchants and that ran counter to the assumptions behind the official, paternalist attitude.

Private charity was not confined to poor relief. It also served to remodel the entire educational system of England. Many schools disappeared as a result of the dissolution of the monasteries and chantries, and although some of these were refounded after Henry VIII's death, his son scarcely deserves his reputation as the patron and benefactor of grammar schools. On the other hand the value of the education given in the older foundations may easily be exaggerated: chantry priests often only taught one or two children to serve at Mass, abbey schools were concerned mainly with training choristers, and even where grammar schools existed they stuck to a medieval curriculum.

Colet had been so dissatisfied with the failure of the new learning to remodel English education that he founded St Paul's School to set an example. But his lead was not followed until the stranglehold of the Church on education had been broken. The second half of the sixteenth century witnessed the founding or re-endowment of a large number of

[1] W. K. Jordan in *Philanthropy in England*. His figures have been challenged by a number of economic historians.

schools by city companies or individual merchants, and in Elizabeth's reign alone £140,000 was contributed for education, over half of it for grammar schools. These schools were usually placed under the control of local bodies, they had full-time schoolmasters, and their curriculum showed at last the influence of Erasmus and the new learning.

The universities also benefited, and the sharp increase in the number of undergraduates from aristocratic and gentry families encouraged a shift in emphasis from theology to the classics. Oxford and Cambridge became training grounds where men were prepared for the service of the state as well as the Church, and the unlettered nobleman or gentleman, who had been so common in the Middle Ages, became the despised exception. As numbers increased, more colleges were needed, and men who had done well out of destroying the old order would often assist in creating the new one: a former treasurer of Augmentations, for instance, who had spent his life disposing of confiscated monastic property, used part of his gains to found Trinity College, Oxford, while a former general surveyor of the same court established Emmanuel College at Cambridge.

Protestantism and Capitalism

Religion provided the impulse to private charity. Poverty and illiteracy had been widespread in pre-Reformation England, but the benefactors of the sixteenth and seventeenth centuries were determined to prove that in a protestant society such evils need not exist. Protestantism, particularly in its extreme form of puritanism, spread rapidly among the merchant classes of England and Europe, and the pursuit of wealth was frequently inspired by fervent anti-catholicism. This did not mean that there were no rich men except protestants. Some of the earliest capitalists in the western world were the Italian financiers who handled papal revenues in the late Middle Ages, while catholic France had given birth to the enormously rich Jacques Cœur and catholic Germany to the wealthy banking family of Fugger.

Protestant communities were not necessarily rich: Scotland, for instance, became strongly Calvinist, but remained poor and backward throughout the entire Tudor and Stuart period. The wealth of English and Dutch merchants came primarily from the fact that their countries were at the centre of the new trading world, but protestantism gave them freedom to exploit their opportunities without fear of censure. The leading reformers—Luther, Calvin and Zwingli—were as strict

F*

as St Thomas Aquinas in their condemnation of usury, but the core of protestantism was to be found in the appeal to individual conscience and the assertion that each man was responsible for his own salvation. The rejection of ecclesiastical authority weakened the barriers which custom and religion had erected against the pursuit of wealth, and the individual was left free to work out his own values.

The protestant emphasis was upon the motives that inspired actions rather than on the actions themselves. 'Good works', in the catholic sense of saying a certain number of prayers, going on a pilgrimage or performing some other outward action, were dismissed as useless superstitions. Salvation, it was held, came from the heart, and if the motive was pure it purified the action. As John Donne, the poet who became Dean of St Paul's, said in one of his sermons: 'to have some thing to do, to do it, and then to rejoice in having done it: to embrace a calling, to perform the duties of that calling, to joy and rest in the peaceful testimony of having done so: this is christianly done; Christ did it. Angelically done; angels do it. Godly done; God does it.'

The protestant emphasis upon the holiness of everyday life extended to money-making which was, after all, one of the main occupations of men in the sixteenth as in other centuries. But the pomp of the world, which had corrupted the Roman Church, was unacceptable to puritans. They advocated a sober, thrifty life, devoid of ostentation and sometimes so plain that it was harshly philistine, yet by practising these virtues many puritans became wealthy. They opposed the corruptive influence of money by contributing generously to charity, but since they believed in predestination it was but a short step to assume that God, who had elected certain of His creatures to eternal blessedness, had given them prosperity as a sign of their election. It also followed that poverty might well be a sign of divine displeasure. Poor men must be given every chance to improve their position, but those who remained at the bottom of the ladder must have been put there by God—or so at least it seemed to many puritans—as an awful warning of the consequences of sin and as a foretaste of damnation. This puritan sanctification of worldly success, even though it was tempered by the creation of charitable institutions, was opposed to the Tudor and early Stuart assumption that the state, divinely guided through the lay ruler, was an organic society in which every member had his essential contribution to make. The tension between these conflicting ideologies was the background to the political and religious disputes of the early seventeenth century, that eventually exploded into civil war.

8

Ireland and Scotland in the Sixteenth Century

IRELAND

Henry VII and Kildare

WHEN Henry VII came to the throne only the Pale, the small area around Dublin, was under direct control of a royal Deputy. The rest of the country was in the hands of great families, chief among which were the Butlers and Fitzgeralds, descended from the Anglo-Norman adventurers of the twelfth century. The Lord-Deputy in 1485 was the Earl of Kildare, one of the leading Geraldines (Fitzgeralds), who had held the same office under Edward IV and was a Yorkist sympathiser. Henry Tudor would no doubt have liked to remove him from office, but there was no obvious person to put in his place, and his control of Leinster, as well as his connexions with many of the leading Irish families, made him extremely powerful.

Kildare's loyalty was tested early on in the new reign when Lambert Simnel landed at Dublin in May 1487, claiming to be the Earl of Warwick, the Yorkist heir to the throne. Kildare and his associates were apparently taken in by the pretender, Simnel was crowned King as Edward VI in Dublin Cathedral, and an Irish contingent sailed with the Yorkist expedition to England. The revolt came to an end at the bloody battle of Stoke, and Henry had to decide how to deal with Ireland. Full-scale invasion would have been far too expensive an operation, since Ireland had little to offer an English King. Its chief importance was as a base from which the enemies of the Tudor dynasty could launch their attacks, and all that Henry required was an assurance from the Irish lords that they would remain loyal to him. Sir Richard Edgcumbe was sent to Ireland with five hundred men to administer an oath of loyalty. Kildare took this and remained in office as Lord-Deputy, but his acceptance did not spring from a change of heart and when the next pretender, Perkin Warbeck, appeared in 1491, Kildare accepted him as King.

Although Warbeck soon quitted Ireland to try his fortune in Scotland, Henry could not ignore the fact that he might return and establish himself as King there. A small English army was therefore despatched to Ireland and in 1492 Henry dismissed Kildare from the Deputyship, replacing him by an adherent of the rival Butler family. The Earl, who had used his office to consolidate his power, made his way at last to England, where he pleaded for Henry's mercy. He was well received at Henry's court, but with Warbeck still threatening invasion the King could not afford to trust any Irishman and he therefore appointed a member of his household, Sir Edward Poynings, as Deputy and sent him off to Ireland with a thousand men. Poynings summoned a Parliament, which met in December 1494 and passed 'Poynings' Law' by which no Irish Parliament was, in future, to meet until the King of England had given his approval to the summons and had scrutinised all proposed legislation.

Poynings achieved the main object of his mission by securing Ireland against Warbeck, and when the pretender arrived off the Irish coast and attempted to take Waterford he was beaten off. But the cost of keeping an army in Ireland was too much for Henry, and once the danger was past he restored Kildare to the Deputyship. The Earl remained ruler of Ireland—or, rather, of the Pale and the Fitzgerald sphere of influence outside it—until his death in 1513, when he was succeeded by his son. After the failure of the two Yorkist conspiracies he was content to remain loyal to the Tudors, and Henry left him largely free to govern as he wished. From the King's point of view it was an economical solution, but it left the Irish leaders apparently as powerful as they had been at the beginning of his reign.

Henry VIII and the Kingdom of Ireland

The process of unification, for which Henry VIII and his ministers were responsible, was bound eventually to affect Ireland. The Earl of Kildare, son of Henry VII's Deputy, was left in office until 1519, but frequent complaints were made about his arrogance and the way in which he used his office to advance the interests of his family. Matters were brought to a head when Kildare was accused of intriguing with the King's foreign enemies, and the decision was taken to replace him by an English noble. The Earl of Surrey, given the title of Lord-Lieutenant, set out with five hundred men and orders to establish effective royal rule throughout Ireland, to unify and anglicise the Irish Church, and to make sure that taxes were collected. But such a policy demanded, as the first Tudor had discovered, a great deal more money than the English treasury could afford. Surrey pleaded for more support: 'I and the treasurer', he wrote, 'with all the captains of the King's retinues here have not amongst us all £20 in money', and he estimated that six thousand men and £10,000 a year would be the minimum required to

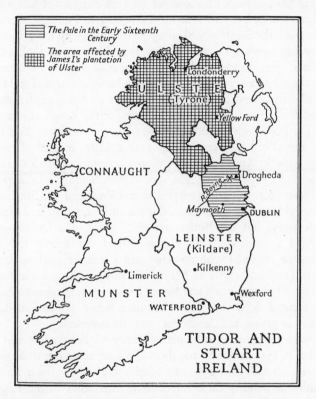

carry out his task. Rather than face this, Henry returned to a policy of indirect rule. In 1522 Kildare's rival, the Earl of Ormonde, head of the house of Butler, was appointed Deputy. Kildare himself remained under arrest in London.

For the next ten years the Deputyship and other high offices alternated between Fitzgeralds and Butlers as the King tried to play one group off against another. Kildare was too powerful for this policy to be entirely successful, but the Butler challenge did reduce his authority, and the Geraldines in Leinster were increasingly restive at what they regarded as an English attempt to undermine their influence. In 1529 Henry decided that the moment had come to try direct intervention once again. He appointed his young son, the Duke of Richmond, Lord-Lieutenant of Ireland, and the following year he sent over Sir William Skeffington, a soldier and administrator of the Poynings type, as Lord-Deputy. Skeffington did his job well, but his very independence of Irish connexions made him susceptible to the intrigues of Kildare, who had been allowed to return to his native land as a gesture of concilia-tion towards the Geraldines. Skeffington was faced with the old problem of needing more men and money than Henry could afford, and the King again abandoned direct rule and made Kildare his Deputy.

By this time, however, the relationship between England and Ireland had radically altered, because of the English rejection of papal authority. Ireland had always been a possible base for the King's enemies, and with the Pope and the Emperor plotting to overthrow him Henry could not afford to take risks. In 1534 Kildare, accused of being in league with the King's many enemies, was summoned to England and imprisoned in the Tower. His son, 'Silken Thomas', called on the Geraldines to revolt and appealed to the Pope and the Emperor for military aid. It looked as though English authority in Ireland would be blown away, but the Butlers remained loyal, and Dublin—which depended upon trade with England—held out against the rebels. Skeffington returned with an army and a train of artillery, stormed 'Silken Thomas's' castle at Maynooth and slaughtered most of the garrison. Thomas himself and five of his uncles were taken to England and executed as traitors. Since Thomas's father, the Earl of Kildare, had died in prison, the Geraldines were left leaderless.

Now that Ireland lay at his mercy Henry might have imposed direct rule, but in 1535 he was far too short of money to be able to do this. He returned, instead, to a policy of conciliating the chieftains. In return for titles of nobility these surrendered their lands to the King and received them back again as fiefs, to be held by military-tenure. They were also given a share of monastic lands, for an Irish Parliament, which met after the suppression of the Geraldine revolt, passed all the Reformation statutes, including those which ordered the dissolution of the monasteries. Further changes were made in the structure of Irish life. Private armies were declared illegal, English law and customs were imposed upon the whole country, and in June 1541 the culmination of this policy was marked by the Irish Parliament's recognition of Henry as King of Ireland.

Elizabeth and the Irish Rebellion

Henry VIII's solution of the Irish problem worked well on the surface, although Irish revenues never covered all the expenses of administration. There was no great love for the Pope in Ireland, and most of the bishops as well as the landowners accepted the Act of Supremacy. When, in 1542, Jesuit missionaries arrived in Ulster they met such a chilly welcome that they sailed on to Scotland. The doctrinal changes of Edward VI's reign were, however, far less acceptable to the Irish, and the attitude of the clergy was in general similar to that of the Archbishop of Armagh, who had supported royal supremacy, but declared that 'he would never be a bishop where the holy Mass was abolished'. The accession of catholic Mary as Queen was therefore welcomed, but Ireland remained only nominally under English control and the clash of family interests continued to dominate Irish affairs.

The flood of Marian exiles returning from the Continent after Elizabeth became Queen helped to establish a living, protestant Church in England, but the same was not true of Ireland. There the effect of the Henrician reformation had been to destroy the Catholic Church without putting anything in its place, and Ireland became a fertile field for the activities of catholic missionaries as England swung further and further away from the old faith. Missionaries arrived in increasing numbers during Elizabeth's reign and by their activities they not only revived the Roman Church in Ireland but also fostered something like national sentiment and linked it, inextricably, with loyalty to the Pope.

Elizabeth's policy in Ireland was defensive—she was concerned only to ensure that the country should not be used as a jumping-off point by her enemies. Trouble was already brewing in Munster, where the Fitzgeralds and Butlers were, as usual, at loggerheads, and the Deputy's support of the Butlers drove James Fitzmaurice Fitzgerald into open rebellion in 1569. Fitzmaurice appealed to the Pope and the King of Spain for help, but by the time their meagre supplies arrived the rebellion had collapsed. Fitzmaurice fled to the Continent and returned to Ireland in 1579 with a mixed force of Spanish and Italian troops, financed by the Pope. For several years revolt smouldered in Munster, since Elizabeth could not afford a major expedition, and Spanish men and money kept the rebels going. Not until 1583 was

Munster finally subdued, after a ruthless campaign which brought starvation to the Irish peasants, whom Spenser described 'creeping forth upon their hands, for their legs could not bear them. They looked like anatomies of death. They spake like ghosts crying out of their graves. They did eat the dead carrions, happy where they could find them.'

Henry VIII had introduced English law and customs into Ireland, but this had not anglicised the Irish or made them more law-abiding. Under Mary the experiment had been tried of settling English colonists in Ireland, and although this and a similar experiment in Ulster early in Elizabeth's reign were failures, the idea of replacing the disloyal and turbulent Irish by English citizens was too attractive to be lightly abandoned. Ireland was, in any case, a suitable field for English colonising activities, nearer at hand than Virginia and strategically more important. Burghley and Ralegh therefore drew up a plan, based upon Ralegh's proposals for a settlement in the New World, by which four hundred thousand acres of Munster were confiscated and distributed to English tenants. Settlement was a slow business as famine, disease and incompetence took their toll, but it was extended to Connaught and gradually undermined the Irish way of life. It seemed as though Elizabeth would complete the work that Henry VIII had begun of incorporating Ireland into the English sphere of administration and influence.

Only Ulster stood out against this English infiltration. The leader there was Hugh O'Neill, Earl of Tyrone, who built up as powerful a position as that which the Fitzgeralds had earlier established in Kildare. O'Neill demanded liberty of worship for Roman Catholics and the preservation of chieftain rule, and when the Queen refused to grant these he appealed to Philip of Spain for help. Philip sent money and also prepared an armada which sailed in 1596, in spite of the combined attack which Howard and Essex made on Cadiz in that year. The armada was turned back by storms before ever it reached Ireland, but the prospect of foreign aid ignited Irish nationalism and produced a major rebellion. English settlers were driven out of Munster in the south, while in the north an English army was crushingly defeated by O'Neill at the battle of the Yellow Ford. Only the Pale and some of the coastal towns remained loyal to the Crown.

Elizabeth, who had already spent a million pounds on Ireland to little effect, was reluctant to pour more money away on a military campaign. But the threat of an independent Ireland under Spanish patronage was too real to ignore, and Essex, appointed Lord-Lieutenant in 1599, was despatched with about twenty thousand men—the largest army ever to be sent to Ireland in the Tudor period. Essex's campaign, however, was a failure, for the Earl was far more concerned with his enemies at the Queen's Court than with those who faced him in Ireland. He could not risk defeat, yet he did not have enough men to make a swift victory certain. Instead of fighting O'Neill he negotiated a truce which left the Irish leader in control of Ulster, and he promptly returned to England to put his case to the Queen.

Elizabeth refused to recognise the truce, and replaced her tarnished favourite by Charles Blount, Lord Mountjoy. He avoided pitched battles and waged a war of attrition instead, destroying the rebels' supplies and consolidating his gains by establishing powerful garrisons. By the autumn of 1601 Munster had been pacified and Mountjoy was ready to deal with O'Neill in Ulster, when news reached him that four thousand Spanish troops had landed at Kinsale. The success of Mount-joy's pacification was demonstrated by the marked lack of support given to these 'liberators', and when O'Neill marched south in an attempt to link up with them he was heavily defeated. Early in 1602 the Spaniards surrendered and were allowed to return home. With them went the last hopes of the rebels, and in March 1603 O'Neill laid down his arms.

O'Neill's surrender completed the Tudor conquest of Ireland. He was treated generously and allowed to keep his lands, as were most of the other Irish lords, but they had to accept the suzerainty of the English Crown. Their authority was slowly replaced by that of the English common law, supplemented by the conciliar Court of Castle Chamber in Dublin, but no change took place in religion. The stubborn Irish adherence to the old faith was a perpetual challenge to English supremacy and a source of conflict in the future. Just as fundamental, in the long run, was the effect of Irish resistance on the constitutional history of England, for as Dietz has commented: 'If the royal necessity of appealing for subsidies to Parliament at certain intervals was the chief factor in maintaining the vigorous life of that institution in Tudor times, how greatly England is indebted for her constitutional development and freedom from autocracy to the royal determination and necessity to subdue the Irish to English rule'.[1]

[1] F. C. Dietz, *English Public Finance, 1558-1642*, p. 48.

SCOTLAND

James IV

The principal difference between Scotland and Ireland in the sixteenth century was that Scotland had been for many years a united kingdom under the rule of its own kings. James IV, who came to the throne in 1488, was typical of the 'new monarchs' in the way in which he used the royal council to enforce his will throughout his entire kingdom, and called men to serve him regardless of their descent. James was an ambitious ruler, determined that his country should play a more prominent role in European politics, and he seized on Perkin Warbeck as an instrument for this purpose. But if James hoped to make Warbeck a puppet king he was disappointed, and the failure of his attempted invasion of England encouraged him to come to terms with Henry VII. The truce of 1499 was extended into a 'perpetual peace' in 1502, and in the following year James married Henry's eldest daughter, Margaret.

Peace between the two kingdoms lasted for the rest of Henry's VII's reign, but the accession of the hot-blooded and ambitious Henry VIII in 1509 transformed the situation. Henry was contemptuous of the Scots and determined to take up again the struggle with France, to whom the Scots were bound by the 'auld alliance'. By 1512 England and France were at war, and Henry crossed the Channel to lead his armies in person, leaving the defence of England to the Earl of Surrey. in August 1513 James IV began his advance towards the south, but the Scottish invasion was not unexpected and Surrey had made good preparations. The two armies met at Flodden, south-west of Berwick, early in September, and in a hard-fought battle that lasted well into the night the Scots were overwhelmed. James IV himself was killed, with the flower of the Scottish nobility and about ten thousand of his troops, and the northern kingdom was left in the hands of a boy king, James V.

James V

Henry's sister Margaret, who had taken as her second husband a Scottish nobleman, the Earl of Angus, was regent of Scotland, but she was so unpopular with Angus's enemies that in 1515 they took up arms and drove her across the border into England. The Duke of Albany, heir to the throne, who had recently arrived from France, was named as regent in her place. Henry VIII schemed for Albany's removal, since he did not want a hostile Scotland threatening him at a time when he was planning a renewal of his war against France. Throughout 1522 there was trouble on the border, and the following year an English army carried out a series of savage raids. Albany tried to rally the Scots lords and lead them against England, but fear of another Flodden paralysed effective action and in 1524 Albany returned, disgusted, to France. This left the way clear for Margaret and the anglophil group of lords who, in 1524, declared that James V was of age and therefore capable of ruling in his own right.

The Reformation did not have such a profound effect upon Anglo-Scottish relations as on those between England and Ireland, but it complicated the situation by making France the champion of Scottish catholics. Henry VIII had tried to persuade his Scottish nephew to join in the attack upon the Church, but James remained loyal to the old faith, particularly as he had been allowed to divert to secular purposes some of the revenues of the Church. In January 1537 he married a French princess, and after her untimely death he took as his second wife Mary, daughter of the Duke of Guise, the head of one of the greatest catholic houses in France. Henry VIII was faced with the unpleasant prospect of a francophil catholic kingdom on his northern frontier just at the moment when he was planning to invade France. Since persuasion had failed he had recourse to force, and in 1542 the Duke of Norfolk led a punitive expedition into Scotland. When the Scots counter-attacked in November 1542 they were heavily defeated at Solway Moss, and James, who was already ill, did not long survive the disgrace. In December he died, leaving as heir his baby daughter, Mary, only a week old, who now became Queen of Scots.

English Intervention in Scotland

The death of James V brought to power the Earl of Arran, leader of the anglophil protestant party among the Scottish nobles. Henry saw an opportunity of extending Tudor sovereignty to Scotland, as he had already done to Wales and Ireland, and negotiations were set on foot for a marriage between Mary and Henry's heir, Prince Edward. These negotiations were successfully concluded in 1543, and the terms were formally set out in the Treaty of Greenwich. But Henry's arrogance, particularly when it accompanied a proposal that would mean the eventual end of Scottish independence, was resented in Scotland, and Arran was under strong pressure to renounce the agreement. Eventually he gave way, and admitted Cardinal Beaton, leader of the francophil, catholic party, to his council. Shortly afterwards the Treaty of Greenwich was denounced and the alliance with France reaffirmed.

Henry showed his fury at what he regarded as deception by sending Hertford with an army into Scotland, with orders to devastate the country. Hertford did his job well and left Edinburgh and Leith in flames behind him as he returned to England. The immediate effect of this vengeful policy was to close Scottish ranks against the aggressor, but the division between catholics and protestants was too deep to be permanently healed. John Knox was the leader of the protestants, whom he had imbued with his own particular band of Calvinist fanaticism, and he looked to England for support. While an English fleet cruised off the Scottish coast the protestants could maintain themselves in power, but when, following Henry's death, the ships were withdrawn, the catholic party, supported by French arms, quickly triumphed. Knox himself was sent to the galleys and many of his followers were imprisoned. Hertford, now Lord Protector Somerset, gathered supplies for a counter-stroke. In September 1547 he invaded Scotland with an army of twenty thousand men, supported by a powerful fleet, and routed the Scots at the battle of Pinkie. It was, however, a hollow victory. The defeated Scots were driven into the arms of France and only a permanent military occupation of the whole of Scotland, on a scale far greater than anything England could afford, would have prevented this. Somerset's expensive expedition had served to show only that Scotland could never be effectively conquered: the best policy for England was to exploit the differences between the Scottish leaders and wait for the anglophil party to return to power.

The English army remained in Scotland until 1549, when Somerset withdrew it for use in open war against France. The Scots, meanwhile, had agreed that their young Queen should marry the heir to the French throne, and in July 1548 Mary was sent across the Channel to the court of St Germain. For the next ten years Scotland was under French influence, particularly after 1554 when the Queen Mother, Mary of Guise, was appointed regent, and many of the highest positions in Church and state were given to Frenchmen. The consequence was growing dissatisfaction among the Scots, who came to detest the French so heartily that even the prospect of English influence seemed preferable.

The protestants increased in strength and profited from their appeal to national pride, that 'the liberty of this our native country may remain free from the bondage and tyranny of strangers'. In 1557 the leading protestant nobles signed an agreement to form 'The Congregation of Christ', to work for the establishment of the reformed religion in Scotland, and they were enormously strengthened when, in 1559, John Knox returned from exile.

By the time Knox returned a protestant sovereign was once again ruling in England. Elizabeth and her chief minister Cecil might have ignored the appeal of their Scottish co-religionists had it not been that the political situation made English intervention imperative, for in July 1559 Mary's husband became King of France. It looked as though France and Scotland would be united, and the danger to England was increased by the fact that Mary was the catholic claimant to the English throne and had publicly asserted her title.

In Scotland the Queen-Regent had decided to take action against the protestants who were a threat to her rule, but her military preparations drove the Lords of the Congregation to open rebellion. They occupied Edinburgh and appealed to England for help, while Mary of Guise remained in a strongly fortified position at Leith, waiting for French reinforcements to arrive. Urged on by Cecil, Elizabeth ordered an English fleet to cut the sea link between Scotland and France, and also issued instructions for assembling an army. By January 1560 the English fleet was anchored in the Forth, and a few months later an English army crossed the border. For Elizabeth the Scottish campaign was simply an extension of the operations against France, and the Treaty of Berwick, signed in February 1560, said nothing about religion, and committed the Scots lords to accept Mary's rule as long as Mary recognised their liberties. But English intervention, although far from glorious where military operations were concerned, was decisive, even in the religious sphere. In July 1560, by which time the Queen-Regent was dead, the Treaty of Edinburgh committed both France and England to withdraw their forces from Scotland, and left the religious question to be decided by a Scottish parliament. This met in August 1560 and marked the triumph of the Reformation in Scotland. The authority and jurisdiction of the Pope were abolished, Mass was forbidden and orders were given to enforce a protestant confession of faith.

In December 1560 Francis II died, and in the following year his widow, Mary, returned to her Scottish kingdom. She found a very different situation from the one she had left twelve years before. Then the catholic Scots were fighting for their religion and their national independence against English invaders, but now the French were regarded as the main threat to Scottish independence, and the government of the country was in the hands of the protestant, anglophil group. Mary, although a catholic, agreed to maintain the reformed religion, but the question of the Queen's marriage was a major problem, as in England. The protestants were afraid that she would marry one of her own religion, and as Knox told the Scottish parliament, 'whensoever the nobility of Scotland, professing the Lord Jesus, consents that an infidel—and all papists are infidels—shall be head to your sovereign, ye do so far as in ye lieth to banish Christ Jesus from this realm, ye bring God's vengeance upon the country, a plague upon yourself, and perchance ye shall do small comfort to your sovereign'.

Elizabeth was as anxious as Knox that Mary should marry a protestant, and put forward her own favourite, Robert Dudley, Earl of Leicester. Mary declared her willingness to marry Leicester if Elizabeth agreed to recognise her as heir to the English throne, but this was a condition that Elizabeth found totally unacceptable. The Queen of Scots therefore turned her attentions to Lord Darnley, who was, like herself, a great-grandchild of Henry VII. When the English Privy Council heard about this, it protested that a marriage between Mary and Darnley 'would be unmeet, unprofitable, and perilous to the amity between the queens and both realms'. The Councillors were no doubt thinking that such a match would double Mary's claim to the English throne and seem like a direct challenge to Elizabeth, but there was nothing they could do about it. Once Mary was set on a course she never allowed political considerations to divert her, and in July 1565 she married Darnley.

The protestant lords, led by the Earl of Moray and supported by Elizabeth, rose in rebellion against Mary, but the Queen and her husband gathered their followers and chased the rebels across the border into England. The marriage, however, did not go well, for Darnley was insufferably arrogant and stupid, as Mary quickly discovered. She turned for comfort to her secretary, the Italian David Rizzio, who was rumoured to be her lover. Darnley, wounded in his pride, plotted with Mary's enemies, the protestant lords, who promised to accept him as king-consort if, in return, he would admit them to the council and get rid of Rizzio.

The first part of the plan was put into operation in March 1566, when Darnley and his associates dragged Rizzio from the Queen's presence and stabbed him to death. Shortly afterwards Moray and the exiles returned.

The Queen never forgave Darnley, even though she dissembled her feelings. In June 1566 she gave birth to a son, Prince James, but there was no reconciliation between her and her husband. Instead, she drew closer to one of the protestant lords, the Earl of Bothwell, and it was at Bothwell's suggestion that Darnley, who had been ill, was sent to convalesce in a house called Kirk o'Field. In February 1567 the house was destroyed by a violent explosion, and Darnley was found, strangled, in the grounds. Public opinion assumed—perhaps too easily —that Bothwell was the murderer. As for Mary, even though she may not have been forewarned of Darnley's murder, she took no steps to investigate it, and in April she allowed herself to be abducted by Bothwell. The following month Mary and Bothwell (who had obtained a divorce from his wife) were married in a protestant ceremony at Edinburgh. By her actions Mary had forfeited public respect, and she was powerless in face of a rising of the protestant lords, led by Moray. In June 1567 she was captured and forced to abdicate in favour of her son, James. A year later she was a refugee in England, poised at the beginning of the long descent that was to bring her at last to Fotheringay and the scaffold.

James VI

With Mary out of the way, Knox and the protestants consolidated their position. The structure of the Roman Catholic Church was allowed to remain because the Crown and aristocracy had succeeded in diverting part of its wealth into their own pockets, and preferred this arrangement to Knox's more idealistic scheme to confiscate Church lands and use them to endow a protestant ministry. But although the old Church was outwardly preserved, all ministers were required, by 1573, to subscribe to a puritan confession of faith, and bishops, although appointed by the Crown, had to be approved by a panel of protestant ministers.

The mid-1570s saw the puritan movement enter a more intense phase in both England and Scotland. Knox died in 1572, but two years later Andrew Melville returned from Geneva and published his *Book of Discipline*. In this he went even further than the English puritans, by affirming that the Church was entirely independent of the state, responsible only to God, and bound to discipline the lay ruler if he transgressed. St Thomas Becket would certainly have approved of such an attitude, but it was diametrically opposed to the anti-clericalism and assertion of lay supremacy which had characterised the English Reformation, and it was unacceptable to James, who had a high opinion of the royal dignity and certainly did not intend to be dictated to by puritan ministers.

James was inspired to take up the struggle against the puritan church—the Kirk—by Esmé Stuart, who arrived in Scotland in 1579 and quickly became the young King's favourite—the first of a long line. The influence of Stuart, whom James created Duke of Lennox, was resented not only by the Kirk but also by the protestant nobles who were afraid that James might be won over to catholicism. A plot was made, and successfully carried out, to kidnap James and hold him prisoner while Lennox was expelled. Not until June 1583 did James escape from captivity and re-establish his authority, by which time Lennox was dead.

The young King built up his position with great care and skill, and by 1584 he was ready to take the offensive. Melville and many puritan ministers fled to England to escape arrest on charges of treason, and a parliament which met in that year passed the 'Black Acts', making the King head of the Church. The assemblies of the Kirk were not to meet without royal permission, nor were their decisions to be valid without royal approval. Government of the Church was to be in the hands of bishops appointed by the Crown, and ministers were forbidden to discuss affairs of state from the pulpit.

James looked for support to Elizabeth, and in 1586 a treaty was concluded which gave the Scottish King a pension of £4,000 a year and bound the Queen to accept him as her successor, provided he did not, by some act of ingratitude, show himself to be unworthy of the English Crown. James was certainly in need of the pension, for his own revenues were meagre, and at the time of his marriage to Anne of Denmark in 1589 one observer wrote that the King 'has neither plate nor stuff to furnish one of his little half-built houses, which are in great decay and ruin. His plate is not worth £100, he has only two or three rich jewels, his saddles are of plain cloth.' So anxious was James to preserve both the English pension and the right of succession that he made no protest when his mother, Mary, was executed. She had, in any case, played little part in his life since he was a baby, and the catholic claim to the throne, which she embodied, was just as much of a threat to James as to Elizabeth.

For the last ten years of his reign in Scotland James was occupied in consolidating his authority against the catholic earls, on the one hand, and the puritan Kirk, on the other. His aim was to exalt the royal dignity, as the Tudors had done in England, and make it the focus of national unity, but he met strong opposition from the leaders of the Kirk. The outspoken Andrew Melville, who had returned from exile in England, told the King that he was 'but God's silly vassal' and countered James's claim to supremacy with the assertion that 'there are two Kings and two Kingdoms in Scotland. There is Christ Jesus the King and his Kingdom the Kirk, whose subject King James VI is, and of Whose Kingdom not a King nor a lord, nor a head, but a member.' Yet in spite of the determined opposition of puritan ministers James gradually extended his control over the Church. He encouraged the moderates by holding general assemblies away from extremist Edinburgh, and in 1600 he appointed a number of bishops, who were given seats in parliament even though they had no clear function in the government of the Church.

As Elizabeth's life drew to a close, James waited impatiently for the news of his accession. To an outsider like himself, Elizabeth seemed to be a rich, powerful monarch, supreme in Church and state, and he took the language of Tudor absolutism at its face value. He knew that the Queen had difficulties, particularly with Parliament, but he knew also that she had managed to overcome them, and he was confident that he, with his lifelong experience of kingship, would be at least as successful, and probably more so. He left Scotland without real regret, for, as he told the Hampton Court Conference, he was happy to be in 'the promised land, where religion was purely professed, where he sat among grave, learned and reverend men—not, as before, elsewhere, a King without state, without honour, without order, where beardless boys would brave him to his face'.

9

Elizabeth I and the Church of England

Elizabeth I

ELIZABETH was an attractive young woman of twenty-five when she came to the throne. She was no classical beauty—her nose was too pronounced and her hair was reddish rather than golden—but she had character and intelligence as well as a commanding personality, and she knew how to charm men to her service. She was also well educated, for her tutors, John Cheke and Roger Ascham, had given her a good grounding in the classics and divinity as well as in several modern languages. And yet she was no pedant. The liveliness of her wit and the sharpness of her tongue were to become famous, and her speeches are models of their kind—involved and convoluted in the manner of the day, but full of salty comments and passages of magnificent rhetoric.

Although a young woman, Elizabeth was experienced in the ways of the world. At an early age she had seen her mother taken away from her to be executed, and in Mary's reign she had come under the shadow of the axe herself. These and other experiences had taught her the art of being devious—of concealing her policy and shifting responsibility for her actions on to other shoulders. She was a maddening woman to work with, because her volatile imagination could never rest content with any single solution to a problem, but was always exploring other possibilities. And yet, while her advisers at times despaired, they came to admire the sheer toughness of Elizabeth's character, that made her a force to be reckoned with in an age of male supremacy, and turned her reign into a personal triumph that dazzled her contemporaries, haunted the political imagination of Stuart England, and survives as a legend to this day.

Elizabeth had inherited her father's exalted conception of the nature of kingship, and believed that God had made her head of the body politic so that she might guide her subjects into the right paths. Like her half-sister, Mary, she was proud and stubborn, but she had an ebullient self-assurance that the late Queen had never known, and the Spanish ambassador reported, two weeks after Elizabeth's accession, that 'she seems to me incomparably more feared than her sister was, and she gives her orders and has her way as absolutely as her father did'.

Elizabeth also had a genuine love for her subjects, and in the relationship between her and her people there was an element of romance that went a long way towards sublimating those instincts which would normally have found expression in love for a husband and children. The Queen's advisers assumed that she would quickly marry, but this was not Elizabeth's intention. One reason for this was that all the time she remained single she could use the prospect of her marriage as a trump card in the game of diplomacy, to be brought out when hostile coalitions were threatening her. Another, and more powerful, reason was her reluctance to share power with a husband, for as the Scots ambassador told her, 'ye think that if ye were married ye would be but Queen of England, and now ye are King and Queen both. Ye may not suffer a commander.'

Elizabeth did, in fact, come near to marriage with Robert Dudley, son of the Duke of Northumberland and grandson of Henry VII's notorious minister. But Dudley was already married, and although this impediment was removed in September 1560 when Amy Robsart, his wife, was found dead in her house at Cumnor Place, the rumours of Dudley's complicity were too widespread for Elizabeth to ignore. She continued to love Dudley, and in October 1562, when she was lying desperately ill with smallpox and was not expected to recover, she recommended his nomination as Lord Protector of the Realm. But when she recovered she did not marry him.

Her illness brought the question of the succession into prominence. The Queen's early death would almost certainly have been followed by a disputed succession, for the obvious heir, Mary Stuart, had been married to the King of France,[1] England's enemy, and was also a Roman Catholic. It was doubtful whether the leading English protestants would have accepted another catholic ruler after their experience of Mary Tudor's reign, but they wanted, above all, to put an end to uncertainty by persuading the Queen to nominate her successor. Elizabeth, however, would not do this. She had had experience of

[1] Mary's husband, Francis II, died in 1560.

being a 'second person' herself in Mary's reign, and knew how intrigues sprang up around the heir to the throne. She also knew 'the inconstancy of the people of England, how they ever mislike the present government and have their eyes fixed upon that person that is next to succeed. *Plures adorant solem orientalem quam occidentalem.*'[1] Her attitude was selfish, for she had to gamble on staying alive long enough for the succession problem to solve itself. The gamble paid off, but there was no reason why it should have done so. The early deaths of Edward VI and Mary suggest some physical weakness in the Tudor inheritance, and what natural causes failed to do the assassin's knife might well have accomplished. It is hardly surprising that the early Parliaments of Elizabeth repeatedly petitioned her to marry and have an heir of her own, or at least to nominate a successor.

The Religious Settlement

Elizabeth's own inclinations and the fact that in Roman Catholic eyes she was an illegitimate usurper pointed to some sort of protestant settlement. The Queen's aim was to preserve the unity which her father and her grandfather had given England, by creating a Church to which all her subjects could belong. Whatever the differences between catholics and protestants they had at least their nationality in common, and Elizabeth hoped to unite them in a Church similar to that of Henry VIII, catholic in its ritual, protestant in its doctrines and looking for guidance not to Rome, Geneva or Zürich, but to the ruler of England.

Unfortunately, Elizabeth's unfanatical attitude towards religion was not shared by the majority of her more important subjects, many of whom were intolerant protestants of the sort later to be known as puritans. Prominent in this group were the returned exiles who, during their time on the Continent, had gone beyond the provisions even of the 1552 Book of Common Prayer. The English congregation at Geneva, which eventually attracted to itself about a quarter of all the exiles, had come under Calvin's influence: its members regarded the communion service as purely commemorative, and they rejected 'papist practices' such as kneeling at communion, signing with the cross, observing saints' days, and using the ring in marriage. The effect of the exile was to bring English protestantism into the main stream of

[1] 'For the most part they worship the rising rather than the setting sun.'

European reformed thought and practice, and to reveal the weakness of an isolated English Church.

The first Parliament of Elizabeth's reign included over a dozen returned exiles, and this 'Puritan Choir', as Sir John Neale calls it,[1] took the lead in the debates on the religious settlement. Elizabeth apparently intended, at first, merely to restore royal supremacy and communion in both kinds while she prepared an eventual settlement on the lines of the 1549 Prayer-Book. Her proposals were unacceptable to the extremists, who rushed through a Bill permitting the use of the 1552 Book. At the very beginning of her reign, then, Queen and Commons were locked in a bitter struggle that set the pattern for the years that were to follow.

The outcome was a compromise. Elizabeth reluctantly accepted the 1552 Book, but insisted on a number of changes to make it more acceptable to catholics and moderates. The Black Rubric, for instance, was dropped, as was the petition to be delivered 'from the Bishop of Rome and all his detestable enormities', while in the communion service the wording of the first Prayer-Book, which implied the real presence, was added to the commemorative phrases of the second Book. Perhaps most important of all, for its short-term consequences, was the clause in the Act of Uniformity which insisted that 'such ornaments of the church and of the ministers thereof shall be retained and be in use as was in the Church of England by authority of Parliament in the second year of the reign of King Edward the Sixth'. This harmless sounding provision, to which Elizabeth attached so much importance that, according to Archbishop Parker, without it she would not have accepted the amended Book, was a calculated blow at the puritans. It meant that all clergy were now obliged to wear a surplice for ordinary church services, and—most galling of all to the extremists—'a white alb plain, with a vestment or cope' for the administration of the holy communion.

The Elizabethan Settlement was legalised by the Act of Supremacy and the Act of Uniformity. The first of these restored the royal supremacy over the Church, although Elizabeth was described as 'Only Supreme Governor of this realm . . . as well in all spiritual or ecclesiastical things or causes as temporal'—a sop to those who thought that a woman could not be 'Supreme Head of the Church'. The Act ordered all office-holders to take an oath accepting the supremacy, and the principle of compulsion was also applied in the Uniformity Act,

[1] *Elizabeth I and Her Parliaments, 1559–1581*, p. 91.

where it was laid down that every person should attend his parish church on Sundays and holy days, on pain of a shilling fine for every absence.

When the oath of supremacy was administered to the bishops they refused to take it, even though they included men such as Bonner and Tunstall who had, in their younger days, accepted Henry's claim to headship over the Church. The bishops had to be replaced, but parish priests offered little resistance, and out of a total of nearly seven thousand only some three hundred were deprived of their livings. Generally speaking the government was not concerned to impose conformity on parish priests, as long as they did not actively oppose the new régime, and in 1566 the Dean of Durham complained that 'many papists enjoy liberty and livings who have neither sworn obedience to the Queen nor yet do any part of their duty towards their miserable flocks'.

The returned émigrés, who had looked forward to building a new Jerusalem in their native land, found the Elizabethan compromise far from satisfactory, since it preserved many practices which they regarded with abhorrence. Yet Elizabeth needed the cooperation of these men, since only with their enthusiasm, purified and hardened by years of exile, could she build a really strong Church in England. They, similarly, felt the need to serve in the new Church, for fear that if they stayed out they would leave the door open for the catholic wolf to come in. Most of the émigrés eventually decided, as Grindal wrote several years later, 'not to desert our churches for the sake of a few ceremonies—and those not unlawful in themselves'. Grindal himself became Bishop of London, while other returned exiles were appointed to the sees of Ely, Worcester, Winchester and Durham. It was perhaps to counter this continental influence that Elizabeth chose as Archbishop Matthew Parker, who had spent Mary's reign in hiding in England. Parker, now over fifty, was a link with the early days of the Reformation—he had been a member of the 'Little Germany' group at Cambridge—and he epitomised that continuity of the reformed tradition which was lacking among the exiles.

William Cecil

Cambridge provided the Queen not only with her Archbishop but also with her chief secular adviser, for in one of the first actions of her reign she appointed William Cecil, now thirty-eight years old, as her principal Secretary. Cecil came from a family that had made its way in the world by service to the Crown. His grandfather, a Welshman, had fought for Henry Tudor at Bosworth, and his father held a minor position in the Court of Henry VIII. The Cecils were not numbered among the great families of medieval England: they were new to power—as new as the Tudors—but they had established themselves as country gentlemen at Stamford in Lincolnshire and were moving into the upper levels of society.

At Cambridge William Cecil met not only many of the future leaders of Elizabethan England but also Edward VI's tutor, John Cheke, whose sister he married. He was thereby linked with the third generation of English humanists, and he shared their concept of an organic society in which every section of the community had its part to play. His second wife, Mildred, whom he married in 1545, linked him with another powerful section of society—the puritans. She was a puritan herself, the daughter of a Marian exile, and two of her sisters took good puritan husbands. The third married Nicholas Bacon, future Lord Keeper and father of Francis Bacon, the statesman and philosopher. Whether Cecil liked it or not, he was being brought into the pattern of family relationships that lay barely concealed beneath the surface of Elizabethan political life, and frequently disrupted or distorted it.

Cecil entered Parliament in 1543, when he was only twenty-one, and was sufficiently well known by the time Henry VIII died to be chosen by Somerset as his private secretary. At Somerset's fall he was imprisoned for a time, but he transferred his allegiance to Northumberland, whose overt puritanism no doubt appealed to him, and received his reward in the shape of a knighthood, large grants of Crown lands, and a formal appointment as one of the two Secretaries of State. He managed to survive Northumberland's fall, but gave up the Secretaryship after Mary's accession and lived in semi-retirement, superintending the building of his great house at Stamford. He kept in touch with Princess Elizabeth, however, and when she came to the throne Cecil emerged again into public life and resumed his role as Secretary. The Queen, when she appointed him to this key office, told him: 'This judgement I have of you, that you will not be corrupted by any manner of gift, and that you will be faithful to the state, and that without respect of my private will you will give me that counsel which you think best'; and although in the early years of the reign Cecil could not take Elizabeth's confidence in him for granted, he soon established a close relationship with her that lasted until his death.

Cecil did not reconstruct the administration as Thomas Cromwell had done. He found the institutions he needed ready to hand, but by his long tenure of power he made sure that the more valuable features of the Cromwellian reorganisation were incorporated into the permanent structure of English government. The Privy Council, cut down to manageable size again, remained the nerve-centre of the administration for the next hundred years, while under Cecil and his successor, Walsingham, the Secretaryship regained much of its Cromwellian significance.

One of the more important offices in the administration, however, owed little to Cromwell. The Lord Treasurer, as the man who was responsible for the financial organisation of the Tudor state, was a key figure in government. Elizabeth continued in office the Marquis of Winchester, who had originally been appointed in 1550. He had been responsible for reforming the Exchequer and incorporating within it the new courts which Cromwell had created, and the reformed Exchequer was a very much more efficient body than its medieval predecessor had been—though it was liable, like all Tudor and Stuart institutions, to periodic lethargy and incompetence.

On Winchester's death in 1572 Cecil himself accepted the white staff which signified his appointment as Lord Treasurer, and he and his son Robert—who succeeded him after a short break—occupied this important office for the next forty years. This long period of stability encouraged the growth of bureaucracy (though on a scale that by modern standards was primitive and ludicrously inadequate) which freed the Lord Treasurer from part, at least, of his routine work and made it possible for him to become, if other circumstances were favourable, the effective head of the administration.

William Cecil was certainly Elizabeth's chief minister, and he had a capacity for political analysis which was beyond the Queen. Elizabeth was an empirical conservative who made up her mind as she went along and was temperamentally opposed to change. William Cecil (and Robert after him) was far more aware of long-term considerations and could see problems in relation not only to the personal ambitions of the men and women around them but also to the needs of the state. Elizabeth was lucky to find, in this painstaking, tenacious, intelligent and loyal servant the complement to her own volatile temperament.

The Puritan Attempt to remodel the Church

Cecil's puritan sympathies helped to make the Elizabethan Settlement at least temporarily acceptable to the returned exiles and their supporters. These men also assumed that they would not be compelled to act against their consciences, and that the settlement would soon be modified in a way that would please them. The first Prayer-Book of Edward VI's reign had, after all, soon been followed by a more radical one, and they saw no reason to suppose that the same thing would not happen under Elizabeth. They concentrated their hopes on Convocation, which met in 1563, where they introduced a number of puritan articles proposing the abolition of those practices of which they and the continental reformed churches disapproved. These proposals, however, were defeated by the narrowest possible margin, fifty-nine votes to fifty-eight, and the puritans therefore shifted their attack to Parliament, where their relentless pressure and effective organisation created a situation unlike anything that Elizabeth's predecessors had ever experienced.

Elizabeth was determined to enforce conformity. 'We will have no dissension or variety,' she told Archbishop Parker, 'for so the sovereign authority which we have under Almighty God would be made frustrate and we might be thought to bear the sword in vain.' Parker listed a number of requirements—they included the wearing of correct vestments and the observation of the prescribed rites and ceremonies—to which he demanded the assent of his clergy, and when the Queen refused her official authorisation—she always preferred to shift the blame for unpopular measures—he issued them as his *Advertisements*. About forty London clergymen were deprived of their livings for refusing to accept these, and puritan sympathisers all over the country were alarmed.

The effect of Parker's action was to change the attitude of the puritans towards episcopacy. Just as monarchical power, which the early reformers had elevated as a protection against papal claims, had come to be regarded as an impediment to further reform, so the authority of bishops was now challenged. 'What talk they', wrote one pamphleteer, 'of their being beyond the seas in Queen Mary's days because of the persecution, when they in Queen Elizabeth's days are come home to raise a persecution?' The reply to this was given by Pilkington, who had led the exiled congregation at Frankfurt and was now Bishop of Durham. 'We are under authority', he said, 'and can innovate nothing without the Queen; nor can we alter the laws. The only thing left to our choice is whether we will bear these things or break the peace of the Church.'

The attitude of Elizabeth and her bishops was that vestments and other 'outward signs' were *adiaphora*, matters indifferent, to be regulated by the lay power. The puritan reply was that if such matters were inessential the government should not bother to enforce its views. All depended ultimately on whether the Church was self-governing or subject to the lay power, and just as this fundamental issue was beginning to emerge a new figure appeared on the scene: Thomas Cartwright, in the lectures he gave at Cambridge in 1570 as Lady Margaret Professor of Divinity, declared that the structure of the Church of England was contrary to that prescribed by Scripture.

The correct model, according to Cartwright, was that which Calvin had established at Geneva. Every congregation should elect its own ministers in the first instance, and control of the Church should be in the hands of a local presbytery, consisting of the minister and the elders of the congregation. The authority of archbishops and bishops had no foundation in the Bible, and was therefore unacceptable. Cartwright's definition lifted the puritan movement out of its obsession with details and threw down a challenge which the established Church could not possibly ignore. The counter-attack was led by John Whitgift, Master of Trinity College, Cambridge, and Regius Professor of Divinity in the university. With the support of William Cecil, Cambridge's Chancellor, Whitgift amended the constitution of the university in such a way that the heads of colleges, who were less given to radical views, became the effective rulers. They deprived Cartwright of his chair in December 1570, and the puritan spokesman left, appropriately enough, for Geneva.

Cartwright's expulsion did not check the puritan revolt, since he had only put into clear terms what many people were already thinking. In some places puritans were coming together privately to use a form of service more acceptable than the 'papist' Prayer-Book, and in London the lead was taken by John Field, himself a clergyman, who acted as a link between the puritan congregations and their sympathisers in Parliament. The puritan position was strengthened by the publication of a papal Bull of deposition against Elizabeth in 1570. All Roman Catholics were now potential enemies of the state and, conversely, puritans could claim to be the only true patriots. When Parliament

met in 1571 a puritan member, Walter Strickland, introduced a Bill
to reform the Book of Common Prayer. This was a clear invasion of
the Queen's prerogative, and the Councillors in the Commons advised
the House to go no further. But they were up against men who would
let nothing stand in the way of religious truth: such matters, said one
member, were God's—'the rest are all but terrene, yea trifles in comparison'. Strickland was summoned before the Privy Council and
ordered to absent himself from the House, but members raised such an
outcry against what they claimed was an infringement of their privilege
of free speech that he was quickly restored to them.

The session of 1571 had shown how the puritans were shifting their
attack from matters of detail—*adiaphora*—to the central question of
who should govern the Church. It seemed as though the pattern of the
Henrician Reformation was to be repeated all over again: since the
Church refused to reform itself, the lay power—Parliament this time
—would take the initiative. Field and his associates drew up a plan of
action, and when Parliament reassembled in 1572 a Bill was introduced
giving puritan ministers the right to leave out whatever bits of the
Prayer-Book they regarded as inadmissible. Elizabeth, who thought
that the Church had already been too radically reformed, refused to
allow the initiative to pass out of her hands. She declared that, in future,
no Bills on religion were to be introduced into the Commons without
her express approval.

The puritans had failed to win over Convocation, and now the
parliamentary way to reform had been closed to them: their only
hope seemed to lie in self-help. In the *Admonition to Parliament* which
he wrote in 1572, Field went far beyond a mere repetition of the old
grievances and came much nearer a total rejection of the Church of
England, based as it was upon 'an unperfect Book, culled and picked
out of that popish dunghill, the Mass Book, full of abominations'.
Cartwright returned briefly to England to elaborate his views on an
alternative and more satisfactory system of Church organisation, and
for several years he fought a bitter pamphlet war with Whitgift.
The orthodox view, as presented by Whitgift, was that the Bible, while
containing everything that was necessary for salvation, did not lay
down any blueprint for the government of the Church, and he
declared his conviction that 'there is no such distinction between the
Church of Christ and a Christian Commonwealth as you and the
papists dream of'. His association of puritanism with catholicism is
revealing, since they were both of them versions of clericalism.

Roman Catholic priests and puritan ministers were alike in that they rejected any lay authority over the Church. In this they ran counter to the spirit of the Henrician Reformation, which took the nation as its unit and affirmed the spiritual purpose of secular society.

The Anglican Church would have been insupportable to the puritans had it not been for the fact that among its rulers were many sympathisers. The Queen herself hated puritans, who, she said, 'were greater enemies to her than the papists', but her Council included not only moderate puritans like Cecil and Leicester, but also more extreme ones like Sir Walter Mildmay, who founded a puritan college at Cambridge, and Sir Francis Walsingham. The bishops, also, although they put their loyalty to the Queen foremost, were much nearer the puritan viewpoint than their Stuart successors: even Archbishop Parker told Cecil that he cared nothing for 'cap, tippet, surplice or wafer-bread or any such'. Parker's successor, Edmund Grindal, who became Archbishop in 1575, was strongly puritan in his sympathies, and particularly encouraged the 'Prophesyings' in which clergy and laity met together to expound the Bible. The main object of these was to improve the standard of learning of parish priests, but Elizabeth preferred an ignorant and docile clergy to an educated and intransigent one.

The lead in Prophesyings was taken by the puritans—one famous meeting-place was the house of Peter Wentworth, who caused Elizabeth more trouble in Parliament than any other member—and the Queen ordered Grindal to put an end to these gatherings. Grindal took the astonishing step of refusing to obey, and in a long letter explaining his action he urged the Queen to leave Church matters to the bishops in the same way that she left legal matters to her judges, and not 'to pronounce too resolutely and peremptorily, *quasi ex authoritate*, as ye may do in civil and external matters'. The outraged Queen suspended Grindal from office, and herself ordered the suppression of Prophesyings. Nevertheless, they continued, for the bishops, even if they did not actively encourage them, were prepared to turn a blind eye. As for the Councillors, on whom the Queen depended for carrying her will into effect, their attitude is indicated by the fact that Leicester was Field's patron and that Walsingham, who was patron of the English church at Antwerp, appointed Cartwright as its minister.

While puritanism was taking an increasingly presbyterian form in the 1570s, there were some who asked themselves why an individual who had broken with Rome should submit himself to the authority of either bishop or presbyter. Such an attitude was implicit in protestantism, which took its impetus from the revolt of individual conscience against an organised Church, and even in the early days of the Reformation there had been radical groups, like the Anabaptists, to whom the authoritarianism of Luther and Calvin was just as repellent as that of the Pope. There were Anabaptists in England, but they were few in number and of little influence. The English Independents, who shared many of the same assumptions, looked for inspiration not to the Continent but to Cambridge, that deep well of nonconformity.

It was a Cambridge man, Robert Browne, who in 1582 wrote the *Treatise of Reformation without Tarrying for Any*, in which he declared that every congregation was self-sufficient and did not need any form of central guidance or authority. The Anglican Church was, he declared, hopelessly corrupt, its ministers 'turned back after babbling prayers and toying worship . . . after popish attire and foolish disguising, after fastings, tithings, holy days and a thousand more abominations, and their feet do stick fast in the mire and dirt of all popery, that they cannot get out'. Browne's teaching, with its undertones of anarchy, was anathema to the government, and in 1583 two members of his sect were hanged for treason since they denied the royal supremacy. Browne himself was eventually reconciled to the Anglican Church, and spent the remaining forty years of his life as a country parson. But from his protest was to grow that tough and individualistic form of puritanism that reached its apogee with Cromwell's army.

By the early 1580s the Anglican Church had come of age and was no longer the temporary expedient it had seemed to be when Elizabeth ascended the throne. It had found able defenders, among them Bishop Jewel who, in his *Apology*—written at Cecil's suggestion, and published in 1562—maintained that the Anglican Church was a true Church and not merely a compromise between two extremes. Catholics and puritans alike had to accept the fact that the Church of England had taken root and was unlikely to shift its position. Even among the bishops there was far less inclination towards puritanism after the generation of Marian exiles died out, and the end of their influence may be dated to 1583, the year of Grindal's death. The new men, such as John Aylmer who became Bishop of London in 1577, had no difficulty in reconciling the claims of conscience with their acceptance of royal supremacy, and the spread of presbyterianism, with its implied rejection of episcopacy, hardened their attitude. They were not necessarily hostile to Calvinism, but they did not regard Geneva as being any more infallible than Rome. As Whitgift said, later in the century, 'I reverence Mr Calvin as a singular man and worthy instrument in Christ's Church, but I am not so wholly addicted unto him that I will condemn other men's judgements that in divers points agree not fully with him, especially in the interpretation of some places of the Scripture, when as, in my opinion, they come nearer to the true meaning and sense of it in those points than he doth'.

The Roman Catholics and Foreign Policy

The puritans were not the only opponents with whom Whitgift had to deal, for the Elizabethan Church was also threatened by the Roman Catholic revival. Elizabeth had been careful not to persecute the catholics, for she was a tolerant woman, who did not wish, in her own words, 'to open windows into men's souls'. She frequently intervened to moderate the extremism of her Councillors and bishops, and even in the years of persecution that followed the Armada she showed her lack of bigotry by staying with Viscount Montague at Cowdray, though his house was a notorious catholic centre.

Roman Catholics were, like all her subjects, bound to attend their parish churches on pain of a shilling fine, but this degree of compulsion was mild compared with the ferocious penalties imposed on religious nonconformists by other countries, both protestant and catholic. Many catholics believed they could attend anglican services without endangering their souls, and holy communion was celebrated rarely enough for them to be able to absent themselves without courting bankruptcy. In many parts of the country local justices turned a blind eye to absence from church, and as late as 1578 the Council declared that 'sundry persons being in commission of the peace within divers counties have of late years forborne to come to the church to any common prayer and divine service; whereby not only is God dishonoured and the laws infringed, but very evil example given to the common sort of people'.

The aim of Elizabeth and Cecil was not to wipe out Roman Catholicism by violent suppression but to let it die a natural death through lethargy and outward conformity, and in this they came very near to success. As long as English catholicism remained isolated from the Continent it was not much of a threat to the Elizabethan Church or state. This meant that from the beginning of the reign the treatment of

English recusants was dependent upon the political situation in Europe, and only with the rise of Spain did they become victims of a persecution that was more political than religious. For the first ten years of Elizabeth's reign France, with her ally Scotland, was the main enemy, but in 1562 the political situation in Europe was transformed by the outbreak of the French wars of religion. For the next twenty years French influence fluctuated violently as aristocratic families, at the head of religious factions, struggled for supremacy. In the peaceful interludes between bouts of fighting the French monarchy attempted to resume its European role, and this, as well as ingrained habits of thought, blinded the English to the fact that a dramatic shift in the balance of power had taken place.

With the decline of France, Philip II of Spain emerged not only as the greatest catholic prince in Europe but also as the chief threat to English independence, and as if to emphasise this he moved an army into the Spanish Netherlands in August 1567 to crush the Calvinist revolt that was smouldering there. Elizabeth could hardly ignore such a move, even though it was not directed against her. For one thing a powerful army in the Netherlands was always a potential threat to England, and, for another, the rebels in question were fellow-protestants who looked to the Queen of England for support. Elizabeth had to offer at least token assistance to the rebels, and yet by so doing she would anger Philip of Spain.

The most acceptable solution, from her point of view, would have been a return to the *status quo* before Philip's intervention, and she urged him to withdraw his troops and restore to the Netherlands the semi-autonomy that had kept them quiet during his father's reign. But she reckoned without Philip's stubbornness, and she could not, in any case, hold back the tide of religious fanaticism that was threatening to sweep away Spanish rule in the Low Countries. She tried to put pressure on Philip by encouraging the rebels, by allowing her sailors to prey on Spanish shipping, and by confiscating the bullion from a Spanish convoy that took shelter in English ports in December 1568. She hoped to go far enough to force Philip to reconsider his policy, but not so far that he would turn the full force of his anger against her. In the long run she failed, but it was a superhuman task and she did at least manage to postpone open war for twenty years.

The Northern Rebellion

By 1568 England and Spain were already drifting apart, and when, in May of that year, Mary, Queen of Scots, arrived in England as a refugee, she immediately became a focus for Spanish intrigue. Elizabeth did not want the catholic claimant to the English throne so near at hand, but she could hardly use English arms to reimpose Mary's rule on the protestant Scots, nor could she allow Mary to take refuge in the courts of England's enemies, the Kings of France and Spain. There was no alternative to keeping the Queen of Scots prisoner in England until such time as she could return peacefully to her own kingdom, and this was what Elizabeth decided on. Early in 1569 Mary was moved to Tutbury in Staffordshire to start her long captivity.

No sooner had Mary reached Tutbury than the plotting began. Some English nobles of ancient lineage, such as the Duke of Norfolk and the Earl of Arundel, resented the rule of Cecil and other 'new men', and drew up a plan by which Elizabeth should recognise Mary as heir to the English throne and give permission for Norfolk to marry her—thereby ensuring the rule of the 'old' nobility after Elizabeth's death. There was nothing treasonable about this proposal, which, in fact, had the support of many members of the Council. But Norfolk was in touch with the Spanish ambassador, through a Florentine banker named Ridolfi, and he had also played on the discontent of many of the northern lords. These men had particular cause to resent the rule of 'new men', who, through the Council of the North, threatened the supremacy that the Percies, Dacres and other noble families had taken for granted as theirs by hereditary right. The north was not particularly backward—compared with Scotland it was economically advanced—but the older patterns of landownership and dependence there were only slowly changing, and the labour pains of the new society were harsh. Rule from London, which was a week's hard riding away, was resented, for the north had a sense of its own identity and was reluctant to submit to Tudor unification. This separatism, which had found its symbols in the northern earls and its faith in the catholic religion, had caused the Pilgrimage of Grace in Henry VIII's reign. Now, once again, in November 1569, the north rose in revolt. The banner with the Five Wounds of Christ floated above the rebel army as it moved south, and when Durham was occupied the Prayer-

Book was trampled underfoot while the sound of the Latin Mass echoed in the cathedral.

The rebels, led by the Earls of Westmorland and Northumberland, planned to free Mary, Queen of Scots, but apart from that they had no clear aims. They seem to have thought, like Aske, that once they had demonstrated to Elizabeth the folly of trusting 'new men' the Queen would change her ways. They never had any intention of deposing Elizabeth and putting Mary on the throne in her place, and the weakness of the revolt of the northern earls was exactly the same as that of the Pilgrimage of Grace; they had no effective alternative to offer to the existing system.

Elizabeth stood firm and mustered her forces, while Mary was moved south, out of harm's way. Once it was clear that the Queen would not compromise, the rebel army melted away and the leaders fled to Scotland. Before 1569 came to an end the rebellion was finished. The Earl of Northumberland was handed over by the Scots and later executed, while Westmorland spent the rest of his life in exile. Elizabeth's tolerance did not extend to rebels. She gave orders that at least one man should be hanged in every town or village that had contributed recruits to the rebellion, and about eight hundred of the poorer sort were executed: wealthier rebels were allowed to buy themselves off.

The New Catholicism

The northern rebellion failed because the English catholics never rose to support it. The policy of Elizabeth and Cecil was working well, so well in fact that even before the rebellion broke out Pope Pius V had decided that some clear statement must be made to English catholics, to show them where their loyalty lay. In the Bull *Regnans in Excelsis*, published in February 1570, he declared Elizabeth excommunicate and 'deprived of her pretended title to the kingdom. . . . And We do command and charge all and every the noblemen, subjects, people and others aforesaid that they presume not to obey her or her orders, mandates and laws.'

This Bull was not intended as an open challenge to Elizabeth. It was designed to give guidance to catholics, so that when the appropriate moment came—as in the northern rebellion—they should know how to act. In theory Roman Catholics had now to choose between their faith and their loyalty as subjects, but in fact the majority managed to

G*

reconcile these irreconcilables. The government, however, could not be sure of this, and took the justifiable view that every Roman Catholic was a potential traitor. The papal Bull brought to an end the decade of comparative tolerance, and even Philip II commented that 'this sudden and unexpected step will make matters worse and drive the Queen and her friends the more to oppress and persecute the few good catholics remaining in England'.

Although Alva was poised with a large army in the Netherlands, Elizabeth did not doubt her catholic subjects' loyalty. She told Parliament in 1570 that as long as the catholics observed her laws and did not 'wilfully and manifestly break them by their open acts, Her Majesty's meaning is not to have any of them molested by any inquisition or examination of their consciences in causes of religion', and she vetoed a Bill which would have made attendance at the communion service compulsory. Outward conformity was all she insisted on, but she accepted a Bill making it treasonable to procure a papal Bull for the purpose of reconciling her subjects to Rome. This was the first of those Acts which, in response to increasing papal pressure and a rapidly worsening European situation, drove the English catholics into an intolerable position.

The fears of the government were apparently confirmed when, in March 1571, another Ridolfi plot was uncovered, by which Norfolk and the English catholics were to rise in revolt, seize Elizabeth and release Mary, at the same time as a Spanish expeditionary force landed in England. Cecil discovered the details of the plot and struck swiftly. Norfolk was arrested, tried and executed in 1572. John Foxe, his old tutor, attended him upon the scaffold, but Norfolk, although he lived and died a protestant, hardly qualified for inclusion in the *Book of Martyrs*. If he stood for anything other than personal ambition, it was for a lost cause—that of the 'old' nobility against the 'new men' who were taking over control of the English state.

English catholicism, centred as it was on great households in remote areas, stood for order and hierarchy rather than revolution. It appealed, like anglicanism, to moderate men, and for this reason it had to face, also like anglicanism, an extremist movement within its own ranks. The catholic equivalent of the puritans was to be found in the 'new catholics'—the young men who were opposed to lay supremacy and intellectual compromise, and who wanted to see English catholicism linked to the revived and purified Church of Rome which was now counter-attacking all over Europe. The ecclesiastical council which concluded its meetings at Trent, in Italy, in 1563, had clarified catholic doctrines and taken the first step towards improving the administration of the Church and the quality of the clergy, while organisations such as the Society of Jesus and the Inquisition were restoring to the Church of Rome some of the crusading zeal that it had lost. The Popes of the second half of the sixteenth century were a long way removed, in the quality of their lives, from the corrupt world-liness of Julius II, and they were at last giving a lead to the Church, which, had it come earlier, might have channelled the Reformation into less disruptive courses.

The 'new catholics' in England looked to Rome for a lead and put their loyalty to the international Church above the claims of patriot-ism. One of these men, William Allen, established a college at Douai, in the Spanish Netherlands, in 1568, to train priests and send them over to England, where they could preach the old faith with new vigour and, in Allen's words, 'train catholics to be plainly and openly catholics, to be men who will always refuse every kind of spiritual commerce with heretics'. By the time Allen left to take over the English College at Rome in 1585 Douai had produced nearly three hundred priests, and others were also being trained for the English mission by the Jesuits. The success of the seminary priests was striking, and the Bishop of London told Walsingham in 1577 that 'the papists marvellously increase both in numbers and in obstinate withdrawal of themselves from the Church and services of God'.

The priests, and their defenders, claimed that their aim was 'purely religious' and they were instructed to avoid direct entanglement in politics. They were, however, operating in a country in which Church and state were so closely integrated as to be indistinguishable. Nothing in sixteenth-century England could be 'purely religious' any more than it could be 'purely secular', and Elizabeth's government was not alone in seeing the 'new catholics' as a threat to the established social and political order, far more radical in its implications than the older, seigneurial catholicism. The danger was real, for Gregory XIII, who was Pope from 1579 to 1585, made the overthrow of Elizabeth the main object of his policy, and papal patronage was extended to Fitzmaurice's expedition, sent to Ireland in 1579 to provoke rebellion against the Queen's rule.

Just at this moment of tension, the first two Jesuit missionaries, Robert Persons and Edmund Campion, landed in England. Campion, who combined intellectual ability and high moral standards with courage and toughness, declared in an open letter to the Council that he had come 'to cry alarm spiritual against foul vice and proud ignorance, wherewith many my dear countrymen are abused'. Although he denied any intention of interfering in politics, and believed this to be not only desirable but also possible, the government thought otherwise. Their reply took the form of an Act of 1581 'to retain the Queen's Majesty's subjects in their due obedience', which opened a period of severe repression of catholicism in England. Anyone attempting to subvert the loyalty of the Queen's subjects, or to convert them as a means to this particular end, was to suffer death as a traitor, while the run-of-the-mill catholics, who showed their faith by refusing to attend anglican services, were to be fined the crippling sum of £20 for every absence, instead of a shilling as earlier. Seminary priests were hunted down, imprisoned, tortured and frequently executed, and in 1585 an Act was passed declaring that any catholic priest who remained in England was committing treason by so doing.

Altogether one hundred and eighty-three catholics, most of them priests, were executed during Elizabeth's reign—this was the great price that had to be paid for the great achievement of reviving Roman Catholicism in England. Without the courage of these men Elizabeth and Cecil might have achieved their object, and the ferocity with which priests were treated sprang, in part at least, from resentment at their success in undermining the Elizabethan Settlement. Yet if the rulers of England had been tolerant of the 'new catholicism' they would not have survived to regret their error, for the priests moved in the upper ranks of English society, among men who had it in their power to challenge the authority of the Queen's government. The catholic martyrs of Elizabeth's reign were, whether they admitted it or not, politically significant—unlike the ordinary men and women whom Mary Tudor had put to death. Campion, who was captured and executed in 1581, proudly claimed that the catholics were 'as true subjects as ever the Queen had', but the Privy Council found this an insufficient answer to the notorious 'Bloody Question': 'If the Pope or any other by his appointment do invade this realm, which part would you take, and which part ought a good subject to take?' A clearer answer was given by Robert Persons, who wrote a virulent tract against Elizabeth, to be distributed by Spanish troops after they had landed from the victorious Armada.

About half the priests working on the English mission were eventually captured, and half of those captured were sentenced to death.

The government drew a distinction, in practice, between those who were a serious threat and those whose influence was restricted: William Weston, for instance, was not tortured or executed even though he made his prison at Wisbech a catholic centre. As for lay catholics, their treatment depended, as always, on the attitude of the Justices of the Peace in the area where they lived. In the north, which was a catholic stronghold, the Justices frequently ignored recusancy, while in Essex, as in Hampshire, only one catholic paid a regular monthly fine of £20 throughout the second half of Elizabeth's reign. But where fines were levied they could be crippling, and the historian of Sussex gentry families has noted a remarkable correlation between recusancy and economic decline.[1]

War with Spain

Tolerance of Roman Catholics turned to persecution because of the Spanish-catholic threat which grew more menacing throughout the 1570s and 1580s. Elizabeth hoped that the revolt of Holland and the Netherlands against Spanish rule might be ended peacefully, and she welcomed the truce which was agreed on in 1577. But this did not last, and the Duke of Parma began a methodical reconquest of the southern provinces. In April 1584 the leader of Dutch resistance, William of Orange, was assassinated. It looked as though nothing except English intervention could now save the Dutch and make possible the compromise peace that Elizabeth still wanted. At last, therefore, she committed herself, and in 1585 sent Leicester over to the Netherlands with an expeditionary force.

Leicester's force accomplished little, and only the nobility of Sir Philip Sidney, dying on the battlefield at Zutphen, has redeemed his campaign from total oblivion. But the mere presence of an English army in the Netherlands prevented the easy fulfilment of Spanish plans, and forced Philip II to recognise that if his ambitions in Europe were to be achieved he would have to deal with England. Plots against Elizabeth's life were not, of themselves, sufficient: the Throckmorton conspiracy of 1583, for instance, led only to the expulsion of the Spanish ambassador. At the same time, the achievements of English seamen, particularly Drake's raid on the coast of Spain in 1585, showed that Spanish power, so overwhelming on land, could be successfully

[1] J. E. Mousley, 'The Fortunes of Some Gentry Families of Elizabethan Sussex', *Economic History Review*, Vol. 11, No. 3, April 1959.

challenged and defeated at sea. If Philip was to bring his Netherlands policy to a successful conclusion he would have to construct a fleet and strike at England.

As the danger from Spain increased so did the threat offered to Elizabeth's life by Mary, Queen of Scots. Mary had been involved in plotting ever since her arrival in England, and only Elizabeth's reluctance to execute a divinely appointed monarch had saved Mary from sharing Norfolk's scaffold after the exposure of the Ridolfi conspiracy. The assassination of William of Orange was a warning that Philip II and the Pope would not stop short of political murder if it advanced their policy, and Elizabeth, upon whom the defence not only of England but of the protestant cause depended, was the obvious target. In 1584 the Council drew up the Bond of Association, incorporated into a statute the following year, by which the signatories pledged themselves, in the event of a successful attempt on Elizabeth's life, to hunt down and destroy the person in whose name the assassination had been carried out. Mary was not explicitly named, but she was clearly uppermost in the minds of those who flocked to sign the Bond, and in Parliament and the Council the prevailing opinion was that the Queen of Scots should be put to death.

Elizabeth, who knew that the stability of her own throne depended, in the last resort, upon a general reverence for monarchy, was unwilling to execute a fellow-sovereign, and she refused to be convinced of Mary's complicity in the plots against her. It was left to Sir Francis Walsingham to provide irrefutable evidence. In 1586 he discovered a new plot to murder Elizabeth and release the Queen of Scots, with the help of a Spanish army, in which the go-between was a young English catholic named Anthony Babington. Walsingham tapped Babington's correspondence with Mary, and through his agents he prompted the sending of a letter asking for Mary's explicit approval of all the details of the plot, including Elizabeth's assassination. In July 1586 came Mary's reply, giving her full assent. Even Elizabeth could not ignore this evidence, and she gave orders for Mary's trial.

The result of the trial was a formal condemnation of the Scottish Queen, and Parliament petitioned for Mary's execution. But Elizabeth still could not bring herself to this action, which would outrage public opinion in France and Spain and complete the isolation of England. As always she hoped to shift the responsibility for action on to other shoulders, and hinted that Mary's murder would not be displeasing to her. The hint was not taken, but in the end the Council acted on its own initiative and despatched the death warrant to Fotheringay Castle in Northamptonshire, where Mary was held prisoner. On 8 February 1587 she was led out to a scaffold specially constructed in the castle hall and there executed.

Elizabeth was furious when she heard the news, refused to admit Cecil, now Lord Burghley, to her presence, and sent Davison, the Secretary of State who had been entrusted with the warrant, to the Tower. Her anger was genuine, for her ministers, even though they acted in good faith, had disobeyed her trust. But she was too much of a realist not to appreciate the advantages of Mary's removal from the scene. Not least among these was the fact that the new catholic claimant to the English throne was the daughter of Philip of Spain. English catholics, who might have risen in Mary's cause, were unlikely to feel much enthusiasm for a Spanish Queen.

The removal of the Queen of Scots from the political scene made Philip's way plain, for while she was alive he had always been aware that by placing her on the English throne he would be putting England into the orbit of France. Yet even before the news of Mary's execution reached him, Philip had decided to invade England. His plan was for a great fleet to sweep the English Channel and leave it clear for the Duke of Parma and his Spanish infantry—the finest in the world—to cross over from the Netherlands. Throughout 1586 ships were being built and assembled along the Channel coast, and in England the Council ordered the setting up of beacons at prominent places so that news of a Spanish invasion could be quickly transmitted. The Armada was almost ready in 1587 and might have sailed then, had not Drake swooped on Cadiz and destroyed the ships and stores assembled there. In fact it did not leave until May 1588, by which time the great Spanish admiral, Santa Cruz, who might have led it to victory, was dead. His successor was the Duke of Medina Sidonia, who described himself as possessing 'neither aptitude, ability, health nor fortune for the expedition'.

Howard of Effingham, the English commander, and Drake, the Vice-Admiral, wanted to attack the Armada off the Portuguese coast, but bad weather, lack of supplies and the Queen's own wishes, kept them in home waters. By July 1588 the Armada was in the Channel, where William Camden, the antiquary, saw it 'built high like towers and castles, rallied into the form of a crescent whose horns were at least seven miles distant'. Medina Sidonia had about a hundred and thirty ships, carrying more than twenty thousand soldiers and sailors, and he kept them in tight formation which the English could not break up. Howard had about the same number of ships, but they were far more manœuvrable than the cumbrous Spanish ones—'so fast and nimble', wrote Medina Sidonia, 'they can do anything they like with them'. The Spaniards were still thinking in terms of a land battle at sea, while the English used their ships as weapons which they launched against the enemy with guns flaming and then pulled swiftly back again.

Medina Sidonia's orders were to keep his fleet intact until the rendezvous with Parma, and this he managed to do in spite of English attacks. Yet although Philip had provided detailed plans for the expedition, no place had been fixed for the rendezvous, and Parma remained strangely inactive. On the night of 28 July 1588 the Armada anchored off Calais, and Howard at last saw his chance. He sent fire-ships sailing downwind towards the anchored ships, and when the Spaniards saw the burning vessels rushing down upon them they took fright and stood out to sea. Next morning the Aramada was scattered over the waters and the English ships cut in among their cumbersome opponents, doing great damage. They could have done more had they not run out of ammunition, which compelled them to break off the engagement and return to harbour to restock. The lull that followed gave Medina Sidonia the chance to reform his half-moon and stand away northwards to escape.

The battle was, in fact, over, for the Spanish ships were short of ammunition, food and water, and had been so badly damaged by English fire that they would fight no more. Since Howard blocked the return passage south, the Duke had no option but to take his leaking ships north, round the coast of Scotland and Ireland, where rough winds and high seas took a heavy toll. Only half of the great fleet that had set out to humble the protestant English ever returned to harbour, and the enemies of the Catholic Church all over Europe hailed this defeat as a sign of God's blessing on their cause. Elizabeth, too, saw the divine judgement in the success of her arms, for the commemorative medal which she ordered to be struck recorded not the skill of her sailors but the favour of an almighty providence. *Afflavit Deus et dissipati sunt*, it declared, with masterly understatement: 'God blew, and they were scattered.'

The defeat of the Armada did not mean the end of the war. The problem for the English was how to make the most of their supremacy at sea, and opinions were divided. Hawkins wanted to bankrupt Spain by blockading the coast and cutting the vital imports of American silver, while Drake wished to spark off rebellion in Portugal (which Philip had annexed in 1580) by an attack on Lisbon. Drake's plan was adopted, and in April 1589 a fleet carrying twenty thousand men set out for Portugal. The expedition was a complete failure, just like those of the 1620s for which Buckingham was to be so severely criticised. Land and sea operations were not co-ordinated, and more damage was done to the English forces by drink, incompetence and disease than by the Spanish defenders. Vigo was sacked, but apart from that nothing was accomplished. American bullion continued to flow into Spain, Portugal remained a part of the Spanish empire, and the half of the Armada which had returned to port was left in safety to refit.

One of the reasons for the English failure to exploit their victory over the Armada was shortage of money. The Queen's revenues could not meet the heavy demands made on them, especially the cost of the army which Elizabeth despatched to France to fight for Henry of Navarre against the Catholic League and to keep the Spanish forces away from the Channel coast. Not until 1596 were supplies available for another naval expedition. This sailed, under Drake and Hawkins, to revive the glories of former years by attacking the Spanish Main, but the Spaniards had by now built up their defences in the New World and they beat off an English assault on Puerto Rico. The expedition was a blow to English morale in more ways than one, for Hawkins died on the outward voyage and Drake on the way home. Howard of Effingham was still alive, however, and he led an expedition to Cadiz in 1596. This was designed to check the assembly of a second Armada, and was at first brilliantly successful. But although Cadiz was captured and a number of ships destroyed, the victory was not exploited. The Armada was able to sail before the end of the year, but fortunately strong winds and high seas turned it back before it reached England.

Part of the blame for these depressing failures must be attributed to the peculiar organisation of these ventures, which were financed by a number of shareholders, of whom the Queen was only one, more concerned with making a profit than with military success. Sea warfare was, in any case, a secondary consideration for England as for Spain. Elizabeth was not fighting a naval war, as Pitt was later to do, for control of world trade and empire. For her, as for her opponents, the main purpose of the Navy was to guard the flanks of a battle line that stretched from Brittany to the Netherlands. Only on rare occasions, as in 1588, did the sea become for a brief moment the main theatre of war.

10

Elizabeth I and Parliament

Whitgift and the Defence of the Church of England

THE Spanish threat to English independence increased the fervour and militancy of the puritans, who came to regard themselves as the only true protestants. But after 1583 the Queen found a powerful ally against them in the person of her Archbishop, John Whitgift. While he was Professor of Divinity at Cambridge, Whitgift had signed a petition for a modification of the rules governing the dress of the clergy, but when the Queen refused to accept this he obeyed. It was typical of his attitude, for he thought that the primary duty of a priest was to care for his flock and not to consume his energy and his charity in disputes over details. He had a great deal of sympathy with puritan doctrines, and was as much of a Calvinist as Cartwright except on the question of ecclesiastical organisation. But once he had made up his mind that royal supremacy was necessary for the protection of the Church, he enforced it with a vigorous intolerance that matched the puritans' own.

While Whitgift fought the enemies of the Church on both flanks, he also carried out a rearguard action against the lay take-over of ecclesiastical wealth. The Reformation had freed the Church from papal control only to subject it to the landowners, including the greatest landowner of all. Monasteries had controlled the right of appointment to about a third of all the livings in England, and this valuable piece of patronage had passed at the Dissolution to the new owners of monastic estates. So also had the tithes which had been 'impropriated' to the upkeep of the monasteries. This meant that a third of all the tithes paid throughout England now went to lay patrons who passed only a small proportion on to the actual incumbents. The Anglican Church, as Grindal told Elizabeth, had been 'spoiled of the livings which at the first were appointed to the offices of preaching and teaching . . . so as at this day, in my opinion, where one church is able to yield sufficient living for a learned preacher, there be at least seven churches unable to do the same'.

The Queen treated the bishops much as her wealthy subjects treated the lesser clergy, and although the plunder of the Church was carried out more discreetly than it had been under Northumberland, the result was the same. An Act passed in the first year of Elizabeth's reign gave the Queen the temporalities of vacant sees, and the temptation to hold up appointments so as to pocket the profits was too great to resist. The diocese of Oxford was without a bishop for over forty years, Ely for nineteen and Bristol for fourteen, and even when bishops were at last appointed they were often forced to exchange some of their more valuable lands for scattered royal manors or for impropriated tithes, which were difficult to collect and caused much hostility. The Queen and a small group of courtiers were the main beneficiaries: the Earl of Oxford, for instance, had £1,000 a year out of the bishopric of Oxford, while the coal-bearing lands of the bishopric of Durham were leased by the Queen and the Earl of Leicester to Thomas Sutton, who, in spite of the high rent he had to pay, made enough money to found the London Charterhouse.

Not surprisingly the value of bishoprics declined. Durham, which had been worth £2,800 in 1535 was valued at £1,800 forty years later, while Lincoln dropped from nearly £2,000 to under £900. The bishops, as individuals, often did well out of their depleted estates, which they treated as if they were personal property. Archbishop Parker, for instance, spent £500 a year on servants, and Whitgift was usually attended by a hundred retainers when he went on progress. Yet at the bottom of the ecclesiastical hierarchy many parish priests and curates had to live on inadequate tithes or such sums as their patron made available. It was hardly to be wondered at that the quality of anglican clergy at the beginning of Elizabeth's reign was not much better than it had been under Edward VI, when an investigation in the diocese of Gloucester had shown that out of more than three hundred clergy, over half were unable to repeat the Commandments, twenty-seven did not know the author of the Lord's Prayer and ten could not even say it. The best men often preferred one of the lectureships that were being established in increasing numbers by individuals and corporations, usually puritan in their sympathies.[1] As for the remainder, as one clergyman wrote in 1590, 'when they look upon our

---

[1] Lecturers were supported by voluntary contributions and were required to deliver lectures on spiritual subjects, usually in the afternoon or evening.

contempt and beggary and vexation, [they] turn to law, to physics, to trades, or anything rather than they will enter into this contemptible calling'.

Whitgift realised that reform was needed, but believed that it must be done gradually, so as not to shake the structure of the Church at a time when its opponents were waiting to dismantle it. The abuses, however undesirable, had something to be said for them. Impropriated tithes, for instance, swelled the revenues of bishops and university colleges, and pluralism did at least free the occupants of benefices from an obsession with getting their daily bread, and left them more time for spiritual duties. A complete overhaul of ecclesiastical finances was needed, but only Parliament and the Queen were strong enough to carry this out, and these were the big property-owners, the very people who had a vested interest in maintaining the existing state of affairs. Whitgift therefore advised caution. 'The temporalty', he wrote in 1575, 'will not lose one jot of their commodity in any respect to better the livings of the Church. And therefore let us keep that we have. For better we shall not be. We may be worse, and that, I think, by many is intended.'

Not all property-owners were opposed to reform. In Parliament there was a puritan group which wanted to free the church from lay control by transferring to each congregation the responsibility for appointing its own minister, but such a sweeping change would have involved the abolition of the entire ecclesiastical hierarchy, and neither the Queen nor her Archbishop was prepared to abandon a form of ecclesiastical government that had centuries of acceptance behind it. Whitgift intended to carry out piecemeal reform of the existing order at the same time as he enforced conformity, but he was frequently made aware that Councillors and members of Parliament, while urging more speedy reform, would have preferred laxer rule. In 1583, for instance, his order that all the clergy should affirm that the Prayer-Book 'containeth nothing in it contrary to the word of God' caused such a storm of protest that he had to modify the terms of the oath and allow ministers to subscribe that they accepted the Book in so far as it was compatible with the Scriptures. Some three or four hundred ministers refused to make even this modified affirmation, but only a handful of them were deprived.

Whitgift found the Court of High Commission an admirable instrument for his purpose, since it could deal with all matters affecting the Church, except where property was concerned, and it could impose fines and imprisonment as well as spiritual punishments. Whitgift did not create the Court, which had developed from the commissioners appointed to exercise the royal supremacy, but he made it far more active and efficient than it had previously been. The enforcement of conformity by the High Commission aroused protests from puritan gentry and clergy in the southern, midland and eastern counties, and the Council summoned Whitgift to appear before it early in 1584 to answer charges made against him.

The Archbishop, aware of his dignity and of the need to resist lay control, declined to appear, but he modified his tactics in face of the opposition against him, and introduced the *ex officio* oath. This gave any officer of the Church the right 'by virtue of his office' to question a man, on oath, about his beliefs. The common lawyers, who were sympathetic to the puritans and resented the activity of the prerogative courts, challenged the validity of the *ex officio* oath on the grounds that a man should not be compelled to incriminate himself, but it was eventually decided in Cawdrey's Case, in 1591, that the authority of Church courts, based as it was upon the royal prerogative, could not be challenged. Whitgift, meanwhile, went ahead with his relentless investigations, suspending as many as forty-five ministers in a single day in Suffolk.

The puritan sympathisers in the Privy Council protested against Whitgift's policy—Sir Francis Knollys, for instance, who was the Queen's cousin and treasurer of her household, told Burghley how much he grieved 'to see the zealous preachers of the Gospel, sound in doctrine (who are the most diligent barkers against the popish wolf to save the fold and flock of Christ) to be persecuted and put to silence', and Burghley was sufficiently impressed by this complaint to write to the Archbishop in similar terms, asserting that the *ex officio* oath was 'too much savouring of the Romish Inquisition'.

Whitgift, however, would not be deflected from his course, especially as the presbyterian organisation advocated by Cartwright was spreading rapidly. Where suitable ministers could be found puritan congregations were established and elders elected, and by 1582 at the latest *classes*, or conferences, of ministers and elders from several congregations were taking place. This *classis* movement was underground, depending for success on cooperation between sympathetic ministers and magistrates, and was not so much opposed to the existing hierarchical system as completely oblivious of it. But as it reached out for some form of national organisation it threatened the whole pattern of government of the Anglican Church. In 1582, for instance, the first national synod, or general assembly, took place in Cambridge, and another was held at London to coincide with the 1584 Parliament. Field and other London puritans organised the conference and worked out techniques of lobbying political figures, which were to be of immense value to the parliamentary opposition as it developed.

. The fruit of Field's labours was seen in the House of Commons in 1585. When members insisted on discussing religious matters in spite of the Queen's prohibition, she sent for the Speaker and ordered him to allow the debate to go no further. Complaints, she said, were to be made to the bishops or to her Councillors or in the last resort to herself, but 'she will receive no motion of innovation, nor alter or change any law whereby the religion or church of England standeth established at this day'. The temper of the House was such that there were proposals to pass motions rejecting the Queen's command and censuring the Speaker for attending the Queen without the Commons' permission. These angry and extremist proposals came to nothing, but several Bills on Church matters did, in fact, pass through both Houses, and Whitgift had to appeal to the Queen to delay or veto them.

Elizabeth made her anger known against 'some particular persons' who had acted contrary to her direct commandment, but she knew, as well as Whitgift, that the best way to stifle criticism was by reforming the Church from within. Convocation, which met at the same time as Parliament, passed a number of articles designed to deal with the most obvious abuses. Bishops were ordered to insist on stricter standards for ordinands, thereby avoiding the criticism that Burghley had made of the Bishop of Lichfield who ordained 'seventy ministers in one day for money: some tailors, some shoemakers, and others craftsmen. I am sure the greatest part of them are not worthy to keep horses.' Yet even the limited articles of reform that were agreed upon were more counsels of perfection than practical possibilities. The evils of the Church could not be cured overnight, and even if radical reconstruction had been a practical possibility it would, as the critics of the Church realised, have opened the way to total destruction.

The puritan leaders made elaborate preparations for the meeting of Parliament in 1586, and their mastery of political techniques was shown by the letter which the leader of a *classis* at Dedham in Essex wrote to Field: 'I hope you have not let slip this notable opportunity of furthering the cause of religion by noting out all the places of government in the land for which burgesses for the Parliament are to be chosen, and using all the best means you can possibly for ... procuring the best gentlemen of those places, by whose wisdom and zeal God's causes may be preferred.' Field also had ready a survey of the clergy in over two thousand five hundred parishes, covering London and the surrounding counties. This survey, which other evidence suggests is reasonably accurate, reported that in Essex, for example, which contained more than three hundred benefices, over half were held by ignorant and unpreaching ministers. Many of the charges were based upon nothing more substantial than the fact that the minister in question did not live up to the puritan ideal—one was described as 'sometimes a popish priest, a gross abuser of the Scriptures'—but there was sufficient truth in the survey to make it a powerful indictment of the established Church.

Anthony Cope was chosen as the puritan spokesman in the Commons, and in 1587 he introduced a Bill to replace the Prayer-Book by the Geneva *Book of Discipline*, and to sweep away all the ecclesiastical hierarchy. The House, meeting under the shadow of catholic plots and impending war with Spain, was in no mood to compromise, and swept aside the Speaker's protests. Peter Wentworth brought up the whole question of freedom of speech and put a number of leading questions to the Speaker, which, he proposed, should be immediately considered by the Commons. Elizabeth was driven by this puritan attack to action stronger than any she had so far taken. Wentworth, Cope and three other members of the Commons were imprisoned, and the Speaker was told to prevent further discussion of religious matters. Sir Christopher Hatton, one of the Councillors in the House, led a counter-attack, pointing out that a presbyterian system would endanger members' rights of patronage, and the Commons therefore shifted their ground to Church abuses, and set up a committee to consider these. But Elizabeth again intervened and, insisting that the government of the Church was a matter for the royal prerogative alone, stopped any further discussion.

The puritans, blocked in Parliament, were forced back on self-help. Field said: 'Seeing we cannot compass these things by suit nor dispute, it is the multitude and people that must bring the discipline to pass which we desire.' The *classes*, however, were divided. Some wanted to go ahead with erecting a nationwide presbyterian system: others wished to remain still within the fold of the Church of England and to purify rather than abandon it. At this difficult stage, while they were floundering, the tide of events and opinion receded and left them stranded. The defeat of the Armada in 1588 reduced the catholic threat which had made patriotism and puritanism virtually synonymous, and in the same year Field, the organising genius of the movement, and Leicester, one of its most influential patrons at Court, both died. Public opinion was beginning to turn away from puritanism, partly in reaction against the Marprelate Letters, which first appeared in October 1588. These letters were masterpieces of invective, but their unremitting abuse acted like an inoculation and induced its own reaction. Bishops, for instance, were described as 'Right poisoned, persecuting and terrible priests . . . petty anti-Christs, petty popes, proud prelates, intolerable withstanders of reformation, enemies of the Gospel', while the clergy in general were dismissed as 'so many swine, dumb dogs, non-residents . . . so many lewd livers, as thieves, murderers, adulterers, drunkards, cormorants, rascals, so many ignorant and atheistical dolts'. Less violent language might have been far more effective.

Whitgift and his chaplain, Richard Bancroft, were meanwhile developing their own campaign. Puritan leaders were summoned before the High Commission and their papers confiscated, and Bancroft used these documents in an impressive sermon, preached at Paul's Cross in February 1589, in which he exposed the puritan plan to undermine the Church. In 1590 Cartwright himself was imprisoned for refusing to take the *ex officio* oath, and was only released after acknowledging the royal supremacy. Three puritan ministers, including Penry and Udall who were suspected of being the anonymous 'Marprelate', fled to Scotland, and Elizabeth demanded their return in an angry letter which she sent James. 'There is risen both in your realm and mine,' she wrote, 'a sect of perilous consequence such as would have no kings but a presbytery, and take our place while they enjoy our privilege.' Udall just escaped the gallows, but Penry was executed. So were Barrow and Greenwood, the leaders of the Independents.

These harsh measures, and the changing temper of the nation, took the fight out of puritanism. Puritan sentiment still, of course, remained strong, but as a political force it was finished for Elizabeth's reign, and it spent its energies once again on details such as vestments and ceremonies. No longer did it threaten either to remodel the Church of England or to abandon it, and when the Dedham *classis* held its eightieth and last meeting in June 1589, it wrote its own epitaph: 'Thus long continued through God's mercy this blessed meeting, and now it ended by the malice of Satan.'

The comparative ease with which militant puritanism was defeated suggests that it had not taken as deep a hold as its leaders believed. In some ways the amount of attention paid to the puritans, both at the time and ever since, is misleading, because it obscures the truth that puritans remained a minority inside the Church and in the country as a whole. Many people resented puritan fanaticism, and Richard Baxter, describing his boyhood in Shropshire in the early seventeenth century, says that the three or four 'competent preachers'—presumably puritan —who lived in his neighbourhood, 'were the common marks of the people's obloquy and reproach, and any that had but gone to hear them . . . was made the derision of the vulgar rabble under the odious name of a puritan'.

The Church of England, which had been at the beginning of Elizabeth's reign an artificial creation, gradually struck roots that time and habit drove deep into English life, and its increasing strength was reflected in the emergence of an 'anglican group' in the Commons after 1588. The success of the Elizabethan settlement owed much to the Queen herself who, by refusing to permit the slightest change, turned a temporary compromise into a permanent institution. As she told Parliament in 1589, she was 'most fully and firmly settled in her conscience, by the word of God, that the estate and government of this Church of England, as now it standeth in this reformation, may justly be compared to any church which hath been established in any Christian kingdom since the Apostles' times: that both in form and doctrine it is agreeable with the Scriptures, with the most ancient general councils, with the practice of the primitive church, and with the judgements of all the old and learned fathers.'

This position was defended and elaborated by Richard Hooker, who published his *Laws of Ecclesiastical Polity* in the last decade of the sixteenth century. The Church of Christ, he maintained, was a living body which needed constantly to adapt to changing conditions and could not be rigidly tied to a stereotype culled from the Bible. Scripture laid down only fundamentals: the rest were *adiaphora*, to be decided by the lay ruler, and 'it is no more disgrace for Scripture to have left a number of other things free to be ordered at the discretion of the Church, than for nature to have left it unto the wit of man to devise his own attire. . . . Sundry things may be lawfully done in the Church, so as they be not done against the Scripture, although no Scripture do command them, but the Church, only following the light of reason, judge them to be in discretion meet.' By his appeal to age and tradition, Hooker emphasised the historical descent of the English Church and contrasted it with the novel organisation of the puritans, who seemed to think that no pure Church existed until Calvin created it! He also appealed to the senses, and rejected the puritan concentration on impromptu praying and preaching. Ceremonial was an inducement to holiness, he claimed, and so was music 'that carrieth as it were into ecstasies, filling the mind with an heavenly joy, and for the time in a manner severing it from the body'. 'They must', he added, thinking of the puritans, 'have hearts very dry and tough from whom the melody of psalms doth not sometime draw that wherein a mind religiously affected delighteth.'

The increasing vigour of the Anglican Church was shown at Cambridge, previously a puritan stronghold, where Lancelot Andrewes drew large audiences to his lectures in the 1580s, in which he expounded the view that divine grace and human nature, far from being at loggerheads, worked in harmony. In this he was going beyond the position that Whitgift held, for the unofficial Lambeth Articles, drawn up by the Archbishop in 1595, affirmed that God had from eternity predestined some men to life and reprobated some to death. Had these Articles ever replaced the official Thirty-nine they would have let Calvinism into the Church of England by the back door, but Elizabeth was quick to spot the danger. At her command Robert Cecil wrote to Whitgift to tell him 'that she mislikes much that any allowance hath been given by your Grace [in the Articles] of any points to be disputed of predestination (being a matter tender and dangerous to weak, ignorant minds) and thereupon requireth your Grace to suspend them'.

The decline of puritanism as a political force was shown in the Commons, where, in 1593, an Act was passed declaring that anyone who refused to go to church to hear the Prayer-Book service, or who attended an unauthorised religious meeting, should be sent into exile with a warning that if he returned it would be to face a felon's death. There were still puritan sympathisers in the House, but they abandoned the attempt to remodel the Church by statute, and concentrated instead on urging stricter Sunday observance. A Bill 'for the better keeping of the sabbath' was introduced into the 1601 Parliament by (significantly enough) the last of the Marian exiles in the House, but it did not gain the support of the Commons. As a religious and moral force, puritanism was stronger at the end of Elizabeth's reign than it had been at the beginning, but politically speaking it was moribund.

Parliament and Freedom of Speech

Elizabeth summoned ten Parliaments, which met for a total of one hundred and forty weeks, and there were many years in which no session took place. Yet although Parliament was an intermittent assembly, its prestige was high and there was intensive competition for seats in the Commons. The Queen was pressed to create more Parliamentary boroughs, and in the first thirty years of her reign she added sixty-two new members to the House. This was of benefit not to the townsmen but to the gentry who were invading the boroughs and taking over their seats. The influence of land spread right into the heart of Elizabethan towns, and by 1600 two out of every three boroughs were represented by non-residents.

Procedure in the Commons was crystallising, and by the end of the reign Bills were usually read three times, with a committee stage after the second reading. The full House met in the morning from eight to eleven, and divisions were common: the afternoon was reserved for committees. When Parliament was in session members were allowed to speak freely, but it was not certain whether they had the right to initiate discussion. The privilege of 'Freedom of Speech' was highly valued, but its scope was not at all clearly defined, and Elizabeth's reign saw constant dispute between the Queen and her faithful Commons on the distinction between 'liberty' and 'licence'.

Elizabeth was faced, in her early years, with a difficult situation abroad which needed tactful handling, and she was also involved in domestic disputes about the succession and the ecclesiastical settlement. She claimed that all these matters, since they affected her so closely, were not for discussion by the House, but the weakness of such a definition was that these matters were the only ones worth discussing. Members of the Commons resented what seemed to them to be an attempt to limit their freedom of expression. Their House represented the richest and most influential section of the population, and they had acquired, under a boy King and a catholic Queen, a degree of independence which made them unwilling to compromise. Members had no reason to believe in 1559 that Elizabeth would live long and turn into a great Queen. For them she was a weak and feeble woman who must not be allowed to betray her country through inexperience or lack of ability. Elizabeth, of course, viewed the matter differently. She was Henry VIII's daughter, Queen by hereditary right, and determined to be ruler in fact as well as in name. Some sort of clash was inevitable.

When the first Parliament of the reign met, the Queen saw no reason to attempt a definition of freedom of speech, but when the Commons petitioned her to marry she sharply reminded them that it was 'a very great presumption, being unfitting and altogether unmeet for you to require them that may command'. The Commons, undaunted, revived the petition in the 1566 session, inspired to do so by one of the 'puritan choir', and this time linked it with the subsidy Bill. In spite of Elizabeth's message that she was minded to marry, the debate continued, and the furious Queen told a deputation from the Lords that the Commons were very rebels who would never have dared to treat her father in such a fashion.

Through her Councillors Elizabeth sent a message to the House to discontinue the debate, but this brought Paul Wentworth to his feet to ask whether such a commandment 'be a breach of the liberty of the free speech of the House?' This appeal to self-interest rallied the Commons, who drew up a petition in which they described their privilege—in historically inaccurate but deeply felt terms—as 'an ancient laudable custom, always from the beginning necessarily annexed to our assembly'. The petition was never presented, for the Queen withdrew her prohibition, but in her closing speech she told members that while she had no intention of infringing their lawful privileges, neither did she wish their liberty to make her bondage.

Perhaps as a result of this tussle, the Queen made a much more careful definition of freedom of speech when Parliament again assembled in 1571. The Lord Keeper, speaking in her name, told the Commons they would 'do well to meddle with no matters of state but such as should be propounded unto them, and to occupy themselves in other matters concerning the commonwealth'. 'Matters of state' were not defined, but the practice of Elizabeth's reign showed that she included in this category anything that directly affected herself or her prerogative—the succession, for instance, and her own marriage, the royal supremacy over the Church, the conduct of foreign policy, and the regulation of trade. These were all topics on which the Queen needed, like any government, room to manœuvre, and Acts of Parliament—which were the natural conclusions of parliamentary debate—tied her far too rigidly. She could hold up a Bill, or, in the last resort, veto it, but this type of clear-cut decision was always disagreeable to Elizabeth. She wanted the Commons to use the much more flexible procedure of petitioning, since this brought grievances to her attention while leaving her free to decide on the best way of dealing with them. Unfortunately for her the very rigidity of procedure by Bill appealed to members, who *wanted* to tie the Queen's hands. In their concern for the welfare of the Queen and the protestant Church, and in their certainty that they knew best, they favoured the very procedure which was least acceptable to Elizabeth.

The Queen's definition of freedom of speech in 1571 did not prevent Parliament from debating religious matters, for it was in this session that Strickland introduced his Bill for reforming the Prayer-Book,[1] and was promptly summoned before the Council and ordered to absent himself from the House. The Councillors explained that he had been restrained not for anything he had said inside the House but for discussing parliamentary affairs with outsiders—presumably his puritan friends. The Commons, however, were not impressed by this explanation, and another puritan member shifted the debate on to the question of the Commons' privileges, asserting that 'all matter not treason, or too much to the derogation of the imperial Crown, was tolerable there [in the Commons]'. He went on to say that it was proper for princes to have their prerogatives, but that these were 'to be straitened within reasonable limits'. At moments like this Elizabeth's cause would have been lost without her Councillors. It was they who, on this occasion as on many others, 'whispered together. And thereupon the Speaker made this motion, that the House should stay of any further consultation hereupon.' Next morning Strickland was back in his place. The Queen had given way on this particular issue, while still maintaining the principle.

Religion was not the only matter that inflamed the House in this 1571 session. An angry discussion on financial abuses led to the setting up of a committee for grievances—the first of those committees which were later to provide the Commons with an alternative leadership to that offered by the Privy Councillors and enable them to seize the initiative in legislation. The debate saw the maiden speech of Peter Wentworth, brother of Paul, who was to become the great champion of freedom of speech in the Commons. Peter Wentworth was passionately loyal to the Queen, but at the same time passionately devoted to the rights of Parliament, and in his speech he attacked the practice of Councillors reporting debates to the Queen, claiming that discussions in the House should be kept secret even from the sovereign. This extreme view,

[1] See above, Chapter 9, p. 179.

like most of Wentworth's, was not shared by the rest of the House, but by pushing the privileges of the Commons to their logical conclusion he set a precedent that later Parliaments were to follow. The isolated voice of Wentworth in 1571 had become the general opinion of the House half a century later.

Peter Wentworth's great moment came in the 1576 Parliament, when he delivered a speech he had been brooding on for several years. His theme was freedom of expression, and when he considered the forces which endangered this liberty, he put 'rumours and messages' first. The House, he said, was full of rumours such as 'Take heed what you do. The Queen's Majesty liketh not of such a matter. Whosoever preferreth it, she will be much offended with him', and occasionally there were messages 'either of commanding or inhibiting, very injurious unto the freedom of speech and consultation. I would to God, Mr Speaker, that these two [rumours and messages] were buried in hell.' Developing his argument he went on to claim that the Queen was bound to maintain the law and that 'free speech and conscience in this place was granted by a special law, as that without which the prince and state cannot be preserved or maintained'.

Here was novel doctrine indeed: that the Crown had no right to intervene in parliamentary debates. Other members were shocked by Wentworth's outspokenness, particularly when he openly criticised the Queen, and by order of the House he was sent to the Tower. There he stayed for a month until the Queen ordered his release, and one of the Councillors used the occasion of this generous gesture to remind the House that liberty did not mean licence. 'Though freedom of speech', he said, 'hath always been used in this great council of the Parliament, and is a thing most necessary to be preserved among us, yet the same was never, nor ought to be, extended so far as though a man in this House may speak what and of whom he list.'

Elizabeth could never afford to relax in her struggle to keep her wealthy, independent-minded Commons under control, and from 1571 onwards her reply to the Speaker's petition for freedom of speech emphasised that this privilege did not extend to matters of state. She never entered the House of Commons, let alone listened to a debate, but from her palace at Whitehall, Richmond, Nonsuch or Greenwich, she kept a constant watch on parliamentary affairs and despatched those rumours and messages of which Wentworth complained. She was fortunate in having Councillors who were not only loyal to her but were also popular figures in the House. After Cecil

left for the Lords in 1571 leadership in the Commons passed to Sir
Christopher Hatton, who was well supported by three of his colleagues,
Knollys, Walsingham and Mildmay—all three men whose puritan
sympathies made them particularly acceptable to the House. Elizabeth's
policy was never, in any case, merely negative. She appreciated the
fact that the Commons would only proceed by petition if she showed
her willingness to take action, and in 1581, for instance, after a debate
on the abuses of the Church, she sent for the bishops and ordered them
to draw up proposals for reform.

Peter Wentworth returned to the attack in March 1587, prompted
to do so by the Queen's confiscation of Cope's Bill[1] and book. He put
a number of leading questions to the House, which were designed to
interpret the privilege of freedom of speech in the widest possible
manner. Sir John Neale describes these questions as 'comparable, in the
secular sphere, with the theses posted on the church door at Wittenberg by Martin Luther'.[2] Had Wentworth's views been accepted,
the Crown would have been left with no effective control over the
Commons and would have lost the initiative in legislation. The Queen
showed her anger by sending Wentworth to the Tower, where he
remained for the rest of the session. The mood of the House was shown
by the appointment of a committee to search the statute book and see
if the imprisonment of members was legal.

By the time the next Parliament met, in 1589, the Armada had
come and gone, and religion was no longer such a burning issue.
Financial grievances came to the fore instead, and two Bills were
introduced to check abuses concerning the Exchequer and the practice
of purveyance. The Queen informed the Commons that since these
matters affected her closely she would take action herself, and she asked
that four members of Parliament should be chosen to confer with a
group of Privy Councillors and household officials about the best ways
in which to remedy the grievances. In this way she preserved her
prerogative while at the same time satisfying the Commons' urge to
take part in the work of reform, but as Neale comments, 'the Tudor
constitution was by now standing on uncertain foundations: on little
more than the masterful nature and unique personality of an ageing
Queen'.[3]

In 1593, when Parliament met again, Hatton, Mildmay and Walsingham were all dead and a new generation had emerged which did not

[1] See above, p. 199.   [2] *Elizabeth I and Her Parliaments 1584-1601*, p. 156.
[3] Ibid., p. 212.

willingly accept the restraints imposed by the Queen Perhaps for this reason the Lord Keeper's reply to the petition for freedom of speech defined the privilege most carefully. 'For liberty of speech', he said, 'her Majesty commandeth me to tell you that to say "Yea" or "No" to Bills, God forbid that any man should be restrained or afraid to answer according to his best liking, with some short declaration of his reason therein, and therein to have a free voice—which is the very true liberty of the House: not, as some suppose, to speak there of all causes as him listeth, and to frame a form of religion or a state of government, as to their idle brains shall seem meetest. She saith, no King fit for his state will suffer such absurdities.'

Elizabeth was far less tolerant of breaches of her instructions in this session. She sent Peter Wentworth to prison for publishing a tract on the succession, excluded from the House two members who dared to attack the High Commission, and reminded the Speaker that she had the right not only to summon and dissolve Parliament, but also to tell members what they were and were not to discuss. She was, by 1593, sixty years old, and had been ruling England before some of the members of the Commons had even been born. She regarded them as young hotheads, who needed to be disciplined, and she particularly resented 'such irreverence [as] was showed towards Privy Councillors'.

Yet in spite of hotheads the later Parliaments of Elizabeth were never as difficult to control as some of the earlier, puritan ones had been. Young men had their way to make in the world and were aware that a speech in opposition to the Queen's policy could end their chances of promotion. When the Earl of Essex tried to obtain an office for a friend in the Commons he failed because, as he wrote, the Queen 'startles at your name, chargeth you with popularity, and hath every particular of your speeches in Parliament. . . . She stands much upon the bitter speech against Sir Robert Cecil.'

Monopolies replaced the Prayer-Book as the main object of Parliament's attack in the last years of the reign. Monopolies were patents granted by the Queen to a favoured courtier, or sold to a business man, and they gave the holder the sole right to manufacture or trade in a certain commodity. This system, justified as a means of protecting new inventions, was applied to everyday articles simply as a means of raising revenue, and the Commons resented it as a form of indirect taxation. Since monopolies were created by the Queen they fell within the category of 'matters of state', not to be discussed without prior permission. But the Queen—no doubt informed by Robert Cecil,

Burghley's second son and political heir, about the temper of the House—chose to defend her prerogative by taking action herself. She ordered her Councillors to examine all monopolies to see if there were any against the public interest, and the grateful Commons turned their petition of complaint into a thanksgiving address. The Queen, in reply, reminded her 'dutiful and loving subjects' that they must not entrench on her prerogative, which was 'the chiefest flower in her garland and the principal and head pearl in her Crown and diadem'.

Although the Queen cancelled some of the more objectionable monopolies the need for money brought many of the abuses back again, and the last Parliament of the reign, which met in October 1601, returned to the attack. One member called monopolists 'these bloodsuckers of the commonwealth', and told how they brought 'the general profit into a private hand'. 'The end of all', he declared, 'is beggary and bondage to the subject.' Bacon tried to persuade the House not to take direct action itself but to petition the Queen to do so. 'The use hath ever been', he said, 'by petition to humble ourselves unto Her Majesty and by petition desire to have our grievances redressed, especially when the remedy toucheth so nigh in point of prerogative.' But members were in an angry mood, disillusioned by the Queen's failure to take effective action after their earlier petition. When the Speaker tried to switch the debate on to discussion of the subsidy he was shouted down, and several members who tried to speak were unable to make themselves heard in the general confusion. Robert Cecil, who had been, as he reminded the Commons, a member of six or seven Parliaments, said that he had never seen the House in so great a confusion: 'This is more fit for a grammar school than a court of Parliament.'

The Queen realised that her prerogative would be endangered if she clung to monopolies, for they were a real grievance and opposition to them was widespread—Cecil, for instance, reported that while he was in his coach he had heard someone say, 'God prosper those that further the overthrow of these monopolies! God send the prerogative touch not our liberty!' Proclamations were therefore issued cancelling the principal monopolies complained of, and authorising anyone with a grievance to seek for redress in the courts of common law.

Elizabeth had once again preserved the principle by conceding the particular point at issue. Her success as a politician came from a remarkable blend of rigidity and flexibility. She knew when and how to give way gracefully, but she was no trimmer: she maintained the Church

HTSB

of England unaltered against opposition that would have overwhelmed an ordinary person, and she refused to abate one jot of her royal prerogative. Although by the end of the reign the Commons had come much nearer to Wentworth's view of freedom of speech, the initiative in legislation still lay with the Queen. This would have been impossible without her unremitting surveillance of the Speaker and the Councillors who represented her in the Commons. It would also have been impossible had she not known how to win the affections of her subjects. She had a wonderful gift for vivid, racy, memorable prose, and she used this with great skill to charm the Commons, as for instance in her 'Golden Speech' in 1601. 'There will never Queen sit in my seat', she told the members, 'with more zeal to my country, care for my subjects, and that will sooner with willingness venture her life for your good and safety, than myself. For it is my desire to live nor reign no longer than my life and reign shall be for your good. And though you have had and may have many princes more mighty and wise sitting in this seat, yet you never had, nor shall have, any that will be more careful and loving.'

Elizabeth had the art not only of appealing to the emotional bonds that linked her with her people but also of skilfully mixing anger and graciousness. She did not hesitate to rebuke publicly those who had offended her, but for the most part she left this unpleasant task to her 'official' voice—the Lord Chancellor or Keeper, the Archbishop of Canterbury, or one of her Councillors. This left her free, in her own speech, to stress the themes of forgiveness, love and unity. By these means she won her way, 'converting her reign', as Harrington wrote, 'through the perpetual love-tricks that passed between her and her people, into a kind of romance'. Yet her achievement depended very much upon her unique personality, and the fact that she had allowed the Commons to go some way in debating matters of state was to be a stumbling-block to her successors. She was often content to maintain a principle by giving way in practice, but, in a legalistic age, her actions were precedents more binding than her words, as the Stuarts discovered to their cost.

The independence of the Commons was shown in their assertion of other privileges as well as freedom of speech. Their right to release imprisoned members and members' servants by warrant of the mace only, which had led to a brawl in Henry VIII's reign, was confirmed by Smalley's case in 1571, but in Fitzherbert's case (1593) it was decided that the privilege did not apply when the action against a member was initiated by the Crown. The Queen's power to discipline members was considerable, though undefined, but after Strickland's imprisonment in 1571 she was always careful to state that any offending member had been punished for words spoken outside the House and not for any unpalatable opinions expressed during the course of debate. The Commons also took action themselves against offending members, as, for example, when they imprisoned Wentworth for criticising the Queen. This and other precedents made it possible for later Parliaments to assert that they and they alone had authority over their members.

The Financial Problem

Elizabeth must frequently have regretted the existence of Parliament, but she could not do without it, for the effectiveness of Tudor government depended on harmony and consent, and Parliament facilitated this. It turned the ideal of unity into reality by bringing together men from all over England, and it attracted many of the leading figures in Elizabethan society. Among those who assembled in London for the opening of the 1584 Parliament, for instance, were the philosopher and lawyer Francis Bacon, the statesman Robert Cecil, the seaman Francis Drake, the scholar and adventurer Walter Ralegh and the poet Fulke Greville; and the variety and distinction of this list could have been matched in most other Parliaments of the reign. The Queen needed good men for her service, and, like her father, she turned to Parliament to find them.

Most important of all Parliament's functions was the voting of money. The rapid rise in prices was eroding the Crown's income, and Elizabeth needed all the extra supplies of money she could get: the systematic plunder of the Church, for instance, was prompted by more than mere avarice. Although she pursued a cautious foreign policy she could not avoid expense. Intervention in Scotland cost several hundred thousand pounds, the garrison in Ireland consumed £30,000 every year, and the army sent to aid the Huguenots against the Guise faction in 1562 added nearly a quarter of a million pounds to the Queen's bills. By selling Crown lands and borrowing money from City companies she could narrow the gap between income and expenditure, but she depended on parliamentary subsidies to close it. Parliamentary grants were still, in theory, exceptional, and were supposed to be justified by some obvious necessity, but in fact they were becoming part of the ordinary revenue, and were of great value to the Queen. The subsidy of 1563, to take one example, was worth a quarter of a million pounds, and with financial assistance on this scale Elizabeth was able to free herself from debt by 1574.

The cautious policy of the next decade was dictated, in part at least, by a desire to economise, and Burghley, who became Lord Treasurer in 1572, advocated retrenchment at home and restraint abroad. There was nothing spectacular about Burghley's work at the Treasury, but he made the existing financial system operate as well as it could by cutting expenditure on pensions and holding the amount spent on the Court at £40,000 a year. The main source of royal revenue was Customs, which brought in £80,000 a year: Crown lands, in spite of the efforts of Henry VII and Henry VIII, brought in only £60,000. Revenue from Customs increased with the expansion of trade, yet the Crown was becoming steadily poorer when compared with the property-owners who sat in Parliament. The subsidies they voted helped redress the balance, but the commissioners for the subsidy in every county were the leading gentry, and the evidence of the Sussex assessments suggests that they were gradually reducing the rate at which they were taxed. Even if they did not actually cut their assessments, they rarely increased them to take account of new wealth. As Ralegh said in a debate of 1601: 'our estates [which] are £30 or £40 in the Queen's books [are] not the hundredth part of our wealth.'

Burghley managed to accumulate a surplus of £300,000, but the outbreak of open war with Spain quickly swallowed this up and left a yawning gap between income and expenditure which even Parliamentary grants could not plug. Only peace could avert bankruptcy, but although Cecil would have welcomed peace it was hardly attainable at a time when English troops were openly supporting the Dutch in their fight for independence and Henry IV in his struggle for the crown of France. The only effective way of raising large sums of money quickly was by selling Crown lands, and this brought in £126,000 in 1590. A few years later the coastal counties were called on to provide ships at their own expense for the Cadiz expedition, while inland counties were ordered to provide money in lieu. There was opposition to this levy, but the Council was desperate for supplies and in the following year, 1597, had recourse to a forced loan.

Yet whatever was done, the cost of the war was too great for the Tudor financial system, which simply could not cope with the demands made on it. Nothing is more striking than the contrast between the

lofty aims of sixteenth-century statesmen and their limited achievement. They aimed at creating a centralised administration, supreme
over state and Church, and extending its control into every aspect
of English life, but the machinery with which they had to work
had been created to serve the limited needs of feudal monarchy, and
needed radical reconstruction. Elizabeth and Burghley might, between
them, have carried this out but the Queen's temperamental conservatism and the Treasurer's natural caution persuaded them to make the
best of a bad job rather than imperil the hard-won stability of English
society. The *ancien régime* survived, even though it lurched from one
financial crisis to another, but the impoverishment of the Crown upset
the balance which Elizabeth and her great minister were so anxious to
preserve.

The government remained dependent on the cooperation of the
property-owners, and although these men were usually ready to
serve they expected some mark of royal favour, preferably lucrative,
in return. This was particularly true of those who held important
posts in the central government, for the nominal salaries attached to
such offices were pitifully small. The English monarchy had traditionally depended for administration on ecclesiastics who could be
rewarded by advancement in the Church, but the anti-clericalism
released by the Reformation changed this. Bishops remained men of
substance, but the decline of their political importance is reflected in
the fact that no bishop sat in Elizabeth's Council until Whitgift was
appointed to it in 1586. Government, which had formerly been the
preserve of the Church, had been taken over by laymen.

These secular administrators could not be rewarded by advancement
in the Church, yet no Tudor monarch could possibly afford to pay
them a salary commensurate with their rank. It was left to the office-
holder to supplement his official income by fees and gratuities from the
public and occasional favours from the Crown. This practice could
easily lead to corruption, especially when—as in Edward VI's reign—
there was no effective sovereign to hold it in check. The political world
then became an arena in which men fought each other for place and
profit, and not until the 1570s did Elizabeth re-establish royal control.
For the next thirty years she kept a tight hand on the distribution of
royal patronage, and made sure that no single individual or faction came
to monopolise it.

Royal patronage fell into three main categories. First of all there was
the grant of titles of honour, but Elizabeth cut down on these in order

to avoid cheapening them by the sort of lavish distribution that had marked Henry VIII's closing years and the brief reign of his son. She created only ten new peers, and although she was more generous with knighthoods, the title was sufficiently rare to be coveted.

The second category included appointments to offices in the Crown's gift. There were about two hundred positions in the royal household, traditionally reserved for the leading families, and other offices were available in the central administration—the Treasury, the Secretariat and the Court of Wards. The Judiciary also provided many opportunities of profit—though appointment was limited to men trained in the law—and so did the armed forces, whose commanders disposed of temptingly large sums of money. The Queen appointed to many lucrative offices in the Church as well, and she alone could confirm a man's local standing by making him Lord-Lieutenant or Justice of the Peace, or by conferring on him some nominal office—such as stewardship of a royal park or manor—which carried great prestige. Tudor England was a hierarchical society, and a man's place in it at any given moment depended upon the titles, offices and perquisites with which he was endowed. Unfortunately, there were only about a thousand such offices to be distributed among over double that number of claimants.

The third category of patronage included more obvious marks of royal favour, such as gifts and pensions, leases of Crown lands, and monopolies. Direct grants from the Queen were generally confined to a handful of favourites, but they could be a valuable prize—Leicester, for example, had an annual pension of £1,000 and Christopher Hatton was given £400 a year in 1576. Leases of royal estates could be almost as valuable, since Crown lands were usually under-exploited and might be made to yield a big profit to a hard-headed lessee: a typical example was that of the Earl of Essex, who paid £23 a year to the Crown for the lease of Uttoxeter Moors, which he sublet for £167. The Queen could also be occasionally persuaded to exchange some of the scattered manors of the Crown for a more consolidated block belonging to a subject. The new owner could make a handsome profit by selling enough of the manors to cover his purchase price and increasing the rents on those he kept. Monopolies were another valuable (though double-edged) gift in the Queen's possession, and she gave the valuable control of sweet wines successively to her two favourites, Leicester and Essex.

The demand for patronage was insatiable and the range was so wide that the Queen could not deal with it all herself but depended for advice on those around her. These men and women, who knew how to channel the flow of royal favour, were some of the most influential figures in Elizabethan society, and constellations of suppliants clustered round them, for, as one contemporary remarked, 'advancement in all worlds be obtained by mediation and remembrance of noble friends'.

The men who controlled Elizabethan England were enmeshed in this network of patronage. Burghley, for instance, received a mere £400 a year as Lord Treasurer, and complained in 1585 that 'my fees of my treasureship do not answer to my charge of my stable—I mean not my *table*!' But the patronage which this office gave him was worth £1,000 a year, and from 1561 to 1598 he held the far more lucrative Mastership of the Wards. The feudal incidents, of which wardship was the most important, were anachronistic in the sixteenth century, but the Crown refused to part with its valuable rights. Henry VIII had enormously enlarged the range of wardship by insisting that purchasers of monastic property should assume the financial obligations of a tenant-in-chief, and throughout his daughter's reign the Court of Wards was hard at work searching out wardships and arranging their sale.

Guardianship of a ward and his lands was sold at a low price—usually about the annual value of his estate—and the buyer could count on making a big profit. So also could the Master of the Wards, through whom this lucrative form of patronage was channelled. When Sir Edward Coke, to take only one example, bought a valuable wardship from the Crown for £300, he showed his gratitude to Burghley by making him a gift of £1,000. Coke still made a profit from the transaction, since he promptly sold the wardship for £4,000. The real losers in this system were the poor wards, who had to watch their estates being exploited by their guardians until they came of age, and who blamed the Crown for perpetuating such a pernicious practice.

The Queen, although she took the brunt of the blame, was lucky if she received as much as a fifth of the profits of wardship. The remaining four-fifths went to the purchasers and intermediaries. Under Burghley, the Court of Wards provided about £15,000 a year for the Exchequer —a small sum when compared with the total royal revenue, and one that was hardly worth the amount of hostility it caused. After Burghley's death Robert Cecil, the new Master, put up the official price of wardships, bringing it closer to the market value and thereby giving the Queen a larger share—about a third—of the profits. Yet the two-thirds which the Queen never saw were almost as valuable to her as the fees paid in to the Exchequer, since they compensated her more important subjects for the inadequate salaries which they received. If the Queen had taken *all* the profits, and paid her ministers and servants what they were worth, she would have made a heavy loss. Since she could not afford to reform the system, she used it to her advantage, and received a steady income at the same time as she strengthened the golden bonds which bound her more important subjects to her.

Burghley guided the Queen in her patronage policy, but he did not monopolise her generosity. Other courtiers—Ralegh, Hatton and Walsingham among them—could usually make their voices heard, and Elizabeth would please herself where her favourites were concerned. Burghley realised that the success of the Elizabethan system of patronage was in proportion to the number of important families it involved, and he was not concerned to build up a private empire. But in the closing years of his life, when he was anxious to ensure that his political influence would pass to his second son, Robert, he became aware that the Queen's young favourite, the Earl of Essex, was deliberately trying to create a monopoly of power that would exclude the Cecils. Burghley reacted by building up 'Cecil's Commonwealth', and his son continued the process in a less scrupulous fashion. The balance which Elizabeth and Burghley had established was destroyed by this conflict of two family groups. The Queen's affection for Essex did not blind her to his lust for power, but somebody had to replace the ageing Burghley and there was no obvious reason why it should be another Cecil. Unfortunately for the Queen's peace of mind, Essex's bid for patronage came at the very moment when poverty was forcing her to cut down, and without Burghley at hand to spread the profits, however thinly, over the widest possible surface, the stability of Elizabeth's middle years gave way to bitter and disruptive conflict.

The struggle was for big stakes, since royal favour and high office opened the way to great wealth—greater than anything that might be built up out of land alone, or the law, or trade. Burghley constantly complained that he had spent all his fortune in the Queen's service, but he did so well out of fees, gratuities, and other 'fringe benefits' which power brought with it that he became one of the richest landowners in England, built two enormous palaces at Stamford and Theobalds, left £15,000-worth of plate behind him, and established his family so securely in the upper ranks of English society that it remains there to this day. Such was the prize that tempted Robert Devereux, second Earl of Essex.

The young favourite depended for his success upon the Queen, and although Elizabeth had a great affection for Essex she was not unaware of his arrogance, and knew that if he replaced Burghley as her patronage secretary he would use his monopoly for private profit rather than the common good. She also distrusted Essex's popularity. The long peace of her reign had given no opening for glory except at Court, but the war with Spain encouraged the emergence of military heroes, and Essex, who distinguished himself in the Cadiz expedition of 1596, became the idol of the soldiers. The Tudors had never looked kindly on military leaders whose fame might eclipse their own, and Elizabeth was no exception. While Essex was away fighting in Cadiz or in Ireland, his rivals entrenched themselves in the Queen's favour. This drove the Earl to desperate measures, for once it was known that he no longer formed part of that circle of mediators whose goodwill opened the way to royal bounty, the gifts and the adulation offered him by petitioners would be proffered elsewhere. Had he not demanded so much so imperiously the Queen might well have given way, but she had never liked being dictated to and was determined to curb Essex's pride before she gratified his political ambitions.

After his failure to win the Mastership of the Wards, in 1598, Essex accepted command of the army in Ireland. He knew it was a gamble, for, as he wrote to a friend, 'I am not ignorant what are the disadvantages of absence—the opportunities of practising enemies when they are neither encountered nor overlooked; the construction of princes, under whom *magna fama* is more dangerous than *mala*, and *successus minus quam nullus*. . . . All these things which I am like to see, I do foresee.' His forebodings were justified. The Council, either by accident or design, was slow to send supplies, and Essex saw himself committed to a long campaign which would keep him far from the Queen. His rivals had already taken advantage of his absence—Robert Cecil, for instance, had secured appointment as Master of the Wards— and the longer he stayed away the weaker his influence became. In defiance of the Queen's explicit orders he threw up his command in Ireland, even though the rebellion was still alive, returned to England in September 1599, and rode post-haste to Elizabeth at Nonsuch.

The Queen was at first glad to see him, but as she reflected on his disregard of her wishes her anger mounted. 'By God's son', she burst

H*

out to one of her gentlemen, 'I am no Queen! That man is above me. Who gave him commandment to come here so soon?' Essex's valuable monopoly of sweet wines was taken away from him and he was kept prisoner until June 1600 when a special tribunal stripped him of his offices. The pyramid of patronage on which he had been precariously perched collapsed under him, and now he had nothing to hope for.

Out of his anger against those who, he was convinced, had ousted him from Elizabeth's favour, Essex hatched a plot for an armed rising, to take over the government and force the Queen to accept new advisers. It looked as though faction struggles were once again going to lead to civil war, and Essex House became a centre where groups of discontented nobles and gentry, including Shakespeare's patron, the Earl of Southampton, discussed their plans. The Council was alarmed, particularly when Shakespeare's company staged *Richard II* at the Globe—the story of an English monarch who had been deposed because he listened to evil counsellors—and Essex was summoned to appear before it. This challenge sparked off the rising, and on 8 February 1600 the Earl rode into the City at the head of two hundred armed men, crying out, 'For the Queen! For the Queen!' Nobody joined him, but troops were drawn up to block his way. The rebellion was over before it had even begun.

The Essex rising showed how close factional strife had come to destroying Elizabethan harmony. Not for nothing did Edward Coke, who led the prosecution against Essex, hark back to the Wars of the Roses when he prayed that 'this Robert might be the last of his name, Earl of Essex, who affected to be Robert the first of that name, King of England'. Essex was executed, but his removal did not solve the problem of an ageing Queen and an empty treasury, even though by confirming Robert Cecil in power it restored at least a semblance of the order that Burghley had established.

Cecil's supremacy apparently depended on the Queen's life, for James had no love for the Cecils, whom he held responsible for Elizabeth's refusal to nominate him as her successor. In the last years of the Queen's reign Robert Cecil spent £25,000 on land, to cushion his possible fall from power, but at the same time he was working hard to make sure that such a fall would not take place. In 1601 he opened secret negotiations with James and prepared arrangements for the peaceful accession of the King of Scots. James's suspicion changed overnight to warm friendship, and when Cecil sent him the draft proclamation announcing his succession, he made no corrections: this music, he said 'sounded so sweetly in his ears that he could alter no note in so agreeable an harmony'.

By March 1603 the Queen was obviously dying and sat for long periods saying nothing. When, however, Cecil and the other officers of state asked her to name her successor, she was said to have given a sign that she acknowledged James. After that she prayed with Whitgift until she fell into a stupor. Early on the morning of 24 March 1603 she died, and a few hours later, while a messenger rode north as fast as relays of horses could carry him, James was proclaimed King of England.

II

James I

JAMES left Edinburgh in April 1603, and so many Englishmen flocked north to see their new monarch that his journey turned into a triumphal progress. The King showed his pleasure by creating over three hundred knights and by revelling in the entertainments that were provided for him at the great country houses where he stayed. It was early May before he eventually entered London and took up residence at Whitehall.

'King James is England's joy. Say all amen!' wrote one budding poet, and there were many who echoed his delight. They were not simply indulging in flattery, for James's peaceful accession put an end to fears of a disputed succession. As the translators of the Bible recalled, some years later, 'it was the expectation of many, who wished not well unto our Sion, that upon the setting of that bright occidental star, Queen Elizabeth of most happy memory, some thick and palpable clouds of darkness would so have overshadowed this land that men should have been in doubt which way they were to walk. . . . The appearance of Your Majesty, as of the sun in his strength, instantly dispelled those supposed and surmised mists, and gave unto all that were well affected exceeding cause of comfort.'

The Constitutional Problem

James was thirty-seven and the fact that he had two sons seemed to assure an unbroken succession for the future. At first sight he was quite pleasing to look at, with his ruddy complexion and fair hair, but his speech was slurred like that of a drunken man, while his spindly legs and ever-rolling eye robbed him of any natural dignity. Whatever a critical observer might have thought of the new King, however,

James was quite satisfied with himself, confident in his own abilities and convinced that, as an old and experienced ruler, he would be able to deal with the problems facing him.

These problems, although he did not at first realise it, were considerable. The Tudor period had seen a revival of the powers of the Crown, and the creation or resuscitation of instruments like the Courts of Star Chamber and High Commission which, while they were invaluable for preserving order, threatened to limit the freedom which the common law guaranteed to Englishmen—particularly propertied Englishmen. Parliament was the watchdog of the common law, and Elizabeth's reign had seen a number of clashes over the use of the royal prerogative. These disputes were in essence constitutional, but political thought in England had not begun to grapple with the problems facing the modern state, and the explosive anger that came increasingly to characterise these disputes sprang, in part at least, from the frustration of men who felt that something was going wrong with English government but could not lay their fingers on the cause.

A redefinition of the powers of the Crown was needed, for no one could be certain where the frontier was drawn between royal prerogative and the rights of the individual. Elizabeth had avoided any such redefinition, instinctively appreciating that the very uncertainty about the extent of the Crown's authority left a reserve of power in her hands. She relied on her own charm to deal with problems as they arose, and by her skilful choice of Councillors she kept friction to a minimum. Nevertheless, discontent was mounting as her reign drew to a close, and was only held in check by the realisation that the Queen's days were numbered and that the accession of a new monarch would shortly provide an opportunity for a fundamental reassessment. As the Commons told James: 'In regard of her sex and age which we had great cause to tender, and much more upon care to avoid all trouble which by wicked practice might have been drawn to impeach the quiet of Your Majesty's right in the succession, those actions were then passed over which we hoped, in succeeding times of freer access to Your Highness of renowned grace and justice, to redress, restore, and rectify.'

The beginning of a new reign was, traditionally, a time for reassessment, and James was a stranger to England and English institutions. Members of Parliament were not lacking in loyalty or reverence to the Crown, but they knew that their privileges—which they were increasingly coming to regard as synonymous with the liberties of all

Englishmen—might mean nothing to a foreigner. Unless they asserted their rights they might find that their rights had disappeared. In Scotland Roman law prevailed, with its emphasis on the authority of the ruler, while the Scottish Parliament had nothing like the dignity and degree of independence of its English namesake. Many of the lessons that James drew from his Scottish experience were simply not applicable to England, but he did not at first realise this. He had taken Tudor absolutism at its face value and he gloried in the high authority which had now been granted him. There was nothing new in his belief that kings were appointed by God to rule in His name. 'The godly prince' had been the Reformation's substitute for papal authority, and Elizabeth believed, no less than James, that her office was of divine origin. There was widespread acceptance of this assumption, even among those who were later to be prominent in the opposition to James's policies—Pym, for instance, told James in 1621 that 'the image of God's power is expressed in your royal dignity'. But James's insistence on his divine right to rule and on the almost limitless authority appertaining to his exalted position seemed to confirm the fears of the Commons that their privileges would be swept aside, and that common law rights might be swamped by an extension of the prerogative.

James, intoxicated with his new glory and conscious not only of his ability but also of his desire to rule well, was probably unaware of the effect on his politically-conscious subjects of his rhapsodies on divine right. His assumption that all problems could be solved if only they were left to him failed to take account of the constitutional development of England during the previous half century, and of the defects of his own character. James was a man who believed that the expression of goodwill was sufficient in itself: he left the detailed work of administration to men who were often less concerned than he appeared to be with the liberties of his subjects.

In the early years of his reign James was content to rely on many of Elizabeth's former ministers, particularly Robert Cecil, whom he created Earl of Salisbury. Cecil was as industrious as his great father had been, and while James was away from London, indulging his passion for hunting, Cecil worked late into the night writing despatches and memoranda. Yet even Cecil's devoted work could not prevent a clash between James and his first Parliament. One reason for this was that Cecil's elevation to the Lords left him unable to influence the Commons, except through conferences of the two Houses. His absence would not have been so disastrous if James had appointed good men to take his place in the Lower House, but the King did not appreciate the need for this. He assumed that Parliament was only too eager to carry out his bidding, and his Scottish experience taught him to rely on the nobles rather than commoners. During the first session of the 1604 Parliament there were only two Privy Councillors in the Commons, neither of them men of great ability, and as late as 1610 there were still only three. In the absence of effective leadership the Commons organised themselves and by the end of James's reign all important business was transacted in committees controlled by the opposition. Most important of these was the Committee of the Whole House, in which the Speaker vacated the chair, leaving members to speak freely in the knowledge that what they said would not be recorded in the Commons' Journal.

James's first Parliament had been in session only a short time when King and Commons quarrelled over a disputed election. The King ordered the Commons, 'as an absolute ruler', to consult with the judges, showing how little he understood of English constitutional practice. The Commons were not prepared to challenge so direct a command, and agreed to a conference, at which the dispute was settled. But James's use of the word 'absolute' had pinpointed all their vague fears and uncertainties, and they drew up—for their own satisfaction as much as anyone else's—the first great constitutional document of the seventeenth century, *The Form of Apology and Satisfaction*. In this they told the King how grieved they were that he should be so misinformed about their privileges, which, he had declared, all derived from royal grace (and, by implication, could be revoked). They assured him that their privileges were, on the contrary, 'our right and due inheritance, no less than our very lands and goods [and] cannot be witheld from us, denied, or impaired, but with apparent wrong to the whole state of the realm'. They assured James of their devotion to him and of their trust in his judgement, but they pointed out that rights which might not be necessary under a good King like himself ought nevertheless to be preserved for protection against a possible bad one. This remarkable document was never formally presented to the King, though he probably saw a copy of it, but the mere fact that the Commons drew it up shows a degree of political awareness and sophistication far beyond anything that could have been expected fifty years earlier. It was forced out of the Commons from the conviction that, as they said, 'the prerogatives of

princes may easily and do daily grow; the privileges of the subject are
for the most part at an everlasting stand'.

James was bewildered by this cold wind, following so swiftly
upon the warmth that had greeted his accession. In Scotland, he told
the Commons, 'I was heard not only as a King but, suppose I say it,
as a counsellor. Contrary, here nothing but curiosity from morning to
evening to find fault with my propositions. There all things warranted
that came from me. Here all things suspected.' His resentment was
understandable—even though he failed to appreciate that the Commons were criticising not his lack of good intentions but his lack of
knowledge—and Parliament's refusal to act on James's proposal to
unite the kingdoms of England and Scotland showed how narrow-
minded members could be. Unfortunately the opening years of the
reign did nothing to allay the suspicions that had grown up, for shortage of money drove the King to assert his prerogative in a way that
seemed to confirm all that the property-owners feared.

The Financial Problem

Elizabeth had died in debt, but James never appreciated the need for
economy. After the poverty of his Scottish kingdom, England seemed
a land flowing with milk and honey, and he spent lavishly as befitted
a mighty monarch. The conclusion of peace with Spain in 1604 led to
the reduction of expenditure on the army and navy, but James's
personal extravagance, combined with the continuing price rise,
plunged the Crown deeper and deeper into debt. In 1610 it was
estimated that the King had given £10,000 in annual pensions and
almost £100,000 in cash to his Scottish favourites alone, and by that
date he was over half a million pounds in debt and overspending at the
rate of £100,000 a year. When Parliament first met, the subsidy
granted in 1601 had still two years to run, and James had no occasion
to ask for money, but in 1606 subsidies were formally requested. There
was some opposition to these, on the grounds that the King should live
of his own in peacetime, and protests were made against grievances
such as purveyance which amounted to indirect taxes on the subject.
Three subsidies were eventually granted, but although the Commons
convinced themselves of their own generosity the sum was hopelessly
inadequate compared with the debts of the Crown. What James needed
was not only a large grant in order to pay off his debts, but an increase
in his permanent revenue as well. For a solution to this crucial prob-

lem he turned to Salisbury, whom he appointed Lord Treasurer in 1608.

Salisbury had seen enough of James to know that any substantial reduction in royal expenditure was out of the question: he was therefore forced to increase the King's income by exploiting all available resources. One of these was Customs, and in 1608 Salisbury issued a new Book of Rates, and also added 'Impositions' to the standard charges. His action did not pass unchallenged, for earlier Impositions had already led to a test case brought by John Bate, a merchant trading with Turkey, in 1606. The case came before the Barons of the Exchequer Court, where it was decided in favour of the Crown. But more important than the verdict was the language used by Chief Baron Fleming. He claimed that the royal prerogative comprised two distinct types of authority. The first, or ordinary prerogative, was that which the King exercised through the courts of common law, by appointing judges to decide questions of ownership and to protect his own legal rights as well as those of his subjects. But in addition to this ordinary prerogative, the King had, said Fleming, an extraordinary or absolute prerogative, which operated for the public benefit outside the range of common law. Impositions were imposed, according to Fleming, not to raise revenue but to regulate the flow of trade for the national good. The ports belonged to the King, and he had power to open or close them at will. Such matters came within the sphere of the absolute prerogative and could not therefore be challenged in the courts of common law.

When Parliament reassembled in 1610 it debated the legality of Impositions. Able Councillors might have steered the Commons away from so explosive a topic, but in the absence of any effective royal representatives the leadership of the House passed to 'opposition' leaders, of whom the most important at this stage was Sir Edwin Sandys. When James sent a message through the Speaker ordering the Commons 'not to dispute of the King's power and prerogative in imposing upon merchandises' the Commons replied that it was 'an ancient, general, and undoubted right of Parliament to debate freely all matters which do properly concern the subject and his right or state; which freedom of debate being once foreclosed, the essence of the liberty of Parliament is withal dissolved'. A generation earlier, when Peter Wentworth had put forward this sweeping interpretation of freedom of speech, the House had refused to follow him. The protestation of 1610 showed that what had formerly been an extreme view had now become general, and in the debate which followed several speakers came within striking distance of the concept of sovereignty—of a power within the state which is superior to all other powers. Whitelocke, for instance, pointed out that in England the King was sovereign but that his power was twofold: he could act alone and he could act through Parliament. 'And if of these two powers in the King, one is greater than the other and can direct and control the other, that is *suprema potestas*, the sovereign power, and the other is *subordinata*. It will then be easily proved that the power of the King in Parliament is greater than his power out of Parliament, and doth rule and control it. . . .'

To modern ears this sounds like an unqualified assertion of Parliamentary sovereignty, but in 1610 very few people were thinking in such terms. The general assumption was that government was a matter for cooperation between various bodies all in basic agreement upon fundamentals. Not until 1642 were the Commons at last forced to recognise that harmony no longer existed, and even then, although they wielded sovereign power, they still claimed to be doing so in the name of King and Parliament.

Whitelocke was not the only Englishman in the first decade of the seventeenth century who approached the concept of sovereignty. John Cowell, Professor of Civil Law at Cambridge, also dealt with it in *The Interpreter*, a dictionary of legal terms which he published in 1607. 'And of these two', he wrote, 'one must needs be true, that either the King is above the Parliament—that is, the positive laws of his kingdom —or else that he is not an absolute King.' Since the King was, by Cowell's definition, 'above the law by his absolute power' it followed that Parliament was a subordinate body, and Cowell observed that some people—he was careful not to commit himself—thought that subsidies were granted to the King because he chose to consult Parliament about the making of law instead of acting, as he had a perfect right to do, alone.

The 1610 Parliament, already angered by Impositions, condemned Cowell's doctrines out of hand. In this, however, they were joined by the King, who objected to any attempt to define his powers, but agreed that he had no authority to make laws alone or to take subsidies without Parliamentary consent. The question of money dominated this Parliament, for Salisbury, in his attempt to find a solution for the King's financial problems, had proposed a bargain to the property-cwners who controlled the Commons. He offered, in the King's name, to abolish the hated charges of wardship, purveyance and Impositions, in return for an increase in the Crown's permanent revenue.

The 'Great Contract', which Salisbury proposed, was an attempt at fundamental reorganisation of the Stuart financial system, and had it succeeded English history would have taken a very different course in the seventeenth century. But negotiations broke down because neither side was prepared to trust the other. The King wanted to be assured of alternative sources before he agreed to abolish feudal incidents; the Commons, on the other hand, were afraid that if they took the lead by voting the King additions to his permanent revenue, he would postpone abolishing feudal incidents and thereby provide himself with enough money to rule without Parliament. Discussions continued for some time, and tentative agreement was reached on a land tax of £200,000 a year to compensate the King. But Salisbury wanted a lump sum in addition, to wipe out the King's accumulated debt. The Commons stuck at this, and Salisbury was caught between their intransigence and the resentment of the King, who felt that he had compromised his dignity by haggling over the value of his rights. James was so angry that he dissolved Parliament in January 1611 without waiting for any settlement on the Great Contract, and he wrote to Salisbury in bitter terms: 'your greatest error hath been that ye ever expected to draw honey out of gall, being a little blinded with the self-love of your own counsel in holding together of this Parliament, whereof all men were despaired, as I have oft told you, but yourself alone.'

Failure and the ingratitude of his sovereign probably hastened Salisbury's death in 1612. He had made a fortune out of service to the Crown, but he had at least served it well. After him administration fell into the hands of men whose main concern was personal profit, and the flood-gates were opened to corruption on such a massive scale that it undermined the moral foundations of government and brought about a widespread revulsion against the Court. By the 1620s the term 'Country' was in common use to describe all those who despised and distrusted the 'Court-caterpillars' eating up the revenues of the state, who looked back to the great days of Queen Elizabeth which they wished to revive by anti-Spanish, anti-papist policies, and who felt that they stood for all that was best in the English tradition.

The Religious Problem

The anti-papalism of the 'Country' was intensified by the spread of Roman Catholic influence at Court, and found a focus for its discontent in puritanism. When James came to the throne the puritans were, and wished to remain, an integral part of the Church of England. There was no obvious need to separate from the Church, since a considerable degree of latitude was permitted in matters of ceremony and doctrine. The puritans were those members of the Church of England, lay and clerical, who were pressing for a further degree of moderate reform to bring the Church as a whole closer to the pattern set by the reformed churches on the Continent, and they hoped that the arrival of a Scottish King, coming from a country where puritanism had firmly established itself, might be their opportunity.

The accession of a new sovereign had been, for the last three reigns, the occasion for a redefinition of religious policy, and when James was presented with the Millenary Petition, containing a list of detailed reforms which the puritans hoped to see made law, he decided on a conference as a prelude to an agreed settlement. James had a natural interest in theology and he was not blind to the weaknesses of the English Church. He wanted to diminish pluralism and non-residence, recognising that an active preaching minister in every parish was the best way in which to strengthen the Church, and he realised the need to limit the powers of laymen acting in ecclesiastical courts.

The puritans asked for little more than this. They did not want to abolish episcopacy or to set up a 'Genevan Presbytery' in England. The Millenary Petition, it is true, included the almost traditional puritan demands for abolishing, or at least not insisting on, such practices as the sign of the cross in baptism, wearing caps and surplices, using the ring in marriage services, or bowing at the name of Jesus, but an active preaching ministry would have gone a long way to satisfying the puritans, and in this they could hope for assistance from James.

The anglican bishops were reluctant to meet puritan representatives in a formal debate, protesting that to do so would be to recognise that puritan ministers were, in a sense, their equal, and would therefore undermine the basis of episcopal authority. But James, who was not besotted with bishops any more than with presbyters, insisted that the conference should take place, and in January 1604 the delegates assembled at Hampton Court. In the three days' debate that followed,

James emphasised that episcopal authority should be maintained, and he refused to make the detailed changes in ceremonial that the puritans asked for, on the grounds that there was no condemnation of such practices in the Scriptures. Neither would he agree that puritan ministers should be 'associated' with the bishops in their work an governing the Church, for this smacked too much of the presbyteriof system that had challenged his authority in Scotland. 'I will think of this matter seven years,' he burst out, 'before I resolve to admit of a presbytery, and by that time happily I may wax fat and if then I think it behoveful for me to have any to stir me up and awaken me, I will then have a presbytery by me.'

As long as the structure of the Anglican Church was not tampered with, however, James was prepared to make concessions for the sake of unity. On the last day of the conference he announced that committees of bishops and Councillors would be appointed to devise means to improve the value of livings and cut down non-residence and plural-ism, to make minor changes in the Prayer-Book, and to limit the powers of laymen in Church courts. The puritan reaction to this was favourable, but, as so often with James, words were never translated into action. Having decided what ought to be done, he assumed that it would be done. But the committees charged with carrying out the detailed work were dominated by the bishops, who were opposed to any concessions, and by emphasising the difficulties and delaying decisions they managed to postpone the execution of James's orders until such time as the King had lost interest. The only major result of the Hampton Court Conference was the Authorised Version of the Bible, which rapidly became a major influence not only upon the language but also upon the thought of seventeenth-century Englishmen. Nothing else was achieved in the way of reconciliation, and the puritans felt that they had been tricked and betrayed. The bishops, by their stubbornness, had done much to create the very anti-episcopal feeling which they feared.

Yet the bishops, although they may have been shortsighted, acted from the best motives, believing that the Church of England, having established its foundations, needed a long period of stability in which to carry out its essential work of propagating the Christian faith. For the puritans the Anglican Church was a framework for worship, which should be modified to meet changing needs, but for Archbishop Bancroft and many of his colleagues it was not simply a convenient second-best but a God-given solution to the problem of protestant ecclesiastical organisation, and one that might eventually set a pattern for the whole Christian world.

Bancroft died in 1610, and his death marks the break with the Elizabethan Church in the same way as Salisbury's marked the end of the Elizabethan state. He was succeeded as Archbishop by George Abbott, who was far more sympathetic to the puritans but had none of their energy or passionate conviction. For twenty-two years Abbott let things slide. Where good preaching ministers were appointed it was usually as a result of local initiative, and little was done to improve livings or to tackle non-residence and pluralism. The corruption that rotted the Jacobean state rotted the Church as well.

The puritans were not the only people who had looked to a new monarch for fairer treatment. The same was true of the Roman Catholics, and they had good reason to be hopeful, for James was not an intolerant man by nature and shortly before his accession he had been in correspondence with one of the leading English catholics, Henry Howard, later Earl of Northampton, and had promised him that 'as for the catholics, I will neither persecute any that will be quiet and give but an outward obedience to the law, neither will I spare to advance any of them that will by good service worthily deserve it'. The King was, for once, as good as his word, and catholics enjoyed a degree of tolerance they had not known for a long time. They took comfort from the fact that James's wife, Anne of Denmark, was an avowed catholic, and as the memory of persecution receded many catholics who had hitherto kept their religious beliefs strictly to themselves now came out into the open. One contemporary commented: 'it is hardly credible in what jollity they now live. They make no question to obtain at least a toleration, if not an alteration of religion, in hope whereof many who before did dutifully frequent the church are of late become recusants.'

The defenders of the established order were alarmed by the revelation of catholic strength in England at a time when protestantism was being pushed on to the defensive throughout Europe. They advised James to take a less tolerant attitude, for fear that the Church (and with it the throne) of England should be swept away by the papists, and James accordingly ordered the enforcement of the penal laws in February 1605. The catholics, like the puritans after the Hampton Court Conference, felt bitterly betrayed, and out of their resentment grew the fantastic design to blow up the Houses of Parliament with all the royal family.

Fortunately for James the plot was discovered in time, and Guy Fawkes and his associates were executed. Yet the conspiracy had little permanent effect on James's policy. Catholic priests were ordered to choose between death and exile, but as for secular catholics, they were soon as free as they had been before the Plot. The effect on the English imagination was much more striking. Catholic plotters became part of popular mythology and the terror they aroused went so deep into protestant hearts that it is still exorcised every November by burning poor Guy in effigy. The history of England in the seventeenth century is incomprehensible without taking into account the hysterical anti-catholicism that coloured popular attitudes: to call a man a papist was to accuse him of the vilest perfidy and treachery.

Members of Parliament certainly did not share James's tolerant attitude. In 1610 they petitioned him to allow his 'natural clemency to retire itself and give place to justice, and . . . to see the laws made against Jesuits, seminary priests, and recusants (of what kind and sort soever) to be duly and exactly executed'. Perhaps they had a better appreciation than James of the threat that revived Roman Catholicism offered to protestantism all over Europe, not excluding England. They were also aware that while catholics were tolerated, puritans were being persecuted. After the failure of the Hampton Court Conference, Convocation ordered the enforcement of conformity, and about ninety puritan ministers were ejected from their livings. The puritans, who put the number of their evicted brethren at three hundred, complained to the King, but James, who could see no reason why they should not trust to his good intentions, lost patience with them. 'I have daily more and more cause', he told Salisbury, 'to hate and abhor all that sect, enemies to all Kings and to me only because I am a King.'

After Salisbury's death there was no single minister who had the King's confidence. The Privy Council which, under Salisbury, had consisted of about twenty members—only a little above the figure for Elizabeth's reign—increased in size until, by the time of James's death, it numbered thirty-five. This enlargement was, as Edward VI's reign had shown, a sign of weakness, for factions developed within the Council, and the opposing groups were more concerned with spiting each other than with keeping watch over the administration. The Earl of Northampton was the leader of one faction, composed mainly of catholics and members of his own family—the Howards—and the temporary ascendancy of this group was confirmed when he brought

Robert Carr into it. Carr was one of the Scotsmen who had accompanied James to England in 1603, and his good looks soon brought him to the notice of the King, who was peculiarly susceptible to a certain type of masculine charm. Place-seekers quickly realised that if they were to succeed in their quest they would have to please the favourite, and Carr grew rich on the 'gifts' he received from them as well as from James. By 1613 Carr, who was created Earl of Somerset in that year, was at the height of his power, and the Spanish ambassador reported that after meetings of the Privy Council 'the King resolveth all business with him alone'.

Parliament and the Common Law

Somerset and the Howards found no difficulty in making money for themselves, but, not surprisingly, the King's debts mounted. By 1614 the outstanding debt was nearly £900,000 while the annual deficit was £50,000, and the 'protestant' group in the Council urged James to summon Parliament. The Howards opposed this, since they feared that any Parliament would be strongly anti-papist and anti-Spanish, but the King's poverty left little apparent alternative.

The 'Addled' Parliament, which met in April 1614, was, as its name implies, an inglorious failure. If the King had appointed Councillors in time to prepare the business of the Commons, and had been ready to make concessions on major grievances such as Church reform, monopolies and purveyance, he might have achieved some positive results, but in fact he only appointed a new Secretary of State shortly before Parliament met (the office had been vacant since Salisbury's death), and although Sir Ralph Winwood, a staunch protestant, was in many ways a good choice for this key office, he had no parliamentary experience to guide him. In the absence of any effective leadership from the Crown, opposition leaders like Sir Edwin Sandys and Sir Dudley Digges were able to divert the House to discussion of grievances—including the unfounded charge that James had meddled in the elections.

The King had been reluctant to summon Parliament at all—it was an institution that he disliked and never understood—and when the Howards, delighted with its failure, urged him to dissolve it, he agreed. The Spanish ambassador, Sarmiento (later Count Gondomar), who had almost as much influence over James as Carr, hinted that if he did order a dissolution Spanish financial support might be forthcoming, and James clutched at this straw. In early June he dissolved Parliament, which had accomplished nothing, and showed his anger with the Commons by summoning six members before the Council and accusing them of making seditious speeches. Three of them were sent to the Tower, where they remained for a year until they signed submissions, and James would no doubt have liked to do the same to many other members of the Commons. That House, he told Sarmiento, 'is a body without a head. The members give their opinions in a disorderly manner. At their meetings nothing is heard but cries, shouts and confusion. I am surprised that my ancestors should ever have permitted such an institution to come into existence. I am a stranger, and found it here when I arrived, so that I am obliged to put up with what I cannot get rid of.'

James was as much of a stranger to common law—that peculiarly English institution—as he was to Parliaments. For him the King was source of all laws, for, as he said, 'Kings sit in the throne of God, and thence all judgement is derived'. But for many Englishmen the common law was as old as, if not older than, the monarchy, and embodied the wisdom of countless generations of their forefathers. It was not to be lightly challenged or changed, and they resented any suggestion that the power of Kings could override so venerable an inheritance.[1]

This attitude found its most formidable defender in Sir Edward Coke, Chief Justice of Common Pleas and the most famous lawyer in England. For Coke common law was 'the golden metwand and measure to try the causes of the subjects and [to protect] his Majesty in safety and peace', and he was quite prepared to oppose the Crown when he thought that the law was threatened. Dispute arose, among other things, over proclamations. The 1610 Parliament had complained about the multiplication of these, 'by reason whereof there is a general fear conceived and spread amongst your Majesty's people that proclamations will by degrees grow up and increase to the strength and nature of laws'. James referred this matter to the judges, and they, led by Coke, gave as their opinion 'that the King by his proclamation cannot create any offence which was not an offence before' and 'that the King hath no prerogative but that which the law of the land allows him'. These observations show how close were the links between the common lawyers and Parliament—many of whose members had spent some time at one or other of the Inns of Court. They also show how

[1] See below, Chapter 14: 'The Movement of Ideas'.

Coke wished to make the common law the arbiter of the constitution. But to this there was one major objection: the King could not change the law, but he could change the judges who interpreted that law. James showed his awareness of this when, in 1616, he dismissed Coke from his Chief Justiceship.

The Rise of Buckingham

The dissolution of the Addled Parliament had done nothing to solve the King's financial problems, and James's extravagance—he spent over £100,000 on his daughter's marriage—made matters worse. The Howards were still in power, and one of their number, the Earl of Suffolk, was made Lord Treasurer in July 1614. The anti-Spanish faction in the Council, however, led by Archbishop Abbot, was plotting to bring the Howard ascendancy to an end. Somerset, the King's favourite, was identified with the Howard interest, but Abbott argued that if James was to have a favourite he might as well have a 'protestant' favourite. In 1614, therefore, he introduced George Villiers, the handsome twenty-two-year-old son of a Leicestershire knight, to the King. Abbott's plan succeeded beyond all expectations. Early in 1616 Villiers was knighted, made Master of the Horse and given a pension; later that year he became Viscount Villiers and was given an estate to maintain his new dignity. In 1617 he was created Earl of Buckingham, in the following year he became a Marquis, and by 1623 he was Duke of Buckingham and the most important man in England.

Buckingham's rise meant the fall not only of the old favourite but also of Carr's patrons, the Howards. Northampton had died in 1614, but Nottingham (who, as Lord Howard of Effingham, had led the English fleet against the Armada) was forced to resign his position as Lord High Admiral to Buckingham, while Suffolk was persuaded to give up the Treasurership in 1618. For the rest of the reign the direction of policy and the control of royal patronage were in the hands of the new favourite, and James, in an astonishing declaration to the Council in 1617, declared his enslavement to the young man. 'I, James, am neither a god nor an angel but a man like any other. Therefore I act like a man, and confess to loving those dear to me more than other men. You may be sure that I love the Earl of Buckingham more than anyone else, and more than you who are here assembled. I wish to speak in my own behalf and not to have it thought to be a defect, for Jesus Christ did the same and therefore I cannot be blamed. Christ had his John and I have my George.'

Buckingham was no more scrupulous than Somerset where money was concerned, and the line between legitimate perquisites and bribery, which had never been easy to determine, virtually disappeared during the years of his ascendancy. Anything was for sale—Crown lands, offices in the King's gift, even titles of honour. James had already cheapened the prestige of knighthood by the lavish grants he made in the opening years of his reign, and it was common knowledge that the dignity was for sale. Ben Jonson was imprisoned for making a character in one of his plays say (in a broad Scottish accent, perhaps, not unlike the King's?) 'I ken the man weel. He's one of my £30 knights', and another dramatist wrote

> But now, alas, it's grown ridiculous,
> Since bought with money, sold for basest prize,
> That some refuse it, which are counted wise.

As the prestige of knighthood declined the need arose for a more respectable title, and the dignity of baronet was created in 1611, open to anyone who would pay £1,000 to maintain thirty soldiers in Ireland. But by 1622 baronetcies were being sold for £250 apiece, and the prestige declined with the price. The same was true of peerages. In the last thirty years of her reign Elizabeth had created only one new peerage, and the pent-up demand caused by social change led to pressure on James to be more generous. At first James was comparatively restrained in his grants, but after Buckingham's rise to power peerages were sold for cash, and the number of peers increased from just over eighty in 1615 to almost one hundred and thirty by 1628.

Sale of titles on this lavish scale cheapened them and brought into disrepute not only the buyer but the seller. Stuart England was a hierarchical society, and although the sale of honours was, in a way, no more than a formal recognition of shifts in position that had already taken place, it affronted all those who believed that a man's place in the community should not be decided simply by the amount of wealth he had. The 'Country', which held aloof from such practices and therefore could not benefit by them, came increasingly to feel that the Court, which in Elizabeth's day had been the focus of English life, was something alien and extravagant. They echoed the opinion of Sir Walter Ralegh who wrote:

Say to the Court, it glows
And shines like rotten wood.

Ralegh, whose *History of the World* appealed to puritans because it demonstrated the will of God working through human society, was one of the heroes of the 'Country'. James distrusted him, because Ralegh stood for a vigorous anti-Spanish policy in the Elizabethan tradition, and held him prisoner in the Tower on a trumped-up charge of treason. From 1613 onwards, under the influence of Sarmiento, James moved closer and closer to Spain, hoping to arrange a marriage between his second son, Charles, and the King of Spain's daughter. Such a match would not only link the Stuarts with the most powerful dynasty in Europe: it would also, James believed, encourage the reconciliation of protestants and catholics and thereby contribute to that general pacification which he hoped to bring about. It would also bring a welcome dowry into the royal coffers.

Negotiations dragged, however, and James allowed himself to be persuaded by the 'protestant' party in the Council to let Ralegh sail to the Spanish Main to search for the city of gold which he hoped to find there. The marriage negotiations immediately sprang to life, but one of the preconditions was that James should break with Ralegh and all he stood for. When Ralegh returned empty-handed from his search the sentence of death passed against him in 1603 (on a charge of conspiring against the King) was carried out.

The Spanish Match

James was eager to arrange the Spanish match, because the peace of Europe was seriously threatened. The catholic Habsburg emperors were, by long custom, also Kings of protestant Bohemia, but in 1618, on the death of the Emperor Mathias, the Bohemian nobles renounced the allegiance they had sworn to his heir, Ferdinand, who was known to be a bigoted catholic, and offered their throne instead to a protestant German prince, Frederick of the Palatinate. Frederick, who had married James's daughter Elizabeth, accepted the offer and became a hero in England where he was seen as the champion of protestantism against the revived Roman Catholic Church. It was clear that Ferdinand, who became Emperor himself in 1619, would not meekly accept this act of rebellion, and war was inevitable.

In England public opinion was strongly in favour of Frederick, particularly when the Spanish Habsburgs agreed to help their Austrian cousins by attacking the Palatinate from the Spanish Netherlands. James could have put himself at the head of an anti-Habsburg crusade and thereby made himself really popular for the first time in his reign, but this would have meant abandoning all his hopes for peace and for a Spanish marriage. He allowed himself to be gulled by Gondomar into believing that if he kept England out of the war the King of Spain would restrain the Emperor from taking the Palatinate—though Frederick would have to give up Bohemia. James was not an old man, but senility was already sapping him of vitality. He could not bear the thought of war, and regarded his son-in-law not as a protestant champion but as an impetuous young man who must pay for his folly. 'The Palatine', he told Gondomar, 'is a godless man and a usurper. I will give him no help. It is much more reasonable that he, young as he is, should listen to an old man like me, and do what is right by surrendering Bohemia, than that I should be involved in a bad cause.'

Yet although James poured out his resentment against his rash son-in-law, he could not ignore the need to make some preparation in case England should be involved in war. Money was, as always, the problem, and the only hope of solvency lay in a Parliament. By the time James's third Parliament met in 1621, Frederick had been driven from his newly acquired kingdom by imperial troops, while England was in the throes of an economic depression. These circumstances did not augur well, and the Commons were in a very critical mood. As usual there were no adequate Councillors to act as the King's representatives in the Lower House, and the leaders of the Commons launched an attack on the monopolists who were (so members asserted) waxing fat at the expense of the country as a whole. To deal with these powerful offenders they revived the practice of impeachment, which had not been used since the 1450s, and sent Sir Giles Mompesson, one of the most notorious monopolists, before the Lords. The success of this manœuvre encouraged the Commons to strike at bigger game, and they accused the Lord Chancellor, Francis Bacon (recently created Viscount St Albans) of bribery. The charge was undoubtedly just, even though the taking of bribes was almost standard practice. But the Commons wanted a scapegoat, and in Bacon they were condemning the widespread corruption in James's administration, for which, it was generally assumed, Buckingham was responsible. The Commons did not yet dare to openly attack the King's favourite so they struck at Bacon instead, implying by their action that great officers of state were not absolved by their position from giving an account of their actions. The Lords found Bacon guilty, and ordered that he should be fined and imprisoned and should never again hold public office.

Parliament had voted two subsidies, and the King, despairing of getting more, adjourned it. But the need for money remained as pressing as ever. Although James disapproved of his son-in-law's action, he could hardly stand by while Frederick was being driven not only from Bohemia but from his native land, the Palatinate, as well. There was no question, at this stage, of sending troops, but large sums of money were despatched to Frederick, and further Parliamentary grants were essential if the King was to avoid bankruptcy. In November 1621, therefore, Parliament was recalled—though James, feeling old and ill, went off to Newmarket to be away from it all.

The Commons, under the leadership of Sir Edward Coke, plunged into a debate on foreign affairs and named Spain as the major enemy. They drew up a petition to James urging him 'to pursue and more publicly avow the aiding of those of our religion in foreign parts' at a time when a 'strange confederacy of the princes of the popish religion' was threatening the very existence of protestantism. And to check the enemy within the gates they demanded that the recusancy laws should be strictly enforced, and that 'our most noble Prince [Charles] may be timely and happily married to one of our own religion'.

Foreign affairs were traditionally 'matters of state', not to be discussed by Parliament without the sovereign's permission, and James took the same attitude as Elizabeth, writing to the Speaker to order that the House should not 'presume henceforth to meddle with anything concerning our government or deep matters of state, and namely not to deal with our dearest son's match with the daughter of Spain'. Elizabeth would have stopped here, but James went further and elaborated the general principle that 'we think ourself very free and able to punish any man's misdemeanours in Parliament, as well during their sitting as after'.

An inhibition of this sort, coming from Elizabeth, would have caused grumbling in the House, but with the Councillors and Speaker to guide debate and with the Queen herself at hand to charm as well as to frown, the incipient rebellion would have been checked. James, however, had no good Councillors in the Commons, he was too far away to play any effective part in moderating the temper of the House, and by moving from the particular to the general he seemed to be denying the principles upon which the privileges of the Commons were based. The situation, also, was very different from anything that had been known in Elizabeth's reign. No one had doubted the Queen's ardent protestantism and her willingness to support the cause of the reformed religion against Spain, but the same was not true of James. His plan for peaceful negotiations might have had much to recommend it, but the Commons felt that a critical stage in the religious struggle had opened and that the time for diplomacy had passed.

In reply to James's inhibition, therefore, the Commons drew up another petition, which they despatched to Newmarket with a delegation from the House. King and Commons had drifted so far apart that they were negotiating almost as separate powers, as James recognised when he ordered his servants to 'bring stools for the ambassadors!' In their petition the Commons protested that they never meant 'to encroach or intrude upon the sacred bounds of your royal authority, to whom and to whom only we acknowledge it doth belong to resolve of peace and war and of the marriage of the most noble Prince your son', but they asked for answers to their requests for the enforcement of the penal laws and other matters. They also took occasion to remind James that their privilege of freedom of speech was 'our ancient and undoubted right, and an inheritance received from our ancestors' which they trusted the King would never attempt to infringe.

James, in his reply, informed the House that 'we are an old and experienced King, needing so such lessons' as they were giving him. He pointed out, with justice, that 'in the body of your petition you usurp upon our prerogative royal and meddle with things far above your reach, and then in the conclusion you protest the contrary—as if a robber would take a man's purse and then protest he meant not to rob him'. As far as the privileges of the House were concerned, he would have preferred the Commons to say that they 'were derived from the grace and permission of our ancestors and us', but he gave his word that he would maintain them 'as long as you contain yourselves within the limits of your duty'.

The Commons had shown at the beginning of the reign how strongly they felt about their privileges—not simply out of pride but because freedom of debate seemed to be the best security against possible attempts at absolutism. James's reply stung them to the Protestation of December 1621, which was formally entered in the Commons' Journal. In this they declared that 'arduous and urgent affairs concerning the King, state, and defence of the realm and of the Church of England, and the maintenance and making of laws, and redress of mischiefs and grievances which daily happen within this realm, are proper subjects and matter of counsel and debate in Parliament; and that in the handling and proceeding of those businesses every member of the House of Parliament hath, and of right ought to have, freedom of speech to propound, treat, reason, and bring to conclusion the same'. The ghost of Peter Wentworth must have nodded approvingly at this triumphant assertion of the beliefs for which he had earlier suffered. Historically speaking the Commons' claim was false, but under the guise of an appeal to the past they were really making a claim about the present, and although James sent for their Journal and solemnly tore out the offending page, he could not so easily destroy the economic strength and religious fervour which gave the Commons their power.

Not surprisingly James dissolved Parliament and went ahead with his plans for a Spanish match. Meanwhile, until such time as the longed-for dowry should wipe out his accumulated debt, he looked for salvation to a protégé of Buckingham's, Lionel Cranfield, a London merchant who had already made a name for himself on the various reform commissions appointed to try to cut down expenditure. Cranfield was made Lord Treasurer in 1621, and created Earl of Middlesex in the following year. He could do little about the accumulated debt but he set himself to wipe out the annual deficit, and in this he was remarkably successful. He realised that one of the main reasons for the Crown's poverty was that too many of its revenues were diverted into the pockets of pensioners and place-holders, and he therefore persuaded the King to agree that in future no pensions would be granted without the Lord Treasurer's approval. He cut salaries and existing pensions where possible, raised the rent charged to the Customs farmers, and began exploiting Crown woodlands.

By these and similar measures Middlesex managed to reduce, if not eliminate, the annual deficit by the end of 1623, but only at the cost of angering most of the important men in the kingdom. Office-holders and pensioners bitterly resented the interruption of the golden flow; Buckingham felt insulted and betrayed when he found that the curb on royal generosity applied to him as well; the 'Country', so strong in the Commons, resented the apparent success of this man who might make the King independent of Parliament; while the King himself, who was by nature generous and extravagant, fretted under restraint. Middlesex made money out of service to the Crown, but hatred and ingratitude were his only other rewards.

Such economies as Middlesex made were soon wiped out by increasing expenditure on defence preparations and on the missions which James's diplomacy involved. Among the most expensive of these missions—its total cost was over £100,000—was the voyage which Buckingham and Prince Charles made to Spain in an attempt to bring the marriage negotiations to a head. The King was opposed to this journey on the grounds that it would merely encourage the Spaniards to raise their terms, but he could not resist the combined pleading of his son and his favourite. When news of the mission became public it aroused widespread distrust in England and increased the hatred that was already felt for Buckingham.

These forebodings were premature. Charles and Buckingham were treated with great formality but negotiations made only slow progress. The Infanta declared that she would go into a convent rather than marry a protestant, while the Spanish minister, Olivares, insisted that James should promise to repeal the penal laws before Spain made any binding commitments. James was so anxious to have the two young men return safely home that he agreed to this demand, and in July 1623 ordered the Privy Councillors to bind themselves by oath to suspend the penal laws and not reimpose them. But Charles was becoming disillusioned with the Spaniards, especially when he found that they were not prepared to do anything effective to restore Frederick to the Palatinate. In September 1623 he and Buckingham left Spain, having signed the marriage articles, but their previous enthusiasm for a Spanish policy was turning into suspicion and anger. Their change of front was confirmed by the reception that awaited them in England. All the foreboding that had been felt at the prospect of a Spanish princess changed to exultation when the travellers returned empty handed. Charles and Buckingham were the heroes of the hour, and in a service of thanksgiving at St Paul's the choir sang the anthem 'When Israel came out of Egypt, and the house of Jacob from amongst the barbarous people'.

War

Buckingham, who had no profound principles and clutched at popularity where he saw a chance of it, was now as eager for war as he had previously been opposed to it. James was bullied into summoning Parliament, and when it met, the King invited members to discuss foreign affairs. The Commons were in a violently anti-Spanish mood, and their attitude was expressed by Sir John Eliot who proclaimed 'Spain is rich. Let her be our Indies, our storehouse of treasure!' The Commons wanted a naval war against Spain on the Elizabethan model, and although they protested their desire to help the Palatinate it was not clear how they intended to do so. For them the great war which had opened on the continent was a struggle between the forces of light and the forces of darkness. Strategy was unimportant. If the papist enemy was struck in Spain he would reel in Germany. They had little understanding of the nationalist ferment at work in Europe, which was eventually to set catholic France against catholic Spain, neither did they appreciate that the Palatinate had to be relieved in Germany and not in Cadiz. The narrowness of their approach was demonstrated by one member who said 'the Palatinate was the place intended by his Majesty. This we never thought of, nor is it fit for the consideration of the House in regard of the infinite charge.'

The King had asked for six subsidies and twelve fifteenths—about £800,000—for the proposed war, but the Commons, appalled by this sum, voted only three subsidies and three fifteenths, which they believed would be sufficient to fight a naval war. Buckingham would have been well advised to commit Parliament to a much larger supply before embarking on an aggressive policy, but now that he was determined on war he did not stop to haggle. He no doubt assumed that more money would be forthcoming when the armies clashed and victory sent spirits soaring. Meanwhile, to increase his popularity with the Commons, he acquiesced in their attack upon Middlesex. The Lord Treasurer was impeached on charges of 'bribery, extortion, oppression, wrong and deceit', but the real concern of the Commons was to get rid of 'this strange and prodigious comet which', in Eliot's words 'so fatally hangs over us'. James tried to save the Treasurer, and warned Charles that 'he would live to have his bellyful of Parliaments', but Buckingham was tired of Middlesex's economising and was happy to throw him to the wolves.

With Middlesex out of the way there were no obstacles in the path of the war party except the King, and he left policy to Charles and Buckingham, making only occasional protests. James had been, as he told the Commons, 'all the days of my life a peaceable King', but having reluctantly agreed to war he promised that the money voted for it should be in the hands of treasurers appointed by the House. Not content with this abdication of his prerogative rights he went on to assure the House that he would not 'treat nor accept of a peace without first acquainting you with it and hearing your advice, and therein go the proper way of Parliament in conferring and consulting with you in such great and weighty affairs'.

One of James's last actions was to agree to a marriage between his son and the daughter of Henry IV of France. The French, like the Spaniards, demanded the repeal of the penal laws, and although James had promised the Commons that he would never accept such a condition, he gave way to Buckingham's insistence as he had done at the time of the negotiations with Spain. There is something pathetic about the picture of James in these closing days of his life, senile beyond his years, seeing the dangers that war offered to those he loved yet unable to do anything effective about it. James was vain and often silly, but he had a love of peace and a genuine goodwill which endeared him to his subjects, and even those members of Parliament who took the lead in criticising his policies protested their loyalty to him. It was not James they opposed but the people who took advantage of his generosity and gullibility to build private empires at the public cost. The other quality that redeemed James was his common sense, even though he rarely made this a guide to action. He saw more clearly than Charles and Buckingham where their adventurous policies would lead them, and he warned his favourite that 'you will find that in this fit of popularity you are making a rod with which you will be scourged yourself'. The truth of this became only too apparent after March 1625 when, on the death of his father, Charles I became King of England.

12

Charles I

CHARLES, only twenty-four when he came to the throne, had a gravity and dignity far beyond his age. For the first twelve years of his life he had been a younger son, overhadowed by his brother Henry, the friend of Ralegh and the man on whom the hopes of the 'Country' were fixed. But Henry died in 1612 and from then onwards the heir was Charles—shy, reserved, with an impediment in his speech that made him a man of few words. This reticence remained with him all his life, and he told his first Parliament how grateful he was that the business on hand required so little explanation, 'for I am neither able to do it, nor doth it stand with my nature to spend much time in words'. This brevity was a welcome change from the effusiveness of James, and Sir John Eliot reported that 'both the sense and shortness of this expression were well liked, as meeting with the inclination of the time, which wearied with the long orations of King James that did inherit but the wind'.

One characteristic which Charles had acquired from his father was a profound respect for his own position. He believed that kings were directly responsible to God alone for their actions, and that the prerogatives of the Crown could not be taken away by human means. No puritan had a stronger sense than Charles of the constant presence of God, and for him politics were an aspect of morality: 'I cannot', he said 'defend a bad, nor yield in a good cause.' This moral rigidity was welcome after the laxness of James's régime, and an immediate change came over public life. Charles put a stop to the sale of titles, and cut down the tasteless extravagance of the Court. He lived splendidly and surrounded himself with a collection of pictures and works of art that showed an exquisite taste, but he never lapsed into vulgarity. His high seriousness matched that of the 'Country' members of Parliament, and he might have won their approval had it not been for the circumstances of his accession. Unfortunately, he was bound to Buckingham, whom the Commons were coming to hate, and to a war which he could not afford to fight. When these led him into conflict with the Commons, he took criticism of his policies and his advisers as a personal affront, and, while he admitted his responsibility to God, denied that he or his servants were accountable to the House of Commons.

Charles did not appreciate the necessity for managing Parliament any more than his father had done, and Buckingham was so intoxicated by his spell of popularity during the 1624 session that he did not bother to brief the Councillors in the Commons when a new Parliament assembled in 1625. The result was that private members took the lead, and the House, after voting only two subsidies for the prosecution of the war, concentrated its attention on grievances. Members wanted to know what had happened to the money voted the previous year—which they had then described as 'the greatest aid which was ever granted in Parliament to be levied in so short a time'—and they complained about the continued exaction of Impositions. To show how strongly they felt about this tax, which they chose to regard as llegal in spite of the judges' favourable decision in Bate's case, they took the unprecedented step of cutting the King's ordinary revenue. By long tradition Parliament voted the King the Customs duties— Tonnage and Poundage—for life, but in 1625 the Commons made the grant for one year only. This was the sort of action that deeply offended Charles. Tonnage and Poundage, he believed, were his *by right*; he rejected the limited grant and continued to collect the duties by virtue of his prerogative.

Parliament and Foreign Policy

When the second session of Parliament opened at Oxford, more care was taken to present the Crown's case to the Commons. Buckingham had built up a 'grand alliance' and needed money to finance it. The subsidies voted by the 1624 Parliament had been spent on equipping an expedition for the relief of the Palatinate, under Count Mansfield. Charles was negotiating with the Dutch, who were once again at war with Spain; he had promised the King of Denmark £30,000 a month to fight for the protestant cause in north Germany; and he claimed that since Parliament had promised to finance the war it must do so now.

The Commons, however, were not prepared to make further grants. One reason for this was their insularity. They could safely deny their King the means to raise an army because they were defended by what Cromwell was later to call 'a great ditch': continental assemblies could not afford to be so uncooperative when great armies were crossing their frontiers. But the Commons were not blindly uncooperative. They knew that, under the stress of war, the power of princes was daily growing, and as Sir Robert Phelips said in the 1625 Parliament: 'we are the last monarchy in Christendom that retain our original rights and constitutions.' Apart from such general considerations, the Commons did not trust the King—or rather Buckingham—to make good use of whatever money they voted. Even while they were meeting at Oxford the remnants of Mansfield's disorganised rabble were straggling back from Europe, where they had accomplished nothing, and there was little to suggest that any further expeditions would be more successful. They therefore refused to vote additional subsidies until their grievances had been redressed, and Charles promptly dissolved Parliament.

The Commons claimed that they wanted a sea war against Spain, and Buckingham decided to provide just this in the shape of an expedition against Cadiz. Money was raised by holding back the payment of wages, by pledging the credit of the Crown, and by consuming the £120,000 paid by France for Henrietta Maria's dowry. The counties were ordered to raise troops at their own expense and to provide equipment, and ten thousand men—mostly gaolbirds and vagabonds—were somehow collected for the expedition. The lack of organisation, of adequate supplies, and of any clear strategy, did not promise much hope of success, yet Buckingham cannot be entirely blamed for this. Combined expeditions were notoriously difficult to arrange, as the Elizabethans had found to their cost and as Cromwell was to discover thirty years later. England had neither a professional army nor a professional navy, and the marvel is that the troops were actually embarked and eventually landed on the Spanish coast. There they captured a fort and marched on Cadiz, but before ever they reached the town the heat, the lack of food and the abundance of local wine had turned the army into an undisciplined rabble. Any attack was now out of the question. The troops—or as many of them as were in a fit state—were re-embarked, and the ships sailed back to England with their cargo of sick, starving and dying men. Sir John Eliot saw some of the remnants landed at Plymouth and never forgot the shame of it. Until that time he had been part of the Buckingham 'empire', but now he turned against his patron.

The need for money forced the King to summon his second Parliament in 1626, but it met under the shadow of the Cadiz fiasco, and Eliot, whose passionate devotion to his country and his King frequently led him, like Peter Wentworth, far beyond the bounds of discretion, launched a bitter attack on those responsible for the failure. 'Our honour is ruined,' he thundered, 'our ships are sunk, our men perished, not by the sword, not by an enemy, not by chance, but . . . by those we trust.' Eliot himself had no doubt where the responsibility lay. The King's revenues, he declared, were 'consumed as well as the treasures and faculties of the subject. . . . But the harvest and great gathering comes to one who must protect the rest, and for his countenance draws all others to him as his tributaries.' At Eliot's suggestion the House refused to consider the King's request for subsidies until their grievances, including the greatest grievance of all, should be remedied.

Charles had few friends, but he was unswervingly loyal to those he had. He knew that Buckingham had spent much of his own money, as well as energy, in preparing the expedition, and he regarded the Commons' criticism not only as grossly unjust but as a criticism of himself, the King, who had entrusted Buckingham with the direction of affairs. He told the Commons in reply to their address: 'certain it is that I did command him to do what he hath done therein. I would not have the House to question my servants, much less one that is so near me', and two weeks later he summoned both Houses to Whitehall where he warned them that liberty must not be confused with licence. He understood, he told them in words that are very reminiscent of those used by Elizabeth, 'the difference betwixt council and controlling, and between liberty and the abuse of liberty'. He assured them that 'never any King was more loving to his people nor better affectioned to the right use of Parliaments', but he reminded the Commons that since they had encouraged him to go to war they were morally bound to support him in it. 'Now that you have all things according to your wishes and that I am so far engaged that you think there is no retreat, now you begin to set the dice and make your own game. But I pray you be not deceived. It is not a parliamentary way, nor is it a way to deal with a King.' If Parliament acted responsibly, by voting supplies and enabling the war to be continued, the King would, he said, redress grievances, but they must play a constructive and cooperative role. If not, he warned them, 'remember that Parliaments are altogether in my power for their calling, sitting and dissolution. Therefore as I find the fruits of them good or evil they are to continue or not to be.' The threat was unmistakable.

The Commons would not accept Charles's interpretation of their actions. What he regarded as sterile and destructive criticism, they believed was the expression of their main function—to expose grievances and petition the King to remedy them. In the remonstrance which they drew up at Eliot's suggestion they affirmed 'that it hath been the ancient, constant and undoubted right and usage of Parliaments to question and complain of all persons, of what degree soever, found grievous to the commonwealth in abusing the power and trust committed to them by their sovereign', and to demonstrate their rights they went ahead with a formal impeachment of the Duke of Buckingham.

Throughout these proceedings Eliot protested his loyalty to the King. 'In nothing,' he said, 'we intend to reflect the least ill odour on his Majesty or his most blessed father of happy memory.' The aim of the Commons was, he declared, to protect the honour of the King by removing all those who threatened to eclipse his royal glory, and of these Buckingham was the worst. 'His profuse expenses, his superfluous feasts, his magnificent buildings, his riots, his excesses—what are they but a chronicle of his immense exhausts out of the Crown revenues? No wonder then the King is now in want, this man abounding so. And while he abounds the King must still be wanting. . . .' Eliot, carried away by his feelings, went on to compare the hated favourite with Sejanus, the adviser of the tyrannical emperor Tiberius. 'If the Duke is Sejanus,' said Charles, when the comparison was reported to him, 'I must be Tiberius', and he determined to dissolve Parliament rather than let the attack on Buckingham continue.

Since Parliament had never voted the four subsidies for which the King asked, no improvement had taken place in the royal finances. Charles therefore ordered that a forced loan should be raised by collecting from householders and others what they would have paid if the parliamentary subsidies had been voted. When the Lord Chief Justice, Sir Randolph Crew, questioned the legality of what was, in effect, unparliamentary taxation, Charles dismissed him, and he ordered the imprisonment of those who refused to pay. These included Eliot, John Hampden and Sir Thomas Wentworth.

The loan brought in nearly a quarter of a million pounds, but aroused widespread resentment. So did the demand that coastal towns should provide ships at their own charge for the royal service, and that counties should provide free billeting for troops raised for another expedition which Buckingham was planning. England had blundered into war with France and Buckingham intended to give support to the protestant inhabitants of La Rochelle, who were in revolt against their sovereign. Since the Cadiz expedition had been blamed on him, even though he had not been present, Buckingham decided to lead the attack on La Rochelle in person.

The expedition was almost as disastrous as the first. Shortage of money was partly to blame, for although nearly a million pounds were raised from the loan, from sale of Crown lands, and from pawning the Crown jewels, the money was not enough to provide all the ships, troops and equipment that were necessary. Mismanagement and corruption also played their part in ensuring failure. The island of Rhé, off the French coast, was occupied as a base from which to relieve La Rochelle, but French troops soon drove the English from their positions, and although Buckingham fought bravely he had to retreat to the ships, losing many of his men. By November the remnants of the expedition had straggled back to Portsmouth, and as the news of another failure spread, anger against Buckingham increased to dange, point. Denzil Holles, one of the leaders of the Country in Parliamentr declared that 'since England was England she received not so dishonourable a blow', and his was no isolated voice. Only Charles struck a different note, when he assured Buckingham that 'with whatsoever success ye shall come to me, ye shall ever be welcome'.

The Duke had still not given up hope of organising a successful expedition. Part of his charm consisted in his optimism, his belief that fortune which had raised him from comparative obscurity to so great a height would not desert him now. He persuaded Charles to summon another Parliament, but before this was done the seventy or so gentlemen who had been imprisoned for refusing to pay the forced loan were released. During their imprisonment the prerogative had won another victory, for when a test action—the case of the Five Knights—was brought before the Court of King's Bench to determine whether the King had any right to imprison without showing good cause, the judges upheld the imprisonment.

When Parliament met, the leaders of the Commons were determined to obtain from the King some guarantee of the subjects' rights. Eliot wanted to concentrate on defending the privileges of Parliament, but as Pym said later in the session 'the liberties of this House are

I*

inferior to the liberties of the kingdom'. Because of Eliot's narrowness, the lead passed to one of the members for Yorkshire, Sir Thomas Wentworth, who had suffered imprisonment for refusing to pay the forced loan. Wentworth believed that evil counsellors had 'extended the prerogative of the King beyond the just symmetry which maketh a sweet harmony of the whole'. What was needed, he said, was a new Magna Carta, a new definition of the rights of the subject, which should restore the balance of the constitution and enable King and Parliament to work in harmony once again.

At Wentworth's suggestion the House voted five subsidies to show that they appreciated the Crown's needs. Then they went ahead with a Bill to define the liberties of the subject—not those which the King had granted out of grace, but those which belonged to the subject *by right*. Their hopes were dashed when the King made it known that he would not accept any new law on this matter, but Coke suggested that although they might not proceed by Bill there was no reason why they should not draw up a petition. His suggestion was immediately taken up, and out of it emerged the *Petition of Right*, one of the most important constitutional documents of the whole Stuart period, which looked back to the *Form of Apology and Satisfaction* at the beginning of the century and forward to the *Bill of Rights* at the end.

In this petition it was requested that such practices as unparliamentary taxation, imprisonment without good cause, the billeting of troops and the imposition of martial law, should henceforth be declared illegal, and although Charles did his best to avoid formally committing himself to this, he eventually agreed to do so at a joint meeting of both Houses. The petition was read and Charles pronounced the formula '*Soit droit fait comme il est desiré.*' This gave the petition the force of law and made it binding on the courts, thereby marking the first decisive check to the legal extension of prerogative power.

The session had not been as harmonious as its outcome might imply. Charles's reluctance to assent to the petition had aroused discontent, and he was still defending the man whom Coke openly named as 'the Duke of Buckingham, the grievance of grievances'. Eliot had taken the lead again in drawing up a remonstrance against Buckingham and against the illegal collection of Tonnage and Poundage, and tempers were rising when, in June 1628, Charles decided on prorogation. Before dismissing the Houses he reminded them that 'I owe an account of my actions to none but to God alone', and that the Petition of Right had only confirmed existing liberties, not created any new ones.

Just over a month later, while the King was at prayers in a house outside Portsmouth, the news was brought him that Buckingham had been assassinated. The Duke had been preparing yet another expedition, when John Felton, who had taken part in the Cadiz fiasco, stabbed him to death. Charles concealed his emotion in public, but there can be little doubt that he regarded the leaders of the Commons as the real murderers of his friend.

Buckingham's death may have relieved the Commons but it did not make them more cooperative. The King, now that he had agreed to the Petition of Right, expected members to show their goodwill by voting him Tonnage and Poundage, but the opposition leaders— Denzil Holles, Valentine and Eliot—wanted to postpone this until further grievances, particularly the religious ones, had been removed. One figure was conspicuously absent from their ranks. Wentworth, disillusioned by the negative attitude of the Commons, had agreed to take office under the Crown. He believed that harmony now depended upon cooperation, and that the Commons' persistent pursuit of grievances was making any government impossible.

The King was coming rapidly to the same conclusion. In March 1629 he decided on an adjournment, but the opposition leaders were determined not to leave until they had made their views known. When the Speaker rose to declare the adjournment, Holles and Valentine forced him back into his chair, while Eliot made a passionate attack on papist influences at Court, and called on the House to pass three resolutions. When the clerk refused to read these, Holles did so himself. They asserted that anyone advising the King to collect Tonnage and Poundage, or paying such a tax, or proposing innovations in religion, should be reputed 'a betrayer of the liberties of England and an enemy to the same'. Only when the House had acclaimed these resolutions did the adjournment take place.

Charles never recalled this Parliament. As for the men who had led the Commons in such unprecedented action, Eliot, Valentine and Holles were tried before King's Bench and sentenced to imprisonment until such time as they acknowledged their fault. Valentine remained in prison until January 1640; Eliot stayed there until his death in 1632; Holles alone managed to escape abroad. For the next eleven years Charles ruled England without Parliament. There is no reason to suppose that he never intended to summon it again, but he wanted time to show how beneficial royal government could be when it was given a chance to operate freely.

Laud and the Church

The vigour of this revived royal administration was felt most strongly in the Church. The late sixteenth and early seventeenth centuries had seen a general drift towards puritanism in the Church of England, since the bishops' authority was weakened by lay attacks on their property and by the poor quality of many of the parish clergy. In James's reign, however, a reaction set in among some of the higher clergy, inspired by Andrewes, who deplored the way in which the puritans, by their insistence on a preaching ministry, had come to reject the traditional conception of the Church as the body of God on earth, preserving in its liturgy and sacraments a visible link with spiritual realities. This movement was not confined to England; in Holland, for instance, a similar reaction had taken place against the aridity and novelty of puritan attitudes. The Dutch theologian Arminius had played a leading part in this movement towards traditionalism, and the followers of Andrewes were given the name 'Arminians' by their puritan opponents.

The leader of the Arminians was William Laud, son of a Reading clothier, who took his first big step towards high office when, by his skill in debate, he persuaded Buckingham's mother not to join the Roman Catholic Church. The Duke made him his chaplain, and from then on Laud moved in Court circles. His rise might have been more rapid but for the attitude of James I, who said of him: 'He hath a restless spirit and cannot see when matters are well, but loves to toss and change and bring things to a pitch of reformation floating in his own brain.' This was, like many of James's insights, most perceptive, but the restlessness which he disliked appealed to Charles I, who realised that only a man with Laud's energy and even intolerance could bring about the necessary reform of the Anglican Church. In 1627 Laud was made a Privy Councillor, in 1628 he was appointed to the see of London, and in 1633 he became Archbishop of Canterbury. No man, except Wentworth, was more closely identified with the period of Charles's personal rule, and when that rule collapsed Laud collapsed with it.

Laud concentrated first on the bishops, ordering them not to part with their lands on long lease, nor to make a quick profit by ruthless exploitation of natural resources. When sees fell vacant he secured the appointment of men who had his own high ideals and, if possible some of his own intolerance, and he urged bishops to extend their control over puritan lecturers and to impose uniformity in their dioceses.

As for the lower clergy, he encouraged them to hold up their heads instead of accepting a position of social inferiority, and by generous gifts to Oxford University, of which he was Chancellor, he tried to improve the quality of candidates for ordination. His efforts, coming on top of those made by Whitgift, Bancroft and others, did have a marked effect in raising standards. In the diocese of Worcester, for example, the proportion of graduates among the clergy rose from under twenty per cent in 1560 to over eighty per cent by 1640, and much the same was true of other dioceses. By appointing parish clergy to the bench of Justices, and by upholding them in their disputes with local gentry, Laud did much to undo the neglect of the previous half century. He had a high view of the responsibilities of the Church, and believed, like Becket, that the clergy were a special order of men, chosen by God for the most important of earthly tasks. Their social inferiority hindered them and their work, and Laud would no doubt have agreed with his colleague Bishop Wren who declared that he 'hoped to live to see the day when a minister should be as good a man as any Jack Gentleman in England'.

Many gentlemen, of course, resented this threat to their own local sovereignty: a kingdom shared with the parish priest lost half its charm. Puritan writers, who had their own reasons for hating bishops, delighted in attacking what Prynne called 'tyrannising lordly prelates raised from the dunghill', and one of the reasons why Laud was so sensitive to these attacks and punished them so savagely was that they struck at his whole conception of the clergy as a spiritual élite.

Laud's aims ran counter to the ingrained anti-clericalism which had marked the English Reformation, and they implied a threat not only to the social supremacy of the landowning classes, but to their property as well. Church reform was held up by shortage of money, yet a large amount of Church money went into the hands of lay impropriators who used it either to enrich themselves or to appoint puritan ministers or lecturers. Laud was not the first Archbishop to hope that these impropriated tithes might be recovered for the Church. Bancroft had put forward a scheme in 1610 for extending the payment of tithes to all property—commercial and industrial as well as agricultural—and for buying back impropriated tithes with funds provided by Parliament. His scheme, which would have re-endowed the Church in the same way as Salisbury was seeking to re-endow the state, failed for the same reason—Parliament's unwillingness to provide the money. Now Laud hoped to achieve the same end by other means.

Laud's attitude, briefly, was that lay impropriators were morally bound to provide an adequate sum for the maintenance of the parish priest, and he encouraged the bishops to sue for their rights. Church courts were convenient instruments for this purpose, but the prohibitions issued by the common law courts were a major obstacle, even though the King ordered in 1638 that such prohibitions were not to be issued without the Archbishop's consent. Laud therefore turned to the Privy Council for support, and many a recalcitrant landlord found himself summoned before this august assembly and browbeaten for his refusal to part with his tithes. Such actions did not increase the popularity of the Council or the prerogative courts, and Clarendon described how 'persons of honour and great quality' who regarded courts of law as guarantors of the existing social order, never forgot 'the shame which they called an insolent triumph upon their degree and quality and levelling them with the common people'.

Laud was not only concerned to recover impropriated tithes: he also wanted to make sure that they were used for the right purpose, and for this reason he suppressed the 'Feoffees for Impropriation'—a puritan body which raised over £6,000 to buy up impropriations and use the income to improve the stipend of 'godly' ministers and lecturers. It was these ministers and lecturers—particularly strong in urban areas where tithes were difficult to collect and clergy depended largely on voluntary contributions—who were the main obstacles to Laud's plan to restore ceremony and a uniform liturgy—the 'beauty of holiness'—to the Church. He checked them by extending episcopal control and by insisting that certain minimum requirements be observed. Among these was the regulation that the communion table should be moved to the east end of the church and there protected by rails 'one yard in height and so thick with pillars that dogs may not get in'. This deeply offended puritans, who were so anxious to avoid any suggestion of venerating the sacraments that they frequently placed the holy table in the body of the church, where it served as a hatstand: Laud was not exaggerating when he complained that "tis superstition nowadays for any man to come with more reverence into a church than a tinker and his bitch come into an ale-house'. He also insisted on the wearing of the surplice, and on bowing at the name of Jesus.

Laud has been painted, with justice, as a narrow fanatic, but without his stubbornness the Church of England might well have been captured by rigid Calvinism, equally narrow and even more fanatical. Like Elizabeth, Laud was not concerned to make windows into men's souls as long as they outwardly conformed, and he would have liked to include the puritans in a single, comprehensive, national Church. In the early days of the Reformation Starkey had declared that ceremonies and traditions were *adiaphora*, 'matters indifferent', which the state might regulate to suit its own convenience. Laud took his stand on the same ground, accepting the authority of the Bible in questions of faith but insisting on his duty, as well as his right, to regulate matters on which the Scriptures were silent. 'Unity cannot long continue in the Church,' he said, 'when uniformity is shut out at the church door. No external action in the world can be uniform without some ceremonies. . . . Ceremonies are the hedge that fences the substance of religion from all the indignities which profaneness and sacrilege too commonly put upon it.'

Laud's measures angered the puritans and turned them against the bishops. Some puritans outwardly conformed, some carried on in their old ways until they were hauled before the Court of High Commission, while others broke away from the Church and took themselves and their congregations into exile in Holland or America. Laud and the bishops were so closely identified with the administration that 'puritan' became a general term to describe those who had any complaints against the government. Landowners, for instance, might not be particularly puritan but they would resent the commissions which were set up to enquire into and break down enclosures, particularly as the fines paid by offenders went towards a fund for the repair of St Paul's, which Laud hoped to make the symbol of revived anglicanism. He was firmly convinced that the clergy should take an active part in government and should aim at securing social justice. 'You must not measure preaching,' he said, 'by a formal going up into the pulpit. For a bishop may preach the Gospel more publicly, and to far greater edification, in a court of judicature or at a council table, where great men are met together to draw things to an issue, than many preachers in their several charges can.'

He set an example himself by constantly sitting in the Star Chamber and on the Court of High Commission. Star Chamber had been a popular court, but the puritan hatred of the bishops gradually came to include the court they controlled. Elizabeth had been careful to allow only one bishop at a time to sit in Star Chamber, but after 1630 there were three, and they were some of the most active members of the

court. As puritan attacks on the bishops became more public, Laud
used Star Chamber to punish the offenders, and in so doing he gave it
the unjustified reputation for savage sentences that still endures. In
most cases that came before the court, fines were inflicted—not
usually crushing, and rarely collected in full. Corporal punishment was
reserved for those who, by slandering great men, had brought the
Church or royal government into disrepute. This explains the harsh
treatment of Prynne, Burton and Bastwicke in 1637. They had
published libels against the bishops and were sentenced to stand in the
pillory, have their ears cropped and spend the rest of their lives in
prison. Such harshness had the opposite effect from what Laud intended. The three men were treated as heroes, and property-holders
were more impressed by Prynne's words than by his fate: 'you see,'
he declared from the pillory, 'they spare none of what society or
calling soever. None are exempted that cross their own ends. Gentlemen, look to yourselves. You know not whose turn may be next.'
    Puritans were particularly resentful of the fact that while they were
persecuted Roman Catholics were treated tolerantly. Only a small
proportion of catholic laymen were recusants, since the penalty for
refusing to attend anglican services—a fine of £20 a month—was still
in force, and Charles, who could not afford to neglect any source of
income, made about £15,000 a year from recusancy fines. The
incidence of these fines varied from county to county, but there is no
doubt that the greatest degree of toleration was to be found at Court,
where Henrietta Maria presided over an influential catholic circle.
Catholics were to be found even within the government itself, for in the
1630s Lord Treasurer Portland, Chancellor of the Exchequer Cottington
and Secretary Windebanke were all adherents of the old faith. Charles
could not suspend the penal laws, in spite of his father's promise at the
time of the marriage negotiations, but he issued individual dispensations to the more important of his catholic subjects, and he welcomed
a papal agent to his Court in 1636. Catholic circles, particularly on the
Continent, had hopes that England might be restored to the Church
of Rome, and a cardinal's hat was offered to Laud as an inducement.
There was little foundation for such hopes, since Charles and Laud
were convinced anglicans, hoping for the reunification of all the
Christian churches but not at the cost of major concessions either to
right or to left. To puritans, however, unprepared to make fine distinctions between papists and Arminians, anything short of persecution
of Roman Catholics was a sign of apostasy from the protestant faith.

Wentworth and the Policy of 'Thorough'

In the eleven years of non-parliamentary rule Laud was closely associated with Sir Thomas Wentworth, created a viscount in 1628 and appointed Lord President of the Council of the North. Parliament and the King were not so far apart that to serve the one was to betray the other, and Wentworth never regarded himself as an enemy of representative institutions—he had, after all, been an active and far from subservient member of the House of Commons. But by temperament he was autocratic, and he appreciated more than many of his fellow members that if the subjects' liberties could be defended only by crippling the government, the subject might well find that he had no liberties left to defend. Under the impact of the price rise, the expansion of commerce, and the development of industry, the English economy was being transformed and many of the old landmarks, by which society had orientated itself, were being swept away. The 'political nation' depended for its power, its wealth and its culture upon the acquiescence of the mass of the people who were undernourished and underprivileged, and if the authority of government were relaxed, discontent might lead to social ferment and disruption. 'The authority of a King', said Wentworth, 'is the keystone which closeth up the arch of order and government which contains each part in due relation to the whole, and which, once shaken . . . all the frame falls together in a confused heap of foundation and battlement, of strength and beauty.'

By early 1631 Wentworth and Laud were on close terms and were working together to make the King's will effective. Commissions were appointed to see that the poor law was carried out, to devise some better treatment for the punishment and relief of debtors, and to check the expansion of London, while other commissions enquired into abuses in the administration and initiated reforms. For a time the Privy Council acquired an Elizabethan vigour and kept a close watch on local government—much to the resentment of the peers and gentry who were inclined to regard any attempt at central control as tyranny.

This programme, which Wentworth and Laud christened 'Thorough' —the carrying-through of policies which were not new but had been long neglected—was more effective as an irritant of the landowners than as an instrument of social justice. To have been really efficient it would have needed a highly trained, regularly paid bureaucracy of the sort which Richelieu was creating in France. But the

English civil service, which had been reasonably efficient under the
Tudors, had developed into a self-perpetuating oligarchy, more
interested in its own privileges and profits than in speedy and in-
expensive administration. The rot that set in during the closing years of
Elizabeth, and spread rapidly under James, could not easily be checked.
The household consumed forty per cent of all the peacetime revenue
of the Crown, and efforts at economy were impeded by what Wentworth and Laud called 'Lady Mora'—the greed, lethargy and sheer
incompetence which blunted the edge of administration by every
conceivable kind of delay.

Wentworth himself was not free from the corrupting influence which
he was trying to combat. Although he opposed pluralism he held on to
the Lord Presidency even when he was appointed Lord-Deputy of
Ireland in 1632, and he used his high position in the state to increase
his income from about £6,000 in 1628 to nearly £23,000 ten years
later. Few of his actions were dishonest, but many of them took place
in that borderland between legitimate and illegitimate, permissible
and impermissible, where Bacon, Cranfield and others had fallen.
But although Wentworth made money out of serving the Crown, he
did at least devote all his enormous energy and talent to that service.
In Ireland he imposed royal authority on the English settlers who had
become virtually independent, he brought the Irish Parliament to heel,
he improved the financial administration, and he called to account
great men like the Earl of Cork who had previously had the government in their pocket.

Wentworth's rule in Ireland was a try-out for the policy of
'Thorough' which he advocated in England, and his success there gave
English property-holders considerable cause for alarm. Laud had
encouraged the English bishops to sue for recovery of tithes which had
fallen into lay hands, but in Ireland Wentworth took the initiative
himself in recovering, for Church and Crown, lands which had been
alienated during the previous half century of disturbance. When the
common lawyers, always defenders of property-rights, opposed him,
Wentworth secured letters patent from Charles giving the prerogative
Court of Castle Chamber final authority in matters affecting the
Church. Royal power was, of course, less restrained in Ireland than in
England, since there was no strongly entrenched gentry class to oppose
it, but English landowners, most of whom had some property which
had at one time or another belonged to the Church, feared that they
themselves might one day be called to account before a prerogative

court in which the defences carefully constructed by the common law would be of little asistance to them.

Charles's personal government, then, in spite of its laudable aims of social justice and efficient administration, was only really successful in alienating the property-owners on whose cooperation, in the last resort, it depended, and on driving them into the arms of the puritans. The same was true of his foreign policy. The 'Country' wanted an aggressive naval war against Spain but Charles had learned the lesson that Parliament would never pay for war except on terms that would be incompatible with the maintenance of royal prerogatives, and in 1629 he had made peace with both France and Spain. From then on the policy of the Court became distinctly pro-Spanish, and this met with the approval not only of catholics and their sympathisers but also of people like Wentworth, who was close to the puritans in his religious attitude but who wanted peace with Spain because this was the only way to keep the King's government solvent.

In 1630 Charles made an agreement to mint Spanish silver in England and to send it in English ships to Antwerp where it would be used to pay the armies fighting the Dutch. This apparent desertion of the protestant cause outraged the 'Country', but Charles never shared their enthusiasm for continental protestantism. When Gustavus Adolphus, King of Sweden and the great hope of the protestants, was killed, a parliamentary diarist wrote 'never did one person's death in Christendom bring so much sorrow to all true protestant hearts—not our godly Edward's, the Sixth of that name, nor our late heroic and inestimable Prince Henry, as did the King of Sweden's at this present'. Charles's only reaction was to forbid public mourning for the King's death. His marked lack of enthusiasm was not due to any profound awareness of the declining importance of religious motives in the Thirty Years War: it was the result of his natural sympathy for the great European monarchies, of which Spain was still the outstanding example.

The advocates of a more active policy took as their heroine Charles's sister, Elizabeth of Bohemia, the 'Winter Queen'. She lived in the Hague, on a pension from the Dutch government, still hoping that one day the Palatinate might be recovered either for her eldest son Charles Louis, or for her younger son, Prince Rupert. In 1637 Charles Louis visited England to try to persuade Charles to join Holland in attacking Spain, but the King would not be deflected from his peaceful policy by family considerations. The young Elector Palatine found a

warmer welcome among Charles's opponents, particularly the
directors of the company which had been set up to establish a colony
on Providence Island in the Spanish West Indies, for use as a base from
which puritan buccaneers could prey on Spanish shipping, like latter-
day Drakes. But the Providence Island Company was not of importance only in colonial affairs—in which, indeed, it was conspicuously unsuccessful. Meetings of the directors provided an opportunity
for some of Charles's leading opponents to keep in touch and make
plans for the future. Among the shareholders of the company were
the puritan lords Warwick, Saye, and Brooke. John Hampden, a
country gentleman of enormous wealth, was another of the shareholders: the solicitor was Oliver St John and the secretary was John
Pym.

Hampden and St John became public figures when, in 1637, they
were involved in the Ship Money case. The King wished to raise a
fleet to defend English merchants against the Dunkirk privateers and
the Barbary corsairs (from North Africa) who infested the seas. This
was no mere excuse, for in the first Parliament of the reign one member
had complained that 'pirates come into our sea and take our ships at
our door', and in 1631 the Barbary corsairs had sacked Baltimore on the
Irish coast. In 1634, therefore, the King sent out writs to the seaports,
ordering them to supply ships at their own expense for the royal
service. The demand for ships was, to some extent, a formality.
London provided them, but the other towns preferred to pay money
instead. In 1635 the demand for ships was repeated, but this time it was
extended to inland counties, on the grounds that 'that charge of
defence which concerneth all men ought to be supported by all.'
This device proved so lucrative that ships, or money in lieu, were
demanded every year, and the King had, in fact, added a new tax to
his revenue without obtaining parliamentary consent for it.

Such an invasion of property-rights did not go unchallenged, and in
1637 John Hampden invited a test case by refusing to pay. The case
aroused interest all over England, and the speech made by St John,
who defended Hampden, centred on the argument that if the King
could force his subjects to contribute taxes at his pleasure their property
would be at his mercy. But the judges, as in Bate's case and the case of
the Five Knights, were not well placed to consider the broader implications of the King's action. The King had stated that an emergency
existed and that by virtue of his absolute prerogative he was empowered to levy contributions from his subjects without waiting for

their formal consent. Sir Robert Berkeley, Chief Justice of the King's bench, upheld this, and declared 'that it is a dangerous tenet, a kind of judaizing opinion, to hold that the weal public must be exposed to peril of utter ruin and subversion rather than such a charge as this, which may secure the commonwealth, may be imposed by the King upon the subject, without common consent in Parliament'.

Berkeley was careful to state that the King's absolute prerogative applied only in cases of emergency, and that in the normal course of affairs he would raise money solely through Parliament. But who was to decide when an emergency existed? The common law could give no guidance on such a subject, and Berkeley could only assume that the King must be relied on not to abuse his trust. Not all his colleagues were so confident of the King's intentions, however, and the degree of resistance which Charles's policies had aroused is indicated by the fact that out of twelve judges, five gave their verdict in Hampden's favour. For Charles it was a pyrrhic victory.

Ship Money, all of which was spent on the navy, brought in a total of nearly three-quarters of a million pounds before the Long Parliament put an end to it, but the cost in goodwill was high. The same is true of other sources of revenue which were exploited. The Courts of Wards which, under James I, had provided about £20,000 a year, yielded over £80,000 in 1640, and in that year Impositions, benefiting from the revival of trade consequent upon peace, brought in more than £140,000 compared with £36,000 in the early 1630s. The rent charged to the Customs farmers was increased, monopolies were exploited, and old devices such as distraint of knighthood were revived. In 1634 a survey of royal forests was begun, and areas which had been out of the scope of the forest law for many centuries were now brought within it again. Men who had disafforested or enclosed land in these areas were brought before the forest courts and fined for breaking the special laws which governed these game reserves. The common law courts were once again powerless to prevent this sudden change in the status of a man's property.

The result of these and other measures was that the Crown's annual income gradually came to equal and sometimes exceed its expenditure, particularly after William Juxon, Bishop of London, was appointed Treasurer in 1636. His appointment was another sign of increasing clerical influence in political life, and Laud was delighted. 'No church-man', he wrote, 'had it since Henry VII's time. I pray God bless him to carry it so that the Church may have honour and the King and state contentment by it.' Juxon had many of Laud's virtues. He was hard-working, honest, and not interested in personal gain, and above all he was a good administrator. But even though he did much to restore the royal finances, he could not wipe out the huge backlog of debt, and the surplus on current expenditure was only achieved by borrowing money on the security of future revenues—a practice that steadily diminished the proportion of annual income actually available to the Crown.

In the 1630s England seemed to be, on the surface, a happy and prosperous country, particularly when compared with the war-torn Continent. In 1629 Rubens arrived and was enchanted with 'a people rich and happy in the arts of peace'. He began work on the designs for the magnificent painting with which he decorated the ceiling of Inigo Jones's Banqueting House in Whitehall, and a few years later the Flemish painter Van Dyck started his series of portraits of the King and members of his Court. 'Charles I', in the words of one historian, 'was the most enthusiastic and discerning patron of the arts to grace the English throne and he assembled a collection of pictures and works of art unequalled in the history of English taste.'[1] Such an achievement, however, was unlikely to endear Charles to his puritan subjects, and it was dependent, like the whole of his régime, on the preservation of peace. By a strange irony Charles himself, abetted by Laud, brought this peace to an end.

The Destruction of Prerogative Monarchy

In October 1636 the King ordered a new service-book, modelled on the English Prayer-Book, to be brought into general use in Scottish churches. His aim was to extend to Scotland the uniformity of worship which Laud was already imposing in England, and perhaps to continue that process of integrating the two kingdoms which his father had begun. But when, in July of the following year, the Book was used for the first time in St Giles's Cathedral, Edinburgh, it provoked a riot. 'The mass is entered among us!' shouted one woman, another flung her stool at the preacher, and soon the whole cathedral was in an uproar. The revolt spread quickly, and found support and leadership among the Scottish nobles who feared that the King's next step would be the confiscation of such of their lands as had formerly belonged to the Church. Puritanism, in its presbyterian form, was much stronger in

[1] Margaret Whinney and Oliver Millar, *English Art 1625-1714*, p. 1.

Scotland than in England, and thousands of people, encouraged by their ministers, flocked to sign the National Covenant, in which they pledged themselves to defend their system of worship.

Charles gave himself a breathing-space by suspending the new service-book, but at the same time he prepared to use force and ordered the trained bands of the northern counties to be called to arms. Years of peace had, however, left the country unprepared for war, and the Lord Admiral reported to Wentworth that 'the King's magazines are totally unfurnished of arms and all sorts of ammunition, and commanders we have none either for advice or execution; the people through all England are generally so discontented. . . . I think there is reason to fear that a great part of them will be readier to join with the Scots than to draw their swords in the King's service.'

By December 1638 Charles's patience was exhausted. He appointed the Earl of Essex—son of Elizabeth's favourite—as commander of his army in the field, and went north to join it at York. But even Charles was forced to realise, when he saw the ragged collection assembled under his colours, that he could not possibly beat the Scots, who were commanded by men who had made their name and fortune as professional soldiers on the Continent. In June 1639, therefore, he agreed to the Pacification of Berwick, by which both armies were to be disbanded while a Scottish Parliament and Assembly of the Kirk were to advise on what action should be taken to restore peace. It was at this moment that Charles, realising the need for a strong man, overcame his distrust of Wentworth and summoned him back from Ireland. 'Come when you will,' he wrote, 'ye shall be welcome to your assured friend, Charles R.'

Wentworth advised the summoning of Parliaments in England and Ireland as well as Scotland, arguing that the traditional enmity between England and Scotland would rouse members in defence of their native land. In the Scottish Parliament and Assembly members voted, as was to be expected, for the abolition of episcopacy—which the King would never accept—but the Irish Parliament, well managed by Wentworth, set a better example by voting over £150,000 for the King's needs. Yet if Wentworth thought that the English Parliament, which met in April 1640, would be as amenable as the Irish one, he was swiftly disillusioned.

The King depended for the presentation of his case to the Commons on the recently appointed Secretary, Sir Henry Vane, who had little skill in parliamentary tactics and was envious of Wentworth. His fumbling gave an opportunity to John Pym. This bull-necked west countryman had been born four years before the Armada, and grew up hating Spain and longing to restore not only the aggressive policies but also the constitutional harmony (as it seemed to him in retrospect) of Elizabeth's reign. The King had proposed that subsidies should be voted in the first session of Parliament and that grievances should be left until the second, but Pym, who feared that once subsidies had been granted there would be no second session, insisted that grievances should be redressed first. His attitude alarmed the Court, particularly as it was rumoured that he and other leading members of the 'Country' were in touch with the Scots and intended to take up their cause in the English Parliament. Wentworth, who had just been created Earl of Strafford, was in favour of keeping Parliament in session, but the majority of the Privy Councillors were against him and in May 1640 the King dissolved this Short Parliament only three weeks after it had first met. By this hasty action Charles lost a good chance of coming to some sort of agreement with the parliamentary leaders, for the Commons and Lords, while they insisted on the need for reform, were not so intransigent as they were later to become.

Although Parliament had been dissolved, the King ordered Convocation to continue sitting. This clerical assembly voted £20,000 a year for the cause of the King and Church, and it also passed a number of canons defining the doctrines of the Anglican Church in an extremely Arminian manner. Particular offence was given by the order that all clergymen, teachers and doctors should take an oath to maintain the government of the Church by 'archbishops, bishops, deans and archdeacons, etc.', for no one could be sure what was included in that final significant abbreviation. The 'Etcetera Oath' united the puritans against the bishops at the very moment when the authority of both King and bishops was being seriously challenged.

Strafford urged the King to go ahead with military operations against Scotland, and meanwhile began negotiations with Spain, proposing that in return for an enormous loan English ships should be provided to guard Spanish transports carrying men and money to the Netherlands. Negotiations broke down, however, when the Dutch made it clear that they would regard such a commitment by England as a hostile act, and the King had to rely on what resources Juxon could make available to him. These were not sufficient to fight a major campaign, especially since throughout the country there was general reluctance to provide men and money for the King's service.

The Scots crossed the border and occupied the northern counties without meeting any effective resistance, and even Strafford, who had earlier believed that the King's benevolent rule had made royal government popular, was forced to realise the hopelessness of the situation. 'Pity me,' he wrote to a friend, 'for never came any man to so mightily lost a business. The army altogether unexercised and unprovided of all necessaries. That part which I bring now with me from Durham the worst I ever saw. Our horse all cowardly, the country from Berwick to York in the power of the Scots; an universal affright in all men; a general disaffection to the King's service; none sensible of his dishonour. In one word, here alone to fight with all these evils, without anyone to help.'

The King, in desperation, decided to summon a great council of peers to meet him at York, where they would be free from the influence of puritan London, to give him their advice. When the peers met, all they could suggest was a truce with the Scots, to last until such time as another Parliament could settle the affairs of the kingdom. Writs were accordingly sent out, and on 3 November 1640 members of both Houses assembled in London for what was to be the last Parliament of Charles's reign. The King could not, this time, risk an early dissolution, for the terms of the truce negotiated with the Scots were that their army should remain in possession of Northumberland and Durham and receive £850 a day until a final settlement was agreed upon. Not until Parliament had guaranteed repayment of any moneys advanced were the City authorities prepared to raise a loan to pay the Scots.

Pym, who was once again the effective leader of the Commons, was determined on a ruthless policy, and told Edward Hyde, a fellow member, that 'they must be of another temper than they were the last Parliament. They must not only sweep the house clean below, but must pull down all the cobwebs which hung in the tops and corners.' The only man Pym feared was Strafford, but Strafford did not arrive in London until Parliament had already been sitting a week, and by the time he was ready to take his seat in the Lords, the Commons had already drawn up articles of impeachment against him. The great minister was sent off to the Tower to await trial, and in the following month he was joined there by Laud, also impeached.[1] Other members of the King's administration fled abroad rather than face the revenge of the Commons. They included the Lord Keeper, Finch, who had

[1] Laud remained in the Tower until his execution in January 1645.

played a prominent part in the collection of Ship Money, and Secretary Windebanke.

Strafford was accused of subverting 'the fundamental laws of the kingdom', and in his person the whole of the King's government during the eleven years without Parliament was on trial. The Commons were acting as defenders of the common law against the absolute prerogative, but the weakness of their case was that although they were convinced that the absolute prerogative was illegal, they could not *prove* it to be so. During his trial, which took place before the Lords in March and April 1641, Strafford defended himself very ably and insisted that he had not planned to build up a tyranny in England but only to restore the balance of the constitution. 'I did ever inculcate this', he declared in his final speech; 'the happiness of a kingdom consists in the just poise of the King's prerogative and the subject's liberty, and ... things should never be well till these went hand in hand together.'

It eventually became clear that the Lords—who had no love for Strafford, but were not prepared to abdicate their responsibilities as judges—would not find the minister guilty of the charges made against him. Pym therefore changed his tactics and introduced a Bill of Attainder into the Commons. It was in this instance a political rather than a legal weapon. It simply declared Strafford's guilt without giving him any chance to reply, and its use was a belated recognition by Pym that the King's prerogative rule, however oppressive, had not been actually illegal.

The Bill passed the Commons—where many of the members were already beginning to absent themselves—and was sent to the Lords. While they considered it, London was in a fever of excitement. The official government of the City was royalist, particularly as many of the big merchants who controlled it had lent too much money to the King to risk deserting him now. But the City members, led by Isaac Pennington, were radical, and they were linked with the highly organised puritan movement that flourished around such churches as St Antholin's and St Stephen's, Coleman Street. The puritan radicalism of this part of London had been demonstrated by the triumphal reception accorded Burton and Prynne on their release from prison in November 1640, and by the support given to Pennington's 'Root-and-Branch Petition' calling for the abolition of episcopacy. Pym had close links with these puritan parishes and with the Scottish commissioners who had been sent to negotiate a peace treaty and who lived in a house adjoining St Antholin's. When he wanted reinforcement for his policies he had only to give the word and the apprentices of this quarter, often led by their puritan masters, would flock to Westminster to terrorise the more moderate members of Parliament.

This mob—which was far from an undisciplined rabble—crowded the approaches to the House of Lords while the debate on the Bill of Attainder was taking place. The King was playing for time and was deliberately courting the moderates. He demonstrated his change of heart by arranging a marriage between his elder daughter Mary and the Prince of Orange; he appointed Oliver St John as Solicitor-General and he took as his chief adviser the moderate Earl of Bedford. It was at Bedford's suggestion that Charles proposed to address the Lords and remind them that if they condemned Strafford they would be undermining the law and the social structure on which their own privileged position depended. But Bedford fell suddenly ill, and the King, left alone to make his speech, simply told the Lords that he would never consent to the Bill of Attainder. If he hoped by this declaration to set an example, he had badly miscalculated. All he had done was to release the Lords from their responsibility, for they were now persuaded that even if they passed the Bill Charles would veto it. While the crowds surged outside, the small number of lords who were able and willing to attend the House debated Strafford's fate. The Bill passed by twenty-six votes to nineteen.

Charles had promised Strafford that if he came to London he would not be harmed. But now, from the Tower, Strafford wrote to the King releasing him from his promise: 'to set Your Majesty's conscience at liberty, I do most humbly beseech Your Majesty (for prevention of evils which may happen by your refusal) to pass this Bill.' Charles had to weigh the life of his minister against the danger to himself and his Crown, and it was only after long and agonising deliberation that he gave his assent. 'My Lord of Strafford's condition', he said, 'is happier than mine.' Strafford went to his execution on 11 May, looking up at Laud's window as he passed to receive the Archbishop's benediction. A huge crowd had gathered to witness the end of Black Tom and one of them described how 'many that came up to town on purpose to see the execution rode in triumph back, waving their hats and with all expressions of joy through every town they went crying 'His head is off! His head is off!' Laud was one of the few people who mourned Strafford's death, and he permitted himself a rare criticism of the King who had brought this about: Strafford, he wrote, 'served a mild and gracious prince, who knew not how to be, or be made, great'.

The destruction of Strafford opened the way to the destruction of the prerogative. Bills were passed abolishing the Courts of Star Chamber and High Commission, declaring Ship Money illegal, forbidding distraint of knighthood, and limiting the royal forests. Another Bill made a temporary grant of Tonnage and Poundage and Impositions to the King, but declared that the earlier collection of these taxes by the prerogative power had been illegal. By these acts Parliament left the common law supreme and unchallenged in England; but although the initiative in bringing about this transformation came from the Commons, the Bills were submitted as usual to the Lords and the King. 'Parliament' did not yet mean 'The House of Commons', and Pym maintained as firmly as Henry VIII that he was carrying through a restoration and not a revolution.

The King could not get rid of Parliament, even though he had now made peace with the Scots, because he had given his assent to a Bill forbidding the dissolution of the two Houses without their own consent. He therefore decided to go north, to visit his other kingdom and see if he could win the Scots over to the support of his cause. Pym was reluctant to see the King 'escape' from London, where Parliament and the puritans were so strongly entrenched, and his forebodings seemed justified when crowds of people flocked to cheer Charles in the towns and villages through which he passed. This triumphant reception reminded Charles how much support he still had. The veneration for monarchy, and the habit of loyalty, were deeply ingrained in the English people, and the Commons had been careful to direct their attacks not against the King but against the 'evil counsellors' who perverted his good intentions. Now that the King had got rid of these evil men, it seemed to many of his subjects that his reign could continue happily. Few of them were thinking in terms of civil war.

The Approach to Civil War

While the King was in Scotland news came that the catholics in Ireland had risen in revolt against the English settlers and were massacring them. This immediately precipitated a crisis in the relationship between Charles and Parliament. Rebellion, particularly one so horrible, demanded speedy repression, but this could only be carried out by an army, and the head of the armed forces was the King. Pym and his friends had no reason to trust the King, or to think that he had really accepted the legislation of 1641 and had no intention of overthrowing it when the situation changed. How could they be sure that an army raised to quell the Irish catholics, and officered by men whom the King had chosen, would not be turned against the English Parliament? Pym's answer was a proposal that the King should choose only such men as Parliament approved of.

This proposal met with opposition from the moderates in the House, who were now beginning to organise themselves under the leadership of Edward Hyde. Up to this point civil war had not been feasible, because no one would have fought for the King: the 'political nation' was united against him. But many members who had opposed prerogative government were prepared to trust the King now that he had changed his ways. They were also increasingly concerned at the religious radicalism of Pym's supporters. They had shared with the puritans the desire for reform, but they had no wish to see the structure of the Church or state of England altered. Pym had come out in support of the Root-and-Branch Bill, proposing the total abolition of episcopacy, and although the Commons had dropped this measure in favour of more urgent ones, the problem of church reform remained acute. The moderates now rallied round Hyde and tried to call a halt to the revolution before it went too far. Hyde's attitude was, quite simply, that the King *must* be trusted, otherwise any government on the traditional pattern would be impossible. But Pym, who also wished to preserve the traditional constitution, believed that the revolution must be carried to the point where the King could not reverse it. To remind members that they were dealing with an untrustworthy man, he drew up a long list of all the grievances for which the King had been responsible, and presented these to the House as the *Grand Remonstrance*. But although this document was mainly concerned with reciting the past, it made some drastic proposals for the future. The King was asked to join with the Commons in depriving the bishops of their votes in Parliament and in referring the whole question of church reform to a committee of divines. He was also asked to take as counsellors only 'such persons . . . as your Parliament may have cause to confide in'.

Pym must have known that the Grand Remonstrance would split the Commons, but he was prepared to take this risk to preserve the gains of the revolution. Hyde—who was, like Pym a common lawyer— led the moderates in defence of the constitution. 'Take heed', he said later, 'of removing landmarks and destroying foundations. Whilst you insist upon these you have a place to fix your feet upon. . . . Abandon your principles and there is no judge of reason left but plurality of voices and strength of hands.' Debate went on all through the winter afternoon and late into the night, and the division was not called until one o'clock. 159 members voted in favour of the Remonstrance, 148 against: Pym had won by eleven votes. The moderates immediately claimed the right to enter a protest, and members sprang to their feet reaching for their swords. 'I thought we had all sat in the valley of the shadow of death,' wrote one of them, 'for we, like Joab's and Abner's young men, had catched at each other's locks and sheathed our swords in each other's bowels, had not the sagacity and great calmness of Mr Hampden, by a short speech, prevented it.'

The Grand Remonstrance was regarded, at the time and later, as a test case, to determine whether the revolution should go forward or stand still. The member for Cambridge, Oliver Cromwell, told Falkland that if it had not been passed 'he would have sold all he had the next morning and never seen England more, and he knew there were many other honest men of the same resolution'. Hyde despaired of winning the Commons over to moderation, and offered his services to the King, hoping to prevent Charles from making mistakes which would widen the gulf between him and Parliament.

But Hyde was not the King's only adviser. The Queen and Lord Digby were urging Charles to take action before it was too late, and they reminded him that the Militia Bill, which passed the Commons in December, would take away his control of the Lords-Lieutenant and Deputy-Lieutenants who commanded the trained bands of the counties —the only military force in England. The King was alarmed, too, by the loss of London. In November 1641 the Lord Mayor and civic authorities had given him an official welcome on his return from Scotland, but in the elections for the Common Council which took place the following month the radicals won control. From then on the government of London was effectively on the side of Pym and Parliament.

When the Commons reassembled after the Christmas break, in January 1642, Pym set out to goad the King into violent action before the moderates should increase their strength. He took advantage of the fear aroused by the catholic rebellion in Ireland to inflame feelings against the Queen, who was herself a catholic and might well be— or so it was suggested—in league with her co-religionists. Rumours were spread that the Queen was about to be impeached, and these had the desired effect. Charles, torn between the moderates and the extremists, tried to follow both courses simultaneously. On 2 January he offered the Chancellorship of the Exchequer to Pym, and when Pym refused he gave the office to Culpeper, one of Hyde's supporters. Another of the moderates, Viscount Falkland, renowned for his integrity and his love of peace, was persuaded by his friend Hyde to take office as Secretary. But unknown to these new members of his Council the King was also preparing a *coup d'état*. On 3 January he accused Lord Mandeville and five members of the House of Commons —John Pym, John Hampden, Arthur Haslerig, Denzil Holles and William Strode—of subverting the fundamental laws by attempting to destroy his rightful prerogatives and by aiding his Scottish enemies.

The next day the King, with a bodyguard of soldiers, marched to the Commons and made his way into the House. 'By your leave, Mr Speaker,' he said, 'I must borrow your chair a little', and stepping on to the dais he scanned the rows of faces to see if the five members were among them. When he realised that they had fled, he turned to the Speaker and demanded to know where they had gone. But William Lenthall, in an uncharacteristic moment of greatness, fell on his knees and answered: 'May it please Your Majesty, I have neither eyes to see nor tongue to speak in this place but as the House is pleased to direct me, whose servant I am here.' Charles knew then that his coup had failed. 'Well,' he said, 'since I see all the birds are flown, I do expect from you that you shall send them unto me as soon as they return hither', and he made his way out of the House amid a clamour of voices and shouts of 'Privilege! Privilege!'

The five members, who had been warned that Charles was contemplating the use of force, were in fact in the City, where the puritan radicals of the parish of St Stephen's, Coleman Street, had given them refuge. Charles drove to the City and called on the Common Council to hand over the fugitives so that they might stand trial, but the City would not abandon its heroes, and angry crowds surged round the King's carriage as he drove, empty-handed, back to Whitehall. London was becoming too dangerous a place for Charles to stay in, and on 10 January he left for Hampton Court. Next day the five members returned in triumph to Westminster.

War was not yet inevitable. There were extremists on both sides— Pym and his followers in the Commons, and the Queen and her circle at Court—but there were also moderates, who hoped to build a bridge between King and Parliament. Hyde, for instance, stayed in London and regularly attended the Commons, even though he was acting as Charles's adviser and drafted most of the King's replies to messages

sent him by the House. Both Lords and Commons contained many
men who were anxious for peace and reconciliation, and Hyde hoped
to win their support for the King by committing Charles to a policy
of moderation. The King, however, could not afford to ignore the
real threat that Pym represented, and it was not simply weakness of
character that drove him from time to time to listen to the advocates
of a stronger policy.

It was at the suggestion of the Queen's party that the King appointed
the Earl of Newcastle governor of Hull—one of the major ports and
arsenals of the kingdom. But Pym got wind of this and sent Sir John
Hotham to Hull with orders to hold it for Parliament. After this rebuff
the King turned again towards the moderates, and in February he sent
the Queen to Holland, out of harm's way. At Hyde's suggestion he
agreed, in principle, that Parliament should nominate Lords-Lieutenant
to control the militia, as long as a time limit was set to this innovation.
He also gave his assent to the Bill excluding bishops from the Lords,
and authorised Parliament to go ahead with its proposals to reform the
Church.

Hyde hoped that this conciliatory attitude might form the basis for
a *rapprochement*, but Pym still distrusted the King's intentions, and
knew that the Queen's party, though temporarily out of favour, could
easily take control again. Both sides wished to argue only from positions of strength, and were unable, or unwilling, to see that such an
attitude implied capitulation by one or other group. At Pym's prompt-
ing the Commons rejected the King's reply to the Militia proposals as
inadequate, and published their own Militia Bill as an ordinance,
requiring obedience to it on the grounds that the King's 'public will'
was expressed not in royal proclamations but in the actions of 'his'
Parliament. By issuing the Militia Ordinance the leaders of the Commons had clearly exceeded the powers which traditionally belonged to
Parliament, and they were now as much of a threat to the fundamental
laws of the kingdom as the King had earlier been.

Parliament made its terms known in the Nineteen Propositions sent
to the King at York in June 1642. In these they demanded that the two
Houses should control appointments to the highest military and civil
offices, that the Church should be reformed, and that the protestant
cause in Europe should be actively supported by England. Acceptance
of such terms would have meant for the King total capitulation, but
the parliamentary leaders felt certain he would have to accept them in
the end because he had no alternative. They were in a position of

strength, and they were dictating terms from it. Charles and Hyde now agreed that the only chance of a compromise agreement rested in strengthening the royal position. In June, therefore, the King sent out Commissions of Array to the Lords-Lieutenant of every county, ordering them to ignore the Militia Ordinance and to call out the trained bands for the King's service. On 22 August Charles raised his standard at Nottingham.

13

Civil War and Interregnum

Roundheads and Cavaliers

IN June 1642 the Commons felt certain that the King would have to accept their demands because he would find no one to fight for him; yet four months later Charles was advancing on London with an army of thirteen thousand men. From that time to the present day the problem of who fought for whom, and why, has intrigued historians and defied any clear-cut explanation. As far as the ordinary soldier was concerned, pay and the chance of plunder, as well as traditional loyalties, seem at first to have been the main incentives, and when captured he was usually quite willing to change sides. But the 'upper class', the 'political nation', which had been united against the King in 1640, split for a variety of reasons, and none of the general explanations is entirely satisfactory.

For Gardiner, the great nineteenth-century historian of the Stuart period, the dispute was primarily one of ideas, with the champions of religious liberty fighting side by side with defenders of constitutional government in opposition to the Crown. This interpretation has been challenged, but not by any means entirely overthrown. There seems little doubt, for instance, that the majority of those who loved the Church of England were to be found in the King's armies when war came, whatever their private reservations about Charles's political ambitions, while the parliamentary armies, on the other hand, were overwhelmingly puritan. But twentieth-century historians, writing under the shadow of Marx, find the explanation of the civil war solely in terms of religion insufficient, since it takes no account of economic realities which underlay and, it is presumed, helped mould the attitudes of the property-owners who led the struggle. For Marxists proper the civil war was the revolt of the up-and-coming capitalist gentry against the feudal aristocracy who were clinging to power and could only be dislodged by violence, and the victory of the gentry was an essential part of the process whereby England was transformed from a feudal-agricultural society into a capitalist-commercial one.

This interpretation was strengthened by the study which R. H. Tawney—not himself a Marxist—made of the gentry, showing how they had been increasing in wealth and influence as a result of their acquisition of monastic lands, and it seemed to explain why the economically advanced south and east, led by London, supported Parliament, while the commercially backward north and south were predominantly royalist.

The weakness of the Marxist hypothesis is that the gentry were not capitalist nor were the aristocracy feudal. There were capitalists in England, but they were to be found among the richer City merchants, who did not play a major role in the revolution and, in the early stages at any rate, supported the Crown. There were also a few aristocrats who might be legitimately described as 'feudal', because they could call up armies of retainers to fight for them. The Earl of Derby was one of these, and he, it is true, supported Charles I; but the Earl of Northumberland, head of the great house of Percy and one of the most powerful magnates in England, was to be found on the side of Parliament. Such men were, in any case, exceptions, for the long period of Tudor rule had seen the decline and disappearance of feudalism (except as a money-raising device). It had also seen the disappearance of the feudal aristocracy: the majority of English nobles in 1640 came from gentry families that had been elevated to the peerage only during the preceding hundred years. There was no great gulf fixed between the gentry and the aristocracy in birth, wealth or custom. John Hampden, for instance, was a mere gentleman, but he was richer than most of the nobles, and after the attempt on the Five Members a thousand of the tenants from his Buckinghamshire estates marched to Westminster to offer their services to Parliament. Hampden also had at least eighty relatives in the Long Parliament, but they did not form a united group and they included not only Oliver Cromwell but the King himself!

The interpretation of the civil war as a class struggle precipitated by economic changes fits neatly into the preconceptions of our own class-conscious, highly industrialised society. Yet there is no convincing evidence that economic changes brought about the civil war, or that the English revolution significantly changed the pace at which capitalism was advancing. Only the eye of faith can discern all the capitalists on one side and all the reactionaries on the other, for England was not an industrial state in 1640 and a man's position in society depended far more upon birth and geography than it does today. There were only

The area supporting
Parliament in 1642-43

Newcastle

imp
Battle
Marston Moor   • YORK
                    Hull   *important*

•Preston *Adwalton*
           Moor

•Nantwich   Nottingham   •Newark

Shrewsbury

                 Naseby *imp. batle*
Worcester•   •Newmarket
              Holmby House
         Edgehill•
Gloucester•   •The Rye
                            House
              Oxford•   LONDON
              Roundway
                Down   Brentford
Bristol•   Newbury• •Cheriton
    •Sedgemoor   Arundel•

              Exeter•
                          •Carisbrooke
Braddock
 •Down
   •Plymouth   ENGLAND DURING
                      THE CIVIL WAR

two classes—the 'haves' and the 'have-nots'—and the war was brought about by a division among the 'haves', not by a take-over bid from the 'have-nots'—though this came later.

Professor Trevor-Roper put forward quite a different interpretation, though one that was also based on property. According to him the revolt was led by the declining or 'mere' gentry—those who had no access to office, the law or trade, and were determined to break the power of the 'Court' gentry, who supplemented their landed wealth from these other sources. Oliver Cromwell comes to mind immediately as an example of a 'mere' gentleman who managed not simply to break his way into the gilded circle but to make himself the centre of it, and on a lesser scale it seems likely that as the war progressed the leadership of the county committees, which organised the supply of men and money for the parliamentary armies, fell increasingly into the hands of men whose families had not formerly been numbered among the élite of their county.

Yet this interpretation, attractive as it is, does not accord with some of the most important evidence. The Court gentry were not, as Professor Aylmer has shown, a homogeneous group: when war came some supported one side, some the other, and the choice seems to have been dictated by personal convictions. The Roman Catholics were declining gentry, if only because of the heavy recusancy fines they had to pay, but they were to be found in the King's armies. The parliamentary leaders included some of the most prosperous landowners in England, while on the other hand the 'mere' gentry of the north and west placed their money and lives at the King's disposal.

Professor Trevor-Roper has also put the English revolution into its European context, pointing out that the 1640s saw rebellions in France, Holland, Spain, Portugal and Naples. He suggests that these upheavals marked the end of the Renaissance monarchies in Europe—monarchies which had flourished as papal power declined and had extended their authority by creating bureaucracies which were at first efficient but later became top-heavy and a burden on the society which they exploited. Hatred of parasitic Courts resulted in a puritanism of the right as well as the left, embracing not only the moral indignation of Pym and Cromwell but the devotion to duty of Laud and Strafford as well. It was, suggests Professor Trevor-Roper, the failure of these monarchies to streamline their administration that caused the 'Country' to revolt. Other historians, commenting on this view, have emphasised the gap between the far-reaching aims of the Renaissance monarchies and the inadequate means at their disposal, which resulted in bungling and oppressive government, bad enough in time of peace and prosperity, but insupportable during the wars and economic crises of the 1640s.

It seems that no all-embracing explanation has, as yet, been found of the motives which governed the actions of men forced to choose between conflicting loyalties when civil war came. This is hardly surprising, since human beings are complex creatures, not simply puppets who respond to the jerking string. In a sense it is true to say that Pym, by opposing the prerogative monarchy and urging an anti-Spanish policy, was merely protecting his investment in the Providence Island Company, but to concentrate on this alone would be to ignore his very real idealism, his passionate concern for individual liberty, as he conceived it, and for religious freedom. Hyde, by supporting the King, believed he was preserving the rule of law which guaranteed all property, his own included, but he abandoned his estates and went into exile rather than come to terms with the revolutionaries.

Every member of the 'political nation' had to steer his way through a mass of conflicting arguments, and personal considerations were often the deciding ones. Loyalty to the Crown persuaded Sir Edmund Verney to take up arms for Charles though, as he said, 'I do not like the quarrel and do heartily wish that the King would yield and consent to what they desire; so that my conscience is only concerned in honour and gratitude to follow my master. I have eaten his bread and served him near thirty years, and will not do so base a thing as to forsake him.' But dislike of Charles was just as powerful a motive as loyalty. In 1642, at any rate, parliamentarians and royalists wanted much the same thing. The dispute was over the *means* by which constitutional government might be restored and preserved, and under any other King but Charles it might have been resolved without fighting: the search for deeper motives should not blind us to the fact that the civil war was, in a very real sense, a clash of personalities.

The Civil War

When Charles found he had an army at his disposal his strategy was dictated by the need to strike at London, the richest city in the kingdom and the nerve-centre of his enemies. In mid-October he left Shrewsbury and moved south-east towards the capital, taking with him his twenty-three-year-old nephew Rupert, younger son of the Winter Queen, who repaid Charles's indifference towards his Palatinate relatives by coming to fight for him. Rupert was a brilliant soldier and the glamour of his name acted as a magnet, drawing men to the King's service. The Earl of Essex, who commanded the parliamentary army, marched out to meet the King, and the two armies clashed at Edgehill. In this first big engagement of the war the pattern was set for many of the later encounters. Rupert's cavalry, on one wing, charged right through their opponents and disappeared into the distance. But the Roundhead cavalry, on the other wing, broke the royalist line and captured the King's standard. By the time Rupert returned with his exhausted cavalry the infantry of both sides were fighting it out unaided and when night fell neither side had won a decisive advantage. The King was ready to give battle again next morning, but Essex drew off his men and left the road to London open.

Rupert was all for a swift advance on the capital, but the King, shocked by the slaughter he had witnessed and realising for the first time what war entailed, moved only slowly south-east, and let Essex march round him and enter London first. There the Earl mobilised the citizens for their defence and marched them out to Turnham Green—then a small village surrounded by market gardens whose hedges provided good cover against attack. By early November the King's army had reached Brentford, which Rupert captured and fired, but there his advance stopped. Winter was drawing in, and the approaches to London were so heavily defended that savage fighting would have been needed to break through. Rupert, thinking in military terms, might have been prepared for this, but the King did not wish to make himself master of a ruined city. His aim was to demonstrate his strength and force his opponents to negotiate with him as an equal, and the Edgehill campaign had achieved just this. He therefore drew back his troops and established his headquarters at Oxford.

In London discontent was spreading. The King controlled Newcastle and had cut the supply of coal to the capital, where just over half the Commons and about a fifth of the Lords exercised power in the name of King and Parliament. Theatres were closed, food was dear and fuel prohibitively expensive, and the failure to obtain the swift victory which Pym had predicted revived the peace party in Parliament. Early in 1643 Parliamentary commissioners arrived at Oxford to negotiate the terms of a settlement, on the basis of abolition of episcopacy and acceptance by the King of the Militia Ordinance. Hyde urged the King to accept these demands as a basis for negotiation, but Charles, elated by the news that his forces in the west had been victorious at Braddock Down, rejected Hyde's advice. He had realised, as Parliament was later to do, that armies raised to make negotiation possible opened the way to *total* victory, after which no negotiations would be necessary.

The King's rejection of negotiations confirmed Pym's prediction and strengthened his authority in the Commons. He was by no means unchallenged master of this assembly. Holles—who, as one of the five members, had no reason to love Charles—was in favour of peace at almost any price, while at the other extreme there were men like Henry Marten who was prepared to fight until the King was destroyed. Between these two wings came the mass of members, and Pym had to move skilfully to avoid antagonising them and to secure the passing of the measures which he believed were necessary for financing the war. He persuaded the House to order the confiscation of all property belonging to royalists in areas controlled by Parliament, and to impose a regular weekly assessment throughout the kingdom for the maintenance of the parliamentary armies. Pym could count on the support of London, where his ally Isaac Pennington had been elected Lord Mayor in 1642, but City opinion was as divided as that in the House of Commons. The richer merchants were in favour of peace and gave a sympathetic ear to royalist propaganda, but there was also a radical group which set up its own committee and took as its hero Sir William Waller, the parliamentary commander in the west, rather than Essex, whom it accused of not wanting to win the war.

Both sides used the winter of 1642-43 to improve their organisation. The King ordered the sequestration of the estates of parliamentary sympathisers, and also imposed a regular assessment on the counties under his control. He was not desperately short of money. His richer supporters made generous gifts to the royal coffers as well as raising men at their own expense, and Oxford and Cambridge colleges sent the King much of their plate. But the defection of the fleet, which, under the Earl of Warwick, had declared for Parliament, was a serious blow, since it meant that the King could not collect Customs from the ships entering London and other big ports. For arms he depended on the capture of local arsenals and on supplies from abroad. Hull would have been a valuable acquisition, not only as a port but as a well-stocked magazine, yet even without it the King managed to import considerable quantities of small arms from Denmark, France and particularly Holland. When the Queen came back to join her husband in 1643 she brought a shipload of munitions with her.

As winter came to an end in 1643 the King planned to renew his advance on London, but this time it was to be carried out by three armies. The Earl of Newcastle was to strike down from the north and Sir Ralph Hopton was to push past Waller into the southern counties, while the King and Rupert broke out of Oxford.

At first all went well. Newcastle brought Sir Thomas Fairfax and his army to battle at Adwalton Moor in June and heavily defeated them. Yorkshire was now under effective royal control, and siege was laid to Hull. In the following month Waller's entire army was virtually wiped out at the Battle of Roundway Down, outside Devizes, and by September, Hopton had pushed as far east as Arundel. But the greatest victory of all was won in the west. Rupert had been sent to besiege Bristol, the second largest port in the kingdom, which was too powerful and dangerous a roundhead stronghold to be left in the rear of the advancing cavalier armies. In July he took the city by storm and the news sent royalist spirits soaring.

These defeats shook Pym's position in Parliament, where proposals for peace on terms which were little short of capitulation were only narrowly rejected. The war party in the Commons, with support from the radicals in the City, now took the lead and campaigned for the removal of Essex. Pym may have had reservations about Essex's military ability, but he could not afford to desert the Earl. Essex, Pym and Hampden had stood for a negotiated peace, even though they were unwilling to negotiate until they were in a position of strength, but Hampden was killed early in 1643 in a skirmish outside Oxford, and as far as Pym could see only Essex stood between him and a victory for the 'war party'. He persuaded the Commons to give Essex command of an army, to be raised largely from the London trained bands, which should march north-west to block the King's advance. He also persuaded them that new forces must be brought in to redress the balance in Parliament's favour. The Scots, who had earlier come to the help of the English Parliament, were alarmed by the King's successes and were ready to march south if only terms could be agreed on. At Pym's suggestion parliamentary commissioners, of whom the most influential was Sir Henry Vane the Younger, son of Charles's former Secretary, were sent to Edinburgh to arrange a treaty with the Scots.

This was almost Pym's last service to the parliamentary cause, for he was a dying man, but he managed to complete his reorganisation of the financial system by getting the Commons to agree that an Excise should be levied on wine, sugar and other articles. Pym never fought in the armies, but no man did more to make sure of Parliament's victory in the civil war. He provided the money, without which no army could have been raised, and he called in the Scots when they were most needed. But more important even than these was the way in which he steered Parliament between the two extremes and kept alive in 1642 and '43 the principles which had guided it in 1640. Pym's death in December 1643 removed from the scene the one man who might have made sure that those principles found expression in the peace that followed victory.

Pym lived long enough to know that his faith in Essex had been justified. Charles had decided not to advance on London until Gloucester had been captured, and Essex marched to the city's relief. The King called off the siege, but moved rapidly round Essex's army and took up his position at Newbury between the Earl and London. The battle of Newbury, which took place in September, might have been decisive, for a royalist victory would not simply have opened the way to London but would also have increased the dissensions in Parliament itself. Essex, however, handled his men well, and although the King was not defeated he drew off his forces during the night, leaving the parliamentary army to return home in triumph.

By the end of 1643 neither side had obtained any definite advantage over the other. The King's triple advance on London had broken down, but from his headquarters at Oxford he was still well placed to renew the attack in the following year. The parliamentary armies on the other hand, although they had not won glory in the field, had managed to contain the royal forces. Stalemate had, in fact, been reached, and both sides were looking for ways out of it. The King was hoping for reinforcements from Ireland where his commander, the Earl of Ormonde, had signed a truce with the rebels in September 1643. The first troops from Ireland were already arriving at Bristol, but the King hoped that the trickle would soon turn into a flood. Charles was also, on Hyde's advice, preparing to appeal to all moderate men by summoning a Parliament to Oxford. This body, which assembled early in 1644, consisted of about thirty peers and over a hundred members of the Commons, and Hyde hoped that it would serve as a reminder and a guarantee that the King had abandoned all thought of ruling by virtue of his absolute prerogative.

The Westminster Parliament had also extended its appeal by setting up an Assembly of Divines to discuss religious differences and make recommendations about a settlement of the Church. There was no question of continuing episcopal government, for the Scots demanded as the price of their military intervention that the Church should be reformed on a puritan pattern. Parliament committed itself to this by taking the Solemn League and Covenant, by which members swore to 'endeavour the extirpation of popery, prelacy . . . and whatsoever shall be found to be contrary to sound doctrine and the power of godliness', and to reform religion 'according to the word of God and the example of the best reformed churches'. The Scots assumed that by subscribing to the Solemn League and Covenant the English had subscribed also to a presbyterian settlement on the Scottish model. But not all puritans were presbyterians. Vane, for instance, who had carried through the negotiations with the Scots and had persuaded them to trust him, was deeply opposed to presbytery, and when the Committee of Both Kingdoms was set up in January 1644, as a coordinating body for the direction of the war, only six of the twenty-one members were staunch presbyterians.

In 1644 the tide of war began to turn against the King. The Scots crossed the border in January with an army of twenty thousand men and drove the Earl of Newcastle back towards York, and in the same month Fairfax, in a sudden swoop from Yorkshire across to the west, fell on the troops who had just landed from Ireland and captured most of them at Nantwich. In March the King's western army was virtually annihilated as a separate force by Waller's victory at Cheriton, in Hampshire, and it became even more important for Charles to save his northern army which was now bottled up in York. Charles therefore despatched Rupert to York, with orders to act as quickly as possible. 'I command and conjure you,' he wrote, 'by the duty and affection which I know you bear me, that, all new enterprises laid aside, you immediately march, according to your first intention, with all your force to the relief of York.'

Rupert had about fifteen thousand men and was outnumbered by his opponents, for the Scots had been joined by the army of the Eastern Association under the Earl of Manchester, and the northern army under Fairfax. As the Prince advanced the investing forces drew off and marched to intercept him, but in a brilliant manœuvre Rupert swung round them and entered the city that Newcastle had so gallantly defended. Newcastle wanted to rest his tired men, but Rupert, conscious of the King's command, insisted on an immediate engagement.

The two armies drew up on Marston Moor outside York, on 2 July 1644. Cromwell and the cavalry of the Eastern Association were on one wing of the parliamentary army, Fairfax and the northern cavalry on the other, while the Scottish infantry were concentrated in the centre. In the royalist army, Rupert commanded the cavalry opposite Cromwell, Lord Goring was in charge of the other wing, while the centre was composed of Newcastle and his infantry. The day was drawing to a close and Rupert, deciding there would be no fighting until the morning, allowed his troops to break ranks. Cromwell saw his opportunity, charged, and drove Rupert's cavalry from the field. As he did so, Goring's horse advanced to the attack, and broke right through Fairfax's cavalry. Everything now depended on the speed with which either side could exploit its victory, and here the advantage went to Cromwell who had trained his men not to scatter in pursuit but to rein in their horses and wait for further orders. Newcastle's infantry were gradually overcoming their Scottish opponents when Cromwell brought his cavalry back on to the battlefield, swept away the remnants of Goring's horse, and attacked Newcastle's men from the flank.

The Yorkshire infantry refused to give way and were cut down where they stood. With them died the King's hopes of holding the north. York, which Charles regarded as one of the brightest jewels in his crown, surrendered to Fairfax, the Earl of Newcastle fled to the Continent, and Cromwell wrote to the Speaker to tell him that 'truly England and the church of God hath had a great favour from the Lord in this great victory given to us, such as the like never was since this war began. . . . God made them as stubble to our swords.'

Parliament could have won the war after Marston Moor if its armies had been united and had been commanded by men determined on victory. But Essex was entangled with the King's forces down in Cornwall, while Manchester was playing for time. He had been an opponent of the King from the early days, and had been named (as Lord Mandeville) along with the five members as an enemy to the Crown. But like Pym, Manchester had fought only to make a negotiated peace possible, and he realised that victory now would give authority not to those who agreed with him—like Holles, who had been carefully excluded from the Committee of Both Kingdoms— but to the radicals, led by Cromwell, St John and Vane. In the circumstances he preferred to do nothing, and Parliament lost the initiative it had gained after Marston Moor.

Cromwell, who was now emerging as one of the most important figures on the parliamentary side, brought a formal complaint against Manchester before the House of Commons, and he and Vane were probably behind the plan to introduce a Self-Denying Ordinance by which members of Parliament would lay down their military commands in order to permit the remodelling of the army. The Commons were as divided as ever. The peace party, to which Essex and Manchester pinned their hopes, was in favour of a negotiated peace and a presbyterian system of worship, while on the other wing Vane, St John and the 'Independents'—as they were coming to be called—wanted a solution which would leave the puritan sects free, within the framework of a national church, to worship as they pleased. To win over the presbyterians and the mass of members who belonged to neither extreme, Vane agreed that the Directory of Worship, drawn up by the Assembly of Divines, should be used in place of the Prayer-Book, but the price he demanded for this was reform of the army. He knew that if he could place the army under control of his sympathisers, no paper agreements could bind him.

The Lords held up the Self-Denying Ordinance until they knew the outcome of negotiations with the King which were taking place at Uxbridge. These broke down, however, because the King refused to abandon episcopacy, and the Lords then accepted both the Self-Denying Ordinance and the ordinance which created the New Model Army. Sir Thomas Fairfax was to be head of the New Model, and he gave the command of the cavalry to Cromwell, who was given temporary exemption from the operation of the Self-Denying Ordinance. So far Vane and Cromwell had succeeded: they had got rid of Essex and Manchester and were about to create an army which would bring total victory.

The New Model was a national army, as distinct from the various county associations which had hitherto fought the war, and in creating it Parliament was unwittingly bringing together the representatives of the common people whose voice had not so far been heard. But the New Model's military significance must not be overestimated. It had been in existence only a few months when the King was finally defeated at Naseby, and in that battle it was the steadiness of Cromwell's cavalry—mostly drawn from the eastern counties, and renowned for their discipline long before the New Model was first thought of—which won the day. Naseby lies north of Oxford, and it was there that on 14 June 1645 Fairfax brought Rupert and the King to battle. Rupert again succeeded in driving his opponents from the field, but Cromwell, on the other flank, broke the royalist cavalry and then turned to take the infantry in the flank. When Rupert returned with his exhausted horsemen he could only look on helplessly as the King's last army was destroyed.

Charles knew after Naseby that it was only a matter of time before he had to surrender. Rupert urged him to accept Parliament's terms and preserve at least something from the wreck, but the King replied: 'speaking either as a mere soldier or statesman I must say there is no probability but of my ruin. Yet as a Christian I must tell you that God will not suffer rebels and traitors to prosper, nor this cause to be overthrown. .... A composition with them at this time is nothing else but a submission, which, by the grace of God, I am resolved against, whatever it cost me.' He still hoped that troops might arrive from Ireland, or that Montrose's astonishing successes in Scotland might eventually save him, but by the spring of 1646 he could fight no more, and in May he rode in to the Scottish camp outside Newark and gave himself up.

The Scots tried to make Charles accept the Covenant and agree to the establishment of a presbyterian system in his three kingdoms, but Charles was obdurate in defence of the Anglican Church. His captors were in a dilemma. They could not stay in England now that the war was over, especially as Parliament made haste to pay what was owing to the Scottish troops; neither could they risk taking the King back with them to Edinburgh, where he might become a focus of discontent. After much hesitation they decided to hand him over to Parliament, and in February 1647 Charles was removed to Holmby House in Northamptonshire.

Independents, Presbyterians and Levellers

Parliament had won the war, but only by creating a national army which had become a power in its own right and which was linked with radical movements all over England. The New Model was not the highly disciplined, regularly paid, godly collection of saints in arms that some of its admirers would have us believe. One observer said he thought 'these New Modellers knead all their dough with ale, for I never see so many drunk in my life in so short a time', and the majority of soldiers were far more concerned with recovering their arrears of pay and securing indemnity for illegal actions committed under the necessity of war than with constitutional or religious questions. There were a number of army chaplains, preaching an austere doctrine of salvation for the elect, but generally speaking the presbyterians had neglected the New Model, and the greatest of them, Richard Baxter, had—to his subsequent regret—declined an invitation to serve as chaplain to Cromwell's regiment.

The lack of authorised preachers had given an opportunity to ordinary soldiers who felt within them a sense of mission to gather some at least of their comrades around them and expound their belief that all men were potentially saints: all that was necessary, they said, was to listen to the voice of God which came to every man without the aid of any intermediary. These Independent congregations were not good for discipline, but their influence in the army was considerable —much greater, probably, than their numbers warranted—particularly as these lay preachers demanded not only religious toleration but arrears of pay as well.

Independency was almost as old in England as puritanism. In Scotland the reformed church had united to oppose the Crown and had found in the rigid presbyterian organisation the strength it needed. But in England puritans had accepted the state Church as long as it left them free to preach, and wherever local congregations had contributed money to pay a lecturer or to augment the stipend of their parish priest they had, in effect, created an Independent, or semi-Independent, congregation. Laud had tried to suppress these and had thereby turned the Independents into haters of episcopacy, but he had not made them embrace presbyterianism. Having suffered under the tyranny of bishops they were not eager to submit themselves to the autocratic rule of elders and presbyteries. The Independents had no positive views on Church government. Any organisation was acceptable to them as long as it left them free to preach and to worship as they wished.

Independent congregations had long flourished in London, and they were a breeding ground for democratic ideas. If all men are equal in the eyes of God, why should they not be equal in the eyes of the law and the government? These democratic stirrings were given expression by John Lilburne, who came from a family of Durham gentry and had been apprenticed to a London clothier in the 1630s. Lilburne had openly opposed Laud, and had suffered whipping and imprisonment for his outspokenness. He fought as a Lieutenant-Colonel in the army of the Eastern Association, but as the war continued Lilburne became increasingly disillusioned with members of Parliament who, he felt, were fighting to save their own privileges rather than to establish a free society in England. He drew up a programme for annual Parliaments, payment of members and the vote for all householders—a programme calculated to appeal to small property-holders, not to the landless man, but one that in the context of seventeenth-century society was revolutionary.

The aims of the Levellers, as they came to be called, appealed to the Independent congregations of the New Model who saw in them the secular expression of their religious beliefs, and Lilburne's pamphlets had a wide circulation among the soldiers. They were not welcome to the Independents in the Commons, however, who had much to gain from the existing social system. If Independent members were forced to choose between presbyterian tyranny and Leveller anarchy they would usually choose the former, and many Independent members were, for this reason, to be found acting as elders in the presbyterian State Church established by Parliament. They had supported Vane when he created the New Model, but when they realised what a monster he had brought to birth they deserted him and joined the presbyterian members. The right wing now had a majority in the House, and their main aim in March 1647 was to get rid of the army as swiftly as possible.

Had Parliament treated the soldiers generously and given them their arrears of pay, the army might have been disbanded without difficulty. But money was in short supply because members, in their haste to send the Scottish army back home and get the King into their own hands, had used all available funds to settle their outstanding accounts with the Scots. They could only offer promissory notes to the English soldiers, and this ungenerous treatment turned the leaders of the Independent congregations into spokesmen for the whole army.

The key figure in the dispute was Cromwell, for he was a member of Parliament and at the same time a soldier—the very combination that the Self-Denying Ordinance had been designed to prevent. Cromwell was no democrat—'I was by birth a gentleman,' he declared later, 'living neither in any considerable height nor yet in obscurity'— but he had considerable sympathy with the soldiers from the puritan eastern counties who had fought so well for him, particularly as he shared their religious attitude and had formed, with them, an Independent congregation. Cromwell had no wish to see Parliament impose an intolerant presbyterianism, and some years earlier, when he had written to the Speaker to announce the capture of Bristol, he had described how 'presbyterians, Independents, all had here the same spirit of faith and prayer, the same pretence and answer. They agree here, know no names of difference. Pity it is it should be otherwise anywhere. . . . As for being united in forms, commonly called uniformity, every Christian will for peace-sake study and do as far as conscience will permit. And from brethren in things of the mind we look for no compulsion but that of light and reason.'

Cromwell was working for a reconciliation between Parliament and the army, much to the disgust of Lilburne who assumed that the Lieutenant-General had abandoned his principles and was 'being led by the nose by two unworthy earthworms, Vane and St John'. Lilburne encouraged the Levellers in the army to appoint representatives, or 'Agitators', to put their point of view to the officers. Parliament, increasingly alarmed by these symptoms of radicalism, was desperately trying to reach a settlement with the King and the Scots, and was rewarded when, in May 1647, Charles agreed in principle to accept both presbyterianism and parliamentary control of the militia for a limited number of years.

In order to implement this settlement Parliament ordered the army to dissolve immediately, but the soldiers were by now on the point of rebellion, and Cromwell, fearing what might happen if they were left leaderless, decided to join them. To prevent any further negotiations between the King and Parliament he agreed that Cornet Joyce should be sent with a troop of cavalry to Holmby, to keep close watch over Charles. When Joyce arrived, however, he decided that the safest thing would be to remove the King to a place where he could be more easily controlled, and on 4 June he set off with him for Hampton Court. Meanwhile, the representatives of the army, meeting at Newmarket, had subscribed to the Solemn Engagement, binding themselves not to disband until their demands had been met. Cromwell joined them and agreed that an Army Council should be set up of two officers and two agitators from each regiment, and it was this body which formally accused eleven members of Parliament, including Holles, of planning to raise a new army and call in the Scots to overthrow English liberties. When Parliament rejected these charges the army marched towards London and had got as far as St Albans when it heard that the eleven members had fled.

The agitators wanted an immediate occupation of the City, but Cromwell and his fellow officer Henry Ireton realised that a solution by force would be no permanent solution, and they tried to restrain the army until some constitutional settlement could be arrived at. But their hand was forced by the City apprentices, who poured into the House of Commons and held the Speaker down in his chair while they called for the upholding of the Covenant and the return of the eleven members. Over fifty anti-presbyterian members of the House fled to the army, asking for protection, and in August the troops moved into the City and occupied it.

The future pattern of English government now depended on the army, and in October the Levellers and the officers debated their proposals in a remarkable series of meetings at Putney. The Levellers put forward the *Agreement of the People*, demanding that the old system of government by King, Lords and Commons should be scrapped and replaced by a new and just one. The *Agreement* called for annual Parliaments and equal electoral districts, manhood suffrage for all except servants and the poor, the reduction of tithes, abolition of restraints on trade, and liberty of conscience. The Army Levellers declared that in this *Agreement* they were speaking for the people as a whole, not just the property-owners who were represented in Parliament: 'we are not,' they claimed, 'a mere mercenary army, hired to serve any arbitrary power of a state, but called forth . . . to the defence of our own and the people's just rights and liberties.'

Ireton, who was the spokesman for the officers, would not agree to such far-reaching proposals. 'I think we ought to keep to that constitution that we have,' he replied, 'because it is the most fundamental we have, and because there is so much reason, justice and prudence in it.' Society, thought Ireton, existed to preserve property, and in the *Heads of the Proposals* he put forward suggestions for a settlement which would retain parliamentary rule and confine the vote to ratepayers. He was supported by Cromwell, who reminded the Levellers that if they insisted on their new form of government there was nothing to stop other innovators insisting on theirs: 'while we are disputing these things, another company of men shall gather together and put out a paper as plausible perhaps as this. . . .' Such a plethora of proposals would lead, he assured them, only to anarchy.

The Putney debates broke up without any conclusion being reached, and Cromwell ordered the agitators to return to their regiments. The time had come, he thought, to restore discipline to the army before the presbyterians in Parliament should be able to take up negotiations again with the King and the Scots and decide on the details of the proposed settlement. When the Levellers tried to renew the debate at a meeting of the army at Ware, Cromwell rode among the soldiers with his sword drawn, arrested three ringleaders, and promptly had one of them shot. This firm action stopped the revolt. The majority of the army preferred to trust Cromwell rather than risk their lives for the Levellers.

Shortly before this meeting took place, in November 1647, Charles escaped from Hampton Court, fearing that the extremists in the army might make an attempt on his life, and fled to Carisbrooke Castle in the Isle of Wight. From there he opened negotiations with Parliament and the Scots, hoping that with the help of a Scottish army and the presbyterian members of the Commons he might reverse the verdict of the civil war. Cromwell, who had earlier been prepared to trust the King, would do so no longer. He suspected that agreement between the King and Parliament would be at the expense of the Independents and that Charles would promise anything in order to sow dissension among his enemies, holding it no crime to break faith with traitors. In January 1648 Cromwell denounced the King to the Commons as 'so great a dissembler and so false a man that he was not to be trusted', and persuaded them to break off negotiations. Many of the presbyterian members—those, that is, who did not trust the army —quitted Westminster and left the Independents and the army to face the challenge of the second civil war which broke out in April 1648. In south-east England and in Wales royalist risings took place, and petitions were sent in to Parliament from Kent and Surrey demanding the restoration of the King. If the Scots had been ready to move, the risings might have challenged the parliamentary régime, but Fairfax had time to subdue Kent, while Cromwell put down the Welsh rising before going north to deal with the Scots.

While the army was occupied in suppressing the revolts, many of the presbyterian members returned to Westminster and reopened negotiations with the King. They were counting on a Scottish victory, but in August Cromwell routed the Scots at Preston, and wrote to Parliament calling on members to recognise that 'this is nothing but the hand of God', and warning them that they should 'take courage to do the work of the Lord in fulfilling the end of your magistracy [and] in seeking the peace and welfare of the people of this land'. The Commons, however, ignored this warning and paid no attention to the remonstrance of the army officers demanding that the King should be brought to trial. Their commissioners were with the King at Newport, and they hoped to present Cromwell, on his return, with a *fait accompli*. They reckoned without Ireton and the Levellers. These were temporarily united to prevent the establishment of a presbyterian régime, and in early December Ireton led his troops into London. When the presbyterian members arrived at the House of Commons to take their seats as usual they found Colonel Pride at the door, with orders to exclude them. Only a rump of army supporters, some seventy all told, was allowed to enter.

The Rump in spite of its unrepresentative character, proudly declared in January 1649 'that the people are, under God, the original of all just power', and 'that the Commons of England, in Parliament assembled, being chosen by and representing the people, have the supreme power in this nation'. Armed with this sovereign authority the Rump went ahead with plans to bring the King to trial, and voted by twenty-six votes to twenty that a High Court should be set up for this purpose. Cromwell, Ireton and the officers were the real force behind these proceedings. They despaired of coming to terms with Charles because they knew that he would not hold himself bound by any promise he made to them and would continue his game of trying to set Scots against English, presbyterians against Independents, and Parliament against the army. The execution of Charles would not solve the problem but it would at least simplify it.

The court, under the presidency of John Bradshaw, an obscure lawyer, opened in Westminster Hall on 20 January 1649. Never before had an English King been put on trial by his subjects, and the mere fact that the trial was possible shows how far Parliament's political thinking had advanced since the early years of the war when it still claimed to be fighting not the King but his evil advisers. The charge against Charles was that 'being admitted King of England, and therein trusted with a limited power to govern by and according to the laws of the land' he had wickedly designed to erect 'an unlimited and tyrannical power'. Charles never showed to better advantage than at this, the supreme moment of his life. Throughout the proceedings he conducted himself with a calm dignity that impressed even his opponents, and he steadfastly refused to acknowledge the jurisdiction of the court. He took his stand on the known laws. If, he said, the army could set up a court and impose its will by force, 'I do not know what subject . . . can be sure of his life or anything that he calls his own. . . . I do plead for the liberties of the people of England!'

As the King refused to acknowledge the court, Bradshaw proceeded to pronounce judgement 'that he, the said Charles Stuart, as a tyrant, traitor, murderer and public enemy to the good people of this nation, shall be put to death by severing of his head from his body'. Fifty-nine judges were persuaded to sign the death warrant, and by their authority a scaffold was constructed outside the Banqueting House that Inigo Jones had built in Whitehall. An enormous crowd gathered there on the afternoon of 30 January, when the King was led out to die, but only those near the scaffold heard Charles declare that he died in the cause of law and the Church. 'For the people,' he said, 'truly I desire their liberty and freedom as much as anybody whomsoever, but I must tell you that their liberty and freedom consist in having of government—those laws by which their life and their goods may be most their own. It is not for having share in government, Sirs; that is nothing pertaining to them. A subject and a sovereign are clean different things.' As for the Church, 'I declare before you all that I die a Christian according to the profession of the Church of England as I found it left me by my father.'

There was no jubilation, as at Strafford's execution. The vast crowd was silent until they saw the execution axe swing in the air 'at the instant whereof', according to one eye-witness, 'there was such a groan by the thousands then present as I never heard before and desire I may never hear again'. By the manner of his death Charles went far towards wiping out the memory of his eleven years' prerogative rule For the anglicans he was a saint, for the royalists a martyr who had sacrificed his life to protect the old constitution against the abuse of arbitrary power. Cromwell may have been right in believing that the execution of the King was a political necessity at the time, but he created a spectre that was to haunt his own régime and bring it to dust.

The Rule of the Rump

The Rump, having got rid of the King, abolished the monarchy and the House of Lords as well, and set up a Council of State, of which Cromwell was the first chairman, to carry on the government. The Levellers felt bitter at what they regarded as this betrayal. The execution of the King had, they felt, left the way clear for a remodelling of the English constitution on the lines of *The Agreement of the People*, but instead of this they saw an unrepresentative collection of property-owners taking steps to preserve their hold on power indefinitely. 'We were before ruled by King, Lords and Commons,' complained the author of one pamphlet, 'now by a General, a Court Martial and House of Commons. And we pray you what is the difference?'

Cromwell was alarmed by the revival of Leveller agitation in the army, and by the proliferation of sects like the Fifth Monarchists, who wanted the reign of Christ to begin with the rule of the godly, and the 'True Levellers', or Diggers, who believed in agrarian communism and set up a community at St George's Hill, Weybridge. He realised that a period of firm government was needed to give the country a chance to recover from the strain of civil war, and he believed that 'there is more cause of danger from disunion amongst ourselves than by anything from our enemies'. He put down the revolts in the army by force, executing the leaders, and summoned Lilburne before the Council of State where that irrepressible champion of popular liberties heard him thumping his fist 'upon the council table until it rang again, and saying, "I tell you, Sir, you have no other way to deal with these men but to break them in pieces. . . . If you do not break them, they will break you." '

This was the virtual end of the Leveller movement, though Lilburne, in prison and out, continued to preach the good cause. It seems unlikely that, in the conditions of mid-seventeenth-century England, agrarian democracy could ever have worked. The landowners were so power-ful, the mass of the people so poor and uneducated, that even if a Leveller régime had been established it would almost certainly have collapsed or come under the control of men who would have exploited it for their own ends. Yet in the Levellers one can hear the voice of a section of the community—the yeomen—which was usually mute. They were not 'common people'—Lilburne for instance was as proud of his gentry family as Oliver Cromwell—but they show how deeply radical idealism had penetrated into English society. It is difficult not to feel sympathy with Lilburne, when in prison in the Tower, who told one of his visitors: 'I had rather choose to live seven years under old King Charles's government (notwithstanding their beheading him as a tyrant for it) when it was at the worst, before this Parliament, than live one year under their present government that now rule. Nay, let me tell you, if they go on with that tyranny they are in they will make Prince Charles have friends enough not only to cry him up but also really to fight for him, to bring him into his father's throne.'

From August 1649 until the spring of the following year Cromwell was in Ireland,[1] restoring order to that unfortunate country and forcing it to accept the authority of the new rulers of England. He returned in time to deal with a new threat from Scotland. The Scottish leaders were deeply shocked at the King's execution. Charles was King of Scotland, yet they had not been consulted about the proposal to put him on trial, even though the English Parliament had joined with them, in the Solemn League and Covenant, in swearing 'to preserve and defend the King's Majesty's person and authority'. In February

[1] See below, p. 410.

1649 they proclaimed Charles's son King of Scotland, on condition that he signed the Covenant, and a Scottish army was prepared once again for an invasion of England.

Cromwell went north to check the Scots before they should have a chance of crossing the border. In September 1650 he found himself hemmed in close to the sea at Dunbar, with little prospect of survival, let alone victory, but with great skill he extricated himself from this position, caught the Scots at a disadvantage and sent their army flying. By December he had occupied Edinburgh, and his advance was halted not by his opponents but by illness, which brought him close to death and kept him off the battlefield until the summer of 1651. The Scots used this pause to reform their army, and in August 1651 Charles II, with Scottish troops, struck south across the border and occupied Worcester. There Cromwell caught him on 3 September and in a hard-fought battle put an end to royalist hopes. For Cromwell it was, in his own words, 'a crowning mercy'. The young King had to make his way, disguised, to the south coast, where he took ship for France, and he left behind him a country which, however unsettled, could offer no effective opposition to Cromwell and the Rump.

Now that peace had been restored to England Cromwell assumed that the members of the Rump would vote for the dissolution of Parliament, and make way for a new and more representative body to decide on a settlement of Church and state. But the Rumpers saw no reason to abdicate their authority. New elections might open the way to a royalist revival or, which would be almost as bad, might produce a Parliament so divided that it would be at the mercy of the Army leaders. They distrusted Cromwell's power and reputation, and they were convinced of their own ability to govern. This was not merely vanity, for the Rump, through its committees, ruled well and set on foot reform of the law and the Church. Cromwell, in fact, when he came to power, took up much of the work which the Rump had inaugurated, and carried it forward. His real objection was not to the policy or the ability of the Rump: his anger was directed at what seemed to him to be efficiency without idealism, government without morality. He could not believe that a great war had been fought and an ancient monarchy overthrown simply to give power to a handful of men who had come to stand for nothing but themselves.

He had little enthusiasm for the war with protestant Holland which broke out in 1652. The Dutch had been shocked by the execution of Charles I, and the envoys sent by the Rump to arrange for a union of the two republics were publicly insulted. The failure of negotiations inflamed the latent antagonism between the two countries that had its roots in economic competition, and the Rump passed the Navigation Act of 1651,[1] which was designed to cripple Dutch trade. In the war which followed, the English navy, led by Robert Blake—son of a Bristol merchant, and the greatest sailor since Drake—came into its own. In a number of hard-fought engagements the Dutch fleet was defeated and the coast of Holland blockaded. When the Dutch admiral, Tromp, tried to break out in July 1653, his ships were routed and he himself was killed. By that time Cromwell had taken charge of English government, and both sides were ready for peace.

Success in battle gave leadership to the war party in the Rump, and there was no further talk of dissolution. But the high level of taxation which was demanded made the Rump increasingly unpopular. So did the failure to provide a religious settlement which should guarantee freedom of worship, and the Independents now pinned their hopes on Cromwell. Milton spoke for all these when he hailed 'Cromwell, our chief of men' and reminded him that

> . . . yet much remains
> To conquer still; peace hath her victories
> No less renowned than war; new foes arise,
> Threatening to bind our souls with secular chains.
> Help us to save our conscience from the paw
> Of hireling wolves whose Gospel is their maw.

Cromwell was not long in answering this call to action. When, in April 1653, he heard that the Rump was planning to increase its numbers through by-elections instead of risking a general appeal to public opinion, he strode off to the House, calling on his guards to follow him. Once inside he listened to the debate for a while, his anger mounting until he could sit still no longer. Rising to his feet he shouted at the assembled members: 'Come, come! I will put an end to your prating. You are no Parliament. I say you are no Parliament. I will put an end to your sitting.' As the members continued to sit in their places, stupefied, Cromwell called his troops into the House and told them to clear it. Speaker Lenthall was hustled from his chair so quickly that he left the mace—the symbol of civil authority—behind him. When Cromwell caught sight of it he told one of his soldiers to 'take away this bauble', but he could not so easily destroy the Long

---

[1] See below, p. 314.

Parliament. Its memory remained as a perpetual challenge to the so-called Parliaments of the Interregnum, constantly reminding them that their authority was based on nothing more legitimate than naked power, for as Bradshaw proudly told Cromwell: 'you are mistaken to think that the Parliament is dissolved, for no power under heaven can dissolve them but themselves. Therefore take you notice of that.'

Oliver Cromwell

Oliver Cromwell was descended from Henry VIII's minister Thomas Cromwell, through a nephew who had done well out of the Dissolution of the Monasteries and had taken his uncle's name as a sign of gratitude. Oliver was born in 1599 to a branch of the family that had settled in Huntingdon, and his early links were all with East Anglia —that part of England where unemployment and Dutch influence encouraged the growth of radical puritanism. He was not by any means a rich man, and he was certainly not a courtier. He was, in fact, a typical adherent of the 'Country', looking back nostalgically to the great days of Queen Elizabeth and praying that England might once again humble the might of Spain and lead a crusade for the defence of protestantism. In 1627 he was a burgess for Huntingdon, but not until the Long Parliament did he really make his name. In that Parliament he sat as one of the members for Cambridge, and a fellow member described him as 'very ordinarily apparelled, for it was a plain cloth suit which seemed to have been made by an ill country tailor. His linen was plain and not very clean, and I remember a speck or two of blood upon his little band, which was not much larger than his collar. His hat was without a hat-band. His stature was of a good size, his sword stuck close to his side, his countenance swollen and reddish, his voice sharp and untunable, and his eloquence full of fervour.'

The war showed Cromwell to be a natural leader of men, and it also brought out the radical streak in him. He was a conservative, in that he wanted to preserve as much of the old order as possible, but he also recognised that merit took no account of wealth or breeding. At times he could use Leveller language, as on the occasion when he told Manchester that he hoped to live to see the day when there was not a nobleman left in England, but he also had a Strafford-like awareness of the need for government and of the precariousness of the foundations on which English society rested. His enemies accused him of hypocrisy, because he would preach radicalism and practise autocracy, yet in a way he was more consistent than they were: he believed, not without reason, that he alone had the will and the power to carry through a reformation of the state, and he was reinforced in this conviction by his awareness of a divine calling.

For Cromwell, as for so many of his contemporaries, human society existed only to make possible the carrying-out of God's will. If God had called him to bring order into the state and toleration into the Church, how could he give up his power to men who, he was convinced, were more selfish and less able than he was? The crux of the matter was religion. Cromwell believed, from his own experience, that every man had it within him to be a saint. The Church must therefore be organised in such a way as to remove the barriers between men and God. A Parliament of property-owners would have insisted on a hierarchical organisation with control vested in themselves, but this would have destroyed the religious liberty for which, in Cromwell's view, the war had been fought. If religious liberty could only be preserved at the cost of military dictatorship he was prepared to be a dictator.

Before resorting to dictatorship, however, he hoped to find a constitutional basis for his rule, and to help him in this task he summoned representatives of the Independent congregations to meet at Westminster. When this 'Parliament of Saints'[1] met, Cromwell left it to formulate its own opinions, not appreciating that the success of Elizabeth, whom he so much admired, had depended on the Councillors acting as a link between the executive and the legislature. In the absence of effective guidance the House fell under the control of extremists, particularly Fifth Monarchists, and went about the task of reform so whole-heartedly that it threatened to leave little of the old foundations. The members of the assembly were mainly merchants and lesser gentry and did not have the reverence for property-rights that had characterised earlier Parliaments. Many of the measures they passed were admirable, particularly those designed to relieve debtors, speed up probate proceedings, and establish civil marriage, but proposals to abolish the Court of Chancery and to put an end to tithes struck at the vested interests of lawyers and property-holders. Cromwell declared that the effect of such measures was to 'fly at liberty and property. . . . Who could have said that anything was their own if

---

[1] Often known as the 'Barebones Parliament', after one of its most prominent members, Praise-God Barbon (Barebones), a London leather-seller and Independent minister.

they had gone on?' He also resented the fact that an assembly which he had summoned to prepare the ground for a final settlement had taken upon itself the mantle of Parliament and was acting not as an advisory body but as a sovereign power. The pace of reform was so great—twenty-six Acts were passed in under six months—that the moderates in the assembly decided to bring its sessions to a close before irreparable damage was done. Meeting early one morning, in a thin House, they called for the dissolution of the 'Parliament of Saints' and left Cromwell once again to govern alone.

Still seeking a constitutional basis for his rule, Cromwell turned to one of his generals, John Lambert, and accepted the *Instrument of Government* which he had drawn up. This document declared 'that the supreme legislative authority . . . shall be and reside in one person and the people assembled in Parliament. The style of which person shall be the Lord Protector of the Commonwealth of England, Scotland and Ireland.' The Lord Protector, with the assistance of a Council of State, was to be responsible for administration and foreign affairs, but although he was provided with a permanent revenue to maintain his household and the armed forces, he was dependent on Parliament for any extra supplies. Parliament, according to the Instrument, was to be summoned at least once every three years and was not to be dissolved without its own consent until it had sat for a minimum of five months. The Protector could hold up Bills for twenty days, but after that time they were to become law with or without his consent, unless they were contrary to the principles laid down in the *Instrument*.

When he accepted this constitution, Cromwell took the first step towards turning his régime back to the traditional pattern of English government. The *Instrument* contained a number of safeguards designed to prevent any recurrence of arbitrary rule, but otherwise it was a conservative document. The franchise was restricted to those who held property worth £200, and the number of borough members was reduced while that of the knights of the shire was increased to a level which would give them a majority in the House. It was hoped by this means to produce a Parliament of independent-minded country gentlemen of the sort Cromwell admired.

In December 1653 Cromwell was solemnly installed as Lord Protector in a service at Westminster Abbey, and in the following April he and his family took up residence in the old royal palace at Whitehall. Parliament did not meet until September, and for eight months Cromwell and the Council of State ruled alone, issuing ordinances which had the force of law. In these ordinances, which provided for the continuing reform of the administration of justice and liberty of worship for all except catholics and anglicans, Cromwell showed how he would have liked Parliament to deal with the problems facing it. But when Parliament assembled in September 1654 it immediately attacked the *Instrument of Government* and claimed for itself supreme authority in the state.

The Protectorate Parliament was, in theory, an entirely new institution, not connected with previous Parliaments and depending for its existence and authority not upon ancient custom but upon the *Instrument of Government.* Yet members made it clear that they regarded themselves as the guardians of the parliamentary tradition. They elected William Lenthall, who had presided over the Commons in the Long Parliament, as Speaker of their House, and they ordered the mace—which Cromwell had scorned when he dismissed the Rump—to be brought in by the Long Parliament's Sergeant-at-Arms. Nearly a hundred former members of the Long Parliament were to be found in the first Parliament of the Protectorate, and among them were about forty republicans who regarded Cromwell as the betrayer of the revolution and were determined to cripple his autocracy if they could not bring it to an end.

The Lord Protector had his supporters in the House—they included Councillors of State, household officials and members of his own family—but he failed, once again, to give them the leadership they needed. This was the opportunity for Haslerig and his fellow republicans to assert the sovereignty of Parliament by challenging the validity of the *Instrument of Government.* Cromwell's reply was to surround the House with soldiers while he called on members to recognise four fundamentals—government by a single person and Parliament; liberty of conscience in religion; joint control of the armed forces; and no perpetual Parliaments. The extremists withdrew from the House rather than consent to such terms, but the members who remained were still suspicious of the Protector and his policy of religious tolerance. By January 1655 Cromwell could bear with them no longer and dissolved Parliament. 'Is there not yet upon the spirits of men a strange itch?' he angrily demanded. 'Nothing will satisfy them unless they can put their finger upon their brethren's consciences, to pinch them there. . . . What greater hypocrisy than for those who were oppressed by the bishops to become the greatest oppressors themselves so soon as their yoke was removed!'

The dissolution of Parliament meant that the constitutional problem remained unsettled. Yet the need for some sort of solution had never been greater, for there was widespread discontent in the country as a whole, and Cromwell's secretary, the able John Thurloe, reported that a royalist revolt was being planned. Penruddocke's rising actually took place in March, and was easily crushed, but it convinced Cromwell of the need for a period of strong government. He grouped the counties into eleven military districts, each under the control of a major-general, and he ordered that the expense of this should be met by a temporary ten per cent decimation tax on all royalist estates. These two measures did much to remove from his régime what little basis of popular support it had created. The royalists, without whose goodwill (or at least acquiescence) no permanent settlement could be made, were confirmed in their enmity by this tax on estates which had already suffered so much; the gentry resented the major-generals' challenge to their local supremacy; while the mass of the people were alienated by the way in which soldiers pried into their private lives and equated puritanism with joyless austerity.

The outbreak of war with Spain in 1656 made another Parliament necessary, since Cromwell's administration was already in debt and there was no money to spare. The Protector's annual income was about £1,500,000—twice as much as Charles I's—but it was not enough to pay for the armed forces and the administration even in peacetime. Cromwell was driven, like the Stuarts before him, into punishing those who challenged his right to raise money. When George Cony, a silk merchant, refused to pay Customs in November 1654 on the grounds that these duties belonged to the Protector only by virtue of the *Instrument of Government*, which had never been approved by Parliament and therefore had no validity, Cromwell ordered that he and his lawyers should be imprisoned until they dropped their plea. Two judges had earlier been dismissed for questioning the authority of the *Instrument*: now one of the Chief Justices resigned rather than be party to such high-handed treatment, which seemed to echo Bate's case and the Ship Money trial.

War had broken out with Spain by the time Parliament met in September 1656. The Council of State excluded nearly a hundred members whom it regarded as trouble-makers, and another sixty refused to take part in debates as a protest against this arbitrary action. The two hundred or so members who remained voted £400,000 for the war, but they showed their disapproval of Cromwell's religious policy by inflicting a savage punishment on James Naylor, a Quaker accused of blasphemy. The moderates in the House, among whom were many of the older members who had fought in the early stages of the civil war and clung to the ideals of Pym and the Long Parliament, wanted Cromwell to detach himself from the army by taking the Crown and re-establishing constitutional monarchy. But the younger members—particularly those who were connected with the household and administration—wanted 'Thorough' government, carried out by the army and paid for by a permanent decimation tax on royalists. The moderates only just managed to defeat these proposals, but they followed up their success, in March 1657, by presenting the *Humble Petition and Advice* to Cromwell. In this they formally requested him to put an end to constitutional disputes and to provide for the succession by taking the office and title of King.

Cromwell took time to consider this offer. He was not blind to the considerable advantages of becoming King, but he had to consider opinion in the army, and this was strongly opposed to such a change. Some of the generals had ambitions of their own, and did not want to be ruled out of the succession in favour of Cromwell's family, while among the junior officers and soldiers there were many who felt that the war had been fought to overthrow monarchy and that any return to kingship would be a betrayal. Kings were too closely associated with bishops for puritans to feel happy about such a change, and as for anglicans and royalists they would have no more regard for a usurper King than for a Lord Protector. What weighed most with Cromwell, however, was the realisation that many honest men, 'men that will not be beaten down with a carnal or worldly spirit', would not welcome the advent of King Oliver. In a confused speech, which showed his genuine uncertainty, Cromwell therefore declined the Crown and begged the Commons 'that there may be no hard thing put upon me —things, I mean, hard to them [men of goodwill] that they cannot swallow'.

Although Cromwell refused the crown he accepted the rest of the Humble Petition. This gave him the right to nominate his successor and to appoint members of a 'second house' of Parliament—in other words to restore the old constitution in all but name. This amounted to a confession that the régime had failed to solve the constitutional problem of how to transfer the basis of power from naked force to something more representative. It was also a commentary on the history of the previous twenty years. The civil war had been fought because the traditional constitution, with its assumption of harmony between an hereditary executive and an elected legislature, did not seem to guarantee the liberties of the subject, yet the Interregnum had shown that no other constitution could command even the limited degree of acceptance that centuries of use had given the old one.

The last Parliament of the Commonwealth assembled in January 1658, and in spite of the fact that members were not admitted until they had taken an oath of loyalty to the régime, squabbles broke out immediately between the Commons and the Lord Protector. Members attacked the authority of the 'other house', and poured scorn on the newly created titles of nobility. The republicans in the Commons would not forgive Cromwell for overthrowing the Long Parliament, and were determined to make good their claim that sovereignty lay with the elected representatives of the people, whatever army-inspired constitutions might say. Cromwell, tired and ill, lost patience with this fractious assembly and dissolved Parliament after it had sat for little more than two weeks. He had come, like Charles I before him, to believe that the House of Commons was dominated by selfish men determined to have no government rather than one of which they disapproved. When the Commons protested against this abrupt conclusion to their meeting, Cromwell appealed, like Charles, to divine sanction. 'Let God judge', he challenged them, 'between you and me' to which some of the republican members replied 'Amen'.

The Achievements of the Protectorate

The Protectorate left little permanent mark on English life, yet it was not without its achievements. In domestic affairs, Cromwell found his reforming impulses hamstrung by parliamentary opposition—and there was no fundamental change in the structure of English social life or of the administration. Personnel was changed—at Oxford and Cambridge, for instance, puritan heads of colleges were appointed—but institutions were preserved. Plans to create new universities led only to the creation of a college at Durham, while reform of the Court of Chancery, which was long overdue, foundered on the vested interest of common lawyers. As for the Church, the parochial system and the hated tithes were preserved, but Triers were appointed to consider all candidates for ordination, while Ejectors removed any clergy held to be unworthy of their office. Cromwell was as tolerant as he could be without endangering public order. Roman Catholics were not allowed to worship publicly, but were rarely persecuted; anglicans were forbidden to use the Prayer-Book, but frequently did so; and the sects were left free to worship as they pleased, provided they did not become 'a busybody in other men's matters and a stirrer-up of sedition'. The Jews were also allowed to return to England, and generally speaking a considerable degree of latitude was permitted in the expression of religious beliefs—far more in fact than Parliament approved of.

Cromwell's greatest achievement was to restore the prestige of hi country abroad. He hoped to build up an alliance of protestant powers and to encourage the expansion of English trade, assuming that what was good for England was good for protestantism as a whole. He put an end to the war with Holland which the Rump had begun, and tried to negotiate a union between the two countries. He also concluded treaties with Denmark, reopening the Baltic to English shipping, and with Portugal, giving English traders freedom of access to Portuguese colonies. Cromwell also decided on war with Spain, to revive the glories of Elizabeth's reign and to wipe out the humiliation of Buckingham's Cadiz expedition. In December 1654 an expedition was sent to the West Indies, where it failed, much to Cromwell's chagrin, to capture Hispaniola, but compensated for this by occupying Jamaica.

Cromwell recognised the importance of sea power to Britain, and turned the navy into a full-time regular service with a ladder of promotion and standard rates of pay. He left Robert Blake in charge of the fleet, which carried out an arduous but successful blockade of the Spanish coast all through the winter of 1657 and, in April of the following year, destroyed a Spanish treasure fleet in the bay of Santa Cruz. Blake died on the journey back to Plymouth, but his skill had given England command of the sea.

Yet however great Cromwell's achievement was in restoring the prestige of England, his desire for a protestant crusade and his encouragement of buccaneering expeditions against Spain were anachronistic in contemporary Europe—the Europe of Richelieu, in which power politics had replaced religion as the basis for relationships between states, and in which France was rising to dominance as Spain declined. Equally anachronistic was Cromwell's ambition to give England once again a bridgehead on the Continent. In this, however, he was successful, for English troops fought side by side with the French at the Battle of the Dunes in June 1658, and acquired Dunkirk, previously a Spanish possession, as their reward.

Cromwell had to pay a high price for English glory, and much of the trouble between the Protector and his Parliaments came from their reluctance to meet the cost of his adventurous policy. When he was installed as Protector, Cromwell cut the monthly assessment, which had first been imposed by the Long Parliament to pay its forces in the civil war, but he could not afford to abolish it altogether. He continued to collect Tonnage and Poundage and the excise, yet even so his revenue was insufficient. By 1656 the gap between income and expenditure had been reduced to £250,000, but war with Spain widened it to over £1,000,000. City merchants and financiers, who had suffered from the Long Parliament's failure to meet its obligations, were not prepared to advance more money to the Protector, and Cromwell was faced with the choice of bankruptcy or parliamentary grants on conditions that were unacceptable to him. 'The position of the Protectorate early in 1659', comments one historian, 'was similar in many financial respects to the position of Charles I in 1640',[1] and this financial weakness accounts in part for the collapse of the Protectorate after Cromwell's death.

The Restoration

In 1658 George Fox, the Quaker, went to visit the Lord Protector at Hampton Court, and described how 'I saw and felt a waft of death go forth against him and when I came to him he looked like a dead man'. Cromwell died on 3 September 1658, the anniversary of the battle of Worcester, having named his son Richard as his successor. Richard had never been a soldier, and the army had no respect for him. The generals, particularly Fleetwood and Lambert, forced him to retire into private life, and to cement their alliance with the republicans they recalled the Rump—that remnant of the Long Parliament which had survived Pride's purge and could claim to be the only legitimate authority in England. When the Rump reassembled, however, members showed that they had lost none of their old spirit, and they determined to demonstrate the superiority of duly-constituted civil authority to mere military power by disbanding the army. Such a proposal met with no support from the generals, whose position depended solely on the number of soldiers they could command, and in October 1659 Lambert once more used troops to drive out the Rump.

[1] H. J. Habakkuk, 'Public Finance and the Sale of Property during the Interregnum', *Economic History Review*, Vol. 15, No. 1, August 1962.

North of the border, however, General Monck had one of the finest armies in Britain, and he was ready to use this to prevent anarchy. The news from London convinced him of the need for action, for commercial life in the capital was being brought to a standstill by frequent clashes between unpaid troops and the citizens. Monck was in touch with Fairfax—who had retired from public life soon after the execution of the King, in which he played no part—and Fairfax agreed to use his prestige to win over malcontents from Lambert's army and use them to hold Yorkshire for Monck. The plan worked well. Monck and his army crossed the border unopposed and made a triumphal progress to London where the Rump had already reassembled. In February 1660 Monck ordered that the members whom Pride had excluded should be invited to return to their places in the Commons, and when the augmented House met it voted that the Long Parliament, after twenty years of existence, should at last be legitimately dissolved.

The tide of royalism was now flowing strongly, for the experience of military dictatorship, particularly under generals as incompetent as Fleetwood and Lambert, had created a strong desire for the restoration of legitimate authority. Cromwell had brought back the old constitution: all that was missing was the old reigning family. When elections for a new Parliament were held in March, the republicans were routed, and the last obstacle to a restoration was removed when Charles II, at Monck's suggestion and with the help of his Chancellor, Edward Hyde, published a declaration from Breda promising a general pardon, liberty of conscience, and the determination of all disputed matters 'in a free Parliament, by which, upon the word of a King, we will be advised'.

Fairfax, who had done more than any man alive to defeat Charles I, headed the commission which Parliament sent to The Hague to greet Charles II and invite him to return to the kingdom from which he had so long been absent. In May 1660 the King arrived in London, where that staunch anglican John Evelyn described how 'the ways were strewed with flowers, the bells ringing, the streets hung with tapestry, fountains running with wine. I stood in the Strand', he added, 'and beheld it and blessed God. And all this was done without one drop of blood shed, and by that very army which rebelled against him.' The irony of it all was not lost upon the new King, for he was heard to observe that since his subjects were obviously so delighted to see him back it was doubtless his own fault that he had been absent so long.

14

Early Stuart England

Local Government

UNDER the early Stuarts as under the Tudors the government of every county was in the hands of a comparatively small group of families who owed their position to birth and land. Members of the aristocracy were automatically men of influence in their shire, but they were associated in the work of administration with the upper gentry, who were often connected with them by marriage and derived their status not so much from wealth as from tradition and the fact that they were willing to accept public office. These upper gentry usually provided the Deputy-Lieutenants, who were chosen from among the Justices of the Peace and were the effective rulers of the counties. Below them came a larger group of middling gentry from whose ranks the other Justices of the Peace were drawn. Below these again were the lesser gentry, who served, if at all, in the lower ranks of the administration—as coroners or escheators, to take two of the most common examples—and the lesser gentry merged almost imperceptibly into the yeomen. In theory yeomen were freeholders who farmed their estates, but in fact the term was often used for the richer copyholders. The lines that separated one section of society from another were not hard and fast, particularly in the lower levels, and a person might be described as a yeoman at one time and as a gentleman at another. But every county was a hierarchy, made up of smaller hierarchies, and although the historian often finds it difficult to define a man's status, it was usually clear enough to his contemporaries.

The aristocracy and gentry in every county were mostly of recent origin, even though they invented pedigrees that took them back to the Conqueror. There were few families in England that could claim more than a hundred and fifty years of local predominance: the majority had climbed to power after the Reformation by taking over land that had formerly belonged to the Church. Yet however recent their establishment the local rulers firmly controlled county life, and their families were interlinked by ties of marriage. Many of them had followed the same pattern of education, at the universities or Inns of Court, and the more important ones had sat as county or borough members at Westminster. But although every county was linked, administratively, with London, its society was largely self-contained, and very few families maintained a permanent town house. Sir Henry Hyde, Clarendon's father, never went to London after he attended Queen Elizabeth's funeral, even though he had thirty more years of life ahead of him, and his wife never once visited the capital. London was becoming increasingly a social magnet, but many gentlemen were content to pass most of their time on their country estates, enjoying the pleasures of the chase and of reciprocal hospitality.

The head of every county was the Lord-Lieutenant, usually a nobleman and a Privy Councillor into the bargain, who might well be in charge of more than one county. He was the commander of the trained bands of the county—the local militia—and he was the link between the local authorities and the central government.

Because the Lords-Lieutenant were frequently away from their counties, local administration fell into the hands of the Deputy-Lieutenants, originally appointed by the Crown but now nominated by the Lord-Lieutenant from among the ranks of the Justices of the Peace. The number of Deputy-Lieutenants varied from county to county but was usually about ten or twelve, and these men, who had all the duties of a Justice of the Peace to perform, had also to carry out the orders of the central government. In time of war they would have to raise troops for the King's service and collect money for their equipment and maintenance, while in peace-time they were supposed to see that the militia was regularly assembled and trained.

The maids-of-all-work in county administration were the Justices of the Peace. The great men in the shire, including the bishop, if any, and members of the cathedral chapter, were appointed to the bench as a matter of course, and the office itself, in spite of the work it entailed, was highly prized not only as a mark of distinction within the county but as a link, however tenuous, with that source of all honour and profit, the Court. The J.P.s were first and foremost judges, and dealt with a variety of crimes. They passed serious criminal cases on to the justices of assize, but minor matters they dealt with themselves, either at Quarter Sessions or in the more frequent smaller meetings that were eventually to be formalised as Petty Sessions. In addition to being judges the J.P.s were also administrators, having had, in the words of one contemporary, 'not loads but stacks of statutes . . . laid upon them'. They were responsible for supervising poor relief, keeping roads and bridges in repair, licensing and controlling alehouses, regulating wages according to the Statute of Artificers, and deciding who should be responsible for looking after illegitimate children. In their legal work they were advised and assisted by the Clerk of the Peace, a full-time official, usually a professional lawyer, who was responsible for keeping the records of Quarter Sessions, and had a small clerical staff under him. In their administrative duties they were dependent upon the unpaid services of local constables, churchwardens and overseers of the poor.

Twice a year the Justices of the Peace met one of the High Court judges on assize and had to give him an account of their work. The judge, on his return to London, would pass on the results of his examination to the Privy Council, which thereby kept in touch with the county administration and was able to gauge its efficiency. The Council also sent orders to the Justices, and these increased in number and regularity after Charles's accession. In 1631 the Council issued the *Book of Orders*, laying down in great detail the responsibilities of J.P.s. They were instructed to meet every month and to make regular reports to the sheriff, who, in turn, was to pass these reports on to the assize judge. They were told to take particular care over the enforcement of the poor law, since the commercial and agricultural depression of the 1620s had enormously increased the number of unemployed and vagabonds. The Council kept up this pressure on J.P.s until about 1635, when the improving economic situation as well as natural lethargy checked the flow of conciliar letters. Nevertheless, the period of Charles's rule without Parliament saw a prolonged attempt to bring a measure of uniformity into local administration and to make the Council what it had been in Tudor times—a powerful and tireless watchdog.

The Justices of the Peace had increased in authority at the expense of the sheriff, but that officer was still responsible for arranging parliamentary elections, serving writs, empanelling juries and executing punishments. The sheriff served for a year only, and during his period of office he was not allowed, in theory, to leave the county—as Charles remembered in 1625 when he 'pricked' a number of opposition leaders as sheriffs in order to keep them out of the House of Commons. The sheriff's office was not coveted, since it was expensive— he had to pay his own staff—kept a man out of politics, and entailed a great deal of work. This was particularly the case after 1635 when the sheriff was made responsible for apportioning and collecting Ship Money. Collecting taxes was a difficult enough task at any time, but the unpopularity of Ship Money put the sheriff in an impossible position. As a local magnate he would be reluctant to take legal action against his fellows, and yet he was made personally liable for any deficiencies in the amount he had been ordered to collect. If his task was difficult in 1635 it became impossible by 1640, when refusal to pay was widespread. The sheriff might conceivably have coped with opposition only from small men, but gentry and aristocracy combined to block the will of the government. The whole episode served to show just how much the King's administration in the localities depended upon the cooperation—or at least the acquiescence—of the land-owners.

The civil war disrupted communications between central and local government, but Cromwell's accession to power saw their renewal. The regulation of wages, prices and apprenticeship was once again supervised by the Council (this time the Council of State), and efforts were made to prevent speculators from buying up food at a low price and hoarding it until they could sell at a profit. Cromwell had no prerogative courts to enforce his will, but he had an army at his disposal. Not until after the Restoration could local landowners breathe freely and rule the localities more or less as they wished.

Trade and Finance

England's major export in the sixteenth century was woollen cloth, but by about 1614 the growth of continental industries was limiting the demand for English cloth of the older heavier type known as shortcloth. Lower prices would have increased the English share of the European market, but the industry was already as efficient as it could reasonably hope to be, and in the absence of any technological advance price was determined by wages and quality. As the market shrank, cloth workers were laid off, wages were reduced, and in the older centres of manufacture such as the Cotswolds and west country unemployment and poverty caused great hardship and led to frequent rioting.

The end of the boom period for English cloth manufacturers was marked by Aldermen Cockayne's project in 1614. Cockayne, who was a member of the Eastland Company, pointed out that the Merchant Adventurers, who controlled the English trade in shortcloths, exported mainly 'white', or unfinished, cloth, which was dressed and dyed in Germany and the Low Countries. If, argued Cockayne, this work were done at home, unemployment would be checked and English profits would rise. The scheme met with royal approval, in 1614 the privileges of the Merchant Adventurers were suspended, and a new company—the 'King's Merchant Adventurers'—was set up to handle the trade in finished cloth to the Continent.

The government was hoping to encourage English exports, thereby increasing the Customs revenue, but Cockayne's motives were more doubtful. He had made no preparations for marketing the finished cloth, and it soon became apparent that he and his associates were far more interested in breaking the monopoly of the Merchant Adventurers and transferring it to themselves than in changing the pattern of the English cloth industry. The whole project was based upon the assumption that England had a monopoly of the continental market, but this was not the case. Foreign countries reacted by forbidding the import of dressed cloth from England, and the only result of the scheme was to disrupt the English cloth industry and give its continental rivals an advantage which they never lost. The King cancelled Cockayne's concession in December 1616 and restored the Merchant Adventurers to their former privileged position, but by that time the damage was done.

For ten years after 1614 the cloth industry, and with it English commerce as a whole, was in a slump. Exports to Germany and the Low Countries fell, and by 1622 the amount of cloth shipped from English ports was only forty per cent of what it had been in 1614. Riots were reported from the west country and from East Anglia, and in 1624 Parliament debated the sad state of English trade and tried to find a cure for its ills. One answer it gave was the Statute of Monopolies of 1624, which placed all monopolies under the control of the common law courts, except for those grants designed to protect the inventors of new processes against imitation. The statute was aimed mainly at the monopolies granted by James I to his favourites, but there was also a free trade lobby in the Commons which was opposed to the restrictive activities of the trading companies—particularly the Merchant Adventurers—and believed that if trade were thrown open to all comers it would flourish. They were responsible for the decision that the Merchant Adventurers' monopoly should in future be limited to the export of white cloth only.

The causes of the 1620s slump are not easy to diagnose. One of the most important seems to have been currency depreciation in Germany and eastern European countries following the outbreak of the Thirty Years War. English merchants could not afford to accept at their face value coins which in England and Western Europe would have been worth far less, and they therefore put up their prices. This gave local manufacturers an enormous advantage, and for several years, until recoinage became effective, English cloth priced itself out of the German market.

Although the trade in shortcloths steadily declined, there was a big expansion in the production and export of the so-called 'New Draperies'. These were lighter cloths—bays, says and perpetuances—more suitable for warmer climates, and they found a ready sale in Mediterranean countries. Spain was an important market for the New Draperies, particularly after the signing of peace in 1604, and James's pro-Spanish policy, whatever objections were made to it on religious and emotional grounds, was good for trade. Italy was another important market, particularly the free port of Leghorn, and the New Draperies also found a ready sale in the Levant. Piracy in the Mediterranean was a major problem, and although an English fleet under Sir Robert Mansell attacked the Barbary Corsairs in 1620, it was not until Blake's Mediterranean expedition of 1654 that piracy was really brought under control. That expedition also showed how important an English fleet in the Mediterranean could be to English policy in general, and what had started originally as a measure of trade protection soon developed into a regular weapon of diplomacy.

Piracy was not confined to the Mediterranean. In the Channel and North Sea the 'Dunkirkers' preyed on shipping, and the Eastland merchants organised convoys for their ships. The wars against Spain and France, which lasted from 1625 to 1630, seriously disrupted trade in the New Draperies and brought unemployment to East Anglia, which was one of the main centres of production. It may be that too much cloth was being produced, for even after the restoration of peace the East Anglian industry remained depressed, and discontent was increased by the poor harvests of 1630 and 1631, with the subsequent increase in grain prices.

Depression continued through the 1630s, and unemployment and poverty combined with puritanism to spread disaffection in the eastern counties. The emigrants who left Essex and Suffolk for Holland and the New World were inspired by hatred of Laudianism, but years of slump also played their part in making men decide to break with their native land. It was a misfortune for Charles that his eleven years of personal government coincided with economic depression. The attack on Impositions and the refusal to pay Tonnage and Poundage were not merely political protests: the margin of profit on trade in these years was so narrow that taxation could wipe it out.

By the time civil war came in 1642 the export of New Draperies equalled, in value, the export of shortcloths, and this reflected an important extension of the range of English trade. Shortcloths were associated with the European market, but the New Draperies were sent to America, the Levant, Africa, India—in short, all over the world. This expansion was not confined to England. In the new markets as in the old, English merchants found that they were up against competition from the Dutch who, because they had few natural resources of their own, specialised in carrying the goods of other nations. In the struggle for trade, diplomacy often came to the aid of the merchants. In 1648, for instance, the Dutch persuaded the King of Denmark to sell them the right for their ships to pass through the Sound without paying toll, and six years later the Sound was closed to English shipping. Dutch and English merchants were rivals also in the East Indies, where they were struggling for control of the empire which Portugal was too weak to hold. In 1623 seven English merchants were tortured and executed at Amboyna, and when the news of this 'massacre' reached England it caused a public outcry and created a desire for revenge that was not satisfied until the first Dutch War.

Economic depression at home and the struggle for markets abroad encouraged English governments to adopt a policy of protection which reached its peak with the Navigation Acts. This policy, which Adam Smith called 'Mercantilism' because it protected the interests of the merchant at the expense of the consumer, was condemned by nineteenth-century economists, who knew from their own experience that free trade brought prosperity and therefore dismissed mercantilism as an irrational desire to build up a favourable balance of trade so that bullion would pour into the country instead of flowing out of it. To the twentieth century, which has abandoned free trade, mercantilism is far more comprehensible, but we perhaps exaggerate the self-consciousness of early seventeenth-century governments in this

L*

respect. They did not pursue a consistent policy, neither did they have a staff of professional economists to advise them: they reacted to changing situations with a number of piecemeal measures that can only be interpreted as a philosophy of trade by treating them as a whole and filling in the gaps with hypotheses.

Foreign trade was encouraged because it stimulated employment and helped develop merchant shipping which, before the time of Cromwell, provided the country's navy in time of war. Unemployment was a perpetual problem for early Stuart administrators, because men who had no work were easily goaded into riots, which were difficult to put down. English industry, it is true, was expanding, but with the exception of cloth it still played a very small part in the economic life of the nation.

A further advantage of encouraging exports was that if these could be made to exceed the volume of imports a favourable balance of trade would be created and silver would flow into the country. As Thomas Mun wrote in 1630: 'The ordinary means to increase our wealth and treasure is by foreign trade, wherein we must ever observe this rule—to sell more to strangers yearly than we consume of theirs in value. For that part of our stock which is not returned to us in wares must necessarily be brought home in treasure.'

For this reason the government preferred to organise trade through companies which could be easily controlled, rather than throw it open to all comers. Silver was not wanted simply to hoard and gloat over. In the absence of credit facilities it was the only internationally acceptable medium of exchange, and without it trade could not be carried on. It was essential also for domestic industry, since the wool manufacturers had very little capital to spare. They could afford to pay their workers only if they received money for the cloth they sold: no silver meant no money, and no money meant unemployment.

The Dutch were generally blamed for the fact that English trade, in spite of the abundant natural resources on which it could draw, was not expanding fast enough. James and Charles both made belligerent gestures towards the Dutch, and claimed supremacy in the narrow seas, but nothing effective was done until the passing of the Navigation Act in 1651. This measure was designed to cut the Dutch out of the carrying trade with England, and it ordered that all goods coming into the British Isles should be carried in British or colonial ships or in ships belonging to the country in which the goods originated. The Act could not be rigidly enforced because there was not enough English shipping available, and it was only a contributory cause of the war with Holland which broke out in the following year, but it demonstrates more clearly than any other measure the way in which the government was prepared to put the full weight of its authority behind the merchants, and it cleared the ground for subsequent Navigation Acts which went far towards giving England that supremacy in foreign trade upon which her political greatness was to be based.

Under the early Stuarts there were close links between the government and the more influential members of the merchant community, as was shown by the appointment of one of their number, Lionel Cranfield, to be Lord Treasurer. The 'Country' interest campaigned for war against Spain and alliance with Holland, but the merchants who controlled the great chartered companies were generally in favour of a peaceful policy and would have agreed with Strafford that war tended 'to the decay of trade and losing entrance to the enlargement thereof that hath of many years been open to us'.

These merchant magnates were also linked to the Crown by mutual need. They wanted the privileges, including monopoly rights, that only the King could give them, while the King needed the loans that only they could raise. James and Charles borrowed large sums of money both from individuals and from privileged groups, which included the Livery Companies and the City Corporation. Repayment was a slow business that dragged on for many years—long after the dates originally fixed. In 1628 the Crown was so deeply in debt to the City that it handed over £350,000 worth of land on condition that a further cash advance of £100,000 was made. Delays in repayment did the Crown's credit much harm, and both bribery and threats were used to persuade potential lenders to part with their money. Sir Baptist Hicks, for instance, who was made a viscount in 1628, paid little or nothing for his title because he had already lent so much to the Crown; but companies which declined to meet the King's request for financial aid might find their charters confiscated and their privileges transferred to rival organisations, while individuals would find themselves subjected to the sort of treatment that one courtier advocated: they were like nuts, he said, that 'must be cracked before one can have any good of them, and then too at first they appear dry and choky, but bring them to the press, they yield a great deal of fat oil'.

One of the most lucrative privileges in the gift of the Crown was the grant of the Customs farm. Early in James's reign it was decided that Customs should no longer be collected by royal officials but should go to a private company which paid a fixed rent for its rights. The advantage of this was that the Crown got a regular revenue while the Customs farmers made a substantial profit over and above the rent. As trade expanded and profits increased the government could, of course, increase the rent, but even so the Customs farmers did well out of the transactions—so well, in fact, that they became one of the main sources of loans for the Crown. In the crisis year of 1640 they advanced well over £100,000 to the King, who could not save them from the subsequent anger of the Long Parliament, and they were to be found, not unnaturally, among the supporters of the Crown as the dispute between King and Parliament developed.

The Customs farmers may serve as a reminder that in the civil war 'the merchants' were not all on the side of Parliament. Where London was concerned—and it was far and away the most important centre of trade and finance in England—there was no such thing as a 'merchant community' with common interests. Some merchants had profited from royal intervention, some had suffered, but when the time came to take sides, considerations such as religion, that often ran counter to economic interests, played an important part in determining the choice that was made.

The Movement of Ideas

The English Revolution cannot be defined simply in terms of politics, economics or religion. It came about as a result of the stresses produced in English society by challenges to accepted authority in nearly every aspect of life and thought. The authority of the Pope had been overthrown at the Reformation; the supremacy of Aristotle was challenged by Bacon and the scientists; the self-sufficiency of the European continent crumbled as new worlds emerged out of the eastern and western oceans; and the very idea of authority was undermined by the insistence on the primacy of the individual conscience. Contemporaries were aware, in a general sense, of what was happening, but their reactions were varied. Some welcomed change as a liberating force, while others clung even more firmly to established landmarks and determined to defend them. Yet it is not possible to divide men simply into progressives and reactionaries. A conservative in politics might well be impatient of tradition when it stopped him putting his rents up, while a scientist who gloried in overthrowing outmoded conceptions might be found, like William Harvey, serving in the King's armies when civil war came.

The monarchy in England became associated with reaction, inefficiency, and eventually defeat, but there was nothing inevitable about this. Many European countries were faced with problems similar to those of England, and they adopted a despotic, monarchical solution. There was no reason in 1603 to suppose that such a solution might not work in England, and this seems to have been the view of Francis Bacon. In spite of the fact that he was a common lawyer and was to be appointed Attorney-General in 1613, Bacon was no opponent of the prerogative. He saw the need to regulate the life of the state in such a way that natural resources might be used to the full, and only the Crown, he thought, had the necessary authority for this task. He was inclined to regard Parliaments—particularly early Stuart Parliaments—as obstacles to efficient government, and he identified the common law with his hated rival Edward Coke—both of them, he thought, hidebound by precedent and unable to adapt to the needs of a new age. Like Strafford after him he believed that the job of government was to get things done, and that individual rights, although they were not to be wantonly overthrown, should be held below the point where they became an obstacle to administrative efficiency.

Bacon demonstrated his attitude by championing the Court of Chancery, which was not bound by precedent and which acted as the King's conscience, remedying defects of the common law by the application of common sense. Coke challenged the right of Chancery to change the decisions of common law courts, but Bacon had the King's support and his view, in the short run, triumphed. If only James had been blessed with political ability and strength of character to match his intelligence, royal government might have become what Bacon wanted it to be—a powerful machine at the heart of a centralised state. Unfortunately James had only the outward trappings of a philosopher king, but even so Bacon chose to serve him, hoping that he would not merely make himself rich but would also help to bring about that administrative efficiency without which centrifugal forces, represented by sectional and local interests, would pull the state apart.

Opposed to Bacon was Sir Edward Coke who believed that the common law, whatever its imperfections, represented the accumulated wisdom of countless generations and came close to that fundamental law which held all levels of society in their place. 'So dangerous a thing it is', he told the Commons, 'to shake or alter any of the rules or fundamental points of the common law, which in truth are the main pillars and supporters of the fabric of the commonwealth [that it is better] to leave all causes to be measured by the golden and straight mete-wand of the law and not to the incertain and crooked cord of discretion.' By 'discretion' Coke meant the prerogative power, and shortly after he became Chief Justice he informed the Commons of a maxim that 'the common law hath admeasured the King's prerogative'.

Coke did not deny that the King, by virtue of his position, had certain special rights, but he believed that these were provided by the common law, of which the judges were guardians. If the extent of the King's prerogative were disputed, let it be submitted to the judges, for these were the men who, by virtue of their long study and specialised training, were best fitted to draw the line between the prerogatives of the Crown and the rights of the subject. Coke bitterly opposed the claim that the King had an absolute prerogative which operated outside the sphere of common law and was not determinable by it, and he resisted attempts by the Crown to make the judges part of the executive. In 1616, for instance, James ordered that the judges should not give judgement in any matters which concerned the prerogative, however indirectly, until they had consulted with the King and his Council. Eleven of the twelve judges eventually accepted this view, but not Coke. He preferred dismissal to surrender.

The common law could not, in spite of Coke's claims, act as a fundamental law. This was demonstrated when the first two Stuarts did what Coke wanted and submitted disputes over the prerogative to the common law courts. They were not bound to do this, and James pointed out at the time of Bate's case that it was a considerable concession on his part to permit prerogative matters to be settled outside prerogative courts. His willingness to do so came from the fact that he, and Charles after him, were convinced that their actions were not simply politically advisable but also morally and legally right. Their confidence was justified, for the judges' decisions were favourable to the Crown. Many people, at the time and since, have attributed these decisions to the partiality of the judges and their fear of dismissal, yet early Stuart judges were not, generally speaking, servile courtiers: they were genuinely puzzled men who had been trained to consider not the general principles involved in the cases before them but the precise legal issues. By their training, and by the nature of the common law, they were unsuited to decide constitutional questions. What appeared to be questions of law were, in reality, questions of power, and their final answer was to be found not in the courts but in Parliament and on the battlefield.

The relationship between Parliament and the common law was far from straightforward. Both Houses claimed the right to act as courts in cases which involved their own privileges, but there was no regular channel of appeal from the courts of common law to the 'High Court of Parliament'. If Parliament wanted to give a decision it could do so only by passing a statute which would either change the law or make it more explicit, but statutes required not only the agreement of the two Houses but the assent of the King as well. The King's power, moreover, was not confined to veto: he could also intervene at any stage in the discussion of a matter which concerned his prerogative, and forbid debate to continue. This is why the Commons became so tenacious of their privileges, particularly the privilege of freedom of speech, under the first two Stuarts. Without this privilege they could not even embark upon the discussion of constitutional matters, let alone bring them to the point of statutory definition.

James and Charles claimed that the privileges of the Commons derived from the King's grace and were revocable. The Commons could have replied that whatever the origin of their privileges they were too valuable to part with, but this would have meant abandoning their most cherished preconceptions. Most members of the Commons had received some training in the common law and adopted a reverential attitude towards precedent. They assumed, in fact, that what was old was right, and it was but a short step from this to the assumption that what was right must therefore be old. The privileges of Parliament, they argued, were undoubtedly theirs of right: they must therefore have a respectable antiquity. To find support for their belief they consulted the records—those, for instance, which were stored at the Tower, or those in private collections such as that which the great antiquary Sir Robert Cotton made freely available to his friends in the Commons—and from their studies they derived a view of history which served as a basis for the claims they were making in the present.

This view, briefly, was that England had originally been a community of Anglo-Saxon freeholders who met together in frequent Witenagemots, or Parliaments, to settle disputes and consider matters of general interest. This free community had been overthrown by William the Conqueror, who established monarchical despotism in England, but the tradition of liberty survived, preserved in the common law, and encouraged the English to continue the fight against the Conqueror and his descendants. Over the course of centuries they had won back for themselves many of the liberties of which defeat had deprived them, and their great moment of triumph had come with Magna Carta, when the 'Norman' John was forced to concede that in future no freeman should be proceeded against except by due course of law.

Parliament and the common law were both, according to this view, older than the monarchy, and when James told the Commons that their privileges were derived only from the grace of his predecessors he was, so members assumed, ignoring the fact that parliamentary privileges existed before there were Kings of England to grant them. When, in the 1620s, the shadow of the Conqueror seemed once again to threaten free institutions, the Commons had recourse to another Magna Carta to defend the rights which had their grounds in the common law and were therefore, as Coke told the House in 1621, 'beyond the memory or register of any beginning, and the same which the Norman Conqueror found within the realm of England'.

Coke was not alone in his belief that the Commons were taking up the struggle which their Anglo-Saxon forefathers had begun. Sir Benjamin Rudyerd, for instance, declared that he would be glad to see 'that old decrepid law Magna Carta—which hath been kept so long and lien bedrid as it were—I shall be glad to see it walk abroad again with new vigour and lustre', and Pym, speaking in support of the Petition of Right, reminded the Commons that 'there are plain footsteps of those laws in the government of the Saxons. They were of that vigour and force as to overlive the Conquest—nay to give bounds and limits to the Conqueror.'

The victory of Parliament was a victory for the common law, and on the day of Strafford's execution the Commons ordered that the second part of Coke's *Institutes*—a commentary on the common law which Charles had suppressed because it left no room for the prerogative—should be published. But the law defended only free men, and there were men in England who felt they were not free. Lilburne and the Levellers believed as firmly as Coke that Anglo-Saxon liberty had been destroyed by the Conqueror, but unlike him they regarded the common law as the means by which William had imposed the Norman yoke on the shoulders of his enslaved subjects. They wanted a return to first principles by calling on the people—the source of law—to reclaim the freedom that belonged by right to *all* men, not simply the holders of property, and to remodel the state now that the Norman monarchy had at last been dissolved. The Diggers went one stage further and asserted that since all property-rights derived only from the Norman yoke, and had been abolished with the monarchy, they were now free to take the land which was rightfully theirs. Cromwell put down the Levellers and Diggers but not until after the Restoration could property-holders sleep peacefully in their beds, secure in the knowledge that the common law once against protected them not only from the greed of Kings but also from the anger of the common people.

Coke and many of his contemporaries used the past as a storehouse of precedents which they could plunder for the benefit of the present, but the study of historical records also helped to further the intellectual revolution that was taking place in England. John Selden, for instance, in his *History of Tithes*, showed that these payments were not of divine origin, as the Laudians claimed, but had been imposed and collected only where secular law had so ordained. Selden, with his enormous learning and his insistence that interpretations must not be stretched beyond the limits of evidence, was typical of what was to become the scientific approach to knowledge. The Scots divines in the Westminster Assembly were baffled by this indomitable man who pricked their speculations with the rapier of his knowledge. 'It may read so in your little pocket Bibles with the gilt leaves', he would tell them, 'but the Hebrew reads thus . . .'

Selden had been on the fringe of that circle of gifted men which met at Falkland's house, Great Tew, to discuss religious and philosophical questions in a comparatively dispassionate manner, and to try to arrive at the truth not by emphatic assertion but by considering the evidence and weighing it carefully. The Great Tew circle, which included Hyde, was anglican in tone, but its attitude reflected the secularisation of thought which the scientific revolution[1] brought with it, for the desire to disentangle the facts of any situation from the mass of assumptions that surrounded it had one of its main sources of inspiration in Bacon who, in such books as the *Novum Organum* of 1620, rejected medieval assumptions about the nature of the universe, and urged experiment and research.

Bacon was not a practising scientist himself, but he was the patron and protector of those who were, and he tried to persuade James to establish a centre where scientists could meet and exchange information, thereby liberating themselves from the dead hand of the past. James had no money for such a project, nor did he appreciate the need for it, but Gresham College in London provided a convenient and

[1] For a fuller discussion of the scientific revolution, see below, Chapter 19.

congenial meeting place, and it was there that in 1645 the group from which the Royal Society was to be formed began its meetings.

The Baconians, who wanted to free the pursuit of knowledge from the orthodoxies which impeded it, had many links with the puritans and the parliamentary opposition in the years before the civil war. They shared the puritan distrust of Laud's insistence on uniformity, and they shared with the leaders of the Commons a desire for freedom of speech. Yet this was largely a marriage of convenience, and it is surely an exaggeration to say, as one historian does,[1] that 'the civil war ... was fought between rival schools of astronomy, between Parliamentarian heliocentrists and Royalist Ptolemaics'. Men were not neatly divided into adherents and opponents of the scientific method, and acceptance of royal authority was not confined to those who believed that the earth was at the centre of the universe. A puritan theocracy would have been no more acceptable to the scientists than an anglican or Roman one, and the significance of the civil war is that by discrediting all forms of theocracy it left men free to pursue their speculations unhindered.

[1] Christopher Hill, *The Intellectual Origins of the English Revolution*, p. 118.

15

Charles II

CHARLES II—'a long, dark man, above two yards high', as the round-heads had described him when they were searching for him after Worcester—arrived in London on his thirtieth birthday, having spent the years of his adult life in exile. The experience of poverty, humiliation and danger had taught him to take a cynical view of human behaviour and to value every man only for what he could get out of him. Where Charles I had been stiff and reserved, Charles II was easy and friendly and charmed all who spoke to him, until they discovered, in Burnet's words, 'how little they could depend on good looks, kind words and fair promises, in which he was liberal to excess because he intended nothing by them but to get rid of importunities and to silence all farther pressing upon him'. Charles had not known security since he was a young child, and now that providence had restored him to his throne he was determined, as he told his brother James, not to set out on his travels again. He valued a quiet life and would have approved of the attitude of the Renaissance Pope who commented, after the news of his election, 'Now that God has given us the papacy, let us enjoy it'. Charles was determined to enjoy the monarchy, and his skill as a politician came from the fact that he was prepared to sacrifice almost anything—advisers, friends, principles, even religion—in order to preserve his throne.

The Restoration Settlement. I: The Constitution

The King's chief adviser was his Lord Chancellor, Edward Hyde, created Earl of Clarendon in 1661. Hyde was a common lawyer who came from a gentry family and had made his name by leading the moderates in the Long Parliament. After the defeat of the cavaliers he joined the young King in exile, and he, more than anyone else, had schooled Charles II in the art of government and had kept him faithful to the Church of England. Charles had no firsthand experience of kingship; he relied upon Hyde, and for the first years of his reign was content to leave government largely in the Chancellor's hands.

Unfortunately for Hyde the political world of the 1640s, which he had known so well, had vanished beyond recall. Even in those years his hopes of preserving a constitution on the Elizabethan model, balanced nicely between the prerogative of the King and the rights of the subject, had been anachronistic. The relationship that had kept Elizabeth and her Parliaments in precarious balance depended upon personal, religious and economic factors which were constantly changing. What had been possible in 1590 was no longer possible in 1640, yet twenty years later Hyde still hoped to restore government by King, Privy Council, Lords and Commons on the old pattern. The result was that, in constitutional matters at any rate, the Restoration solved none of the problems that had led to civil war: 'at the best, it put them again on the agenda, to be reconsidered under the new circumstances.'[1]

The Crown and the traditional pattern of government were restored, but the clock was put back only to 1642. Those Acts to which Charles I had given his assent, however reluctantly, remained in force, and Star Chamber and the other prerogative courts were never restored. The King could still issue proclamations, but for the execution of his will he was now entirely dependent upon the courts of common law. Nothing was said about the judges, whose tenure still remained conditional upon the King's good will, nor was the King's authority to dispense with the operation of the law in particular cases limited or abolished. The prerogative monarchy, in short, was not restored, but certain prerogative powers were left to the Crown. These had been of no great importance in earlier reigns, but with the destruction of the major part of the prerogative the little that was left became of critical significance.

The Restoration Settlement. II: Land

Parliament restored to the Crown and Church all the lands that had been taken from them during the Interregnum. As for private individuals, they were left to fend for themselves. So much land had

[1] T. F. T. Plucknett, 'The Restoration and the Constitution', *The Listener*, 30 June 1960.

changed hands in the previous two decades that Parliament despaired of unravelling the legal intricacies and arriving at a just solution. It resolved that land which had been confiscated should be restored to the original owner, but passed no general Act to enforce this. Returning cavaliers had to try to come to an arrangement with the occupier of their estates, failing which they could sue for possession. Law suits, however, were expensive, and the aggrieved cavalier could not always be sure that judgement would be given in his favour. Noblemen were in a stronger position, since they could more easily obtain private Acts of Parliament and they had the powerful backing of the House of Lords which issued direct orders to sheriffs, commanding them to see that confiscated lands were returned to their original noble owners.

This settlement was not as unfair as it seems to be at first glance. Many cavaliers who had been forced to sell their lands or had allowed them to be confiscated and sold by the state had managed to buy them back again before the Restoration took place, while others found that the new owners were content to become rent-paying tenants in 1660 rather than risk expropriation. Most royalists got their land back, before or after the Restoration, though the cost of recovery sometimes led to financial collapse in succeeding generations. It is remarkable how few of the leading Commonwealth families managed to establish themselves on confiscated estates, and the redistribution of land during the Interregnum cannot be compared, in its effects, with that which followed the dissolution of the monasteries.

It remains true, however, that a number of royalists who had parted with their land as a consequence of their devotion to Charles I never regained it, and turned into sour-faced critics of Charles II. The Convention Parliament passed an Act of Indemnity and Oblivion, pardoning all those who had taken part in the revolution—except certain named individuals, of whom only one, Sir Harry Vane, was actually executed. This was a wise measure of clemency and reconciliation, but embittered cavaliers were not slow to point out that the restoration of the monarchy, for which they had waited so long, had produced indemnity for the King's enemies and oblivion for his friends.

The Restoration Settlement. III: Finance

Restored royal lands gave the King a source of income independent of Parliament, but this was far from adequate to meet all the costs of administration: constant land sales from the 1530s onwards had frustrated the attempt of Henry VII to base the wealth and power of the Crown primarily upon this source. A committee of the Commons was set up to consider the costs of government and to decide what additional supplies ought to be voted by Parliament. This committee estimated that the Crown would need £1,200,000 a year, of which lands would provide a mere £100,000. Customs would, it was thought, bring in £400,000; the rest was to be provided by an excise which it was hoped would produce £400,000 a year, and a number of minor duties. Half the excise was voted to the Crown in perpetuity, in return for the abolition of the hated feudal dues. The Court of Wards had not been abolished until 1646 and in theory could have been revived by the restored monarch, but Charles and Clarendon, who knew how much bitterness had been created by feudal tenures, were content to abandon them in return for a permanent grant, thereby fulfilling, fifty years too late, the contract which Salisbury had proposed in 1610.

The abolition of feudal tenures symbolised the end of Tudor monarchy, for the King could never again hope to make himself independent of Parliament by soaking the landowners. The representatives of the landed interest who sat in Parliament had at last recognised their responsibility to provide compensation for the Crown, but the excise which they voted fell on beer, cider and tea—not on land. In this way they neatly converted a direct land tax into an indirect imposition on the consumer, and as if to emphasise their triumph they refused to abolish copyhold tenure, which was also a survival from the feudal past. Copyholds left tenants very much at the mercy of their lords, and were at least as oppressive to the lower levels of society as wardship had been to the upper levels. But the Restoration saw the triumph of the landowners and of their interests. They abolished restraints upon themselves but kept restraints upon their subordinates. Since the Privy Council, deprived of the prerogative courts, could no longer effectively coerce oppressive landlords, the country squire really came into his own and ruled like an independent prince over his particular locality.

Parliament voted additional sums of money in order to disband the army, but the King retained Monck's regiment for his own use, and this—the Coldstream Guards—became the nucleus of a regular army which, in spite of complaints from Parliament, kept going until the long war against France turned it from a dangerous luxury into a tolerated necessity. No extra sums were voted, however, to meet the

debts of the Crown—either those which Charles had contracted
during his exile or those incurred by Charles I, which his son intended
to honour. The new King started his reign, therefore, with a heavy
burden of debt, and to make matters worse it soon became apparent
that the income of £1,200,000 which Parliament had intended to
provide would not in fact be produced by the taxes voted.

It is sometimes maintained that Parliament deliberately starved the
Crown of supplies, to make sure that no king would ever again be
able to rule without the regular assistance of his 'faithful Commons'.
There may be some truth in this so far as the Convention was concerned, since that assembly included many members who would have
liked to impose conditions on the King as the price of his restoration.
But the Convention was dissolved in December 1660, and the new
Parliament which met in May 1661 was full of young cavaliers, more
royalist than the King himself. This Cavalier Parliament voted the
Crown an additional Hearth Tax in 1662 and was anxious to strengthen
rather than weaken the monarchy. A new settlement, much more
royalist than the first, might have been possible had it not been for the
restraining hand of Clarendon, who devoted himself, as always, to the
establishment of parliamentary, not absolute, monarchy.

The Commons were also hampered by the fact that however generous their intentions they did not have sufficient material available
about the yield of taxes: the statistical age was only just beginning.
The Treasury was hopelessly inefficient, and Charles made matters
worse by appointing the aged Earl of Southampton as Lord Treasurer.
Southampton was a man of integrity and good intentions, and the
Treasurership was the reward for the faithful service he had given
Charles I, but something more than loyalty was needed to galvanise
the Exchequer into activity and to give the King a true picture of his
financial position. The opportunity was missed, and by the time
Charles learned how near he was to bankruptcy the goodwill of the
Commons had changed to indifference if not hostility.

The Restoration Settlement. IV: The Church

The restoration of the King meant the restoration of the Anglican
Church. During the Interregnum many incumbents—perhaps as high
a proportion as seventy per cent—had come to terms with Cromwell
and had kept their livings by agreeing not to use the Prayer-Book and
not to preach against the new political order. More important, so far

as the restoration was concerned, were those men who refused to conform and who went either into exile or into the houses of cavalier families, to keep the tradition and ceremonies of the Church alive in readiness for happier days. Many of these men were products of the Laudian reform of the Church, and valued order, decency and ceremony as highly as Laud himself had ever done. They included men like Gilbert Sheldon, who had been educated in Laud's own university of Oxford, and their devotion to the ideals for which Charles I and his Archbishop had died assured Laudianism of victory even at its darkest moment, when the Church of England had apparently ceased to exist. By taking refuge in country houses the Laudians helped to convert the squires to anglicanism and to produce the generation of young cavaliers who dominated the Parliament which met in 1661 and who were devoted to the Church of England in a way that their fathers had never been.

Those clergy who went into exile showed a constancy equal to Sheldon and the others who stayed at home. A century earlier the Marian exiles—creators of a Church that had barely established itself —had fallen under the influence of continental religious practices, and had brought radical ideals back to England when they returned in 1559. But the Caroline exiles were confident in their anglican faith and unimpressed by the varieties of religious practice, Roman Catholic or protestant, which they encountered on the Continent. For them the years of exile meant a confirmation of all they had earlier taken for granted, and they returned to England more strongly anglican than when they had left.

The anglicans in exile were enormously strengthened by the support of Edward Hyde, the King's right-hand man. Hyde had earlier been a critic of episcopacy, and he never shared Laud's political ambitions, which came too near theocracy for his liking. But political Laudianism had died with the Archbishop, and Hyde found himself strongly in sympathy with the principles of royal supremacy, hierarchical government and uniformity, which characterised latter day Laudians. The young King had no strong religious opinions and in 1650 he agreed to accept the Covenant and to pose as a presbyterian in return for Scots support. But Charles's experiences in Scotland taught him a lesson which he did not forget. He found, as his grandfather James I had found, that the Scottish elders were not only intolerable but were a grave threat to royal supremacy. After the defeat of Worcester Charles never again flirted with presbyterianism; neither did he go to the other extreme, for when he discovered that the Queen Mother, Henrietta Maria, was trying to convert his younger brother to Roman Catholicism, he acted swiftly and put an end to the attempt. There is no reason to suppose that Charles II ever loved the Anglican Church as his father had done, but he was sufficient of a realist to know that adherence to it offered him the best chance of regaining his throne.

As Restoration turned from a dream into reality in 1659, Hyde worked towards a moderate settlement. He knew that the puritans were still strong in Parliament and that fear of intolerant anglicanism would hold them back more than any other consideration from accepting the monarchy. It was to quieten their fears that Charles, on his Chancellor's advice, issued the Declaration of Breda in which he promised 'a liberty to tender consciences and that no man shall be disquieted or called in question for differences of opinion in matter of religion'.

No sooner had the King been restored than dispossessed anglican clergy began demanding back their livings from puritan incumbents. In many cases the puritans left without difficulty, recognising that the tide had turned against them, but where disputes occurred they were decided by the local magistrates, who were usually anxious to demonstrate the warmth of their anglicanism. The Convention Parliament debated religious matters, hoping to arrive at a settlement which would bind the King to toleration, but members were frustrated by their own lack of unity. There were many presbyterians and Independents in the House, but the civil war had left bitterness between them, and although by coöperation they might have preserved some of the gains made during the Interregnum they preferred to bicker and thereby lost the initiative to the 'Court managers' in the House—the men who had the King's ear and were in daily touch with Clarendon. These 'managers' were concerned to prevent the Convention from arriving at any statutory settlement of religion until such time as the Anglican Church had been firmly re-established. This was already happening. While parish priests once again conducted their services according to the Book of Common Prayer, bishops began to restore discipline to their dioceses and to eject remaining puritan incumbents. The King set the tone in his chapel at Whitehall where one observer reported that 'there are twelve singing boys provided, and a pair of organs setting up where Noll's seat was', and new appointments to the episcopal bench put the leadership of the Anglican Church firmly into the hands of the Laudians. Juxon, who had attended Charles I on the scaffold and had been Laud's colleague on the Council, was elevated to the Archbishopric of Canterbury. He was old and ailing, however, and the real leader of the Church was Gilbert Sheldon, who became Bishop of London and, in 1663, formally succeeded Juxon as Archbishop.

While the Independents, in Parliament and elsewhere, were prepared to accept restored anglicanism as long as they were left free to worship in their own way, the presbyterians hoped to come to a compromise agreement which would move the anglican church nearer to their position. Negotiations between the bishops and the leaders of the presbyterians continued throughout the summer of 1660 and in October the King issued his first Declaration on Ecclesiastical Affairs, in which he ordered that bishops should be assisted in ordination and excommunication by representatives of the parish clergy, and that no one should be persecuted for refusing to use the Prayer-Book. The presbyterians were delighted by these concessions, and their representatives in Parliament, led by the indomitable Prynne, tried to make them into a statute. The cavaliers, aided by some of the Independents, just managed to defeat this manœuvre, and from that moment onwards the presbyterian cause was lost. The puritan failure to unite had given victory to the anglicans, and the Convention was dissolved before the question of the religious settlement could be reopened. Hyde gave tongue to triumphant anglicanism in his closing speech to the Convention, when he warned the opponents of 'the best and the best reformed Church in the Christian world' that 'God would not so miraculously have snatched this Church as a brand out of the fire, would not have raised it from the grave after He had suffered it to be buried so many years . . . to expose it again to the same rapine, reproach and impiety'.

Although Hyde welcomed the triumph of anglicanism he still hoped that reconciliation could be effected between the puritans and the established Church. As a sign of goodwill bishoprics were offered to three of the puritan leaders, Baxter, Calamy and Reynolds, but only Reynolds accepted; Baxter was far less ready for compromise, and his intransigent attitude largely accounted for the failure of the Savoy Conference, which opened in April 1661. The bishops were sincere in their desire to create a comprehensive and inclusive Church, which should be, as under Elizabeth, the Church of all the English people, but Baxter badly overplayed his hand, on the assumption that it was up to the presbyterians to state their terms and that all concessions would come from the anglican side. He ignored the fact that the Anglican Church had now been fully restored and, with the Cavalier Parliament whole-heartedly behind it, was no longer dependent upon presbyterian support.

While negotiations between the two sides stumbled into deadlock, the bishops produced their revision of the Prayer-Book. A number of minor alterations were made in the hope that puritan objections would be met, but in fact Baxter declared that the new Book was even less acceptable than the old. It was this new Book which was incorporated in the Act of Uniformity of 1662, and all ministers were required not only to use the Book before the following St Bartholomew's Day but also to make public declaration of their 'unfeigned assent and consent to all and every thing contained and prescribed in and by the Book'. They were also ordered to acknowledge 'that it is not lawful, upon any pretence whatsoever, to take arms against the King', and to renounce the Solemn League and Covenant as 'an unlawful oath . . . imposed upon the subjects of this realm against the known laws and liberties of this kingdom'.

Clarendon felt that the Commons had gone too far in their anglican enthusiasm, and he persuaded the Lords to accept an amendment allowing any minister to perform by deputy those parts of the service which went against his conscience. The Chancellor was concerned, as always, with the problem of public order, and was anxious not to drive the puritans into open rebellion, but the Commons would permit no concessions and threw out the amendment. St Bartholomew's Day was awaited with some trepidation by both sides, but it came and went quietly enough, and Pepys recorded in his diary that the presbyterian clergy had 'gone out very peaceably, and the people not so much concerned therein as was expected'.

Just under a thousand ministers were, in fact, deprived of their livings, and joined the seven hundred who had been already evicted since the Restoration. The puritans blamed Clarendon for their eclipse, and accused him of professing toleration while he prepared an anglican take-over, but they probably exaggerated both his intolerance and his far-sightedness. Clarendon had no means of knowing how ineffective the presbyterians would be. He moved carefully, testing opinion at each step and counselling moderation where he thought that civil disorder might be provoked. He was probably as surprised as anyone by the violence of the anglican reaction that set in during the early part of 1661 and produced the Cavalier Parliament.

It was this Parliament which confirmed the victory of the Anglican Church by passing the series of acts known collectively as the Clarendon Code—although Clarendon was not responsible for them. The Corporation Act of 1661, designed to break the puritan hold on municipal government, ordered that all mayors, aldermen, town clerks and other officials should publicly declare that they renounced the Solemn League and Covenant and accepted the principle of non-resistance. The Conventicle Act of 1664 made it an offence for any person to attend a service other than that prescribed by the Prayer-Book, and gave Justices of the Peace authority to break into private houses if they thought that illegal conventicles were being held there. In spite of this legislation puritan assemblies continued, and were often presided over by former ministers, ejected from their livings. The Five Mile Act of 1665 was aimed at these men, and made it an offence for ejected ministers to come within five miles of any corporate town.

One motive behind the Clarendon Code was revenge on the puritans for the suffering and indignities they had inflicted on the Anglican Church. Another was fear. London and the provinces were full of unemployed ex-soldiers who had nothing to hope for from the restored monarchy and who were inclined to puritanism of one sort or another. The Clarendon Code was a police measure, designed to hold these dangerous forces in check, for it was assumed, in the words of a contemporary ballad, that

> A Presbyterian is such a monstrous thing
> That loves democracy and hates a King.

Persecution, however, as the Roman Catholics had shown in the previous century, can rarely wipe out faith, and puritan congregations continued to meet and worship. The King wanted to unite his subjects and was temperamentally opposed to persecution, but although he issued a Declaration of Indulgence in December 1662, reminding Parliament of the commitment he had made in the Declaration of Breda and asking it to make statutory provision for the relief of dissenters, he could not make his wishes prevail. The anglican gentry in Parliament had learned to hate the puritans and were determined that they should never again threaten the supremacy of the landowners.

The Church of England's abandonment of comprehension marks the end of the Tudor and early Stuart ideal of the united Christian society of which Church and state should be but two faces. The ideal of comprehension was not formally renounced until the settlement of

1689 and attempts at reconciliation continued on and off until that date, but the Church could never again claim to represent the English people. It became increasingly the Church of the squires and lost touch with labouring men and women. It also lost its dominant position in politics, and after 1664, when Sheldon agreed with Clarendon that the clergy should no longer tax themselves but should contribute at the same rate as the laity in Parliament, Convocation did not meet for a quarter of a century. The bishops as individuals remained important in the House of Lords, and they set a high standard of learning and of piety, but the Church as a whole was declining as a moral, political and religious force.

Clarendon

Clarendon's administration consisted of old cavaliers, like himself, Ormonde and Southampton, and former Commonwealth men like Manchester, the Lord Chamberlain; Monck, created Duke of Albemarle and appointed Captain-General for life; and Ashley Cooper, who became Chancellor of the Exchequer in 1661. Clarendon, the Lord Chancellor, was no mere figure-head. Because he had the ear of the King he was the chief minister and dominated the Privy Council, to which decisions on a whole host of matters, major and petty, were referred.

Clarendon's conservatism was particularly dangerous where Parliament was concerned. He recognised the need for the Council to give a lead in the Commons, and at the beginning of the reign he 'had every day conference with some select persons of the House of Commons' to consult together 'in what method to proceed in disposing the House'. Yet although he was prepared, like Elizabeth, to watch over debates and to intervene where necessary, Clarendon had no intention of building up a 'King's party' in the Commons. He regarded Parliament as an extension of the King's Council, called to discuss matters of major interest and to vote money, but not to take any regular part in the government of the country. He had been out of England during those years when the Long Parliament had learned, through its committees, the arts of administration, and he did not realise that the divided society, revealed in 1642, was to be a permanent feature of English political life. In 1660 there was a superficial appearance of unity, but the fissure between Court and Country, anglicans and dissenters, supporters of divine right and opponents of absolutism, ran too deep to be healed. National unity could no longer be taken for granted, and if the King's government was to be carried on efficiently the 'King's men' in the House of Commons would have to be organised. Clarendon was not prepared to do this dirty work, but other politicians were less scrupulous.

These 'others' included ambitious courtiers and young members of Parliament who saw in the aged Chancellor a barrier to their own advancement. The Cavalier Parliament had not been long in session before an opposition group began to form in the Commons. The Chancellor was not popular. Ardent cavaliers blamed him because he had made the constitutional settlement too moderate, while dissenters accused him of making the religious settlement too extreme. Many people were jealous of his wealth and of his exalted position. Clarendon's daughter Anne had married James, the heir to the throne, and courtiers commented with acid tongues on the obscure country lawyer who had wormed his way into the royal family itself. The Chancellor was also blamed for selling Dunkirk—which Cromwell had acquired—to France, even though it cost far more to keep up than it ever brought in. Public opinion showed itself when the mob rioted outside the great house he was building in Piccadilly and broke its windows.

Clarendon was a far finer character than any of his critics, but they were more in tune than he was with the amoral, cynical and witty tone of Restoration England. Even the King, although he valued Clarendon's loyalty and wisdom, had no love for him and preferred the company of younger, more amusing men and women—particularly women. He was prepared to keep Clarendon in office as long as the administration functioned smoothly, but when the second Dutch War revealed appalling corruption and inefficiency, he hastily got rid of him.

War was forced on Clarendon by the younger men, like Thomas Clifford and Henry Bennett, who had the Commons behind them. The Dutch were hated as commercial rivals whose trading empire and control of the European carrying-trade threatened to block the expansion of the English economy. War against Holland offered the prospect of rich prizes, and young cavaliers hoped to show that the restored monarchy could acquit itself just as honourably as the Commonwealth when it came to fighting. The self-confidence engendered by the Restoration had developed into aggressiveness, and the widespread desire for war was reflected in the results of by-elections which brought a steady flow of new members into the Commons—members who had no love for the pacific Chancellor, and therefore increased the number of his enemies in the House.

The war party looked to the King rather than Clarendon, and believed that they had the Chancellor in a cleft stick. If the war went well, they, as the instigators, would take the credit for it. If it went badly they would put all the blame on Clarendon. Charles forced Clarendon to include some of the younger men in his administration by appointing Clifford to the Privy Council and by giving seats on the Treasury Commission to him and Ashley. Everything now depended on the outcome of the war.

Fighting between the Dutch and the English in America and Africa created the situation that led to a formal declaration of war in March 1665. At first English arms were triumphant. James, the Lord High Admiral, routed the Dutch fleet in the battle of Lowestoft in June 1665, and killed the enemy admiral, Opdam. But this victory was not followed up, and the Dutch made such a good recovery that a year later they pounced on a squadron commanded by Prince Rupert, and in the Four Days Battle sank about twenty ships and would have done even more damage had not Albemarle arrived with the rest of the fleet in time to save his fellow admiral from destruction.

While the navies grappled in the Channel and the North Sea, two natural disasters fell on England. In May 1665 the first signs were observed of bubonic plague, which spread with frightening rapidity in the narrow, smelly streets and rat-infested slums of London. In the heat of the summer thousands of people died every month, and all who could afford to do so fled from the polluted city. Houses where the plague had struck were closed up, with a red cross painted on their door and the inscription *Lord have mercy on us*, while at night carts rumbled through the deserted streets, gathering up the dead and tumbling them into pits for common burial.

In September 1665 the plague claimed over thirty thousand victims, but after that it began slowly to decline as the survivors developed immunity. Hardly had life in the City returned to normal, than the Great Fire broke out. It started in September 1666 in a baker's shop in Pudding Lane, not far from the place where the Monument now stands, and for three days and nights it burned its way westward, fanned by a strong breeze. Pepys, who watched it all, describes the 'poor people staying in their houses as long as till the very fire touched them, and then running into boats, or clambering from one pair of stairs, by the water-side, to another', and as darkness fell he saw the fire spread 'in corners and upon steeples, and between churches and houses, as far as we could see up the hill of the City, in a most horrid, malicious, bloody flame. . . . The churches, houses, and all on fire, and flaming at once; and a horrid noise the flames made, and the cracking of houses at their ruin.'

Charles went down to the City and supervised the blowing up of houses to make a fire break. Little could be done, however, until the wind dropped and the fire burned itself out. By that time the old City of London had been destroyed, and the great church of St Paul, which Laud had struggled to restore, was a hollow shell. Over thirteen thousand houses and nearly ninety churches had been ruined by the fire, and the homeless citizens camped out in the fields that stretched towards the villages of Highgate and Hampstead. After the first shock was over, various plans were drawn up and submitted to the King for the rebuilding of the City in a more rational, and more grandiose, manner. The most famous of these came from the hand of Sir Christopher Wren, who was commissioned to rebuild St Paul's and many parish churches, but in the end little was done to alter the ground plan of the medieval City. It survives to this day, in spite of a second devastation, a monument to the enduring power of property-rights over acts of man and God. Minor changes of some significance were, however, made. The height of houses was regulated and a minimum width was laid down for principal streets. Charles also ordered that the new City should be built of brick and stone and not of inflammable wood.

Those who believed that plague and fire had been sent by God to punish a wicked and blasphemous people, sought for a scapegoat. The honeymoon years which followed Charles's restoration were now over and in the country as well as in Parliament there was increasing criticism of the profligate Court and of Clarendon's administration. If the war with Holland had ended in triumph, public opinion might have swung round once again in the King's favour, but there was no hope of this since the King could not afford to equip the fleet for the campaign of 1667. In the early part of that year peace negotiations were opened with the Dutch at Breda, while the greater part of the English fleet was paid off and sent to lie idly at anchor in the Medway. It was there that the Dutch found it in June 1667 when, with magnificent effrontery, they sailed up the river, burnt three English ships and towed away two others, including the *Royal Charles*, the flagship of the fleet. The *Royal Charles*, originally the *Naseby*, had been rechristened by Charles when it brought him back from his long exile. Its humiliating capture pointed the contrast between the efficiency and warlike strength of Cromwell's reign and the maladministration and weakness that seemed to be inextricably associated with the Stuarts. When Albemarle went down to Chatham to see to the defence of the naval base there, he found a shortage of guns, ammunition, timber, cordage —everything, in fact, which the base existed to supply.

Charles realised that a scapegoat would have to be provided, for the tide of criticism was washing round the throne itself and Pepys recorded a rumour that 'the night the Dutch burned our ships the King did sup with my Lady Castlemaine [one of his mistresses] and there were all mad in hunting of a poor moth'. Clarendon was the obvious victim. He was head of the administration which had been responsible for failure in war, and he was already unpopular because of the sale of Dunkirk. He was also blamed for marrying Charles to a Portuguese princess, Catherine of Braganza, who had failed to produce an heir. She had brought with her as dowry Bombay and Tangier, which were so expensive to maintain that Clarendon was considering selling them. Pepys describes how, when the news of the Medway humiliation reached London, a crowd of 'rude people' demonstrated outside the Lord Chancellor's new house and painted a gibbet on his gate, with 'these three words writ: "Three sights to be seen, Dunkirk, Tangier and a barren Queen." '

Charles could hardly dismiss Clarendon before peace was concluded with Holland, but this was accomplished in July 1667 when, by the Treaty of Breda, the *status quo* was restored—except in America, where the Dutch colony of New Netherland was transferred to England. The King was longing to get rid of Clarendon and dismissed him shortly after the signing of peace. He was tired of the old man who reproached him for his mistresses, rebuked him when he did not take the advice of the Privy Council, opposed his scheme for toleration, and had deliberately (or so it was suggested) limited the revenue that Parliament voted him so that he should not be able to undermine either the constitutional monarchy or the established Church.

Clarendon's dismissal did not satisfy the young men in the Commons who wanted to make sure that the fallen Chancellor would never again be able to threaten them. They decided on impeachment, and rallied their forces in the Commons. They could count on the presbyterian sympathisers, who hated the intolerant anglicanism with which Clarendon was associated, and on the independent country gentlemen who saw in the Chancellor the embodiment of Court corruption and intrigue. They could also count upon the eighty or so holders of office at Court, who had entered the House in one or other of the numerous by-elections and were tied to Charles by bonds of patronage that Clarendon had regarded as unworthy of his consideration. Clarendon was prepared to face his accusers, confident in the knowledge that he had done nothing illegal, but when it became clear to him that the King had united with his enemies in the Commons to destroy him, he realised the futility of opposition and fled to France. The King allowed him to keep his titles and the profits of his estates, but Parliament passed an Act of perpetual banishment against him. The man who, more than any other person, had brought about the Restoration spent the rest of his life in exile, reflecting on the vanished virtues of an earlier age and recording them for posterity in the *History of the Rebellion and Civil Wars in England*, which remains to this day one of the finest pieces of historical writing in the English language.

The CABAL

The politics of the next few years are associated with the CABAL— Sir Thomas Clifford, appointed Treasurer of the Household; Anthony Ashley Cooper, Baron Ashley, who kept his post as Chancellor of the Exchequer; the Duke of Buckingham, son of Charles I's favourite; Henry Bennet, Lord Arlington, one of the Secretaries of State; and John Maitland, Earl of Lauderdale, who ruled Scotland for the King. In this ill-assorted group Arlington and Lauderdale were the oldest members, but the other three were in their late thirties or forties, some twenty years younger than Clarendon, and representatives of a new political generation. In spite of its name the CABAL was never a united body and members had little more than their initials in common. The main division was between Arlington and Clifford,[1] who were in favour of an anti-French, pro-Dutch foreign policy, and Buckingham and Ashley, who were more inclined to France than to Holland. Members were united only in their ambition and in their opposition to Clarendon and all that he stood for. They disliked the cumbersome Privy Council, preferring more intimate and less formalised consultations. They also had little affection for the Church of England: Clifford and Arlington were Roman Catholic sympathisers, Lauderdale was a former presbyterian, Ashley had close links with the dissenters, and

---

[1] Clifford's catholic sympathies inclined him towards France, but as Arlington's protégé he could not, at this stage, risk his prospects of advancement by advocating such a policy.

Buckingham had married the daughter of Fairfax, the puritan leader of the parliamentary armies in the civil war.

Nothing would be farther from the truth than to imagine that the members of the CABAL came together at regular Cabinet meetings to advise the King on policy. Charles listened now to one, now to another, and played on personal rivalries in such a way that he was free to pursue his own desires. His experience with Clarendon had taught him never again to become the pawn of a statesman, but although he kept a careful watch on government, and attended meetings of councils and committees, he was not suited by temperament to the working out of general policies. He preferred an empirical approach, and the CABAL served as a screen behind which he could shift from one course of action to another. With Ministers who could never be sure of the King's confidence, and a King who was pursuing no consistent course, it is not surprising that English policy lost any clear sense of direction. As one historian has commented: 'By pitting his ministers against each other [Charles] did not secure control for himself, but merely ensured that nobody should be in control at all.'[1]

The European political situation was dominated by the ambitions of Louis XIV of France. One of Louis' main aims was to extend France's frontier to the 'natural' boundary of the Rhine, but to do this meant taking over the Spanish Netherlands, thereby imperilling the independence of Holland. Had Charles been entirely free to act as he pleased he would probably have allied with France. He admired and envied Louis, the 'Sun King', and his French mother and his years of exile in France had given him considerable affection for that country.

Unfortunately for Charles he had to consider English public opinion, particularly as expressed in Parliament. The Commons disliked the Dutch as commercial rivals, but they were coming to dread the French, who symbolised absolutism, catholic intolerance, and an aggressive expansionism—economic as well as political—that threatened England just as Spain had done a century earlier. Charles could not afford to do without the Commons, and had to tread warily to avoid offending their susceptibilities, particularly after the outcry caused by failure in the Dutch War. In 1665 the Commons had begun the practice of appropriating supplies for specific purposes, and in 1667 they appointed the first of many committees to audit public accounts. Charles needed all the goodwill he could muster if he was to preserve his control over policy from the grasp of the Lower House. Therefore,

[1] Andrew Browning, *English Historical Documents*, vol. VIII, p. 8.

while he kept in secret touch with Louis he encouraged Arlington to go ahead with plans for a league against France, and these reached fruition in January 1668 when the Triple Alliance was signed between England, Holland and Sweden. In this treaty the three powers agreed to terms they would impose upon France and Spain, in order to restore peace to Europe. Louis was in fact already negotiating peace terms, considerably to his own advantage, and the Triple Alliance was, from this point of view, stillborn. But the popularity of this 'Protestant League' in England gave Charles a breathing space; it also increased his value in the eyes of Louis XIV who, Charles hoped, might be tempted to buy him off at a handsome price.

Early in 1669 James, Duke of York and heir to the throne, disclosed to Charles, Clifford and Arlington that he had become a convert to the Roman Catholic faith. Charles took this opportunity of declaring that he also would like to promote the catholic faith in England, and asked for advice on how best to do so. As a result of the discussions that followed, new negotiations were opened with France, which led to the signing of the secret Treaty of Dover in May 1670. Charles agreed to assist Louis in war against Holland in return for a French subsidy. Payment of this, however, was to be dependent upon Charles's conversion to catholicism, and in the second clause of the treaty it was recorded that 'the King of England, being convinced of the truth of the Roman Catholic religion, is resolved to declare it and to reconcile himself with the Church of Rome as soon as the state of his country's affairs permit. He . . . will avail himself of the assistance of the King of France who . . . promises to pay to the King of England the sum of two million *livres tournois*, the first half payable three months after ratification of the present treaty, the other half three months later. In addition, the King of France undertakes to provide, at his own expense, six thousand troops for the execution of this design, if they should be required. The time for the declaration of catholicism is left entirely to the discretion of the King of England.'

The true significance of the secret treaty of Dover has remained a matter for controversy ever since it was signed. Charles was inclined towards catholicism and died in the Roman Catholic faith, but his lack of any fervent religious convictions makes it difficult to believe that spiritual considerations alone prompted his action. Yet Charles declared that he was anxious to announce his conversion, and he was only held back from doing so by the French insistence that Holland should be dealt with first.

Financial considerations no doubt played a big part in determining the King's attitude. The Commons had made big grants for the Second Dutch War, but these fell short of the real cost by £1,500,000 and the King was desperate for money. Yet the total sum offered by Louis XIV amounted to less than £170,000, a ridiculously small amount for a commitment on Charles's part which, if it became generally known, would jeopardise his throne. It may be that he was influenced by the pleadings of his favourite sister, Henrietta ('Minette'), Duchess of Orleans, who was a devout catholic and came over to Dover specially to speed negotiations, yet Charles did not usually allow affection to warp his political judgement. Perhaps the best explanation is that the King, faced with an increasingly critical Parliament which would obviously never solve his financial problem, clutched at the straw held out by Louis XIV, taking comfort from the fact that the timing of his conversion was a matter for himself alone.

Buckingham and the 'protestant' members of the CABAL knew nothing of these secret clauses. They were fooled by the 'open' Treaty of Dover, signed in December 1670, which contained only the provisions relating to joint war on Holland. Parliament knew nothing, of course, about either treaty, foreign affairs being reserved by long practice for the King's consideration alone. When the two Houses reassembled in October 1670 they assumed that the protestant league created by the Triple Alliance was still the keystone of Charles's foreign policy and showed their approval of it by voting subsidies estimated to bring in £800,000, as well as an additional excise. The success of the government was partly due to the skilful way in which Clifford, working on Arlington's behalf, had organised the 'King's men' in the Commons. The lesson was not lost on one of Buckingham's protégés, Sir Thomas Osborne, nor on the King himself who, some time later, reported that in this session the majority of the Commons 'were tied to his interests either by offices or by pensions'.

From April 1671 until February 1673 Parliament was in prorogation while the King made his preparations to put the Treaty of Dover into effect. The parliamentary grant enabled him to set out the fleet but did nothing to reduce the backlog of accumulated debt with which he was burdened. Much of his annual revenue was mortgaged in advance to his creditors, but with the approach of war the King needed all the money he could lay his hands on. In January 1672, therefore, by the Stop of the Exchequer, he put an end to repayment of loans and took all the revenue into his own hands. He offered to pay his creditors interest on their loans, but no longer bound himself to repay the principal. Not surprisingly the royal government lost the confidence of merchants and business men by its action, and found it even more difficult to raise fresh loans. The idea of a national debt had not yet gained general acceptance, and only became practical politics after Parliament had taken over the responsibility for national finance.

The Stop of the Exchequer was followed, in March 1672, by the Declaration of Indulgence, suspending the penal laws against Roman Catholics and dissenters. Roman Catholics were now free to worship privately, while dissenters could hold public services as long as they obtained an official licence. The Declaration was of great importance for the dissenters, since it acknowledged the failure of persecution to stamp them out, 'it being evident by the sad experience of twelve years that there is very little fruit of all those forcible courses', and many dissenting churches date their existence as organised congregations from 1672. On the surface the King was merely fulfilling the promise he had made at Breda, before his restoration, but the Declaration may also have been intended as a possible first stage in the attempt to reimpose catholicism on England.

Public opinion—the opinion, that is to say, of the politically articulate —was moving gradually towards acceptance of the principle of toleration, but there was widespread opposition to Charles's action. For one thing it implied that the King had power to suspend the operation of statute law and, for another, it was issued at a time when rumours about the King's private leanings encouraged the suspicion that the main aim of the Declaration was not to relieve protestant nonconformists so much as to prepare the way for a Roman Catholic restoration.

The success of the King's policy now depended upon the outcome of the third Dutch War which opened in March 1672, when Louis XIV's preparations were complete. Charles did his best to win support for his plans. Lauderdale was made a duke, Arlington an earl, and Clifford a baron, while Ashley was given the Earldom of Shaftesbury. It was at this date also that Sir Thomas Osborne, who had shown his financial ability as Treasurer of the Navy, was appointed to the Privy Council. Arlington, who opposed the war, dropped into the background. The leading members of the administration were Clifford and Shaftesbury, who had a deep interest in commercial matters, regarded the Dutch as dangerous rivals, and valued the policy of toleration. In November 1672 Shaftesbury was made Lord Chancellor, while Clifford was given the white staff of the Lord Treasurer.

The plan of campaign was that French troops, with a small English contingent, would be responsible for land operations, while the English fleet, aided by a French squadron, would attack the Dutch at sea. The opportunity to win a decisive victory, which would have opened the coast of Holland to invasion, came in May 1672 when the Earl of Sandwich, commanding the English fleet, joined battle with De Ruyter in Solebay (Southwold Bay) off Suffolk. Both sides fought stubbornly, but Sandwich was killed after his flagship blew up and the Dutch fleet was able to withdraw, battered but intact.

Meanwhile, on land, the French invasion of Holland had met with rapid success and had driven the Dutch to sue for peace. The terms dictated by Louis were, however, so humiliating that the Dutch preferred to continue fighting. The republican leaders were assassinated and the Prince of Orange was recalled to power to meet the emergency. He ordered the dykes to be cut, and the French advance slowed to a halt in a slough of mud.

Charles could not fight the war without parliamentary grants, and the two Houses assembled in February 1673. Shaftesbury made his famous *Delenda est Carthago* speech, declaring that 'the States of Holland are England's eternal enemy both by interest and inclination', and the Commons proposed to vote generous supply, but only on condition that the King abandoned his claim to suspend the laws. In an address to Charles they asserted that 'penal statutes, in matters ecclesiastical, cannot be suspended but by Act of Parliament', and when the King assured them in his reply that he did not 'pretend to the right of suspending any laws wherein the properties, rights or liberties of any of his subjects are concerned', they told him that his answer was 'not sufficient to clear the apprehensions that may justly remain in the minds of your people'.

Buckingham and Clifford advised Charles to protect his prerogative by refusing to withdraw the Declaration, and Lauderdale even suggested the use of Scottish troops to enforce the royal will, but Arlington urged the King to abandon not only the Declaration but the whole pro-French, anti-Dutch policy of which it was a part. In order to win Shaftesbury over to his view, Arlington revealed to him the details of the secret Treaty of Dover, and from this moment onwards the Lord Chancellor, angry at the way in which he had been deceived, began to move away from the 'Court' and appeal to the 'Country'—all those who distrusted the papist tendencies at Whitehall and wanted to see the re-establishment of what they thought to be traditional English virtues.

Charles cancelled the Declaration in March 1673, and Parliament voted £1,250,000 for the war, but only after it had also passed the Test Act, banning from office all who refused to take the sacrament according to the Church of England and to make a public declaration against transubstantiation. The aim of the Act was to put an end to rumours of papists in high places, and to make it clear that the Commons were voting money only for a 'protestant war'. When, however, it became law, the rumours were given unexpected confirmation. James resigned his office as Lord High Admiral, and Clifford gave up the Treasury.

Danby

The King had not abandoned his catholic policy, but he saw the need to temporise. The parliamentary grant was swallowed up by war expenditure, and shortage of money remained acute. Charles, casting round for someone to replace Clifford, picked on Sir Thomas Osborne, who had shown his financial ability as Treasurer of the Navy. In July 1673 Osborne was given the white staff.

Osborne's aim, like that of Lionel Cranfield half a century earlier, was to achieve a short-term balance between income and expenditure, but the major source of expenditure was war, and the new Treasurer was not yet powerful enough to bring about a major change in policy. His position was improved, however, when Parliament assembled in the autumn of 1673, for members were strongly critical of France and wanted to see the war brought to a close. Any chance of a decisive victory was lost in August of that year when, at the Battle of the Texel, the French squadron withdrew from the fight. Prince Rupert, the English commander, put all his anger into his despatches: 'it was the plainest and greatest opportunity ever lost at sea', he wrote. 'It wanted neither signal nor instruction to tell him [the French admiral] what he should then have done—the case was so plain to every man's eye in the whole fleet.' Parliament took up the complaint against France, refused to vote supply, protested against a standing army, martial law and compulsory billeting of troops, and expressed its anger at the action of James who had taken a Roman Catholic princess, Mary of Modena, as his second wife after the death of Anne Hyde.

Now that Parliament had refused to aid the King, the Lord Treasurer became the key figure in the administration, for it depended on him whether the government went bankrupt or attained a precarious solvency. Osborne had many of the virtues of Clarendon, but he was also to become a skilled parliamentary manager. He wanted a protestant foreign policy, to turn the Commons' hostility into cooperation and thereby prepare the ground for a final parliamentary solution of the financial problem. Meanwhile, he cut down on pensions and salaries, and made honesty and economy his aims. His ability as a financial administrator gradually won him the King's support, especially as none of the other CABAL ministers had anything to offer. Clifford had committed suicide, Shaftesbury had gone over to the opposition, Arlington had no clear policy, and as for Buckingham he was

> A man so various that he seemed to be
> Not one, but all mankind's epitome:
> Stiff in opinions, always in the wrong,
> Was everything by starts and nothing long;
> But in the course of one revolving moon
> Was chemist, fiddler, statesman and buffoon.[1]

Shaftesbury was dismissed from the Lord Chancellorship in November 1673—'It is only laying down my gown and putting on my sword', he commented—and Heneage Finch, a lawyer and ally of Osborne, became Lord Keeper in his place. Arlington stayed in office long enough to negotiate the Treaty of Westminster, which brought about a separate peace between England and Holland in February 1674, but resigned his Secretaryship later in the year. Osborne was gradually attaining a primacy in the King's counsels unparalleled since the fall of Clarendon, and in June 1674 he was created Earl of Danby.

The new earl was a Yorkshire landowner, but the wealth of his family came from the business acumen of his great-grandfather, the descendant of a small gentry family who had taken up the cloth trade in London and had risen to be Lord Mayor. During the civil war the Osborne estates had been sequestered and the strain of raising money to buy them back hastened the death of Danby's father in 1647.

Danby himself was only fifteen at the time, and the heavy responsibility which fell on him helps to explain the toughness of his character. He was that comparatively rare combination—the Tory squire turned politician. Like his fellow squires he had come to support the Church of England and hate the puritans, to suspect popery and corruption at Court, and to see the hopes of English greatness residing in harmony between a protestant King and an anglican Parliament. Danby was one of the 'young cavaliers' who had led the attack on Clarendon in the

[1] Dryden: *Absalom and Achitophel.*

M*

Commons, but he shared many of Clarendon's ideals and devoted himself to the task of committing Charles to an anti-French, protestant policy which would, he hoped, win the King the confidence and financial support of the Commons.

Danby was inclined at first to rely upon the attractiveness of his policy to win the favour of the House of Commons, but in this he reckoned without Louis XIV. The emergence of England as an active protestant champion threatened to check French expansion, and Louis was ready to use French money to bribe members of Parliament and encourage them to an open breach with the executive. It is unlikely that the money paid by Louis or by anyone else created changes of opinion in the Commons: its effect was to persuade those who were already critical of government policies to organise themselves. The opposition in Parliament had good enough reasons for its attitude without French gold. Charles's continued flirtation with France made the Commons suspicious of him, and members were not ready to trust Danby. How could they be sure that the King and his chief minister were not plotting to deceive Parliament once again, by persuading it to vote money for a protestant war that would in fact be used to establish a French-style, catholic absolutism?

If Charles had stood firmly behind Danby, harmony between King and Parliament might eventually have been achieved. Mutual confidence was all that was lacking, and time could have built this. There is no reason to suppose that Charles was deliberately working *against* such a reconciliation. Those who picture the King as a Machiavellian intriguer, juggling men to suit his long-prepared designs, surely do him a disservice. Charles's main aim was to keep his throne and live comfortably, and he was prepared to embrace a protestant policy if this would achieve the required result; Louis XIV, at any rate, was sufficiently convinced of Charles's change of heart to spend thousands of pounds on frustrating Danby's plans. But Charles II did not want to be caught in the same trap as his father, who had committed himself to war at the Commons' request, only to find, as he told them bitterly, that '[now] I am so far engaged that you think there is no retreat . . . you begin to set the dice and make your own game'. The King therefore kept up the secret link with Louis as an insurance in case Danby should not succeed. Unfortunately, by doing so he created an atmosphere of suspicion that ensured Danby's failure.

Throughout 1675 Danby tried to reach agreement with Parliament, and began organising the King's men in the Commons as Clifford had done before him. Pensions and offices were carefully distributed, and the nucleus of a royalist 'party' was created. This produced a natural reaction. By emphasising that certain members were *in* the golden circle of Court patronage it encouraged the *outs* to organise themselves. The hard core of the Commons remained, as always, the independent, uncommitted country gentlemen, but on either wing there were organised groups, neither of them strong enough to command a majority, but each working constantly to win over a sufficient number of the uncommitted to give it victory.

Parliament did not meet in 1676. The King, despairing of agreement, was moving closer to France, while Danby was reinforcing his position by extending the range of patronage. Fortunately for him his economy measures were beginning to take effect, and a revival of trade—helped by the fact that England was at peace while the Dutch and French were still fighting—increased the yield of Customs and Excise.

When the Cavalier Parliament met for its fifteenth session in February 1677 Danby and the Court party were well organised, and the Commons voted £600,000 for the Navy as well as renewing the additional excise originally granted in 1670. The voting of supply on this scale was a major victory for Danby and might have led to closer cooperation between King and Parliament had it not coincided with news of a big French offensive against the Dutch. The Commons petitioned Charles to make a firm alliance against France and promised him further supply once he had declared war. Charles wanted the grant *before* he committed himself so irrevocably, but the Commons would not agree to this: their attitude was expressed by the member who recalled 'that example of Harry the Seventh, who got aids for the war and presently struck up a peace'. This was the testing moment for Danby's policy, and he came within an ace of success. But the King would not take the decisive step until he was sure of supply, and consequently the session petered out in acrimonious exchanges, the King reminding the Commons that 'should I suffer this fundamental power of making peace and war to be so far invaded (though but once) as to have the manner and circumstances of leagues prescribed to me by Parliament, it is plain that no prince or state would any longer believe that the sovereignty of England rests in the Crown'.

Danby, in an effort to reassure the Commons, persuaded the King to agree to a marriage between William of Orange, the protestant champion, and James's daughter Mary, and in January 1678 he followed this up with a treaty between England and Holland by which both sides

agreed to impose peace on Louis, if necessary by force. Parliament
reassembled in January 1678 and members were once again called on to
vote supply to the Crown so that a protestant policy could be put into
effect. But everything hinged upon the actual declaration of war, and
Charles shrank from this. He was afraid, as he told one of his advisers,
that the Commons 'had a mind to engage him in a war and then leave
him in it, unless they might have their terms in removing and filling of
places'. The Commons, on the other hand, were afraid that if they
voted money they might be putting an end to their effectiveness. As
one member said, 'the States of France gave the King power to raise
money upon extraordinary occasions till their next meeting. And they
never met more.'

Even Danby seems to have despaired, at this stage, of winning the
Commons over, and he could offer no effective alternative to a French
alliance. At the King's command he wrote to the English ambassador
in Paris, Ralph Montague, ordering him to go ahead with negotiations
for a French subsidy. This was the situation when, in September 1678,
Titus Oates—a turncoat Jesuit and liar of the first quality—and his
associate Israel Tonge, laid before a protestant magistrate the details
of the Popish Plot.

The Popish Plot

Oates claimed to have secret information that the Pope had ordered the
Jesuits to overthrow the government of England, kill the King, and
place his brother James on the throne. French troops were to be used to
carry out this design, and it was to be accompanied by a general
massacre of protestants. This fantastic story came at just the right
moment, for the rooted suspicion of catholics that had existed in an
acute form since the Gunpowder Plot had been inflamed by rumours
about the King's secret policy. There *was*, in fact, a popish plot—
though not the one Oates claimed to know about—and this explains
why Oates's revelations were believed by people who were not
ordinarily so gullible.

What lingering doubts there might have been about the truth
of Oates's story were swept away when the protestant magistrate,
Sir Edmund Berry Godfrey, was found dead on Primrose Hill. The
mystery of his death remains unsolved to this day, but it was immediately assumed that the papists had killed him to prevent further disclosures. By the time Parliament met in October, London was in a

ferment, and nothing was discussed but the Plot. Oates had accused Coleman, the Duke of York's secretary, of being implicated, and when Coleman's papers were searched, copies were discovered of letters to foreign correspondents, describing enthusiastically the 'mighty work' of 'subduing a pestilent heresy which has domineered over part of this northern world a long time'.

Before the end of 1678 Shaftesbury had taken up Oates and made himself the champion of the Plot. Shaftesbury was a great Dorset landowner, with big commercial connexions, especially with the colonies. He was a skilful politician, unscrupulous but not unprincipled, and his close friend and adviser was John Locke, who was already at work on the *Two Treatises of Government* in which he provided a philosophical basis for Shaftesbury's belief that government depended on an implied contract between the property-owners and the ruler, a contract which became invalid if the ruler attempted to deny his obligations and turn himself into an absolute monarch. Shaftesbury was not a republican. He was in favour of limited monarchy and had been prominent among those who urged Cromwell to take the crown. He saw in James a threat to everything he believed in, and took advantage of the anti-catholicism inflamed by the Plot to try to force Charles to accept legislation excluding James from the throne. To do this he built up a powerful party in Parliament, linked with the Green Ribbon Club in London and with its branches throughout the country. Pamphlets were published, Pope-burning processions organised, and public opinion marshalled in such a manner that the opposition in Parliament became for a few years a party in the modern sense, with a political programme and national organisation. And at the centre, working tirelessly to achieve the single end of exclusion, was Shaftesbury, small in stature, great in his ambitions. Dryden, in *Absalom and Achitophel*, has left an unforgettable picture of him:

> For close designs and crooked counsels fit.
> Sagacious, bold, and turbulent of wit,
> Restless, unfixed in principles and place,
> In power unpleased, impatient of disgrace;
>   ......
> A daring pilot in extremity,
> Pleased with the danger when the waves went high,
> He sought the storms; but, for a calm unfit,
> Would steer too nigh the sands, to boast his wit.

The opposition won their first victory when Montague, now a member of the Commons, was persuaded to reveal to a shocked House the details of Danby's negotiations for a French subsidy. This seemed to confirm that Danby, while pretending to be a supporter of the protestant interest, had all the time been working to destroy it, and the Commons voted his impeachment. Rather than risk further disclosures the King prorogued Parliament, and in January 1679 he at last dissolved it. The Cavalier Parliament had been in existence for nearly eighteen years, during which time the Crown had built up its influence in such such a way that long parliaments seemed to be almost as much of a danger to the liberty of the subject as no parliaments. The opposition had been clamouring for dissolution and now they were rewarded.

The election was, as always, fought over local rather than national issues, but when the new Commons assembled in March 1679 it became clear that the majority of members were strongly exclusionist. Parliament immediately revived Danby's impeachment, and the fact that the King had given him a pardon under the great seal only added to their indignation. The Treasurer was clearly of no more use to the King. In March he resigned his office, and in the following month the House of Lords committed him to the Tower to await trial.

Charles now made a bid for broader support by enlarging the Privy Council and restoring it to the position it had earlier held. The period after the Restoration had seen the emergence of a smaller body, sometimes called the Cabinet Council, which was more fitted, as Charles explained, for the 'secrecy and dispatch that are necessary in many great affairs'. Now, however, he made Shaftesbury Lord President of a Council that included not only courtiers and officials, like the Earl of Sunderland, but also such opposition leaders as Essex and Russell. By doing this Charles hoped to divide the opposition leaders from their followers and avoid the mistake that his father had made in a similar situation in 1641.

The Commons voted £200,000 to disband the army, then passed a Bill excluding James from the throne and providing that the Crown should pass to the next in succession, as though James had been dead. Tempers were rising, and memories of an earlier conflict were revived when John Hampden's grandson was chosen to introduce the Exclusion Bill to the House. Shaftesbury was busy whipping up anger against James, whom he described as 'heady, violent and bloody, who easily believes the rashest and worst of counsels to be most sincere and hearty. . . . His interest and designs are to introduce a military and arbitrary government.' Charles, however, stood firm. He offered to accept statutory limitations on his brother's authority, but not exclusion. When Parliament went ahead with exclusion he dissolved it, with nothing accomplished except the Habeas Corpus Act, designed to protect the subject against arbitrary imprisonment.

A new Parliament was due to meet in October 1679, but Charles prorogued it before it even assembled. He realised now that his enemies would not compromise, and he determined to fight them. Shaftesbury was dismissed from the Council in October, and the King turned for advice to Sunderland and two commissioners of the Treasury— Laurence Hyde, Clarendon's second son, and Sidney Godolphin. He was playing for time, in hopes that the passions aroused by Shaftesbury's exploitation of the Plot would die down. Shaftesbury, of course, concentrated on keeping passions alive. While Oates's victims were condemned and executed, a flood of pamphlets called on the landowners to protect their own interests. 'If any men who have estates in abbey lands desire to beg their bread and relinquish their habitation and fortunes to some old, greasy, bald-pated abbot,' wrote one pamphleteer, 'then let them vote for a popish successor and popery!'

When the new Parliament at last met, in October 1680, a second Exclusion Bill was introduced and passed the Commons. It was careful not to name the alternative successor to James, however, for the opposition was divided on this issue. Some members wanted Mary, James's daughter and wife of William of Orange; others, including Shaftesbury, wanted Charles's illegitimate son, the Duke of Monmouth. The decisive debate came in the Lords, where Charles had two big advantages. The first was the fact that he was always present at debates, standing with his back to the fireplace, noting the points made by successive speakers, and now and again making an effective interjection. The second was the conviction of the Earl of Halifax that limitations, of the sort proposed by Charles, were a better bet than exclusion. During the course of the heated debate Halifax rose to speak sixteen times, and his pleading, combined with Charles's presence, was effective. The Lords rejected the Bill by thirty-three votes.

In January 1681 Charles dissolved Parliament and summoned a new one to meet at Oxford, away from the London mob and the influence of the Green Ribbon Club. He also dismissed Sunderland,

who had lost his nerve and come out in favour of exclusion, and made
Halifax his chief adviser. The opposition—or the Whigs, as they
were coming to be called, to distinguish them from the Tory anglicans
—were still in a commanding position, and rode into Oxford with their
bands of retainers, confident of victory. Shaftesbury was counting on
the fact that the King would have to give way or go bankrupt. What
he did not know was that the revival of trade was bringing the royal
revenue up to and even above the figure of £1,200,000 originally
intended by the Commons. Charles had also been promised a small
pension by Louis XIV who was at last alarmed by the success of the
opposition and realised that to maintain deadlock and keep England
impotent in international affairs, he would have to switch his support to
the King.

In his opening speech to the Oxford Parliament Charles emphasised
that he had taken his stand on law, and that if the rules governing
succession were changed no man's property would be safe. He offered
to accept any limitations on James that Parliament would propose,
but made it clear that he would never accept exclusion. Whether he
was genuine in his offer of limitations was never put to the test, for
Shaftesbury clung to exclusion, convinced that if sufficient pressure was
put on the King he would eventually give way. 'If you are restrained
only by law and justice,' he said to Charles in the Lords, 'rely on us and
leave us to act. We will make laws which will give legality to a measure
so necessary for the quiet of the nation.' 'Let there be no delusion,'
replied the King. 'I will not yield, nor will I be bullied. Men usually
become timid as they become older. It is the opposite with me, and for
what may remain of my life I am determined that nothing will
tarnish my reputation. I have law and reason and all right-thinking
men on my side. I have the Church [here he pointed to the bishops]
and nothing will ever separate us.'

The Commons insisted on going ahead with exclusion. On 28 March
Charles went to the Lords as usual, with his crown and robes following
secretly in a sedan chair. Both Houses were taken by surprise when the
King appeared robed and crowned and commanded their presence
before him. The Whigs still expected victory, but Charles announced
the dissolution of Parliament. Had his enemies been warned they might
have organised, and had they been in London they might have taken
the initiative into their own hands. Charles, however, had his Life-
Guards at Oxford and made it clear that he would fight if necessary.
The Whig bluff had been called. The country would not follow

Shaftesbury into the horrors of another civil war. The Whig lords and their retinues talked violence, but in the end they dispersed peaceably, while the King returned speedily to London.

The Royalist Reaction

After the fever of the Plot, apathy set in, of which the King took full advantage. Shaftesbury was arrested on a charge of high treason and brought before the grand jury of Middlesex. The Whig sheriffs of London, who were responsible for choosing the jury, had done their work well, however, and the Earl was acquitted. He called on Monmouth to raise London in revolt while he spread rebellion throughout the country, but the Whig moment had passed and Shaftesbury was lucky to escape to Holland where he died the following year. In June 1683 the other Whig leaders were accused—justly or unjustly—of planning to assassinate Charles at the Rye House, near Hoddesdon, on his way back from the races at Newmarket. The Earl of Essex committed suicide after his arrest: Russell and Sidney were tried, condemned and executed.

Charles remodelled the judicial bench, to make sure that it would not oppose his will, and in 1683 appointed Jeffreys as Chief Justice. With the judges behind him the King took action against the municipal corporations, the strongholds of the Whigs, to ensure that when Parliament met again it should not be dominated by his enemies. Parliamentary boroughs derived their corporate existence and their privileges from royal charter, but in many cases they carried out functions for which there was no specific authorisation. They were now subjected to *Quo Warranto* investigations, to determine by what right they claimed the powers they used. Many boroughs preferred to surrender their charters rather than risk legal investigation. As for the others, they crumpled before the majesty of the law. Even London, the greatest corporation of all, was punished for its refusal to condemn Shaftesbury, by being called upon to defend its privileges in the King's Bench. Judgement was given against it, and an order was made 'that the franchise and liberty of London be taken into the King's hands'. Charles was pleased to restore all the rights of his capital city, but only on condition that no official should in future be elected without his consent. The same condition was imposed on hundreds of other boroughs throughout the kingdom. The King now controlled the borough governments which elected the majority of members of the House of Commons.

This was a solution to the constitutional problem that had been anticipated in 1660, but had not been fully developed.

The closing years of Charles II's reign were the Indian summer of
the Stuarts. Tories replaced Whigs in county administration as well as
in the boroughs, and from pulpits throughout the land the sinfulness of
resistance to the will of a divinely appointed monarch was preached.
So secure was the King that when, under the terms of the Triennial
Act of 1664, another Parliament became due in 1684, he deliberately
flouted the law and did not summon it. Halifax protested, but there
was no general outcry. The ubiquitous and time-serving Sunderland
came back as Secretary in 1682, and was joined in 1684 by Godolphin.
The year 1684 also saw the release from the Tower of Danby and
the Roman Catholic peers imprisoned there at the time of the Popish
Plot. Danby, however, was not recalled to office. The anglican-
parliamentary policy for which he stood was dead, so far as Charles
was concerned, and the King came to lean more and more upon his
brother James.

It was James who, in February 1685, when the King had a stroke
and was obviously dying, sent for a Roman Catholic priest to receive
him into the Church of Rome. At this late stage, therefore, Charles at
last carried out the promise he had made in the Treaty of Dover to
declare himself a catholic. As for the second part of his promise, to
restore the Roman Catholic faith in his kingdom, he left this, by default,
to his brother James.

Charles had kept his throne and preserved his prerogative intact
by a combination of good luck and good judgement. By showing up
the weaknesses of the Restoration settlement he prepared the way for
the constitutional changes of 1689, but these might never have come
about had Charles been succeeded by a ruler as flexible and as tolerant
as himself. The irony of Charles's reign lies in the fact that his greatest
success carried the seeds of failure in it: by safeguarding the succession
of his brother James he ensured the destruction of the monarchy and
dynasty he had so skilfully preserved.

16

The Glorious Revolution

'Iꜰ it had not been for his popery he would have been, if not a great, yet a good prince.' In these words Bishop Burnet pithily and accurately summed up James II. The new King had much to be said in his favour. He was honest and hard-working, and he wanted to see his country become once again a major power in Europe—not for him the dependence on France that had come to characterise Charles II. He had, it is true, an exalted view of kingship which would sooner or later have brought him into conflict with Parliament, but he shared so many of the attitudes of the Tory squires who dominated the Commons that he could probably have arrived at a *modus vivendi* with them. Yet he threw away all his advantages because of his determination to secure at least toleration for his fellow catholics. He might have been content with toleration, but the prevailing suspicion of popery made any move towards relaxing the penal laws seem like the first step towards a restoration of the Roman Catholic religion. Suspicion of James's intention was reinforced by knowledge of his character. Lauderdale observed that he 'loves, as he saith, to be served in his own way, and he is as very a papist as the Pope himself, which will be his ruin. . . . If he had the empire of the whole world he would venture the loss of it, for his ambition is to shine in a red letter after he is dead.'

Towards a Catholic England. I: Toleration

James hoped at first to gain toleration for Roman Catholics by the cooperation of the anglican Tories, and he assured the Privy Council that he would 'preserve this government both in Church and state as it is now by law established. I know the principles of the Church of England are for monarchy, and the members of it have showed themselves good and loyal subjects. Therefore I shall always take care to defend and support it.' The composition of James's first ministry showed that he meant what he said. The Lord Treasurer was Laurence Hyde, now Earl of Rochester, and the Lord Privy Seal was Henry Hyde, second Earl of Clarendon. These two brothers, James's relations by marriage, were pillars of the Anglican Church, and so were Godolphin and Halifax, who retained his post as Lord President of the Council. Only Sunderland, who managed to keep his Secretaryship, was lacking in any real enthusiasm for the Church of England.

Sunderland prepared for the election of Parliament with considerable thoroughness, sending letters to Lords-Lieutenant and influential noblemen asking them to make sure that only the 'well-affected' were returned. He was helped by the fact that the remodelling of the municipal corporations had brought them under much closer royal control, and when Parliament met it turned out to be the most loyal that any Stuart ever had the pleasure to encounter. Even James reckoned there were only about forty members of whose devotion he could not be certain.

James's opening speech to Parliament when it assembled in May 1685 was not a model of tact. He warned members not to vote him small sums from time to time in hopes that they would thereby ensure the regular summons of Parliament: such a proceeding would, he said, 'be a very improper method to take with me. . . . The best way to engage me to meet you often is always to use me well.' Far from resenting this tone, Parliament responded by treating James very well. He was voted for life all the revenues that Charles II had been given, which were estimated to be worth £1,500,000 a year now that trade was expanding, as well as an extra £400,000 a year for a period of eight years. James was in the happy position of enjoying a revenue of a little under two million pounds, and this enabled him, at a later date, to dispense with Parliament altogether.

In June 1685, a month after Parliament had assembled, the Duke of Monmouth landed in the west country to raise a protestant rebellion. The loyalty of Parliament was reflected throughout England, for nobody of any consequence joined the rebels. Monmouth could command the support only of poor men who had nothing to hope for from the existing system, and who may genuinely have believed that their religion was in danger. Without the cooperation of the landowners, however, the rebellion was stillborn. Monmouth led his peasants against the royal forces encamped on Sedgemoor, but his

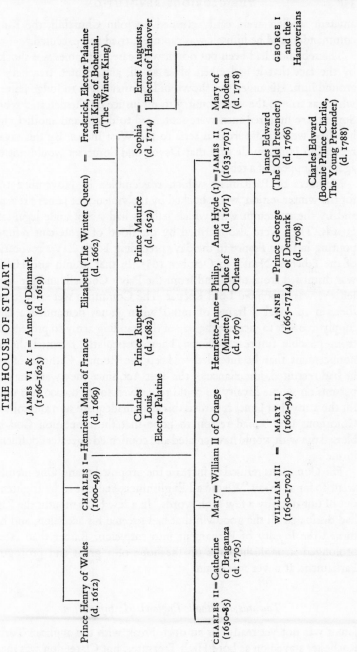

THE HOUSE OF STUART

JAMES VI & I = Anne of Denmark
(1566-1625)   (d. 1619)

Prince Henry of Wales   CHARLES I = Henrietta Maria of France   Elizabeth (The Winter Queen) = Frederick, Elector Palatine
(d. 1612)   (1600-49)   (d. 1669)   (d. 1662)   and King of Bohemia.
                                                                                                 (The Winter King)

Charles   Prince Rupert   Prince Maurice   Sophia = Ernst Augustus,
Louis,   (d. 1682)   (d. 1652)   (d. 1714) Elector of Hanover
Elector
Palatine   GEORGE I
                                                         and the Hanoverians

CHARLES II = Catherine   Mary = William II of Orange   Henrietta-Anne = Philip,   ANNE = Prince George   Anne Hyde (I) = JAMES II = Mary of Modena
(1630-85)   of Braganza   (Minette)   Duke of   (1665-1714) of Denmark (d. 1671)   (1633-1701)   (d. 1718)
            (d. 1705)   (d. 1670)   Orleans   (d. 1708)

                          WILLIAM III = MARY II   James Edward
                          (1650-1702)   (1662-94)   (The Old Pretender)
                                                                                                   (d. 1766)

                                                                                                   Charles Edward
                                                                                                   (Bonnie Prince Charlie,
                                                                                                   The Young Pretender)
                                                                                                   (d. 1788)

amateur soldiers were easily crushed by John Churchill, the King's commander, and he himself was captured, tried and executed.

The rebellion had been put down with ease, but James was shocked by the fact that it had taken place at all, and scented treachery all around him. His anger was shown in his instructions to Judge Jeffreys, who was sent to the west country to do justice on the defeated rebels. Some three hundred men were sentenced to death, and another eight hundred were transported as serfs to the West Indies. By this savage repression James made sure that Devon and Somerset would not rise again in support of a rebel.

Members of Parliament, which reassembled in November 1685 for the winter session, were shocked by the violence of James's revenge and by the contempt with which Jeffreys had swept aside legal safeguards. They were also alarmed by the flood of protestant refugees pouring in from France in the days preceding Louis XIV's revocation of the Edict of Nantes in October 1685. In that month also Halifax was dismissed from office and from the Privy Council, and the hated Jeffreys was appointed Lord Keeper. The Commons were not, therefore, in so loyal a frame of mind when James demanded a large supply in order to increase the size of the standing army to protect him from possible future rebellions. They particularly resented the announcement that he intended to keep the Roman Catholic officers he had recruited, in defiance of the Test Act, since they were the only persons on whose loyalty he could rely. Even so £700,000 was voted for the army, but James regarded this as an inadequate sum and told the Commons that 'I had reason to hope that the reputation God has blessed me with would have created and confirmed a greater confidence in me'.

The Commons refused to increase the proposed grant. One member went so far as to say 'We are all Englishmen, and not to be frightened out of our duty by a few high words.' In a few brief months the King had dissipated all the goodwill that had greeted his accession, and had turned the loyalty of Parliament into suspicion. Rather than face a prolonged struggle he gave up the hope of a grant and prorogued Parliament. It never met again.

Towards a Catholic England. II: Infiltration

James was not yet ready for an open break with the anglican Tories. Rochester stayed on as Lord High Treasurer, but Clarendon was made

Lord-Lieutenant of Ireland, and his place as Lord Privy Seal was taken by Sunderland, who retained his Secretaryship. Sunderland was by now the King's chief minister, in fact if not in name, and the 'Cabinets' which met at his house were far more important in policy-making than the Privy Council. These Cabinets had no formal existence and no fixed membership; they could therefore include Roman Catholics, and Father Petre, James's Jesuit confessor, was a frequent attender.

Since the anglican Tories refused to cooperate with James in his plans for catholic toleration, the King used his dispensing power to infiltrate Roman Catholics into the Church, the army, the universities and the royal administration. There was some doubt, however, whether the King had sufficient authority to dispense with statute law. The matter was brought to a head through a test case in 1686 when Edward Hales, a Roman Catholic officer who had refused to take the oaths prescribed under the Test Act, defended himself on the grounds that he had a royal dispensation. Eleven of the twelve judges maintained that the dispensation was valid, and Chief Justice Herbert, giving judgement, delivered himself of the opinion 'that the Kings of England are sovereign princes; that the laws of England are the King's laws; that therefore 'tis an inseparable prerogative in the Kings of England to dispense with penal laws in particular cases and upon particular necessary reasons . . . [and] that this is not a trust invested in or granted to the King by the people, but the ancient remains of the sovereign power and the prerogative of the Kings of England, which never yet was taken from them, nor can be'.

This momentous judgement, with its insistence on the inalienable prerogative, meant that there was now no legal barrier preventing James from carrying out his policy of Romanisation. He anticipated trouble from the Church, however, and to make his task easier he set up, in July 1686, a body of Ecclesiastical Commissioners to discipline clergy who opposed his will. The Ecclesiastical Commission was not a court, neither did it have jurisdiction over laymen, but it bore a sufficiently close resemblance to the hated Court of High Commission, which the Long Parliament had abolished, to encourage the belief that James intended to use the same instruments as his father. Among the first persons to be dealt with by the commissioners was Compton, Bishop of London, who had refused to take the required action against one of his clergy for preaching an anti-catholic sermon. For this offence Compton was suspended from his functions—a clear warning to any other bishop who was considering resistance.

The dismissal of Clarendon and Rochester in January 1687 marked the end of James's attempt to achieve his aims through cooperation with the Tories. He now turned to the Whigs, whose links with the dissenters might make them more receptive to a policy of toleration. In April 1687 the first Declaration of Indulgence suspended the penal laws against catholics and dissenters, and in the following months James ordered the release from prison of leading nonconformists, and asked them for their cooperation. Some of them, including William Penn, the Quaker founder of Pennsylvania, believed (with some reason) that James was sincere in his advocacy of toleration, but most treated it with suspicion. They were more impressed by Halifax's observation, in his *Letter to a Dissenter*, that 'you are therefore to be hugged now, only that you may be the better squeezed at another time'.

One of the biggest problems facing James was the shortage of Roman Catholics of sufficient ability and experience to fill key positions in the government of the Church and state. The anglicans had long monopolised the universities, which existed to train young men for these tasks, and in the spring of 1687, therefore, James began putting pressure on Oxford and Cambridge to admit papists. When Cambridge refused to give a degree to a Benedictine monk, the Ecclesiastical Commission deprived the Vice-Chancellor of his office; and when the fellows of Magdalen College, Oxford, refused to elect a Roman Catholic head, James eventually turned out all twenty-five of them and appointed catholics in their place. Magdalen became, to all intents and purposes, a seminary for training the future rulers of catholic England.

If James had been content to move gradually he *might*, conceivably, have achieved his aims. But in 1687 he was fifty-four and could not count on having many more years to live. He knew that his death would lead, like that of Mary Tudor, to a reversal of all the work he had done, for he had no son to succeed him and the heir to the throne was his protestant daughter Mary, wife of William of Orange. More rapid and sweeping Romanisation was needed, but for this he required the cooperation of Parliament which alone could pass and repeal the necessary statutes. In July he declared the dissolution of the prorogued Parliament and ordered Sunderland to make the necessary preliminary preparations for a new one.

Before Parliament could meet, a further remodelling of local government was carried out, to remove the anglican Tories whom Charles II had appointed to buttress his throne. Since catholics were not avail-able in sufficient numbers, and the Whigs were as hostile as the Tories, James had to appoint many people who had no personal standing in their localities. The leading local families were, not surprisingly, outraged, and one Yorkshire squire who had served Charles II and James II loyally wrote of his astonishment at the new Justices of the Peace for his county. 'The first', he said, 'can neither write nor read, the second is a bailiff . . . and neither of them have one foot of freehold land in England.' By challenging the authority of the land-owners, who were the natural supporters of monarchy, James was preparing his downfall.

Many of the anglican leaders, including Danby, Nottingham and the Bishop of London, were already in touch with William of Orange. The Dutch prince had been careful not to offend James, and at the time of the Monmouth rebellion had returned the English troops in his service so that they might be used against the rebels. But as James's reign went on its headstrong course, William came to fear that the King would be driven into increasing dependence on France, to save him from the anger of his own subjects. William had devoted his life to fighting France and checking the ambitions of Louis XIV. He was not prepared to stand by while England became, once again, a French satellite, but he bided his time, like most of the English leaders, hoping that the eventual death of James would solve all problems.

In a further bid for dissenter support in the forthcoming Parliament, James issued a second Declaration of Indulgence in April 1688, and ordered the anglican clergy to give this the maximum publicity by reading it from their pulpits. Archbishop Sancroft and six of his fellow bishops petitioned James against this order, and the King promptly commanded their arrest and trial on a charge of seditious libel. Excite-ment was mounting in London, and the bishops became, perhaps for the first time, popular heroes. But before their trial began, a major blow was struck at protestant hopes. James's wife, Mary of Modena, after several miscarriages, at last gave birth to a son.

The Glorious Revolution

The birth of a Prince of Wales meant that the death of James would be followed not by the accession of the protestant Mary but by the rule of another catholic King. The anglican leaders showed their bitterness by refusing to accept that James Edward was in truth the King's son.

While James hailed the birth of his child as a signal mark of divine favour, his opponents spread the rumour that the baby had been smuggled into Mary's bed in a warming-pan and had no drop of royal blood in him. Whether or not they really believed their story is of little importance. Its significance is that it gave them an excuse to disregard the principles of non-resistance which they professed, and to take action against James in order to preserve the 'legitimate' succession of his daughter Mary. On 30 June the Seven Bishops were acquitted by a London jury, and while bonfires were being lit in the streets Admiral Russell slipped quietly away on the first stage of his journey to Holland. He took with him an invitation to William of Orange to invade England and defend those who, they feared, would be 'every day in a worse condition than we already are, and less able to defend ourselves'.

The seven signatories of the invitation were rebels only in a narrow sense. They included two former Roman Catholics, Shrewsbury and Lumley; two staunch anglicans, Danby and the Bishop of London; and three Whigs, Devonshire, Russell and Sydney. All these men were, if not nobles themselves, closely connected with the nobility, and knew that rebellion might lead to the destruction of the social order upon which their property and their privileges depended. Yet absolute monarchy of the type James was planning to introduce was a more immediate threat and one that they felt impelled, out of self-preservation, to meet. William had made it clear that he was willing to assist them: all he needed was some assurance of support. Such an assurance was contained in the invitation, where William was informed that 'there are nineteen parts of twenty of the people throughout the kingdom who are desirous of a change and who, we believe, would willingly contribute to it if they had such a protection to countenance their rising as would secure them from being destroyed'.

James heard that naval and military preparations were being made in Dutch ports, but he was not inclined to take the rumours seriously. He had lavished money on the navy, which was one of the finest in Europe, and he had a standing army of some twenty thousand men. He seemed to rest confident that William would not be foolhardy enough to attempt so dangerous an enterprise, and that if he did he would be easily crushed. James also doubted whether William would dare leave Holland denuded of troops in face of the threat from France. He decided to let events take their course, and in August issued writs for a general election. By October, however, James had become convinced that the threat was real. He cancelled the writs, but made a bid for popular support by dissolving the Ecclesiastical Commission and restoring charters to those boroughs that had forfeited them.

There was no widespread movement of revolt against James. Danby planned to raise rebellion in Yorkshire as soon as he heard of William's landing—which, he assumed, would take place on the north-east coast—and other conspirators had made similar preparations, but the prevailing mood was one of hesitancy, and it looked as though success would depend upon the speed with which William arrived.

As October drew to a close, with William still in Holland, Louis became convinced that the right moment for an invasion attempt had passed. He therefore moved his army towards the Rhine for operations against the Palatinate. But on 1 November William at last set sail, and was blown down the Channel by the 'protestant wind' which stopped the English fleet from coming out. On 5 November, the day on which deliverance from an earlier catholic threat was being celebrated, he landed in Torbay.

The west country had learnt its lesson after Monmouth's rebellion, and there was no general rising in William's favour. He would have done better, from a military point of view, to land in the north, but he had no wish to become the puppet of the English nobles. In the west country he was at least his own master, but as the days passed and the country remained apathetic he began to wonder whether he had made a mistake. He was saved by James's inaction. The King was not a coward, but rebellion unnerved him and he never used the fine army he had created. The officers, many of whom were wavering in their allegiance, took James's hesitation as a sign of weakness and began deserting to William. Among the first to go was John Churchill, the King's friend and commander of the royal army, and after him the trickle turned into a flood.

Halifax, Nottingham and Godolphin remained with the King and persuaded him to summon Parliament, dismiss Roman Catholics from office and declare an amnesty for all those who had risen against him. They then, at James's command, met William and suggested that he should return to Holland as the objects of his mission had been accomplished. But William had no intention, at that stage, of going home. He continued his advance on London, and James, obsessed by the thought of the fate that had befallen Charles I, fled from the City. After an unsuccessful first attempt, he managed to find a boat which took him across the Channel, and on Christmas Day 1688 he landed in France.

The Revolution Settlement

The flight of James left the way clear for William to take over the government of England. The representatives of the aristocracy (who had made the Revolution) advised the Prince to summon an assembly and in January 1689 the Convention—a Parliament in all but name—met in London. The Revolution had been carried out by Whigs and Tories, but the two sides were split over the question of a constitutional settlement. The Tories insisted that since the monarchy was hereditary the throne was not, and could never be, vacant. James was still King, but regents should be appointed to act in his name. This was the solution that Charles and Halifax had put forward in 1680, and it was accepted by the House of Lords. The Commons, however, with its Whig majority, resolved that James, by his flight, had abdicated the throne, which was therefore vacant.

The dispute between the two Houses might have produced deadlock, but the Tories gave way. Their plan for a regency depended on finding a regent, and in this they failed. Danby hoped that Mary might act as regent, with her husband as uncrowned prince-consort, but Mary soon disillusioned him: 'she would take it', she wrote, 'extreme unkindly if any, under a pretence of their care of her, would set up a divided interest between her and the Prince.' As for William, he let it be known that he would never consent to be his 'wife's gentleman-usher': either he must be offered the throne or he would shake the dust of England off his feet and leave the ungrateful nobles to defend themselves as best they could against James and Louis. The Tories bowed to the inevitable, but salved their consciences to some extent by insisting that the Crown should be offered jointly to William and Mary. In a ceremony that took place in the Banqueting House—the place from which Charles I had stepped out to execution forty years earlier—William and Mary were formally proclaimed King and Queen.

In 1660 Charles II had been restored without conditions and, as a consequence, had been able to upset the balance of the constitution which was the ideal of English statesmen. The leaders of Parliament were determined that this should not happen a second time, and they made the offer of the Crown follow upon the monarch's acceptance of a *Bill of Rights*.

This document was a commentary on the constitutional history of the whole Stuart period and marks the triumph of principles enunciated in the *Form of Apology and Satisfaction* and the *Petition of Right*. Most of the provisions were inspired by the events of the preceding twenty years, but some looked further back. The suspending power was declared illegal, while the dispensing power was to operate only in those cases where statutory provision was made for it. The Ecclesiastical Commission 'and all other commissions and courts of like nature' were declared 'illegal and pernicious', and so was 'the raising or keeping a standing army within the kingdom in time of peace, unless it be with consent of Parliament'. The levying of money, except by parliamentary grant, was condemned, and the right of subjects to petition the King was upheld. As for Parliament, the 'election of members', it was stated, 'ought to be free'; while a century of dispute, much of it violent, was concluded in the declaration 'that the freedom of speech, and debates or proceedings in Parliament ought not to be impeached or questioned in any court or place out of Parliament'.

Since William and Mary were childless, the *Bill of Rights* also had to make arrangements for the succession. This was done by the provision that the Crown should pass after the sovereigns' deaths to Mary's sister Anne and her heirs—except in the unlikely event of children being born to William and Mary. The Stuart claim was terminated by the declaration 'that all and every person and persons that is, are, or shall be reconciled to, or shall hold communion with, the see or Church of Rome, or shall profess the popish religion, or shall marry a papist, shall be excluded and be for ever incapable to inherit, possess, or enjoy the Crown and government of this realm'.

Three other Acts completed the Revolution settlement. The Mutiny Act, passed for a year at a time, gave the King authority to impose military discipline on the armed forces raised 'during this time of danger . . . for the safety of the kingdom [and] the common defence of the protestant religion'. The Toleration Act, which was the reward of the dissenters for not responding to James's assurances, freed nonconformists from the operation of the penal laws as long as they took the oath of loyalty and the declaration against transubstantiation. The penal laws themselves were not repealed, merely suspended, and the dissenters, like the Roman Catholics, were still barred from public life. The anglican Tories, who had abandoned 'their' King, were all the more determined to preserve the privileged position of 'their' Church, and the grudging concession made in the Toleration Act marked the limits beyond which they would not go.

The Triennial Act, the third of this trilogy, was not passed until

1694, because of William's resistance to the invasion of his prerogative. It met the twin dangers of no Parliaments and perpetual Parliaments by providing that in future a new Parliament should meet not more than three years after the dissolution of its predecessor, and that 'no Parliament whatsoever, that shall at any time hereafter be called, assembled, or held, shall have any continuance longer than for three years only at the farthest'.

The striking thing about the Revolution settlement was its moderation. It did not establish parliamentary government. The King was left free to choose and dismiss his ministers as well as his judges, and he could summon, dissolve, prorogue and adjourn Parliament as he thought fit, provided he did not transgress the provisions of the Triennial Act. Nothing was said about placemen in the Commons, nor was the King's prerogative in foreign affairs brought into question. The 'glory' of the Revolution consisted in its conservatism: it kept the traditional constitution and made only minor adjustments to bring it back into balance. Parliament was to be a regular and important part of government and so was the King, but neither, alone was to be supreme. 'Parliamentary sovereignty' (in the sense of the two Houses acting alone), 'party government', and 'democracy', were none of them envisaged by the makers of the Revolution—except with a shudder. The great landowners who had risen to power in the century and a half that followed the Dissolution conceived of the constitution of England on the lines that Shaftesbury had proposed and that Locke was actively propagating—as a contract between governor and governed, which would preserve order without threatening property-rights.

William and the Tories

William III was a man who inspired affection in few people. His constant struggle against ill-health left him short-tempered, and he concealed his feelings beneath a cold mask of indifference. The controlling passion of his life was the destruction of French power, and to this he devoted all his energy. Because England was essential to the fulfilment of his plan he had taken the English throne, but he had no love for the country he ruled and usually spent half of every year out of it. In his high views of the prerogative he came close to the Tories, but they could never forgive him the fact that he had driven out the legitimist King, and they could not focus on him the devotion they had given to the divinely appointed Stuarts.

The Whigs, on the other hand, although they were no great lovers of monarchy, felt that William ought to rely on them because they had, on a long-term view, made possible the sequence of events that led to his accession. Their attitude was expressed by Shrewsbury—a moderate Whig, who would have preferred the King's government to be above parties—when he warned William against reliance on the Tories. 'I shall make no difficulty', he said, 'to own my sense that Your Majesty and the government are much more safe depending upon the Whigs ... than [on] the Tories who, many of them, questionless would bring in King James, and the very best of them I doubt have a regency still in their heads. For although I agree them to be the properest instruments to carry the prerogative high, yet I fear they have so unreasonable a veneration for monarchy as not altogether to approve the foundation yours is built upon.'

The Tories only tolerated William because they had no alternative to him. Mary, with her charm and vivacity, was far more popular than her husband (to whom she was devoted) and provided some of the warmth in which he was so conspicuously lacking. The Tories comforted themselves with the thought that she was a Stuart, and would be succeeded by the devoutly anglican Anne. Meanwhile, they made one of their main objects the defence of the Anglican Church against the dangerous combination of a calvinist King and low church–dissenter Whigs. The anglican clergy had accepted the change of dynasty with surprisingly little fuss, in spite of the fact that they had been more fervent than anybody else in preaching the evils of resisting monarchical authority. Only four hundred non-jurors, including five of the famous Seven Bishops, gave up their livings rather than take the oath of allegiance to the new sovereigns.

The position of the non-jurors was quite logical. They had sworn to obey James, and believed that no power on earth could absolve them from that obligation. Fortunately for William most of the clergy were closer in spirit to the Vicar of Bray than to the non-jurors, and he filled the vacancies on the episcopal bench with latitudinarians who would act as a valuable counter-weight in the House of Lords to the high Tories. But the Anglican Church was the poorer without the non-jurors, among whom were numbered many of its most saintly men—high church puritans whose insistence that everyday life must be sanctified by spiritual awareness and the practice of devotion was not again to be the hallmark of the Church of England until the days of Keble. Their immediate political significance was small, but they acted as a constant reminder to the Williamite-Tories of ideals which had been abandoned. The fervent anglicanism of the Tories in the reigns of William and Anne was inspired, in part at least, by the desire to justify themselves to the non-jurors and to their own consciences.

William had no wish to be either 'King of the Whigs' or 'King of the Tories', and his first administration was balanced carefully between the two groups. Halifax, who was not really committed to any party, held the important office of Lord Privy Seal, while the Tory Danby was Lord President of the Council. One Secretary of State was Daniel Finch, second Earl of Nottingham and son of Heneage who had been Danby's ally in the reign of Charles II. Nottingham was a devout anglican, but his Tory fervour was offset by the Whiggish leanings of the other Secretary, Shrewsbury. These ministers did not form a united 'Cabinet' with a common policy. Their job was to serve the King and to advise him when necessary. Policy-making was William's prerogative, and one that he exercised to the full. He was his own chief minister, and used his Dutch favourite, William Bentinck, Earl of Portland, as the link between him and his administration.

In May 1689 William declared war on France, and he hoped that the country would unite behind him. But the Whigs in Parliament were bitter at what they regarded as the King's betrayal of their cause, and were determined to take revenge on all those who had made possible the despotism of the later Stuarts. They annulled the sentences passed against Russell and Sidney at the time of the Rye House Plot, and were pressing ahead with a proposal to confine borough government to men of their own persuasion when William, disillusioned and disgusted by their partisan behaviour, dissolved Parliament in January 1690.

War

The long war with France, which opened in 1689, had a profound effect on English politics. The army was expanded from eight thousand to over eighty thousand, and its annual cost rose to over £2,500,000— more than double Charles II's nominal revenue. William enjoyed a permanent income 'inherited' from James II, which covered his civil expenditure, but he depended entirely upon Parliament to provide the enormous sums needed for war. The practice of voting these annually was more important than any statute in ensuring that the two Houses sat regularly from winter to spring of every year. In law, there was nothing to stop William ruling without Parliament, except for a brief meeting every three years, and he had no greater affection for this representative institution than had James I or Charles II. It was the war that compelled King and Parliament to work together and to translate into practice that theoretical balance which had been so long the ideal of English statesmen. William could not redress the balance in his favour, as the later Stuarts had done. He had to fight hard to preserve his prerogatives, and the strain of war gradually eroded the power of the Crown and upset the balance in the opposite direction. But while William lived, King and Parliament worked if not in harmony at least in reluctant cooperation.

Halifax resigned in February 1690 and Danby became the dominant figure (under the King) in an administration that was increasingly Tory. He used all his old arts of parliamentary management, noting of one member 'not willing to lose his place', and of another 'I think hath a pension', and his seven 'managers' in the House of Commons kept in touch with the 'King's men' and ensured a reasonably smooth passage for finance Bills and other important government measures. Yet Danby never had the full support of the Tory country gentlemen, who found the heavy land tax, levied for the war, a crippling burden. From their stronghold in the Commons they attacked the government for fighting expensive land campaigns instead of winning prizes at sea, for permitting corruption to divert national wealth into private pockets, and for failing to bring the war to a close.

Danby suffered from this resentment and could offer little in the way of victory. William was bogged down in siege warfare in the Netherlands and could not break the French stranglehold. In July 1692 he had to abandon Namur to the enemy, and a year later he was heavily defeated at Landen. At sea the French won command of the Channel in the summer of 1690, after the Battle of Beachy Head, and although they were heavily defeated two years later at the battle of La Hogue—which put an end to James's hopes of invasion—the credit for this went to the Whig Admiral Russell and not to the Tory ministry. Russell was so uncooperative that he was replaced by a trinity of Tory admirals, but these only succeeded in bringing the administration into even greater discredit by permitting the French to wipe out the Levant Company's convoy in May 1693 and inflict losses estimated at £1 million.

What William demanded of his ministers was that they should keep on good terms with Parliament so that the supply of money which kept his armies and navies in action should not dry up. Danby had been

NTSB

successful at first, but by 1693 he had lost his touch. One of the reasons for this was that the men he relied on to manage the Commons were not as efficient at the job as he himself had been. But Danby's failure was not simply one of management. The 'Court party' in the Commons was always a small group, and flourished when the political temperature was low. When, on the contrary, members were stirred by great causes, they were less susceptible to bribery, family connexions and all the other influences that tugged at them. The country gentlemen wanted an end to heavy taxation, and the only hope of this lay in an end to the war. They blamed Danby for military and naval reverses which destroyed hopes of an early peace, and they bitterly attacked the placemen in the House who, they were convinced, were the sole reason why an inefficient, unsuccessful and corrupt administration remained in power.

Danby suffered from the effects of the Glorious Revolution which had made Parliament more powerful but left the King in charge of policy. As the King's representative in Parliament he had to take the blame for William's actions; yet as Parliament's representative to the King he had to bear the brunt of royal anger against parliamentary criticism. While the King chose his ministers regardless of their following in the Commons, this situation was bound to recur. The ultimate solution was for the King to accept as ministers the representatives of the predominant parties or groupings in the Commons, but this implied a tacit surrender of prerogative powers, and William was unwilling to consider it.

The King's defence of his prerogative added to the resentment felt in Parliament. In 1692, for instance, he vetoed a Bill making the judges' tenure dependent on their good behaviour instead of on royal pleasure (though he had no objection to this in practice); in March 1693 he vetoed a Triennial Bill, and in January of the following year he refused to accept a Bill to exclude placemen from the House of Commons. Altogether William used his veto five times where Charles II had used it twice and James II not at all. This shows that liaison between Crown and Parliament was not as good as it ought to have been, for skilful management of both Houses might have diverted discontent into relatively harmless channels before it reached the stage where the veto had to be used.

The decline of the Privy Council was partly responsible for the unsatisfactory state of the linking mechanism between King and Parliament. Under Elizabeth, members knew that Councillors were, in fact as well as in name, the sovereign's advisers, and were familiar with her policies. Under William they could not be sure of this. The King was out of the country for half the year, and even when he was in it allowed few men into his confidence. During his absences a small committee, called the Cabinet Council, handled government business and tendered advice to Mary, but from about 1695 onwards this 'Cabinet' continued meeting even when the King was in England. William himself was frequently present, and it was at these small, informal assemblies that the decisions were taken which transformed his policy into action.

Members of Parliament knew, of course, that such meetings went on, but resented the fact that because of the uncertain membership of these 'Cabinets' they could never be sure who to blame for measures of which they disapproved. The King, by the conventions of the constitution, could do no wrong: his ministers had to take the blame for his mistakes. But how could Parliament know which minister to blame when government was carried out through secret committees of fluctuating composition? The advantage of the Privy Council was that its membership was formal and defined, but nobody could be sure whether or not he had a 'right' to attend a Cabinet Council—and there were other meetings which did not have even the limited degree of formality towards which the Cabinet Council was moving. The confusion to which this situation could give rise was shown in 1694 when Lord Normanby claimed a right to sit on *all* councils on the grounds that William had promised him this privilege. The King, however, replied that 'it is true that I did promise my lord Normanby that when there was a Cabinet Council he should assist at it, but surely this does not engage either the Queen or myself to summon him to all meetings which we may order on particular occasions . . .?'

William and the Whigs

The Place Bill which William vetoed in 1694 was the work of the Tory country gentlemen in the Commons, and a constitutional crisis was only prevented by William's conciliatory reply to their protest, in which he assured them that 'no prince ever had a higher esteem for the constitution of the English government than myself, and . . . I shall ever have a great regard to the advice of Parliaments'. This quarrel persuaded William that in spite of his high views of monarchy he could no longer depend on the Tories. The Whigs might be, as he suspected, neo-republicans, but they were at least in favour of the war, and it was this consideration which prompted the King to broaden the basis of his administration by including more Whigs—a process that over the course of the next few months turned a predominantly Tory ministry into one that was mainly Whig.

Although William was forced to abandon the Tories he did not wish to become the prisoner of the Whigs. What he needed, as always, was a non-party man who would put the interests of the Crown above everything else. He therefore turned to Sunderland, who had served many causes but committed himself to none, and whose attitude to party was summed up by the observation—delivered in the languid drawl for which he was famous—'What matter who saarves His Majesty so long as His Majesty is saarved?' Sunderland took over from Danby the task of 'managing' the placemen in the Commons, and it was at his insistence that the King eventually agreed in November 1693 to part with Nottingham. Danby, created Duke of Leeds, was kept in office to preserve a semblance of continuity and to avoid antagonising the Tories, but he was no more than a figurehead.

The important members of the reformed administration were Russell, appointed First Lord of the Admiralty in May 1694, Charles Montagu, who became Chancellor of the Exchequer, and Shrewsbury, who accepted office once again as Secretary of State. Russell and Montagu were members of the JUNTO, the group of influential Whig leaders who were whole-heartedly in favour of the war and who commanded a big following in the Commons. Other members of this group were John Somers, John Trenchard and Thomas Wharton, and they were the spiritual descendants of Shaftesbury's Whigs. Russell, for instance, was cousin to the Whig peer who had been executed for his alleged involvement in the Rye House plot; Wharton's father had been one of the leaders of the opposition to Charles II in the House of Lords; while Trenchard had been a fervent exclusionist and supporter of Monmouth. For William, alliance with such men was at best a marriage of convenience, but as Sunderland pointed out 'it was very true that the Tories were better friends to monarchy than the Whigs were, but then His Majesty was to consider that he was not their monarch'.

The reformed administration suffered from the disadvantage of all mixed ministries. Because it contained a number of Tories, the Whigs were dissatisfied and clamoured for complete control. At the same time the Tories were horrified that the King's government should be largely in the hands of enemies to monarchy and the Anglican Church. If party allegiances had been clear-cut, disputes could have been settled by a mere counting of heads, but party feeling was only one of several influences that played on the Commons and made it so difficult to control. Personal feelings about the war and about the Church were of great significance in determining a man's attitude; but so were his family relationships, his involvement in one or other of the aristocratic 'connexions', and his hopes of holding an office of profit or a commission in the armed forces.

The complexity of political patterns is suggested by the emergence of the Harley–Foley grouping, which came to be called the New Country Party. Foley was a moderate presbyterian, who had been an exclusionist under Charles II and a Whig in the Convention Parliament. Harley came from a gentry family with puritan leanings, and had been tutored by no less a person than Richard Baxter, the founding father of English nonconformity. Both Foley and Harley were Whigs in 1690, but four years later, as a predominantly Whig ministry took over the policy of the Tories and came out in support of the war and all that it entailed, they moved into opposition. They took up the traditional 'Country' attitude of suspicion towards the Court and attacks on placemen and corruption, and they were joined by many Tories who shared the same assumptions. The New Country Party resented the way in which ministers who had formerly served the cause of Stuart absolutism were gaining power under William III and using the same methods to preserve their authority. A typical 'Country' pamphlet referred contemptuously to the placemen 'voting always the same way and saying always the same things, as if they were no longer voluntary agents but so many engines merely turned about by a mechanic motion, like an organ where the great humming basses as well as the little squeaking trebles are filled but with one blast of wind from the same sound-board'. In April 1695 the opposition mounted an attack on the Duke of Leeds who symbolised corruption in their eyes, and William had to prorogue Parliament to stop the impeachment of his minister.

Fortunately for the King the war in the Netherlands had taken a turn for the better, and in August 1695 William achieved his greatest success when he recaptured the fortress of Namur. The favourable climate of opinion produced by this victory persuaded him to dissolve Parliament, in hopes that a less fractious assembly would be elected. The new Parliament was not, in fact, any more friendly towards

William than the old one had been, particularly as the death of Mary in December 1694 left the King as sole ruler. But in February 1696 a Jacobite plot to assassinate William was discovered, and in the reaction against this William acquired, for the first time, some semblance of popularity. An association was formed, on the model of the one that had been set up to protect Elizabeth, and an Act of 1696 declared that William was *rightful and lawful King*—terms which the Tories, with their scruples about hereditary succession, had kept out of the legislation which followed the Revolution. Throughout the summer of 1696, fears of a Jacobite invasion stifled the critics of the war, and the JUNTO became increasingly powerful. In 1697 Somers was made Lord Chancellor, Russell was created Earl of Orford, and Montagu became First Lord of the Treasury.

Harley and the opposition did not abandon their attacks on the administration, but they had to concentrate on matters other than the war. One obvious target was the lavish grants of land made by the King to his Dutch favourites out of confiscated Jacobite estates in Ireland. The opposition demanded that these grants should be revoked, and denounced them as examples of the way in which the wealth of the country was being squandered while the landowners, under the burden of heavy taxation, were bleeding to death. The squires in the House of Commons, however Tory in their attitude, were also prepared to join with Harley and the dissident Whigs of the New Country Party in attacks on the Bank of England. This had been created in 1694, and much of its capital was subscribed by City merchants and financiers who were Whig in sympathy. These men were doing well out of the war, making big profits on the supply of arms, ammunition and clothing to the armed forces, and the smaller landowners bitterly resented the fact that the proceeds of the Land Tax, which they paid at so great a cost in suffering, should pass through the Bank of England into the pockets of the Whigs. They supported Harley's scheme for a Land Bank, to function in the same way as the Bank of England but with its capital provided mainly by landowners. The Bill setting up the Land Bank received the royal assent in April 1696, but the scheme was stillborn. The City magnates and big landowners who had invested in the Bank of England had no intention of supporting a rival institution, and the squires alone were too poor to raise more than a few thousand pounds. The failure of the Land Bank became just one more item in the balance sheet of resentment.

The Whig JUNTO remained in power as long as the war lasted, but in May 1697 peace negotiations opened and in the following September the Treaty of Ryswick brought the war to a close. Both sides agreed to return their conquests, and Louis XIV announced his acceptance of William as King of England, and his abandonment of the Jacobite cause.

Harley and the New Country Party welcomed the end of the war and proposed that the army should be immediately reduced to seven thousand men. William, who realised that the Peace of Ryswick was only a truce and that Louis XIV had not abandoned his ambitions, struggled to preserve at least four times that number, but he could not win over the squires in the Commons who, when they chose to unite —and they were united on this issue—could be sure of a majority. Sunderland, afraid of a revengeful Tory attack on him, insisted on leaving the King's service in December 1698, and the King was left without a link between himself and the JUNTO ministers. The Whig leaders knew that their predominance was threatened, and demanded guarantees from William in the shape of a Secretaryship for Wharton. But William never liked being dictated to, particularly by Whigs. He was drawing close to John Churchill, Earl of Marlborough and a favourite of Princess Anne, and felt that he could dispense, if needs be, with the services of the JUNTO.

Succession Problems

Under the terms of the Triennial Act, Parliament was dissolved in July 1698. In the new Commons which met in December of that year the Tories and New Country Party had a majority and immediately demanded a reduction in the army. William was so disgusted at their parochial attitude that he drafted a speech of abdication, in which he proposed to tell them that since they had 'so little regard to my advice that you take no manner or care of your own security, and expose yourselves to evident ruin by divesting yourselves of the only means for your defence, it would not be just or reasonable that I should be witness of your ruin'.

William never delivered the speech, for England was more than ever essential to the fulfilment of his plans. The problem of the Spanish Succession still dominated European politics, and in 1698 William had concluded a secret Partition Treaty with France and Holland. It was agreed that Louis' grandson, Philip, should have the southern Italian possessions of Spain, while the Archduke Charles, younger son of the

Emperor, was to have north Italy. The great bulk of the Spanish Empire—Spain itself, the Netherlands and America—was to go to the Emperor's grandson, the Electoral Prince of Bavaria. In this way the Spanish Empire would be prevented from passing into the hands of Louis and shifting the balance of power in Europe decisively in France's favour. In January 1699, however, while William was engaged in bitter dispute with Parliament, the Electoral Prince died, and the question of the Spanish Succession was once again wide open. It was for this reason that William decided to keep his crown and try to arrive at some *modus vivendi* with his turbulent Parliament.

Since Parliament was strongly Tory in sentiment a Tory ministry offered the best chance of harmony, but the King had first to disembarrass himself of the JUNTO without giving them such offence that they would decline to serve again, if he needed them. The JUNTO ministers were therefore turned out of office one by one. Orford resigned from the Admiralty in May 1699, Montagu left the Treasury commission in the following November, but Somers held on to his office as Lord Chancellor until April 1700. His dismissal cleared the way for a Tory ministry, and only just in time, for the Commons were getting out of control. In April 1700 they passed a Bill revoking all the grants William had made of Irish estates, and threatened to attaint the King's Dutch favourites. Rumours of dissolution were in the air, mobs gathered outside Parliament, and at Harley's suggestion the Commons carried on their debate behind locked doors. The King, angry and embittered, decided to accept the Bill without resisting, but he prorogued Parliament rather than agree to a formal request that he should employ no foreign advisers except Prince George of Denmark, husband of Anne.

This Parliament did not meet again, for William dissolved it in December. Before summoning another he made approaches to the high Tories and the New Country Party, hoping that a ministry based on these two interests would be able to lead the Commons into a constructive solution of the urgent problems that had to be dealt with. In March 1700 William had secretly concluded a second Partition Treaty, giving the Archduke Charles, Spain, America and the Netherlands, while France was to have all the Spanish possessions in Italy. Six months later, however, in October 1700, the King of Spain at last died, and left a will bequeathing all his vast possessions to Philip on condition that the crowns of France and Spain were never united. Louis decided to accept the will on behalf of his grandson, and there were no obvious grounds for objecting to this decision since it fulfilled the main aim of the partition treaties—namely, the separation of the French and Spanish empires. William, however, was convinced that Louis would ignore the provision about keeping the two crowns apart, and would try to present Europe with a *fait accompli*. He could not risk struggles with Parliament while such a threat hovered on the horizon.

William also had to deal with a succession problem nearer home, and one that could be solved only by statute. In July 1700 the Duke of Gloucester, Princess Anne's only surviving child, died, and since it was certain that Anne would have no more children, steps had to be taken to assure the succession. Only William, a sick man, and Anne, a sick woman, stood between England and the prospect of a Jacobite restoration.

By the time a new Parliament met in January 1701 the administration had again been reformed. Rochester was now Lord-Lieutenant of Ireland, Godolphin was First Lord of the Treasury, and Harley was nominated for election as Speaker. William, in these closing years of his reign, had come to rely on the two men who had served Charles II in a similar capacity after the collapse of the Popish Plot. The Tories were, of course, delighted, but the Whigs could be excused for wondering why the Glorious Revolution had ever taken place.

The Rochester–Harley combination was successful in pushing the Act of Settlement through Parliament, thereby ensuring—as far as statute alone could do—an undisputed succession after Anne's death. But Harley could not control the extreme Tories, and they were largely responsible for adding provisions to the Act which were deliberately critical of William and the practices that had grown up during his reign. As far as the succession was concerned, the Act of Settlement provided that the Crown should pass, on Anne's death, to the Electress Sophia of Hanover, daughter of Elizabeth of Bohemia, 'the Winter Queen', and granddaughter of James I. The heirs of Sophia were to inherit the throne after her death, Roman Catholic claimants were specifically excluded, and it was ordered that in future every monarch should be a communicant member of the Church of England.

This last provision was an implied criticism of William; so were the clauses requiring that 'this nation be not obliged to engage in any war for the defence of any dominions or territories which do not belong to the Crown of England, without the consent of Parliament', and that no future sovereign should leave the country unless he had first obtained parliamentary permission. To prevent Dutchmen, Germans or any

N*

other foreigners from playing, in future, the key role that they had filled under William, it was ordered that no person born outside the British Isles should be capable of enjoying 'any office or place of trust, either civil or military, or to have any grants of lands'.

As for the true-born Englishmen who were held to have betrayed their honour by serving as the King's retainers in the Commons, the triumphant Tories decreed 'that no person who has an office or place of profit under the King, or receives a pension from the Crown, shall be capable of serving as a member of the House of Commons'. Government by 'Cabinets' was forbidden by the provision that 'all matters . . . which are properly cognizable in the Privy Council by the laws and customs of this realm, shall be transacted there', and to prevent the King from interfering with the course of justice it was ordained that judges should in future be appointed *Quamdiu se bene gesserint*, and that 'no pardon under the Great Seal of England be pleadable to an impeachment by the Commons in Parliament'.

In some ways the Act of Settlement was a rounding-off of the Revolution settlement, but the clauses about placemen and the Privy Council reflect the opposition of the 'Country' members to changes in constitutional practice over which they had no control.[1] They wanted to stabilise the constitution, to fix it in the mould which Clarendon had created. The purpose of the placemen clause was not to separate the executive from the legislature, since most ministers were peers and would not be affected by the restriction, but simply to weaken the power of the Crown and preserve the balance which a future King might, like the later Stuarts, try to upset.

The attempt to keep placemen out of the Commons continued well into the eighteenth century, and was successful in so far as it reduced the number of officials allowed to engage in active political life. But the rigid exclusion of all office holders was hardly practicable, and would have left the Commons dangerously divorced from the real centre of political life. The ultimate solution was to be found by tackling the problem from the other end and abolishing the sinecures which had made possible the worst features of the system of patronage.

The passing of the Act of Settlement did not produce the harmony between Crown and Parliament for which William had hoped. News of the Partition Treaties had leaked out, and the Tory squires, furious at the way in which they had been committed behind their backs, showed their anger by proposing to impeach the leading members of

---

[1] These clauses were later modified. See below, p. 390.

the JUNTO. But while the Commons were working themselves into a fury over the defence of their constitutional liberties, a much more real and more dangerous threat was growing in Europe. Louis XIV had sent his troops into the Spanish Netherlands, officially to aid his grandson but in fact to annex them to France. Even a peace-lover like Harley was beginning to talk of a 'necessary war', and the feeling of the country was indicated by a petition presented to the Commons in April 1701 by representatives of the Gentlemen of Kent. In this petition the Commons were asked to vote supplies to the King so that he could form his alliances before it was too late. The indignant members, outraged at this criticism of their public spirit, committed the delegates to prison, but they could not so easily stifle public opinion. Robert Walpole was a member of this Parliament, and one of his Norfolk correspondents, writing to him in May, assured him that 'our people . . . seem pleased with the sentiments of the Grand Jury of Kent [and] think this time ought not to be neglected to make haste to secure ourselves and allies'.

The Lords refused to accept the Commons' articles of impeachment against the JUNTO leaders, and a violent dispute between the two Houses was only averted by William's dissolution of Parliament in November 1701. In September of that year he and Marlborough had been in Holland, building up a coalition against France, and their work came to fruition in September with the signing of the Grand Alliance. By the terms of this agreement, England, Holland and the Empire bound themselves to force Louis to accept partition of the Spanish Empire. Philip was to be left in possession of Spain and America, but the Archduke Charles was to have the Italian territories and the Spanish Netherlands. France was not to be allowed to monopolise trade with the New World, nor were the crowns of France and Spain to be united.

English opinion, which was already turning in favour of war, swung whole-heartedly behind William when, on the death of James II in September 1701, Louis recognised his son, the Old Pretender, as King of England. This was a direct violation of the Treaty of Ryswick. It was also an insult to the English people and Parliament, since it implied that they had no right to decide the succession to the English throne. It was in the heated atmosphere created by this challenge that the general election of December 1701 took place.

When William's last Parliament met, the Commons were almost evenly balanced between the Tories and the New Country Party on one wing and the adherents of the Whig JUNTO on the other. The Tories still felt bitter over what they regarded as William's betrayal of them, but all groups, Tory and Whig, recognised the necessity for war. The King, in his opening speech, reminded them that 'the eyes of all Europe are upon this Parliament. All matters are at a stand till your resolutions are known. . . . If you do in good earnest desire to see England hold the balance of Europe and to be indeed at the head of the protestant interest, it will appear by your right improving the present opportunity.' Parliament responded to this appeal, and assured William that 'all true Englishmen, since the decay of the Spanish monarchy, have taken it for granted that the security of their religion, liberty and property, that their honour, their wealth and their trade depend chiefly on the measures to be taken from time to time against the growing power of France'.

William made the details of the Grand Alliance known to both Houses, so that they should not be able to complain, as they had done over the Partition Treaties, of being committed without their approval. There was general agreement among members that the terms of the Alliance were in the interests of Britain, since they offered the prospect not only of a check to French expansion but also of security for British trade in the Mediterranean and West Indies. The Commons showed their approval by voting that an army of forty thousand soldiers should be raised, and they passed an Act of Attainder against the Pretender: there was no room, at this moment, for Jacobite scruples about legitimacy.

William had already appointed Marlborough to command the troops being assembled in Holland and was looking forward to joining them there, but as he was riding from Kensington Palace to Hampton Court in February 1702 his horse stumbled on a molehill and threw him. He died the following month, aged fifty-one—much to the delight of the followers of 'James III', who raised their glasses to toast the Jacobite mole: 'the little gentleman in black velvet'. But the mole had done his work too late. William died only after he had committed England to war, and the reign of his successor witnessed the triumph of all he had fought for.

17

Queen Anne

ANNE was the last of the Stuarts and had all the pride and stubbornness of her family. She was only thirty-seven when she came to the throne, but youth had long ago deserted her. She was crippled by gout and dropsy, which made public appearances agony, yet Anne believed that God had given her the throne and she was determined not to evade the responsibilities that went with this high trust. She had disliked William, referring to him in her private correspondence as 'Mr Caliban', and proudly assured her first Parliament that 'I know my heart to be entirely English'. Yet she shared William's exalted view of the prerogative, and struggled throughout her reign to prevent the Crown from becoming the pawn of any political group or party. One of her ministers wrote, 'she will be Queen of all her subjects and would have all the parties and distinctions of former reigns ended and buried in hers', and Anne herself described her aim as that of having 'my liberty in encouraging and employing all those that concur faithfully in my service, whether they are called Whigs or Tories'.

The fact that Anne was a Stuart was not simply a matter of interest: it was a political factor of the first importance. Since 1688 the Tories had been longing for a monarch on whom they could focus their loyalty, and who would preserve those twin pillars of society— the royal prerogative and the Anglican Church. Anne seemed to fit these requirements exactly. In spite of her size and stupidity she had a natural dignity, and as a Stuart by birth she emphasised her hereditary right to the throne and once again exercised those sacred functions which her predecessor—whose title was more obviously dependent upon parliamentary grant—had allowed to lapse. She revived, for instance, the practice of touching for the Queen's evil—to the benefit, it is to be hoped, of many of her subjects, including the young child who was to become famous as Dr Johnson—and she asserted her headship over the Church of England which God had committed to her care. 'My own principles', she informed Parliament, 'must always keep me entirely firm to the interests and religion of the Church of England, and will incline me to countenance those who have the truest zeal to support it.'

Marlborough and Godolphin

The Marlboroughs came to power with Anne, for Sarah Churchill, the Earl's wife, was the Queen's intimate friend and adviser. Marlborough himself was the son of Sir Winston Churchill, a royalist squire who had been impoverished by the civil war, and he had risen to power by service at Court, where at an early age he had become page to James II.[1] Marlborough played a major part in the suppression of Monmouth's rebellion, but in 1688 he led the deserters into William's camp. The shock of his friend's betrayal accounts in part for the lack of resistance that James made to the invader, but William, although he rewarded Marlborough with an earldom, was not disposed to take him into his confidence. The new King despised traitors and suspected that Marlborough, having betrayed one sovereign, would be just as ready to betray another. He may have been jealous of Marlborough's military ability and he certainly resented the fact that the Earl was held in such high esteem by Anne. The nadir of their relationship came in 1692 when Marlborough spent several months as a prisoner in the Tower of London, on suspicion of treasonable correspondence with James, but some years before William died the two men were reconciled, and in 1702 Marlborough was ready to take over the task that William had left unfinished. His ally in the political world was Sidney Godolphin, his son-in-law, and while Marlborough was engaged in fighting the Queen's enemies on the Continent, Godolphin looked after affairs at home and persuaded Parliament to vote the vast sums of money needed to finance war on a scale greater than anything England had yet known.

The Tories believed that with the accession of Anne they had come into the promised land, and the first administration of the reign seemed to confirm all their hopes. Rochester and Nottingham, both staunch anglicans, were respectively Lord-Lieutenant of Ireland and Secretary

[1] Marlborough's sister, Arabella, was one of James's mistresses, and bore her lover a son who became, as Duke of Berwick, one of the finest marshals in the French Army.

of State, while Somers, Halifax and Orford, the representatives of the JUNTO, were dismissed from the Privy Council.

The administration was, however, only superficially Tory, for the key figures in the government were Marlborough and Godolphin, who were neither of them party men. Their main concern was the prosecution of the war, and while they hoped that cooperation with the Tories would be the best means of achieving victory, they were prepared to work with the Whigs if necessary. They were a long way removed, in sympathy, from Rochester and Nottingham, who made the preservation of the Anglican Church their main interest and were anxious to put an end to the practice of occasional conformity.[1]

The high Tories were also in favour of fighting the war mainly at sea, and Nottingham told Marlborough that he was 'biast by an opinion that we shall never have any decisive success nor be able to hold out a war against France but by making it a sea war, and such a sea war as accompanies and supports attempts on land'. Such a strategy appealed to the Tory squires because it held out the prospect of capturing prizes—which could be used to offset the cost of war—and did not involve the maintenance of enormously expensive armies. As for the second part of Nottingham's statement, there was widespread agreement among all groups that naval operations in support of English trade were to be encouraged. What Marlborough objected to was the assumption that the two concepts were mutually exclusive, and that if the war was fought at sea it could not simultaneously be fought on land. He was convinced that the French would only be ultimately defeated after the overthrow of their armies in the field. He was also convinced that he alone could bring about such a consummation.

In May 1702 Anne dissolved the Parliament which she had inherited from William, and issued writs for a general election. The campaign that followed was not fought on party lines: about half the total number of seats were uncontested, and in those constituencies where an electoral battle took place, local interests and family influence were at least as important as national issues. In the new House of Commons the combination of the Marlborough–Godolphin connexion with the high Tories and Harley's New Country Party gave the ministry a majority, but not one on which they could rely, since the coalition was based on personal attitudes which were constantly shifting.

---

[1] Protestant dissenters who wished to take part in public life occasionally attended anglican services and received the sacrament in order to evade the penalties prescribed in the Test Act.

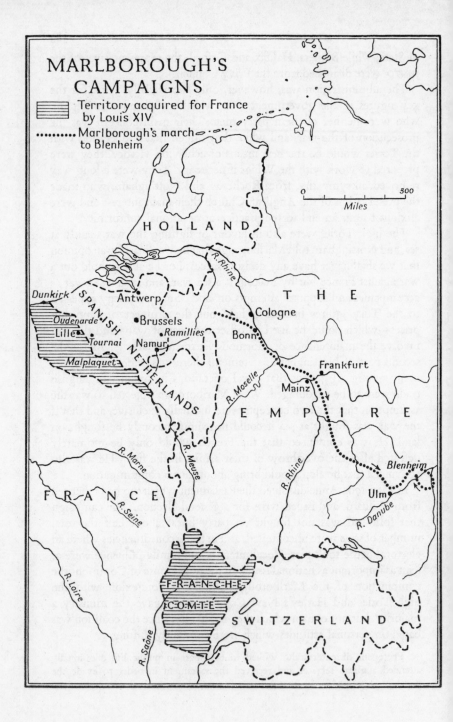

MARLBOROUGH'S CAMPAIGNS

▤ Territory acquired for France
   by Louis XIV

•••••• Marlborough's march
        to Blenheim

0 _____ 500
       Miles

HOLLAND

R. Rhine

Dunkirk

SPANISH

Antwerp

Oudenarde

Lille

Brussels

Ramillies

Tournai

Namur

NETHERLANDS

Malplaquet

Cologne

Bonn

THE

Frankfurt

R. Moselle

Mainz

EMPIRE

R. Meuse

R. Marne

R. Rhine

Blenheim

FRANCE

R. Seine

Ulm

R. Danube

R. Loire

FRANCHE-COMTÉ

R. Saône

SWITZERLAND

War against France was formally declared by England and Holland in May 1702, and Marlborough took charge of operations in the Netherlands. He was hampered by the Dutch political representatives on his staff, who were terrified of losing the war and preferred inaction to the taking of risks, but in spite of this he managed to capture a number of important strongholds and to push the French out of the valleys of the Lower Rhine. His success, in striking contrast with William's early failures, made Marlborough a public hero, the Commons voted that he had 'retrieved the ancient honour and glory of the English nation', and the Queen made him a duke.

The high Tories were suspicious of Marlborough's success since it confirmed their fears that England was going to expend the wealth of her landowners in a continental war. They had favoured an attack upon Spain, and although an expedition against Cadiz had been a miserable failure, their self-confidence was revived when they heard that the returning fleet had come across some Spanish treasure-ships in Vigo Bay and sent them to the bottom. Rochester was already on bad terms with Godolphin, whom he suspected of being lukewarm in his opposition to occasional conformity, and an open break came in February 1703 when Godolphin persuaded the Queen to dismiss her uncle.

Nottingham remained a thorn in the Lord Treasurer's flesh, however, since he and Sir Edward Seymour—the leader of the high Tories in the Commons—were threatening to divide Parliament and the country by their passionate advocacy of a Bill to prevent occasional conformity. Marlborough confessed to Sarah that though he felt 'bound not to wish for anybody's death . . . should Sir Edward Seymour die it would be no great loss to the Queen nor the nation', but Seymour remained obstinately alive, and in December 1703 the Commons passed the Occasional Conformity Bill by a big majority. Marlborough and Godolphin felt obliged to vote for the Bill in the Lords, since they knew the Queen was in favour of it, but they were relieved when the House threw it out.

Nottingham remained a member of the administration until April 1704, when his demand that Whig members of the Privy Council should be expelled brought matters to a head. Marlborough and Godolphin seized their opportunity, for Nottingham had been, in the Duke's words, 'so impertinent as to join with Sir Edward Seymour and others to obstruct business'. Anne was anxious to keep this pillar of the established Church, but was persuaded not to give in to his blackmail. Nottingham therefore resigned, and Seymour, who was dismissed from the Council, went with him. The brief reign of the high Tories had come to an end, and the moderate Tories who supported Harley were brought in to fill the gap. Harley himself took Nottingham's place as Secretary, while his protégé, Henry St John, was appointed Secretary-at-War.

The war aims of the allies had been significantly changed by the Methuen treaty, signed with Portugal in May 1703. Portugal agreed to join in war against France, and also made Lisbon available as a British naval base, but demanded that the Archduke Charles should be sent to the Peninsula, with a force of allied troops, to try to establish himself on the throne of Spain. When William had signed the Grand Alliance he had not envisaged giving Spain to the imperial claimant, since this would have opened the way to the reunification of the Habsburg empire—a prospect almost as alarming as the union of the Spanish and French crowns. But by the Portuguese Treaty England became committed to a campaign in the Peninsula that was to keep the war dragging on long after it should have been over. The Tories at first welcomed this Peninsular commitment, but when they realised that it meant a longer, not a shorter, war, they came to oppose it.

Hopes of a speedy end to the war rose in 1704 when Marlborough won the first of the magnificent victories which destroyed the legend of French invincibility and marked the re-emergence of Britain as a major military power. Marlborough hoped to avoid siege warfare of the type that had hamstrung William by an advance down the Moselle, and had persuaded his reluctant Dutch allies to agree to this. But in the heart of Europe French armies were threatening Vienna, and the Emperor sent urgent appeals for help. Marlborough knew that if Vienna fell and the Empire was knocked out of the war the chances of allied success would be slender; but he also knew that the Dutch would never consent to sending their troops hundreds of miles away from their homeland. The Duke therefore had resort to deception and allowed it to be assumed that he was preparing an attack down the Moselle while in fact he was in secret communication with the imperial commander, Prince Eugene, planning a surprise campaign on the Danube.

Marlborough left Holland at the beginning of May with an army of over fifty thousand men, about half of whom were paid for by Britain, although only nine thousand were actually British. For three months he marched south-east, following the course of the Rhine, then suddenly and secretly switched his army towards the Danube. On 13 August 1704 the British and French armies, evenly matched so far as numbers and equipment were concerned, faced each other on either side of the Nebel, a small stream that ran into the Danube by the little village of Blenheim, not far from Augsburg. The French front was protected by marshes, but Marlborough personally directed his main offensive across these, while a holding attack was delivered by the British troops on the twelve thousand or so enemy who were concentrated in the village. Marlborough had trained his cavalry to charge full out, with their swords drawn, instead of using them as mounted musketeers in the continental fashion. As the French centre weakened under repeated blows, the cavalry pressed home their advantage and broke right through. From that moment onwards the battle was won, although it was not until late in the afternoon that the Duke could at last find a moment to scribble a hasty note to his wife. 'I have not time to say more,' he wrote, 'but to beg you will give my duty to the Queen and let her know her army has had a glorious victory. Monsr. Tallard [the French commander] and two other generals are in my coach, and I am following the rest. . . .'

Marlborough had saved Vienna and had thereby saved the Grand Alliance. He had also made British arms more feared on the Continent than they had been since the days of Henry V. Even before he left England he had been a popular hero, but on his return he was idolised. The Emperor made him a prince of the Empire, while Anne presented him with the royal manor of Woodstock, just outside Oxford, and commissioned Sir John Vanbrugh to build a palace for him there at her own expense.

The Godolphin-Harley ministry was enormously strengthened by Marlborough's victory, which temporarily stifled criticism and discontent. The high Tories, led by Rochester and Nottingham, looked around for another hero, who could be used to dim Marlborough's glory and that of the ministry to which he belonged. They found such a man in Admiral Rooke, who had been responsible for the capture of Gibraltar ten days before Blenheim was fought. Marlborough himself welcomed this achievement. He was aware, like William before him, of the importance of naval operations in the Mediterranean, and appreciated that British supremacy there would not only afford protection to commerce but would also influence the outcome of the Peninsular campaign. The high Tories, however, managed to give the impression that the Duke was interested only in the military operations in the Netherlands, and that every victory won at sea was a blow to his reputation. Daniel Defoe, who was employed by Harley as a government propagandist and sounder of public opinion, reported from Bury St Edmunds that Rooke was 'exalted above the Duke of Marlborough; and what can the reason of this be, but that they conceive some hopes from this that their high church party will revive under his patronage?'

In the winter session of 1704 the high Tories pressed home their attack by reviving the Occasional Conformity Bill, and proposed that, it should be 'tacked' to the Supply Bill in order to ensure its passing the Lords. The supporters of the ministry defeated this proposal, but the untacked Bill passed the Commons and was sent up to the House of Lords who followed the lead given by Marlborough and Godolphin and rejected it. The Commons were furious, but could hardly claim that the Lords had acted unconstitutionally. They vented their anger by taking up the cause of William White, mayor of Aylesbury. White was a Tory, and had struck off many Whig voters from the electoral roll, confident that when the case came before the Commons—who claimed the sole right to decide disputed elections—the Tory majority in the House would uphold him. However, one of the deprived electors, Matthew Ashby, was encouraged by the Whig leaders to bring an action against White, and this eventually came, by way of appeal, to the Upper House. The Lords decided in Ashby's favour, on the grounds that while the Commons undoubtedly had authority to decide disputed elections they had no right to deprive a man of his vote, which was a piece of property. The Commons had already decided in favour of White, and when a number of other Aylesbury men followed Ashby's example the House ordered them to be arrested for breach of privilege. The situation was made even more explosive when the prisoners appealed to the House of Lords to uphold a writ of Habeas Corpus and order their release. The Commons had long resented the increasing power of the Lords, and now it seemed as if the Upper House was going to sit in judgement on those privileges which the Commons valued more than anything else. Tempers rose to such a pitch that government business came to a halt, and Anne had to put an end to this unedifying conflict by dissolving Parliament in April 1705.

The Drift towards the Whigs

The opposition of the high Tories drove Marlborough and Godolphin towards the Whigs, but they were not yet willing to bring the JUNTO lords into the administration. They allied instead with the Duke of Newcastle, a moderate Whig with vast estates and therefore considerable electoral influence, who was appointed Lord Privy Seal in April 1705. Forunately for the government coalition the Tories were split between the extremists and the centre group. The extremists were nicknamed 'Tackers' since they were in favour of tacking the Occasional Conformity Bill on to the vote of supply, and they took as their cry 'The Church in Danger'. The Church *was*, in fact, in danger. William had appointed many low church bishops, and Convocation, which only began its regular meetings again in 1701, was split between an upper house dominated by low churchmen and a lower house in which the high churchmen were in the majority. The Church had become a department of state, and its authority, like that of the dissenting churches, was being eroded by the spread of rationalism and the decline of enthusiasm. Yet although the high Tories were sincere in their desire for a rejuvenated, authoritarian Arminian Church, the main object of their campaign was to embarrass the government, and in this they were unsuccessful. As a result of the election the government coalition controlled more seats in the Commons, and the number of 'Tackers' was cut by almost half.

The Queen hoped to arrest the drift of her government towards the Whigs, and to keep herself free, as far as possible, from party ties. She wrote to Godolphin urging him to find a moderate Tory for the post of Lord Chancellor: 'I must own to you,' she continued, 'I dread the falling into the hands of either party, and the Whigs have had so many favours showed them of late that I fear a very few more will put me insensibly into their power, which is what I'm sure you would not have happen to me, no more than I. . . . I do put an entire confidence in you, not doubting but you will do all you can to keep me out of the power of the merciless men of both parties.' Godolphin, however, although he shared the Queen's ideals, had to look to his majority in the Commons, and for this the support of the moderate Whigs was essential. The Queen had to contain her fear and indignation and agree to the appointment of a Whig as Lord Chancellor. She did not blame Godolphin for forcing this choice on her, but incidents such as these gradually undermined the confidence between the Queen and her chief minister, and inclined her to look for support to other men— Harley, for instance, who wrote in 1706: 'I have no obligation to any party . . . I know no difference between a mad Whig and a mad Tory. . . It will be very hard ever to bring the nation to submit to any other government but the Queen's. In her they will all centre.'

When Parliament met for the winter session of 1705 the high Tories temporarily abandoned occasional conformity and instead tried to embarrass the government by a proposal that the Electress Sophia should be invited to take up residence in England. They knew that Anne would resent any such suggestion since, like Elizabeth before her, she did not wish to share her prestige with another, or to be constantly reminded of her own mortality. They calculated that the government would have to choose between the unwelcome alternatives of offending the present Queen, by supporting the proposal, or alienating the future Queen by opposing it. Godolphin and Harley, however, supported by the Whig JUNTO, neatly turned the flank of this attack by rejecting the proposal but at the same time passing the Regency Act to ensure the smooth succession of the Electress Sophia or her heir. The Act provided that, on the death of Anne, the Privy Council should immediately assemble and 'with all convenient speed cause the next protestant successor entitled to the Crown . . . to be openly and solemnly proclaimed'. The opportunity was also taken to modify some of the constitutional provisions of the Act of Settlement, by repealing the clause requiring all government business to be dealt with by the Privy Council, and by modifying the prohibition on placemen in the Commons by permitting members who accepted office—with the exception of newly created offices and certain named posts—to be re-elected.

Military operations had made little progress in 1705. In the Mediterranean area Gibraltar had survived a six-month siege, and in October 1705 'King Charles', with the assistance of allied troops, had captured Barcelona. In tentative peace negotiations that took place between Holland and France during the summer the allies had formally committed themselves to support of Charles's claims, and Marlborough wrote to the Dutch to remind them that 'England can like no peace but such as puts King Charles in the possession of the monarchy of Spain.'

In the Netherlands and central Europe Marlborough had been unable to exploit the victory of Blenheim. He always had difficulty in persuading his allies to sink their individual fears and differences and to leave him free to determine strategy. When the military situation was unfavourable they turned to the Duke for support and gave him all the authority he required, but after a victory they became over-confident and stubborn. This accounts for the two-year cycle of success followed by stagnation that prevented a speedy end to the war.

By the spring of 1706, however, a major French offensive on all fronts had united the allies behind Marlborough, and in May of that year the Duke won his second great victory at Ramillies in the Spanish Netherlands. 'The consequence of this battle', he wrote to Godolphin, 'is likely to be of greater advantage than that of Blenheim, for we have now the whole summer before us, and with the blessing of God I will make the best use of it.' As the allied forces swept south, capturing 'so many towns . . . that it really looks more like a dream than truth', Marlborough began to hope for an early peace, and told Sarah to hurry on the building of Blenheim Palace so that they could move into it as soon as the war was over. Antwerp, Ostend and Brussels were all captured, and by the time the campaigning season came to an end the allied armies were poised for an advance into France itself.

1706 had also been a year of success for the allies in Italy, where Prince Eugene had expelled the French and proclaimed Charles as King. In the Peninsula Barcelona held out against French attempts to recapture it, and an allied force from Portugal struck into the heart of Spain and actually captured Madrid. This gave an opportunity for 'King Charles' to turn his claim to the Spanish throne from an inflated gesture into actual fact, but Charles was slow to take advantage of it, and did not decide to go to Madrid until it was too late. He distrusted the English commander, the volatile Earl of Peterborough— another Tory idol—and had none of the personal magnetism that might have persuaded the Spanish people to rally round him. The allied aim to place Charles on the throne of Spain came increasingly up against the difficulty that the Spaniards had accepted Philip as their sovereign, and were not prepared to tolerate anyone else. Spain was ideal country for guerrilla warfare, in which the native inhabitants excelled, and the military balance moved even further against the allies when the Duke of Berwick returned to Spain to take command of the French and Spanish forces there.

The parliamentary session which opened in the winter of 1706 saw the Godolphin–Harley administration pushed further towards the Whigs. The Regency Act had settled the succession as far as England was concerned, but relations with Scotland were so bad that a union of the two crowns seemed the only way of averting a disputed succession and possible war between the two kingdoms. The Whigs were in favour of union, but the Tories dreaded the prospect of Scottish presbyterians arriving to sit as members of the Commons, and were opposed to giving formal recognition to the puritan Church of Scotland. Once again the opposition of the high Tories drove Godolphin, against his will, into the arms of the Whigs. The Whig leaders, however, demanded concrete rewards for their support, and insisted that one of their number, the third Earl of Sunderland, should be appointed Secretary of State. The Queen was opposed to Sunderland in person and in principle. 'All I desire', she declared, 'is my liberty in encouraging and employing all those that concur faithfully in my service, whether they are called Whigs or Tories; not to be tied to one nor the other.'

Such sentiments as these were to be expected from Clarendon's granddaughter, but the Queen was no longer entirely free to choose her servants as she wished. The demands of the war made parliamentary cooperation essential, and this could only be achieved by the support of the Whigs. Sarah, Duchess of Marlborough, who was a close friend of Godolphin, put pressure on Anne to accept Sunderland. She knew that no compromise was possible, for Sunderland had told her that he and the JUNTO had 'come to our last resolution in it, that this, and what other things have been promised, must be done, or we and the Lord Treasurer must have nothing more to do together about business'. Anne reluctantly gave way and in December 1706 appointed Sunderland Secretary of State for the southern department: Harley remained in charge of the northern department. But although the Queen had bowed to the inevitable she resented the pressure put upon her, and her feelings were not mollified by Sarah's tactless observation that 'it looks like infatuation that one who has sense in all other things should be so blinded by the word Tory'.

Robert Harley did not approve of the drift towards the Whigs, and he was already establishing direct links with the Queen, behind Godolphin's back. The intermediary in these was unwittingly provided by the Duchess of Marlborough who introduced into the Queen's presence Abigail Hill, Mrs Masham. The ambitious Abigail swiftly replaced Sarah in the Queen's confidence, and by the winter of 1707 the embittered Duchess was describing to one correspondent how she never had 'the honour to speak of anything but what concerns my own offices, and in that I can't prevail—all which is compassed by the black ingratitude of Mrs Masham, a woman that I took out of a garret and saved from starving!' Mrs Masham was the friend of Harley, and through her a relationship was established that gradually began to undermine Godolphin's authority.

Godolphin sensed that his position was becoming less secure, and was shocked when, in the summer of 1707, he learned that the Queen had nominated two Tories for election as bishops without consulting him. The JUNTO lords were furious, because two extra Tory votes in the House of Lords could make a big difference, and they refused to believe Godolphin's protestations of innocence in the affair. Anne, encouraged by Harley and Mrs Masham, stood firm, and Godolphin was appalled by the thought that her actions would alienate the Whigs and thereby impede the voting of supplies for the war when Parliament assembled in the winter. 'The liberties of all Europe and the glory of your reign', he reminded the Queen, 'depend upon the next session of Parliament. This being truly the case, what colour of reason can incline your Majesty to discourage and dissatisfy those whose principles and interest lead them on with so much warmth and zeal to carry you through the difficulties of the war?'

The Queen eventually agreed to make some Whig bishops, in order to cancel out the Tory advantage—thereby demonstrating the extent to which Church appointments, even under a devout monarch, had become a matter for political wrangling. The Whigs were not satisfied, however, and kept up the pressure on Godolphin, while the high Tories pursued their own vendetta against the chief minister. At the battle of Almanza in April 1707 the allied forces in Spain were heavily defeated by the Duke of Berwick, while in the Netherlands a combination of Dutch caution and allied bickering prevented Marlborough from exploiting the favourable situation created by Ramillies. The high Tories blamed defeat in Spain upon the inadequate supply of troops, and in December 1707 Rochester and Nottingham formally proposed that several thousand men should be transferred from the Netherlands to the Peninsula. Their allies in the Commons followed up this proposal by demanding to know why less than nine thousand English troops had actually been present at Almanza when Parliament had appropriated supply for thirty thousand.

By January 1708 Godolphin and Marlborough had decided to throw in their lot with the Whig JUNTO. They were beginning to suspect Harley's treachery, they were exhausted by the perpetual struggle against the high Tories, and they realised that Whig cooperation was essential, especially as the Union with Scotland, brought about in 1707, had added to Whig strength in the Commons. The JUNTO had always been in favour of Marlborough's conduct of the war and had now openly committed themselves to the principle of

'No peace without Spain'. There seemed little reason for keeping them out of the administration except Anne's dislike of party rule—by which she seemed to mean, more often than not, Whig party rule. Anne was prepared to get rid of Godolphin rather than accept the Whigs, and tried to persuade Marlborough to serve under Harley, but the Duke refused to do so after 'the treacherous proceedings of Mr Secretary Harley to Lord Treasurer and myself'. Since Anne could not possibly, at that stage, dispense with the services of Marlborough, she had to let Harley go instead. Harley resigned in 1708, St John went with him and Robert Walpole, a moderate Whig who was on good terms with the JUNTO, became the new Secretary-at-War.

In May 1708, after the administration had been reformed, a general election was held. War fervour had been revived by the repulse of a French invasion attempt two months earlier, and this helped the Whigs—both the moderates and the JUNTO. Many Tories, including St John, lost their seats, and Walpole, in a letter to Marlborough, reported that 'the Whigs have had the advantage very much. I believe by the most modest computation there are near thirty more Whigs chosen in the room of Tories than Tories in the room of Whigs, which makes them in Parliament stronger by double that number.'

By the time the election was held the war had entered its seventh year, and there was still no prospect of peace. The land tax remained high, indirect taxation fell heavily on poor and rich alike, and war-weariness was spreading. In July 1708 Marlborough defeated the French for the third time, at Oudenarde, but was persuaded by Eugene not to advance on Paris until the great fortress of Lille had been captured. The siege lasted until December, when Lille at last capitulated, and Marlborough extended the campaigning season long beyond its normal course by capturing Ghent and Bruges in January of the following year.

These victories were welcomed in England, particularly by the Whigs, but the Tory squires were longing for peace and could not understand why, after three major triumphs, Marlborough had still not been able to bring the war to a close. They suspected him of wanting to be another Cromwell, rising to supreme power through a standing army, and they came to believe that he was deliberately prolonging the war for his own personal advantage. In the Mediterranean theatre Port Mahon, in Minorca, had been captured in September 1708, and provided an invaluable naval base, but the war in the Peninsula was going badly and there seemed little prospect of

Charles ever taking over the effective government of 'his' kingdom.

The Tories, who had originally urged the claims of the Peninsular campaign in preference to those of the Netherlands, had now swung into opposition to it. St John gave expression to their feelings when he angrily told Harley that the ministers' plan to raise yet more regiments 'is to my apprehension downright infatuation, and what I am glad of. They hasten things to a decision, and our slavery and their empire are put upon that issue. For God's sake let us be once out of Spain!'

As the Tories became more and more clamorous in their desire for peace, the JUNTO demanded a bigger share in the government, and insisted that Somers should be given a post. Anne held out against this demand, but in October 1708 the death of her husband prostrated her with grief and broke her resistance. Somers was appointed Lord President of the Council and Wharton was made Lord-Lieutenant of Ireland. Godolphin and Marlborough, who had started off as Tory ministers, were now to all intents and purposes the heads of a Whig administration. But public opinion was turning in favour of the Tories and against the war, and discontent was increased by the severe winter of 1708-9, when the Thames froze and prices soared.

The strain of war was felt in France as well as England, and in the spring of 1709 Louis sued for peace. He offered to accept the transfer of the whole Spanish empire to Charles of Austria, except for those places that should be claimed by England or Holland, as long as Philip was compensated for the loss of his Spanish crown by being given territories somewhere else—preferably in Italy. These terms represented total defeat for France and would certainly have been acceptable to William III. But the allies insisted that Louis should join them in driving his grandson out of Spain if the young man refused to leave of his own free will. Even Marlborough was shocked at such terms, commenting that 'if I were in the place of the King of France, I should venture the loss of my country much sooner than be obliged to join my troops for the forcing of my grandson', yet he did nothing to moderate them. Marlborough's enemies had some truth in their argument that he was deliberately prolonging the war, for although the Duke longed for peace he conceived only of a military solution. He was prepared to go on fighting until the French surrendered unconditionally, and his victories only confirmed him in the belief that such a solution was possible. He was not an opponent of peace, but he was in fact an obstacle to a *negotiated* peace.

By the summer of 1709 the allies had at last pushed into France, and

in September Marlborough captured Tournai. The same month saw
the last of the great battles of the war, and Marlborough's last triumph,
at Malplaquet. But this was a pyrrhic victory, for the allies lost more
than the French, and the flower of the Dutch infantry was wiped out.
If the French defended every inch of their soil with the determination
they had shown at Malplaquet the war would turn into a holocaust,
and the Tories were already talking about the 'butcher's bill'. Marlborough knew that his position was being undermined, but was also
convinced, with good reason, that if he were dismissed there would be
no more allied victories. The planning of strategy and negotiations
with allies were long-term projects that demanded a greater measure of
security than Marlborough could be certain of. He was therefore
toying with the idea of asking to be made Captain-General for life,
although he knew that his enemies would see in this proof of his
ambitions to be a military dictator. In the autumn of 1709 he at last
formally demanded the life tenure of this high office, but Anne
refused to comply. She, like the Tories, was tired of the war and disillusioned with the man who seemed able to win everything except
peace.

As bitterness between the Whigs and the Tories—the war party and
the peace party—increased, so both sides took up more and more
extreme positions. The Tories came to identify themselves with the
Anglican Church and the cause of monarchy, and minimised the part
they had played in the Glorious Revolution, preferring to emphasise
the continuity between the age of Charles I and that of his granddaughter. Their attitude was made explicit when, on Gunpowder
Day 1709, Dr Sacheverell preached a sermon in St Paul's Cathedral.
Sacheverell was a noted high Tory, and took as his text, 'In peril among
false brethren'. The Church of England, he said, had had 'her pure
doctrines corrupted and defiled; her primitive worship and discipline
profaned and abused; her sacred orders denied and vilified; her priests
and professors (like St Paul) calumniated, misrepresented and ridiculed;
her altars and sacraments prostituted to hypocrites, deists, socinians
and atheists', and he implied that this tragic decline was due to the
resistance that had been offered to the Stuart monarchy in 1688. The
only hope, he was convinced, lay in 'an absolute and unconditional
obedience to the supreme power in all things lawful', and he insisted
on 'the utter illegality of resistance upon any pretence whatsoever'.

The Whigs, who had almost convinced themselves that they alone
carried out the Revolution, took up the challenge thrown down by

Sacheverell, and all the pent-up party strife was concentrated on this single issue. The Whig majority in the Commons decided to impeach Sacheverell, and Walpole was one of the managers of the trial which took place in Westminster Hall, where Charles I had defended the same twin causes of monarchy and the Church sixty years earlier. Sacheverell was accused of maintaining 'that the necessary means used to bring about the said happy Revolution were odious and unjustifiable', and Walpole, speaking for the prosecution, denounced the doctrine of non-resistance. He agreed that violent opposition to government should never be declared legal, but countered this by the assertion that 'the doctrine of unlimited, unconditional, passive obedience was first invented to support arbitrary and despotic power'.

The trial excited enormous public attention. Sir Christopher Wren had been commissioned to build galleries for the fashionable world and a box for the Queen—who was in daily atttendance—and outside the Hall the Tory mob gave itself up to the congenial task of burning down dissenters' meeting-houses. They even threatened to burn that Whig stronghold, the Bank of England, and the Horse Guards had to be called out to save the nation's treasure.

Sacheverell was condemned, but the punishment inflicted upon him —he was forbidden to preach for three years, and his sermon was ordered to be burnt by the common hangman—was so light that it amounted to a victory. The trial had shown just how strong Tory sentiment was, and this helped persuade Anne to remodel her ministry. The leading Whig ministers were gradually removed, and the Queen turned for support to that middle group of moderate Whigs and moderate Tories, of which Harley was a leading member. In April 1710 the last meeting between Anne and the Duchess of Marlborough took place, and the beginning of a new era, in which the Marlboroughs should no longer be dominant, was signalled by the appointment of the moderate Shrewsbury as Lord Chamberlain.

Godolphin complained to Anne about the way in which she had 'taken a resolution of so much consequence to all your affairs both at home and abroad, without acquainting the Duke of Marlborough and me with it till after you had taken it', but the Queen did not listen to him. Her policy was guided now by Robert Harley and his inter-mediary, Mrs Masham, and Harley appealed, as always, to those who put service to the Crown and state before consideration of party. 'As soon as the Queen has shown strength and ability to give the law to both sides,' he declared, 'then will moderation be truly shown in the exercise of power without regard to parties only.' In June, Sunderland, who was the vital link between his father-in-law, Marlborough, and the Whig JUNTO, was dismissed from office, and finally, on 8 August, the Queen sent a curt message to Godolphin, ordering him to break the white staff that had given him authority not only as Lord Treasurer but also as chief minister of the Crown. In September Rochester was appointed Lord President in place of Somers, and St John was made Secretary.

Harley, the Tories and Peace

Only after she had demonstrated her attitude by dismissing the Whigs did Anne dissolve Parliament and order a general election. The result was a Tory landslide, which shocked Harley as much as it surprised him. He had hoped to build a ministry of moderates, free from the extremists of both wings, but now he was dependent for his majority upon a House of Commons in which the high Tories were extremely powerful. By encouraging the Queen to get rid of the Whigs he had made himself the prisoner of the Tories. Marlborough saw the danger of this when he wrote that if Harley could, by allying with the Whigs, form 'a party stronger than that of the Tories, he would do it tomorrow. But the Tory party (or rather the Octobrists) is so strong in the Lower House that it is to be feared that Harley, who will always sacrifice everything to his ambition and private interests, will be obliged, if he is to keep his place, to devote himself to them and to embrace all their schemes.'

The Octobrists were the hundred and fifty or so high Tories who formed themselves into the October Club and demanded the dismissal of all Whigs, the impeachment of Whig ministers and the condemnation of occasional conformity. Harley skilfully placated this right wing by supporting measures of which it approved, as long as they did not restrict him. He persuaded the House, for instance, to reject a Place Bill, but he gave his support to an Act making a minimum land qualification necessary for members of Parliament. The Tories hoped that this measure would exclude from the Commons the landless business men of whom they disapproved, but the Act was stillborn, for temporary conveyances of land in the months preceding a general election enabled propertyless candidates to ignore the spirit of the law while observing its letter. In January 1711 Tory love of the Church of England was given practical expression in a Bill authorising government funds for the building of fifty new churches in London, and a committee was set up to investigate public accounts and (so the Tories hoped) to produce evidence of Whig defalcation.

The main aim of the Tories was, of course, peace, and even Marlborough agreed that 'besides the draining our nation both of men and money almost to the last extremity, our allies do by degrees so shift the burthen of the war upon us that, at the rate they go on, the whole charge must at last fall on England'.

There was little hope of a military solution, for Marlborough could neither bring the French to battle nor risk a laborious campaign of sieges, while in Spain an allied army which had sent hopes soaring by its capture of Madrid was cut off in December 1710 and its English rearguard forced to surrender. Even before this news reached England, peace negotiations had been opened between England and France, and Harley's envoy informed his French counterpart that 'we will no longer insist on the entire restoration of the monarchy of Spain to the House of Austria, or, if we do, it will be weakly and *pro forma*, and we shall be content provided France and Spain will give us good securities for our commerce; and as soon as we have got what we need and have made our bargain with the two crowns, we will tell our allies'.

The significance of this message was clear. Harley had abandoned the policy of 'No peace without Spain' and was prepared to negotiate terms with France behind the backs of England's allies. This was betrayal, but the only alternative was to continue fighting indefinitely until Louis agreed to the Austrian demand that he should assist in expelling his grandson from Spain. The absurdity of such a condition became even more apparent when, in April 1711, the Emperor died and was succeeded by 'King Charles'. There was no point in continuing the war merely to add Spain to the already vast possessions of the House of Austria, thereby reuniting the Empire that Charles V had divided a hundred and fifty years earlier.

In April 1711 the Queen showed her approval of Harley's policies by creating him Earl of Oxford and appointing him Lord Treasurer. The administration was Tory, but only moderately so, and the high Tories were already showing their discontent at the way in which they were being excluded from power. Oxford was prepared to cooperate with Marlborough until peace was signed, but he and the Duke fell out over the provisional terms drawn up by St John and the French in September 1711. By these terms France recognised the protestant succession in England, agreed to the cession of Gibraltar, Port Mahon and Newfoundland, and conceded English merchants a monopoly of the valuable slave trade with Spanish South America. The Netherlands, like the Italian possessions of Spain, were to go to the Empire, except for a barrier of fortress towns to protect the Dutch against further French aggression, and it was formally agreed that the crowns of France and Spain should never be united.

These terms were very satisfactory from England's point of view. Port Mahon and Gibraltar would give the English navy control of the Mediterranean and encourage the expansion of English commerce into Italy and the Levant; Newfoundland would give English fishermen a privileged position in the valuable fishing banks; while the slave trade monopoly, though nominally limited to thirty-three years, might well be extended indefinitely. The Lord Treasurer also saw in this last provision an opportunity to free himself from dependence on the Whig Bank of England, for he set up a South Sea Company which was to have the sole right to the South American trade as long as it took over part of the national debt.

English pleasure at the proposed terms was not shared by Austria and the Dutch, who felt they had been betrayed; nor were the German princes pleased at a settlement which left France as a potential menace to their security. Marlborough made himself the spokesman of the allies and it was to counter this powerful criticism that Oxford called on Swift to write the pamphlet which appeared in November 1711 under the title of *The Conduct of the Allies*. In this brilliant and savage piece of propaganda Swift built up a distorted, but convincing, interpretation of the war. It had been started, he said, by a united nation in order to ensure the partition of the Spanish Empire. But Marlborough and the Whigs had become infatuated with military glory and with the prospect of their own continual enrichment, and had turned a deaf ear to French offers conceding all their original demands. They had deliberately kept the war going, not only in the Netherlands but in Spain, where they had undertaken commitments which they had no intention of meeting. The only gainers from these long years of exhaustion were the Whig profiteers and the foreign allies who had bled the English squirearchy to death while they waxed fat.

The Conduct of the Allies sold over eleven thousand copies within a month of its appearance, and provoked a pamphlet war more violent than anything seen since the days of the Popish Plot. The Whigs, in their struggle to defeat the proposed terms of peace, made an unholy alliance with Nottingham and the high Tories. They committed themselves, at last, to accepting the Occasional Conformity Bill, while the Tories promised to support the principle of 'No Peace without Spain'. In December 1711 the Occasional Conformity Bill, which imposed penalties on any office-holder found attending a dissenting service, became law, and the House of Lords passed a resolution against peace without Spain. But Harley and the moderate Tories in the Commons had closed their ranks in face of the common danger and were ready, with the Queen's support, to counter-attack. On the last day of 1711 Anne dismissed Marlborough by a note which was so curt that the Duke tossed it into the fire; in January of the following year Walpole was impeached on a charge of corruption; and to ensure the acceptance of peace terms by the Lords, Anne created twelve new peers.

Now that the Tory government was secure at home, it could go ahead in bringing peace to Europe. In January 1712 a conference opened at Utrecht, and the chief English negotiator was Henry St John, a descendant of the Earls of Warwick and a member of the same family as Oliver St John who had been Pym's ally against absolute monarchy. Henry St John was not a lover of absolutism, but he saw an opportunity of replacing Oxford as the Queen's chief minister if he made himself the leader of the high Tories. Anne herself disliked and distrusted St John, and in July 1712 she refused his request for an earldom and created him Viscount Bolingbroke instead. Bolingbroke resented this slight—'I remain clothed with as little of the Queen's favour as she could contrive to bestow' he commented bitterly—but the opposition of Anne only made him the more determined to force himself into a commanding position in the administration. He was impelled by ambition, and time was never given him to show what use he might have made of the power he so ardently desired. 'I am afraid', he wrote many years later, 'that the principal spring of our actions was to have the government of the state in our hands; that our principal views were the conservation of this power, great employments to ourselves and great opportunities of rewarding those who had helped to raise us, and of hurting those who stood in opposition to us. . . . I believe few or none of us had any very settled resolution.'

Bolingbroke, who echoed Swift's criticism of the conduct of England's allies, felt no obligation towards them. He was afraid that military success would encourage the Dutch to raise their terms, and for this reason he sent a message to Marlborough's successor in command of the British army, giving him 'the Queen's positive command to . . . avoid engaging in any siege, or hazarding a battle, till you have further orders from her Majesty. I am at the same time directed to let your Grace know that the Queen would have you disguise the receipt of this order; and her Majesty thinks that you cannot want pretences for conducting yourself so as to answer her ends without owning that which might, at present, have an ill effect if it was publicly known.' He added as an afterthrought: 'I had almost forgotten to tell your Grace that communication is given of this order to the Court of France. . . .'

Bolingbroke was, in fact, treating the French as allies and the allies as enemies. In July 1712 English troops were withdrawn from active service, leaving Eugene to be heavily defeated, and in the following October Bolingbroke notified the French of Eugene's plan of attack so that they could take the necessary counter-measures. This sort of treatment, combined with her own exhaustion, drove Holland to accept the terms drawn up by England and France, and in April 1713 the war was formally concluded by the signing of the treaties of Utrecht. Only the Emperor held out for another year, until he too was obliged to come to terms.

St John and the Succession

A general election held in the summer of 1713 confirmed the Tories in possession of power. Now that the war was over the succession was the major political issue. In law there was no succession problem, since the heir to the throne was the Electress Sophia of Hanover. But Sophia was an ageing woman, not expected to live long, and it seemed certain that the Crown of Great Britain would therefore pass to her son, Prince George. The disadvantage of this arrangement from the Tory point of view was that George was one of the German princes who had taken a prominent part in the war against France, and he regarded the 'English Peace' as a betrayal of all he had fought for. George was in touch with Marlborough and the Whigs, and the general assumption was that his accession would be followed by Whig rule.

Such a prospect did not appeal to the Tories, and many of them, including Bolingbroke, were flirting with the idea of bringing back the Stuart line in the person of the Old Pretender, James Edward, the 'warming-pan baby'. The biggest obstacle to this was James's Roman Catholic religion, especially since the young man, in spite of considerable pressure put upon him, refused to renounce his faith. James would return to England as a catholic King, or he would not return at all.

Bolingbroke was not so besotted with the Stuarts that he believed their restoration was possible even without a change of religion. He knew that the country would not accept another catholic King, yet he also knew that the accession of George of Hanover would mean the end of his political career. He therefore struggled for power, hoping, as he later said, 'to break the body of the Whigs, to render their supports useless to them, to fill the employments of the kingdom down to the meanest with Tories. We imagined that such measures, joined to the advantages of our numbers and property, would secure us against all attempts during [the Queen's] reign, and that we should soon become too considerable not to make our terms in all events which might happen afterwards.'

For the fulfilment of this plan Bolingbroke needed control of royal patronage, but this was vested in Lord Treasurer Oxford. Bolingbroke had therefore to drive Oxford from power, and to do it speedily, so that he could push Tories into all the key posts before Anne died. He knew that time was short, and he deliberately whipped up high Tory feeling so that he could force the issue. In the last years of Anne's reign, with the Tories torn between two leaders, with rumours of treachery in the air, and with the Whigs fighting every move to deprive them of the reward which would follow George's accession, political passions rose to fever height.

Oxford had no policy except that of staying in power and keeping Bolingbroke out of it. He had always been averse to preconceived ideas, and told Swift 'that wisdom in public affairs was not . . . the forming of schemes with remote views, but the making use of such incidents as happen'. Unfortunately for him there were no 'incidents' of which he could make use. He did not seriously consider working for a Stuart restoration, he hoped vaguely to come to terms with the Whigs and the Hanoverians, and he dulled his anxiety by drinking more and more heavily.

In June 1714 Bolingbroke led the high Tories in their campaign to put down dissenting academies, and to restrict teaching to persons holding a licence from the bishop of their diocese. The Schism Act was introduced into the Commons to give effect to these proposals, and Bolingbroke hoped that Oxford, who had good reason to think well of nonconformist teachers, would oppose it and thereby discredit himself with the Queen and the Tories. But Oxford, although he proposed amendments to the Bill when it reached the Lords, did not vote against it, and he counter-attacked by persuading the Queen to issue a proclamation denouncing James Stuart and offering a reward of £5,000 to anyone who captured him, should he attempt to land in Britain.

Anne was slowly turning against her Treasurer, but Oxford was still in power when Parliament was prorogued in July 1714. Swift described the Tory ministry as 'a ship's crew quarrelling in a storm, or while their enemies are within gunshot', and it was true that by mid-July the situation had become critical, for Anne fell ill and was not likely to recover. Bolingbroke was frantic in his efforts to oust Oxford, and bitter quarrels took place between the two men in the presence of the dying Queen. Eventually, on 27 July, Anne dismissed her Lord Treasurer, but she did not immediately offer the white staff to Bolingbroke.

Before the Queen could make up her mind her illness took a turn for the worse. The Cabinet, reinforced by two Whig members who had not attended since the making of the Peace of Utrecht, decided against Bolingbroke, and recommended to the Queen that the moderate Whig Duke of Shrewsbury should be appointed Treasurer. Bolingbroke, hoping to make the best of a situation that was rapidly slipping out of his control, headed the procession of Councillors which made its way to the dying Queen to obtain her consent to this appointment. Shrewsbury became Lord Treasurer on 30 July, and early on the morning of 1 August Anne died at Kensington Palace. She had lived long enough to deprive Bolingbroke of any chance of success and to ensure the smooth accession of George I. 'The Earl of Oxford was removed on Tuesday,' Bolingbroke recorded in his diary, 'the Queen died on Sunday. What a world is this, and how does fortune banter us.'

18

Ireland, Scotland, and Overseas Possessions in the Seventeenth Century

IRELAND

The Plantation of Ulster

THE Tudors had imposed English rule on Ireland by force. The problem facing James was how to establish his authority on something more durable and less expensive. One method, which had already been tried with some success, was to dispossess the Irish landlords and replace them by English settlers, but this had caused rebellion in the closing years of Elizabeth's reign. Hugh O'Neill, Earl of Tyrone, who had led the rebellion, had been pardoned, but he and his fellow chieftain, the Earl of Tyrconnel, both felt apprehensive about the fate that might be reserved for them by the protestant English government, and in 1607 they fled to France rather than obey a summons to England.

The 'Flight of the Earls' left Ulster open to plantation, and the Crown took over the six northern counties, confiscating most of the land and offering it, in small parcels, to English and Scots 'undertakers', who had to agree, as one of the terms of their tenure, to accept only British settlers as tenants. Like so many Stuart enterprises, the plantation of Ulster was only a partial success. Ireland was in such a disturbed state, and land titles were so uncertain, that settlers were not forthcoming in any considerable numbers. By 1628 there were only some two thousand British families in Ulster, and many of the 'undertakers' had allowed the original Irish tenants to stay on. The two most successful features of the scheme were associated with Scotland and London. Scottish presbyterians, suffering from a shortage of land in their own country, were prepared to try their fortunes in Ireland, and as their numbers slowly increased they turned Ulster into a

Calvinist enclave and gave it a flavour, quite different from the rest of Ireland, which has endured to this day. The contribution of London came through the City corporation, which decided to invest money in establishing a major port in Ulster, and achieved a remarkable success by creating Londonderry.

The dispossessed Irish landowners, the great majority of them Roman Catholic, found themselves paupers and outlaws in their own country. They were, as one of their bishops described them, 'excluded from all hopes of restitution or compensation, and are so constituted that they would rather starve upon husks at home than fare sumptuously elsewhere. They will fight for their altars and hearths, and rather seek a bloody death near the sepulchres of their fathers than be buried as exiles in unknown earth and inhospitable sand.' These men, joined by the former retainers of chiefs who had been expropriated or had gone into exile, took to the hills and lived a life of plunder, waiting for the moment to come when they should at last be restored to their own.

The Anglo-Irish, or 'Old English', landowners were not affected by the plantation of Ulster. These men, descendants of settlers who had come to Ireland before the Tudor period, shared the Roman Catholic faith of the Irish, but were conscious of their origins and their social status and were not, at this stage, prepared to make common cause with their co-religionists against the New English—the government officials, soldiers and 'adventurers', who, with the blessing of the royal administration, were taking over Irish estates.

The Old English began to suffer as James gradually extended his plantation policy. They were also angered by the creation of a Court of Wards for Ireland in 1622, which represented a threat not only to their property but also to their religion, since it was part of the policy of the court to bring up all wards as protestants. By the time Charles I came to the throne the loyalty of the Old English had been strained almost beyond endurance, but the outbreak of war with Spain made it essential for the King to secure his position in Ireland. Negotiations took place between Lord-Deputy Falkland (father of Clarendon's friend) and representatives of the Irish landowners, and agreement was reached in 1628. The landowners agreed to pay the King £120,000 on condition that the enforcement of the oath of supremacy was relaxed and that security of land titles was guaranteed to anyone who had held his estates for sixty years.

The King accepted these terms, and made his concessions as an act of grace. It was intended that these 'Graces' should be given the authority of Parliamentary statute, but this had not been done by the time Falkland left Ireland in 1629. Falkland had hoped to establish the King's authority in Ireland by an alliance with the Old English, but he was frustrated by the New English who were strongly entrenched in the Irish administration. These men, of whom the most influential was Richard Boyle, Earl of Cork, regarded Falkland's dismissal as a triumph and looked forward to a period of cooperation and profit-sharing with the new Deputy. Unfortunately for them the new Deputy was Thomas Wentworth.

Lord-Deputy Wentworth

Wentworth was determined to extend the plantation system and the authority of the King in Ireland, and to this extent he was in agreement with the New English. But he had nothing except contempt for Cork and his colleagues, whom he regarded as 'a company of men most intent upon their own ends that ever I met with'. He was determined that Charles's rule in Ireland should be based not upon any group or faction but upon the goodwill of the people as a whole, assuming that the firm, impartial, uncorrupt administration which he intended to establish would command obedience by its own obvious virtues and would bring under its sway not only the Irish and Old English but the New English as well.

The authoritarian attitude of the new Deputy was clearly shown when the Irish Parliament assembled in 1634. Wentworth had taken great trouble to make sure that the protestants were in a majority, and had briefed the Councillors on their role. The Old English wanted confirmation of the Graces, but Wentworth would not consider a bargain. 'It is far below my great master', he told them, 'to come at every year's end with his hat in his hand, to entreat you that you would be pleased to preserve yourselves', and he insisted that the first session should be devoted to considering the needs of the Crown. Only in the second session, after Parliament had shown its goodwill, would he be prepared to consider grievances.

The Old and New English were both interested in winning security for their title-deeds and hoped to make certain of this by a generous vote of supply. They accordingly granted the King six subsidies, and then waited hopefully for the announcement of the promised reforms. But Wentworth would not agree that sixty years' tenure should give security, nor was he prepared to grant official recognition to the hold-ing of office by Roman Catholics. He had good reason to believe that the Crown and the Anglican Church had both been deprived of a great deal of land during the previous hundred years, and he did not wish any investigation into the legality of title-deeds to be held up by statutory barriers. He was thinking mainly of the New English, whose methods in land-grabbing had often been very doubtful, but by his refusal to confirm the Graces he alienated the Old English as well.

Wentworth realised that the common law courts would defend property rights in Ireland as in England. He therefore secured from the Crown letters patent giving the Court of Castle Chamber authority to make final decisions in matters affecting the Church. With this weapon he prepared to restore to the Crown and Church many estates of which they had been cheated. The biggest offender in this respect was the Earl of Cork, and Wentworth had a list of all Cork's property drawn up so that the title-deeds could be examined and if necessary disproved. Some of these deeds went back to the reign of Elizabeth, when Cork had first arrived in Ireland, and the Earl fought a bitter battle, with no quarter given, to preserve his property. He was forced to disgorge some of his possessions, and although he eventually won a favourable verdict, after Wentworth's fall, in the short run his fate served as a warning to all the other New English landowners.

Wentworth was not deterred by opposition. He was convinced that his policy in Ireland was the right one and that it would ultimately redound to the credit of the King. He also took pride in the fact that, as a result of his strong government, Irish trade was flourishing. Piracy round the coasts was put down, communications were improved and the linen industry was encouraged. Wentworth had a direct interest in the success of such measures, since he had taken over the Customs farm and was doing well out of it. He condemned the abuse of office by other men, but he was not free from it himself—although he could claim that his own enrichment served to increase the wealth and authority of the King he represented. Certainly, by the time he left Ireland in 1640, Wentworth was convinced of the success of his policy, for he declared that the Irish were 'as fully satisfied and as well affected to his Majesty's person and service as can possibly be wished for'.

The events of the next few years were to show how wrong the great Deputy had been in the estimate of his achievement. Wentworth had done nothing to solve the basic problems of Ireland. He had hoped to smother all discontents in the blanket of royal authority, but such a solution—assuming that it could ever have worked—would have needed a much longer time than Wentworth had at his disposal. When the Lord-Deputy left Ireland he had succeeded only in angering *all* the various groups. The Irish and Anglo-Irish hated him because he had refused to give them security of tenure and had extended the system of plantation; the New English loathed him because he had shown up their corruption and attacked their hold on office; while the presbyterians in the north detested him because he had tried to impose Laudian anglicanism and had ordered them to take the 'black oath' to obey royal commands unconditionally.

The Irish Rebellion

The discontent which Strafford had held in check boiled to the surface after his departure when, in October 1641, the native Irish rose in rebellion against the new settlers in Ulster and massacred them. The Old English were torn between the appeal to their faith and the appeal to tradition, but in the end their faith proved stronger and they threw in their lot with the rebels. Successive English governments had done nothing to keep their allegiance, and they saw in the growing strength of the puritans in England a menace to their own position.

Londonderry and a few other towns held out in Ulster, while in the Pale loyalist forces were commanded by the Earl of Ormonde—head of the Butlers, one of the oldest and greatest of the Old English families, but a protestant as a result of his upbringing as a royal ward. Ormonde appealed to England for reinforcements, but King and Parliament were in deadlock and there were few troops to be spared. Parliament proposed that ten million acres of Irish land should be confiscated and the best of it used to repay those who would advance money to the state for the suppression of the rebellion. The King accepted this proposal, but by the summer of 1642 both sides were preparing for war and Ireland was left to fend for itself.

The Irish rebels were guided by the Roman Catholic bishops, who set up the Confederation of Kilkenny, with a supreme council of two members from each province, pledged to carry on the war until Roman Catholicism was accepted as the official religion of Ireland. The Confederation controlled most of the country, except for pockets of resistance in Ulster and the Pale. Ormonde was still the nominal commander of all the protestant forces, but his primary loyalty was to the King,

O*

and Charles was constantly urging him to come to terms with the rebels so that his forces could be transferred to England.

In September 1643 Ormonde agreed to a cease-fire—the 'Cessation' —with the rebels, but little came of this. The Scots army in the north ignored the Cessation and subscribed to the Solemn League and Covenant, while the Munster protestants called on Parliament for support. Ormonde was betrayed even by the King, for Charles was in secret negotiation with the rebels, and gave the impression that if only they would come to his assistance he would accept their terms.

The Old English leaders in the Confederation were anxious for agreement with the King, partly out of loyalty and partly because they saw in a royal victory the best chance of toleration for their catholic religion. The Old English were in a strong position on the supreme council, and early in 1646 came to terms with Ormonde. But in June of that year the Confederate forces in Ulster, under the leadership of the Irishman O'Neill, heavily defeated the Scots. O'Neill was now the chief man in the Confederation, and dissolved the supreme council. He distrusted Charles, and insisted that the demands of the Roman Catholic Church must be met in full before any pact was made with the King. Not until January 1649, by which time the royal cause was lost, did Ormonde and the confederates accept the Treaty of Kilkenny, guaranteeing religious toleration and an independent Parliament for Ireland.

Cromwell and Ireland

Just over six months after the signing of the abortive Treaty of Kilkenny Cromwell landed in Ireland with twelve thousand men. He had been shocked, like all his contemporaries, by the reports of massacre and atrocities committed in Ulster, and was determined to exact vengeance. In September he assaulted Drogheda, after the garrison had refused to yield, and took the town by storm. 'Being thus entered,' he proudly recorded, 'we refused them quarter, having the day before summoned the town. I believe we put to the sword the whole number of the defendants. I do not think thirty of the whole number escaped with their lives. Those that did are in safe custody for Barbados.' He had no reason to anticipate criticism of his actions from the English Parliament, but he made his position clear. 'I am persuaded', he wrote, 'that this is a righteous judgement of God upon those barbarous wretches, who have imbrued their hands in so much innocent blood.'

The slaughter at Drogheda was followed by the destruction of the garrison at Wexford, for Cromwell—who shared the general English ignorance about Ireland—never realised that most of the troops fighting against him had earlier fought *against* the rebels.

Cromwell left Ireland after nine months, leaving Ireton and Ludlow to complete the conquest. Ormonde fled into exile, O'Neill died, and by May 1652 Ireland lay prostrate before the English invaders. The conquerors' terms were set out in the Act for Settlement of Ireland, which provided that every Irish landowner, protestant or catholic, should lose his estates unless he could prove that he had shown 'constant good affection to the interests of the commonwealth of England'. There was nothing new about this policy. It marked the extension to the whole of Ireland of the system of plantation that had previously been applied only to parts, and it resulted in a gigantic change of land-ownership. Protestant landowners might, with luck, hold on to part at least of their estates, but the majority of the eight thousand catholic landlords were expelled from their property. They were replaced by English soldiers, who accepted land in compensation for arrears of pay, and by the 'adventurers' who had loaned money to the government in order to make the reconquest of Ireland possible. Parliament and Cromwell had between them completed the work that the Tudors had begun. They had turned catholic Ireland into a country dominated by protestant landlords.

The confiscation and redistribution of land was the most durable achievement of Cromwell in Ireland. He also established a union between England and Ireland, and summoned thirty Irish representatives to sit in his Parliaments, but neither this measure nor the establishment of free trade between the two countries survived the Restoration.

The Restoration Settlement

Charles II was faced with a land problem in Ireland even more intractable than that with which he had to deal in England. He promised to confirm the titles of existing owners and at the same time to restore to their estates all those who had been evicted for fighting on the royalist side, but as Ormonde wryly commented, 'there must be new discoveries of a new Ireland, for the old will not serve to satisfy these engagements!' An Irish Parliament, summoned in 1661, passed the Act of Settlement, which left existing owners secure in the possession of their estates, promised restitution for evicted protestants, and made grudging provision for Roman Catholics who could be shown to have suffered for the King's cause. As Ormonde had foretold, however, there was not enough land to meet this settlement, and four years later an Act of Explanation was passed, requiring the Cromwellian settlers to part with a third of their property in order to compensate land-hungry claimants, and ordering that in all disputes between catholics and protestants, the latter were to have the benefit of the doubt.

This solution of the land problem satisfied the protestants since it confirmed their ascendancy, but the catholics felt, with reason, that they had been robbed, and they continually agitated for the repeal of the Act of Settlement. As far as religion was concerned, however, they had much to be thankful for. Ormonde returned to Ireland as Lord-Lieutenant, and although he was a devout anglican he was prepared to obey Charles II's orders and turn a blind eye to catholic practices. Roman Catholic clergy were allowed to move freely about the country, schools and monasteries were set up, and the Mass was openly celebrated. There was less tolerance of dissenters, however, and in Ulster the bishops began evicting presbyterian ministers. Persecution continued, on and off, until the Declaration of Indulgence of 1672, which opened a new era for the nonconformists in Ireland as in England.

Prosperity helped to keep discontent at a safe level. Cattle-raising turned out to be a profitable enterprise and became the basis of Irish wealth. English commercial jealousy resulted in the exclusion of Irish cattle from England, but continental markets remained open and a flourishing trade was built up with them. Ormonde also continued Wentworth's policy of fostering the linen industry which, since it did not obviously compete with English manufactures, was relatively free from restrictive tariffs.

It is possible that Charles II intended to try out in Ireland the re-establishment of the Roman Catholic Church which he had in mind for England. But whatever his long-term plans, he never attempted anything more than toleration. James went much further, and ordered Tyrconnel, who replaced Clarendon as Lord-Lieutenant in January 1687, to weed out protestant officers from the Irish Army, appoint Roman Catholic judges, and generally repeat in Ireland the policy that was being pursued in England. Tyrconnel was so successful that when the Glorious Revolution took place in England, Ireland remained loyal—except for the Ulster protestants, who proclaimed William as King and were driven by Tyrconnel to take refuge in Londonderry.

The Penal Laws

James landed in Ireland in March 1689, and two months later he met the 'Patriot Parliament', which was dominated by Roman Catholics. This Parliament proceeded to establish liberty of conscience, and to repeal the hated Act of Settlement. In theory the land question was once again wide open, but in fact little could be done until James had achieved control over the whole country. In April 1689 he laid siege to Londonderry, but the city stubbornly held out until relieved by an English fleet. More than ships were needed, however, if Ireland was to be regained for the protestants. Danby urged William to take action before it was too late, but the King, who was eager to fight France in the Netherlands, regarded Ireland as a minor irritant. He authorised the despatch of an expedition to Ireland in August 1689, but it was not until June of the following year that he himself took control. The decisive encounter between the two Kings came a month later, at the Battle of the Boyne, and it resulted in the defeat of James, who gave up the struggle and retired to France. William and the protestant cause had triumphed, and in October 1691, Limerick, the last Irish stronghold, surrendered.

By the terms of the Treaty of Limerick, which put an end to fighting, Irish soldiers were to be free to take service in the armies of France, while Roman Catholics were to enjoy 'such privileges as are consistent with the laws of Ireland, or as they did enjoy in the reign of King Charles II'. The military articles of the Treaty of Limerick were duly observed, and English ships were provided for 'the flight of the wild geese'—the departure into voluntary exile of thousands of Irish catholic soldiers. The Irish Parliament, however, once again under the control of the protestant landlords, refused to ratify the civil articles. The protestants were determined to monopolise power, and they could not do this if catholics were allowed to take part freely in public life. They were prepared to tolerate the open exercise of the catholic religion, but only on condition that catholics accepted a position of permanent social and political inferiority.

During the reigns of William and Anne Irish Parliaments passed the penal laws which confirmed the protestant ascendancy. Roman Catholics were excluded from Parliament, the civil service, the armed forces, local government and the law. They were not allowed to educate their children at universities, nor were they free to acquire land.

The estates of a Roman Catholic landowner were to be divided, after his death, among all his children, unless the eldest became a protestant, in which case he was to have the entire property. These and other restrictive measures could not be rigidly enforced, but they did succeed in crippling the catholic Irish and keeping them out of public life throughout the eighteenth century. The transformation that the Tudors had started and Cromwell had accelerated was completed by the penal laws, and a legacy of hatred and violence was handed down to future generations.

SCOTLAND
James VI

James VI of Scotland, who became James I of England, hoped that the union of crowns would shortly be followed by a statutory union of peoples. He persuaded both the English and the Scottish Parliaments to set up commissions to consider this question, but in the end dislike between the two countries, and England's fear that her commercial supremacy might be weakened by Scottish competition, brought the negotiations to nothing. The only crumb of comfort came with the judgement given in 1606, in Calvin's case, that persons born in either of the two kingdoms after the date of James's accession to the English throne should have dual nationality.

When James left his native land he was full of expressions of regret and of his longing to return, but in fact he went back only once, and for the greater part of his reign Scotland had to be content with an absentee King. James boasted that he ruled Scotland with his pen, and it is true that government was carried out by the Scottish Privy Council, acting on orders from the King. The Scottish Parliament was of little account. It met only occasionally and its agenda was prepared by the Lords of the Articles, who were, in effect, royal nominees.

From London, James continued the fight to check the power of the presbyterian Kirk in Scotland. In 1606 Andrew Melville, one of the most determined of the puritan leaders, was sent into exile, and in the same year the Scottish bishops were strengthened by a statute restoring to them revenues that had earlier been transferred to the Crown. Four years later a Court of High Commission, on the English pattern, was set up to impose royal authority on the Church, and the position of the Scottish bishops was confirmed when they were formally con-secrated by their English brethren. James presumably hoped to persuade his Scottish subjects to accept the same form of Anglican Church government that buttressed his authority in England, but he moved carefully and took his time. In 1618, by the Five Articles of Perth, the King ordered the observance of certain practices in the Scottish Church, including kneeling to receive the sacrament. This last provision caused uproar among the puritan Scots, who regarded it as synonymous with popery, and although James did not cancel the Articles he did not insist on their rigid enforcement. The same was true of the Prayer-Book which was drawn up, at his command, in 1619. It was left to Charles I and his Archbishop to carry the battle against the Kirk into its next phase.

Charles I and Scotland

One of the reasons for James's success in Scotland was that he kept the nobles and the Kirk apart by playing on the jealousies between them. Charles, however, pushed the two groups together at the very outset of his reign by the Act of Revocation, which asserted the right of the Crown and Church to resume any lands which had been taken from them since the Reformation. Charles had no intention of immediately dispossessing all the nobles—most of whom, like their English counterparts, held Church lands—but it was his ultimate aim, as Wentworth was showing in Ireland, to counter-attack the forces of secularism and greed which had undermined royal and spiritual authority. The ministers of the Kirk were not impressed by the prospect of having lands restored to them; they were far more concerned about the threat which Arminianism represented, and they began to look upon the nobles as possible allies.

Open revolt came when Charles went ahead with his father's plan to impose a new Prayer-Book on the Scottish Church. The Scots bishops had been consulted about drawing up the Book, but it was never submitted to the Scottish Parliament or to the General Assembly of the Kirk. The Scots detested it not simply because it was 'popish' but also because it was imposed upon them by an alien power: it was an insult to Scottish nationalism as well as the Scottish Church. The uproar in St Giles's Cathedral that greeted the introduction of the Book sparked off a general rising, and all classes united in signing the Covenant, by which they swore to uphold the honour of the King, but to resist all popish innovations.

The Covenanters were organised by John Leslie, Earl of Rothes, whose family held many estates which had previously belonged to the Church, and he was assisted by the Earls of Argyll and Montrose. Charles's chief adviser in Scotland was the Marquis of Hamilton, and the King ordered him to play for time while he mustered an army. 'I expect not anything can reduce that people, but only force', he wrote. 'I give you leave to flatter them with what hopes you please . . . till I be ready to suppress them.' Suppression was out of the question, however, for Charles had no effective army, and he therefore instructed Hamilton to suspend the Prayer-Book (a mere formality, since it was not being used) and to summon a General Assembly of the Kirk.

The Assembly opened in November 1638, but no bishops were present. The Covenanters had spread the rumour that the bishops were to be tried for 'crimes' they had committed, and this had the desired effect of keeping them away from the Assembly. Hamilton realised that he could do nothing with this collection of ministers and lay elders, and decided on a swift dissolution. The Assembly, however, refused to dissolve. Members allowed Hamilton to depart, but they stayed in session themselves, annulled the Articles of Perth and the Prayer-Book, and declared the abolition of episcopacy.

Both sides were now preparing to fight, and the Scots chose Alexander Leslie, a veteran of the Thirty Years War, to command their forces. Charles's raw levies could not stand up to such troops, and in June 1639 the King accepted the Pacification of Berwick, by which he agreed to leave all matters in dispute to the decision of the Scottish General Assembly and Parliament. But when these bodies assembled, in August, they proved to be as intransigent as their predecessors. The General Assembly confirmed the abolition of episcopacy and ordered all Scots to take the Covenant, while the Parliament, in which the Covenanters were strongly represented, broke with its servile past and insisted on its right to appoint the Lords of the Articles. Charles might have been prepared to accept a temporary abandonment of episcopacy, but he would not consent to its total abolition. Negotiations between the two sides came to nothing, and the Scots had recourse to arms again. In August 1640 the Covenanting army crossed the border into England and by the end of the month had occupied Newcastle.

The Scots remained in possession of the northern English counties until the Long Parliament met and drew up terms of peace. The King agreed to withdraw his condemnation of the Covenant and Covenanters, to remove his garrisons from Scotland and to hand over Edinburgh Castle, and in return the Scots agreed to recall their troops from England. Charles was now hoping to gain a party for himself in Scotland, anticipating that Scottish troops might one day be useful in defending him against the English Parliament. On his visit to Scotland in 1641 he tried to win over his former opponents by distributing honours among them. Argyll, for instance, was made a marquis, while Alexander Leslie, the Scottish commander, was created Earl of Leven. This policy of conciliation did not, however, pay off. The Covenanters were very powerful and not disposed to put their trust in Charles's apparent change of heart. Montrose, it is true, was anxious for a reconciliation with the King, but he was outmanœuvred by Argyll who, in spite of his marquisate, was using all his influence to cement the coalition against Charles.

The Covenanters were far more likely to support Parliament than the King, but after sparking off the civil war they held aloof until the closing months of 1643. Their aim was to establish presbyterianism in England, thereby giving themselves the sort of religious security that Charles had tried to obtain by imposing episcopacy on Scotland, but the Long Parliament, having just thrown off one ecclesiastical despotism, was unwilling to subject itself to another. English puritans had never wholeheartedly accepted the political implications of Calvinism, and preferred an erastian settlement to any form of theocracy. They were only persuaded to agree on terms with the Scots after Charles had come within an ace of winning the civil war. The Scots were confidently awaiting the plea for help that Pym made shortly before his death, convinced that God had used the weapon of defeat to bring the English to their senses. For them the Solemn League and Covenant was the first step in the creation of a presbyterian England, but for Vane and many other members of the Long Parliament it was mainly a military alliance, with doctrinal undertones that were best left undiscussed.

A Scottish Covenanting army, under the Earl of Leven, invaded England early in 1644 and played a major part in the campaign that eventually brought Charles I to defeat. But while the Covenanters were marching south, Montrose, now completely disillusioned with his fellow-rebels, raised a rebellion in the Highlands and won a series of astonishing victories. If Charles could ever have reached him, or could have sent troops to him from Ireland, defeat would have been staved off, but the war in England was going too badly for any men to be spared, and Montrose had to fight alone. His luck and his skill enabled him to survive until September 1645, but in that month he was heavily defeated at Philphaugh and had to flee to the Continent.

Cromwell and Scotland

The Scots failed to come to terms with Charles I, after he surrendered himself to them in 1646, and eventually handed him over to Parliament. But they had sworn, in the Covenant, to protect the honour and person of the King, and became increasingly alarmed by the news which reached them from England. When Charles escaped from the army and fled to Carisbrooke they were ready to open negotiations with him again, and the King eventually agreed to accept presbyterianism for three years in return for Scots support. This 'Engagement', as it was called, led at last to Scottish intervention on the King's side, but the Covenanters still distrusted Charles and were unwilling to give him their full assistance unless and until he took the Covenant. The 'Engagers', unable to depend upon the Covenanting army, had to raise their own troops, and it was their force, badly trained and badly led, which Cromwell swept away at the battle of Preston in August 1648.

A year later, however, Covenanters and Engagers had united against England. They were shocked by the execution of Charles I and by the failure of the republican government to establish presbyterianism in England, and when Charles II agreed to accept the Covenant they proclaimed him King. It was an unhappy alliance. Charles had to abandon Montrose to the revengeful fury of the Covenanters, who executed him, and he was plagued by Scottish divines anxious to probe into the secrets of his soul and assure themselves that his 'conversion' was genuine. In fact it was far from genuine, but Charles preferred a Covenanting Crown to no Crown at all, and the Scots were quite confident that, with the Lord on their side, they would humble the proud Parliament and at last impose 'the godly religion' on England.

Their certainty, their self-confidence and their hopes were shattered at Dunbar. They had appealed to the Lord and the Lord had spoken! The defeat at Worcester, which came a year later, in September 1651, merely confirmed the verdict. Scotland was now, like Ireland, prostrate before the English invader, and the conquest that Cromwell had started was completed by General Monck.

During the Interregnum, Scotland remained under military rule, and although it was formally integrated into the united republic which Cromwell established, the thirty Scottish representatives who sat at Westminster were in fact the nominees of the army. Cromwell left the presbyterians undisturbed in their worship, but insisted that toleration should be shown towards the sects. The ministers of the Kirk did not thank him for his lack of fanaticism, and opposition to the Protectorate was increased by the heavy taxation needed to maintain the army. Monck observed in 1657 that 'the Scots are now as malignant as ever they were', and the Restoration was welcomed in Edinburgh as in London.

The Restoration Settlement

The short-lived union of England and Scotland was ended in 1661, as was freedom of trade between the two countries, and presbyterians were once again subjected to persecution. The bishops returned, conventicles were forbidden, and illegal assemblies were put down by force. The Scottish Parliament could offer no resistance to these measures because it was once again under the control of Crown-appointed Lords of the Articles, and after formally annulling all the legislation of the Interregnum and voting the King a considerable annual revenue, it was dissolved. Scotland was henceforward ruled by the Privy Council, under the direction of the King's commissioner in Edinburgh.

The policy of repressing the puritans lasted until 1666, when it provoked the Pentland Rising. This minor rebellion was easily put down, but it persuaded Charles to abandon persecution and to accept Lauderdale's proposals for increasing toleration. Lauderdale, who was Secretary for Scotland throughout the greater part of Charles's reign, was a former presbyterian, and he wanted to put an end to religious and factional strife by elevating royal authority, as Wentworth had done in Ireland forty years earlier. The Letter of Indulgence of 1669 allowed ejected ministers to return to their livings, as long as they agreed to accept episcopacy, and the number of conventicles increased. But Lauderdale, who had hoped to quieten passions by a policy of toleration, was alarmed to find that he had opened the way to a revival of the power of the Kirk. Rather than risk a renewed challenge to royal authority he began repression once again. In 1670 a new Act against conventicles was passed, and in the years that followed troops were once more employed to suppress illegal assemblies. The Covenanters, despairing of any improvement in their condition, rose in rebellion in 1678 and murdered James Sharp, the oppressive Archbishop of St Andrews. But they had no clear plan, their hastily raised army was no match for the trained English troops, and they were crushed by Monmouth at the Battle of Bothwell Bridge in May 1679.

Monmouth persuaded his father to get rid of Lauderdale and to be lenient in his treatment of the rebels, but Lauderdale was succeeded by James, Duke of York, who immediately brought the machinery of government under close control. All officials were required to renounce the Covenant and to take an oath of non-resistance, and the Scottish Parliament was persuaded to pass an Act recognising that differences of religion could not prevent a legitimate heir from succeeding to the throne of Scotland. James's opponents had to suffer silently or to emigrate, but in the south-west of the country perpetual guerrilla warfare was waged between the dissident Cameronians and English troops.

James was pleased with the success of his policy in Scotland, which encouraged him in his belief that firm rule was the answer to all problems. When Argyll—son of the first marquis, who had been executed after the Restoration—tried to raise a rebellion against the new King in 1685, he found no support, and suffered the same fate as his father. Even James's policy of Roman Catholic infiltration aroused little protest, especially as it was accompanied by toleration for dissenters. Scotland took no part in the Glorious Revolution, and not until February 1689 did a Convention of Estates, meeting at William's invitation, recognise the new English sovereigns as monarchs of Scotland.

Scotland and the Glorious Revolution

Although the Scots had not joined in expelling James, they took advantage of the Revolution to secure their religious and constitutional liberties. The 'Claim of Right' went further than the English Bill of Rights by asserting that Parliament was justified in deposing any ruler who violated the law, and when the Convention was formally declared a Parliament it forced William to agree that the Lords of the Articles should be abolished. As for the Church, episcopacy was abandoned, ministers who had been ejected by the Stuarts were restored, and a General Assembly of the Kirk was summoned for the first time since 1653. The contrast between the treatment of Scotland and of Ireland could not have been greater. In Scotland the Revolution marked the triumph of all the Scots had struggled for, whereas in Ireland it meant defeat and humiliation for the Roman Catholic population. The key to the difference lies in the fact that Scottish puritanism had never affronted English susceptibilities in the same way as Irish catholicism, and there had been no attempt to establish plantations in Scotland. While Ireland had been divided by Tudor and Stuart rule, Scotland had remained united.

Although the accession of William and Mary had been accepted by the greater part of Scotland, the Jacobites found many supporters among the Highlanders, and in July 1689 they defeated William's troops at Killiecrankie. But the rebels could not hold together for a long campaign and by 1690 the pacification of the Highlands was well under way, with Fort William being constructed as a base from which to complete operations. Highland chiefs were offered a free pardon if they made their submission to William, but some of the King's advisers felt that an example should be made of one of the more recalcitrant clans, to overawe the others. The Macdonalds of Glencoe were chosen as victims and in February 1692 troops from Fort William, who had been billeted on the Macdonalds, suddenly turned on their hosts and murdered them. Many of the intended victims escaped, but the chief and thirty of his followers were slaughtered. It is doubtful whether William himself had any knowledge of what was intended, but the massacre of Glencoe poisoned relations between him and his Scottish subjects.

Bad feeling was also stirred up by the Navigation Acts, which treated the Scots as foreigners where trade was concerned. Scotland was not rich in natural resources, but in the face of English jealousy Scottish merchants looked to their own salvation. In 1695 a Bank of Scotland was successfully created, and in the same year the Scottish Parliament authorised the establishment of a company to trade with Africa and the Indies. It was hoped that this company would be a joint venture between England and Scotland, for many English merchants who were excluded from trade with the East by the monopoly of the East India Company hoped to find an outlet for their capital and enterprise in the Scottish company. The English Parliament took up the question, however, inspired not so much by love of the East India Company as by fear of Scottish competition, and threats of impeachment persuaded English merchants to pull out of the scheme.

The Scots, smarting under a sense of betrayal, decided to go ahead on their own. About £200,000 was raised by a national effort, and it was decided to send an expedition to establish a settlement at Darien, on the Isthmus of Panama. This plan was foolhardy, in face of the

terrible climate and of the fact that Darien was claimed by the Spaniards. William was engaged in complicated diplomacy over the
Spanish succession, and the last thing he wanted was an overt act of
hostility against Spain. He therefore instructed neighbouring English
colonies to give no assistance to the Scottish venture, and by April
1700, after three expeditions had been decimated by disease and Spanish
opposition, the Scots gave up. The money which had been subscribed,
and which had meant a heavy sacrifice for a poor country like Scotland, had been dissipated without result, and the Scots put the blame
for their failure firmly on England.

The Union

The Darien fiasco had shown up the weakness of William's position.
As King of England he was opposed to the project, while as King of
Scotland he might have been expected to support it. The only way in
which to prevent the recurrence of this split personality was to unite
the legislatures of the two countries, but William died before he could
accomplish this. Anne continued his work and immediately appointed
commissioners to treat for union, but little progress was made, for the
English were determined to keep the Scots out of their commercial
empire, and negotiations were eventually broken off. The Scottish
Parliament showed its anger against this unfriendly treatment by
emphasising the isolation thrust upon Scotland. By the Act anent
Peace and War, passed in 1703, it declared that Scotland should not be
automatically committed to war or peace by English policies, but
should arrive at its own decisions, and in the following year the Act of
Security laid down that Scotland would not accept the Hanoverian
Succession unless her constitutional, economic and religious liberties
were guaranteed.

The English Parliament riposted with the Aliens' Act, ordering that
all Scots were to be treated as foreigners and that trade between the
two countries was to come to an end. But the prospect of a Hanoverian
successor arriving in England at the same time as the Old Pretender
landed, with a French army, in Scotland, was more than English
ministers could bear. The Aliens Act had already opened the way to a
solution by providing that its terms should not come into effect if the
Scottish Parliament appointed commissioners to treat for union. This
invitation was taken up, terms were swiftly agreed, and in 1707
England and Scotland were formally combined into Great Britain.

The Union confirmed the Hanoverian succession. It also opened the trade of England to all British subjects. The Scots kept their own established presbyterian Church, their own law and, for a time, their own Privy Council, but they lost their Parliament. They were compensated for this by being given forty-five seats added to the Lower House of the Parliament sitting at Westminster, as well as sixteen representative peers in the Upper House. The Scots agreed to share the burden of the National Debt, but in return for this they were given a lump-sum payment of £400,000, to be used to compensate those who had suffered from the Darien disaster—thereby removing, it was hoped, at least one source of Anglo-Scottish hostility.

The terms of the Union have been criticised on the grounds that they gave Scotland inadequate representation in the British Parliament, but the commercial provisions were generous and were quickly exploited by Scottish merchants. The Union did not, of course, lead to the immediate end of friction. The period of Tory rule at the end of Anne's reign put severe strains on the new relationship, since the government insisted on restoring the rights of lay patrons in Scotland and of permitting episcopal worship there. Bitterness reached such a point that in 1713 a motion to dissolve the Union was only narrowly defeated in the House of Lords, but the following year saw the triumph of the Whigs, who had framed the original agreement and were determined to maintain the Union. It has survived to the present day, bringing incalculable advantages to both sides and showing that the politicians of Anne's reign could act with far-sighted generosity when self-interest and protestantism combined.

OVERSEAS POSSESSIONS
Virginia

Elizabethan attempts to found a colonial empire failed because of lack of persistence. Money and energy that might have enabled infant settlements to survive were spent on fighting the Spaniards and preying on their treasure-ships, but the conclusion of peace with Spain shortly after James's accession made resources available again for attempts at establishing plantations overseas. These were commercial ventures, inspired in part by economic nationalism, for it was hoped that the colonies might make England self-sufficing by producing the naval stores and 'Mediterranean' goods which she could not produce herself. Good settlers were not at first easy to find, but the economic depression which set in about 1620 created unemployment and acted as a spur to emigration; so also did the persecution of the puritans, which became more severe after Laud's rise to power.

The first big attempt at colonisation in the Stuart period was directed towards Virginia, where Ralegh had pointed the way. Ralegh sold his patent for colonising Virginia to a group of London business men who included Sir Thomas Smythe, son of the chief Customs farmer and himself a prominent member of the Merchant Adventurers, the Levant Company and the Muscovy Company. Smythe believed that colonisation could be a profitable business, and he was the moving spirit behind the formation of the Virginia Company in 1606. In December of that year three ships, the *Susan Constant*, *Godspeed* and *Discovery*, set sail from London, carrying almost a hundred and fifty settlers. They arrived in Chesapeake Bay in May 1607, sailed up the river which they named after King James, and established a settlement at the site which was eventually to become Jamestown.

For many years the future of the colony hung in the balance. The swampy site and hostile Indians accounted for many deaths, and the settlers were dependent on the supplies which reached them from England. A Royal Council of Virginia had been set up in England during the first flush of enthusiasm, but as it became clear that no easy fortunes were going to be made, the King lost interest, and in 1609 he issued a new charter making the Virginia Company the proprietors of the colony.

Money for the venture came from 'adventurers' who bought shares in the company; the cost of transportation was paid either by the settlers themselves, who were then free to start up their own farms as soon as they arrived, or by the Company, in which case the assisted person had to agree to work for the community for a number of years. By 1617 the colony was firmly established, and had made tobacco its staple crop. Unfortunately for the Company, the habit of smoking developed only slowly, and met with the disapproval of the King. Profits were never sufficient to repay adventurers the money they had invested, and new capital was consequently hard to attract. Smythe was unpopular with many of the shareholders, who blamed him for the lack of profits, and he was also opposed by some of the leaders of the parliamentary opposition who saw in Virginia a chance to put their own principles into practice. By 1619 Smythe had been pushed out of office and Sir Edwin Sandys, that doughty champion of the privileges of the House of Commons, became Treasurer in his place.

Sandys's rule lasted only a few years, but it led to the summoning of the first representative body ever to meet on American soil. The general assembly of Virginia, elected by the settlers themselves, met in July 1619 and again the following year, and this movement towards self-government, which Sandys had encouraged, survived his fall. In 1624, after complaints that the administration of the Virginia Company was more concerned with politics than commerce, the Crown confiscated the Company's charter and assumed direct control itself. A royal governor was despatched, but he had orders to continue summoning the representative assembly, and it was also made clear that settlers, being under the authority of the English Crown, were to enjoy the law and liberties that belonged to Englishmen at home.

New England

Just over a year after the little fleet had sailed from London for Virginia, a group of Nottinghamshire puritans, who could not find it in their consciences to give outward conformity to the practices of the Church of England, emigrated to Holland and there established a spiritual community. But in spite of the tolerance that Holland offered, they missed their native land and hoped that they might one day be able to live, if not in England, at least among Englishmen. The Virginia Company, prompted by Sandys, gave them a licence to settle in the New World, a joint-stock company was set up, and in September 1620 the Pilgrim Fathers set sail from Plymouth in the *Mayflower*. Out of more than a hundred passengers only thirty-five were members of the original separatist congregation: the rest of the emigrants had come direct from England and did not all share the puritan attitudes of their colleagues. No provision had been made for the separate government of this community, since it was assumed that it would come under the jurisdiction of the authorities in Virginia, but the more responsible emigrants drew up the 'Mayflower Compact', in which they agreed to set up a civil administration, if necessary, make their own laws and see to the enforcement of order. This foresight was wise, for the Pilgrim Fathers landed well to the north of Virginia and established their settlement at Plymouth. They managed to survive, though conditions were hard, and they made sufficient profit, by sending corn, timber and furs to England, to buy out the shareholders who had remained at home. By this means they created the first self-contained, self-governing English community in America.

The Pilgrim Fathers had begun the colonisation of New England and in 1629 they were followed by another puritan congregation, which had obtained a separate charter for itself as the 'Company of the Massachusetts Bay'. These new settlers founded Salem, and they shortly copied the example of the Plymouth settlers by deciding that 'the whole government, together with the patent for the said plantation, be . . . legally transferred and established to remain with us and others which shall inhabit upon the said plantation'. In 1630 John Winthrop, elected governor of the company and colony, set sail for Salem, taking with him not only the charter itself but a thousand new emigrants. These men were nearly all religious refugees, and they paid their own passage. Poor men had to go to the southern colonies and sell their labour to pay off their debt, but the New England colonists were, from the beginning, men of substance and of independent spirit.

During the reign of Charles I some sixty thousand emigrants left the shores of England, and of these about a third went to New England. The ideal of the puritan settlements in New England was not religious toleration but a different form of intolerance from that which obtained in England itself. In Massachusetts, government was confined to elders of the Church, who constituted only about one-fifth of the adult males, and anyone who objected to the rule of this theocratic oligarchy was expelled.

The intolerance of Massachusetts led to the foundation of a number of other colonies. One group of dissident settlers hived off and established themselves in Connecticut. Another group followed the irrepressible Roger Williams, champion of religious liberty, who was driven out of Massachusetts for declaring that the civil government had no authority in religious matters. In 1636 Williams took refuge among the Indians, and he insisted on treating them as equals and on buying from them land on which he might establish a new, and free, settlement. The community which he set up developed eventually into the self-governing colony of Rhode Island.

By the time civil war broke out in England, the colonies of North America were firmly established and already valued their virtual independence of the mother country. Further south, across the gap formed by the Dutch colony of New Netherland, Virginia had been joined by Maryland, created in 1632 by the Roman Catholic Lord Baltimore, and named in honour of Charles I's Queen. The northern colonies made their living out of agriculture and the trade in fish, furs and naval stores, but in Virginia and Maryland tobacco and cotton were the main crops. These were ideally suited for cultivation on big plantations, and because immigrant labour was not readily available for such work negroes were imported from West Africa. The New England settlements had built up a flourishing trade by supplying the plantation colonies with food, and they worked in close co-operation with the Dutch merchants and shipowners of New Netherland.

The West Indies

Of the islands off the American coast, Bermuda was the first to be settled by the English. Sir George Somers, sailing out to Virginia with fresh emigrants in 1609, was wrecked on the 'Somers Islands', but he found life there very agreeable and sent back reports which not only inspired Shakespeare to write *The Tempest* but also encouraged the formation of the Somers Islands Company. Further south, in the Caribbean, the first English settlement was on St Kitts, discovered in 1624, but in the following year an English ship returning home came across the uninhabited island of Barbados, and declared it annexed to the English Crown. Sir William Courteen, partner in an Anglo-Dutch trading concern, provided the funds for the settlement of the island and began a profitable trade in tobacco, but his rights were challenged by one of James I's Scottish favourites, the Earl of Carlisle, who had been given a patent creating him proprietor of the 'Caribee Islands'. Carlisle was not personally interested in colonisation, but he hoped that profits from the West Indian plantations would help pay off his debts, and he fought a prolonged legal battle which eventually confirmed his ownership. For some years Barbados and other West Indian islands concentrated on the production of tobacco and cotton, but by the time the civil war broke out they had begun the cultivation of sugar cane on a large scale.

Cromwell and the Colonies

The colonies took no direct part in the civil war, and although the sympathies of the New England settlements were clearly with Parliament their main objective was the preservation of their freedom of action. The puritan triumph in England caused a second big wave of emigration—this time of royalists, most of whom went to the southern colonies. Others settled in Barbados and Antigua, and royalist predominance in the southern colonies explains why after the execution of

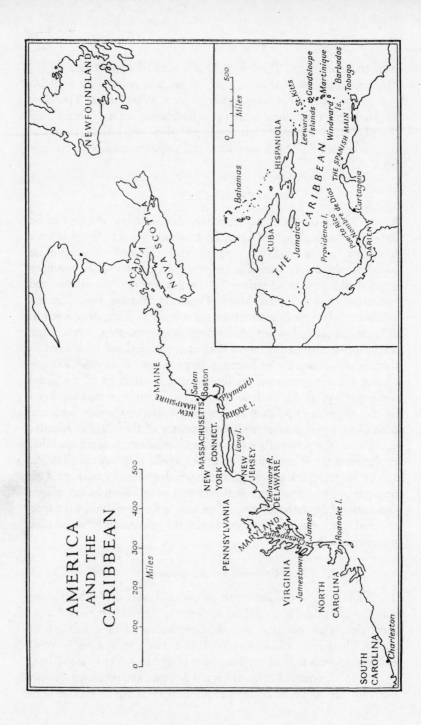

AMERICA
AND THE
CARIBBEAN

Miles
0   100   200   300   400   500

NEWFOUNDLAND

ACADIA

NOVA SCOTIA

MAINE
NEW HAMPSHIRE
Salem
Boston
Plymouth
MASSACHUSETTS
RHODE I.
NEW YORK
CONNECT.
Long I.
NEW JERSEY
PENNSYLVANIA
Delaware R.
DELAWARE
MARYLAND
Chesapeake
R. James
Jamestown
VIRGINIA
NORTH CAROLINA
Roanoke I.
SOUTH CAROLINA
Charleston

Miles
0   500

Bahamas
CUBA
THE JAMAICA
Jamaica
HISPANIOLA
Leeward Islands
St. Kitts
Guadeloupe
Martinique
Windward Is.
Barbados
Tobago
CARIBBEAN
Providence I.
Porto Rico
Nombre de Dios
THE SPANISH MAIN
Cartagena
DARIEN

Charles I, the governments of these settlements recognised Charles II as King.

The English Parliament, having won its long struggle against the King, was not prepared to lose control of the West Indian and southern mainland colonies, which were so valuable for English trade. In 1651 Sir George Ayscue was sent with a fleet to restore obedience, and this he did without any difficulty. His expedition was a striking demonstration of the effect of sea power, especially when used against settlements that were entirely dependent upon oceanic trade. Cromwell hoped to use the Commonwealth navy not simply to enforce obedience but to extend the area of English sovereignty in the West Indies. He realised that this would be to his country's economic advantage, and the idea of uprooting Spanish power in that area appealed to the Elizabethan in him. He had already been involved with the company that attempted to establish a puritan settlement on Providence Island, but this was far too near the mainland coast, and the settlers had been driven out by the Spaniards in 1641. Cromwell's expedition, despatched in 1654, failed in its main objective of capturing Hispaniola, but it added Jamaica to England's colonial empire.

The governments of the Interregnum took the first big steps towards breaking the Dutch monopoly of trade in the American region, and of knitting together the commerce of England and her colonies. Early Stuart governments had not been entirely neglectful of colonial needs: the first committee of the Privy Council for Foreign Plantations, for instance, had been set up in 1634, and as early as 1621 James had ordered that colonial tobacco should be sent only to England and that, in return, the growing of tobacco in England should be forbidden. In 1651 these *ad hoc* measures were gathered together in the Navigation Act, which was intended to stimulate the growth of English shipping and to push the Dutch out of the privileged position they had won for themselves during the civil war period.

The Restoration of Royal Authority

Post-Restoration governments continued the policy of commercial integration, and completed the process of driving out the Dutch by taking over the colony of New Netherland in 1664. Expansion continued also to the south and north of Virginia, though the settlers for these new colonies were drawn from Europe and the existing settlements rather than from England, where the growth of trade and industry was creating a demand for labour. In 1663 a group of courtiers, including Clarendon, Albemarle and Ashley, was given proprietorship over the area which they named Carolina. They intended to produce Mediterranean goods there—wine, oil and fruit—but the project was not a great success, smuggling flourished more than viticulture, and by 1700 there were only two small settlements which eventually developed into the separate colonies of North and South Carolina.

To the north of Virginia, Pennsylvania was colonised after William Penn had been given proprietary rights in 1681. Penn was the Quaker son of one of the admirals who had commanded Cromwell's Hispaniola expedition, and Charles II granted him territory in the New World to cancel out a debt owed by the Crown to the admiral. The colony was at first settled by Quakers, glad to escape from religious persecution in England, and Penn's high ideals were reflected in the framing of an elaborate constitution and in the careful design of the city of brotherhood, Philadelphia, which he built by the Delaware river. Soon, however, the Quakers were outnumbered by other immigrants, who refused to accept Penn's direction and gradually took over control of the colony themselves.

The distance between England and America, and the conditions of life in the New World, promoted the growth of popular assemblies and self-government. The Navigation Acts, however, made some sort of central control imperative, in order to see that the regulations were not evaded, and under Charles II and James II an attempt was made to bring the colonies more effectively under royal authority. The weapon of *Quo Warranto*, which had been used with such effect against the English corporations, was also employed to bring the American settlements to heel. In 1684 the charter of Massachusetts was declared forfeit; two years later similar action was taken against Connecticut; and in 1687 Rhode Island was also turned into a Crown colony. James consolidated the northern settlements into a single dominion of New England, and appointed a governor for the whole area, with orders to suppress popular assemblies and to rule through a nominated council.

America and the Glorious Revolution

Autocracy, in New England as well as old, was ended by the Glorious Revolution. Most of the colonies had their charters restored, although in the case of Massachusetts the rule of the Church elders was brought to an end. The attempt at central control was abandoned, but further steps were taken to enforce the Acts of trade. In 1697 colonial Customs officials were given the same rights of search as their English counterparts, and governors of colonies were required to take an oath to enforce the Navigation Acts on pain of £1,000 fine for negligence. The following year saw the setting up of Vice-Admiralty courts, which worked without juries and were therefore specially suitable for dealing with smuggling cases, since public opinion, as expressed through juries, was usually on the side of the offender.

The wars against Holland and France were fought in America as well as Europe, and several settlements changed hands. But ultimately the fate of colonies depended on the outcome of war in Europe, and the effect of Marlborough's victories was felt even on the far side of the Atlantic. The Treaty of Utrecht transferred to England the French settlements of St Kitts, Newfoundland and the Hudson Bay region, and set the stage for the last act of the colonial conflict, that was to take place in the eighteenth century. By the time the Treaty of Utrecht was signed, the British possessions stretched unbroken along the east coast of America, and included many of the more important West Indian islands. The total population of this whole area, including negroes, was about 350,000—less than the number of people living in London and only about one-fifteenth of the total population of England. Yet these figures, though relatively small, represent an astonishing achievement on the part of a small country, and although the English colonies had usually been a disappointment to the early speculators who hoped for swift rewards, they brought enormous wealth to the Britain over which Anne ruled, and confirmed Hakluyt's prediction that 'this western voyage will yield unto us all the commodities of Europe, Africa, and Asia, as far as we were wont to travel, and supply the wants of all our decayed trades'.

Africa and India

The settlement of the New World led to the development of trade with Africa, and the years that followed the Restoration saw the establishment of a number of British trading stations on the west coast. In 1664 Fort James was founded on an island in the river Gambia, and the Treaty of Breda of 1667 transferred to England the Dutch settlement at Cape Coast Castle. These posts, and others like them, served as warehouses for human cattle, where negro slaves were held before being sent on the appalling journey which, for those who survived, ended in slavery.

Further east, English traders had made settlements in India. When Charles II came back to his throne England did not actually *own* any Indian territory; the various trading stations, or 'factories', were held on lease from native rulers. This situation was changed by Charles's marriage to a Portuguese princess and by the breakdown of imperial government in India. Catherine of Braganza brought with her, as dowry, the port of Bombay, and this possession of the King of Portugal passed into outright English ownership. Charles II found it too expensive to maintain and in 1668 handed it over to the East India Company, who later made it their headquarters.

The Company was concentrating on the development of its Indian links, leaving the East Indies to Holland, but it looked for protection to the Mogul emperors. This protection declined as the emperors lost effective control of the great empire which they ruled, and long before Aurungzeb died in 1707 the Company had taken measures for its own defence. Royal charters from Charles II and James II had already given it authority to form alliances, declare war and make peace, issue coins, and carry out many other functions which were normally the preserve of sovereign powers. The trading company was, in fact, being slowly transformed into a sovereign state in India, and in 1687 the directors ordered the governor of Surat to 'establish such a polity of civil and military power, and create and secure such a large revenue . . . as may be the foundation of a large, well-grounded, sure English dominior in India for all time to come'. When this declaration was made it was little more than a statement of intention, and the years that followed saw bitter disputes between members of the Old and the New East India Companies.[1] Not until a united company was once again established in 1708 could trade and diplomacy take advantage of the disintegration of central authority in India to establish British influence no foundations that were to last for nearly two hundred and fifty years.

[1] See below p. 434.

19

Late Stuart England

Trade and Finance

THE years following the restoration of Charles II saw a rapid increase in the rate at which English commerce expanded. In the Tudor and early Stuart period English trade had been based upon the export of wool and woollen cloth to Europe, and by the time civil war broke out more distant markets had been opened for the New Draperies in India, the Levant and America. Until the Restoration, then, English industry and English trade were wool; everything else was incidental. After this date, the pattern of English commerce was transformed as oceanic trading routes and overseas possessions were exploited to make England the centre for an increasingly valuable business in re-exports, which gave London the sort of dominance in world trade that Antwerp and Amsterdam had attained in the previous century.

By 1700 nearly a third of all English imports came from outside Europe, and about half of these were re-exported—at a profit, of course. This was partly due to the opening up of new sources of supply, but it would have been impossible without the lowering of prices and the growth of a mass market. Tobacco, for instance, which in the early years of the century had been a luxury, costing at least twenty shillings a pound, became the indulgence of all classes as its price dropped to under a shilling a pound. There was consequently an enormous increase in the amount imported. Virginia and Maryland, for example, which had despatched a mere twenty thousand pounds to England in 1619, sent twenty-two million pounds in the last year of the century, and colonial production was being constantly expanded to meet an apparently insatiable demand.

The same pattern was followed in the sugar trade, though here the expansion was not so dramatic. The Portuguese colonies in South America held a virtual monopoly of sugar exports until the 1640s, and it was not until James II's reign that sugar from the British West Indies began pouring into London and from there to all the major European centres. The third important item in this flourishing re-export trade was calicoes, which the East Indian Company began importing in considerable quantity. These fine cotton cloths, well suited to the style of living of an elegant age, were particularly valued by fashionable ladies of late-Stuart and early-Georgian England, and their taste was shared by their contemporaries throughout Europe.

The government was alarmed by the threat which foreign textiles offered to the native woollen industry and did its best to protect the home product. The export of wool was forbidden, so that English clothmakers should have first call on the raw material available, and in 1678 the dead as well as the living were called on to maintain England's greatest manufacture, by an Act ordering that all shrouds should be made of wool. These and other measures no doubt helped to check the decline of the cloth industry, but the salvation of the cloth merchants came in the end from their own efforts. They could not hope for a big expansion of their trade with hot regions like India, China and the Levant, but they exploited colder markets and sent increasing quantities of woollen goods to northern Europe and the American colonies. Although cloth no longer accounted for ninety per cent of English exports it was still more important than any other single item.

The spice trade lost its significance as tastes changed and more fresh meat became available in the winter, but tea and coffee both made their appearance in post-Restoration England, and quickly became popular. The East India Company flourished, but its monopoly was threatened by interlopers and resented by City merchants who did not belong to it. This jealousy found expression in the decision taken by Parliament in 1698 to create a new company, but the representatives of the old one fought a stubborn battle to preserve their privileges and in 1709 the two bodies were amalgamated once again into a single East India Company.

Although Parliament had been, in the early seventeenth century, an opponent of monopoly companies, its increasing power did not lead to free trade. In fact the post-Restoration period saw the creation of a number of new chartered companies—the Royal African Company, for instance, which bought slaves from West Africa and shipped them to the West Indies where they were exchanged for sugar; and the Hudson's Bay Company, which was formed to exploit the fur trade of North America. The general assumption, in an age when first the

Dutch and then the French offered such a threat to the expansion of English trade, was that only organised groups of merchants could hope to raise the capital and provide the services necessary to ensure this expansion.

As far as trade to and from the American colonies was concerned, a monopoly was granted not to any specific company but to English merchants as a whole. The Staple Act of 1663 required the colonies to send 'enumerated' goods—of which the most important were sugar, tobacco and cotton—only to England, and forbade them to buy European goods until these had first been imported into England. This legislation was designed to protect English merchants against the Dutch, who were strongly entrenched in the carrying-trade both between one colony and another and between the colonies and Europe. Nothing effective, however, could be done while the Dutch held colonies on the North American mainland, and while the number of English ships was insufficient to cope with the demands made on them. Shortage of ships and sailors prompted the Navigation Act of 1660 which closed several loopholes in the 1651 Act by requiring that foreign-built ships in English ownership should be registered, and that English ships should have predominantly English crews. These measures presumably contributed to the great expansion of English shipping after 1660 and prevented the diversion of men and capital to less protected occupations. As for the Dutch colonies, these were conquered in the fighting that preceded the outbreak of the Second Dutch War, and by the Treaty of Breda were annexed to the English Crown.

The expansion of English commerce made London one of the focal points of world trade, and brought not only wealth but elegance to the capital city. The London of Pepys and Defoe was a long way removed from the London that Shakespeare had known. After the Restoration it extended westwards into the area around Piccadilly and Jermyn Street, while in the early eighteenth century Edward Harley, son of Anne's Lord Treasurer, perpetuated his family's name and fortune by building Harley Street, Oxford Street and other fashionable thoroughfares on the open spaces that surrounded Tyburn. The streets of London were broader and cleaner after the Great Fire; hackney coaches and sedan chairs made travelling much more comfortable; theatres were crowded by the fashionable world, anxious to see the latest productions of Dryden, Congreve, Wycherley and Farquhar; and coffee-houses provided meeting places not only for the ladies and gentlemen of London 'society' in the narrower sense, but also for business men. One of these coffee-houses—that started by Edward Lloyd—was a favourite haunt of shipowners, and gradually developed into the headquarters of marine insurance in England, while other coffee-houses were associated with particular political groups or with men of letters.

Lloyds was one example of the way in which the merchants of London were gradually providing the financial mechanism demanded by a great trading community. The merchants were also responsible for persuading the government to establish a national bank. Ever since Charles II had declared, in 1672, his inability to repay his debts unless special parliamentary provision was made, but had offered the regular payment of interest, a national debt had existed, but public opinion was reluctant to accept such an innovation, especially when it was involved with the shaky financial system of the Stuart monarchs. The long war against France, however, made government borrowing on a big scale inevitable, and in 1694 a Bill was passed authorising the establishment of a national bank. Subscribers guaranteed to raise £1,500,000 and advance the entire sum to the government, in return for the regular payment of interest. The money was quickly raised, the Bank was an immediate success, and the key role played by the City is indicated by the fact that among the first directors were no fewer than seven future Lord Mayors. The Bank was given permission to issue its own notes as long as the total of these did not exceed the sum originally advanced to the government, and three years later, after the failure of the Land Bank, Parliament confirmed the Bank of England in its privileged position, and made the forging of its notes a felony. To make sure that the resources of the Bank were never used to finance monarchical despotism it was laid down that no advances were to be made to the government without the express approval of Parliament, and the combination of a parliamentary security with assurance against royal intervention persuaded the merchant classes at last to contribute to the needs of the state on a scale that would have been impossible while Charles II or his brother was on the throne.

The Bank of England did not take over the existing national debt, although from time to time government bonds were transferred to it, but it made the *idea* of a national debt acceptable—even though it was hoped, and assumed, that the government would eventually return to solvency. The government, in fact, made a remarkable effort to meet its financial obligations by taxation rather than borrowing. The excise was a major source of revenue, and was gradually extended from beer and cider to many other commodities and articles in daily use. By 1715 it brought in £2,300,000 compared with £1,700,000 from the Customs, and the total revenue by that date was over five and a half million pounds—nearly five times as much as it had been under Charles II. Yet taxation even on this scale could not meet the cost of Marl-borough's campaigns in the Netherlands, war in the Peninsula, and naval operations in the Channel and Mediterranean. By the time Anne died the national debt stood at more than thirty-six million pounds, and interest charges on it consumed three-fifths of the annual revenue.

The main source of government income was the Land Tax, which had superseded the older subsidy during the Commonwealth period. Originally levied on all forms of property, the tax had come to bear more and more heavily on landowners, and each county was ordered to provide a stated share of the total sum. A shilling in the pound yielded about £500,000, and when the tax stood at four shillings in the pound, as it did throughout most of the war years, it became an intolerable burden and contributed to the decline of the smaller land-owners, which marked the post-Revolution period.

The government's interest in the economy was not confined to taxation. In 1660 a Council for Trade was set up to advise the Privy Council on commercial matters, and to work in cooperation with another Council for Foreign Plantations (colonies). These two bodies survived until 1665, when they were replaced by standing committees, but the triumph of the CABAL brought to power men who were much more interested in commerce than Clarendon had been, and in 1668 a new Council for Trade was set up, which, by 1673, had also become responsible for plantations. Shaftesbury was active on this body, of which John Locke was Secretary, and in its few years of life it began the important process of collecting and interpreting statistical informa-tion. This Council lasted only two years, when it was again replaced by committees of the Privy Council, and not until 1696 was a perma-nent Board of Trade set up, to keep in touch with the merchants and to advise the government on commercial policy.

Administration by committees was a feature of the post-Restoration period. The success of this system had been demonstrated during the rule of the Rump, and jealous Kings and apprehensive Parliaments were both inclined to prefer committees to single persons who were liable to become too powerful. The key figures in the administration before 1660 were the two Secretaries of State, but their importance was increasingly overshadowed by that of the Treasury, which gradually extended its control over other departments. The Lord Treasurer was a powerful minister, as Danby and Godolphin showed, and the Treasury was occasionally put into commission—a practice that became regular after the death of Anne. Under the stress of war, departments which had previously been of little importance acquired a new significance. The Secretary of the Admiralty, for instance, was responsible for seeing that the supplies appropriated by Parliament and the instructions given by the Secretaries of State were put into effect as far as the navy was concerned, while the Secretary-at-War carried out a similar range of duties in connexion with the army. The industrious Samuel Pepys, who was Secretary of the Admiralty under James II, built up an efficient departmental administration out of virtually nothing, and under William III William Blathwayt, the Secretary-at-War, became almost as important as the Secretaries of State.

All these departments were grossly understaffed by modern standards —the Secretaries of State, for instance, had only about a dozen clerks to help them and had to write most of their letters themselves—while the Treasury was handicapped by its addiction to Roman numerals and medieval tally-sticks. Nevertheless, the years between 1660 and 1714 witnessed the development of an administrative machine far more complex than anything envisaged by, for instance, Thomas Cromwell, and one that, because of its complexity, was no longer under the immediate control of the King. No single minister controlled it either, for the Lord Treasurer (or, when the office was in commission, the First Lord of the Treasury) had not yet obtained the position of primacy which Walpole was to secure; but the collection and expenditure of public moneys were the most important governmental functions, as the Commons recognised when, in 1713, they passed a standing order giving the government sole right to initiate financial business in Parliament. While Anne was alive the emergence of a Prime Minister was hardly possible, but the half-century which followed her death showed that the minister who controlled the financial policy of the government could, in certain circumstances, become more important even than the sovereign.

The various committees and councils for trade were largely responsible for drawing up and enforcing the Acts which regulated commerce, and for initiating a deliberate policy of encouraging exports. Many duties on outgoing goods were abolished, and in the case of corn the earlier attempts at protection gave way to an export subsidy in 1673. The year 1699 saw the abolition of export duties on woollen goods, and in 1709 the duty on coal was removed. These changes were designed not only to encourage British exporters and produce a favourable balance of trade', but also to speed the growth of British shipping, since it was bulk cargoes, like coal and corn, that offered the biggest profits, as the Dutch had earlier discovered.

The freeing of trade was accompanied by the freeing of industry, though here the process was negative rather than positive. In theory the Elizabethan laws regulating apprenticeship were still in force, and the various companies which controlled every industry were responsible for seeing that they were put into effect. In fact, however, the authority of the companies was declining, and the apprenticeship laws were moribund, except as an administrative convenience where paupers were concerned. The Livery Companies survived in London, but their members were recruited by patrimony rather than by occupation, and they were more concerned with social functions and City government than with the close supervision of particular trades. The law courts might have acted as a barrier, by enforcing the apprenticeship regulations, but since the days of Coke they had been increasingly opposed to interference in the free running of the economy.

The apprenticeship laws had attempted to impose a strait-jacket on English industry, and were the product of an age when men were plentiful and jobs were scarce. This was no longer true in the late seventeenth century. The rise in population had apparently been checked, while the demands of a wealthy community encouraged industry to expand. The use of machines such as the stocking-frame and the gig-mill, which had earlier been prohibited on the grounds that they put weavers out of work, was now encouraged, and experiments were taking place to harness steam power to the needs of industry. In 1712 the first steam pump, invented by Savery and Newcomen, was installed in a coal mine, and by the time George I came to the throne several more were at work. The exploitation of deeper seams was made necessary by the demand for coal. London alone burnt a quarter of a million tons a year, and the shortage of wood encouraged manufacturers to use coal instead. The iron and steel industry remained dependent upon charcoal, because the sulphur contained in coal made the metal brittle, but even here future developments were anticipated, for some time during Anne's reign a Quaker ironmaster, Abraham Darby, turned coal into coke, which he used to feed his blast furnaces.

In agriculture no major developments took place in the seventeenth century, except in Suffolk where, by the time Charles II was restored, the cultivation of turnips on a large scale had been started. Turnips were planted in late summer, after the harvest had been gathered, and were used throughout the winter as cattle-feed. This practice made the wholesale slaughter of animals at the approach of winter unnecessary, and it gradually spread to neighbouring counties. Some of these, such as Norfolk, had improvements of their own to offer—the use of lime, marl and manure to recover sandy soils for instance, and the growing of clover and other grasses.

Late Stuart England was, generally speaking, a country in which the way was being prepared for the agrarian and industrial changes that were to transform English society in the following century. New techniques were being tried out. Old restrictions were being swept away. Most important of all, the growth of great estates and the expansion of foreign trade were making possible the accumulation of capital on such a scale that it could eventually finance revolutionary changes.

Political and Scientific Thought

The end of the Stuarts coincided with the decline of fanaticism in politics and of intolerance in religion. The temperature of eighteenth-century politics remained, generally speaking, well below boiling-point, and although Roman Catholics and dissenters still suffered from civil disabilities, they were free to worship as they pleased. Superstition declined, along with enthusiasm, and 1712 saw the last occasion on which an English court convicted a woman of witchcraft. Public attitudes were gradually becoming more humane, as was shown by the foundation of the Society for the Reformation of Manners in 1691, and much of the fervour that had previously gone into the persecution of heretics (of one sort or another) at home now went into the conversion of pagans abroad. The expansion of trade brought with it greater knowledge of the world that lay outside Europe, and societies such as those for Promoting Christian Knowledge (1698) and the Propagation of the Gospel (1701) were set up to provide missionaries for the conversion of the heathen.

The case against religious intolerance was put most convincingly by John Locke, who, in his *Letters on Toleration*, demonstrated its in-effectiveness as a means of conversion, and emphasised that true religion consisted in 'the inward and full persuasion of the mind'. 'I cannot be saved', he added, 'by a religion that I distrust and by a worship that I abhor.' Locke's tolerance and his sense of reality were also reflected in his political writings, which were so much in tune with the new age that they became a sort of secular gospel.

Locke's immediate predecessors had been mainly concerned to find a philosophical justification for absolutism, reflecting in this—as did Locke at a later date—the age in which they lived. Thomas Hobbes, for instance—who was born in the year of the Armada, frequented the Great Tew circle, and was appointed tutor in mathematics to the future Charles II—put forward in his *Leviathan* the doctrine that self-preservation is the basis of society. 'The condition of man', he wrote, 'is a condition of war of everyone against everyone', and in the state of nature which preceded the establishment of civil society there were 'no arts, no letters, [only] continual fear and danger of violent death; and the life of man, solitary, poor, nasty, brutish and short'. To free themselves from this terrible condition, human beings had (so Hobbes maintained) abdicated all their rights to the ruler—whether one man or a group—and the sovereign was justified in commanding *absolute* obedience, since any criticism of his authority would threaten to throw society back into the condition of primitive anarchy from which it had so laboriously raised itself.

Hobbes's view shocked his contemporaries, who had not grasped the nettle of sovereignty as firmly as he had. Cavaliers distrusted him because he seemed to justify power, no matter how that power had been acquired, while roundheads disapproved of his theories because they could be taken as a defence of royal absolutism. Even Locke, who wrote under Hobbes's shadow, declined to attack the *Leviathan* directly, for fear that he should become involved in the unsavoury reputation of its author. Instead he took as his target the doctrine of divine right, as expounded by Sir Robert Filmer in his *Patriarcha*, written during the Interregnum, but not published until 1680.

Locke took a far more optimistic view of human nature than Hobbes or Filmer. He believed that men were born with certain rights which belonged to them as individuals. They had a right to life and to liberty, and because they had added their labour to the raw material that nature provided, they had a right to the property so created. Locke agreed with Hobbes that the basis of society was contractual, but where Hobbes had imagined primitive men contracting to abandon all their freedom of action to a sovereign power, Locke conceived of

P*

them making a bargain. They would agree to obey the sovereign because by so doing they could better preserve their natural rights. But if the sovereign himself became a threat to those rights, then the contract was automatically dissolved and the obligation of obedience annulled. 'A government', he wrote, 'is not free to do as it pleases . . . the law of nature stands as an eternal rule to all men, legislators as well as others.'

Locke was no republican. Like his friend and patron, Shaftesbury, he thought that limited monarchy would strike the happy mean between tyranny and anarchy, but he was concerned above all that the community should be the ultimate arbiter. Government had been created by and for the people, and the people should decide what form of government they wanted at any given time.

Such a bare outline cannot, of course, do justice to the subtlety of Locke's argument, but it does suggest why the two *Treatises on Government* were so influential in post-Revolution England. A representative institution existed in England—though in fact it was hardly representative!—and it was dominated by people who did not need to be told that society existed to preserve property-rights. The owners of property were the real victors of the political revolutions of the seventeenth century, and they found in the writings of Locke a theory which not only justified their assumption of power, but made it seem all but inevitable. Locke, in short, was appropriated by the Whigs, and came to power with them.

The even tone of Locke's writings, the absence of passion and the appeal to common sense, were, like latitudinarian attitudes in religion, the heralds of the age of reason. Nothing contributed more to the triumph of reason than the progress of science, for by calling established truths into question and subjecting them to critical examination, the scientists increased the prestige and the self-confidence of man as a rational being.

The scientific revolution which began with the sixteenth century was a European phenomenon to which Englishmen made a number of important contributions. They were not among the first to challenge accepted explanations of the structure of the universe, but the Scotsman John Napier produced in 1614 the first tables of logarithms which were used by Kepler in his work on ellipses, and Queen Elizabeth's physician, William Gilbert, published a book *On the Magnet and Magnetic Bodies and that Great Magnet the Earth* which so impressed Galileo that he gave a detailed account of it in his *Dialogues*.

The first major English figure in the scientific revolution was not, however, a practising scientist. Francis Bacon made himself the propagandist of the scientific method, and constantly urged the need for experiment and research. 'We cannot command nature', he said, 'except by obeying her', and he realised that the laws of nature could not be discovered unless men were left free to challenge accepted ideas and to suggest alternative hypotheses. Scientists working in Europe were not always left free after the Counter-Reformation got going: Giordano Bruno, for instance, who envisaged an infinite universe with an infinity of solar systems, was convicted of heresy and executed in 1600, while Galileo, in his closing years, was put under restraint. Bacon's achievement was to give science a programme and to make it respectable. The high position that he held, and the fame of his name, were a shelter behind which enquiring men could pursue their re-searches, and the freedom given to scientific speculation in England may account for the fact that by the late seventeenth century London had become the capital of the scientific, as well as the commercial, world. It was Bacon's hope that academies would be formed where scientists could exchange information, for he recognised the paramount import-ance of communications to the spread of knowledge. No such academy was founded during his lifetime, but the Royal Society acknowledged him as its spiritual founder, and his picture appears next to the bust of Charles II in its official history.

In spite of Bacon and of the isolated achievements of such men as William Harvey, the discoverer of the circulation of the blood, English scientists did not come into their own until after the Restoration. Charles II was interested in mathematics and experimental science, and gave his patronage to the Royal Society which was formed in 1660. Among the early members of this distinguished body were Robert Boyle—son of Strafford's old enemy, the Earl of Cork—who was the first person to make a quantitative test of the elasticity of air, and Robert Hooke, who gave the first detailed description of a micro-scope and of the observations he had obtained by using one.

Most famous of all members of the Royal Society was Sir Isaac Newton, who fitted the isolated segments of scientific knowledge into a coherent pattern. Copernicus had shifted the earth from the centre of the universe, where Ptolemy had placed it; Galileo had confirmed, by his own observations, that heavenly bodies did not revolve around one fixed centre; while Kepler had discovered that the planets moved in ellipses and not circles. These men between them had destroyed the old picture of the universe, but had not succeeded in putting anything in its place. As John Donne, the Jacobean poet, complained:

> The sun is lost, and th' earth, and no man's wit
> Can well direct him where to look for it.
> 'Tis all in pieces, all coherence-gone;
> All just supply, and all relation.

It was left to Newton to restore coherence to the universe. Born in 1642, the year of Galileo's death, he studied at Cambridge under the mathematician Isaac Barrow, and eventually succeeded to Barrow's chair. During the Great Plague, Newton left Cambridge, like most of his contemporaries, and returned home to Lincolnshire. It was during this enforced vacation that he worked out the principles which were to form the basis of his system. He combined Kepler's laws and the observations of Galileo into a single theory of gravitation, and showed that the same force which makes an apple fall to the ground sends the heavenly bodies swinging on their courses.

The extension of scientific knowledge transformed older and traditional attitudes in much the same way, and at the same time, as protestantism and the expansion of trade broke up the fabric of medieval Christendom. The destruction of the old order with nothing to replace it would almost certainly have led to reaction, but the success of the scientists in creating a new synthesis had the opposite effect— it encouraged criticism and experiment, and it produced a veneration for the faculty of human reason that ushered in the Enlightenment. Intellectual self-confidence and pride in the ability of man brought about a climate of thought in late Stuart England very different from that which had prevailed half a century earlier, and its effect was felt in all departments of life. Intolerance gradually gave way to tolerance, and problems which had previously been the preserve of prejudice were now brought under the dispassionate purview of the scientist and the statistician, the philosopher and the historian.

The early scientists were not irreligious—on the contrary, they regarded their discoveries as leading to a new awareness of God— but intensity of religious faith declined as a result of their overthrow of long-accepted truths. Fanaticism did not vanish overnight, as the high Tories of Anne's reign demonstrated, but the prevailing tone of society was sceptical and indifferent. Deism—belief in God, but denial of revelation—became fashionable among the upper classes of eighteenth-century England, and God Himself was relegated to the position of 'prime mover', the force which had originally set the universe in motion but which played little part in ordinary human life.

In politics as in religion the eighteenth century brought with it a period of calm. This was partly a reaction against the passionate and at times violent enthusiasm which had produced revolution and civil war, but it was only possible because the upheavals of the seventeenth century had solved the constitutional problem. For two hundred years, ever since the break-up of the medieval state and the Reformation had between them destroyed most of the traditional assumptions about legitimate authority, the rule of the divinely appointed lay prince had seemed, in England as in the rest of Europe, the best safeguard against chaos. But absolutism was an experiment which failed in England, and it was the older, medieval institutions and attitudes—such as Parliament, common law and the belief in natural rights—which survived into the new age. The two revolutions, the long war against France and the devotion of James II and his descendants to the Church of Rome, made the property-owners in Parliament the effective rulers of England, and now that they had won supremacy it was in their interest to keep the political temperature as low as possible. Content in the security that earlier struggles had given them, they could afford to look back with Olympian detachment on the passions of their fathers, and coolly assert the virtues of moderation and tolerance.

For forms of government let fools contest;
Whate'er is best administered is best.
For modes of faith let graceless zealots fight;
He can't be wrong whose life is in the right.
In faith and hope the world will disagree,
But all mankind's concern is charity.[1]

English Society in the Late Stuart Period

The triumph of the property-owners was reflected in the attitude towards the poor. Up to the civil war the royal Council had frequently intervened in the localities to give the poor a measure of security, but after 1660 the problem of poverty was left almost entirely to the Justices of the Peace and to private charity. The Act of Settlement of 1662 was the last major piece of legislation on this subject before the nineteenth century, and it did little more than confirm the

[1] From Alexander Pope, *An Essay on Man*.

provisions of the Elizabethan code. Asserting that 'the necessity, number, and continual increase of the poor . . . is very great and exceeding burthensome', it declared that paupers were to be the responsibility of their native parish, and that if any dared to wander they were to be returned to their last place of settlement, for fear that otherwise they would become an intolerable burden on the more prosperous areas.

The able-bodied poor were to be set to labour in workhouses, but the aged and enfeebled were left to fend for themselves. Their lot was eased by the numerous charitable foundations established during the previous hundred years, and many more almshouses were founded during the reigns of William III and Anne. The prosperous landowners and merchants of late Stuart England were not unmindful of their responsibility, and frequently left sums of money in their wills to be devoted to charitable purposes, but society as it was then organised could not hope to do more than relieve the outward symptoms of poverty. In good times the poor probably managed to struggle along, but a hard winter often meant death from malnutrition and cold.

Agricultural labourers, even though they were not destitute, normally lived near the poverty line. Their wages were low, their living conditions primitive, and they depended on communal grazing rights and the collection of brushwood to keep themselves going. Urban workers were no better off, and could not count even on the occasional benevolence which the country squire bestowed on his tenants. Justices of the Peace were still theoretically responsible for fixing wages, and occasionally did so, but they were usually more concerned with holding wages down than with enforcing a minimum. Strikes and combinations were illegal under common law, and in 1706 the Leeds Quarter Sessions heavily fined some cloth workers who had agreed among themselves to demand a penny-halfpenny an hour for their work, when the current official rate was only one penny.

The smaller landowners were suffering from the effects of heavy war taxation, and from the gradual decline in their social position. Game laws forbade any freeholder with land worth less than £100 a year to hunt even over his own property, and the contrast grew steadily greater between the aristocratic landowners who lived like princes in the great mansions, filled with the treasures of the earth, which they were building for themselves, and the squires and yeomen who looked on resentfully or beggared themselves in an attempt to keep up. Bitterness between the aristocracy and the smaller gentry gave an edge to political differences, and kept up the Whig-Tory struggle in the localities long after it had ceased to have any real meaning at the centre.

The clergy, who from the economic point of view counted as smaller landowners, were gradually improving their social position. Now that the Church of England had become the Church of the land-owners there was no shortage of recruits for it, and most of these were men who had been educated at the universities. The value of livings remained low, however, and pluralism was common. Poorly paid curates were all too frequently left in charge of parishes, while the holder of the living acted the part of a country gentleman or served as chaplain to some great household. Queen Anne showed her affection for the Church, and her appreciation of its needs, by surrendering the First Fruits and Tenths which Henry VIII had originally annexed to the Crown. The income from this source was used as 'Queen Anne's Bounty', to supplement the income of poorer clergy, but there was still an enormous gap between the average incumbent earning about fifty pounds a year and some of the wealthier bishops who lived like princes on five thousand.

The greater bishops, the greater merchants, the greater landowners —these were the people who ultimately profited from the social and political changes of the sixteenth and seventeenth centuries. The Stuart attempt to give the central government control over local affairs had brought such discredit on this practice that it was not repeated. The landowners were left free, like the late medieval barons, to rule the areas over which their influence extended, and their mansions became the administrative centres from which the localities were run. They could usually depend on sources other than land to swell their incomes, offset the demands of taxation, and provide capital for expansion. The profits of trade, for instance, enabled Sir Josiah Child, a prosperous East India merchant, to build his great house at Wanstead; the profits of office—amounting in this case to £40,000—provided the Earl of Nottingham, after six years as Secretary of State, with the capital he required to build his mansion at Burley-on-the-Hill; even war could be turned to profitable account, as the Duke of Marlborough discovered when a grateful Queen and country presented him with Blenheim Palace and an extensive estate as a thank-offering for his services on the battlefield.

The vacuum left by the contraction of royal authority was every-where filled by the great landowners, and their influence extended even into that stronghold of the squirearchy, the House of Commons.

Parliament met regularly after 1689, and ambitious men were now prepared to devote not only much of their time but also much of their money to securing a seat. The cost of 'influencing' a county electorate could be enormous, but even in boroughs the price of votes was rising to the point where only very rich men could afford to compete. Peers could not themselves be members of the Commons, but they gradually came to control the electors who chose these members. By an ironic twist of fate, the gentry House of Commons, which had successfully led the struggle against absolutism, lost its own independence in the moment of victory.

Bibliography

The following list is a selection from the more important books and articles published during the last twenty years. Fuller bibliographies are contained in BURSTON, W. H., and GREEN, C. W., *Handbook for History Teachers*, 1962.

Names of journals are abbreviated as follows:

AmHR: The American Historical Review
BIHR: The Bulletin of the Institute of Historical Research
CHJ: Cambridge Historical Journal
EHR: The English Historical Review
EcHR: The Economic History Review
H: History
HJ: The Historical Journal
JEH: The Journal of Ecclesiastical History
JMH: The Journal of Modern History
LQR: The Law Quarterly Review
P & P: Past and Present
TRHS: The Transactions of the Royal Historical Society

1. GENERAL

The relevant volumes of the *Oxford History of England* (Oxford University Press):

VII. MACKIE, J. D. *The Earlier Tudors 1485-1558.* 1952.

VIII. BLACK, J. B. *The Reign of Elizabeth 1558-1603.* 2nd edn. 1959.

IX. DAVIES, GODFREY. *The Early Stuarts 1603-1660,* 2nd edn. 1959.

X. CLARK, G. N. *The Later Stuarts 1660-1714,* 2nd edn. 1961.

ASHLEY, MAURICE. *England in the Seventeenth Century.* 2nd edn. Penguin, 1960 *(Pelican History of England).*

AYLMER, G. E. *The Struggle for the Constitution 1603–1689*. Blandford, 1963.

BELL, H. E. and OLLARD, R. L., ed. *Historical Essays 1600–1750*. A. and C. Black, 1963.

BINDOFF, S. T. *Tudor England*. Penguin, 1950 (*Pelican History of England*).

CARUS-WILSON, E. M., ed. *Essays in Economic History*. 2 vols. E. Arnold, 1954, 1962.

CLARK, G. N. *Three Aspects of Stuart England*. Oxford University Press, 1960.

ELTON, G. R. *England under the Tudors*. Methuen, 1955.

FISHER, F. J., ed. *Essays in the Economic and Social History of Tudor and Stuart England*. Cambridge University Press, 1961.

HEXTER, J. H. *Reappraisals in History*. Longmans, 1961.

HILL, CHRISTOPHER. *Puritanism and Revolution*. Secker, 1958.
—— *The Century of Revolution 1603–1714*. Nelson, 1961.
—— *Society and Puritanism in Pre-Revolutionary England*. Secker, 1964.
—— ed. *The European Crisis 1560–1660*. Routledge, 1964.

KEIR, D. L. *The Constitutional History of Modern Britain*. 6th edn. A. and C. Black, 1961.

KENYON, J. P. *The Stuarts*. Batsford, 1958.

MCILWAIN, C. H. *Constitutionalism Ancient and Modern*. Rev. edn. Cornell University Press, 1947.

MORRIS, CHRISTOPHER. *The Tudors*. Batsford, 1955.

PIPER, DAVID. *Catalogue of Seventeenth Century Portraits in the National Portrait Gallery 1625–1714*. Cambridge University Press, 1963.

TREVOR-ROPER, H. R. *Historical Essays*. Macmillan, 1957.

WEDGWOOD, C. V. *Poetry and Politics under the Stuarts*. Cambridge University Press, 1960.

WILLIAMS, PENRY. *Life in Tudor England*, Batsford, 1964.

WILLIAMSON, J. A. *The Tudor Age*. 3rd edn. Longmans, 1965.

WILSON, CHARLES. *England's Apprenticeship, 1603–1763*, Longmans, 1965.

WOODWARD, G. W. O. *Reform and Resurgence 1485–1603*, Blandford, 1963.

Articles printed in volumes mentioned in Section I are not listed separately in later sections.

2. THE EUROPEAN CONTEXT

The volumes so far published of the *New Cambridge Modern History* (Cambridge University Press):

I. POTTER, G. R., ed. *The Renaissance 1493-1520.* 1957.
II. ELTON, G. R., ed. *The Reformation 1520-1559.* 1958.
V. CARSTEN, F. L., ed. *The Ascendancy of France 1648-1688.* 1961.

The volumes so far published in *The Rise of Modern Europe* series, edited by W. Langer (Harper: Hamish Hamilton):

GILMORE, MYRON P. *The World of Humanism 1453-1517.* 1952.
FRIEDRICH, CARL J. *The Age of the Baroque 1610-1660.* 1952.
NUSSBAUM, FREDERICK L. *The Triumph of Science and Reason 1660-1685.* 1953.
WOLF, JOHN B. *The Emergence of the Great Powers 1685-1715.* 1951.

CHADWICK, OWEN. *The Reformation* (Pelican History of the Church), Penguin, 1964.
CRAGG, C. R. *The Church and the Age of Reason* (Pelican History of the Church), Penguin, 1960.
HAZARD, PAUL. *The European Mind 1680-1715.* Penguin, 1964.
ELTON, G. R. *Reformation Europe 1517-1559.* Collins, 1963 (*Fontana History of Europe*).
WILLIAMS, GEORGE H. *The Radical Reformation.* Weidenfeld & Nicolson, 1962.

3. THE ARTS

The Pelican History of Art includes:

SUMMERSON, JOHN. *Architecture in Britain 1530-1830.* 1955.
WATERHOUSE, ELLIS. *Painting in Britain 1530-1790.* 1953.
WHINNEY, MARGARET. *Sculpture in Britain 1530-1830.* 1964.

The Oxford History of English Art includes:

MERCER, ERIC. *English Art 1553-1625.* 1962.
WHINNEY, MARGARET, and MILLAR, OLIVER. *English Art 1625-1714.* 1957.

4. EDWARD IV and HENRY VII

BAYNE, C. G. *Select Cases in the Council of Henry VII*. Selden Society, Volume 75, 1958.

CHRIMES, S. B. *Lancastrians, Yorkists, and Henry VII*. Macmillan, 1964.

COOPER, J. P. 'Henry VII's Last Years reconsidered', *HJ*, 2, 1959.

ELTON, G. R. 'Henry VII: Rapacity and Remorse', *HJ*, 1, 1958.

—— 'Henry VII: A Restatement', *HJ*, 4, 1961.

HAY, D. 'Late Medieval—Early Modern', *BIHR*, 25, 1952.

LANDER, J. R. 'The Yorkist Council and Administration', *EHR*, 73, 1958.

—— 'The Council 1461-1485', *BIHR*, 32, 1959.

—— 'Attainder and Forfeiture 1453-1509', *HJ*, 4, 1961.

SOMERVILLE, R. 'Henry VII's "Council Learned in the Law"', *EHR*, 54, 1939.

WOLFFE, B. P. 'The Management of English Royal Estates under the Yorkist Kings', *EHR*, 71, 1956.

—— 'Henry VII's Land Revenues and Chamber Finance', *EHR*, 79, 1964.

5. HENRY VIII

BROOKS, F. W. *The Council of the North*. Historical Association Pamphlet G.25. 1953.

DICKENS, A. G. *Thomas Cromwell and the English Reformation*. English Universities Press, 1959. (*Teach Yourself History*).

—— *Lollards and Protestants in the Diocese of York 1509-1558*. Oxford University Press, 1959.

—— *The English Reformation*. Batsford, 1964.

ELTON, G. R. *The Tudor Revolution in Government*. Cambridge University Press, 1953.

—— *Star Chamber Stories*. Methuen, 1958.

—— *Henry VIII*. Historical Association Pamphlet G.51. 1962.

HUGHES, PHILIP. *The Reformation in England*. Hollis and Carter, 1950, 3 vols.

KNOWLES, DAVID. *The Religious Orders in England. Volume III: The Tudor Age*. Cambridge University Press. 1959.

PARKER, T. M. *The English Reformation to 1558*. Oxford University Press, 1950 (*Home University Library*).

PRESCOTT, H. F. M. *Man on a Donkey* [Robert Aske]. Eyre and Spottiswoode, 1953.

RIDLEY, JASPER. *Thomas Cranmer*. Oxford University Press, 1962.

RUPP, G. *Studies in the Making of the English Protestant Tradition*. Cambridge University Press, 1947.

ZEEVELD, W. G. *The Foundations of Tudor Policy*. Harvard University Press, 1948.

———

ASTON, MARGARET. 'Lollardy and the Reformation', *H*, 49, 1964.

COOPER, J. P. 'The Supplication against the Ordinaries Reconsidered', *EHR*, 72, 1957.

ELTON, G. R. 'The Evolution of a Reformation Statute (The Act in Restraint of Appeals)', *EHR*, 64, 1949.

—— 'The Commons' Supplication against the Ordinaries', *EHR*, 66, 1951.

—— 'Thomas Cromwell's Decline and Fall', *CHJ*, 10, 1951.

—— 'Parliamentary Drafts 1529-1540', *BIHR*, 25, 1952.

—— 'King or Minister?', *H*, 39, 1954.

—— 'The Political Creed of Thomas Cromwell', *TRHS*, 1956.

—— 'The Statute of Proclamations', *EHR*, 75, 1960.

—— 'The Tudor Revolution? A Reply', *P & P*, 29, 1964.

HODGETT, G. A. J. 'The Unpensioned Ex-Religious in Tudor England', *JEH*, 13, 1962.

KOEBNER, R. '"The Imperial Crown of this Realm"', *BIHR*, 26, 1953.

RICHARDSON, W. C. 'Some Financial Expedients of Henry VIII', *EcHR*, 7, 1954-55.

STONE, LAWRENCE. 'The Political Programme of Thomas Cromwell', *BIHR*, 24, 1951.

WILLIAMS, PENRY, and HARRISS, G. L. 'A Revolution in Tudor History?', *P & P*, 25, 1963.

WOODWARD, G. W. O. 'The Exemption from Suppression of Certain Yorkshire Priories', *EHR*, 76, 1961.

YOUINGS, JOYCE. 'The Council of the West', *TRHS*, 1960.

6. EDWARD VI AND MARY

BINDOFF, S. T. *Ket's Rebellion*. Historical Association Pamphlet G.12. 1949.

CHAPMAN, HESTER. *The Last Tudor King*. Cape, 1958.

EMMISON, F. G. *Tudor Secretary: Sir William Petre at Court and Home.*
Longmans, 1961.

PRESCOTT, H. F. M. *Mary Tudor.* 2nd edn. Eyre and Spottiswoode, 1952.

———

BERESFORD, M. W. 'The Poll Tax and Census of Sheep', *Agricultural
Historical Review*, 2, 1954.

DICKENS, A. G. 'The Edwardian Arrears in Augmentations Payments
and the Problem of the Ex-Religious', *EHR*, 55, 1940.

GRIEVE, HILDA. 'The Deprived Married Clergy in Essex 1553-1561',
TRHS, 1940.

7. TUDOR BRITAIN

A. *Economic*

BERESFORD, M. W. *The Lost Villages of England.* Lutterworth Press, 1954.

BOWDEN, P. J. *The Wool Trade in Tudor and Stuart England.* Macmillan,
1962.

CAMPBELL, MILDRED. *The English Yeoman.* Merlin Press, 1959.

RAMSEY, PETER. *Tudor Economic Problems.* Gollancz, 1963.

THIRSK, JOAN. *Tudor Enclosures.* Historical Association Pamphlet
G.41. 1959.

———

BERESFORD, M. W. 'The Common Informer, the Penal Statutes and
Economic Legislation', *EcHR*, 10, 1957-58.

BRENNER, Y. S. 'The Inflation of Prices in Early Sixteenth Century
England', *EcHR*, 14, 1961-62.

ELTON, G. R. 'An Early Tudor Poor Law', *EcHR*, 6, 1953-54.

—— 'State Planning in Early Tudor England , *EcHR*, 13, 1960-61.

GOULD, J. D. 'The Price Revolution Reconsidered', *EcHR*, 17, 1964.

HOSKINS, W. G. 'Harvest Fluctuations and English Economic History
1480-1619.' *Agricultural Historical Review*, 12, 1964.

B. *The Nobility and Gentry*

FINCH, M. E. *The Wealth of Five Northamptonshire Families, 1540-1640*,
with an introduction by H. J. Habakkuk. Northants Record
Society, 1956.

SIMPSON, ALAN. *The Wealth of the Gentry 1540-1640.* Cambridge
University Press, 1961 (*East Anglian Studies*).

WAKE, JOAN. *The Brudenells of Deene.* Cassell, 1954.

COOPER, J. P. 'The Counting of Manors', *EcHR*, 8, 1955-56.

HABAKKUK, H. J. 'The Market for Monastic Property 1539-1630', *EcHR*, 10, 1957-58.

MILLER, H. 'Subsidy Assessments of the Peerage in the Sixteenth Century', *BIHR*, 28, 1955.

MOUSLEY, J. E. 'The Fortunes of Some Gentry Families of Elizabethan Sussex', *EcHR*, 11, 1958-59.

STONE, LAWRENCE. 'The Nobility in Business', in *The Entrepreneur*. Papers presented at the Annual Conference of the Economic History Society in April 1957.

TREVOR-ROPER, H. R. 'The Gentry 1540-1640', *EcHR*, Supplement 1, 1953.

YOUINGS, JOYCE. 'The Terms of Disposal of Devon Monastic Lands', *EHR*, 69, 1954.

C. *Puritanism and Capitalism*

GREEN, ROBERT W. *Protestantism and Capitalism: the Weber Thesis and its Critics*. Harrap, 1959 (*Problems in European Civilisation*).

JORDAN, W. K. *Philanthropy in England 1480-1660*. Allen and Unwin, 1959.

MARLOWE, JOHN. *The Puritan Tradition in English Life*. Cresset Press, 1956.

SAMUELSSON, KURT. *Religion and Economic Action*. Heinemann, 1961.

BURRELL, SIDNEY A. 'Calvinism, Capitalism, and the Middle Classes: some Afterthoughts on an Old Problem', *JMH*, 32, 1960.

KEARNEY, HUGH F. 'Puritanism, Capitalism and the Scientific Revolution', *P & P*, 28, 1964.

LUETHY, HERBERT. 'Once Again: Calvinism and Capitalism', *Encounter*, January 1964.

D. *Exploration and Overseas Trade*

ANDREWS, K. R. *Elizabethan Privateering*. Cambridge University Press, 1964.

CARUS-WILSON, E. M. and COLEMAN, OLIVE. *England's Export Trade 1275-1547* [statistics]. Oxford University Press, 1963.

PARRY, J. H. *The Age of Reconnaisance 1450-1650*. Weidenfeld and Nicolson, 1963.

RAMSAY, G. D. *English Overseas Trade during the Centuries of Emergence.*
    Macmillan, 1957.

ROWSE, A. L. *The Expansion of Elizabethan England.* Macmillan, 1955.
—— *The Elizabethans and America.* Macmillan, 1959.

WILLAN, T. S. *Studies in Elizabethan Foreign Trade.* Manchester Univer-
    sity Press, 1959.

WILLIAMSON, J. A. *The Age of Drake.* 3rd edn. A. and C. Black, 1952.

E. *Scotland and Ireland*

BECKETT, J. C. *A Short History of Ireland.* Rev. edn. Hutchinson, 1958
    (*University Library*).

CURTIS, E. *History of Ireland.* 6th edn. Methuen, 1950.

DICKINSON, W. C., and PRYDE, G. S. *Scotland from the Earliest Times to
    1603.* Nelson, 1961.

FALLS, C. *Elizabeth's Irish Wars.* Methuen, 1950.

MCROBERTS, DAVID, ed. *Essays on the Scottish Reformation 1513-1625.*
    Burns Oates, 1962.

QUINN, D. B. 'Henry VIII and Ireland', *Irish Historical Studies*, 12, 1961.

F. *Political Thought*

MORRIS, CHRISTOPHER. *Political Thought in England: Tyndale to Hooker.*
    Oxford University Press, 1953 (*Home University Library*).

SIMON, JOAN. *The Reformation and English Education. P & P*, 11, 1957.

8. ELIZABETH I

A. *Political*

BINDOFF, S. T., ed. *Elizabethan Government and Society.* Athlone Press,
    1961.

HURSTFIELD, JOEL. *The Queen's Wards.* Longmans, 1958.
—— *Elizabeth I and the Unity of England.* English Universities Press,
    1960 (*Teach Yourself History*)

JENKINS, ELIZABETH. *Elizabeth the Great.* Gollancz, 1958.

MATTINGLY, GARRETT. *The Defeat of the Spanish Armada,* Cape, 1959.

NEALE, SIR J. E. *The Elizabethan House of Commons.* Cape, 1949.
—— *Elizabeth I and Her Parliaments 1559-1581.* Cape, 1953.
—— *Elizabeth I and Her Parliaments 1584-1601.* Cape, 1957.   .
—— *Essays in Elizabethan History.* Cape, 1958.

READ, CONYERS. *Mr Secretary Cecil and Queen Elizabeth.* Cape, 1955.
—— *Lord Burghley and Queen Elizabeth.* Cape, 1960.

ROWSE, A. L. *The England of Elizabeth*. Macmillan, 1950.

WILLIAMS, NEVILLE. *Thomas Howard, Fourth Duke of Norfolk*. Barrie and Rockliff, 1964.

WILLIAMS, PENRY. *The Council in the Marches of Wales under Elizabeth I*. University of Wales Press, 1958.

———————

CROSS, M. CLAIRE. 'An Exchange of Lands with the Crown 1587-1588', *BIHR*, 34, 1961.

MACCAFERY, W. T. 'Elizabethan Politics: the First Decade 1558-1568', *P & P*, 24, 1963.

B. *Religious*

BROOK, V. J. K. *Whitgift and the English Church*. English Universities Press, 1957 (*Teach Yourself History*).
—— *A Life of Archbishop Parker*. Oxford University Press, 1962.

CARAMAN, PHILIP. *John Gerard: the Autobiography of an Elizabethan*. 2nd edn. Longmans, 1957.
—— *The Other Face: Catholic Life under Elizabeth I*. Longmans, 1960.
—— *Henry Garnet 1555-1606*, Longmans, 1964.

KNOX, S. J. *Walter Travers: Paragon of Elizabethan Puritanism*. Methuen, 1962.

PORTER, H. C. *Reformation and Reaction in Tudor Cambridge*. Cambridge University Press, 1958.

WATKIN, E. I. *Roman Catholicism in England from the Reformation to 1950*. Oxford University Press, 1957 (*Home University Library*).

9. THE EARLY STUARTS
A. *Political*

AYLMER, G. E. *The King's Servants: the Civil Service of Charles I*. Routledge, 1961.

BARKER, W. A. *Religion and Politics in the Seventeenth Century*. Historical Association: *Aids for Teachers* series, No. 2. 1957.

BELL, H. E. *An Introduction to the History and Records of the Courts of Wards and Liveries*. Cambridge University Press, 1953.

BOWEN, C. D. *The Lion and the Throne* [Sir Edward Coke]. Hamish Hamilton, 1957.

BRAILSFORD, H. N. *The Levellers and the English Revolution*, ed. Christopher Hill. Cresset Press, 1961.

BRUNTON, D., and PENNINGTON, D. H. *Members of the Long Parliament.* Allen and Unwin, 1954.

HEXTER, J. H. *The Reign of King Pym.* Harvard University Press, 1941.

HILL, CHRISTOPHER. *The English Revolution 1640.* Lawrence and Wishart, 1949.

HULME, HAROLD. *The Life of Sir John Eliot 1592-1632.* Allen and Unwin, 1957.

JUDSON, M. A. *The Crisis of the Constitution.* Rutgers University Press, 1949.

KEARNEY, H. F. *The Eleven Years Tyranny of Charles I.* Historical Association: *Aids for Teachers* series, No. 9. 1962.

KEELER, MARY F. *The Long Parliament.* American Philosophical Society, 1954.

MOIR, T. L. *The Addled Parliament of 1614.* Oxford University Press, 1958.

MOSSE, G. L. *The Struggle for Sovereignty in England.* Michigan State College Press, 1950.

PEARL, VALERIE. *London and the Outbreak of the Puritan Revolution.* Oxford University Press, 1961.

STONE, LAWRENCE. *The Crisis of the Aristocracy 1558-1641.* Oxford University Press, 1965.

TAWNEY, R. H. *Business and Politics under James I* [Lionel Cranfield]. Cambridge University Press, 1958.

WEDGWOOD, C. V. *The King's Peace 1637-1641.* Collins, 1955.

—— *The King's War 1641-1647.* Collins, 1958.

—— *Thomas Wentworth, First Earl of Strafford: A Revaluation.* Cape, 1961.

—— *The Trial of Charles I.* Collins, 1964.

WILLSON, D. H. *King James VI and I.* Cape, 1956 (*Bedford Historical Series*).

WORMALD, BRIAN. *Clarendon.* Cambridge University Press, 1951.

———————

AYLMER, G. E. 'The Last Years of Purveyance', *EcHR*, 10, 1957-58.

—— 'Attempts at Administrative Reform 1625-1640', *EHR*, 72, 1957.

—— 'Office-Holding as a Factor in English History 1625-1642', *H*, 44, 1959.

BATHO, G. R. 'The Payment and Mitigation of a Star Chamber Fine', *HJ*, 1, 1958.

CARTER, CHARLES H. 'Gondomar: Ambassador to James I'. *HJ*, 7, 1964.

COOPER, J. P. 'The Fortunes of Thomas Wentworth, Earl of Strafford', *EcHR*, 11, 1958-59.

—— 'Differences between English and Continental Governments in the Early Seventeenth Century', in Bromley, J. S., and Kossmann, E. H. *Britain and the Netherlands*. Chatto, 1960.

FRASER, I. C. H. 'The Agitation in the Commons, 2nd March 1629'. *BIHR*, 30, 1957.

HABAKKUK, H. J. 'The Sale of Confiscated Property during the Interregnum', *EcHR*, 15, 1962-63.

HAMMERSLEY, G. 'The Revival of the Forest Laws under Charles I', *H*, 45, 1960.

HINTON, R. W. K. 'The Decline of Parliamentary Government under Elizabeth I and the Early Stuarts', *CHJ*, 13, 1957.

HULME, HAROLD. 'The Winning of Freedom of Speech by the House of Commons', *AmHR*, 61, 1956.

MCILWAIN, C. H. 'The English Common Law as a Barrier against Absolutism', *AmHR*, 49, 1943.

STONE, LAWRENCE. 'The Inflation of Honours', *P & P*, 14, 1958.

WILSON, CHARLES. 'Economics and Politics in the Seventeenth Century' (a review of Christopher Hill: *Century of Revolution*), *HJ*, 5, 1962.

ZAGORIN, P. ' "Court" and "Country" in the Early Seventeenth Century'. *EHR*, 77, 1962.

B. *Religious*

BABBAGE, S. B. *Puritanism and Richard Bancroft*. S.P.C.K. for the Church Historical Society, 1962.

HALLER, WILLIAM. *Liberty and Reformation in the Puritan Revolution*. Columbia University Press, 1955.

—— *Foxe's Book of Martyrs and the Elect Nation*. Cape, 1963.

HILL, CHRISTOPHER. *Economic Problems of the Church, from Archbishop Whitgift to the Long Parliament*. Oxford University Press, 1956.

MARCHANT, R. A. *The Puritans and the Church Courts in the Diocese of York 1560-1642*. Longmans, 1956.

TREVOR-ROPER, H. R. *Archbishop Laud 1573-1645*. 2nd edn. Macmillan, 1962.

WELSBY, PAUL A. *George Abbot, The Unwanted Archbishop, 1562-1633*. S.P.C.K., 1962.

YULE, G. *The Independents in the English Civil War*. Cambridge University Press, 1958.

_____

CURTIS, MARK. 'The Hampton Court Conference and Its Aftermath', *H*, 46, 1961.

FRYER, W. R. 'The High Churchmen of the Earlier Seventeenth Century', *Renaissance and Modern Studies*, 5, 1961.

KENNEDY, D. E. 'The Jacobean Episcopate', *HJ*, 5, 1962.

C. *The Civil War*

BURNE, A. H., and YOUNG, PETER. *The Great Civil War*. Eyre and Spottiswoode, 1959.

EVERITT, A. M. *The County Committee of Kent in the Civil War*. Leicester University Press, 1957.

GREGG, PAULINE. *Free-Born John* [John Lilburne]. Harrap, 1961.

PENNINGTON, D. H. and ROOTS, I. *The Committee at Stafford 1643-45*. Manchester University Press, 1957.

SOLT, LEO F. *Saints in Arms*. Stanford University Press, 1959.

TAYLOR, PHILIP A. M. *The Origins of the English Civil War*. Harrap, 1960 (*Problems in European Civilisation*).

WOOLRYCH, AUSTIN. *Battles of the English Civil War*. Batsford, 1961.

D. *Oliver Cromwell*

ASHLEY, MAURICE. *The Greatness of Oliver Cromwell*. Hodder and Stoughton, 1957.

—— *Oliver Cromwell and the Puritan Revolution*. English Universities Press, 1958 (*Teach Yourself History*).

—— *Financial and Commercial Policy under the Cromwellian Protectorate*. 2nd edn. F. Cass, 1962.

HILL, CHRISTOPHER. *Oliver Cromwell*. Historical Association Pamphlet G.38. 1958.

PAUL, ROBERT S. *The Lord Protector*. Lutterworth Press, 1955.

WOOLRYCH, AUSTIN. *Penruddocke's Rising*. Historical Association Pamphlet G.29. 1955.

_____

TREVOR-ROPER, H. R. 'Oliver Cromwell and His Parliaments', in Pares, R., and Taylor, A. J. P. *Essays Presented to Sir Lewis Namier*. Macmillan, 1956.

10. EARLY STUART ENGLAND

A. *Economic*

ASHTON, ROBERT. *The Crown and the Money Market 1603-1640.* Oxford University Press, 1960.

HECKSCHER, ELI. *Mercantilism.* 2 vols. 2nd edn. Allen and Unwin, 1955.

SUPPLE, B. E. *Commercial Crisis and Change in England 1600-1642.* Cambridge University Press, 1959.

WILSON, CHARLES. *Profit and Power.* Longmans, 1957.

—— *Mercantilism*, Historical Association Pamphlet G.37. 1958.

BRENNER, Y. S. 'The Inflation of Prices in England 1551-1650', *EcHR*, 15, 1962-63.

FARNELL, J. E. 'The Navigation Act of 1651, the First Dutch War and the London Merchant Community', *EcHR*, 16, 1963-64.

FISHER, F. J. 'London's Export Trade in the Early Seventeenth Century', *EcHR*, 3, 1950-51.

GOULD, J. D. 'The Trade Depression of the Early 1620s', *EcHR*, 7, 1954-55.

HINTON, R. W. K. 'The Mercantile System in the Time of Thomas Mun', *EcHR*, 7, 1954-55.

RAMSAY, G. D. 'Industrial Laisser-Faire and the Policy of Cromwell', *EcHR*, 16 (1st Series), 1946.

B. *Social*

BARNES, T. G. *Somerset 1625-1640.* Harvard University Press, 1961.

MATTHEW, DAVID. *The Social Structure in Caroline England.* Oxford University Press, 1948.

—— *The Age of Charles I.* Eyre and Spottiswoode, 1951.

NOTESTEIN, W. *The English People on the Eve of Colonisation 1603-30.* Hamish Hamilton, 1954.

—— *Four Worthies.* Cape, 1956.

SCHENK, W. *The Concern for Social Justice in the Puritan Revolution.* Longmans, 1947.

SIMPSON, ALAN. *Puritans in Old and New England.* University of Chicago Press, 1956.

WILLCOX, W. B. *Gloucestershire 1590-1640.* Yale University Press, 1940.

ALLAN, D. G. C. 'The Rising in the West 1628-1631', *EcHR*, 5, 1952-53.

HOSKINS, W. G. 'The Rebuilding of Rural England 1570-1640', *P & P*, 4, 1953.

LASLETT, PETER. 'The World We have Lost.' Three talks printed in *The Listener*, 7, 14, 21 April 1960.

C. *The Movement of Ideas*

COLTMAN, IRENE. *Private Men and Public Causes: Philosophy and Politics in the English Civil War*. Faber, 1962.

FARRINGTON, B. *Francis Bacon*. Lawrence and Wishart, 1951.

FUSSNER, F. SMITH. *The Historical Revolution: English Historical Writing and Thought 1580-1640*. Routledge, 1962.

GOUGH, J. W. *Fundamental Law in English Constitutional History*. Oxford University Press, 1955.

GREENLEAF, W. H. *Order, Empiricism and Politics*. Oxford University Press, 1965.

HILL, CHRISTOPHER. *Intellectual Origins of the English Revolution*. Oxford University Press, 1965.

POCOCK, J. G. A. *The Ancient Constitution and the Feudal Law*. Cambridge University Press, 1957.

———

HILL, CHRISTOPHER. 'William Harvey and the Idea of Monarchy', *P & P*, 27, 1964.

SIMON, JOAN. 'The Social Origins of Cambridge Students 1603-1640', *P & P*, 26, 1963.

STONE, LAWRENCE. 'The Educational Revolution in England 1560-1640', *P & P*, 28, 1964.

11. CHARLES II AND JAMES II

BOSHER, ROBERT S. *The Making of the Restoration Settlement 1649-1662*. A. and C. Black, 1951.

BROWNING, ANDREW. *Thomas Osborne, Earl of Danby 1632-1712*. 3 vols. Jackson, Glasgow, 1951.

BRYANT, ARTHUR. *Samuel Pepys*. 3 vols. Collins, 1947-49.

DAVIES, GODFREY. *The Restoration of Charles II 1658-1660*. Oxford University Press, 1955.

FOXCROFT, H. C. *A Character of the Trimmer* [George Savile, Marquis of Halifax]. Cambridge University Press, 1946.

JONES, J. R. *The First Whigs: The Politics of the Exclusion Crisis, 1673-83*. Durham University: Oxford University Press, 1961.

KEMP, BETTY. *King and Commons 1660-1832*. Macmillan, 1959.

KENYON, J. P. *Robert Spencer, Earl of Sunderland 1641-1702*. Longmans, 1958.

OGG, DAVID. *England in the Reign of Charles II*. 2nd ed. Oxford University Press, 1956.

—— *England in the Reigns of James II and William III*. Oxford University Press, 1957.

TURNER, F. C. *James II*. 2nd edn. Eyre and Spottiswoode, 1950.

ABERNATHY, G. R. 'Clarendon and the Declaration of Indulgence', *JEH*, 11, 1960.

BROWNING, ANDREW. 'Parties and Party Organisation in the Reign of Charles II', *TRHS*, 1948.

FURLEY, O. W. 'The Whig Exclusionists: Pamphlet Literature in the Exclusion Campaign 1679-81', *CHJ*, 13, 1957.

FURLEY, O. W. 'The Pope-Burning Processions of the Late Seventeenth Century', *H*, 44, 1959.

HAVIGHURST, A. F. 'The Judiciary and Politics in the Reign of Charles II', *LQR*, 66, 1950.

JONES, J. R. 'Political Groups and Tactics in the Convention of 1660', *HJ*, 6, 1963.

ROBERTS, CLAYTON. 'The Impeachment of the Earl of Clarendon', *CHJ*, 13, 1957.

THIRSK, JOAN. 'Sales of Royalist Lands 1652-1659', *EcHR*, 5, 1952-53.

—— 'The Restoration Land Settlement', *JMH*, 26, 1954.

WALKER, J. 'The Censorship of the Press during the Reign of Charles II', *H*, 35, 1950.

WHITEMAN, ANNE. 'The Restoration of the Church of England', in Nuttall, G. F., and Chadwick, Owen. *From Uniformity to Unity 1660-1962*. S.P.C.K., 1962.

WITCOMBE, D. T. 'The Cavalier House of Commons: Session of 1663', *BIHR*, 32, 1959.

12. WILLIAM III AND ANNE

BAHLMAN, D. W. R. *The Moral Revolution of 1688*. Yale University Press, 1957.

EHRMAN, J. *The Navy in the War of William III 1688-1697.* Cambridge University Press, 1953.

EVERY, G. *The High Church Party 1688-1718.* S.P.C.K., 1956.

FOOT, M. *The Pen and the Sword* [Pamphlet warfare in the reign of Anne]. Macgibbon and Kee, 1957.

PLUMB, J. H. *Sir Robert Walpole: the Making of a Statesman.* Cresset Press, 1956.

SOMERVILLE, DOROTHY H. *The King of Hearts: Charles Talbot, the Duke of Shrewsbury.* Allen and Unwin, 1962.

STRAKA, GERALD M. *The Revolution of 1688—Whig Triumph or Palace Revolution?* Harrap, 1962 (*Problems in European Civilisation*).

SYKES, N. *From Sheldon to Secker.* Cambridge University Press, 1959.

WALCOTT, ROBERT. *English Politics in the Early Eighteenth Century.* Oxford University Press, 1956.

CARTER, JENNIFER. 'Notes on Cabinet Records of William III's Reign', *EHR*, 78, 1963.

DAVIES, GODFREY. 'The Fall of Harley in 1708', *EHR*, 66, 1951.

LASLETT, PETER. 'The English Revolution and Locke's Two Treatises of Government', *CHJ*, 12, 1956.

PLUMB, J. H. 'The Organisation of the Cabinet in the Reign of Queen Anne', *TRHS*, 1957.

ROBERTS, CLAYTON. 'The Growth of Ministerial Responsibility to Parliament in Later Stuart England', *JMH*, 27, 1956.

THOMSON, M. A. 'Parliament and Foreign Policy 1689-1714', *H*, 38, 1953.

—— 'The Safeguarding of the Protestant Succession 1702-1718', *H*, 39, 1954.

13. LATE STUART BRITAIN

A. *Economic (including Overseas Trade)*

BAXTER, STEPHEN B. *The Development of the Treasury 1660-1702.* Longmans, 1957.

CLAPHAM, JOHN. *The Bank of England, Volume I: 1694-1797.* Cambridge University Press, 1944.

COLEMAN, D. C. *Sir John Banks, Baronet and Businessman 1627-99.* Cape, 1963.

DAVIES, K. G. *The Royal African Company*, Longmans, 1958.

DAVIS, RALPH. *The Rise of the English Shipping Industry in the Seventeenth and Eighteenth Centuries*. Macmillan, 1962.

RICHARDS, R. D. *The Early History of Banking in England*. Frank Cass, 1958.

SCHUMPETER, ELIZABETH. *English Overseas Trade Statistics 1697-1808*. Oxford University Press, 1960.

THORNTON, A. P. *West India Policy under the Restoration*. Oxford University Press, 1956.

WARD, W. R. *The English Land Tax in the Eighteenth Century*. Oxford University Press, 1953.

PARES, RICHARD. 'Merchants and Planters', *EcHR*, Supplement, 1960.

B. *Social*

HABAKKUK, H. J. 'Daniel Finch, Second Earl of Nottingham: His House and Estate', in Plumb, J. H., *Studies in Social History*. Longmans, 1955.

JOHN, A. H. 'The Course of Agricultural Change 1660-1760', in Pressnell, L. S., *Studies in the Industrial Revolution*, Athlone Press, 1960.

KERRIDGE, E. 'Turnip Husbandry in High Suffolk', *EcHR*, 8, 1955-56.

PLUMB, J. H. 'Sir Robert Walpole and Norfolk Husbandry', *EcHR*, 5, 1952-53.

—— 'The Walpoles, Father and Son', in *Studies in Social History*, see above.

C. *Science and Religion*

ARMITAGE, ANGUS. *Copernicus and the Reformation of Astronomy*. Historical Association Pamphlet G.15. 1950.

BOAS, MARIE. *Robert Boyle and Seventeenth Century Chemistry*. Cambridge University Press, 1958.

—— *The Scientific Renaissance 1450-1630*. Collins, 1962.

BUTTERFIELD, HERBERT. *The Origins of Modern Science 1300-1800*. Bell, 1949.

CRAGG, G. R. *From Puritanism to the Age of Reason*. Cambridge University Press, 1950.

—— *Puritanism in the Period of the Great Persecution 1660-1688*. Cambridge University Press, 1957.

QTSB

HALL, A. RUPERT. *The Scientific Revolution*. Longmans, 1954.
—— *From Galileo to Newton 1630–1720*. Collins, 1963.

KEARNEY, HUGH F. *Origins of the Scientific Revolution*. Longmans, 1964 (*Problems and Perspectives in History*).

KOYRÉ, ALEXANDRE. *From the Closed World to the Infinite Universe*. Johns Hopkins Press, 1957.

TOULMIN, STEPHEN, and GOODFIELD, JUNE. *The Fabric of the Heavens*. Hutchinson, 1961.

WESTFALL, RICHARD S. *Science and Religion in Seventeenth Century England*. Yale University Press, 1958.

———

ESPINASSE, MARGARET. 'The Decline and Fall of Restoration Science', *P & P*, 14, 1958.

MASON, S. F. 'Science and Religion in Seventeenth Century England' *P & P*, 3, 1953.

D. *Scotland and Ireland*

DONALDSON, GORDON. *Common Errors in Scottish History*. Historical Association Pamphlet G.32. 1956.

KEARNEY, H. F. *Strafford in Ireland 1633–1641*. Manchester University Press, 1959.

PRYDE, G. S. *Central and Local Government in Scotland Since 1707*. Historical Association Pamphlet G.45. 1960.
—— *Scotland from 1603 to the Present Day*. Nelson, 1962.

WEDGWOOD, C. V. *Montrose*. Collins, 1952.

———

CAMPBELL, R. H. 'The Anglo-Scottish Union of 1707. II. The Economic Consequences', *EcHR*, 16, 1963–64.

SMOUT, T. C. 'The Anglo-Scottish Union of 1707. I. The Economic Background', *EcHR*, 16, 1963–64.

E. *Political Thought*

CRANSTON, MAURICE. *John Locke*. Longmans, 1957.

GOUGH, J. W. *John Locke's Political Philosophy*. Oxford University Press, 1950.

PETERS, RICHARD. *Hobbes*. Penguin, 1956 (*Pelican Philosophy Series*).

APPENDIX I

1. *English Monarchs*

HOUSE OF YORK

Edward IV   1461-1483 (in exile 1470-71)
Edward V   1483 (murdered in the Tower)
Richard III   1483-1485 (killed at Bosworth)

HOUSE OF TUDOR

Henry VII   1485-1509
Henry VIII   1509-1547
Edward VI   1547-1553
Mary I   1553-1558
Elizabeth I   1558-1603

HOUSE OF STUART

James I   1603-1625
Charles I   1625-1649 (executed)
Charles II   1649-1685 (in exile until 1660)
James II   1685-1689 (fled the country in 1688)
William III
 & Mary II   1689-1702
Anne   1702-1714

*Q

2. *English Parliaments*

EDWARD IV

1461 November–1462 May
1463 April–1465 March
1467 June–1468 June
1470 November–?1471 April
1472 October–1475 March
1478 January–February
1483 January–February

RICHARD III

1484 January–February

HENRY VII

1485 November–1486 March
1487 November–December
1489 January–1490 February
1491 October–1492 March
1495 October–December
1497 January–March
1504 January–April

HENRY VIII

1510 January–February
1512 February–1514 March
1515 February–December
1523 April–August
1529 November–1536 April (the Reformation Parliament)
1536 June–July
1539 April–1540 July
1542 January–1544 March
1545 November–1547 January

EDWARD VI

1547 November–1552 April
1553 March–March

MARY I

1553 October–December
1554 April–May
1554 November–1555 January
1555 October–December
1558 January–November

ELIZABETH I

1559 January–May
1563 January–1567 January
1571 April–May
1572 May–1583 April
1584 November–1585 September
1586 October–1587 March
1589 February–March
1593 February–April
1597 October–1598 February
1601 October–December

JAMES I

1604 March–1611 February
1614 April–June (the Addled Parliament)
1621 January–1622 February
1624 February–1625 March

CHARLES I

1625 May–August
1626 February–June
1628 March–1629 March
1640 April–May (the Short Parliament)
1640 November–1660 March (the Long Parliament. Purged in 1648
    and expelled in April 1653)

CIVIL WAR AND INTERREGNUM

1644 January–October (summoned by the King to Oxford)
1653 July–December (Parliament of Saints, or Barebones Parliament)
1654 September–1655 January
1656 September–1658 February
1659 January–April
1659 May–1660 March (The recalled Rump)

CHARLES II

1660 April–December (the Convention)
1661 May–1679 January (the Long Parliament of the Restoration, or Cavalier Parliament, or Pensionary Parliament)
1679 March–July
1680 October–1681 January
1681 March–March (the Oxford Parliament)

JAMES II

1685 May–1687 July

WILLIAM III AND MARY II

1689 January–1690 February (the Convention)
1690 March–1695 October
1695 November–1698 July
1698 August–1700 December
1701 February–November
1701 December–1702 July

ANNE

1702 August–1705 April
1705 June–1708 April (became in 1707 the first Parliament of Great Britain)
1708 July–1710 September
1710 November–1713 August
1713 November–1715 January

(Based on the list given in the *Handbook of British Chronology* ed. Sir Maurice Powicke and E. B. Fryde. 2nd edition, 1961).

Index

Peterborough, Charles Mordaunt, Earl of, 391
Petite, John, 90
Petre, Edward, 359
Phelips, Sir Robert, 246
Philadelphia, 430
Philip II of Spain, marriage with Mary, 123–5; 129, 148–9, 160, 183, 186, 189–92
Philip V of Spain, 375–6, 379, 391, 395
Philphaugh, battle of, 417
Pilgrim Fathers, 425
Pilgrimage of Grace, 74–7, 86, 87, 133, 184–5
Pilkington, James, Bp of Durham, 177–8
Pinkie, battle of, 164
Pius V, Pope, 185
Plague, 132, 335
Plymouth, 425
Pole, Reginald, 66, 95, 123, 126, 129, 131
Ponet, John, Bp of Winchester, 119
Pope, Alexander, 445 n
Portland, Richard Weston, Earl of, 256
Portland, William Bentinck, Earl of, 368
Port Mahon, 394, 399–400
Poynings, Sir Edward, 156
Prayer-book, First, 112, 173, 177
Prayer-book, Second, 116–17, 172–13
Preston, battle of, 291, 418
Pride, Thomas, 291
Proclamations, 233
Propositions, the Nineteen, 272
Providence Island, 429
Prynne, William, 253, 256, 266, 330
Ptolemy, 3, 443
Pym, John, 222, 260, 264–72, 277–82, 320, 417

Ralegh, Sir Walter, 149, 160, 211, 212, 216, 235–6, 424
Ramillies, battle of, 391
Rates, Book of, 130, 225
Redman, Richard, Abbot of Shap, 70
Remonstrance, the Grand, 269–70
Renaissance, 2, 3, 9, 66, 70

Requests, Court of, 41, 137
Reynolds, Edward, Bp of Norwich, 330
Reynolds, Richard, 72
Rhode Island, 426, 430
Rice, John ap, 72
Rich, Sir Richard, 96
Richard III, 16–17, 24
Richelieu, Armand-Jean du Plessis, Duke of, 257, 304
Richmond, Henry Fitzroy, Duke of, 41, 46, 158
Ridley, Nicholas, Bp of London, 123, 128
Ridolfi Plot, 186, 190
Right, Claim of, 420
Right, Petition of, 250, 320, 365
Rights, Bill of, 250, 364–5, 420
Rising, the Northern, 184–5
Rising, the Western (1549), 113
Rizzio, David, 166–7
Roanoke, 149
Robsart, Amy, 171
Rochester, Laurence Hyde, Earl of, 351, 356, 358, 360, 377, 382–5, 387, 393, 398
Rooke, Sir George, 387–8
Root and Branch Petition, 266
Roper, William, 29, 90
Roundway Down, battle of, 281
Rowse, A. L., 129
Royal Society, the, 13, 322, 443
Rubens, Peter Paul, 262
Rubric, the Black, 117, 173
Rudyerd, Sir Benjamin, 320
Rupert, Prince, 259, 278–9, 281, 283–6, 335, 344
Russell, Edward, Earl of Orford, 362, 369, 372, 374, 376, 383
Russell, Sir John, 82, 87, 113, 144
Russell, William, Lord, 350, 353, 368

Sacheverell, Henry, 396–7
St John, Henry. See Bolingbroke
St John, Oliver, 260, 267, 284–5, 401
St Kitts, 427, 431
St Paul's School, 152
Salem, 426